A HUMAN RIGHTS-BASED APPROACH TO CONSERVING PROTECTED AREAS IN CHINA

A HUMAN RIGHTS-BASED APPROACH TO CONSERVING PROTECTED AREAS IN CHINA

Lessons from Europe

Miao He

intersentia
Cambridge – Antwerp – Portland

Intersentia Ltd
Sheraton House | Castle Park
Cambridge | CB3 0AX | United Kingdom
Tel.: +44 1223 370 170 | Fax: +44 1223 370 169
Email: mail@intersentia.co.uk
www.intersentia.com | www.intersentia.co.uk

Distribution for the UK and Ireland:
NBN International
Airport Business Centre, 10 Thornbury Road
Plymouth, PL6 7 PP
United Kingdom
Tel.: +44 1752 202 301 | Fax: +44 1752 202 331
Email: orders@nbninternational.com

Distribution for Europe and all other countries:
Intersentia Publishing nv
Groenstraat 31
2640 Mortsel
Belgium
Tel.: +32 3 680 15 50 | Fax: +32 3 658 71 21
Email: mail@intersentia.be

Distribution for the USA and Canada:
International Specialized Book Services
920 NE 58th Ave. Suite 300
Portland, OR 97213
USA
Tel.: +1 800 944 6190 (toll free) | Fax: +1 503 280 8832
Email: info@isbs.com

A Human Rights-Based Approach to Conserving Protected Areas in China
Lessons from Europe

ISBN 978-1-78068-388-1
D/2016/7849/33
NUR 828

British Library Cataloguing in Publication Data. A catalogue record for this book is available from the British Library.

CONTENTS

LIST OF ABBREVIATIONS

Aarhus Convention	Convention on Access to Information, Public Participation in Decision-making and Access to Justice in Environmental Matters
ACCC	Aarhus Convention Compliance Committee
ACEF	All-China Environment Federation
ACHR	American Convention on Human Rights
AMCE	African Ministerial Conference on Environment
Bern Convention	Convention on the Conservation of European Wildlife and Natural Habitats
Birds Directive	Directive 79/409/EEC on the Conservation of Wild Birds
Bonn Convention	Convention on the Conservation of Migratory Species of Wild Animals
CAFF	Conservation of Arctic Flora and Fauna
CBD	Convention on Biological Diversity
CEACR	Committee of Experts on the Application of Conventions and Recommendations
CEDAW	Convention on the Elimination of Discrimination Against Women
CERD	Committee on the Elimination of Racial Discrimination
CJEU	Court of Justice of the European Union
CHRD	Center for Human Rights and Development
CLAPV	Centre for Legal Assistance to Pollution Victims
CI	Conservation International
CIFOR	Center for International Forestry Research
CIEL	Center for International Environmental Law
CoE	Council of Europe
CPC	Communist Party of China
CRC	Committee on the Rights of the Child
CRIN	Child Rights International Network
CUMPM	Communauté Urbaine Marseille Provence Métropole
Directive 96/61/EC	Council Directive 96/61/EC of 24 September 1996 Concerning Integrated Pollution Prevention and Control

Directive 2003/4/EC	Directive 2003/4/EC of the European Parliament and of the Council of 28 January 2003 on Public Access to Environmental Information and Repealing Council Directive 90/313/EEC
Directive 2003/35/EC	Directive 2003/35/EC of the European Parliament and of the Council of 26 May 2003 Providing for Public Participation in Respect of the Drawing up of Certain Plans and Programs Relating to the Environment and Amending with regards to Public Participation and Access to Justice Council Directive 85/337/EEC and 96/61/EC
Directive 2010/75/EU	Directive 2010/75/EU of the European Parliament and of the Council of 24 November 2010 on Industrial Emissions (Integrated Pollution Prevention and Control)
ECHR	European Convention on Human Rights
ECE	Economic Commission for Europe
ECtHR	European Court of Human Rights
EEA	European Environment Agency
EIA	Environmental Impact Assessment
EIA Directive	Council Directive 85/337/EEC of 27 June 1985 on the Assessment of Certain Public and Private Projects on the Environment
EPB	Environmental Protection Bureau
ESRC	Economic & Social Research Council
Espoo Convention	Convention on Environmental Impact Assessment in a Trans-boundary Context
EU	European Union
EUR	Euro
FPIC	Free, Prior Informed Consent
FPP	Forest Peoples Programme
FIELD	Foundation for International Environmental Law and Development
FTE	Full Time Employment
GDP	Gross Domestic Product
GEF	Global Environment Facility
GONGO	Government Organized Non-Governmental Organization
GPRG	Global Poverty Research Group
Habitats Directive	Directive 92/43/EEC on the Conservation of Natural Habitats and of Wild Fauna and Flora

Helsinki Convention	Convention on the Protection of the Marine Environment of the Baltic Sea Area
HRBA	Human Rights-Based Approach
HRS	Household Responsibility System
IAEA	International Atomic Energy Agency
IAITPTF	International Alliance of the Indigenous and Tribal Peoples of the Tropical Forests
ICCPR	International Covenant on Civil and Political Rights
ICESCR	International Covenant on Economic, Social and Cultural Rights
ICERD	International Convention on the Elimination of All Forms of Racial Discrimination
ICRAF	International Center for Research in AgroForestry
ICRW	International Center for Research on Women
IDS	Institute of Development Studies
IIED	International Institute for Environment and Development
ILO	International Labour Organization
INTRAC	International NGO Training and Resource Center
IPE	Institute of Public and Environmental Affairs
IPPC	Integrated Pollution Prevention and Control
IUCN	International Union for Conservation of Nature
MAB	Man and the Biosphere Programme
MEA	Millennium Ecosystem Assessment
MEP	Ministry of Environmental Protection
NGO	Non-Governmental Organisation
NPC	National People's Congress
NRDC	Natural Resources Defense Council
OECD	Organization for Economic Cooperation and Development
OGI	Open Governance Information
OHCHR	Office of the High Commissioner on Human Rights
OSPAR Convention	Convention for the Protection of the Marine Environment of the North-East Atlantic
PAs	Protected Areas
PATF	Protected Area Task Force
PEEN	Pan-European Ecological Network
PEM	Participatory Environmental Management
PoWPA	Programme of Work on Protected Areas
PRC	People's Republic of China
Ramsar Convention	Convention on Wetlands of International Importance
Rio Declaration	Rio Declaration on Environment and Development

SACs	Special Areas of Conservation
SCI	Sites of Community Importance
SEA Directive	Directive 2001/42/EC of the European Parliament and of the Council of 27 June 2001 on the Assessment of the Effects of Certain Plans and Programs on the Environment
SEPA	State Environmental Protection Administration
"Seveso" Directive	Council Directive of 24 June 1982 on the Major-Accident Hazards of Certain Industrial Activities (82/501/EEC), issued on 24 June 1982 and replaced by 87/216/EEC
SFA	State Forestry Administration
SGLA	Sino-Global Legal Alliance
SPAs	Special Protection Areas
SPC	Supreme People's Court
Stockholm Declaration	Declaration of the United Nations Conference on the Human Environment
TNC	The Nature Conservancy
TRI	Toxic Release Inventory
UDHR	Universal Declaration of Human Rights
UN	United Nations
UNCED	United Nations Conference on Environment and Development
UNCF	United Nations Children's Fund
UNCLOS	United Nations Convention on Law of the Sea
UNCSD	United Nations Conference on Sustainable Development
UNDRIP	United Nations Declaration on the Rights of Indigenous Peoples
UNDP	United Nations Development Programme
UN/ECE	United Nations Economic Commission for Europe
UNEP	United Nations Environment Programme
UNESCO	United Nations Educational, Scientific and Cultural Organization
UNFCCC	United Nations Framework Convention on Climate Change
UNFPA	United Nations Population Fund Agency
USD	United States Dollar
Water Framework Directive	Directive 2000/60/EC of the European Parliament and of the Council of 23 October 2000 Establishing a Framework for Community Action in the Field of Water Policy

WCC	World Conservation Congress
WCED	World Commission on Environment and Development
WCPA	World Commission on Protected Areas
WDPA	World Database on Protected Areas
WFFPDSFA	Wild Fauna and Flora Protection Division of the State Forestry Administration
WHC	World Heritage Convention
WHO	World Health Organization
WPC	World Park Congress
WWF	World Wide Fund for Nature

PART I

INTRODUCTION AND BACKGROUND

CHAPTER 1
INTRODUCTION

1.1. RESEARCH BACKGROUND

The relationship between human rights protection and environmental protection is a fascinating, uneasy, and increasingly urgent one. According to Fitzmaurice,[1] there are three main schools of thought. One that supports the view that there are no human rights without an environmental right, another that see the right, both as an already existing or as an emerging one, as a highly questionable proposition, and finally a school that admits the existence of a right to a healthy environment, deriving its existence from other human rights,[2] such as the right to life, the right to health and the right to information.[3] Dinah Shelton, a well-known scholar working in both fields of international human rights law and international environmental law, observes the connection: "*The international community has adopted a considerable array of international legal instruments, and created specialized organs and agencies at the global and regional levels to respond to identified problems in human rights and environmental protection, although often addressing the two topics in isolation from one another.*"[4] What is the real relationship between human rights protection and environmental protection at the international level?

---

1 Fitzmaurice, M. (1999). The right of the child to a clean environment. *Southern Illinois University Law Journal*, 23, pp. 611–656.

2 Fitzmaurice, M. (1999). The right of the child to a clean environment. *Southern Illinois University Law Journal*, 23, pp. 611–656.

3 Shelton, D.L. (1991). Human rights, environmental rights, and the right to environment. *Stanford Journal of International Law*, 28, p. 105.

4 Shelton, D.L. (2009). Human rights and environment: past, present and future linkages and the value of a declaration. In: High Level Meeting on the New Future of Human Rights and Environment: Moving the Global Agenda Forward, Co-organized by UNEP and OHCHR, Nairobi, 30 November – 1 December 2009.

1.1.1. RELATIONSHIP BETWEEN HUMAN RIGHTS PROTECTION AND ENVIRONMENTAL PROTECTION AT THE INTERNATIONAL LEVEL

1.1.1.1. Linkages Between Human Rights Protection and Environmental Protection in International Instruments

The myriad declarations, international conventions and agreements that address human rights and environmental protection – separately and jointly – reflect the international community's recognition that international actors, particularly States, have obligations in these areas, and individuals, as well as groups of peoples, have a number of rights.[5]

In the international sphere, the earlier evolution of human rights law has influenced and sometimes inspired innovations in international environmental law; in turn, the emergence of a concern for the environment has encouraged international lawyers to explore and attempt to understand and utilise the interrelationship and even interdependence of human rights and environmental protection.[6]

From a historical perspective, the 1972 Stockholm Declaration on the Human Environment,[7] which was born in the United Nations Conference on the Human Environment,[8] was the first international instrument to establish an explicit link between human rights and environmental protection. Principle 1 of the Stockholm Declaration proclaims that: "*Man has the fundamental right to freedom, equality and adequate conditions of life, in an environment of a quality that permits a life of dignity and well-being and he bears a solemn responsibility to protect and improve the environment for present and future generations.*"[9] The Conference recognised that economic development, the State of the environment and the health of humanity are all intricately entwined. As these efforts have

5 Soveroski, M. (2007). Environmental rights versus environmental wrongs: forum over substance? *Review of European Community & International Environmental Law*, 16(3), http://onlinelibrary.wiley.com/doi/10.1111/j.1467–9388.2007.00575.x/pdf accessed 9 October 2013, p. 262.

6 Shelton, D.L. A rights-based approach to public participation and local management of natural resources, http://pub.iges.or.jp/modules/envirolib/upload/1503/attach/3ws-26-dinah.pdf accessed 17 February 2014.

7 Declaration of the United Nations Conference on the Human Environment (Stockholm Declaration), adopted on 16 June 1972, UN Doc. A/CONF. 48/14/Rev.1, www.unep.org/Documents.Multilingual/Default.asp?documentid=97&articleid=1503 accessed 23 December 2012.

8 United Nations Conference on the Human Environment ("Stockholm Conference") was held at Stockholm from 5 to 16 June 1972.

9 Declaration of the United Nations Conference on the Human Environment (Stockholm Declaration), adopted on 16 June 1972, UN Doc. A/CONF. 48/14/Rev.1, www.unep. org/Documents.Multilingual/Default.asp?documentid=97&articleid=1503 accessed 23 December 2012.

multiplied, the human rights and environmental protection have undergone a degree of convergence despite differences in priorities and emphases.[10]

Since then, United Nations human rights treaty bodies and regional human rights mechanisms have clarified the normative content and State responsibilities concerning environmental degradation and human rights.[11] In addition, some non-binding but widely accepted declarations supporting the individual's right to a clean environment were adopted. For instance, the 1982 World Charter for Nature[12] was one of the first instruments to recognise the rights of nature and the right to participate in decision-making.

In 1987, the Brundtland Report[13] addressed the need for an integrated approach to development policies and projects that, if environmentally sound, should lead to sustainable economic development in both developed and developing countries.[14] This report led the United Nations to convene a second global conference on the environment in 1992 in Rio de Janeiro, Brazil, under the title United Nations Conference on Environment and Development (UNCED).[15] Two texts adopted at the UNCED have a general scope: the Rio Declaration on Environment and Development (Rio Declaration)[16] and an action programme called Agenda 21.[17] The Declaration indicates that human beings are at the centre of concern for sustainable development, and that they are entitled to a healthy and productive life in harmony with nature.[18] This falls short of proclaiming a right to environment. In addition, some procedural

---

10 Shelton, D.L. A rights-based approach to public participation and local management of natural resources, http://pub.iges.or.jp/modules/envirolib/upload/1503/attach/3ws-26-dinah.pdf accessed 17 February 2014.

11 CIEL (Center for International Environmental Law) (2012). Human rights & environment in the Rio+20 UN Conference on Sustainable Development, www.ciel.org/Publications/Rio+20_IssueBrief_Feb2012.pdf accessed 23 December 2013.

12 UN General Assembly. World Charter for Nature, adopted on 28 October 1982, A/RES/37/7, www.refworld.org/docid/3b00f22a10.html accessed 31 January 2014.

13 United Nations Report of the World Commission on Environment and Development: Our Common Future (Brundtland Report), adopted on 4 August 1987, A/42/427, http://conspect.nl/pdf/Our_Common_Future-Brundtland_Report_1987.pdf accessed 21 June 2012.

14 Anton, D.K. & Shelton, D.L. (2011). *Environmental Protection and Human Rights*. Cambridge: Cambridge University Press, pp. 73–74.

15 The United Nations Conference on Environment and Development (the Rio Summit, Rio Conference, and Earth Summit), held in Rio de Janeiro from 3 to 14 June 1992, www.un.org/geninfo/bp/enviro.html accessed 22 June 2012.

16 Rio Declaration on Environment and Development (The United Nations Conference on Environment and Development, UNCED), adopted in June 1992, A/CONF. 151/26, www.unep. org/Documents.Multilingual/Default.asp?documentid=78&articleid=1163 accessed 22 June 2012.

17 Agenda 21, adopted at United Nations Conference on Environment & Development in Rio de Janeiro in June 1992, http://sustainabledevelopment.un.org/content/documents/Agenda21.pdf accessed 8 June 2012.

18 Pallemaerts, M. (2002). Introduction: human rights and environmental protection. In: Dejeant-Pons, M. & Pallemaerts, M. (Eds.). *Human Rights and the Environment*. Strasbourg (France): Council of Europe Publishing, p. 118.

human rights related to environmental decision-making, such as principle 10 regarding access to information, public participation and access to justice, principle 11 concerning effective environmental legislation and principle 17 referring to environmental impact assessments, were elaborated by the Rio Declaration. Agenda 21 (especially in Chapter 28 of Agenda 21) envisages that local authorities should play a crucial role in fulfilling Agenda 21's objectives.[19] As a community-wide participatory effort to establish a comprehensive action strategy for environmental protection, economic prosperity, and the well-being of local communities, it facilitates implementation of Agenda 21's key objectives through local authorities and their constituent communities.[20] It also addresses full community participation, clear assessment of current conditions, target setting for achieving specific goals, monitoring and reporting.[21] What's more, two important conventions, drafted and adopted before the Conference, were opened for signature at Rio: the United Nations Framework Convention on Climate Change[22] and the Convention on Biological Diversity (CBD).[23, 24]

In the aftermath of Rio, between 26 August and 4 September 2002, the representatives of more than 190 countries met in Johannesburg, South Africa. At the end of the Conference, the participating governments adopted the Declaration on Sustainable Development[25] affirming their will to "*assume a collective responsibility to advance and strengthen the interdependent and mutually reinforcing pillars of sustainable development – economic development, social development and environmental protection – at local, national, regional and global levels.*"[26] It also recognises the loss of biodiversity; the depletion of fish stocks; the progress of desertification; the evident adverse effects of climate

19 Fulfilment of the objectives requires, amongst other types of action, local consultative process, cooperation between local authorities, exchange of information and representation of women and youth in decision-making, planning and implementation process.

20 Du Plessis, A. (2011). Local agenda 21: a rights-based approach to local environmental governance. In: Benidickson, J., Boer, B., Benjamin, A.H. & Morrow, K. (Eds.). *Environmental Law and Sustainability after Rio*. The IUCN Academy of Environmental Law Series. Cheltenham (UK) and Northampton (USA): Edward Elgar Publishing, p. 48.

21 Summarised from United Kingdom initiative on Local Agenda 21, www.gdrc.org/uem/la21/la21.html accessed 9 June 2012.

22 United Nations Framework Convention on Climate Change (UNFCCC), adopted on 9 May 1992 and entered into force 21 March 1994, 1771 UNTS 107; 31 ILM 849, http://unfccc.int/2860.php accessed 8 June 2012.

23 Convention on Biological Diversity (CBD), opened for signature on 5 June 1992 and entered into force on 29 December 1993, [1993] ATS 32/1760 UNTS 79/31 ILM 818 (1992), www.cbd.int/ accessed 8 June 2012.

24 Anton, D.K. & Shelton, D.L. (2011). *Environmental Protection and Human Rights*. Cambridge: Cambridge University Press, pp. 73–74.

25 Johannesburg Declaration on Sustainable Development, adopted in September 2002, A/CONF. 199/20, www.unescap. org/esd/environment/rio20/pages/Download/johannesburg declaration.pdf accessed 9 June 2012.

26 §5, Johannesburg Declaration on Sustainable Development, adopted in September 2002, A/CONF. 199/20, www.unescap. org/esd/environment/rio20/pages/Download/johannesburg declaration.pdf accessed 9 June 2012.

change.[27] There was no comprehensive international environmental agreement addressing these matters in a holistic manner, nor was there a single agency addressing the problems.[28]

In 2011, the UN Human Rights Council in Resolution 16/11 requested the Office of the High Commissioner for Human Rights to conduct a comprehensive study on human rights and the environment. It concluded that the linkage between human rights and the environment was well established and had received significant attention since the 1972 Stockholm Declaration.[29] Later, as the Rio+20 United Nations Conference on Sustainable Development (UNCSD or Rio+20)[30] in June 2012 neared, the international community was once more faced with the challenge of integrating a complex array of environmental, social and economic issues within the umbrella of sustainable development.[31] The Rio+20 conference focused on two main themes: (a) a green economy in the context of sustainable development and poverty eradication, and (b) the institutional framework for sustainable development.[32] However, the Rio+20 process has not adequately taken into account developments in the integration of human rights and the environment.[33]

---

27 §13, Johannesburg Declaration on Sustainable Development, adopted in September 2002, A/CONF. 199/20, www.unescap.org/esd/environment/rio20/pages/Download/johannesburg declaration.pdf accessed 9 June 2012.

28 Anton, D.K. & Shelton, D.L. (2011). *Environmental Protection and Human Rights*. Cambridge: Cambridge University Press, p. 80.

29 CIEL (Center for International Environmental Law) (2012). Human rights & environment in the Rio+20 UN Conference on Sustainable Development, www.ciel.org/Publications/Rio +20_Issue Brief_Feb2012.pdf accessed 23 December 2013.

30 United Nations Conference on Sustainable Development (UNCSD, Rio 2012 or Rio+20), held in Rio de Janeiro on 20–22 June 2012, A/CONF. 216/16, www.uncsd2012.org/ accessed 25 June 2012.

31 Human rights & environment in the Rio+20 UN Conference on Sustainable Development. (2012). Posted on 15 February 2012, https://docs.google.com/viewer?a=v&q=cache:duwm OANP1DkJ:www.ciel.org/Publications/Rio%2B20_IssueBrief_Feb2012.pdf+human+rights +%26+environment+in+the+rio%2B20+UN+conference+on+sustainable+development&hl= nl&gl=be&pid=bl&srcid=ADGEESgb9-b4D3DEx8PYYQBZcQ7z2S5d1umIbUmFJjqhx etn6rfeeOa5GLs2tim9n3fRY3a0EyrLFoGY00iHbYkMnMMZbU1QFUxbXYPjDT6KIfoFlN1n 8Av1DiRVFGR9Lnc3acqLqmuf&sig=AHIEtbTHPwEWsU6nSdAA-I9QDPtPfefk4w accessed 20 March 2012.

32 Human rights & environment in the Rio+20 UN Conference on Sustainable Development (2012). Posted on 15 February 2012, https://docs.google.com/viewer?a=v&q=cache: duwmOANP1DkJ:www.ciel.org/Publications/Rio%2B20_IssueBrief_Feb2012.pdf+human+ rights+%26+environment+in+the+rio%2B20+UN+conference+on+sustainable+development&hl =nl&gl=be&pid=bl&srcid=ADGEESgb9-b4D3DEx8PYYQBZcQ7z2S5d1umIbUmFJjqhxetn6 rfeeOa5GLs2tim9n3fRY3a0EyrFoGY00iHbYkMnMMZbU1QFUxbXYPjDT6KIfoFlN1n8Av1 DiRVFGR9Lnc3acq Lqmuf&sig=AHIEtbTHPw EWsU6nSdAA-I9QDPt Pfe fk4w accessed 20 March 2012.

33 For instance, the January 2012 Zero Draft of the outcome document "The Future We Want" does not recognise the fundamental right to a healthy environment or adequately operationalise the human rights and environment linkage. For detailed information see CIEL (Center for International Environmental Law) (2012). Human rights & environment in the Rio+20 UN Conference on Sustainable Development, www.ciel.org/Publications/Rio+20_ IssueBrief_Feb2012.pdf accessed 23 December 2013.

1.1.1.2. *Relationship Between Human Rights Protection and Environmental Protection in Practice*

In practice, there are five main dimensions of the relationship between human rights protection and environmental protection. Firstly, environmental degradation can cause human rights infringements. Environmental degradation generates further poverty by the exhaustion of natural resources and creates prejudice to the exercise of basic rights, eventually raising new humanitarian issues, such as the case of environmental refugees.[34] Secondly, a good environment would promote the enjoyment of human rights, such as the right to life, the rights to water, food, adequate housing and so on. The protection and improvement of man's environment arise directly out of a vital need to protect human life, to assure its quality and condition, and to ensure the prerequisites indispensable to safeguarding human dignity and human worth and the development of the human personality.[35] It also means that the environment is a prerequisite for the enjoyment of human rights.[36] Thirdly, certain human rights could help to better protect the environment. For instance, access to information, participation in decision-making, and access to justice in environmental matters are key "tools" to prevent environmental harm. Fourth, environmental protection sometimes can infringe upon some human rights. For instance, establishing wildlife reserves may impair the use or value of property.[37] Fifth, neglecting internationally and domestically guaranteed human rights or abusing some human rights could be a trigger for environmental destruction. For instance, when establishing a protected area, neglecting the basic human rights of local people would lead them to do some illegal activities to destroy the natural resources in the protected area. The importance of "local people and communities"[38] in the sustainable management of biological resources is

---

34 Taillant, J.D. (2000). Environmental discrimination. Center for Human Rights and Development (CHRD), www.cedha.org.ar/en/documents accessed 3 May 2011.

35 Pathak, R.S. (1992). The human rights system as a conceptual framework for environmental law. In: Weiss, E.B. (Ed.). *Environmental Change and International Law.* Tokyo (Japan): United Nations University Press, p. 209.

36 UNEP (United Nations Environment Programme). High level expert meeting on the future of human rights and environment: moving the global agenda forward, www.unep.org/environmentalgovernance/Events/HumanRightsandEnvironment/tabid/2046/Default.aspx accessed 30 January 2014.

37 Boyle, A. (2013). Relationship between international environmental law and other branches of international law. In: Bodansky, D., Brunnee, J. & Hey, E. (Eds.). *The Oxford Handbook of International Environmental Law.* Oxford: Oxford University Press, p. 141; Bowen-Jones, E. (2012). Tackling human-wildlife conflicts: a prerequisite for linking conservation and poverty alleviation: a decision-makers guide to financial and institutional mechanisms. Poverty and Conservation Learning Group Discussion Paper No. 6, http://povertyandconservation.info/sites/default/files/PCLG%20HWC%20discussion%20paper_0.pdf accessed 23 January 2014, p. 3.

38 This book normally use "local people and communities" instead of "indigenous peoples" with a narrower scope, except citing the original term of "indigenous peoples" from some agreements or documents.

one that concerns both human rights and environmental protection, two of the fundamental values and aims of modern international society.[39] It is noted that the issue of protecting natural resources and traditional knowledge is one that goes beyond "indigenous peoples" to encompass local people and communities in general. The international community has not adopted a common definition of indigenous peoples,[40] but the term has become a general denominator for distinct peoples who, throughout history, have been pursuing their own concept and way of human development in a given socio-economic, political and historical context.[41] Indigenous peoples are the descendants of the original inhabitants of territories since colonised by foreigners; they have distinct cultures which set them apart from the dominant society; many have, until comparatively recently, had a high degree of control over their development; indigenous peoples have a strong sense of self-identity.[42] Often for centuries, these distinct groups of peoples have tried to maintain their group identity, languages, traditional beliefs, worldviews and ways of life and, most importantly, the control and management of their lands, territories and natural resources with which they have a special connection, and upon which their physical and cultural survival as indigenous peoples typically depends.[43] The "local people and communities" refer to "resident individuals, families, communities" in or nearby a specific territory within or adjacent to an established or proposed protected area. The "local people and communities" contain indigenous peoples, non-indigenous peoples, minority peoples, majority peoples or even a mixed group. They largely rely on the natural resources in this territory for their livelihoods. In order to achieve a fair balance in a concrete situation, the

---

39 Shelton, D.L. A rights-based approach to public participation and local management of natural resources, http://pub.iges.or.jp/modules/envirolib/upload/1503/attach/3ws-26-dinah.pdf accessed 17 February 2014.

40 International Labor Organization Convention No. 169: Indigenous and Tribal Peoples Convention, adopted on 27 June 1989 and entered into force on 5 September 1991, 28 ILM 1382, www.ilo.org/indigenous/Conventions/no169/lang--en/index.htm accessed 1 October 2012. This Convention is a legally binding international instrument open to ratification, which deals specifically with the rights of indigenous and tribal peoples. It does not define who are indigenous and tribunal peoples. It takes a practical approach and only provides criteria for describing the peoples it aims to protect. Self-identification is considered as a fundamental criterion for the identification of indigenous and tribal peoples. More information see www.ilo.org/indigenous/Conventions/no169/lang--en/index.htm accessed 14 July 2014.

41 UN – REDD (2013). Guidelines on free, prior and informed consent. Geneva: UN – REDD Programme Secretariat, www.unredd.net/index.php?option=com_docman&task=doc_download&gid=8717&Itemid=53 accessed 11 July 2014, p. 36.

42 See Shelton, D.L. A rights-based approach to public participation and local management of natural resources. http://pub.iges.or.jp/modules/envirolib/upload/1503/attach/3ws-26-dinah.pdf accessed 18 Aril 2013.

43 UN – REDD (2013). Guidelines on free, prior and informed consent. Geneva: UN – REDD Programme Secretariat, www.unredd.net/index.php?option=com_docman&task=doc_download&gid=8717&Itemid=53 accessed 11 July 2014, p. 36.

rights and interests of all "local people and communities" should be taken into account. Therefore, there is a need to find a better balanced approach to deal with the relationship between human rights protection and environmental protection. The empowerment for local people and communities and the full implementation of the rights would be a major step in both human rights and environmental protection.

Based on the relationship between human rights protection and environmental protection in theory and in practice, some human rights approaches to environmental protection are still being debated.

1.1.2. HUMAN RIGHTS APPROACHES TO ENVIRONMENTAL PROTECTION

The 2011 Office of the High Commissioner on Human Rights (OHCHR) Report notes that "*human rights obligations and commitments have the potential to inform and strengthen international, regional and national policy-making in the area of environmental protection and promoting policy coherence, legitimacy and sustainable outcomes*".[44] There are three theoretical approaches:[45] (1) the environment as a "precondition to the enjoyment of human rights"; (2) human rights as "tools to address environmental issues, both procedurally and substantively"; (3) integrating human rights and the protection of the environment under the concept of sustainable development. However, it is questionable that there are limits to how far human rights law can be used to achieve environmental outcomes and how far, if at all, human rights law applies to transboundary or global environmental harm even if that harm impacts on the life, health, private life or property of individuals or communities.[46] Four popular human rights approaches to environmental protection below are also trying to link human rights protection and environmental protection.

---

44 OHCHR (2011). Analytical study on the relationship between human rights and the environment (OHCHR 2011 Report), published on 16 December 2011, UN Document, A/HRC/19/34, §2, www.ohchr.org/Documents/HRBodies/HRCouncil/RegularSession/Session19/A-HRC-19-34_en.pdf accessed 23 December 2013.

45 OHCHR (2011). Analytical study on the relationship between human rights and the environment (OHCHR 2011 Report), published on 16 December 2011, UN Document, A/HRC/19/34, §§6–9, www.ohchr.org/Documents/HRBodies/HRCouncil/RegularSession/Session19/A-HRC-19-34_en.pdf accessed 23 December 2013.

46 Boyle, A. & Boer, B. (2013). Human rights and the environment. In: the Thirteenth Informal ASEM (Asia-Europe Meeting) Seminar on Human Rights, Copenhagen, Denmark, 21–23 October 2013, http://asef.org/images/docs/13th%20Informal%20ASEM%20Seminar%20-%20Background%20paper%20%28FINAL%29.pdf accessed 1 November 2013, p. 10.

1.1.2.1. *Mobilising the Existing Rights*

Comparatively speaking, human rights protection was "born" earlier than environmental protection.[47] The existing rights at the international level are more comprehensive. The realisation of civil and political rights – including the right to life, expression, political participation, personal liberty, equality, and legal redress – goes a long way toward enabling concerned groups to voice their objection to environmental damage.[48] These rights could be regarded as one of the "preconditions for improving environmental protection", and conversely serious damage to the environment would lead to the arguments for human rights from the public. Take the right to participation as an example, to mobilise the "right to political participation" to the "right to environmental participation" or the "right to participation in environmental matters". While these civil and political rights may contribute to environmental protection principally through guarantees of process and participation, the second generation rights (economic, social and cultural rights) contribute mainly through substantive standards of human well-being.[49] For instance, the right to health may require legislation or policies to prevent environmental degradation; the right to education may raise environmental awareness for the public. The existing systems for implementing and monitoring second generation rights construe these rights rather narrowly, and continue to approach environmental questions only indirectly.[50]

This approach could be regarded as a first step to link human rights protection and environmental protection. However, some arguments on the insufficient linkages between them and inadequate means to interpret them at the national level are being debated.

1.1.2.2. *Reinterpreting the Existing Rights*

Existing rights must be reinterpreted with imagination in the context of environmental concerns which were not prevalent at the time the existing

---

47 According to the Danish Institute for Human Rights research on human rights timeline, 1215 is the year that the Magna Carta (Latin for "the Great Charter") comes into being in England as the first example of a document restricting the power of the king by law. Later, in 1679, the Habeas Corpus Act is passed, in 1689, the bill of rights related to various restrictions of the arbitrary exercise of power by the state. Detailed information see www.humanrights.dk/human+rights/history+and+documents/time+line accessed 24 December 2012.

48 Anderson, M.R. (1996). Human rights approaches to environmental protection: an overview. In: Boyle, A.E. & Anderson, M.R. (Eds.). *Human Rights Approach to Environmental Protection*. Oxford: Clarendon Press, p. 5.

49 Anderson, M.R. (1996). Human rights approaches to environmental protection: an overview. In: Boyle, A.E. & Anderson, M.R. (Eds.). *Human Rights Approach to Environmental Protection*. Oxford: Clarendon Press, p. 5.

50 Anderson, M.R. (1996). Human rights approaches to environmental protection: an overview. In: Boyle, A.E. & Anderson, M.R. (Eds.). *Human Rights Approach to Environmental Protection*. Oxford: Clarendon Press, p. 6.

rights were first formulated.[51] Some recent concepts show this tendency, such as "green economy" and "greening rights". The right to life, for instance, may be deemed to be infringed where the State fails to abate the emission of highly toxic products into supplies of drinking water; if enforcement bodies explicitly recognise such links, then environmental criteria may be incorporated overtly into the monitoring and enforcement of the right to life.[52] It is also interesting to note that, on the one hand, the right to property may be used to protect the environmental quality of land; on the other hand, the right to property could be used by private owners or collective owners to restrict protected areas conservation, which will be discussed in detail in this book later.

However, as Lauterpacht noted in 1949, "*codification which constitutes a record of the past rather than a creative use of the existing materials – legal and others – for the purpose of regulating the life of the community is a brake upon progress*".[53] Indeed, making explicit in a declaration or protocol the greening of existing human rights that has already taken place would add nothing and clarify little.[54] The question therefore is not how to reinterpret the existing human rights, but how much more a new approach would add.

1.1.2.3. A New Human Right: A Human Right to an Environment of a Certain Quality

A human right to an environment of a certain quality, more popularly known as "a right to an environment" (or "a right to a clean and healthy environment"), was created to push towards the effective conservation of natural resources and guarantee human rights (such as right to life) as well. The right to an environment was defined as "*Everyone has the right, individually or in association with others, to enjoy a healthy and ecologically balanced environment.*"[55] How

---

51 Anderson, M.R. (1996). Human rights approaches to environmental protection: an overview, In Boyle, A.E. & Anderson, M.R. (Eds.). *Human Rights Approach to Environmental Protection*. Oxford: Clarendon Press, p. 7.

52 Anderson, M.R. (1996). Human rights approaches to environmental protection: an overview. In: Boyle, A.E. & Anderson, M.R. (Eds.). *Human Rights Approach to Environmental Protection*. Oxford: Clarendon Press, p. 7.

53 UN (1949). Survey of international law in relation to the work of the international law Commission: preparatory work within the purview of Article 18, paragraph 1, of the international law Commission – memorandum submitted by the Secretary-General, GAOR A/CN.4/Rev., §§3–14, http://legal.un.org/ilc/documentation/english/a_cn4_1_rev1.pdf accessed 10 October 2013.

54 Boyle, A. (2012). Human rights and the environment: where next? *The European Journal of International Law*, 23(3), www.ejil.org/pdfs/23/3/2296.pdf accessed 10 October 2013, p. 66.

55 Article 1, Declaration of Bizkaia on the Right to the Environment, adopted by a group of international experts during a seminar promoted by the Provincial Council of Bizkaia and sponsored by UNESCO and the United Nations High Commissioner for Human Rights, at Bilbao (Portugal) on 12 February 1999, 30 C/INF.11, http://unesdoc.unesco.org/images/0011/001173/117321e.pdf accessed 23 December 2013, p. 4. Also see Pallemaerts, M. (2002). Introduction: human rights and environmental protection. In: Dejeant-Pons, M. &

can we give an appropriate definition to a "clean" and "healthy" environment? There is little international consensus on the correct terminology about "a healthy environment".[56] Scientists would need to establish environmental quality standards and threshold levels for polluting activities, which characterise a healthy environment.[57] In practice, the standards for a "clean" and "healthy" environment would vary quite significantly according to different situations in different regions. The most severe argument put forward against the approval of a distinct right to a healthy environment is based on its anthropocentricity.[58] Such a right implies that the protection of the environment is only for the benefit of humans[59] and does not pay enough attention to the environment and other species living on the earth.

Nevertheless, the discussions about the existence of a human right to an environment of a certain quality seem to be difficult to reach an end. It may be argued that existing rights, if fully realised, are so robust in themselves that proposals for new environmental rights are at best superfluous and at worst counter-productive.[60] In addition, how to interpret and implement a right to a clean and healthy environment may result in wide diversities of economic, policy, legal, social and cultural contexts, as different governments or organisations would pursue their own priorities and make their own value judgments. Furthermore, human rights treaties (with the exception of the African Convention on Human and People's Rights[61] and the Protocol of

---

Pallemaerts, M. (Eds.). *Human Rights and the Environment.* Strasbourg (France): Council of Europe Publishing, p. 118.

56 Boyle, A. & Boer, B. (2013). Human rights and the environment. In: the Thirteenth Informal ASEM (Asia-Europe Meeting) Seminar on Human Rights, Copenhagen, Denmark, 21–23 October 2013, http://asef.org/images/docs/13th%20Informal%20ASEM%20Seminar%20-%20Background%20paper%20%28FINAL%29.pdf accessed 1 November 2013, p. 16.

57 Atapattu, S. (2002). The right to a healthy life or the right to die polluted?: the emergence of a human right to a healthy environment under international law. *Tulane Environmental Law Journal*, 16(65), p. 111; Atapattu, S. (2004). The public health impact of global environmental problems and the role of international law. *American Journal of Law & Medicine*, 30 (2&3), p. 302.

58 Atapattu, S. (2002). The right to a healthy life or the right to die polluted?: the emergence of a human right to a healthy environment under international law. *Tulane Environmental Law Journal*, 16(65), p. 113.

59 Taylor, P.E. (1997). From environmental to ecological human rights: a new dynamic in international law? *Georgetown International Environmental Law Review*, 10(309), p. 351.

60 Anderson, M.R. (1996). Human rights approaches to environmental protection: an overview. In: Boyle, A.E. & Anderson, M.R. (Eds.). *Human Rights Approach to Environmental Protection.* Oxford: Clarendon Press, p. 4.

61 Article 24, African Charter on Human and Peoples' Rights (also known as the Banjul Charter), adopted on 27 June 1981, OAU Doc. CAB/LEG/67/3/Rev.5 (1981), reprinted in 21 ILM 58 (1982), www.achpr.org/files/instruments/achpr/banjul_charter.pdf accessed 12 December 2013. The Article 24 says "All peoples shall have the right to a general satisfactory environment favourable to their development."

San Salvador)[62] still do not explicitly guarantee a right to a clean and healthy environment. The Parliamentary Assembly of the Council of Europe had tried and failed twice before (in 1999 and 2003) to integrate a right to environment in the European Convention on Human Rights: in Recommendation 1885, the Parliamentary Assembly recalled its Recommendation 1614 (2003)[63] on the environment and human rights and its Recommendation 1431 (1999)[64] on future action to be taken by the Council of Europe in the field of environment protection, which both proposed adding an environmental component to the European Convention on Human Rights.[65] Therefore, there is uncertainty as to whether a human right related to the environment will ever be recognised.[66]

1.1.2.4. A Human Rights-Based Approach

According to what has been discussed, on the one hand, there is no acceptance of an explicit right to an environment of a certain quality in international human rights law and the international bill of human rights does not include any reference to environmental protection.[67] On the other hand, international environmental law does not allocate procedures of seeking redress comparable to those found in international human rights law.[68]

62 Article 11, Additional Protocol to the American Convention on Human Rights in the Area of Economic, Social and Cultural Rights ("Protocol of San Salvador"), adopted on 14 November 1988, OAS TS No. 69, reprinted in 28 ILM 156 (1989), www.oas.org/juridico/english/treaties/a-52.html accessed 12 December 2013. The Article 11 with header: "Right to a healthy environment" proclaims: " (1) Everyone shall have the right to live in a healthy environment and to have access to basic public services and (2) The States parties shall promote the protection, preservation and improvement of the environment".

63 Council of Europe, Environment and human rights, Parliamentary Assembly Recommendation 1614 (2003), http://assembly.coe.int/Main.asp?link=/Documents/AdoptedText/ta03/EREC1614.htm accessed 14 July 2014.

64 Council of Europe, Future action to be taken by the Council of Europe in the field of environment protection, Parliamentary Assembly Recommendation 1431 (1999), http://assembly.coe.int/Main.asp?link=/Documents/AdoptedText/ta99/EREC1431.htm accessed 14 July 2014.

65 Van de Venis, J. (2011). A human right to a clean and healthy environment: dream or reality in Europe? *Environmental Law Network International*, 1, www.elni.org/fileadmin/elni/dokumente/Archiv/2011/Heft_1/elni_issue_2011-01_van_de_Venis.pdf accessed 14 July 2014, pp. 27–35.

66 Boyle, A. (2012). Human rights and the environment: where next? *The European Journal of International Law*, 23(3), www.ejil.org/pdfs/23/3/2296.pdf accessed 10 October 2013, pp. 613–642.

67 Mowery, L.A. (2002). Earth rights, human rights: can international environmental human rights affect corporate accountability? *Fordham Environmental Law Journal*, 13(343); Taylor, P.E. (1997). From environmental to ecological human rights: a new dynamic in international law?. *Georgetown International Environmental Law Review*, 10 (309); Atapattu, S. (2002). The right to a healthy life or the right to die polluted?: the emergence of a human right to a healthy environment under international law. *Tulane Environmental Law Journal*, 16(65), p. 111.

68 Atapattu, S. (2004). The public health impact of global environmental problems and the role of international law. *American Journal of Law & Medicine*, 30(2&3), p. 298.

The merits of any proposed approach on human rights protection and environmental protection depend on how far an approach deals with fundamental problems and not only addresses what we already know. All the proposed approaches discussed above are aimed at improving protection of human rights and increasing the effectiveness of environmental protection. Despite unsolved problems and an uncertain developmental tendency between human rights protection and environmental protection, the existing linkages between human rights protection and environmental protection could serve as a basis for the establishment of a human rights-based approach to protect the environment. However, there is little literature building these two topics together by a human rights-based approach. Therefore, the theory of a human rights-based approach to conservation together with its added values, as one of important goals in this book, will be explored in detail in the next chapter.

1.1.3. THE VALUE OF PROTECTED AREAS

In the environmental sphere, biodiversity, the natural biotic capital of the earth, is fundamental to the fulfilment of human needs and vital for the survival of this planet.[69] Biodiversity benefits people through more than just its contribution to material welfare and livelihoods.[70] It contributes to security, social relations, health and freedom of choices and actions.[71] Addressing biodiversity loss and poverty are international societal and political goals.[72] The majority of the world's poor live in rural areas[73] where they depend disproportionately on biodiversity for their survival.[74] Therefore, actions to increase income generation from biodiversity can provide incentives for conservation but can also lead to

---

69 Government of India Ministry of Environment and Forests. (2008). National Biodiversity Action Plan. http://envfor.nic.in/downloads/public-information/NBAP-iyb.pdf accessed 8 October 2012.

70 Millennium Ecosystem Assessment. (2005). *Ecosystems and Human Well-being: Biodiversity Synthesis*. Washington D.C.: World Resources Institute. www.maweb.org/documents/document.354.aspx.pdf accessed 22 January 2014, p. 1.

71 Millennium Ecosystem Assessment. (2005). *Ecosystems and Human Well-being: Biodiversity Synthesis*. Washington D.C.: World Resources Institute. www.maweb.org/documents/document.354.aspx.pdf accessed 22 January 2014, p. 1.

72 Sachs, J.D., *et al.* (2009). Biodiversity conservation and the millennium development goals. *Science*, 325, p. 1502. Roe, D. (Ed.) (2010). *Linking Biodiversity Conservation And Poverty Reduction: A State Of Knowledge Review*. CBD Technical Series No. 44. Montreal: Secretariat of the Convention on Biological Diversity, www.cbd.int/doc/publications/cbd-ts-55-en.pdf accessed 20 January 2014.

73 International Fund for Agricultural Development (2010). *Rural Poverty Report 2011*. Rome: International Fund for Agricultural Development.

74 Belcher, B. (2013). Forests, poverty and conservation: an overview of the issues. In: Roe, D., Elliott, J., Sandbrook, C. & Walpole, M. (Eds.). *Biodiversity Conservation and Poverty Alleviation: Exploring the Evidence for a Link*. Chichester (UK): John Wiley & Sons, pp. 87–99.

degradation without the appropriate enabling environment, which involves appropriate rights to the resources, access to information and stakeholder involvement.[75]

As biodiversity becomes rarer and increasingly precious, protected areas – the jewel ecosystems, species, genetic diversity and associated values that societies agree to conserve – are becoming an ever more important focus of interest and concern, delight and conflict.[76] Protected areas are one of the most important land and sea uses on Earth. On a global scale, up to the end of 2011, there are more than 130,709 protected land and marine sites,[77] these areas cover almost 24.2 million square kilometres.[78] Global land protection is estimated to reach 15–29% of the Earth's surface by 2030.[79] A comprehensive, effectively managed and ecologically representative global network of protected areas is crucial to reducing the rate of biodiversity loss.[80] The importance of protected areas is emphasised by international conventions, such as the CBD,[81] the World Heritage Convention (WHC),[82] and the Ramsar Convention.[83] It is also confirmed by international programmes, for instance, the United Nations Educational, Scientific and Cultural Organization (UNESCO)'s Man and the Biosphere (MAB) Programme.[84] All these agreements and programmes are the backbone for the

---

75 Millennium Ecosystem Assessment. (2005). *Ecosystems and Human Well-being: Biodiversity Synthesis*. Washington D.C.: World Resources Institute. www.maweb.org/documents/document.354.aspx.pdf accessed 22 January 2014, p. 12.

76 Borrini-Feyerabend, G., Dudley, N., Jaeger, T., Lassen, B., Broome, N.P., Phillips, A. & Sandwith, T. (2013). *Governance of Protected Areas: from Understanding to Action*. Best Practice Protected Area Guidelines Series No. 20. Gland (Switzerland): IUCN, https://cmsdata.iucn.org/downloads/iucn_governance_1109_1.pdf accessed 26 September 2013, p. xii.

77 World Databases on Protected Areas (WDPA) (2012). Statistics. www.wdpa.org/Statistics.aspx accessed 28 January 2014.

78 World Databases on Protected Areas (WDPA) (2012). Statistics. www.wdpa.org/Statistics.aspx accessed 28 January 2014.

79 McDonald, R.I. & Boucher, T.M. (2011). Global development and the future of the protected area strategy. *Biological Conservation*, 144, pp. 383–392.

80 UNDP. Ecosystems and biodiversity. http://web.undp.org/biodiversity/protected_areas.shtml accessed 5 March 2012.

81 Convention on Biological Diversity (CBD), opened for signature on 5 June 1992 and entered into force on 29 December 1993, [1993] ATS 32/1760 UNTS 79/31 ILM 818 (1992), www.cbd.int/ accessed 8 June 2012.

82 Convention Concerning the Protection of the World Cultural and Natural Heritage (World Heritage Convention), adopted on 16 November 1972 and entered into force on 17 December 1975, 11 ILM (1972) 1358, http://portal.unesco.org/en/ev.php-URL_ID=13055&URL_DO=DO_TOPIC&URL_SECTION=201.htm accessed 8 June 2012.

83 Convention on Wetlands of International Importance (Ramsar Convention), adopted on 2 February 1971 and entered into force on 21 December 1975, amended by the Paris Protocol on 3 December 1982, 11 ILM (1972) 963, www.ramsar.org/cda/en/ramsar-documents-texts/main/ramsar/1-31-38_4000_0__ accessed 8 June 2012.

84 UNESCO (United Nations Educational, Scientific and Cultural Organization)'s Man and the Biosphere Programme, launched in 1971, is an intergovernmental Scientific Programme that aims to establish a scientific basis for the improvement of relationship between people and their environment, www.unesco.org/new/en/natural-sciences/environment/ecological-sciences/man-and-biosphere-programme/ accessed 8 June 2012.

international policy on the establishment and management of protected areas for biodiversity conservation and the sustainable use of natural and cultural resources.[85]

Specifically, protected areas have various values. Firstly, within these areas, genetic diversity is permitted to evolve in response to natural selection pressures.[86] Well-managed protected areas support healthy ecosystems that in turn support healthy people.[87] Protected areas directly and indirectly provide water, food, clothes, shelter, medicines to human beings. Secondly, protected areas provide for life's diversity in safeguarding species and habitats.[88] Each species makes some contributions to the extraordinary variety of living creatures on Earth. Thirdly, protected areas make some contribution on climate change adaptation and mitigation. By conserving unbroken blocks of intact habitat, protected areas increase the ecosystems' resilience to climate change since ecosystems with high biodiversity and intact structural components recover more easily from climatic disturbances.[89] Fourth, protected areas play an important role in reducing vulnerability of communities to disasters, reducing their physical exposure to natural hazards and providing them with livelihood resources to withstand and recover from crises.[90] Fifth, protected areas are the setting for providing some of life's most joyous moments.[91] Protected areas provide the best opportunities for engaging in activities such as sightseeing, walking, camping, canoeing, bird watching, photography, rock

---

85 Task Force on Economic Benefits of Protected Areas of the World Commission on Protected Areas (WCPA) of IUCN, in collaboration with the Economics Service Unit of IUCN. (1998). *Economic Values of Protected Areas: Guidelines for Protected Areas Managers.* Gland (Switzerland): IUCN, https://portals.iucn.org/library/efiles/edocs/PAG-002.pdf accessed 26 January 2014, p. 3.

86 Secretariat of the Convention on Biological Diversity. (2008). Protected areas in today's world: their values and benefits for the welfare of the planet. Technical Series No. 36, Montreal, https://www.cbd.int/doc/publications/cbd-ts-36-en.pdf accessed 20 January 2014, p. 1.

87 Mulongoy, K.J. & Gidda, S.B. (2008). *The Value of Nature: Economic, Cultural and Social Benefits of Protected Areas.* Montreal: Secretariat of the Conservation on Biological Diversity, https://www.cbd.int/doc/publications/cbd-value-nature-en.pdf accessed 21 August 2013.

88 Secretariat of the Convention on Biological Diversity. (2008). Protected areas in today's world: their values and benefits for the welfare of the planet. Technical Series No. 36, Montreal, https://www.cbd.int/doc/publications/cbd-ts-36-en.pdf accessed 20 January 2014, p. 1.

89 Mulongoy, K.J. & Gidda, S.B. (2008). *The Value of Nature: Economic, Cultural and Social Benefits of Protected Areas.* Montreal: Secretariat of the Conservation on Biological Diversity, https://www.cbd.int/doc/publications/cbd-value-nature-en.pdf accessed 21 August 2013.

90 Mulongoy, K.J. & Gidda, S.B. (2008). *The Value of Nature: Economic, Cultural and Social Benefits of Protected Areas.* Montreal: Secretariat of the Conservation on Biological Diversity, https://www.cbd.int/doc/publications/cbd-value-nature-en.pdf accessed 21 August 2013.

91 Secretariat of the Convention on Biological Diversity. (2008). Protected areas in today's world: their values and benefits for the welfare of the planet. Technical Series No. 36, Montreal, https://www.cbd.int/doc/publications/cbd-ts-36-en.pdf accessed 20 January 2014, p. 2.

climbing and many others.[92] These joyous experiences become embedded as a memorable moment and for many, they can be a life-transforming event.[93] Sixth, protected areas often provide ideal conditions for scientific research, both in terms of the topic of study and the surrounding environment, and often maintain perfect and undisturbed places of study.[94] Protected areas feature some of the best and most significant examples of the Earth's geological past, as well as currently active geomorphological processes.[95] For example, scientific research within the protected areas of the Arctic is highly regarded in terms of the problems of climate change and long-range air pollutants.[96] Seventh, protected areas could make a great contribution on poverty reduction, for the reason that "there are no economies without environments, but there are environments without economies."[97] They provide for life's jobs and livelihoods as a traditional destination for the global tourism industry.[98] At the same time these areas protect resources of immense economic value such as water and fisheries.[99] The table below addresses the total economic values of protected areas.

---

92 Lockwood, M., Kothari, A. & Worboys, G. (Eds.) (2006). *Managing Protected Areas: a Global Guide*. London: Earthscan, p. 107.

93 Secretariat of the Convention on Biological Diversity. (2008). Protected areas in today's world: their values and benefits for the welfare of the planet. Technical Series No. 36, Montreal, https://www.cbd.int/doc/publications/cbd-ts-36-en.pdf accessed 20 January 2014, p. 2.

94 Gillespie, A. (2011). *Conservation, Biodiversity and International Law*. Cheltenham (UK) and Northampton (USA): Edward Elgar Publishing, p. 123.

95 Lockwood, M., Kothari, A. & Worboys, G. (Eds.) (2006). *Managing Protected Areas: a Global Guide*. London: Earthscan, p. 108.

96 Conservation of Arctic Flora and Fauna. (2002). *Protected Areas of the Arctic: Conserving a Full Range of Values*. Canada: CAFF(Conservation of Arctic Flora and Fauna) Secretariat, Department of Foreign Affairs, pp. 21–22.

97 European Communities. (2008). TEEB (The Economics of Ecosystems & Biodiversity): An Interim Report. www.teebweb.org/media/2008/05/TEEB-Interim-Report_English.pdf accessed 27 January 2014, p. 13.

98 Secretariat of the Convention on Biological Diversity. (2008). Protected areas in today's world: their values and benefits for the welfare of the planet. Technical Series No. 36, Montreal, https://www.cbd.int/doc/publications/cbd-ts-36-en.pdf accessed 20 January 2014, p. 1. For instance, Australian top eight national parks were estimated to be bringing in 2 (AUD) billion per year with about a quarter of this sum coming from the Great Barrier Reef. See IUCN. (2002). *Sustainable Tourism in Protected Areas: Guidelines for Planning and Management*. Gland: IUCN. p. 25. Another example is Yosemite in the United States, it generates approximately 1.3 (USD) billion per year. See Gillespie, A. (2011). *Conservation, Biodiversity and International Law*. Cheltenham (UK) and Northampton (USA): Edward Elgar, p. 119.

99 Secretariat of the Convention on Biological Diversity. (2008). Protected areas in today's world: their values and benefits for the welfare of the planet. Technical Series No. 36, Montreal, https://www.cbd.int/doc/publications/cbd-ts-36-en.pdf accessed 20 January 2014, p. 1.

Table 1. Total economic values of protected areas[100]

Use values			Non-use values	
Direct use value	**Indirect use value**	**Option value**	**Bequest values**	**Existence values**
Recreation	Ecosystem services	Future information	Use and non-use Values for legacy	Biodiversity
Sustainable Harvesting	Climate stabilisation	Future uses (indirect and direct)		Ritual or spiritual values
Wildlife harvesting	Flood Control			Culture, heritage
Fuel-wood	Ground-water recharge			Community values
Grazing	Carbon sequestration			Landscape
Agriculture	Habitat			
Gene	Nutrient retention			
Education	Natural disaster prevention			
Research	Watershed protection Natural services			

Apart from these tremendous cultural, ecological, spiritual, educational and scientific values that are being better recognised than before, protected areas also benefit users at different scales, from local people who depend on particular species for their livelihood, to nations that depend on abundant freshwater, to the global community that depends on nature's capacity to regulate climate.[101] In a word, protected areas are a vital part of securing human prosperity and quality of life.[102]

100 Barbier, E.B., Acreman, M.C. & Knowler, D. (1997). *Economic Valuation of Wetlands: A Guide for Policy Makers and Planners.* Gland (Switzerland): Ramsar Convention Bureau, www.ramsar.org/pdf/lib/lib_valuation_e.pdf accessed 13 December 2013; Barbier, E.B. (1989). *The Economic Value of Ecosystems: 1 – Tropical Wetlands.* LEEC Gatekeeper Series 89–02. London: London Environmental Economics Centre; Barbier, E.B. (1993). Valuing tropical wetland benefits: economic methodologies and applications. *Geographical Journal,* 1(59), pp. 22–32; Scodari, P.F. (1990). *Wetlands Protection: the Role of Economics.* Washington D.C.: Environmental Law Institute Monograph.

101 Brandom, K. & Bruner, A. (2008). Local benefits of protected areas: perspectives and experiences of conservation International. In: Protected Areas in Today's World: Their Values and Benefits for the Welfare of the Planet. Technical Series No. 36, Montreal: Secretariat of the Convention on Biological Diversity, https://www.cbd.int/doc/publications/cbd-ts-36-en.pdf accessed 20 January 2014, p. 29.

102 Lockwood, M., Kothari, A. & Worboys, G. (Eds.) (2006). *Managing Protected Areas: a Global Guide.* London: Earthscan, p. 41.

1.1.4. RELATIONSHIP BETWEEN HUMAN RIGHTS PROTECTION AND PROTECTED AREAS CONSERVATION

1.1.4.1. Relationship Between Human Rights Protection and Protected Areas Conservation in General

As the world's population grows and the demands for natural resources increase, protected areas become both more important and more threatened.[103] Whether or not these areas are well protected – and many are not – they increasingly face external threats that are difficult or impossible to control.[104] These include climate change, development beyond their boundaries, water limitations and pollution, invasive species, and interrupted wildlife migration corridors.[105] Besides these uncontrollable factors, the "paper park" problem remains, whereby geographic areas may be labelled as some category of protected areas but they do not achieve the promised form of management,[106] for the reasons that it lacks of funding, experts, effectively monitoring and evaluations and so on. More importantly, reconciling economic development with ecological sustainability is a global challenge.[107] In some cases, the declaration of protected areas has actually been a strategy in order to allow the entrance of mining and oil companies without any interference from human populations.[108] Besides these, some dam construction, highway construction, general industrial development

103 Secretariat of the Convention on Biological Diversity. (2008). Protected areas in today's world: their values and benefits for the welfare of the planet. Technical Series No. 36, Montreal, https://www.cbd.int/doc/publications/cbd-ts-36-en.pdf accessed 20 January 2014, p. 2.

104 Secretariat of the Convention on Biological Diversity. (2008). Protected areas in today's world: their values and benefits for the welfare of the planet. Technical Series No. 36, Montreal, https://www.cbd.int/doc/publications/cbd-ts-36-en.pdf accessed 20 January 2014, p. 2.

105 Secretariat of the Convention on Biological Diversity. (2008). Protected areas in today's world: their values and benefits for the welfare of the planet. Technical Series No. 36, Montreal, https://www.cbd.int/doc/publications/cbd-ts-36-en.pdf accessed 20 January 2014, p. 2; Gillespie, A. (2007). *Protected Areas and International Environmental Law.* Leiden (Netherland): Martinus Nijhoff Publishers, pp. 183–206.

106 Millennium Ecosystem Assessment. (2005). *Ecosystems and Human Well-being: Biodiversity Synthesis.* Washington D.C.: World Resources Institute, www.maweb.org/documents/document.354.aspx.pdf accessed 22 January 2014, p. 70.

107 Adams, W.M., Aveling, R., Brockington, D., Dickson, B., Elliott, J., Hutton, J., Roe, D., Vira, B. & Wolmer, W. (2004). Biodiversity conservation and the eradication of poverty. *Science* (306), pp. 1146–1149; Tallis, H., Kareiva, P., Marvier, M. & Chang, A. (2008). An ecosystem services framework to support both practical conservation and economic development. *Proceedings of National Academy of Sciences of the United States of America*, 105, pp. 9457–9464; Barrett, C.B., Travis, A.J. & Dasgupta, P. (2011). On biodiversity conservation and poverty traps. *Proceedings of National Academy of Sciences of the United States of America*, 108, pp. 3907–13912.

108 Fonseca, H. (2004). Protected areas: protected against whom? Oilwatch & World Rain-forest Movement, www.forestpeoples.org/topics/convention-biological-diversity-cbd/publication/2011/protected-areas-protected-against-whom accessed 23 January 2014, p. 27.

and other economic activities also threaten the protected areas conservation.[109] Nowadays, these economic activities are regarded as a major threat to protected areas conservation. However, all these costs were borne by local people and communities in or near protected areas, which are the most relevant parties (rights-holders). The negative effect on the degradation of protected areas affects the whole society and specifically affects local people and communities, who very often depend on the protected areas for their survival.

From the perspective of local people and communities, indigenous peoples inhabit approximately 85% of areas designated for biodiversity conservation worldwide.[110] Although local people and communities normally benefit from protected areas, they sometimes are affected negatively by the establishment of protected areas. For instance, in some cases local people were displaced because of protected areas. There is no consensus on the number of people that have been displaced because of protected areas establishment and management[111] but examples span across Asia, Africa and Latin America. It has been estimated that approximately 50% of all protected areas have been established on lands traditionally occupied or used by indigenous peoples.[112] In Latin America even 80% of protected areas have been superimposed on indigenous territories.[113] Many human settlements have been displaced from their ancestral lands, which have been turned into national parks.[114] In some countries, communities have usage rights, but have lost their territorial rights, since protected areas usually belong to the State.[115] In fact, besides indigenous peoples, non-indigenous

---

109 Gillespie, A. (2007). *Protected Areas and International Environmental Law*. Leiden (Netherland): Martinus Nijhoff Publishers, pp. 206–226.

110 Schmidt, P.M. & Peterson, M.J. (2009). Biodiversity conservation and indigenous land management in the era of self-determination. *Conservation Biology*, 23(6), 1458. DOI: 10.1111/j.1523-1739.2009.01262.x.

111 Adams, M.W. & Hutton, J. (2007). People, parks and poverty: political ecology and biodiversity conservation. *Conservation and Society*, 5(2), pp. 147–183.

112 Desmet, E. (2011). *Indigenous Rights Entwined with Nature Conservation*. Antwerp: Intersentia, p. 14.

113 Amend, S. & Amend, T. (Eds.) (1995). *National Parks without People? The South American Experience*. Quito, Ecuador: IUCN.

114 Fonseca, H. (2004). Protected areas: protected against whom? Oilwatch & World Rain-forest Movement, www.forestpeoples.org/topics/convention-biological-diversity-cbd/publication/2011/protected-areas-protected-against-whom accessed 23 January 2014, p. 27. The establishment of Mantadia National Park in Madagascar is also an example of local people bearing significant costs because of a protected area, and therefore being a potential threat to it. See Task Force on Economic Benefits of Protected Areas of the World Commission on Protected Areas (WCPA) of IUCN, in collaboration with the Economics Service Unit of IUCN (1998). *Economic Values of Protected Areas: Guidelines for Protected Areas Managers*. Gland (Switzerland): IUCN, https://portals.iucn.org/library/efiles/edocs/PAG-002.pdf accessed 26 January 2014, p. 27.

115 Fonseca, H. (2004). Protected areas: protected against whom? Oilwatch & World Rain-forest Movement, www.forestpeoples.org/topics/convention-biological-diversity-cbd/publication/2011/protected-areas-protected-against-whom accessed 23 January 2014, p. 27.

peoples who live in or nearby a specific territory within or adjacent to an established or proposed protected area can also be affected.

There is also widespread recognition that protected areas which cause harm or inconvenience to local groups will be threatened by these groups' non-cooperation or outright resistance.[116] Such non-cooperation or resistance would even destroy protected areas. Indeed, the potential conflicts regarding human rights protection and protected areas conservation for local groups would be difficult to resolve, especially in some developing countries.

Furthermore, it is recognised internationally that local people and communities are not yet sufficiently engaged in the planning of national protected area systems in which they may be affected, or in the identification and management of protected areas.[117] Disenfranchised traditional, local people and communities may actively work against protected areas which do not reflect their interests, or fail to deliver on the promises and/or expectations raised, when the area was given protected status.[118] This problem has appeared within the World Heritage Convention, where between 1986 and 2004, four protected areas were reported to the Committee for the reason that the protected areas were being threatened due to problems with local communities.[119]

What is more, economic valuation of protected areas is a means to an end – better and more informed and balanced decision-making.[120] Unfortunately, better understanding and more accurate quantification of the economic benefits of protected areas is still weakly reflected in both conservation investments, and in the policies, markets and prices which influence the trade-offs and decisions that public policy-makers, local communities, landholders and resource users face when considering protected areas.[121] In fact, local people and communities have been excluded from the protected areas, let alone some reasonable benefit-sharing from protected areas management. For example, in the mid-1990s, less

116 Schmidt-Soltan, K. & Brockington, D. (2004). The social impacts of protected areas. In: The First Global Workshop of World Conservation Congress, Bangkok, 20 November 2004, www.social-impact-of-conservation.net/ accessed 18 August 2011.

117 World Parks Congress (WPC) (2003). Durban, Accord: Action Plan, adopted at the fifth IUCN World Parks Congress, Durban, South Africa, p. 228.

118 Gillespie, A. (2007). *Protected Areas and International Environmental Law.* Leiden (Netherland): Martinus Nijhoff Publishers, pp. 168–169.

119 Gillespie, A. (2007). *Protected Areas and International Environmental Law.* Leiden (Netherland): Martinus Nijhoff Publishers, p. 169.

120 Secretariat of the Convention on Biological Diversity. (2008). Protected areas in today's world: their values and benefits for the welfare of the planet. Technical Series No. 36, Montreal, https://www.cbd.int/doc/publications/cbd-ts-36-en.pdf accessed 20 January 2014, p. 15.

121 Secretariat of the Convention on Biological Diversity. (2008). Protected areas in today's world: their values and benefits for the welfare of the planet. Technical Series No. 36, Montreal, https://www.cbd.int/doc/publications/cbd-ts-36-en.pdf accessed 20 January 2014, p. 15.

than 6% of the tourist income generated at some key Costa Rican national parks accrued to the local communities.[122]

Nevertheless, from the perspective of human rights, the principles of at least "do no harm"[123] and respect for human rights must be observed – local people and communities should not be worse off than what they are already as a result of a conservation initiative.[124] From the perspective of protected areas, protected areas conservation will have higher chances of success if the conservation is supported by local people and communities. As also indicated above, protected areas could strive their potential various values to contribute to poverty reduction at the local level. In this way, local people and communities could also be stimulated their potential roles in preventing illegal activities and conserving protected areas.

A main solution would be that engaging local communities (often economically poor people) in the management of protected areas in which they have traditionally lived, addresses not only an important dimension of poverty but also often provides an effective means of improving protected areas management.[125] In recent decades, there has been a tendency for governments to decentralise responsibilities for protected areas and become more inclusive when identifying priorities, objectives and approaches for natural resources in general and protected areas in particular,[126] although this varies greatly between countries.

---

122 Neumann, R. (1998). *Imposing Wilderness: Struggles over Livelihood and Nature Preservation in Africa*. Berkeley: University of California Press; Weladji, R. (2003). Conflict between people and protected areas. *Oryx*, 37(1), pp. 72–79; Gillingham, S. (2003). People and protected areas: a case study of local perceptions of wildlife, crop damage and conflict, *Oryx*, 37(3), pp. 316–325; Adams, W. (2001). If community conservation is the answer in Africa, what is the question? *Oryx*, 35(3), pp. 193–200; IUCN. (2002). *Sustainable Tourism in Protected Areas: Guidelines for Planning and Management*. Gland (Switzerland): IUCN, p. 25.

123 One of the desired outcomes of protected areas should be to improve or at minimum "do no harm" to the livelihoods of local people living near the protected area. See IUCN World Parks Congress. (2003). https://www.iucn.org/about/work/programmes/gpap_home/gpap_events/gpap_wpc/copy_of_wcpa_wpc_31082012_1316/ accessed 18 August 2011.

124 Scherl, L.M. (2006). Social justice and human rights in conservation: an ethical consideration for future policies and actions. In: IUCN. *Policy Matters – Poverty, Wealth and Conservation*. No. 14, the IUCN Commission on Environmental, Economic and Social Policy (CEESP), pp. 88–92. Also addressing this issue is at the core of a global taskforce on Protected Areas, Equity and Livelihoods of two IUCN Commissions (World Commission on Protected Areas and Commission on Environment, Economics and Social Policy).

125 Secretariat of the Convention on Biological Diversity. (2008). Protected areas in today's world: their values and benefits for the welfare of the planet. Technical Series No. 36, Montreal, https://www.cbd.int/doc/publications/cbd-ts-36-en.pdf accessed 20 January 2014, p. 27.

126 See De Cosse, P. J., Thompson, P. M., Ahmad, I.U., Sharma, R.A. & Mazumder, A.H. (2012). *Protected Area Co-management Where People and Poverty Intersect – Lessons from Nishorgo in Bangladesh*. Bangladesh: United States Agency for International Development. For a detailed analysis of this process for a specific country (Bangladesh). For more general views and examples see: Borrini-Feyerabend, G. (1996). *Collaborative Management of Protected Areas, Tailoring the Approach to the Context*, Gland (Switzerland): IUCN; Borrini-Feyerabend, G., Kothari, A. & Oviedo, G. (2004). *Indigenous and Local Communities and*

1.1.4.2. Relationship Between Human Rights Protection and Protected Areas Conservation in China

On the one hand, it is estimated that approximately two thirds of the world's indigenous peoples are living in Asia, with the majority in India (80–100 million), followed by China (60–80 million) and Indonesia (50–70 million).[127] The real situation in China is more complicated, the most relevant and vulnerable groups in the protected areas establishment and management are mixed groups, normally including "indigenous peoples", minority peoples[128] and majority peoples, even though the term of "indigenous peoples" is not recognised by the Chinese government.[129] China prefer to use the term ethnic minorities when referring to culturally, linguistically and ethnically divergent groups living within the boundaries of the state as the term recognises their difference, whilst simultaneously reinforcing the notion that they are national citizens within one unified territorial nation state.[130] In contrast, the concept of indigenous people has a strong political resonance which actively emphasises aspects of political mobilisation and organisation.[131] There is no official statistic to directly indicate how many people are affected in a positive or negative way by protected areas establishment and conservation in China. The real population

---

Protected Areas: Towards Equity and Enhanced Conservation. IUCN Best Practice Guidelines for Protected Area Series No. 11. Gland (Switzerland): IUCN; Lockwood, M., Kothari, A. & Worboys, G. (Eds.) (2006). *Managing Protected Areas: a Global Guide*. London: Earthscan; Kothari, A. (2006). Protected areas and people: the future of the past. *Parks*, 17(2), pp. 23–34; Lausche, B. (2011). *Guidelines for Protected Area Legislation*, Gland (Switzerland): IUCN.

127 Feiring, B. (2013). Indigenous peoples' rights to lands, territories and resources, published in May 2013, www.landcoalition.org/sites/default/files/DraftILCIndigenousPeoplesPeerReview.pdf accessed 3 August 2013.

128 Officially, besides the Han Chinese majority, the government recognises 55 ethnic minority peoples within its borders. According to China's sixth national census of 2010, the population of ethnic minorities is 113,792,211 persons, or 8.49% of the country's total population. IWGIA (International Work Group for Indigenous Affairs) (2011). Update 2011 – China. www.iwgia.org/regions/asia/china/859-update-2011-china accessed 16 May 2014.

129 The Chinese government does not agree to its concepts and definition as accepted in international fora. The official terminology and preferred usage is "ethnic minorities" or "minority peoples". IWGIA (International Work Group for Indigenous Affairs). Country profile: China. The concept of indigenous peoples in Asia – a resource book/country profiles, www.iwgia.org/images/stories/sections/regions/asia/documents/short-country-profiles/china.pdf accessed 16 May 2014, p. 358.

130 Chaudhry, P. (2012). Ethnic minority development in China and ASEAN countries. In: the sixth China – ASEAN Forum on Social Development and Poverty Reduction in 2012. UNDP & IPRCC. www.cn.undp.org/content/dam/china/docs/Publications/UNDP-CH-HD-Publications-Ethnic-Minority-Development-in-China-and-ASEAN-countries.pdf accessed 20 May 2014, p. 3.

131 Chaudhry, P. (2012). Ethnic minority development in China and ASEAN countries. In: the sixth China – ASEAN Forum on Social Development and Poverty Reduction in 2012. UNDP & IPRCC. www.cn.undp.org/content/dam/china/docs/Publications/UNDP-CH-HD-Publications-Ethnic-Minority-Development-in-China-and-ASEAN-countries.pdf accessed 20 May 2014, p. 3.

in practice is more than the "indigenous peoples" in China (60–80 million) indicated above.

On the other hand, establishing protected areas is the main strategy used for biodiversity conservation in China. The number and total size of protected areas are increasingly growing. From 1995 to the end of 2014, the number of protected areas increased from 799 to 2,729 and the area protected increased from 71.85 million hectares to more than 149 million hectares.[132] The relationship between official protected areas and the people living in or nearby these areas has often fraught with tension and controversy.[133]

1.1.4.2.1. Problems in Protected Areas Conservation in China

Beginning in 1956, China has built a large protected areas system, but has struggled to implement effective management.[134] There remain ongoing problems with administrative authority, unclear regulations, inadequate funding, inappropriate development within protected areas, a lack of professional capacity and more.[135] According to the recommended framework for "Protected Area Law of China" drafted by the Nature Conservation Legislation Research Group[136] on 14 September 2012, there are some main problems concerning protected areas conservation.[137] Firstly, conservation objectives, degrees

---

132 State Environmental Protection Bureau (1996). *National Environmental Statistics of China in 1995.* Beijing: State Environmental Protection Bureau; Ministry of Environmental Protection (MEP) (2011). *Report of Environmental Conditions of China in 2010.* Beijing: Ministry of Environmental Protection. Also see Wu, R.D. (2013). Review of Chinese nature reserves data in the WDPA. In: National Workshop in China. www.unep-wcmc.org/medialibrary/2013/02/19/2aa7df96/Review%20of%20Chinese%20nature%20reserves%20data%20in%20the%20WDPA-%20Yunnan%20University.pdf; http://news.xinhuanet.com/politics/201506/08/c_1115542132.htm accessed 22 August 2015.

133 Desmet, E. (2011). *Indigenous Rights Entwined with Nature Conservation.* Antwerp: Intersentia, p. 14.

134 Zhou, D.Q. & Grumbine, R.E. (2011). National parks in China: experiments with protecting nature and human livelihoods in Yunnan province, Peoples' Republic of China (PRC). *Biological Conservation*, 144, p. 1314.

135 Zhou, D.Q. & Grumbine, R.E. (2011). National parks in China: experiments with protecting nature and human livelihoods in Yunnan province, Peoples' Republic of China (PRC). *Biological Conservation*, 144, p. 1314.

136 The Nature Conservation Legislation Research Group was organised by Yan Xie (解焱) from the Institute of Zoology in Chinese Academy of Sciences (中国科学院动物研究所) and consisted of more than fifty experts in law, biology and other relevant aspects from Universities, NGOs, local governments and so on. Based on examining the existing legal and policy system regarding protected areas, investigating several protected areas in different regions in China, interviewing some experts and local people and other practical works on protected areas, this group wrote the recommended framework for "Protected Areas Law of China" and submitted to the National People's Congress as a proposal. A part of the name list for the experts can be found on http://blog.sina.com.cn/s/blog_7648860901013ugt.html accessed 14 December 2013.

137 The following problems were summarised by Nature Conservation Legislation Research Group. (2012). The recommended framework for "protected area law of China. Issued on 14 September 2012. The purpose of the recommended framework is suggested to develop the

of conservation attention, and management quality vary between different departments. Cooperation between these departments has hardly been achieved. The distribution pattern of protected areas is seriously imbalanced, the connectivity between protected areas is seriously deficient, and the national conservation goals are hardly achieved. Secondly, conservation management in protected areas in general is too weak to prohibit illegal or inappropriate activities that threaten conservation objectives in protected areas. Thirdly, inspection on conservation management units for many protected areas has been very weak, the scientificity and performance of conservation management units did not receive timely and objective assessment as well as rewards and punishments. Fourth, either for conservation or development projects, the communities within and around protected areas have very low involvement and satisfaction. Fifth, there is a lack of operational funds for conservation management in many protected areas. Sixth, nature conservation is isolated from the society.

Under these complicated main problems on protected areas conservation in China, the primary causes could be respectively summarised as:[138] (1) different departments for protected areas conservation lack unified management standards, inspection mechanisms and effective cross-departmental information sharing and exchange mechanism; (2) there is a serious lack of funding for conservation and the enforcement regulation to operate; (3) there is a lack of assessment mechanisms of performance and effective social inspection mechanisms and channels; (4) the externally-led projects of conservation reduce the enthusiasm of local people's participation, low degree of transparency of conservation information has made it hard for local people to get involved in, and what is more, local people cannot fairly share benefits arising from the protection; (5) there is a lack of long-term and stable funding mechanisms for conservation management in protected areas, the business income relied on protected areas have not paid back to the conservation management of protected areas, and more importantly, there is a lack clear and transparent financial management mechanisms; and (6) the role of the public has not been stimulated with regards to protected areas conservation. It is obvious to see that among these problems and causes, how to provide enough funding for protected areas conservation and how to stimulate the potential roles of local people and communities in protected areas conservation are two key issues.

"Protected Area Law of China" for strengthening the integration (coordination) management of different types of protected areas, promoting and building a regulatory framework for the management categories, in order to maintain ecosystem services, protect natural resources and biodiversity, keep ecological balance and promote community development in protected areas. www.unep-wcmc.org/medialibrary/2012/10/03/f6c87f81/Main%20recommendations%20to%20PA%20Law%20of%20China-en.pdf accessed 20 January 2014.

138 The following causes were summarised by the Nature Conservation Legislation Research Group. (2012). The recommended framework for "protected area law of China. Issued on 14 September 2012. www.unep-wcmc.org/medialibrary/2012/10/03/f6c87f81/Main%20recommendations%20to%20PA%20Law%20of%20China-en.pdf accessed 20 January 2014.

As Tyler has pointed out, the three development stages of law are compliance (traditional situation); cooperation (present situation) and engagement (future goal).[139] Local people and communities are regarded as the most relevant parties in the establishment and management of protected areas. In spite of the problems and difficulties above, their rights are at the heart of the "core values" to be evaluated and judged in a society. Therefore, the legal empowerment and engagement of local people and communities will ultimately help to establish the transparency and effective assessment and inspection mechanisms and promote the relevant regulation enforcement, and more importantly help to put the various values of protected areas into reality, including their huge potential economic value. And then these values from protected areas could complement the funding sources to promote protected areas conservation and stimulate the roles of local people and communities, even from the public, in protected areas conservation. In this way, protected areas conservation and the interests of local people and communities could achieve a win-win relationship.

1.1.4.2.2. Examples of Conflicts in Practice in China

As also indicated above, in practice, conserving protected areas might conflict with the utilisation of the resources in protected areas by local people and communities, which is especially true in China where the population in and around protected areas can be more than 60 million people, many of whom depend upon the resources in the nature reserve for their livelihoods.[140] Most protected areas were established in the rural areas, for instance, woodland, lake or mountain areas. More than 77.84% of the total surface of protected areas is located in the western part of China,[141] for instance Xizang province, Xinjiang province and Sichuan province, which are economically poorer than the eastern part of China. There are 600 national level poverty-stricken villages in China, and around three fourth of those villages are near protected areas.[142] What's more, most local people are minority nationalities in China.[143]

---

139 Tyler, T. (2014). Legitimacy in everyday life. In: the seminar Procedural Justice and the Courts: Normative Dimensions. Ghent University, Belgium. 17 January 2014.

140 Zhou, D.Q. & Grumbine, R.E. (2011). National parks in China: experiments with protecting nature and human livelihoods in Yunnan province, People's Republic of China (PRC). *Biological Conservation*, 144, pp. 1314–1321.

141 Xiao, J.H. & Zhou, X.F. (肖建华、周训芳) (2009). Collective land management in protected areas and community co-management contract (自然保护区集体土地管理与社区共管契约). *Seeker* (求索), 2.

142 Zhang, X.L. (张小利) (2007). *Economic Analysis on Poverty Elimination by Tourism Effect* (旅游扶贫效应的经济分析). Dissertation for Master Degree in Fudan University (复旦大学硕士学位论文).

143 WWF (World Wide Fund for Nature) China. (2004). The minutes of the symposium on the co-management with the community in protected areas in China. Issued on 19 May 2004. www.wwfchina.org/pressdetail.php?id=257 accessed 28 February 2013.

On the one hand, lack of suitable compensation and fair benefit-sharing often exacerbates the quality of life of local residents, and results in greater dissatisfaction with wildlife conservation.[144] Such conditions may even lead them to undertake some illegal activities, leading to the deterioration or destruction of protected areas. For instance, because of some forbidden activities in protected areas, peasants living in forest protected areas cannot live on the forest any more. If peasants cannot get possible compensation, they will cut and sell the plants which should be protected.[145] Besides, because of limitations with regards to the scope and intensity of the compensation, the phenomenon of "more protection, heavier burden" appears. In Heilongjiang province, for instance, the local people's income fell by 82% because of the establishment and management of the national Sanjiang protected areas, although some compensation measures have been taken.[146] In Yunnan province, most protected areas with rich biodiversity are also economic poor areas, and/or mountainous areas, and/or ethnic minority areas with fragile ecosystems. There are many constraints for the utilisation of natural resources. The significant income gap between the people living in and outside protected areas cannot be ignored. The burden of conservation falls most heavily on the people living in or near protected areas, as they lost some developmental opportunities, but they cannot get enough compensation.[147] What is more, in the Wolong protected area for giant pandas, the majority of the investments in hotels/restaurants and souvenir shops was from the local government, official staff in the protected area, and some businessmen from outside of the protected area.[148] Most rural households were too poor to invest in ecotourism,[149] and local farmers rarely have enough detailed and timely information to make sound decisions, such

---

144 Maikhuri, R.K. *et al.* (2001). Conservation policy-people conflicts: a case study from Nanda Devi Biosphere Reserve (a world heritage site), India. *Forest Policy and Economics*, 2(3&4), pp. 355–365; Bajracharya, S.B., Furley, P.A. & Newton, A.C. (2006). Impacts of community-based conservation on local communities in the Annapurna conservation area, Nepal. *Biodiversity and Conservation*, 15(8), pp. 2765–2786.

145 China Green Times (2009). How to reform the collective ownership of forest in protected areas. Posted on 26 May 2009, www.caf.ac.cn/news/xwzx/201001/2010-01-08-10-57.html accessed 3 November 2011, in Chinese.

146 According to the investigation in Sanjiang National protected area in January and February of 2013 by Gao Shuo. See Gao, S. (高硕) (2013). Investigation and reflection of local indigenous people's compensation in nature reserves: based on Sanjiang national protected area (关于自然保护区原住民补偿问题的调查与思考 – – 基于对黑龙江三江国家级自然保护区的调查). *Journal of Northeast Forestry University* (东北林业大学学报), 41 (7) (第41 卷第7期), pp. 151–154.

147 China Green Times. (2009). How to reform the collective ownership of forest in protected areas. Posted on 26 May 2009, www.caf.ac.cn/news/xwzx/201001/2010-01-08-10-57.html accessed 3 November 2011, in Chinese.

148 He, G.M. *et al.* (2008). Distribution of economic benefits from ecotourism: a case study of Wolong nature reserve for Giant Pandas in China. *Environmental Management*, 42, p. 1021.

149 He, G.M. *et al.* (2008). Distribution of economic benefits from ecotourism: a case study of Wolong nature reserve for Giant Pandas in China. *Environmental Management*, 42, p. 1023.

as whether to convert their houses into family hotels/restaurants, how much to invest in souvenir shops, and whether to adjust their crops structure to provide appropriate goods for ecotourists.[150] The major obstacles for rural households to invest near protected areas and the key obstacles to employ rural households might be the lack of local involvement in the process of ecotourism policy design and implementation, shortage of financial resources, and poor education.[151] In addition, according to the questionnaire survey on local participation in protected areas of China,[152] the fact that local participation is limited and there is almost no real equality or mutual benefit between protected areas management authorities and local inhabitants is a common problem in the protected areas management in China.[153] There is also no clear provision to justify or require local participation in the country's protected areas ordinance.[154] However, these problems are not unique because they are also found in other areas and countries.[155] Although the situations have been improved in recent years (see 3.1.3), there is still a lot of room for improvement in China.

On the other hand, 17% of the total land and 10% of the sea in China are protected areas,[156] which need at least 0.2 million employees to directly assist with the management of these areas.[157] In practice, more people are needed to indirectly assist with the protected areas conservation (see 1.1.4.3). Because of

150 He, G.M. *et al.* (2008). Distribution of economic benefits from ecotourism: a case study of Wolong nature reserve for Giant Pandas in China. *Environmental Management*, 42, p. 1023.

151 He, G.M. *et al.* (2008). Distribution of economic benefits from ecotourism: a case study of Wolong nature reserve for Giant Pandas in China. *Environmental Management*, 42, p. 1023.

152 Zhuge, R. (2000). Questionnaire survey on local participation into efforts of nature conservation and resources management in nature reserve of China. In: China Man and Biosphere Committee (Eds.). *Study of Sustainable Management Policies for China's Nature Reserve*. Beijing: Scientific and Technical Documents Publishing House, pp. 131–137.

153 Xu, J.Y. *et al.* (2006). Local people's perceptions as decision support for protected area management in Wolong Biosphere reserve, China. *Journal of Environmental Management*, 78, pp. 368–369.

154 Jim, C.Y. *et al.* (2002). Stifled stakeholders and subdued participation: interpreting local responses toward Shimentai Nature Reserve in South China. *Environmental Management*, 30(3), pp. 327–341.

155 e.g. Trakolis, D. (2001). Local people's perceptions of planning and management issues in prespes lakes national park, Greece. *Journal of Environmental Management*, 61, pp. 227–241; Jim, C.Y. *et al.* (2002). Stifled stakeholders and subdued participation: interpreting local responses toward Shimentai Nature Reserve in South China. *Environmental Management*, 30(3), pp. 327–341; Rao, K.S., Maikhuri, R.K. & Saxena, K.G. (2003). Local people's knowledge, aptitude and perceptions of planning and management issues in Nanda Devi Biosphere Reserve, India. *Environmental Management*, 31(2), pp. 168–181.

156 China Talk (中国访谈) (2013). Chinese protected areas legislation: civilian' activities (中国自然保护地法立法：民间在行动). Published on 23 January 2013, http://fangtan.china.com.cn/2013-01/23/content_27770395.htm accessed 12 June 2013.

157 China Talk (中国访谈) (2013). Chinese protected areas legislation: civilian' activities (中国自然保护地法立法：民间在行动), published on 23 January 2013, http://fangtan.china.com.cn/2013-01/23/content_27770395.htm accessed 12 June 2013.

limited funding[158] and lack of professional staff, some illegal activities are not prohibited in due time, for instance building a road or even mining in and around protected areas.[159]

There are also examples of the positive effect of protected areas. For instance, in the Wanglang national protected area, which was established in 1965 in Sichuan province, more than 40% of the benefits from the protected areas management is directly distributed among villagers.[160] Since the villagers' essential interests are consistent with the goal of the protected area management, if there is any illegal activity in and around the protected area, they will actively inform the relevant authority.[161] Another example is the Sanjiangyuan protected area, with 15 million hectares, which provides some of the last remaining habitat for endemic species such as the Tibetan gazelle and the wild yak.[162] However, poaching and overgrazing at some point posed serious threats because of the size of protected areas and lack of enough funding. In November 2006, the Forest Bureau and the local community of Cuochi, which is located inside the Sanjiangyuan protected area, signed a conservation agreement granting the community the right to manage 250,000 hectares of the protected area as a core zone.[163] Since the agreement was signed, the community has regulated grazing patterns and organised patrols to expel illegal hunters.[164] In this way, wild herds of gazelle, yak and antelope are all returning to the area. The community, in turn,

158 According to the statistics from the World Conservation Monitoring Center in 2005, the financial input for every square kilometre of protected areas in China is only less than 70 US dollars, the average financial input for every square kilometre of protected areas in developing countries is more than 157 US dollars. See The Nature Conservancy (2012). Private fund goes into protected areas in Sichuan, published on 26 June 2012, www.tnc.org.cn/news/dongtai/view/524.aspx accessed 13 June 2013.

159 China Talk (中国访谈) (2013). Chinese protected areas legislation: civilian' activities (中国自然保护地法立法：民间在行动). Published on 23 January 2013, http://fangtan.china.com.cn/2013-01/23/content_27770395.htm accessed 12 June 2013.

160 Renmin Net (人民网) (2009). The win-win road for Chinese protected areas (中国自然保护区寻求双赢之路), published on 18 July 2009, http://env.people.com.cn/GB/9676896.htmlaccessed 15 January 2011.

161 Renmin Net (人民网) (2009). The win-win road for Chinese protected areas (中国自然保护区寻求双赢之路), published on 18 July 2009, http://env.people.com.cn/GB/9676896.htmlaccessed 15 January 2011.

162 Brandom, K. & Bruner, A. (2008). Local benefits of protected areas: perspectives and experiences of conservation International. In: Protected Areas in Today's World: Their Values and Benefits for the Welfare of the Planet. Technical Series No. 36, Montreal: Secretariat of the Convention on Biological Diversity, https://www.cbd.int/doc/publications/cbd-ts-36-en.pdf accessed 20 January 2014, pp. 35–36.

163 Brandom, K. & Bruner, A. (2008). Local benefits of protected areas: perspectives and experiences of conservation International. In: Protected Areas in Today's World: Their Values and Benefits for the Welfare of the Planet. Technical Series No. 36, Montreal: Secretariat of the Convention on Biological Diversity, https://www.cbd.int/doc/publications/cbd-ts-36-en.pdf accessed 20 January 2014, pp. 35–36.

164 Brandom, K. & Bruner, A. (2008). Local benefits of protected areas: perspectives and experiences of conservation International. In: Protected Areas in Today's World: Their Values and Benefits for the Welfare of the Planet. Technical Series No. 36, Montreal: Secretariat of

now benefits from a regular supply of medicines for their health post, training for two communal doctors, investment in recovering disappearing traditions, communication through a satellite telephone, and the right to regulate resource use.[165]

According to the statistics from the Changbaishan protected area, the total value of this area is more than 7.8 billion Yuan (about 0.93 billion EUR)[166] per year, among which 6.3 billion Yuan (about 0.75 billion EUR) from its ecological value, 1.05 billion Yuan (about 0.125 billion EUR) from its social value and 0.42 billion Yuan (about 0.05 billion EUR) from its economic value.[167] A similar situation can also be found in the Zhangjiajie National Forest Park and Wulingyuan Scenic and Historic Interest Area. The tourism development in this area promoted economic development for Zhangjiajie City. In 2002, 59% of the city's tax revenues came from tourism and related sectors while in the early 1990s this percentage was about 20%.[168] In 2005, the city's tourism (mainly the tourism to the park and the area mentioned above) related industry accounted for 54.4% of the city's GDP (gross domestic product).[169] The local residents benefit a lot from the tourism development of these protected areas.

However, there are no official statistics systematically showing the total economic value in various protected areas in China. The potential values of these protected areas cannot be neglected. We may conclude from these positive examples on protected areas that the potential roles of local people and communities can really help the protected areas management and a reasonable benefit-sharing from protected areas management would largely stimulate their potential roles.

Significant attention has already been paid to social impact of protected areas – for example there is a body of literature on the key impact of protected areas – which can be negative (e.g. physical displacement, reduced/lost access to land and resources) or positive (e.g. income from tourism, enhanced conservation of essential resources, improved recognition of community conserved areas).[170]

the Convention on Biological Diversity, https://www.cbd.int/doc/publications/cbd-ts-36-en.pdf accessed 20 January 2014, pp. 35–36.

165 Brandom, K. & Bruner, A. (2008). Local benefits of protected areas: perspectives and experiences of conservation International. In: Protected Areas in Today's World: Their Values and Benefits for the Welfare of the Planet. Technical Series No. 36, Montreal: Secretariat of the Convention on Biological Diversity, https://www.cbd.int/doc/publications/cbd-ts-36-en.pdf accessed 20 January 2014, pp. 35–36.

166 According to the exchange rate on 20 June 2014, 1 EUR is equal to 8.4 Yuan, http://huilv.911cha.com/EURCNY.html accessed 20 June 2014. The following statistics all follow this exchange rate.

167 Changbaishan Protected Area Net (长白山自然保护区网). The introduction on Changbaishan protected area (长白山自然保护区介绍), http://211.103.250.141/publicfiles//business/htmlfiles/cbsbhq/jqgk/index.html accessed 20 January 2014.

168 Liu, Y.D. (2005). Strategies on the increase of tourism tax revenues in Zhangjiajie, www.hnce.cn/news/Article_Print.asp?ArticleID=377 accessed 3 March 2011.

169 Liu, Y.W. (2006). Zhangjiajie tourism development with a promising future, www.zjj-trip. com/news/NewsInfo.aspx?ID=3568&pageUp=5 accessed 2 March 2011.

170 Poverty and Conservation Learning Group. (2007). Towards an integrated system for measuring the social impact of protected areas. UNEP-World Conservation Monitoring

There is little literature to pull together the evidence for and against impacts of protected areas on local people and communities in an objective and systematic approach. Thus, how to stimulate the potential roles of local people and communities and change their position from opposing parties to the defender of protected areas in China have become urgent issues, as well as providing them with (legal) means to help to conserve the protected areas against negative human activities.[171]

1.1.4.3. Relationship Between Human Rights Protection and Protected Areas Conservation in Europe

As one of the most environmentally progressive regions of the world, Europe can indeed serve as a guiding light on the path to a more sustainable future.[172]

At the level of the European Union (EU), on the one hand, 20% of the EU's terrestrial area now has a protected status and many of these areas have both a conservation value and a value to local people for purposes such as farming, fishing, recreation and tourism.[173] This can produce a conflict between conservation and existing land use.[174] Since there frequently are conflicts related to the designation and management of protected areas, this could result in failure to achieve national and international conservation objectives.[175]

On the other hand, the Natura 2000 network in the EU, which will be explained in detail in the section of Protected areas conservation in Europe (see 3.2), is the largest coordinated network of protected areas anywhere in

---

Centre: Vision 2020; WCPA/CEESP Taskforce on Protected Areas, Equity and Livelihoods. http://povertyandconservation.info/sites/default/files/Towards%20an%20integrated%20system%20for%20measuring%20the%20social%20impact%20of%20Protected%20Areas.pdf accessed 18 February 2014.

171 He, M. & Cliquet, A. (2013). Sustainable development through a rights-based approach to conserve protected areas in China. *China-EU Law Journal.* DOI 10.1007/s 12689-013-0031-7, http://link.springer.com/article/10.1007%2Fs12689-013-0031-7 accessed 4 November 2013.

172 Bjerler, N. (2004). Do Europeans have a right to environment? In: International Environmental Law – agora session of the Inaugural Conference of the European Society of International Law, Florence, Italy, 13–15 May 2004, www.esil-sedi.eu/sites/default/files/Bjerler_0.PDF accessed 10 October 2013.

173 European Commission (2010). Public participation in nature conservation – making it happen, Science for Environment Policy, DG Environment News Alert Service. Published on 30 September 2010, http://ec.europa.eu/environment/integration/research/newsalert/pdf/211na5.pdf accessed 7 November 2013.

174 European Commission (2010). Public participation in nature conservation – making it happen, Science for Environment Policy, DG Environment News Alert Service. Published on 30 September 2010, http://ec.europa.eu/environment/integration/research/newsalert/pdf/211na5.pdf accessed 7 November 2013.

175 Fauchald, O.K. & Gulbrandsen, L.H. (2012). The Norwegian reform of protected areas management: a grand experiment with delegation of authority? *Local Environment: the International Journal of Justice And Sustainability,* 17(2). DOI 10.1080/13549839.2012.660910, www.fni.no/doc&pdf/OKF-LHG-LE-2012.pdf accessed 11 October 2013.

the world.[176] Natura 2000 provides vital services such as carbon storage, flood prevention, water quality maintenance – estimated to be worth around €200–300 billion per year.[177] In addition, the overall employment opportunities provided by the Natura 2000 network were calculated based on a land-use approach and scaling-up on a per-hectare basis.[178] It was estimated that[179]:

- the value of recreational visits to Natura 2000 sites was €5–9 billion, based on estimates of visitors' willingness to pay;
- the total expenditure related to tourism and recreation supported by Natura 2000 was between around €50 and €85 billion in 2006;
- the expenditure exclusively related to the visitors who have affinity for Natura 2000 sites (i.e. around 21% of visitors to Natura 2000) was between €9 and €20 billion in 2006, generated by around 350 million visitor days;
- The total expenditure provided by tourism and recreation supports between 4.5 and 8 million full time employment (FTE) jobs. The benefits generated by the visitors with affinity to Natura 2000 would support from 800,000 to 2 million FTE jobs, with a total of about 127 million FTE jobs in the EU27 (in 2009),[180] and about 13 million jobs in the tourism sector (in 2008).[181]
- Natura 2000 sites have supported on average about 12 million FTE jobs each year in the EU during the period 2006–2008. This includes about 1.5 million jobs in agriculture, 70,000 jobs in forestry, around 200,000 jobs in fishing, 3.1 million jobs in recreation (excluding employment generated by hotels and restaurants), and 7 million jobs in other industries.

According to Eurostat, median gross annual earnings of fulltime employees across all industries in the EU were €12,236 in 2006.[182] Taking this number as a

176 Janez Potočnik. (2014). Foreword. In: Born, C.-H., Cliquet, A., Schoukens, H., Misonne, D. & Van Hoorick, G. (Eds.). *The Habitats Directive in its EU Environmental Law Context: European Nature's Best Hope?* Routledge, in press, p. 11.

177 Janez Potočnik. (2014). Foreword. In: Born, C.-H., Cliquet, A., Schoukens, H., Misonne, D. & Van Hoorick, G. (Eds.). *The Habitats Directive in its EU Environmental Law Context: European Nature's Best Hope?* Routledge, in press, p. 12.

178 EU (European Union) (2013). The economic benefits of the Natura 2000 network: synthesis report, http://ec.europa.eu/environment/nature/natura2000/financing/docs/ENV-12-018_LR_Final1.pdf accessed 17 October 2013, p. 30.

179 EU (European Union) (2013). The economic benefits of the Natura 2000 network: synthesis report, http://ec.europa.eu/environment/nature/natura2000/financing/docs/ENV-12-018_LR_Final1.pdf accessed 17 October 2013, p. 30.

180 Eurostat. (2010). Employment in Europe 2010 – Statistical annex, http://ec.europa.eu/employment_social/eie/statistical_annex_key_employment_indicators_en.html accessed 17 October 2013.

181 Eurostat tourism database, http://epp. eurostat.ec.europa.eu/statistics_explained/index.php/Tourism_employment#Database accessed 17 October 2013.

182 EU (European Union) (2013). The economic benefits of the Natura 2000 network: synthesis report, http://ec.europa.eu/environment/nature/natura2000/financing/docs/ENV-12-018_LR_Final1.pdf accessed 17 October 2013, p. 31.

basis, 11,870,000 jobs supported by the Natura 2000 network provide incomes of about €145 billion per year.[183]

However, these great achievements cannot be reached in one day. From a historical perspective, the 1979 Birds Directive[184] and the 1992 Habitats Directive,[185] which will be explained in detail in the section of Protected areas conservation in Europe (see 3.2), were adopted in a very top-down fashion with relatively little consultation involving stakeholders and policy actors on the ground who had to implement the Natura 2000 measures.[186] These low levels of consultation and representation triggered high levels of resistance.[187] In response, Member States increasingly resorted to more participatory forms of decision-making.[188] In all cases, it is essential that those who live and work in Natura 2000 sites are closely involved in decisions over their long-term management.[189] From private land owners and users, government authorities, industries, to recreational groups, conservationists, local communities and concerned citizens – everyone has an important role to play in making Natura 2000 a success and in halting the loss of biodiversity.[190] It is obvious to see that the ultimate success of the Natura 2000 network in reaching its set goals depends on the involvement of all relevant stakeholders in maintaining the network. The core issues involved are procedural fairness – allowing people to be part of the process – and community empowerment – enabling people to take an active role in decisions affecting

---

183 EU (European Union) (2013). The economic benefits of the Natura 2000 network: synthesis report, http://ec.europa.eu/environment/nature/natura2000/financing/docs/ENV-12-018_LR_Final1.pdf accessed 17 October 2013, p. 31.

184 Directive 79/409/EEC of 2 April 1979 on the Convention of Wild Birds, OJ L 103, 25 April 1979 (Birds Directive) was replaced by 2009 Birds Directive, http://euro-lex.europa.eu/LexUriServ/site/nl/consleg/1979/L/01979L0409-20070101-nl.pdf accessed 20 October 2012.

185 Directive 92/43/EEC of 21 May 1992 on the Conservation of Natural Habitats and of Wild Fauna and Flora, OJ L 206, 22 July 1992 (Habitats Directive); text of the Directive, with later amendments, see http://ec.europa.eu/environment/nature.legislation.habitatsdirective.index_en.htm accessed 20 October 2012.

186 Keulartz, J. (2009). European nature conservation and restoration policy – problems and perspectives. *The Journal of the Society for Ecological Restoration International*, 17(4), p. 446. DOI 10.1111/j.1526-100X.2009.005666.x.

187 Keulartz, J. (2009). European nature conservation and restoration policy – problems and perspectives. *The Journal of the Society for Ecological Restoration International*, 17(4), p. 446. DOI 10.1111/j.1526-100X.2009.005666.x.

188 Keulartz, J. (2009). European nature conservation and restoration policy – problems and perspectives. *The Journal of the Society for Ecological Restoration International*, 17(4), p. 446. DOI 10.1111/j.1526-100X.2009.005666.x.

189 European Communities. (2009). Natura 2000 – Europe's Nature for You. Luxembourg: Office for Official Publications of the European Communities. http://ec.europa.eu/environment/nature/info/pubs/docs/europe_nature_for_you/en.pdf accessed 20 March 2014, p. 16.

190 European Communities. (2009). Natura 2000 – Europe's Nature for You. Luxembourg: Office for Official Publications of the European Communities, http://ec.europa.eu/environment/nature/info/pubs/docs/europe_nature_for_you/en.pdf accessed 20 March 2014, p. 16.

their lives.[191] Moreover, demonstrating socio-economic benefits arising from the management of protected areas can help to gain support among the different stakeholders.[192] Furthermore, the assessment of these benefits can help to identify and address possible conflicts in a more precise and fair manner.[193]

In the framework of the Council of Europe, which also includes non EU members, the Emerald Network (see 3.2.1), also make a great contribution to biodiversity conservation and economic development in Europe. The Emerald Network is an ecological network of protected areas, which provides a model for conserving biodiversity, based on ecological principles, while allowing a degree of human exploitation of the landscape.[194]

As indicated above, the main solution for involving all relevant stakeholders, especially the local people and communities, would be to empower them some reasonable rights to stimulate their roles in protected areas conservation. From the perspective of human rights, the European Convention on Human Rights (ECHR; formally the Convention for the Protection of Human Rights and Fundamental Freedoms)[195] is more than 60 years old. The European Court of Human Rights (ECtHR)[196] has had exclusive jurisdiction to receive individual applications for a long time. A rich and extensive human rights case law in Europe is unique in international law. It is noted that compared with African human rights jurisprudence and Inter-American human rights jurisprudence, the greatest amount of conservation related cases was found in the European human rights jurisprudence.[197] In addition, the Convention on Access to Information, Public Participation in Decision-making and Access to Justice in Environmental Matters (Aarhus Convention) (1998)[198] was adopted as part of the "Environment

191 Razzaque, J. (2013). Information, public participation and access to justice in environmental matters. In: Alam, S. *et al.* (Eds.). *Routledge Handbook of International Environmental Law.* London and New York: Routledge, p. 138.

192 EU (European Union) (2013). The economic benefits of the Natura 2000 network: synthesis report, http://ec.europa.eu/environment/nature/natura2000/financing/docs/ENV-12-018_LR_Finall.pdf accessed 17 October 2013, p. 46.

193 EU (European Union) (2013). The economic benefits of the Natura 2000 network: synthesis report, http://ec.europa.eu/environment/nature/natura2000/financing/docs/ENV-12-018_LR_Finall.pdf accessed 17 October 2013, p. 46.

194 Jones-Walters, L. & Civic, K. (2013). European protected areas: past, present and future. *Journal for Nature Conservation*, 21, p. 123.

195 European Convention on Human Rights (formally the Convention for the Protection of Human Rights and Fundamental Freedoms), drafted in 1950 and entered into force on 3 September 1953, 213 UNTS, www.echr.coe.int/Documents/Convention_ENG.pdf accessed 12 April 2013.

196 Detailed information see www.echr.coe.int/Pages/home.aspx?p=home accessed 12 April 2013.

197 Desmet, E. (2011). *Indigenous Rights Entwined with Nature Conservation.* Antwerp: Intersentia, p. 352.

198 The UNECE Convention on Access to Information, Public Participation in Decision-making and Access to Justice in Environmental Matters (Aarhus Convention), adopted on 25 June 1998 in the Danish city of Aarhus at the Fourth Ministerial Conference in the "Environment

for Europe" process. It is regarded as the landmark international instrument linking procedural human rights to environmental protection. The Convention and the communications from the Aarhus Convention Compliance Committee (ACCC)[199] provide some valuable principal guidelines for the Member States, including the EU. Therefore, besides the ECHR and the Aarhus Convention, some cases from the ECtHR and the Court of Justice of the European Union (CJEU),[200] and some communications from the ACCC, will be explored as they provide insight into the relationship between protected areas conservation and protection of human rights for local people and communities.

1.1.5. EXISTING APPROACHES TO CONSERVE PROTECTED AREAS

As indicated above, conservation approaches need to fully institutionalise instruments which specifically incorporate economic and equity thinking in order to target development and poverty reduction concerns.[201] Empowering local communities is a key factor for such governance systems to contribute to poverty reduction.[202]

Over the past decade, there have been substantial changes in the governance of protected areas towards wider participation from more stakeholders and local communities.[203] There are also concerns over the proliferation of protected areas managed primarily for purposes other than biodiversity conservation, as such people-centred approaches often ignore the findings of conservation biology and even undermine the creation of conservation-focused protected areas.[204] However, the question remains as to what constitutes an appropriate balance of

for Europe" process, 2161 UNTS 447, www.unece.org/env/pp/introduction.html accessed 10 March 2012.

199 The Aarhus Convention Compliance Committee was established to fulfil the requirement of Article 15 of the Aarhus Convention on review of compliance to establish arrangements for reviewing compliance with the Convention. www.unece.org/env/pp/cc.html accessed 10 February 2014.

200 With the entry into force of the Treaty of Lisbon in 2009, the court's name was changed from the "Court of Justice of the European Communities" to the "Court of Justice of the European Union". More information see European sources online, www.cardiff.ac.uk/insrv/resources/edc/Court%20of%20Justice.pdf accessed 12 April 2014.

201 Secretariat of the Convention on Biological Diversity. (2008). Protected areas in today's world: their values and benefits for the welfare of the planet. Technical Series No. 36, Montreal, https://www.cbd.int/doc/publications/cbd-ts-36-en.pdf accessed 20 January 2014, p. 16.

202 Secretariat of the Convention on Biological Diversity. (2008). Protected areas in today's world: their values and benefits for the welfare of the planet. Technical Series No. 36, Montreal, https://www.cbd.int/doc/publications/cbd-ts-36-en.pdf accessed 20 January 2014, p. 17.

203 Dearden, P., Bennett, M. & Johnston, J. (2005). Trends in global protected area governance 1992–2002. *Environmental Management*, 36(1), pp. 89–100.

204 Locke, H. & Dearden, P. (2005). Rethinking protected area categories and the new paradigm. *Environmental Protection*, 32(1), pp. 1–10.

power in protected areas conservation. Daniels[205] analyses two approaches that are useful in understanding the administration of protected areas. Top-down, centralised approaches raise the risks of imposition, potentially producing local resistance and resulting in the further deterioration of ecosystems. The surrounding communities cannot benefit from the interests of protected areas. The resulting effects have been the involvement of local communities in economic activities that are less sustainable than previously engaged in.[206] Bottom-up, decentralised approaches raise the risks of parochialism, in which local resource exploitation and economic development objectives often override strategic nature conservation objectives.[207] Compared with the government and authorities, the local community usually has few resources and little power to voice their opinions independently.[208] Because of the limitations of local communities, such as educational facilities, the local communities need further guidance when participating in the management. Besides these two approaches, the mixed top-down and bottom-up management approach, which attempts to partially involve local communities in management and administration of protected areas, seems to be reasonable. The resultant effects of such attempts have been the creation of various land uses of the zone, culturally significant and sacred areas and natural resources distribution[209] aimed at enhancing the communities' abilities to support their livelihoods within the confines of the park such as wildlife protection, agricultural fields and livestock management. The approach indeed reduces incidences of the conflicts regarding conserving protected areas and protecting the rights of the community, however, the meaningful involvement[210] of the local people and communities in the conservation of protected areas needs to be effectively guaranteed by law.

---

205 Daniels, A.E. (2002). Indigenous peoples and neotropical forest conservation: impacts of the protected area systems on traditional cultures. *Macalester Environmental Review.* 23 September 2002, http://lueci.clas.ufl.edu/southworth/grad-application/2002_Daniels%20-%20Neotropical%20forest%20conservation%20-%20indigenous%20peoples%20&%20protected%20areas.pdf accessed 19 October 2013.

206 Andrew-Essien, E. & Bisong, F. (2009). Conflicts, conservation and natural resource use in protected area systems: an analysis of recurrent issues. *European Journal of Scientific Research*, 25(1), www.eurojournals.com/ejsr_25_1_12.pdf accessed 3 April 2011, pp. 118 – 129.

207 Jones, P.J.S. & Burgess, J. (2005). Building partnership capacity for the collaborative management of marine protected areas in the UK: a preliminary analysis. *Journal of Environmental Management*, 77(3), pp. 227–243. DOI 10.1016/j.jenvman.2005.04.004.

208 Miao, H., Ouyang, Z., Wang, X. & Song, M. (2000). Management of communities in natural reserves: challenge and solutions. In: The Fourth National Conservation and Sustainable Use of Biological Diversity Seminar Proceedings, http://cpfd.cnki.com.cn/Article/CPFDTOTAL-ZKYS200011001009.htm, www.brim.ac.cn/book/book235_594.pdf accessed 11 November 2010.

209 Arambiza, E. (1995). The Kaa-Iya protected area of the Grand Chaco: a case collaborations between indigenous peoples and conservationists. In: Gray, A. (Ed.). *Indigenous Peoples and Biodiversity Conservation in Latin America.* Copenhagen: EKs-Skolen Trykkrei APS.

210 Meaningful involvement means that: (1) potentially affected community residents have an appropriate opportunity to participate in decisions about a proposed activity that will affect

In addition, since the first International Union for Conservation of Nature (IUCN) World Conservation Congress (Montreal, 1996)[211] recognised the right of indigenous peoples to participate effectively in the management of protected areas, the community-based approach to conservation has been a new approach which was formulated based on the interests of local people. It is accepted that this approach is a relatively effective method to solve the conflicts from international and national experience.[212] However, little consideration is given with regard to how to realise the community-based approach.[213] The essential factor is the empowerment of the people.[214] Without the continuous support of the most relevant groups whose rights have been affected by the establishment and management of protected areas, human impact cannot be reduced, and more importantly protected areas cannot produce more value. If they feel marginalised from the decision-making process, the most relevant groups will not care about various benefits from protected areas. If they are unable to capture benefits from conservation initiatives, protected areas conservation ultimately fails. Only when the rights are ensured will the local people and communities compromise their historical interests and cooperate with authorities to conserve protected areas in order to achieve sustainable benefits. Effective protection depends on a dynamic, territorial approach in which all relevant concerns – culture, human rights, environment and development – are linked in a systematic way.[215]

Therefore, a systematic, dynamic and better balanced way to solve the potential conflicts regarding human rights protection and protected areas conservation, especially the rights of local people and communities, is urgently needed.

---

their environment and/or health; (2) the public's contribution can influence the regulatory agency's decision; (3) the concerns of all participants involved will be considered in the decision-making process; and (4) the decision-makers seek out and facilitate the involvement of those potentially affected. See US Environmental Protection Agency. (2003). Toolkit for assessing potential allegations of environmental injustice, www.epa.gov/compliance/recent/ej.html accessed 18 December 2012.

211 The IUCN World Conservation Congress in Montreal, October, 1996, www.danadeclaration.org/pdf/recommendations24eng.pdf accessed 20 December 2012.

212 Peng, L. (彭莉) (2004) Research on the joint management of the communities in the protected areas (自然保护区中社区"共管"问题初探). In: The Annual Meeting and Academic Seminar of Environmental and Natural Resources Law under China Law Society (中国法学会环境资源法学研究会), Chongqing (重庆), China, July 2004, www.riel.whu.edu.cn/Article.asp?id=26422 accessed 12 December 2011.

213 He, M. & Cliquet, A. (2013). Sustainable development through a rights-based approach to conserve protected areas in China. *China-EU Law Journal.* DOI 10.1007/s 12689-013-0031-7. http://link.springer.com/article/10.1007%2Fs12689-013-0031-7 accessed 4 November 2013.

214 He, M. & Cliquet, A. (2013). Sustainable development through a rights-based approach to conserve protected areas in China. *China-EU Law Journal.* DOI 10.1007/s 12689-013-0031-7. http://link.springer.com/article/10.1007%2Fs12689-013-0031-7 accessed 4 November 2013.

215 Argumedo, A. & Pimbert, M. (2008) *Protecting Farmers' Rights with Indigenous Bio-cultural Heritage Territories: the Experience of the Potato Park.* International Institute for Environment and Development, Association.

1.2. PROBLEM STATEMENT

According to what has been introduced and discussed above, on the one hand, the post-2010 perception of protected areas is clearly reflected in the content of the CBD Aichi Biodiversity Targets[216] which suggest that protected areas are expected to contribute to social benefits by sustaining communities in and around their boundaries.[217] They are expected to make an economic contribution by generating revenue to sustain their own operation, by bolstering local and national economies through tourism, the supply of minor forest products, fish and other resources and through the provision of ecosystem services.[218]

On the other hand, the main conclusion in literature,[219] which deals with local people's acceptance of protected areas, is that local people often associate protected areas more with restrictions than with increased opportunities for themselves.[220] This is mainly because the designation and management of protected areas may sometimes affect or have disadvantages for certain groups of people and their rights with respect to the protected sites and its natural resources. In fact, in many countries, local people and communities depend on the natural resources that protected areas seek to conserve, deriving their livelihoods from these resources and benefiting from ecosystem services.[221] So

216 The tenth meeting of the Conference of the Parties to the Convention on Biological Diversity (CBD), held in Nagoya, Japan in 2010, adopted the Strategic Plan for Biodiversity 2011–2020 and the Aichi Targets. The Aichi Biodiversity Targets consists of Strategic Goal A (address the underlying causes of biodiversity loss by mainstreaming biodiversity across government and society); Strategic Goal B (Reduce the direct pressures on biodiversity and promote sustainable use); Strategic Goal C (To improve the status of biodiversity by safeguarding ecosystems species and genetic diversity); Strategic Goal D (Enhance the benefits to all from biodiversity and ecosystem services); and Strategic Goal E (Enhance implementation through participatory planning, knowledge management and capacity building). See www.cbd.int/sp/targets/ accessed 2 May 2013.

217 Jones-Walters, L. & Civic, K. (2013). European protected areas: past, present and future. *Journal for Nature Conservation*, 21, p. 124.

218 Jones-Walters, L. & Civic, K. (2013). European protected areas: past, present and future. *Journal for Nature Conservation*, 21, p. 124.

219 e.g. McNeely, J.A. & Pitt, D. (Eds.) (1985). *Culture and Conservation: The Human Dimension in Environmental Planning*. London: Croom Helm; Zube, E.H. & Busch, M.L. (1990). Park–people relationships: an international review. *Landscapes Urban Plan*, 19, pp. 117–131; Lucas, P.H.C. (1992). *Protected Landscapes – A Guide for Policy-Makers and Planners*. Gland (Switzerland): IUCN; IUCN. (1993). *Parks for Life: Report of the Fifth World Congress on National Parks and Protected Areas*. Gland (Switzerland): IUCN; McNeely, J.A. (1995). Partnerships for conservation: an introduction. In: McNeely, J.A. (Ed.). *Expanding Partnerships in Conservation*. Washington D.C.: Island Press, pp. 1–10.

220 Wallner, A., Bauer, N. & Hunziker, M. (2007). Perceptions and evaluations of biosphere reserves by local residents in Switzerland and Ukraine. *Landscape and Urban Planning*, 83, p. 105.

221 Borrini-Feyerabend, G., Dudley, N., Jaeger, T., Lassen, B., Broome, N.P., Phillips, A. & Sandwith, T. (2013). *Governance of Protected Areas: from Understanding to Action*. Best Practice Protected Area Guidelines Series No. 20. Gland (Switzerland): IUCN, https://cmsdata.iucn.org/downloads/iucn_governance_1109_1.pdf accessed 26 September 2013, p. 20.

they have a clear interest in being involved in decision-making and negotiating a fair share of the costs and benefits associated with conservation.[222] They will often wish to maintain access to resources, manage human–wildlife conflicts and receive a fair share of the associated economic benefits (such as conservation payments, employment, markets for local products or tourism ventures).[223]

Broadly speaking, issues of ownership and access to resources, rights to participation in decision-making, and regulation of particular types of resource use or discharge of wastes can strongly influence the sustainability of ecosystem management and are fundamental determinants of who wins and who loses from changes in ecosystems.[224] Protected areas management is a typical example. If the relevant rights of local people and communities have been neglected, conflicts occur. Conflict is often at the heart of protected area establishment and maintenance.[225] The poverty-stricken communities have little to lose by ignoring laws on protected areas if no alternative source of living is provided and if enforcement is weak.[226] They would even do some illegal activities to destroy natural resources that should be protected. Nevertheless, conflictual situations are neither positive nor negative but they can be used in a constructive or destructive way.[227] Conflicts should be viewed as an opportunity for constructive change and growth.[228] A growing number of conservation professionals are considering that the good governance of protected areas depends upon the overall power relations between civil society and government, the quality of the government, and the quality of engagement of other actors.[229]

---

222 Borrini-Feyerabend, G., Dudley, N., Jaeger, T., Lassen, B., Broome, N.P., Phillips, A. & Sandwith, T. (2013). *Governance of Protected Areas: from Understanding to Action*. Best Practice Protected Area Guidelines Series No. 20. Gland (Switzerland): IUCN, https://cmsdata.iucn.org/downloads/iucn_governance_1109_1.pdf accessed 26 September 2013, p. 20.

223 Borrini-Feyerabend, G., Dudley, N., Jaeger, T., Lassen, B., Broome, N.P., Phillips, A. & Sandwith, T. (2013). *Governance of Protected Areas: from Understanding to Action*. Best Practice Protected Area Guidelines Series No. 20. Gland (Switzerland): IUCN, https://cmsdata.iucn.org/downloads/iucn_governance_1109_1.pdf accessed 26 September 2013, p. 20.

224 Millennium Ecosystem Assessment. (2005). *Ecosystems and Human Well-being: Biodiversity Synthesis*. Washington D.C.: World Resources Institute, www.maweb.org/documents/document.354.aspx.pdf accessed 22 January 2014, p. 12.

225 West, P., Igoe, J. & Brockington, D. (2006). Parks and peoples: the social impact of protected areas. *Annual Review of Anthropology*, 35, www.annualreviews.org/doi/pdf/10.1146/annurev.anthro.35.081705.123308 accessed 21 May 2014, pp. 251–277.

226 Millennium Ecosystem Assessment. (2005). *Ecosystems and Human Well-being: Biodiversity Synthesis*. Washington D.C.: World Resources Institute, www.maweb.org/documents/document.354.aspx.pdf accessed 22 January 2014, p. 186.

227 Deloges, C. & Gauthier, M. (1997). Community forest and forest resource conflicts: an overview. In: The XI World Forestry Congress, Antalya, Turkey, p. 4.

228 Deloges, C. & Gauthier, M. (1997). Community forest and forest resource conflicts: an overview. In: The XI World Forestry Congress, Antalya, Turkey, p. 4.

229 Lockwood, M., Kothari, A. & Worboys, G. (Eds.) (2006). *Managing Protected Areas: a Global Guide*. London: Earthscan, p. 138.

Respect for the human rights of all parties, as well as for the intrinsic value of nature, is central.[230] As indicated above, the human rights of local people and communities need more attention. Nobody has better insight into the problems and needs of the environment than the very people who live there. In addition, some literature[231] concludes that if local people and communities could gain some reasonable benefits from protected areas conservation, they presumably have an incentive to stop external threats to the protected areas. What is more, involving people at the early stage of decision-making processes creates greater trust in the process and decreases the possibility of later conflicts.[232] In this way, when they feel that they have been respected by the relevant agencies in the protected areas establishment and management, they would show their great potential roles in these activities. However, these facts have not been given enough attention in China. Most research on protected areas in China has tended to focus on flora and fauna and addressed problems from the perspective of reserve managers or governments.[233]

In order to achieve sustainable conservation, legislation and environmental planning should involve local people in the management of protected areas and identify and promote social processes that enable local communities to conserve and enhance biodiversity as a part of their livelihoods.[234] There is growing interest in seeking innovative policy and institutional arrangements for resolving or managing natural resource conflicts in a peaceful and participatory manner.[235]

230 Lockwood, M., Kothari, A. & Worboys, G. (Eds.) (2006). *Managing Protected Areas: a Global Guide*. London: Earthscan, p. 138.

231 Lu, Y., *et al.* (2003). A framework for evaluating the effectiveness of protected areas: the case of Wolong Biosphere Reserve. *Landscapes Urban Plan*, 63, pp. 213–223; Wiesmann, U., Liechti, K. & Rist, S. (2005). Between conservation and development: concretizing the first World Natural Heritage Site in the Alps through participatory processes. *Mountain Research and Development*, 25(2), pp. 128–138; Ormsby, A. & Kaplin, B.A. (2005). A framework for understanding community resident perceptions of Masoala National Park. *Madagascar Environmental Conservation*, 32(2), pp. 156–164; Fraga, J. (2006). Local perspectives in conservation politics: the case of the Ria Lagartos Biosphere Reserve, Yucatan, Mexico. *Landscapes Urban Plan*, 74, pp. 285–295.

232 Birnie, P., Boyle, A. & Redgwell, C. (2009). *International Law and the Environment* (third edition). Oxford: Oxford University Press, p. 288.

233 e.g. Han, N. (2000). A policy study on sustainable management for China's nature reserves. *Journal of Natural Resource*, 15(3), pp. 201–207; Miao, H. (2000). Community participation mechanism of China's nature reserve. In: China Man and Biosphere Committee (Eds.). *Study of Sustainable Management Policies for China's Nature reserve*. Beijing: Scientific and Technical Documents Publishing House, pp. 57–71; Wu, X. *et al.* (2002). Harmonized development of nature reserve and local community. *Rural Eco-Environment*, 18(2), pp. 10–13.

234 Tomicevic, J. & Bjedov, I. (2012). Understanding Linkages between Public Participation and Management of Protected Areas – Case Study of Serbia. In Ishwaran, N. (Ed.). The Biosphere. Published on 14 March 2012, www.intechopen.com/books/the-biosphere/understanding-linkages-between-public-participation-and-management-of-protected-areas-case-study-of-accessed 7 November 2013, p. 140.

235 Castro, A.P. & Nielsen, E. (2001). Indigenous people and co-management: implications for conflicts management. *Environmental Science & Policy*, 4, p. 229.

A balance needs to be achieved that can satisfy the demands of local people while at the same time offering optimal protection of the conservation targets.[236]

However, present popular debates are mainly focusing on the conflicts regarding economic development and environmental protection. Often in conflicts regarding economic and environmental interests the former tend to prevail.[237] Indeed, it is not easy to pursue environmental protection in the dynamic game of economic development and environmental protection, especially in some developing countries where the first priority is to promote economic development to feed the citizens. Thus, how to find a better balance to stimulate all the possible parties to fully work together to guarantee the existing environmental protection is a vitally important issue. The local people and communities are the most relevant parties to protected areas, their potential roles in protected areas conservation could be used as the irreplaceable power against some economic activities that would negatively affect protected areas conservation. From this perspective, there is also a need to find a better way to solve the potential conflicts regarding human rights protection and protected areas conservation, especially for local people and communities. Although some steps for solving the potential conflicts regarding human rights protection and environmental protection have been taken by some countries, there has not yet been much specific attention to the relationship between human rights protection and protected areas conservation.

Moreover, the existing approaches to conserve protected areas mentioned above cannot be used to effectively solve the existing potential conflicts regarding human rights protection and protected areas conservation, especially in some developing countries like China. Therefore, there is an urgent need to explore a reasonable and well-balanced approach to conserve protected areas in China, and some lessons learned from Europe would help to put this approach into practice.

1.3. RESEARCH QUESTIONS

The core research question in this book is how to stimulate the roles of local people and communities and environmental NGOs in conserving protected

---

236 Allendorf, T.D., Smith, J.L.D. & Anderson, D.H. (2007). Residents' perceptions of Royal Bardia national park, Nepal. *Landscape and Urban Planning*, 82, pp. 33–40; McNeely, J.A. & Miller, K.R. (1984). *National parks, Conservation and Development: the Role of Protected Areas in Sustaining Society*. Washington D.C.: Smithsonian Institute Press; Newmark, W.D., Leonard, N.L., Sariko, H.I. & Gamassa, D.G.M. (1993). Conservation attitudes of local people living adjacent to 5 protected areas in Tanzania. *Biological Conservation*, 63, pp. 177–183.

237 De Sadeleer, N., Roller, G. & Dross, M. (2005). *Access to Justice in Environmental Matters and the Role of NGOs: Empirical Findings and Legal Appraisal*. Groningen: Europa Law Publishing, p. 175.

areas in China by analysing and drawing some lessons from Europe. This research will look at the broader European context and at specific EU law. The hypothesis in this book is that, if empowering local people and communities and environmental NGOs to have some appropriate rights, their enthusiasm, local knowledge and power could be regarded as an irreplaceable role in protected areas conservation. Based on this hypothesis, four main human rights, namely the right to property; the right to information; the right to participation and the right to access to justice, in China and in Europe will be introduced and analysed in a theoretical and historical way, and the key different features of the four main human rights in China and in Europe will be pointed out. To substantiate the core research question, some sub-research questions are formulated:

(1) What is the added-value of a human rights-based approach to conservation, according to literature? (Chapter 2 of Part I)
  (a) What are the advantages and challenges of a human rights-based approach to conservation?
  (b) How to implement a human rights-based approach to conservation in theory?
(2) How to solve the potential conflicts regarding human rights protection and protected areas conservation in China according to some principal lessons learned from Europe? The human rights only focus on the right to property, the right to information, the right to participation and the right to access to justice. (Part II)
  (a) What is the existing legal and policy framework for protected areas conservation in China and in Europe? (Chapter 3 of Part II)
  (b) What are the potential conflicts regarding property rights protection and protected areas conservation in China, from a legal perspective? What can China learn from the European legal system concerning property rights, based on the different cultural understandings of property rights in China and in Europe? (Chapter 4 of Part II)
  (c) What are the potential conflicts regarding protected areas conservation and procedural rights protection, namely the right to information, the right to participation and the right to access to justice, in China, from a legal perspective? What can China learn from the European legal system concerning the three procedural rights, based on the different development stages of the procedural rights in China and in Europe? (Chapter 5 of Part II)
(3) How to implement a human rights-based approach in protected areas conservation in practice in China, based on the experiences and lessons learned from the European legal system? What possible adjustments should be made to the Chinese legal and policy system? (Chapter 7).

1.4. ACADEMIC AND SOCIETAL CONTRIBUTION OF THE BOOK

Firstly, recent literature is mainly centred around: (1) whether a human right related to the environment will ever be recognised;[238] (2) several existing approaches[239] to link human rights and the environment; and (3) the uncertain developmental path that human rights protection and environmental protection are involved in. There is not so much information about solving the existing potential conflicts regarding human rights protection and environmental protection from a human rights perspective, let alone the exploration of a more comprehensive approach to solve the potential conflicts regarding human rights protection and protected areas conservation and the stimulation of the potential role of local people and communities in protected areas conservation in a certain developing county. This book will introduce a human rights-based approach to conservation and explore how to implement it for protected areas conservation in China.

Secondly, there is little literature on the potential conflicts regarding human rights protection and protected areas conservation from a legal perspective in China. Furthermore, little attention has been given to the exact meaning of four main human rights (right to property from the substantial perspective; right to information, right to participation and right to access to justice from the procedural human rights perspective) in China. In addition, while much progress on improving human rights protection and protected areas conservation in China has been made since 2010, it still needs more attention. All these issues will be discussed in Part II of this book.

Thirdly, there are numerous articles and books on human rights protection and protected areas conservation in Europe. However, little attention has been paid to demonstrate the lessons to be drawn for China, operating under a different economic, political, social, cultural and legal system. This book will propose some suggestions on how to implement a human rights-based approach to conserve protected areas in China.

Last but not least, instead of only pointing out the differences of the four human rights between China and Europe, this book will respectively clarify the principal reason which caused these differences by introducing and analysing

[238] Boyle, A. (2012). Human rights and the environment: where next? *The European Journal of International Law*, 23(3), www.ejil.org/pdfs/23/3/2296.pdf accessed 10 October 2013, p. 66.

[239] As mentioned in the section of human rights approaches to environmental protection: (1) mobilising existing rights; (2) reinterpreting existing rights; (3) a human right to an environment of a certain quality and so on. For more detailed information see Aminzadeh, S.C. (2006). A moral imperative: the human rights implications of climate change. *Hastings International and Comparative Law Review*, 30, pp. 231–245; Shelton, D.L. (1991). Human rights, environmental rights, and the right to environment. *Stanford Journal of International Law*, 28, p. 105; Greiber, T. *et al.* (2009). Conservation with justice – a human rights based approach. Gland (Switzerland): IUCN Environmental Law Centre, http://data.iucn.org/dbtw-wpd/edocs/eplp-071.pdf accessed 28 October 2011, p. 27.

the different meanings of the four human rights or the different development stages of the four human rights between China and Europe.

1.5. RESEARCH METHODOLOGY AND SOURCES

The research methodology is predominantly a desktop study and legal analysis, complemented with an analysis of case law and a comparative study. The research relied on primary and secondary sources of information. The international and regional instruments, judicial decisions, the Chinese Constitution and the national legislation of China are the primary sources. The secondary sources of information are the sources from textbooks, journal articles, newspapers, books, conference presentation/papers, previous research findings, and reports/articles from non-governmental organisations.

(1) Desktop study and legal analysis: a literature review and legal analysis have been done in three steps. Firstly, the legal sources regarding a human rights-based approach to conservation are analysed to clarify its comparative advantages and challenges and to identify the responsibilities and obligations of the relevant parties. The following documents have been particularly analysed, the Indigenous and Tribal Peoples Convention (1989);[240] the UN Convention on Biological Diversity (CBD) (1992); the Convention on Wetlands of International Importance especially as Waterfowl Habitat (Ramsar Convention) (1971); Agenda 21(1992); the Aarhus Convention (1998);[241] the United Nations Declaration on the Rights of Indigenous Peoples (UNDRIP) (2007).[242] Secondly, the four main human rights in the related legal instruments and their relationship with environmental protection in general, protected areas conservation in particular, are discussed. Thirdly, this book assesses the existing legal system concerning the main human rights (the right to property; the right to information; the right to participation and the right to access to justice) and environmental protection in general, protected areas conservation in particular, from international, European and Chinese levels, and identifies the potential conflicts regarding them.

---

240 International Labor Organization Convention No. 169: Indigenous and Tribal Peoples Convention, adopted on 27 June 1989 and entered into force on 5 September 1991, 28 ILM 1382, www.ilo.org/indigenous/Conventions/no169/lang--en/index.htm accessed 1 October 2012.

241 The UNECE Convention on Access to Information, Public Participation in Decision-making and Access to Justice in Environmental Matters (Aarhus Convention), adopted on 25 June 1998 in the Danish city of Aarhus at the Fourth Ministerial Conference in the "Environment for Europe" process, 2161 UNTS 447, www.unece.org/env/pp/introduction.html accessed 10 March 2012.

242 The United Nations Declaration on the Rights of Indigenous Peoples (UNDRIP), issued on 13 September 2007, UN Doc. A/RES/61/295, www.un.org/esa/socdev/unpfii/documents/DRIPS_en.pdf accessed 30 October 2012.

(2) Case law analysis: an analysis will be made of court cases chosen from the European Court of Human Rights and the Court of Justice of the European Union and cases from different levels of Chinese courts concerning human rights protection and environmental protection. Some important relevant communications on three procedural human rights from the ACCC[243] will also be analysed. Based on these, the potential conflicts are analysed and some possible suggestions for China are proposed.
(3) Comparative study: after the analysis and discussions mentioned above, the book turns to the comparative study of the four human rights in China and in Europe. It briefly explores the various reasons which caused the differences of the four human rights between China and Europe. The principal reason for the differences of each human right in China and in Europe will be clarified.

1.6. SCOPE AND OBJECTIVES

Although a large number of interesting issues regarding human rights protection and environmental protection are valuable for our research, this book has its own scope and objectives. They are clarified in figure 1.

Figure 1

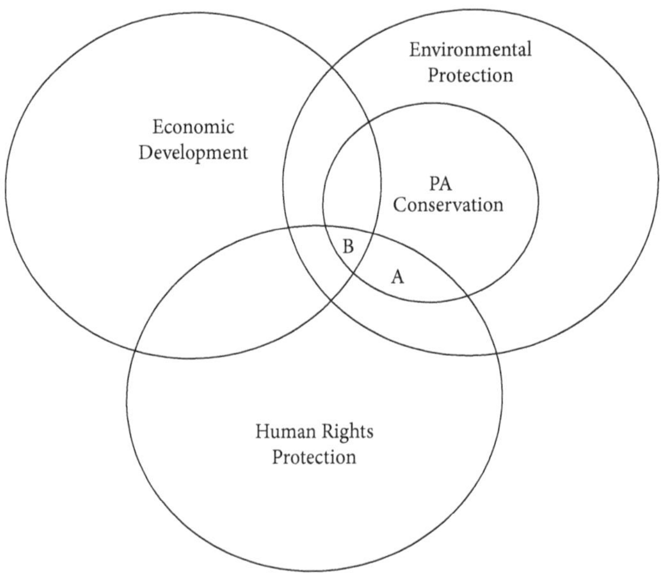

243 The Aarhus Convention Compliance Committee was established to fulfil the requirement of Article 15 of the Aarhus Convention on review of compliance to establish arrangements for reviewing compliance with the Convention. www.unece.org/env/pp/cc.html accessed 10 February 2014.

As shown above, the overlapping parts between any two big circles represent the potential conflicts and possible cooperation between these two parts. The conflicts regarding environmental protection and economic development are difficult to resolve, especially in poverty-stricken rural areas. Economic development often results in habitat destruction, biodiversity loss, and ecosystem degradation;[244] while conservation projects usually preserve natural resources without immediately tangible economic benefits, leading the public to withdraw its support for conservation.[245] It is very difficult to pursue environmental protection if there is a conflict between environmental protection and economic development. So the existing attempts to protect the environment are very precious. The attempts to protect the environment would lead to opposition by the relevant parties, if the attempts would infringe upon their human rights. To better balance human rights protection and environmental protection is a vital premise for stimulating all the potential roles from all the relevant parties in protecting the environment. This book mainly focuses on how to better balance human rights protection and environmental protection in general, protected areas in particular, as shown in the "A" area in the figure above. As shown in the "B" area in the figure above, this book also refers to some potential conflicts and possible cooperation among economic development, human rights protection and protected areas conservation. Specifically, the "B" area represents that: (1) the economic values of protected areas that contribute to promote economic development and improve the livelihood of local people; (2) some economic activities that infringe upon human rights protection and protected areas conservation; and (3) the local people and communities that oppose some economic activities to help the relevant authority to conserve protected areas. This book aims to change these parts from conflict to cooperation, and from infringement to involvement. Figure 2 below explains these step by step.

---

244 Wissel, S. & Wätzold, F. (2010). A conceptual analysis of the application of tradable permits to biodiversity conservation. *Conservation Biology*, 24(2), pp. 404–411; Estes, A.B., Kuemmerle, T., Kushnir, H., Radeloff, V.C. & Shugart, H.H. (2012). Land-cover change and human population trends in the greater Serengeti ecosystem from 1984–2003. *Biological Conservation*, 147(1), pp. 255–263.

245 Wätzold, F. & Schwerdtner, K. (2005). Why be wasteful when preserving a valuable resource? A review Article on the cost-effectiveness of European biodiversity conservation policy. *Biological Conservation*, 123(3), pp. 327–338; Berkes, F. (2007). Community-based conservation in a globalized world. *Proceeding of National Academy of Sciences of the United States of America*, 104(39), pp. 15188–15193; Wissel, S. & Wätzold, F. (2010). A conceptual analysis of the application of tradable permits to biodiversity conservation. *Conservation Biology*, 24(2), pp. 404–411.

Figure 2

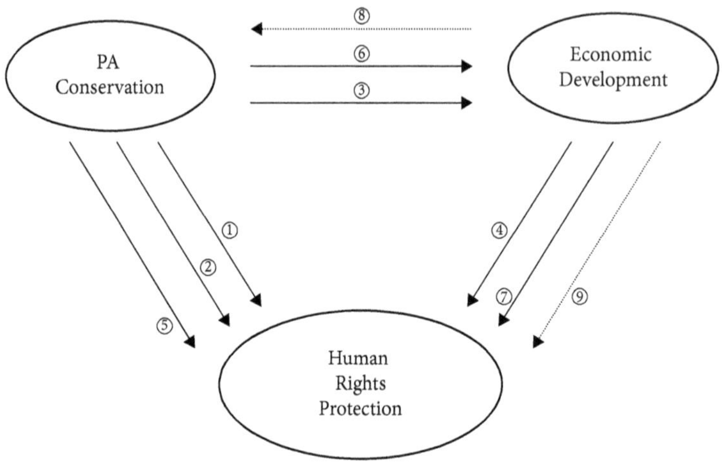

* ① Infringement/conflict; ② Involvement/Cooperation; ③ Promoting; ④ Feedback; ⑤ More cooperation; ⑥ Producing more; ⑦ More feedback; ⑧ ⑨ Infringement

According to what has been discussed on the various values of protected areas (see 1.1.3) and on the examples in China (see 1.1.4.2) (①), the conflict situation changed in a constructive way to cooperation (②) with local people and communities helping protected areas management to produce more values and then undoubtedly promote economic development (③). The appropriate benefit-sharing from the economic development for local people and communities (④) will stimulate their potential enthusiasm and huge roles in protected areas conservation (⑤). This would help protected areas produce more value (⑥) and then more benefit-sharing would be possible for local people and communities. This will certainly promote local people and communities to actively participate in protected areas conservation. They would be granted more rights in protected areas conservation if their local knowledge and power have been adopted by the relevant authorities (⑦). All these aim to avoid the possible infringement of economic development on human rights protection and protected areas conservation (⑧⑨). The key step to achieve this dynamic development among protected areas conservation, human rights protection and economic development is how to change potential conflicts (①) to possible cooperation (②) in a legal perspective. What is more, in order to safeguard protected areas conservation, the potential roles from local people and communities could be regarded as an irreplaceable role in opposing economic activities that would destroy protected areas conservation. A well-balanced human rights-based approach to conservation would promote this dynamic circle to become reality.

Figure 3

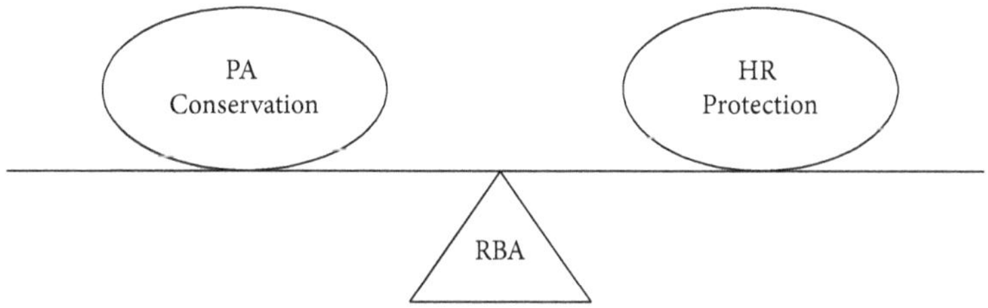

As shown in figure 3 above, a human rights-based approach to conservation would help to realise the well-balanced situation between human rights protection and protected areas conservation, which is explored in detail in this book.

Human rights are best conceived as a language for expressing claims and arguments rather than as an abstract set of universal standards.[246] The human rights in this book mainly refer to the right to property, the right to information, the right to participation and the right to access to justice of stakeholders. The stakeholders are defined as those who are affected or could have a potential to be affected by the establishment and management of protected areas. Normally, those groups refer to the local people and communities, rather than the broader public. However, the status quo of specific rights of local people and communities, together with the NGOs, largely depends on the status quo of a specific human right of the general public. Therefore, the rights of local people and communities will be discussed under the context of the rights of the general public. As for the human rights chosen in this book, the right to property, as a core human right, is based on the economic, policy, social, cultural and legal circumstances. Undoubtedly, the rights of access to information, public participation, and access to justice are essential procedural factors to solve potential conflicts to achieve sustainable development. The reasons why these four human rights have been selected will be further explained in different sections in Part II.

In addition, this book will propose some suggestions on how to solve these conflicts based on assessing the legal system and case analysis (cases from the ECtHR and the CJEU and communications from the ACCC) in Europe. Although the European Convention on Human Rights does not include any provisions on the environment, the European Court of Human Rights has upheld the human rights relevant to the environment in an indirect manner. The case law of the ECHR is considered an authoritative international standard

[246] Twining, W. (2009). Law, justice and rights: some implications of a global perspective. In: Ebbesson, J. & Okowa, P. (Eds.). *Environmental Law and Justice in Context.* Cambridge: Cambridge University Press, p. 88.

regarding the protection of human rights.[247] The description and discussion on the cases from the ECtHR can show a developmental tendency of human rights concerning environmental protection. The Aarhus Convention[248] and its case law from the ACCC reflect how procedural human rights link to the environmental protection. The influence of the Aarhus Convention on EU law on the three procedural human rights further indicate the baselines to solve the potential conflicts regarding human rights protection and environmental protection in the EU. In this context, the case law in the CJEU in this book mainly refer to protected areas conservation. These cases specifically discuss the role of human rights in protected areas conservation. The book also contains two cases from the CJEU further clarifying the right of access to justice. There are a lot of baselines regarding human rights protection and environmental protection in general in the ECtHR, the ACCC and the CJEU.

More importantly, the ECtHR regards a human rights-based approach as a dynamic and evolutive approach. The Court maintains this approach because it finds it is "*of critical importance that the Convention is interpreted and applied in a manner which renders its rights practical and effective, not theoretical and illusory*".[249] The Aarhus Convention is widely accepted as a remarkable legal instrument that links procedural human rights and environmental protection. The communications from the ACCC are also quite useful for solving the potential conflicts regarding human rights and environmental protection. The cases chosen from the ECtHR and the communications from the ACCC in this book are not limited to protected areas conservation for the following reasons. Firstly, the potential conflicts regarding human rights protection and protected areas conservation in China and in Europe are different. Even if referring to the same human rights protection, it is impossible to find two cases that are almost similar to compare. Secondly, compared to the general relationship between human rights protection and environmental protection, a specific relationship between human rights protection and protected areas conservation has received

---

247 Tsukhishvili, N. The case law of the European Court of Human Rights (ECHR): the right of access to public information. Institute for Development of Freedom of Information (IDFI). Published on February 2013. www.idfi.ge/uploadedFiles/files/ECHR%20Case%20Laws%20Analysis%281%29.pdf accessed 12 February 2014.

248 Except for Turkey, San Marino, Russia and Andorra, all the ECHR Member States are the State participants in the Aarhus Convention. https://treaties.un.org/Pages/ViewDetails.aspx?src=TREATY&mtdsg_no=XXVII-13&chapter=27&lang=en#3 accessed 19 April 2014.

249 E.g. ECtHR, Christine Goodwin v. The United Kingdom (2002), App. No. 28957/95, Judgment of 11 July 2002, §74, http://hudoc.echr.coe.int/sites/fra/pages/search.aspx?i=001-60596#{%22itemid%22:[%22001-60596%22]} accessed 12 April 2013; ECtHR, Stafford v. The United Kingdom (2002), App. No. 46295/99, Judgment of 28 May 2002, §68, http://hudoc.echr.coe.int/sites/eng/pages/search.aspx?i=001-60486#{%22itemid%22:[%22001-60486%22]} accessed 14 July 2014; ECtHR, Airey v. Ireland (1979), App. No. 6289/73, Judgment of 9 October 1979, §24, http://hudoc.echr.coe.int/sites/eng/pages/search.aspx?i=001-60486#{%22fulltext%22:[%22airey%20v%20ireland%22],%22itemid%22:[%22001-57420%22]} accessed 14 July 2014.

little attention. This is also true for the ECtHR, even if it has dealt with human rights protection for quite a long time. Thirdly, based on the different economic, political, social, legal and cultural circumstances, it is very difficult to directly transplant a certain law or regulation from Europe to China or vice versa. Fourth, owing to regional diversities, even if a certain law or regulation could solve a specific problem in Europe, we cannot promise that this law or regulation could be implemented well to achieve the similar result in China, or vice versa. Fifth, there is no case law in China, while the ECtHR and the ACCC can provide plentiful cases to discuss, although there are not many cases concerning human rights protection and protected areas conservation. The balancing of qualified human rights is a key practice of the ECtHR. The lessons on how to balance the potential conflicts regarding human rights protection and environmental protection, which are drawn from the ECtHR and the ACCC, will be helpful to solve the potential conflicts regarding the main human rights protection and protected areas conservation in China.

What is more, based on the different contexts between China and Europe and the different meaning or the development stages of the four rights in China and in Europe, the suggestions only set some minimum standards, which could be regarded as some principal baselines or guidelines, for these four human rights to implement a human rights-based approach to conserving protected areas in China.

Last but not least, when exploring the various reasons which caused the differences between the four human rights in China and in Europe, this book discusses some political, economic and cultural factors. In addition, some Chinese policy closely linked with protected areas conservation and human rights protection is also included in this book.

CHAPTER 2

THEORY OF A HUMAN RIGHTS-BASED APPROACH TO CONSERVATION

2.1. A HUMAN RIGHTS-BASED APPROACH AND ITS KEY FEATURES

A new "paradigm" of nature conservation with respect for human rights has recently emerged.[1] The UN Development Program issued a "Statement of Common Understanding"[2] in May 2003, explaining that "*In a human rights-based approach, human rights determine the relationship between individuals and groups with valid claims (rights-holders) and State and non-State actors with correlative obligations (duty-bearers).*"[3] The purpose behind the Statement of Common Understanding was to provide a consistent and coherent definition on the human rights-based approach across all UN agencies, funds and programmes. The human rights-based approach works towards strengthening the capacities of rights-holders to make their claims, and of duty-bearers to meet their obligations.[4] The UN Common Understanding of a human rights-based approach is based on a number of principles, of which empowerment is an important one.[5] The Common Understanding serves to guide processes and outcomes with respect to human rights mainstreaming and in doing so provides practitioners with operational guidance in applying a human rights-based approach in their work. An increasing number of UN agencies are not only integrating human rights into their internal policies, but also actively advocating

1 He, M. & Cliquet, A. (2013). Sustainable development through a rights-based approach to conserve protected areas in China. *China-EU Law Journal*. DOI 10.1007/s 12689-013-0031-7, http://link.springer.com/article/10.1007%2Fs12689-013-0031-7 accessed 4 November 2013.

2 Statement on a Common Understanding of a Human Rights-Based Approach to Development Cooperation (Statement of Common Understanding). Issued in May 2003, www.hrea.org/index.php?base_id=104&language_id=1&erc_doc_id=3107&category_id=44&category_type=3&group= accessed 13 October 2012.

3 The human rights-based approach – statement of common understanding, www.unicef.org/sowc04/files/AnnexB.pdf accessed 20 October 2012, p. 92.

4 The human rights-based approach – statement of common understanding, www.unicef.org/sowc04/files/AnnexB.pdf accessed 20 October 2012, p. 92.

5 Luttrel, C. & Quiroz, S. (2007). Linkages between human rights-based approaches and environment. Published in October 2007, www.poverty-wellbeing.net/resources/sharewebResource_en_1545.pdf accessed 20 January 2011, p. 1.

for human rights through their mandated work. Human rights are fulfilled when the persons involved enjoy secure access to the freedom or resource (adequate health protection, freedom of speech) covered by the right.[6] A human rights-based approach calls for the recognition of the intrinsic link between human rights and development goals, including environmental sustainability. While charity and needs-based approaches focus on the manifestation and immediate causes of problems, a human rights-based approach addresses such causes in a more structural manner.[7]

The term "human rights-based approach" is used by various actors and organisations in different ways. By drawing on the human rights framework – a relatively well developed and widely recognised set of negotiated standards – a human rights-based approach offers a strong standard with which to understand and assess the social implications of conservation practice.[8] A human rights-based approach is generally understood that all rights, including economic, social and cultural rights, are considered indivisible, interrelated and interdependent. However, the human rights-based approach does not necessarily have to be restricted to rights currently recognised in human rights law, but can have a normative component. According to Johnson and Forsyth,[9] "*[a]t the heart of this approach is the notion that governments, donors and societies in general have a responsibility to promote and maintain a minimum standard of well-being to which all people (irrespective of race, class, color, gender and other social groupings) would ideally possess a right. Morally, it is argued that States and societies should recognize and enforce rights that are necessary for 'survival and dignified living'.*"

The main objectives of a human rights-based approach are to[10]:

- strengthen the understanding of rights, i.e. understanding the location, forms and perpetrators of rights violations; recognising who is vulnerable

---

6 UNDP (United Nations Development Programme) (2000). *Human development report 2000.* Oxford: Oxford University Press. http://hdr.undp. org/en/media/HDR_2000_EN.pdf accessed 19 November 2011.

7 Boesen, J. & Martin, T. (2007). *Applying a Human Rights-based Approach – an Inspirational Guide for Civil Society.* Copenhagen: Danish Institute for Human Rights, p. 10. Until 1997, the UN mostly pursued a needs-based approach in its development activities, identifying the basic requirements of beneficiaries. Since then, UN bodies aim to work to fulfil the rights of people. See www.unfpa.org/rights/approaches.htm accessed 8 April 2011.

8 Campese, J. (2009). Human rights-based approaches to conservation: an overview of concepts and questions. In: Campese, J., *et al.* (Eds.). *Human Rights-based Approaches: Exploring Issues and Opportunities for Conservation.* Bogor, Indonesia: CIFOR and IUCN, http://data.iucn. org/dbtw-wpd/edocs/2009-014.pdf accessed 2 February 2011, p. 13.

9 Johnson, C. & Forsyth, T. (2002). In the eyes of the sate: negotiating a 'human rights-based approach' to forest conservation in Thailand. *World Development*, 30(9), pp. 1591–1605.

10 Kapur, A. & Duvvury, N. (2006). *A Human Rights-based Approach to Realizing the Economic and Social Rights of Poor and Social Rights of Poor and Marginalized Women: a Synthesis of Lessons Learned.* International Center for Research on Women (ICRW), www.icrw.org/files/ publications/A-Rights-Based-Approach-to-Realizing-the-Economic-and-Social-Rights-of-Poor-and-Marginalized-Women.pdf accessed 2 February 2012.

and assessing the degree of vulnerability; and recognising existing power imbalances in society;
- ensure accountability and transparency by identifying rights-holders (and their entitlements) and corresponding duty-bearers (and their obligations);
- build capacities for the realisation of rights so that rights-holders can make claims and duty-bearers can meet their obligations;
- facilitate the active and meaningful participation of multiple stakeholders, including people who directly benefit from projects through access to development processes and institutions, improved information, legal redress, and other positive strategies;
- create a sense of ownership of development processes through strategies of empowerment that focus on rights-holders both directly and through their advocates and civil society organisations; and
- encourage the expression of rights through different mediums of communication and interaction with people across regions.

A right entails an obligation on the part of the government to respect, promote, protect, and fulfil it.[11] To respect a right means refraining from interfering with the enjoyment of the right; to protect the right means enacting laws that create mechanisms to prevent violation of the right by State authorities or by non-State actors; to fulfil the right means to take active steps to put in place institutions and procedures, including the allocation of resources to enable people to enjoy the right.[12] The legal and normative character of rights and the associated governmental obligations are based on international human rights treaties and other standards, as well as on human rights provisions in national constitutions.[13] This approach reflects a holistic understanding of the nature of well-being.

---

11 Ssenyonjo, M. (2009). *Economic, Social and Cultural Rights in International Law.* Oxford: Hart Publishing, p. 23; Eide, A. (2001). Economic, social and cultural rights as human rights. In: Eide, A., Krause, C. & Rosas, A. (Eds.). *Economic, Social and Cultural Rights: A Textbook* (second revised edition). Leiden: Martinus Nijhoff Publishers, p. 22; Shue, H. (1984). The interdependence of duties. In: Alston, P. & Tomaševski, K. (Eds.). *The Right to Food.* Leiden: Martinus Nijhoff Publishers, p. 84.

12 UNFPA (The United Nations Population Fund Agency), Human rights principles, www.unfpa.org/rights/principles.htm accessed 20 October 2012.

13 Kapur, A. & Duvvury, N. (2006). *A Human Rights-based Approach to Realizing the Economic and Social Rights of Poor and Social Rights of Poor and Marginalized Women: a Synthesis of Lessons Learned.* International Center for Research on Women (ICRW), www.icrw.org/files/publications/A-Rights-Based-Approach-to-Realizing-the-Economic-and-Social-Rights-of-Poor-and-Marginalized-Women.pdf accessed 2 February 2012.

2.1.1. FEATURES OF A HUMAN RIGHTS-BASED APPROACH

The nature of human rights has been outlined in the Vienna Declaration and Programme of Action as "*all human rights are universal, indivisible and interdependent and interrelated.*"[14] Hence, the nature of human rights states how these rights are to be understood. The human rights principles purport the relevant processes that must take place to ensure the best realisation of human rights. The core part of a human rights-based approach is human rights, thus the human rights-based approach contains the basic features of human rights but more than those features.

(1) *Universality and inalienability.* Human rights are universal and inalienable, the entitlement of all people everywhere in the world. All human beings are entitled to human rights protection independent of the characteristics with which they are born or their own capacities. This requires acknowledging that all rights are universal, meaning that members of disadvantaged groups have the same rights as those in powerful groups.[15] All people everywhere in the world are entitled to human rights. They cannot be given up or taken away. As stated in Article 1 of the Universal Declaration of Human Rights, "*all human beings are born free and equal in dignity and rights.*"[16]
(2) *Indivisibility.* Human rights are indivisible, and all human rights have equal status. Whether civil, cultural, economic, political or social, they are all inherent to the dignity of every person. Consequently, they all have equal status as rights cannot be ranked in a hierarchy.[17] A human rights-based approach is comprehensive in their consideration of the full range of indivisible, interdependent and interrelated rights: civil, cultural, economic, political and social.[18] The realisation of one certain right often depends,

14 United Nations Vienna Declaration and Programme of Action, adopted by the World Conference on Human Rights on 25 June 1993, www.ohchr.org/en/professionalinterest/pages/vienna.aspx accessed 30 October 2011.

15 Cook, P. (1999). Non-discrimination and diversity: the rights of indigenous children (access to basic service and legal protection). A paper submitted to the CRC Day of Discussion on the rights of indigenous Children, International Institute for Child Rights and Development, www.crin.org/docs/resources/treaties/crc.34/IICRD_University_of_Victoria_Canada.pdf accessed 30 October 2011, p. 5.

16 Universal Declaration of Human Rights, adopted on 10 December 1948, UN Doc. A/810 AT 71, UNGA Res. 217 A (III), www.un.org/en/documents/udhr/ accessed 4 November 2011.

17 UN (2003). The Human Rights based approach to development cooperation towards a common understanding among UN Agencies, www.undp. org/content/dam/aplaws/publication/en/publications/environment-energy/www-ee-library/external-publications/un-the-human-rights-based-approach-to-development-cooperation/UN_Common_Understanding_on_Human_Rights-Based_Approach_to_Development_Cooperation_and_Programming.pdf accessed 30 October 2011, p. 2.

18 Singh, B. (2006). Rights Based Approach and Housing for the Urban Poor: an Analysis of the Slum Rehabilitation Schemes in Mumbai. Munich: GRIN Publishing, www.grin.com/

wholly or in part, upon the realisation of others. For example, the realisation of the right to participation may depend, in certain circumstances, on the realisation of the right to education and the right to information.

(3) *Equality (non-discrimination).* As the UN Common Understanding explains: "*all individuals are equal as human beings and by virtue of the inherent dignity of each person. All human beings are entitled to their human rights without discrimination of any kind, such as race, color, sex ethnicity, age, language, religion, political or other opinion, national or social origin, disability, property, birth or other status as explained by the human rights treaty bodies.*"[19] A human rights-based approach requires a particular focus on addressing discrimination and inequality, focusing on marginalised, disadvantaged, and excluded groups.[20] Non-discrimination is about treating like cases similarly and unlike cases differently. The feature of non-discrimination and equality requires paying special attention to those who are more discriminated against, or those who are more negatively affected by unequal distribution of economic, social, political and environmental resources. These groups do not only include "poor people", but also the most vulnerable peoples among the poor, for instance members of low castes, internally displaced persons, indigenous peoples, local businesses and local authorities etc.

(4) *Participation.* According to the UN Common Understanding, "*every person and all peoples are entitled to active, free and meaningful participation in, contribution to, and enjoyment of civil, economic, social, cultural and political development in which human rights and fundamental freedoms can be realized.*"[21] Participation is both a means and a goal and it includes all stakeholders.[22] A human rights-based approach requires a high degree of participation, including from communities, civil society, minorities, indigenous peoples, women and others.[23] This participation must be

---

en/e-book/187187/rights-based-approach-and-housing-for-the-urban-poor#inside accessed 30 October 2011, p. 2.

19 The human rights-based approach – statement of common understanding, www.unicef.org/sowc04/files/AnnexB.pdf accessed 20 October 2012, p. 92.

20 Berman, G. (2008). Undertaking a Human Rights-based Approach: a Guide for Basic Programming – Documenting Lessons Learned for Human Rights-based Programming: an Asia-pacific Perspective – Implications for Policy, Planning and Programming. Bangkok: UNESCO Asia and Pacific Regional Bureau for Education, http://unesdoc.unesco.org/images/0017/001791/179186e.pdf accessed 14 September 2012, p. 13.

21 The human rights-based approach – statement of common understanding, www.unicef.org/sowc04/files/AnnexB.pdf accessed 20 October 2012, p. 92.

22 Berman, G. (2008). Undertaking a Human Rights-based Approach: a Guide for Basic Programming – Documenting Lessons Learned for Human Rights-based Programming: an Asia-pacific Perspective – Implications for Policy, Planning and Programming. Bangkok: UNESCO Asia and Pacific Regional Bureau for Education, http://unesdoc.unesco.org/images/0017/001791/179186e.pdf accessed 14 September 2012, p. 13.

23 UNFPA (The United Nations Population Fund Agency), Human rights principles, www.unfpa.org/rights/principles.htm accessed 20 October 2012.

active, independent, and meaningful.[24] A human rights-based approach pays special attention to creating channels of participation for poor and disadvantaged people, as the ones whose claims are most affected. Creating capacities for effective, free and meaningful participation is a key feature of the human rights-based approach. Participation does not stand for consultation: it must shape and determine the decisions. It requires adequate access to information, adequate organisational capacities, absence of threats, etc. Access to information must be guaranteed both as an end in itself and as a means towards securing participation and accountability.[25] Stakeholder participation must occur during all stages of the project to ensure that issues of rights and obligations are consistently addressed.[26] From the perspective of the human rights-based approach, it is vital that stakeholders be a part of such accountability mechanisms including key rights-holders and key duty-bearers who may need capacities to be developed if they are to play their roles effectively in securing and ensuring accountability.[27]

(5) *Empowerment*. Empowerment is a consequence of appropriate participation.[28] A human rights-based approach offers a more powerful framework by shifting from charity to empowerment. Empowerment is the process by which people's capabilities to demand and use their human rights grow.[29] A human rights-based approach promotes social transformation by empowering people to exercise their "voice" and "agency" to influence the process of change.[30] They are empowered to claim their rights rather than simply

---

24 Orest Nowosad National Institutions Team. A human rights-based approach to development: strategies and challenges, http://nhri.ohchr.org/EN/Regional/Africa/4thConferenceDocuments/Novosad%20Development.pdf accessed 12 December 2011.

25 UNDP (2006). Applying a human rights-based approach to development cooperation and programming: a UNDP capacity development resource. Capacity development group, Bureau for development policy, http://hurilink.org/tools/Applying_a_HR_approach_to_UNDP_Technical_Cooperation--unr_revision.pdf accessed 11 November 2011.

26 UNDP (2006). Applying a human rights-based approach to development cooperation and programming: a UNDP capacity development resource. Capacity development group, Bureau for development policy, http://hurilink.org/tools/Applying_a_HR_approach_to_UNDP_Technical_Cooperation--unr_revision.pdf accessed 11 November 2011.

27 UNDP (2006). Applying a human rights-based approach to development cooperation and programming: a UNDP capacity development resource. Capacity development group, Bureau for development policy, http://hurilink.org/tools/Applying_a_HR_approach_to_UNDP_Technical_Cooperation--unr_revision.pdf accessed 11 November 2011.

28 UNDP (2006). Applying a human rights-based approach to development cooperation and programming: a UNDP capacity development resource. Capacity development group, Bureau for development policy, http://hurilink.org/tools/Applying_a_HR_approach_to_UNDP_Technical_Cooperation--unr_revision.pdf accessed 11 November 2011.

29 UNESCO (United Nations Educational, Scientific and Cultural Organization)/UNCF (United Nations Children's Fund) (2007). A human rights-based approach to education, http://unesdoc.unesco.org/images/0015/001548/154861e.pdf accessed 20 October 2011, p. 10.

30 Rights-based Approach (RBA) to Conservation, https://community.iucn.org/rba1/RBA%20Wiki/conservation.aspx#Question3 accessed 3 December 2011.

wait for policies, legislation or the provision of services.[31] To have a particular right means to have a claim on the duty-bearers (individual or institutions) that should help to collaborate in ensuring access to freedom. This approach takes into account the duties of a full-range of relevant actors, including individuals, communities, States, local organisations and authorities, national institutions, private companies, aid-donors, and international institutions.[32] It strengthens democratic governance by supporting the States to identify and fulfil their responsibilities to all under their jurisdiction.[33] It promotes transparent, fair, equitable, responsive and participatory governance and reduces opportunities for corruption. It also deters the diversion of justice and broadens democratic space for all levels of society. Initiatives should be focused on building the capacities of individuals and communities to hold those responsible to account.[34] The approach aims to give people, especially the vulnerable groups, the power and capabilities to improve their life and influence their own destinies. The human person is at the centre of the process either directly, through its advocates and through national institutions and civil society.[35] An effective human rights-based approach also gives preference to strategies for empowerment of local actors. It then identifies the reason that the root causes including social practices, laws, leadership, institutions and information.[36]

(6) *Accountability and respect for the rule of law.* Rights imply duties; and duties demand accountability.[37] The move from needs to rights, and from charity to duties, also implies an increased focus on accountability. According to the UN Common Understanding, "*States and other duty-bearers are answerable*

---

31 Berman, G. (2008). Undertaking a Human Rights-based Approach: a Guide for Basic Programming – Documenting Lessons Learned for Human Rights-based Programming: an Asia-pacific Perspective – Implications for Policy, Planning and Programming. Bangkok: UNESCO Asia and Pacific Regional Bureau for Education, http://unesdoc.unesco.org/images/0017/001791/179186e.pdf accessed 14 September 2012, p. 13.

32 UNDP (2006). Applying a human rights-based approach to development cooperation and programming: a UNDP capacity development resource. Capacity development group, Bureau for development policy, http://hurilink.org/tools/Applying_a_HR_approach_to_UNDP_Technical_Cooperation--unr_revision.pdf accessed 11 November 2011.

33 Rights-based Approach (RBA) to Conservation, https://community.iucn.org/rba1/RBA%20Wiki/conservation.aspx#Question3 accessed 3 December 2011.

34 UNESCO (United Nations Educational, Scientific and Cultural Organization)/ UNCF (United Nations Children's Fund) (2007). A human rights-based approach to education, http://unesdoc.unesco.org/images/0015/001548/154861e.pdf accessed 20 October 2011, p. 10.

35 Orest Nowosad National Institutions Team. A human rights-based approach to development: strategies and challenges, http://nhri.ohchr.org/EN/Regional/Africa/4thConferenceDocuments/Novosad%20Development.pdf accessed 12 December 2011.

36 Orest Nowosad National Institutions Team. A human rights-based approach to development: strategies and challenges, http://nhri.ohchr.org/EN/Regional/Africa/4thConferenceDocuments/Novosad%20Development.pdf accessed 12 December 2011.

37 OHCHR (2002). Draft guidelines: a human rights approach to poverty reduction strategies. Published on 10 September 2002, www1.umn.edu/humanrts/instree/povertyreductionguidelines.html accessed 28 October 2011.

> *for the observance of human rights. In this regard, they have to comply with the legal norms and standards enshrined in human rights instruments. Where they fail to do so, aggrieved rights-holders are entitled to institute proceedings for appropriate redress before a competent court or other adjudicator in accordance with the rules and procedures provided by law."*[38] A human rights-based approach gives due attention to issues of accessibility, including to the processes, institutions, information and redress or complaints mechanisms – many of which fall clearly within the purview of national human rights institutions.[39] The approach, however, focuses more strongly on relationship between public institutions (at various levels) and civil society, and how to make public institutions accountable to all citizens.[40] It also seeks to raise levels of accountability by identifying "rights-holders" and corresponding "duty-bearers" and to enhance the capacities of those duty-bearers to meet their obligations. The approach stresses that in order to achieve results, clear accountabilities must be set. The value of the approach is that it sets particular entitlements and obligations. The approach starts by assessing specific obstacles that duty-bearers face to exercise their obligations to ensure accountability. It aims to build on claim-holders and duty-bearers' existing strengths and solutions, rather than substituting them. In addition, as for governments, a wide range of other actors should also carry responsibilities for the realisation of human rights, including individuals, local organisations and authorities, the private sector, the media, donors, development partners and international institutions.[41] Accountability derives from the duties and obligations of States and the international community to take steps to respect, protect, promote and fulfil human rights for all people.[42] Accountability does not imply conditionality however, but rather encourages action through cooperation and constructive dialogue.

A human rights-based approach provides a comprehensive set of internationally agreed upon legal standards that promote justice, equality, participation and accountability. The approach requires some changes in social and economic

[38] The human rights-based approach – statement of common understanding, www.unicef.org/sowc04/files/AnnexB.pdf accessed 20 October 2012, p. 92.

[39] Orest Nowosad National Institutions Team. A human rights-based approach to development: strategies and challenges, http://nhri.ohchr.org/EN/Regional/Africa/4thConferenceDocuments/Novosad%20Development.pdf accessed 12 December 2011.

[40] Luttrel, C. & Quiroz, S. (2007). Linkages between human rights-based approaches and environment. Published in October 2007, www.poverty-wellbeing.net/resources/sharewebResource_en_1545.pdf accessed 20 January 2011, p. 1.

[41] UNESCO (United Nations Educational, Scientific and Cultural Organization)/ UNCF (United Nations Children's Fund) (2007). A human rights-based approach to education, http://unesdoc.unesco.org/images/0015/001548/154861e.pdf accessed 20 October 2011, p. 11.

[42] UNESCO (United Nations Educational, Scientific and Cultural Organization)/ UNCF (United Nations Children's Fund) (2007). A human rights-based approach to education, http://unesdoc.unesco.org/images/0015/001548/154861e.pdf accessed 20 October 2011, p. 11.

policies, law, resource allocations, attitudes and behaviours, institutional practices, data and monitoring and in people's participation and empowerment. It enables people to influence government decisions that affect their lives and promotes transparent, fair, equitable, responsive and participatory governance.

2.1.2. A HUMAN RIGHTS-BASED APPROACH TO CONSERVATION

A human rights-based approach to conservation was formally adopted at the fifth IUCN World Parks Congress[43] in Durban in 2003, confirmed at the seventh meeting of the Conference of the Parties to the Convention of Biological Diversity in 2004, and strengthened at the fourth World Conservation Congress in Barcelona in 2008.[44]

The human rights-based approach may be a powerful instrument to combine conservation interests with human rights protection.[45] The debate on a human rights-based approach to conservation that has emerged recently is occurring at a time when conservation thinking is being profoundly changed.[46] Responsible actions mindful of the rights of others, and of obligations to help respect, protect and promote the enjoyment of those rights, also contribute to building a climate of transparency and accountability that enhances the opportunities for long-term conservation.[47] A human rights-based approach to conservation serves as an instrument for addressing the interrelationship between human well-being and environmental objectives, by harmonising nature conservation activities with respect for people's rights.[48] This often includes efforts to make human rights and conservation mutually and positively reinforcing pursuits.[49]

---

43 The IUCN World Park Congresses are ten-yearly events to specifically discuss the issues relevant to protected areas.

44 Desmet, E. (2011). *Indigenous Rights Entwined with Nature Conservation*. Antwerp: Intersentia, p. 15.

45 IUCN arborvitae (2008). Human rights-based approaches to forest conservation. The IUCN Forest Conservation Programme Newsletter, No. 36, www.rightsandresources.org/documents/files/doc_786.pdf accessed 9 November 2011.

46 IUCN arborvitae (2008). Human rights-based approaches to forest conservation. The IUCN Forest Conservation Programme Newsletter, No. 36, www.rightsandresources.org/documents/files/doc_786.pdf accessed 9 November 2011.

47 Springer, J., Campese, J. & Painter, M. (2011). Conservation and human rights: key issues and contexts scoping paper for the conservation initiative on human rights. Published in October 2011, https://community.iucn.org/cihr/Resources/Scoping%20Paper%20_Oct%20final.pdf accessed 30 October 2011, p. 6.

48 Conservation and human rights, www.iucn.org/about/union/commissions/ceesp/topics/rights.cfm#responses accessed 9 November 2011.

49 Campese, J. (2009). Human rights-based approaches to conservation: an overview of concepts and questions. In: Campese, J., *et al.* (Eds.). *Human Rights-based Approaches: Exploring Issues and Opportunities for Conservation*. Bogor, Indonesia: CIFOR and IUCN, p. 8, http://data.iucn.org/dbtw-wpd/edocs/2009-014.pdf accessed 2 February 2011.

The overall aim of a human rights-based approach to conservation is to promote the realisation of conservation with justice.[50] Conservation with justice means that all State and non-State actors planning or engaged in policies, projects, programmes, and activities with potential impact on nature conservation shall secure to all potentially affected persons the substantive and procedural rights that are guaranteed by national and international law.[51] The people who live in high-biodiversity areas are frequently the most vulnerable groups in the country, and they highly and directly rely on ecosystem services and natural resources. The human rights-based approach to conservation requires that all interested stakeholders are provided the right and opportunity to voice their opinions, and have these opinions meaningfully factored into conservation arrangements. Duty-bearers (States, multilateral agencies, business entities, organisations, and individuals) have obligations to respect, protect, guarantee, and promote people's rights and to respect international and national norms concerning conservation.[52] The human rights-based approach is an effective way to reconcile conservation and rights, by integrating rights norms, standards, and principles in policy, planning, implementation, and evaluation to help ensure that conservation practice respects rights in all cases, and supports their further realisation where possible.[53] The two goals should be mutually reinforcing and lead States to adopt and implement a minimum set of public policies, laws and regulations.[54] Providing rights and opportunities requires that projects support locally identified requirements for enabling meaningful participation by all involved and interested stakeholders in conservation efforts.[55] The need for conservation to recognise the rights of those people who are most directly impacted by global conservation initiatives makes that rights-based thinking is not only a question of ethics and social justice but also a practical imperative for saving species and ecosystems.[56] However, the minimum required to free and

---

50 Greiber, T. *et al.* (2009). Conservation with justice – a human rights based approach. Gland (Switzerland): IUCN Environmental Law Centre, http://data.iucn.org/dbtw-wpd/edocs/eplp-071.pdf accessed 28 October 2011, p. vii.

51 Greiber, T. *et al.* (2009). Conservation with justice – a human rights based approach. Gland (Switzerland): IUCN Environmental Law Centre, http://data.iucn.org/dbtw-wpd/edocs/eplp-071.pdf accessed 28 October 2011, p. vii.

52 Greiber, T. *et al.* (2009). Conservation with justice – a human rights based approach. Gland (Switzerland): IUCN Environmental Law Centre, http://data.iucn.org/dbtw-wpd/edocs/eplp-071.pdf accessed 28 October 2011, p. 9.

53 Conservation and human rights, www.iucn.org/about/union/commissions/ceesp/topics/rights.cfm#responses accessed 9 November 2011.

54 Greiber, T. *et al.* (2009). Conservation with justice – a human rights based approach. Gland (Switzerland): IUCN Environmental Law Centre, http://data.iucn.org/dbtw-wpd/edocs/eplp-071.pdf accessed 28 October 2011, p. 9.

55 Conservation and human rights, www.iucn.org/about/union/commissions/ceesp/topics/rights.cfm#responses accessed 9 November 2011.

56 IUCN arborvitae (2008). Human rights-based approaches to forest conservation. The IUCN Forest Conservation Programme Newsletter, No. 36, www.rightsandresources.org/documents/files/doc_786.pdf accessed 9 November 2011.

use the potentiality of these actors is the fulfilment of their basic rights based on the Universal Declaration of Human Rights.[57] A rights perspective provides a framework for examining and addressing the key aspects of power relations that influence people's capacities, rights and responsibilities.[58]

The human rights-based approach to conservation is motivated by two rationales: first, awareness that environmental quality is a prerequisite to ensuring the enjoyment of a host of internationally and domestically guaranteed legal rights and, second, a similar awareness that respect for such rights can lead to better conservation.[59]

2.2. ADVANTAGES AND CHALLENGES OF A HUMAN RIGHTS-BASED APPROACH TO CONSERVATION

2.2.1. ADDED VALUES OF A HUMAN RIGHTS-BASED APPROACH

A human rights-based approach can have significant added value.

- *Aiming at the main objective.* It cannot be doubted that rapid depletion of resources and disturbance of ecological balance affect the living standard of humans and affect, directly or indirectly, the enjoyment of various rights guaranteed to human beings. The main goal of environmental protection is to improve the living environment of the general population.[60] As policies and programmes are formulated, the main objective of these policies and programmes should be fulfilling human rights.[61] Adopting intergenerational equity coupled with an expansion of existing rights, is perhaps the most pragmatic approach to take.[62] A human rights-based approach would –

---

57 Universal Declaration of Human Rights, adopted on 10 December 1948, UN Doc. A/810 AT 71, UNGA Res. 217 A (III), www.un.org/en/documents/udhr/ accessed 4 November 2011.

58 Luttrel, C. & Quiroz, S. (2007). Linkages between human rights-based approaches and environment. Published in October 2007, www.poverty-wellbeing.net/resources/sharewebResource_en_1545.pdf accessed 20 January 2011, p. 1.

59 Conservation and human rights, www.iucn.org/about/union/commissions/ceesp/topics/rights.cfm#responses accessed 9 November 2011.

60 He, M. & Cliquet, A. (2013). Sustainable development through a rights-based approach to conserve protected areas in China. *China-EU Law Journal.* DOI 10.1007/s 12689-013-0031-7. http://link.springer.com/article/10.1007%2Fs12689-013-0031-7 accessed 4 November 2013.

61 OHCHR. Applying a human rights-based approach to climate change negotiations, policies and measures, www.ohchr.org/Documents/Issues/ClimateChange/InfoNoteHRBA.pdf accessed 2 February 2012.

62 Picolotti, R. & Taillant, J.D. (Eds.) (2010). Linking human rights and the environment, www.uapress.arizona.edu/Books/bid1492.htm accessed 2 February 2012.

compared to the existing approach to sustainable development and environmental law – focus less on States and more on individuals, who in fact get hurt or could get hurt by development that is unsustainable or by the disruption of the environment.[63] An obvious gap exists today in the protection of human life and dignity from threats associated with environmental degradation, especially when such threats are a consequence of actions or inactions taken by an individual's own national government.[64] This is what a human rights-based approach to environmental protection can most effectively achieve.[65]

- *Clarifying rights and duties.* A human rights-based approach identifies rights-holders and their entitlements and corresponding duty-bearers, in addition to their obligations towards strengthening the capacities of rights-holders to make their claims and of duty-bearers to meet their obligations.[66] It brings about greater analytical clarity regarding the underlying and broader causes of the multidimensional links between conservation and human rights.[67] By adopting and adhering to common principles and standards, conservation organisations will not only make clear to partner organisations where they stand on human rights, but will also more clearly define the scope of effective responsibility.[68] This will also provide conservation organisations with a basis on which to make decisions about ways to operate in locations with unclear or inadequate governance and rights regimes.[69] Power asymmetries between poor rural communities and conservation agencies – whether they are States or NGOs – must be recognised.[70]
- *Focusing on the most vulnerable.* A human rights-based approach to environmental protection focuses on the most vulnerable and pays special

63 Stand Up for Your Rights. www.standupforyourrights.org/default.asp?pid=49 accessed 1 December 2011.

64 Anton, D.K. & Shelton, D.L. (2011). *Environmental Protection and Human Rights.* Cambridge: Cambridge University Press, p. 142.

65 He, M. & Cliquet, A. (2013). Sustainable development through a rights-based approach to conserve protected areas in China. *China-EU Law Journal.* DOI 10.1007/s 12689-013-0031-7. http://link.springer.com/article/10.1007%2Fs12689-013-0031-7 accessed 4 November 2013.

66 OHCHR. Applying a human rights-based approach to climate change negotiations, policies and measures, www.ohchr.org/Documents/Issues/ClimateChange/InfoNoteHRBA.pdf accessed 2 February 2012.

67 Rights-based Approach (RBA) to Conservation, https://community.iucn.org/rba1/RBA%20 Wiki/conservation.aspx#Question3 accessed 3 December 2011.

68 Roe, D. *et al.* (2010). Conservation and human rights: the need for international standards. Published in May 2010. IIED (International Institute for Environment and Development). www.iied.org/pubs/display.php?o=17066IIED accessed 1 September 2011.

69 Roe, D. *et al.* (2010). Conservation and human rights: the need for international standards. Published in May 2010. IIED (International Institute for Environment and Development). www.iied.org/pubs/display.php?o=17066IIED accessed 1 September 2011.

70 Conservation, human rights & protected areas governance: a field-based workshop in the Baviaanskloof Mega-Reserve. (2007). South Africa, 6–7 July 2007, http://cmsdata.iucn.org/downloads/bav_workshop. pdf accessed 10 October 2012, p. 4.

attention to the rights of the most marginalised people. It promotes local people as rights-holders, meaning that people are the rightful custodians of conservation and responsible actors, not merely passive beneficiaries. Today there is a sophisticated system of rights and duties: one person's entitlement is limited by the entitlement of another person or any duty is justified by the need to ensure everyone's entitlement.[71] The human rights-based approach is also the way to enhance people's power and protect rights which have been ignored or unprotected. Strengthening rights mechanisms enhances the capacity of the poor and marginalised to claim entitlements and push duty-bearers to deliver on their sustainable development commitments.[72] Only by listening to these people, accepting accountability and implementing responsibilities, will we be able to make significant progress towards more sustainable development.[73] It better addresses possible inequalities within and across communities and levels, i.e. avoiding "elite capture".[74] It has already been acknowledged that there are rights that exist but that are not recognised, because the poor are not powerful enough to have them implemented.[75] Arguably, if the poor are strong enough to claim their rights, then there is probably no need for the human rights-based approach.[76] However, for many vulnerable people – including the millions of formally landless rural people – a clear "human right" to land is weak or non-existent.[77]

- *Responding to increasing demands from NGOs, etc.* A human rights-based approach effectively responds to increasing demands from donors, NGOs, communities, social movements, etc., for greater accountability by conservation

---

71 Bosselmann, K. (2011). Property rights and sustainability: can they be reconciled? In: Grinlinton D. & Taylor, P. (Eds.). *Property Rights and Sustainability – the Evolution of Property Rights to Meet Ecological Challenges*. Leiden: Martinus Nijhoff Publishers, p. 28.

72 IBON International. (2012).Reforming global sustainable development governance: a rights-based agenda. IBON International Working Paper. http://rio20.net/wp-content/uploads/2012/02/DRAFT_Reforming-international-susdev-governance-a-rights-based-agenda1.pdf accessed 2 April 2012.

73 He, M. & Cliquet, A. (2013). Sustainable development through a rights-based approach to conserve protected areas in China. *China-EU Law Journal*. DOI 10.1007/s 12689-013-0031-7. http://link.springer.com/article/10.1007%2Fs12689-013-0031-7 accessed 4 November 2013.

74 Rights-based Approach (RBA) to Conservation, https://community.iucn.org/rba1/RBA%20 Wiki/conservation.aspx#Question3 accessed 3 December 2011.

75 Mitlin, D. & Patel, S. (2005). Re-interpreting the human rights-based approach – a grassroots perspective on rights and development. A ESRC Research Group, Global Poverty Research Group (GPRG), Economic & Social Research Council (ESRC), www.gprg.org/ accessed 4 April 2012.

76 Kabeer, N. (2002). Citizenship, affiliation and exclusion: perspectives from the South. *IDS* (Institute of Development Studies) *Bulletin*, 33(2), pp. 12–23.

77 Campese, J. (2009). Human rights-based approaches to conservation: an overview of concepts and questions. In: Campese, J., *et al* (Eds.). *Human Rights-based Approaches: Exploring Issues and Opportunities for Conservation* (p. 20). Bogor, Indonesia: CIFOR and IUCN, http://data.iucn.org/dbtw-wpd/edocs/2009-014.pdf accessed 2 February 2011.

organisations for the efforts of their activities on rights.[78] NGOs can potentially play significant roles in various contexts. One key role is self-regulation – ensuring respect for rights – for purposes of social responsibility as well as to contribute to conservation by reducing conflicts and engaging the substantial capacities of rights-holders and related constituencies.[79] Within the scope of conservation programmes, NGOs can support and promote actions in local contexts to meet the standards and principles of international human rights law. Where existing policy and institutional frameworks are not conducive to this, NGOs can also play roles in promoting improved governance, contributing to improved rights and conservation outcomes.[80] Communities often see international NGOs as having greater power and access to decision-makers.[81]

- *Providing guidance for theory and practice.* A human rights-based approach provides tools for institutions and actors to consider the impact of their policies on the realisation of other rights and development goals.[82] By focusing on individual and collective human dignity, a human rights-based approach can also strengthen the social pillar and the established proper balance and interaction among the economic, social and environmental pillars.[83] From a theoretical perspective, principles and standards derived from international human rights treaties should guide all policies and programming in all sectors and in all phases of the process.[84] From a practical perspective, a human rights-based approach can be used to guide policies and measures. It can inform assessments, and strengthen processes, ensuring access to essential information, effective participation, and the

78 Rights-based Approach (RBA) to Conservation, https://community.iucn.org/rba1/RBA%20Wiki/conservation.aspx#Question3 accessed 3 December 2011.

79 Springer, J., Campese, J. & Painter, M. (2011). Conservation and human rights: key issues and contexts scoping paper for the conservation initiative on human rights. Published in October 2011 https://community.iucn.org/cihr/Resources/Scoping%20Paper%20_Oct%20final.pdf accessed 30 October 2011, p. 15.

80 This approach is reflected in the CIHR Conservation and Human Rights Framework, which includes a principle on encouraging good governance, in addition to those on respecting, support and promoting rights, with particular attention to the vulnerable.

81 Springer, J., Campese, J. & Painter, M. (2011). Conservation and human rights: key issues and contexts scoping paper for the conservation initiative on human rights. Published in October 2011 https://community.iucn.org/cihr/Resources/Scoping%20Paper%20_Oct%20final.pdf accessed 30 October 2011, p. 16.

82 IBON International (2012). Reforming global sustainable development governance: a rights-based agenda. IBON International Working Paper, http://rio20.net/wp-content/uploads/2012/02/DRAFT_Reforming-international-susdev-governance-a-rights-based-agenda1.pdf accessed 2 April 2012, p. 6.

83 IBON International (2012). Reforming global sustainable development governance: a rights-based agenda. IBON International Working Paper, http://rio20.net/wp-content/uploads/2012/02/DRAFT_Reforming-international-susdev-governance-a-rights-based-agenda1.pdf accessed 2 April 2012, p. 6.

84 OHCHR. Applying a human rights-based approach to climate change negotiations, policies and measures, www.ohchr.org/Documents/Issues/ClimateChange/InfoNoteHRBA.pdf accessed 2 February 2012.

provision of access to justice (remedies).[85] It also provides clear criteria with which to design and measure conservation programming and outcomes by drawing on the widely recognised human rights framework.[86] A human rights-based approach is also expected to eradicate poverty and achieve the Millennium Development Goals.[87]

- *Illuminating the underlying causes of impacts of human rights.* Human rights and human rights protection are widely recognised, both at the national and international level as well as in theory and in practice. However, as indicated in the introduction (see 1.1.2.3), a right to a healthy environment is still being debated. To avoid defining what "a good or satisfied environment" is, protecting the environment through a human rights-based approach can be directly under the jurisdiction of all the Courts of Human Rights. What's more, a simple right to environment may not address the complex and technical issues present in environmental problems.[88] A human rights-based approach can illuminate the underlying causes of positive or negative impacts of an activity on people's rights, as well as the impact of the enjoyment or lack of enjoyment on people's rights on conservation efforts, thus allowing better choices in designing and carrying out proposed projects or activities.[89] It also provides a framework for identifying and balancing competing claims – including global public interests and local people's needs – with attention to the minimum standards that cannot be "traded-off".[90] A human rights-based approach also leads to an analysis of responsibilities of actors and institutions when rights are unfulfilled, and thus facilitates in locating accountability and in seeking remedy.[91]
- *Requiring the effort of States and individuals.* Environmental protection requires a concerted effort of the State and the individual. In a welfare State, the government has a duty to control and restrict, if necessary, the access of

85 OHCHR. Applying a human rights-based approach to climate change negotiations, policies and measures, www.ohchr.org/Documents/Issues/ClimateChange/InfoNoteHRBA.pdf accessed 2 February 2012.

86 Rights-based Approach (RBA) to Conservation, https://community.iucn.org/rba1/RBA%20 Wiki/conservation.aspx#Question3 accessed 3 December 2011.

87 UNFPA (The United Nations Population Fund Agency). Human rights principles, www.unfpa.org/rights/principles.htm accessed 20 October 2012.

88 Anton, D.K. & Shelton, D.L. (2011). *Environmental Protection and Human Rights.* Cambridge: Cambridge University Press, p. 145.

89 Greiber, T. *et al.* (2009). Conservation with justice – a human rights based approach. Gland (Switzerland): IUCN Environmental Law Centre, http://data.iucn.org/dbtw-wpd/edocs/eplp-071.pdf accessed 28 October 2011, p. 6.

90 Rights-based Approach (RBA) to Conservation, https://community.iucn.org/rba1/RBA%20 Wiki/conservation.aspx#Question3 accessed 3 December 2011.

91 IBON International. (2012).Reforming global sustainable development governance: a rights-based agenda. IBON International Working Paper. http://rio20.net/wp-content/uploads/2012/02/DRAFT_Reforming-international-susdev-governance-a-rights-based-agenda1.pdf accessed 2 April 2012.

persons to the natural resources of the country.[92] Human rights represent the greatest claim which an individual can have against the State. In other words, environmental law mostly contains obligations of States against each other, whereas human rights law grants individual rights against the State.[93] The necessity of getting the State involved in environmental protection is that it is the only institution capable of restricting access to natural resources and can coordinate human activities on a wide scale to prevent degradation of the environment.[94] The efforts from the individuals and the communities not only can affect some policies and decisions from the government, but can also force the government to fulfil its international commitments and duties.

- *Improving conservation outcomes.* Conservation seeks to provide lasting, flexible and adaptable solutions to the problem of maintaining and improving biodiversity resources in the face of society's expanding economic expectations.[95] It is difficult to achieve a better balance between nature conservation and human rights. The human rights-based approach can enhance conservation outcomes, and those conservation benefits can rightly form part of an organisation's motivation for adopting such approach.[96] The human rights-based approach may improve conservation outcomes by facilitating positive synergies and generally improving the governance of natural resources.[97] It also helps demonstrate the conservation's positive contributions to human rights, including in emerging areas, such as collective and intergenerational rights, and, conversely, increasing understanding of the rights-related risks of not protecting critical natural resources and biodiversity.[98] Human rights promote democracy and social progress and the human rights-based approach can promotes social cohesion, integration and stability. Establishing principles of equity and human rights as integral components of conservation planning and management would enhance

---

92 Picolotti, R. & Taillant, J.D. (Eds.) (2010). Linking human rights and the environment, www.uapress.arizona.edu/Books/bid1492.htm accessed 2 February 2012.

93 www.lund2012.earthsystemgovernance.org/LC2012-paper316.pdf accessed 4 April 2012.

94 Picolotti, R. & Taillant, J.D. (Eds.) (2010). Linking human rights and the environment, www.uapress.arizona.edu/Books/bid1492.htm accessed 2 February 2012.

95 Roe, D. *et al.* (2010). Conservation and human rights: the need for international standards. Published in May 2010. IIED (International Institute for Environment and Development). www.iied.org/pubs/display.php?o=17066IIED accessed 1 September 2011.

96 Campese, J. (2009). Human rights-based approaches to conservation: an overview of concepts and questions. In: Campese, J., *et al.* (Eds.). *Human Rights-based Approaches: Exploring Issues and Opportunities for Conservation.* Bogor, Indonesia:CIFOR and IUCN, p. 13, http://data.iucn.org/dbtw-wpd/edocs/2009-014.pdf accessed 2 February 2011.

97 Greiber, T. *et al.* (2009). Conservation with justice – a human rights based approach. Gland (Switzerland): IUCN Environmental Law Centre, http://data.iucn.org/dbtw-wpd/edocs/eplp-071.pdf accessed 28 October 2011, p. 6.

98 Rights-based Approach (RBA) to Conservation, https://community.iucn.org/rba1/RBA%20Wiki/conservation.aspx#Question3 accessed 3 December 2011.

conservation practice and result in more effective action.[99] The realisation of indigenous peoples' rights largely depends on the sustainable use of biodiversity, and their rights can be used to help to conserve biodiversity effectively. Substantive human rights can be used to achieve goals that are important to biodiversity conservation, while procedural rights can be used to ensure that all stakeholders participate in decision-making, which will in many cases lead to more effective conservation.[100] For instance, the right to life and the right to a healthy environment can reach their full potential only in a rich, diverse, and unspoiled environment. Experience shows better environmental decision-making and implementation when those affected are informed and participate in the process: the legitimacy of the decisions exercises a pull towards compliance with the measures adopted.[101]

2.2.2. CHALLENGES

There is no panacea in the world. An advantage, on the other side of the coin, can be a challenge. A human rights-based approach is beginning to be regarded as a way to achieve and integrate conservation, human rights and social justice. While the benefits of the human rights-based approach for social justice and conservation appear to be many, it is also clear that the question of what the human rights-based approach is, and how such an approach can be operationalised and practically implemented in the conservation arena, remains a challenge.[102] The challenge can be divided into two parts, which are external challenges and challenges inherent to the human rights-based approach itself.

2.2.2.1. External Challenges

There are some external challenges for a human rights-based approach.

---

99 Roe, D. *et al.* (2010). Conservation and human rights: the need for international standards. Published in May 2010. IIED (International Institute for Environment and Development). www.iied.org/pubs/display.php?o=17066IIED accessed 1 September 2011.

100 Kravchenko, S. (2007). Using human rights instruments for biodiversity conservation. IUCN Commission on Environmental, Economic & Social Policy. Issued on 15 July 2007, http://cmsdata.iucn.org/downloads/pm15.pdf accessed 5 May 2011, p. 200.

101 Shelton, D.L. (2002). Human rights, health & environmental protection: linkages in law & practice (A Background Paper for the World Health Organization). Health and Human Rights Working Paper Series No. 1, www.who.int/hhr/Series_1%20%20Sheltonpaper_rev1.pdf accessed 4 September 2011.

102 Campese, J. *et al.* (2008). Rights and conservation in a diverse and sustainable world: a journey at the 2008 IUCN World Conservation Congress. In: A Congress Forum Journey Report, Barcelona, Spain, 5–14 October 2008, http://cmsdata.iucn.org/downloads/rights_and_conservation_journey_report_1_2.pdf accessed 4 April 2011.

- *Challenge from governments' efforts*. Not all governments are fully engaged in long-term conservation efforts or the realisation of human rights,[103] especially in some developing countries. The main goal of the governments from some developing countries is to promote the economic development and to feed the citizens. Thus, on some occasions, short term socio-economic interests drive government decisions on the utilisation of natural resources, without taking into account nature conservation concerns and/or respect for human rights.[104] While human rights standards are established internationally or regionally, the solutions to specific human rights issues are necessarily local and context-based.[105] The human rights-based approach principles can and often are translated into different approaches for different country contexts. It is therefore valuable to reflect on the specifics of the geographic contexts, and particularly their political and cultural context in understanding the methodological approaches adopted in these human rights-based approach projects and their outcomes and impacts on human rights in the short and longer term.[106] To realise human rights in particular solutions should take history, political context, culture, legal system and ecological situations into consideration. There are multiple – or "plural" – sources and conceptualisations of rights, including from statutory system and from customary laws of indigenous peoples and local communities.[107] Normally, States play an important role as human rights duty-bearers, while other actors (such as private companies, NGOs) are also adhering to human rights standards. Owing to poor governance or poor natural resources, States may not always play adequate duty-bearer roles. At the same time, national legislation may not meet the requirements of international law and principles. A human rights-based approach should promote the recognition and respect for local people's own customary laws, processes and institutions

---

103 Greiber, T. *et al.* (2009). Conservation with justice – a human rights based approach. Gland (Switzerland): IUCN Environmental Law Centre, http://data.iucn.org/dbtw-wpd/edocs/eplp-071.pdf accessed 28 October 2011, p. 7.

104 He, M. & Cliquet, A. (2013). Sustainable development through a rights-based approach to conserve protected areas in China. *China-EU Law Journal*. DOI 10.1007/s 12689-013-0031-7. http://link.springer.com/article/10.1007%2Fs12689-013-0031-7 accessed 4 November 2013.

105 Springer, J., Campese, J. & Painter, M. (2011). Conservation and human rights: key issues and contexts scoping paper for the conservation initiative on human rights. Published in October 2011, https://community.iucn.org/cihr/Resources/Scoping%20Paper%20_Oct%20final.pdf accessed 30 October 2011, p. 15.

106 Berman, G. (2008). Undertaking a Human Rights-based Approach: a Guide for Basic Programming – Documenting Lessons Learned for Human Rights-based Programming: an Asia-pacific Perspective – Implications for Policy, Planning and Programming. Bangkok: UNESCO Asia and Pacific Regional Bureau for Education, http://unesdoc.unesco.org/images/0017/001791/179186e.pdf accessed 14 September 2012, p. 3.

107 Springer, J., Campese, J. & Painter, M. (2011). Conservation and human rights: key issues and contexts scoping paper for the conservation initiative on human rights. Published in October 2011, https://community.iucn.org/cihr/Resources/Scoping%20Paper%20_Oct%20final.pdf accessed 30 October 2011, p. 15.

in local contexts on the condition that their goals are to promote a win-win situation between nature conservation and human rights protection.[108]

- *Challenge from global or regional human rights texts.* Global human rights texts are predominantly about human beings. They contain few references to the environment, and efforts to use human rights complaint procedures to protect nature or other species have had only limited success.[109] Human rights law does not mean to protect the environment itself, that is to say, the harm to the environment is not within the jurisdiction of human rights. Biodiversity, ecological integrity and nature cannot only be conserved at the international level; much more practical issues need to be solved at the national level. Conflicts regarding nature conservation and economic development cannot be solved by protecting a single human right. Moreover, problems that cannot be solved by (global) human rights law include climate change issues, the unsustainable use of natural resources, biodiversity loss and other similar global environmental issues.[110] Global human rights law also provides limited reference or experience for developing countries, like China, which wants to solve the conflicts according to the international legal instruments.[111]

2.2.2.2. *Challenges Inherent to the Human Rights-Based Approach Itself*

Some challenges inherent to the human rights-based approach itself will be discussed below.

- *Lack of time, expertise, funding.* The human rights-based approach requires substantial resources including time, expertise, information, and funding to build capacity.[112] It also requires moving outside common boundaries of the conservation area and demands shaping the links between conservation and rights by exploring the broader political and legal system. It is a key and common challenge for any new approach to environmental protection,

---

108 He, M. & Cliquet, A. (2013). Sustainable development through a rights-based approach to conserve protected areas in China. *China-EU Law Journal*. DOI 10.1007/s 12689-013-0031-7. http://link.springer.com/article/10.1007%2Fs12689-013-0031-7 accessed 4 November 2013.

109 Greiber, T. *et al.* (2009). Conservation with justice – a human rights based approach. Gland (Switzerland): IUCN Environmental Law Centre, http://data.iucn.org/dbtw-wpd/edocs/eplp-071.pdf accessed 28 October 2011, p. 7.

110 He, M. & Cliquet, A. (2013). Sustainable development through a rights-based approach to conserve protected areas in China. *China-EU Law Journal*. DOI 10.1007/s 12689-013-0031-7. http://link.springer.com/article/10.1007%2Fs12689-013-0031-7 accessed 4 November 2013.

111 He, M. & Cliquet, A. (2013). Sustainable development through a rights-based approach to conserve protected areas in China. *China-EU Law Journal*. DOI 10.1007/s 12689-013-0031-7. http://link.springer.com/article/10.1007%2Fs12689-013-0031-7 accessed 4 November 2013.

112 Greiber, T. *et al.* (2009). Conservation with justice – a human rights based approach. Gland (Switzerland): IUCN Environmental Law Centre, http://data.iucn.org/dbtw-wpd/edocs/eplp-071.pdf accessed 28 October 2011, p. 7.

especially in a developing country, like China with a quite recently established legal framework.[113]

- *Competition between rights.* Either across groups or within a single group competition may arise, causing the upholding of one right to infringe on another.[114] Human rights are universal, in that they apply equally to everyone, and indivisible, in that they are all considered equally necessary for a secure and dignified life.[115] However, in practice, rights often exist in tension with one another, and different groups of people frequently come into conflict with one another as they exercise their rights. It is generally recognised that the exercise of a person's or group's rights are limited to the extent that they infringe upon the basic rights of others.[116] In the context of natural resources management, where the resources underpinning rights are often limited or declining, this issue of competing rights can be particularly complex.[117] For instance, how can local communities' rights be balanced with environmental rights of a broader public, and the rights of future generations? More specifically, how can the indigenous peoples' traditional lands, territories and resources be balanced with the right to a clean living environment of the public? While a human rights-based approach cannot provide ready answers to these questions, by making these rights issues visible they can provide a useful framework for understanding and negotiating them.[118] When poverty and lack of adequate food are commonplace and people's basic needs are not guaranteed, the priority will

113 He, M. & Cliquet, A. (2013). Sustainable development through a rights-based approach to conserve protected areas in China. *China-EU Law Journal.* DOI 10.1007/s 12689-013-0031-7. http://link.springer.com/article/10.1007%2Fs12689-013-0031-7 accessed 4 November 2013.

114 Greiber, T. *et al.* (2009). Conservation with justice – a human rights based approach. Gland (Switzerland): IUCN Environmental Law Centre, http://data.iucn.org/dbtw-wpd/edocs/eplp-071.pdf accessed 28 October 2011, p. 7.

115 Springer, J., Campese, J. & Painter, M. (2011). Conservation and human rights: key issues and contexts scoping paper for the conservation initiative on human rights. Published in October 2011, https://community.iucn.org/cihr/Resources/Scoping%20Paper%20_Oct%20final.pdf accessed 30 October 2011, p. 13.

116 Greiber, T. *et al.* (2009). Conservation with justice – a human rights based approach. Gland (Switzerland): IUCN Environmental Law Centre, http://data.iucn.org/dbtw-wpd/edocs/eplp-071.pdf accessed 28 October 2011, p. 9.

117 Springer, J., Campese, J. & Painter, M. (2011). Conservation and human rights: key issues and contexts scoping paper for the conservation initiative on human rights. Published in October 2011, https://community.iucn.org/cihr/Resources/Scoping%20Paper%20_Oct%20final.pdf accessed 30 October 2011, p. 14.

118 For further discussion see, e.g., Campese, J. (2009). Human rights-based approaches to conservation: an overview of concepts and questions. In: Campese, J. *et al.* (Eds.). *Human Rights-based Approaches: Exploring Issues and Opportunities for Conservation.* Bogor, Indonesia: CIFOR and IUCN, http://data.iucn.org/dbtw-wpd/edocs/2009-014.pdf accessed 2 February 2011, p. 15; Blomley, T. *et al.* (2009). *From Needs to Rights: Lessons Learned from the Application of Rights Based Approaches to Natural Resource Governance in Ghana, Uganda and Nepal.* Washington, DC: Rights and Resources Initiative.

normally be given to economic development. In practical terms, the frequent presence of competing rights means that correctly identifying the relevant right-holders and duty-bearers, their relationships to one another, and the main underlying challenges or obstacles to full realisation of their rights – including power differences – is a key starting point.[119] This challenge maybe common in many countries.

2.3. RIGHTS AND DUTIES

Modern legal system is a complex system of rights and obligations, including the idea of collective responsibilities.[120] If there is anything that unifies legal system around the world today, it is the ever-growing influence of public law.[121] Without rights and responsibilities, the environment is nothing, legally speaking, but an afterthought in the legal process.[122]

2.3.1. RIGHTS

Rights are at the heart of good conservation governance. Rights, including tenure and resource access, can also help create an enabling environment for people to sustainably manage biodiversity.[123] A human rights-based approach strives to secure the freedom, well-being and dignity of all people everywhere, within the framework of essential standards and principles, duties and obligations.[124] The human rights-based approach to conservation presents tools and methods proposed to reconcile conservation and human rights and

---

119 Springer, J., Campese, J. & Painter, M. (2011). Conservation and human rights: key issues and contexts scoping paper for the conservation initiative on human rights. Published in October 2011, https://community.iucn.org/cihr/Resources/Scoping%20Paper%20_Oct%20final.pdf accessed 30 October 2011, p. 14.

120 Bosselmann, K. (2011). Property rights and sustainability: can they be reconciled? In: Grinlinton, D. & Taylor, P. (Eds.). *Property Rights and Sustainability – the Evolution of Property Rights to Meet Ecological Challenges*. Leiden: Martinus Nijhoff Publishers, p. 27.

121 Sands, P. (2003). *International Environmental Law* (second edition). Cambridge: Cambridge University Press.

122 Bosselmann, K. (2011). Property rights and sustainability: can they be reconciled? In: Grinlinton, D. & Taylor, P. (Eds.). *Property Rights and Sustainability – the Evolution of Property Rights to Meet Ecological Challenges*. Leiden: Martinus Nijhoff Publishers, p. 28.

123 Campese, J. *et al.* (2008). Rights and conservation in a diverse and sustainable world: a journey at the 2008 IUCN World Conservation Congress. In: A Congress Forum Journey Report, Barcelona, Spain, 5–14 October 2008, http://cmsdata.iucn.org/downloads/rights_and_conservation_journey_report_1_2.pdf accessed 4 April 2011.

124 UNFPA (United Nations Population Fund Agency), Human rights principles, www.unfpa.org/rights/principles.htm accessed 20 October 2012.

to realise their positive synergies.[125] The approach supports mechanisms to ensure that entitlements are attained and safeguarded.[126] A human rights-based approach leads to an analysis of constraints to the realisation of rights embedded in power structures.[127] It requires that the rights can be best realised in various social arrangements. Inter-generational rights are a core consideration in the conservation context, including in helping to ensure sustainable resource use to support livelihoods of both present and future generations.[128] Intra-generational rights, and distributive justice between nations and people, are also central, and highly challenging issues at the intersection of conservation and rights.[129] Collective and customary rights, including the rights of indigenous peoples, must also be embraced with the conservation context.[130]

2.3.2. DUTIES

A human rights-based approach reframes the processes and outcomes of sustainable development as entitlements to which people individually and collectively possess an inherent claim.[131] As claims, they yield duties and responsibilities on other actors and institutions to fulfil them.[132] States are usually regarded as core duty-bearers, but the relevant social communities,

125 Campese, J. *et al.* (2008). Rights and conservation in a diverse and sustainable world: a journey at the 2008 IUCN World Conservation Congress. In: A Congress Forum Journey Report, Barcelona, Spain, 5–14 October 2008, http://cmsdata.iucn.org/downloads/rights_and_conservation_journey_report_1_2.pdf accessed 4 April 2011.

126 UNFPA (United Nations Population Fund Agency), Human rights principles, www.unfpa.org/rights/principles.htm accessed 20 October 2012.

127 IBON International (2012). Reforming global sustainable development governance: a rights-based agenda. IBON International Working Paper, http://rio20.net/wp-content/uploads/2012/02/DRAFT_Reforming-international-susdev-governance-a-rights-based-agenda1.pdf accessed 2 April 2012.

128 Campese, J. *et al.* (2008). Rights and conservation in a diverse and sustainable world: a journey at the 2008 IUCN World Conservation Congress. In: A Congress Forum Journey Report, Barcelona, Spain, 5–14 October 2008, http://cmsdata.iucn.org/downloads/rights_and_conservation_journey_report_1_2.pdf accessed 4 April 2011.

129 Campese, J. *et al.* (2008). Rights and conservation in a diverse and sustainable world: a journey at the 2008 IUCN World Conservation Congress. In: A Congress Forum Journey Report, Barcelona, Spain, 5–14 October 2008, http://cmsdata.iucn.org/downloads/rights_and_conservation_journey_report_1_2.pdf accessed 4 April 2011.

130 Campese, J. *et al.* (2008). Rights and conservation in a diverse and sustainable world: a journey at the 2008 IUCN World Conservation Congress. In: A Congress Forum Journey Report, Barcelona, Spain, 5–14 October 2008, http://cmsdata.iucn.org/downloads/rights_and_conservation_journey_report_1_2.pdf accessed 4 April 2011.

131 IBON International (2012). Reforming global sustainable development governance: a rights-based agenda. IBON International Working Paper, http://rio20.net/wp-content/uploads/2012/02/DRAFT_Reforming-international-susdev-governance-a-rights-based-agenda1.pdf accessed 2 April 2012.

132 IBON International (2012). Reforming global sustainable development governance: a rights-based agenda. IBON International Working Paper, http://rio20.net/wp-content/

the private sector and civil society actors, including conservation NGOs, are increasingly being called for more duties for their rights. It is a basic premise of a rights approach that there are rights and rights-holders and relevant duties and duty-bearers which must be upheld. Linking rights and duties in this way can promote to guarantee a balance between competing interests.

By linking rights and obligations at the individual and sub-group levels, in addition to the community/State/NGO levels, the human rights-based approach can provide a powerful addition to an approach that fails to adequately address inequities and vulnerability within and across communities.[133] There may be laws or necessary restrictions to which all people must adhere, but the right is possessed by the individual independent of such rules.[134] Conceived of in this way, the focus may shift from linking responsibilities of rights-holders in where or how they use resources, to ensuring that, even where restrictions in resource use or access must be made to ensure long-term sustainability, basic rights must still be fulfilled.[135] Certainly, the relevant duties cannot be ignored.

2.3.3. ACTORS

A human rights-based approach is in part about changing power relations to increase the capacity of both rights-holders and duty-bearers to realise human rights.[136] The human rights-based approach to conservation follows the principle that the realisation of conservation goals should be accomplished in a relationship between rights-holders and the corresponding duty-bearers.[137]

---

uploads/2012/02/DRAFT_Reforming-international-susdev-governance-a-rights-based-agenda1.pdf accessed 2 April 2012.

133 Filmer-Wilson, E. & Anderson, M. (2005). Integrating human rights into energy and environment programming: a reference paper. Prepared for UNDP. Published in May 2005, www.hurilink.org/tools/Integrating_HRs_into_Energy_and_Environment_Programming.pdf accessed 4 April 2011; Harris-Curtis, E., Marleyn, O. & Bakewell, O. (2005). The implications for Northern NGOs of adopting human rights-based approaches. Occasional Papers Series 41, International NGO Training and Resource Center (INTRAC), www.intrac.org/docs/OPS%2041.pdf accessed 4 April 2011.

134 Campese, J. *et al.* (2008). Rights and conservation in a diverse and sustainable world: a journey at the 2008 IUCN World Conservation Congress. In: A Congress Forum Journey Report, Barcelona, Spain, 5–14 October 2008, http://cmsdata.iucn.org/downloads/rights_and_conservation_journey_report_1_2.pdf accessed 4 April 2011.

135 Campese, J. *et al.* (2008). Rights and conservation in a diverse and sustainable world: a journey at the 2008 IUCN World Conservation Congress. In: A Congress Forum Journey Report, Barcelona, Spain, 5–14 October 2008, http://cmsdata.iucn.org/downloads/rights_and_conservation_journey_report_1_2.pdf accessed 4 April 2011.

136 Conservation, human rights & protected areas governance: a field-based workshop in the Baviaanskloof Mega-Reserve (2007). South Africa, 6–7 July 2007, http://cmsdata.iucn.org/downloads/bav_workshop. pdf accessed 10 October 2012, p. 4.

137 Rights-based Approach (RBA) to Conservation, https://community.iucn.org/rba1/RBA%20Wiki/conservation.aspx#Question3 accessed 3 December 2011.

2.3.3.1. *Rights-Holders*

In a human rights-based approach, every human being is recognised both as a person and as a right-holder.[138] Rights-holders include individuals, groups and communities. They often have the knowledge which enables them to define and assert their rights and to fully participate in conservation activities. Consideration should definitely be given to the rights of all stakeholders. However, it might be necessary to prioritise the most vulnerable right-holders, those who are most affected by conservation measures.[139] A rights-based approach to conservation should at least respect the basic rights of all stakeholders, and at the same time pay more attention to the most vulnerable groups. In addition, rights cannot be unlimited; rights-holders have responsibilities, including not harming other people's rights.[140]

2.3.3.2. *Duty-Bearers*

Duty-bearers may be either State actors (e.g. States, multilateral agencies), or non-State actors (business entities, NGOs, conservation organisations or individuals).[141] States, as primary duty-bearers, are obliged to respect, protect and fulfil the human rights entitlements of individuals, or rights-holders.[142] Although non-State actors may also have substantial influences on rights, direct action against a private enterprise or against some individuals who are responsible for environmental degradation is not part of international human rights procedures.[143] A human rights-based approach has its foundation in the normative framework of international human rights standards and principles. However, States may be held accountable since they ratify international human rights instruments and are responsible for implementing national laws that uphold those obligations.[144]

The human rights-based approach has helped with a shift away from a needs approach based on "charity", to the recognition of the rights of poor people

138 UNFPA (United Nations Population Fund Agency), Human rights principles, www.unfpa.org/rights/principles.htm accessed 20 October 2012.

139 Rights-based Approach (RBA) to Conservation, https://community.iucn.org/rba1/RBA%20Wiki/conservation.aspx#Question3 accessed 3 December 2011.

140 IUCN. Rights and Conservation Journey, www.iucn.org/congress_08/forum/journeys/rights_conservation/ accessed 10 September 2011.

141 Rights-based Approach (RBA) to Conservation, https://community.iucn.org/rba1/RBA%20Wiki/conservation.aspx#Question3 accessed 3 December 2011.

142 Luttrel, C. & Quiroz, S. (2007). Linkages between human rights-based approaches and environment. Published in October 2007, www.poverty-wellbeing.net/resources/sharewebResource_en_1545.pdf accessed 20 January 2011, p. 1.

143 Rights-based Approach (RBA) to Conservation, https://community.iucn.org/rba1/RBA%20Wiki/conservation.aspx#Question3 accessed 3 December 2011.

144 Rights-based Approach (RBA) to Conservation, https://community.iucn.org/rba1/RBA%20Wiki/conservation.aspx#Question3 accessed 3 December 2011.

to entitlements and the obligations on the part of others that are enshrined in law.[145] Local communities are certainly becoming more effective in asserting their rights to negotiate and implement decisions about how conservation needs are balanced across their landscapes – and conservationists need to be able to respond to this.[146] Indeed, there is a pressing need to translate the surfeit of current theory about the human rights-based approach into the practical realities of resource management on the ground, particularly in countries with weak institutions and limited capacity to enforce agreements.[147]

Figure 4. A human rights-based approach and the relationship between duty-bearers and rights-holders[148]

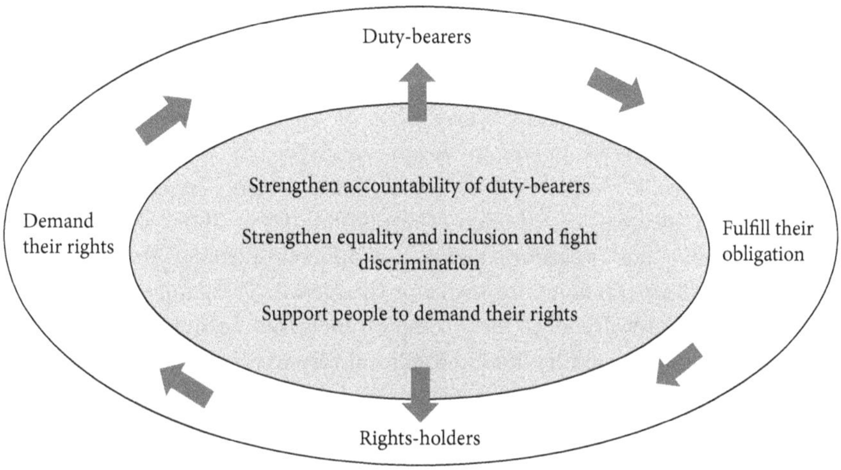

As shown above in figure 4, a human rights-based approach aims to enhance equity through increasing the capacity of rights-holders and duty-bears to realise their own rights. To some degree, a human rights-based approach can be regarded as a strong claim and theoretically cannot be affected by other factors (e.g. State's governance). However, States need to take responsibilities for

145 Luttrel, C. & Quiroz, S. (2007). Linkages between human rights-based approaches and environment. Published in October 2007, www.poverty-wellbeing.net/resources/sharewebResource_en_1545.pdf accessed 20 January 2011, p. 1.

146 IUCN arborvitae (2008). Human rights-based approaches to forest conservation. The IUCN Forest Conservation Programme Newsletter, No. 36, www.rightsandresources.org/documents/files/doc_786.pdf accessed 9 November 2011.

147 IUCN arborvitae (2008). Human rights-based approaches to forest conservation. The IUCN Forest Conservation Programme Newsletter, No. 36, www.rightsandresources.org/documents/files/doc_786.pdf accessed 9 November 2011.

148 Theis. J. (2004). Promoting human rights-based approaches – experiences and ideas from Asia and the Pacific. CRIN (Child Rights International Network), www.crin.org/hrbap/index.asp?action=theme.themeItem&subtheme=6&item=4780 accessed 3 May 2011.

implementing the relevant national duties for the reason that they have ratified international human rights instruments.

The substantive and procedural aspects of an inclusive human rights-based approach can be far more comprehensive than a more general "participatory" or "pro-poor" approach.[149] The human rights-based approach can also enhance accountability by linking rights (and rights-holders) with specific, corresponding obligations (and duty-bearers), including consideration for particularly vulnerable individuals.[150]

2.4. SUBSTANTIVE AND PROCEDURAL RIGHTS

How can the human rights-based approach to conservation both respect the inalienable and indivisible rights and conserve the invaluable and limited natural resources, particularly where poor or vulnerable people depend on these resources? The "*key question is how to assign responsibilities fairly and effectively ... while maintaining an overall human rights-based approach*".[151] The "fair and effective" distribution of responsibilities or duties should respect basic substantive and procedural rights. It is difficult to balance the twin goals, particularly where resources are scarce or threatened. The human rights-based approach cannot resolve all of these complex dilemmas. Secure substantive and procedural rights (including land and natural resource access rights) can help ensure effective ecosystem management, and in return effective ecosystem management can help support substantive rights realisation.[152]

Rights can be categorised into substantive and procedural rights. The former contains the right to food, the right to life, the right to privacy and family life, the right to property, the right to an adequate standard of living, the right to self-determination of people and so on; while the latter includes the right to information, the right to participation, the right to access to justice, the right to substantive redress and so on.

149 Campese, J. (2009). Human rights-based approaches to conservation: an overview of concepts and questions. In: Campese, J., *et al.* (Eds.). *Human Rights-based Approaches: Exploring Issues and Opportunities for Conservation.* Bogor, Indonesia: CIFOR and IUCN, http://data.iucn.org/dbtw-wpd/edocs/2009-014.pdf accessed 2 February 2011, p. 13.

150 Campese, J. (2009). Human rights-based approaches to conservation: an overview of concepts and questions. In: Campese, J., *et al.* (Eds.). *Human Rights-based Approaches: Exploring Issues and Opportunities for Conservation.* Bogor, Indonesia: CIFOR and IUCN, http://data.iucn.org/dbtw-wpd/edocs/2009-014.pdf accessed 2 February 2011, p. 13.

151 Borrini-Feyerabend, G., Kothari, A. & Oviedo, G. (2004). *Indigenous and Local Communities and Protected Areas: Towards Equity and Enhanced Conservation.* IUCN Best Practice Guidelines for Protected Area Series no. 11. Gland (Switzerland): IUCN, p. 12.

152 Campese, J. *et al.* (2008). Rights and conservation in a diverse and sustainable world: a journey at the 2008 IUCN World Conservation Congress. In: A Congress Forum Journey Report, Barcelona, Spain, 5-14 October 2008, http://cmsdata.iucn.org/downloads/rights_and_conservation_journey_report_1_2.pdf accessed 4 April 2011.

2.5. IMPLEMENTING THE HUMAN RIGHTS-BASED APPROACH TO CONSERVATION

Stages in human rights-based programming seek to:

(1) *Focus the problem – causality and obligation analysis.* This step serves to identify different human rights dimensions in the problem, and the specific safeguards (guarantees against actions and omissions) that are insufficiently performing.[153] The problem identified is stated in human rights terms with human rights standards providing a road map to the problem. Questions to be asked are: "*what rights are affected and in what way? whose rights are affected and why? what related impacts are on the human rights of others?*"[154] The answers to these questions concerning different problems may be vary in different regions; it requires analysing the causality focusing on the real problems. The causality analysis aims to achieve consensus on the causes of the problems, the obligation analysis establishes the responsibility of the duty-bearers.[155]

(2) *Target capacity development – empowerment and accountability analysis.* This stage analyses causes of non-performance that relate to capacity problems of (a) claim-holders to claim and exercise rights (empowerment), and (b) duty-bearers to fulfil obligations (accountability).[156] A capacity analysis from the human rights perspective will look at the following issues: responsibility/motivation/leadership; authority; resources; capability to communicate; and the capability for rational decision-making and learning.[157] It aims to build

153 A human rights approach to development – primer for development practitioners (draft) (2003), www.google.be/url?sa=t&rct=j&q=A+Human+Rights+Approach+to+Development+---+Primer+for+Development+Practioners+%28Draft+July+2003&source=web&cd=1&cad=rja&ved=0CCkQFjAA&url=http%3A%2F%2Fwww.crin.org%2Fdocs%2Fresources%2Fpublications%2Fhrbap%2FRBA_training_UNDP_primer.doc&ei=cDCZUMTMCuqM0AXXgYHoDA&usg=AFQjCNGCZTn74rZPh47TvAJ8ansmb7ev7g accessed 4 February 2011.

154 UNDP (2006). Applying a human rights-based approach to development cooperation and programming: a UNDP capacity development resource. Capacity development group, Bureau for development policy, http://hurilink.org/tools/Applying_a_HR_approach_to_UNDP_Technical_Cooperation--unr_revision.pdf accessed 11 November 2011.

155 UNDP (2006). Applying a human rights-based approach to development cooperation and programming: a UNDP capacity development resource. Capacity development group, Bureau for development policy, http://hurilink.org/tools/Applying_a_HR_approach_to_UNDP_Technical_Cooperation--unr_revision.pdf accessed 11 November 2011.

156 A human rights approach to development – primer for development practitioners (draft) (2003), www.google.be/url?sa=t&rct=j&q=A+Human+Rights+Approach+to+Development+---+Primer+for+Development+Practioners+%28Draft+July+2003&source=web&cd=1&cad=rja&ved=0CCkQFjAA&url=http%3A%2F%2Fwww.crin.org%2Fdocs%2Fresources%2Fpublications%2Fhrbap%2FRBA_training_UNDP_primer.doc&ei=cDCZUMTMCuqM0AXXgYHoDA&usg=AFQjCNGCZTn74rZPh47TvAJ8ansmb7ev7g accessed 4 February 2011.

157 UNDP (2006). Applying a human rights-based approach to development cooperation and programming: a UNDP capacity development resource. Capacity development group, Bureau

on existing strengths and solutions of stakeholders and to target weaknesses and vulnerabilities.[158] For duty-bearers this means answering questions as to whether the duty-bearer feels that he should do something about a specific problem, whether he feels or knows that he may take action, and whether he can act.[159]

(3) *Ensure an adequate process.* The guiding principles for rights-based programming are used as an objective guidance to design/implement development strategies and guide indicator setting.[160] This is an effective but complicated way to guarantee that the rights-holders can enjoy their rights; while the duty-bearers can fulfil their obligations. These can be regarded as the principal stages for implementing the human rights-based approach to conservation, more specifically, rights-based programming involves[161]: (1) identifying what specific results should be pursued in line with a human rights framework; (2) identifying their specific claims and obligations; (3) identifying specific capacity problems they face to exercise those claims or fulfil those obligations; (4) designing capacity development strategies accordingly; and (5) ensuring the process respects basic human rights principles.

As for the implementation of the human rights-based approach to conservation, the method can be divided into several steps as follows.

for development policy, http://hurilink.org/tools/Applying_a_HR_approach_to_UNDP_Technical_Cooperation--unr_revision.pdf accessed 11 November 2011.

158 A human rights approach to development – primer for development practitioners (draft) (2003), www.google.be/url?sa=t&rct=j&q=A+Human+Rights+Approach+to+Development+---+Primer+for+Development+Practioners+%28Draft+July+2003&source=web&cd=1&cad=rja&ved=0CCkQFjAA&url=http%3A%2F%2Fwww.crin.org%2Fdocs%2Fresources%2Fpublications%2Fhrbap%2FRBA_training_UNDP_primer.doc&ei=cDCZUMTMCuqM0AXXgYHoDA&usg=AFQjCNGCZTn74rZPh47TvAJ8ansmb7ev7g accessed 4 February 2011.

159 UNDP (2006). Applying a human rights-based approach to development cooperation and programming: a UNDP capacity development resource. Capacity development group, Bureau for development policy, http://hurilink.org/tools/Applying_a_HR_approach_to_UNDP_Technical_Cooperation--unr_revision.pdf accessed 11 November 2011.

160 A human rights approach to development – primer for development practitioners (draft) (2003), www.google.be/url?sa=t&rct=j&q=A+Human+Rights+Approach+to+Development+---+Primer+for+Development+Practioners+%28Draft+July+2003&source=web&cd=1&cad=rja&ved=0CCkQFjAA&url=http%3A%2F%2Fwww.crin.org%2Fdocs%2Fresources%2Fpublications%2Fhrbap%2FRBA_training_UNDP_primer.doc&ei=cDCZUMTMCuqM0AXXgYHoDA&usg=AFQjCNGCZTn74rZPh47TvAJ8ansmb7ev7g accessed 4 February 2011.

161 A human rights approach to development – primer for development practitioners (draft) (2003), www.google.be/url?sa=t&rct=j&q=A+Human+Rights+Approach+to+Development+---+Primer+for+Development+Practioners+%28Draft+July+2003&source=web&cd=1&cad=rja&ved=0CCkQFjAA&url=http%3A%2F%2Fwww.crin.org%2Fdocs%2Fresources%2Fpublications%2Fhrbap%2FRBA_training_UNDP_primer.doc&ei=cDCZUMTMCuqM0AXXgYHoDA&usg=AFQjCNGCZTn74rZPh47TvAJ8ansmb7ev7g accessed 4 February 2011.

Step 1: A situation analysis

In adopting a human rights-based approach, an analysis is required to give priority to those who are deprived in society (usually the poor) and to make factors that empower poor families as an explicit objective.[162] A situation analysis is used to identify immediate, underlying, and basic causes of problems.[163]

(1) Analysing the social background: a situation analysis cannot ignore the existing historical, political, economic and legal circumstances for implementing the human rights-based approach to conservation, as well as the contextually relevant rights and institutions, for instance, international, national and local legal and customary rights.
(2) Identifying stakeholders and duty-bearers: to communicate with all stakeholders, including the potentially affected rights-holders and duty-bearers, is necessary to implement a human rights-based approach to conservation.[164]
(3) Defining a focus: to put a human rights-based approach into practice, a choice must be made whether the protection, fulfilment or promotion of rights is at stake.[165] Acknowledge that rights are context-specific whether working with women, children, the elderly, the disabled, youth or an entire community: a human rights-based approach must adapt to the context in which the rights-holders live.[166]

---

162 UNDP (2006). Applying a human rights-based approach to development cooperation and programming: a UNDP capacity development resource. Capacity development group, Bureau for development policy, http://hurilink.org/tools/Applying_a_HR_approach_to_UNDP_Technical_Cooperation--unr_revision.pdf accessed 11 November 2011.

163 Berman, G. (2008). Undertaking a Human Rights-based Approach: a Guide for Basic Programming – Documenting Lessons Learned for Human Rights-based Programming: an Asia-pacific Perspective – Implications for Policy, Planning and Programming. Bangkok: UNESCO Asia and Pacific Regional Bureau for Education, p. 14, http://unesdoc.unesco.org/images/0017/001791/179186e.pdf accessed 14 September 2012.

164 Greiber, T. *et al.* (2009). Conservation with justice – a human rights based approach. Gland (Switzerland): IUCN Environmental Law Centre, http://data.iucn.org/dbtw-wpd/edocs/eplp-071.pdf accessed 28 October 2011, p. 25.

165 Kapur, A. & Duvvury, N. (2006). *A Human Rights-based Approach to Realizing the Economic and Social Rights of Poor and Social Rights of Poor and Marginalized Women: a Synthesis of Lessons Learned.* International Center for Research on Women (ICRW), www.icrw.org/files/publications/A-Rights-Based-Approach-to-Realizing-the-Economic-and-Social-Rights-of-Poor-and-Marginalized-Women.pdf accessed 2 February 2012.

166 Kapur, A. & Duvvury, N. (2006). *A Human Rights-based Approach to Realizing the Economic and Social Rights of Poor and Social Rights of Poor and Marginalized Women: a Synthesis of Lessons Learned.* International Center for Research on Women (ICRW), www.icrw.org/files/publications/A-Rights-Based-Approach-to-Realizing-the-Economic-and-Social-Rights-of-Poor-and-Marginalized-Women.pdf accessed 2 February 2012.

(4) Identifying applicable legal rights and duties: the identification of relevant rights should include not only local and national law but also regional and international law.[167] Unpacking a right also involves examining the right both from the rights-holder's and duty-bearer's perspective, especially when considering how to uphold a right and for what purpose (e.g. whether to remedy a particular violation or to challenge the status quo).[168]
(5) Searching for potential conflict resolution mechanisms: a dispute resolution process should also be designed and implemented, when appropriate, to help resolve conflicts over whether a proposed project or activity should proceed.[169]

The following are the questions that must be asked in a situational analysis:[170]

- What are the rights violations and denials, which rights are not being realised?
- Who are the poorest and most vulnerable communities and individuals and how can we find out?
- What is the legislative and policy framework and practice that has led to the denial of these rights?

Step 2: Creating transparency

A human rights-based approach requires a shift from providing services to providing information.[171] Access to information about environmental conditions and proposed activities that might affect conservation as well as

167 Greiber, T. *et al.* (2009). Conservation with justice – a human rights based approach. Gland (Switzerland): IUCN Environmental Law Centre, http://data.iucn.org/dbtw-wpd/edocs/eplp-071.pdf accessed 28 October 2011, p. 26.

168 Kapur, A. & Duvvury, N. (2006). *A Human Rights-based Approach to Realizing the Economic and Social Rights of Poor and Social Rights of Poor and Marginalized Women: a Synthesis of Lessons Learned.* International Center for Research on Women (ICRW), www.icrw.org/files/publications/A-Rights-Based-Approach-to-Realizing-the-Economic-and-Social-Rights-of-Poor-and-Marginalized-Women.pdf accessed 2 February 2012.

169 Greiber, T. *et al.* (2009). Conservation with justice – a human rights based approach. Gland (Switzerland): IUCN Environmental Law Centre, http://data.iucn.org/dbtw-wpd/edocs/eplp-071.pdf accessed 28 October 2011, p. 28.

170 Berman, G. (2008). Undertaking a Human Rights-based Approach: a Guide for Basic Programming – Documenting Lessons Learned for Human Rights-based Programming: an Asia-pacific Perspective – Implications for Policy, Planning and Programming. Bangkok: UNESCO Asia and Pacific Regional Bureau for Education, http://unesdoc.unesco.org/images/0017/001791/179186e.pdf accessed 14 September 2012, p. 14.

171 Kapur, A. & Duvvury, N. (2006). *A Human Rights-based Approach to Realizing the Economic and Social Rights of Poor and Social Rights of Poor and Marginalized Women: a Synthesis of Lessons Learned.* International Center for Research on Women (ICRW), www.icrw.org/files/publications/A-Rights-Based-Approach-to-Realizing-the-Economic-and-Social-Rights-of-Poor-and-Marginalized-Women.pdf accessed 2 February 2012.

human rights is a prerequisite to public participation in decision-making and to monitoring governmental and private-sector activities.[172]

(1) Publishing information in an easily accessible way: while it is critical for the proponent of an activity or project to gather and assess relevant information about its potential impacts on conservation and human rights, it is equally important that the information is disseminated to the relevant stakeholders in local languages, where appropriate.[173]
(2) Disseminating specific information regarding legal rights and duties of potential affected persons[174] is an effective way to let all the relevant parties know what they can enjoy and what they must do.

Step 3: Priority-setting and target setting

After step 1 and step 2 have been finished, it is necessary to set priorities and targets when implementing the human rights-based approach to conservation. The priorities will address human rights issues, problems or concerns as they relate to specific groups, communities, or regions of the country facing abuse, exclusion, discrimination or neglect.[175] These are the foundation for preparing a comprehensive and transparent plan for conservation activities, policy decisions, rights implementation and evaluation. It is also a good opportunity to identify the critical potential conservation and human rights impacts, especially for the most vulnerable people.

Step 4: Strengthening the relevant parties' capacities

Capacity-building efforts should be included throughout the project process and more generally integrated into the human rights-based approach to conservation.[176] Efforts to strengthen capacity among duty-bearers should

---

172 Greiber, T. *et al.* (2009). Conservation with justice – a human rights based approach. Gland (Switzerland): IUCN Environmental Law Centre, http://data.iucn.org/dbtw-wpd/edocs/eplp-071.pdf accessed 28 October 2011, p. 28.

173 Greiber, T. *et al.* (2009). Conservation with justice – a human rights based approach. Gland (Switzerland): IUCN Environmental Law Centre, http://data.iucn.org/dbtw-wpd/edocs/eplp-071.pdf accessed 28 October 2011, p. 28.

174 Greiber, T. *et al.* (2009). Conservation with justice – a human rights based approach. Gland (Switzerland): IUCN Environmental Law Centre, http://data.iucn.org/dbtw-wpd/edocs/eplp-071.pdf accessed 28 October 2011, p. 29.

175 UNDP (2006). Applying a human rights-based approach to development cooperation and programming: a UNDP capacity development resource. Capacity development group, Bureau for development policy, http://hurilink.org/tools/Applying_a_HR_approach_to_UNDP_Technical_Cooperation--unr_revision.pdf accessed 11 November 2011.

176 Greiber, T. *et al.* (2009). Conservation with justice – a human rights based approach. Gland (Switzerland): IUCN Environmental Law Centre, http://data.iucn.org/dbtw-wpd/edocs/eplp-071.pdf accessed 28 October 2011, p. 29.

focus not only on legal obligations to uphold rights, but also on fostering views that are sensitive to constructs of gender, class, caste, religion and age – aspects that are particularly significant to the rights of poor and marginalised women and children.[177] Without enough capacities, the relevant parties cannot really participate in the decision-making.

Step 5: Enacting a legislative and regulatory framework

Rights are often viewed with a legalistic context that is more technical than empowering.[178] In most developing countries, the law is not universally applied, known or enforced.[179] It is of vital importance to create and maintain a legislative and institutional framework to implement and monitor the rights protection and conservation activities. The human rights-based approach to conservation requires that State and other duty-bearers change policies, laws and ensure more effective enforcement of laws against rights violations.[180] The key issue is to balance the interests from different parties. Balancing is also regarded by some as "*an irrational and illegitimate renunciation of law in favor of a largely arbitrary judicial discretion, difficult to justify according to the ideals of democracy, respect for human rights, and the rule of law and therefore, ripe for elimination from the legal process*".[181] However, the human rights-based approach to conservation also pays much attention to the legal process, it argues the importance of participation, fair decision-making and other procedural processes.

Step 6: Ensuring participation

Rights-holders need to work with their communities and the State to ensure that their rights are recognised, respected, protected, fulfilled and

177 Kapur, A. & Duvvury, N. (2006). *A Human Rights-based Approach to Realizing the Economic and Social Rights of Poor and Social Rights of Poor and Marginalized Women: a Synthesis of Lessons Learned.* International Center for Research on Women (ICRW), www.icrw.org/files/publications/A-Rights-Based-Approach-to-Realizing-the-Economic-and-Social-Rights-of-Poor-and-Marginalized-Women.pdf accessed 2 February 2012.

178 Kapur, A. & Duvvury, N. (2006). *A Human Rights-based Approach to Realizing the Economic and Social Rights of Poor and Social Rights of Poor and Marginalized Women: a Synthesis of Lessons Learned.* International Center for Research on Women (ICRW), www.icrw.org/files/publications/A-Rights-Based-Approach-to-Realizing-the-Economic-and-Social-Rights-of-Poor-and-Marginalized-Women.pdf accessed 2 February 2012.

179 Care Danmark (2009). Right-based approach guidelines (draft). Published in April 2009, www.careclimatechange.org/files/toolkit/CDK_Rights-Based_Guidelines.pdf accessed 4 February 2011.

180 Theis, J. (2004). Promoting human rights-based approaches – experiences and ideas from Asia and the Pacific. CRIN (Child Rights International Network), www.crin.org/hrbap/index.asp?action=theme.themeItem&subtheme=6&item=4780 accessed 3 May 2011.

181 See Greer, S. (2004). "Balancing" and the European Court of human rights: a contribution to the Habermas-Alexy debate. *Cambridge Law Journal*, 63(2), p. 413.

promoted.[182] Public participation is critical to a human rights-based approach to conservation.[183] The human rights-based approach to conservation can provide a more comprehensive platform or mechanism than general participatory approaches. Where possible, both policy-makers and rights-holders should be consulted in ascertaining the multiple dimensions of non-realisation of human rights and be engaged at the relevant levels in determining the best way to proceed with this work.[184] It is also a good way to provide the formal procedures or mechanisms to secure rights and to guarantee conservation goals. In order to be manageable, this may involve NGOs and governments at the policy level and communities and local government representatives at the local level.[185]

Step 7: Taking reasonable decisions

Rights are interrelated and exist along a continuum; they cannot be fulfilled in isolation.[186] In making the decision, the proponent should keep in mind standards developed by international and national tribunals to review decisions with regards to compatibility with human rights.[187] It is better to conduct a community dialogue and develop village action plans at the grassroots level.[188] In this way, reasonable decisions could be suitable for local practice.

---

182 Kapur, A. & Duvvury, N. (2006). *A Human Rights-based Approach to Realizing the Economic and Social Rights of Poor and Social Rights of Poor and Marginalized Women: a Synthesis of Lessons Learned.* International Center for Research on Women (ICRW), www.icrw.org/files/publications/A-Rights-Based-Approach-to-Realizing-the-Economic-and-Social-Rights-of-Poor-and-Marginalized-Women.pdf accessed 2 February 2012.

183 Greiber, T. *et al.* (2009). Conservation with justice – a human rights based approach. Gland (Switzerland): IUCN Environmental Law Centre, http://data.iucn.org/dbtw-wpd/edocs/eplp-071.pdf accessed 28 October 2011, p. 29.

184 Berman, G. (2008). Undertaking a Human Rights-based Approach: a Guide for Basic Programming – Documenting Lessons Learned for Human Rights-based Programming: an Asia-pacific Perspective – Implications for Policy, Planning and Programming. Bangkok: UNESCO Asia and Pacific Regional Bureau for Education, http://unesdoc.unesco.org/images/0017/001791/179186e.pdf accessed 14 September 2012, p. 15.

185 Berman, G. (2008). Undertaking a Human Rights-based Approach: a Guide for Basic Programming – Documenting Lessons Learned for Human Rights-based Programming: an Asia-pacific Perspective – Implications for Policy, Planning and Programming. Bangkok: UNESCO Asia and Pacific Regional Bureau for Education, http://unesdoc.unesco.org/images/0017/001791/179186e.pdf accessed 14 September 2012, p. 15.

186 Kapur, A. & Duvvury, N. (2006). *A Human Rights-based Approach to Realizing the Economic and Social Rights of Poor and Social Rights of Poor and Marginalized Women: a Synthesis of Lessons Learned.* International Center for Research on Women (ICRW), www.icrw.org/files/publications/A-Rights-Based-Approach-to-Realizing-the-Economic-and-Social-Rights-of-Poor-and-Marginalized-Women.pdf accessed 2 February 2012.

187 Greiber, T. *et al.* (2009). Conservation with justice – a human rights based approach. Gland (Switzerland): IUCN Environmental Law Centre, http://data.iucn.org/dbtw-wpd/edocs/eplp-071.pdf accessed 28 October 2011, p. 32.

188 Berman, G. (2008). Undertaking a Human Rights-based Approach: a Guide for Basic Programming – Documenting Lessons Learned for Human Rights-based Programming: an Asia-pacific Perspective – Implications for Policy, Planning and Programming. Bangkok:

Step 8: Assessing the application of the human rights-based approach to conservation

Since a human rights-based approach to conservation aims to achieve a better balance between nature conservation and human rights protection, the assessment of the application would be better to focus on both environment and rights. Both outcomes and processes are monitored and evaluated.[189] It is worth acknowledging that an environmental impact assessment (EIA) can be an important part of the human rights-based approach to conservation assessment, but not all. This is because the EIA will help assess the environmental impacts of conservation activities but will not take the interrelationship between nature conservation and human rights protection into account. Realising rights is a process and not an end in itself. In order to assess whether rights have been realised or not, it is therefore essential to monitor progress on the creation of such "enabling conditions."[190] While prior steps may have been largely predictive, "*monitoring events and evaluating their performance will hold a mirror to the assumptions that were made at the outset, to see how these assumptions compare with the actual experience*".[191] The assessments of the application of the human rights-based approach can help identify what measures need to be taken for more effective implementation in the next stages. The results should help identify what changes need to be made for a more effective implementation of a human rights-based approach, and ultimately feedback into a cycle of iterative actions and "learning-by-doing" that over time contributes to a more robust and systematic human rights-based approach.[192]

UNESCO Asia and Pacific Regional Bureau for Education, http://unesdoc.unesco.org/images/0017/001791/179186e.pdf accessed 14 September 2012, p. 18.

189 Berman, G. (2008). Undertaking a Human Rights-based Approach: a Guide for Basic Programming – Documenting Lessons Learned for Human Rights-based Programming: an Asia-pacific Perspective – Implications for Policy, Planning and Programming. Bangkok: UNESCO Asia and Pacific Regional Bureau for Education, http://unesdoc.unesco.org/images/0017/001791/179186e.pdf accessed 14 September 2012, p. 29.

190 Kapur, A. & Duvvury, N. (2006). *A Human Rights-based Approach to Realizing the Economic and Social Rights of Poor and Social Rights of Poor and Marginalized Women: a Synthesis of Lessons Learned.* International Center for Research on Women (ICRW), www.icrw.org/files/publications/A-Rights-Based-Approach-to-Realizing-the-Economic-and-Social-Rights-of-Poor-and-Marginalized-Women.pdf accessed 2 February 2012.

191 International Business Leaders Forum and International Finance Corporation (2007). Guide to human rights impact assessment and management road-testing draft. Published in June 2007, www.iblf.org/resources/general.jsp?id=123946 accessed 15 September 2012, p. 58. The experience gained from the road-testing will be used to further refine the guide.

192 Joint UNEP-OHCHR (2002). Human rights and environment issues in multilateral treaties adopted between 1991 and 2001. Background Paper No. 1. In: Expert Seminar on Human Rights and the Environment, Geneva, Swiss, 4–16 January 2002, §§15–16, www.unhchr.ch/environment/bp1.html accessed 11 January 2011.

Where possible, the assessment should address root causes for the non-realisation of rights.[193] These would identify the empowerment and rights-holders' and duty-bearers' capacity. The assessments should be conducted in a manner guaranteeing equality and full participation. The assessments would be better to integrate with social and legal impact assessments.

Step 9: Enforcing rights and providing a legal remedy

When rights have not been respected or harm occurs, Principle 10 of the Rio Declaration provides that "*effective access to judicial and administrative proceedings, including redress and remedy, shall be provided*".[194] The enforcement of rights will largely depend on the national and local legal and policy contexts. If the rights were not enforced well, the legal remedy might help to solve the conflicts. How to provide a legal remedy will depend on the different problems.

2.6. INTERIM CONCLUSION

A human rights-based approach encompasses holistic initiatives to address human risghts and environmental justice. The reasons why a human rights-based approach could help environmental protection can be summarised as follows. Firstly, a human rights-based approach is premised on the assumption that human rights are integrally and symbiotically interrelated, and that human beings have rights by virtue of being human. Rights are inherent attributes of human beings that must be respected in any well-ordered society.[195] The moral weight this concept affords exercises an important compliance pull.[196] Human rights standards and principles guide development to more sustainable outcomes by recognising the links between ecological and social marginalisation, stressing that all rights are embedded in complex ecological systems, and emphasising

[193] UNDP (2006). Applying a human rights-based approach to development cooperation and programming: a UNDP capacity development resource. Capacity development group, Bureau for development policy, http://hurilink.org/tools/Applying_a_HR_approach_to_UNDP_Technical_Cooperation--unr_revision.pdf accessed 11 November 2011.

[194] Rio Declaration on Environment and Development (The United Nations Conference on Environment and Development, UNCED), adopted in June 1992, A/CONF. 151/26, www.unep.org/Documents.Multilingual/Default.asp?documentid=78&articleid=1163 accessed 22 June 2012.

[195] Shelton, D.L. (2011). Human rights and the environment: substantive rights. In: Fitzmaurice, M., Ong, D.M. & Merkouris, P. (Eds.). *Research Handbook on International Environmental Law.* Cheltenham (UK) and Northampton (USA): Edward Elgar Publishing, pp. 265–283.

[196] Shelton, D.L. (2011). Human rights and the environment: substantive rights. In: Fitzmaurice, M., Ong, D.M. & Merkouris, P. (Eds.). *Research Handbook on International Environmental Law.* Cheltenham (UK) and Northampton (USA): Edward Elgar Publishing, pp. 265–283.

provision for need over wealth accumulation.[197] Secondly, this approach is also not limited to just promoting participation. If a successful human rights-based approach is to be developed, this approach must be evaluated against criteria that differentiate the other approaches from efforts to change the system to promote "participation" within the existing conservation management paradigm.[198] Thirdly, at the international level, enforcement of human rights law is more developed than the procedures of international environmental law.[199] The human rights-based approach is a conceptual framework that is normatively based on international human rights standards and operationally directed to promoting and protecting human rights.[200] Under a human rights-based approach, plans, policies and programmes are anchored in a system of rights and corresponding obligations established by international law. In addition, the availability of individual complaints procedures to denounce violations of human rights has given rise to extensive jurisprudence in which the specific obligations of States to protect and preserve the environment are detailed.[201] Fourth, this approach seeks to analyse obligations, inequalities and vulnerabilities and to redress discriminatory practices and unjust distributions of power that impede progress and undercut human rights.[202] This helps to promote the sustainability, empowering people themselves (rights-holders) – especially the most marginalised – to participate in policy formulation and hold accountable those who have a duty to act (duty-bearers). Specifically for protected areas, applying a rights-based approach requires that a stakeholder analysis can accurately identify the different actors, namely the people or organisations that are vital to the success or failure of the protected areas.[203]

---

197 GI-ESCR (The Global Initiative for Economic, Social and Cultural Rights) (2014). A GI-ESCR practitioner's guide, http://globalinitiative-escr.org/wp-content/uploads/2014/03/GI-ESCR-Practitioners-Guide-Human-Rights-Environment-and-Climate-Change.pdf accessed 10 July 2014, p. 2.

198 Alcorn, J.B. & Royo, A.G. (2007). Conservation's engagement with human rights: "traction", "slippage", or avoidance? *Policy Matters*, 15, p. 133. http://cmsdata.iucn.org/downloads/pm15.pdf accessed 27 October 2012.

199 Shelton, D.L. (2011). Human rights and the environment: substantive rights. In: Fitzmaurice, M., Ong, D.M. & Merkouris, P. (Eds.). *Research Handbook on International Environmental Law.* Cheltenham (UK) and Northampton (USA): Edward Elgar Publishing, pp. 265–283.

200 OHCHR. Applying a human rights-based approach to climate change negotiations, policies and measures, www.ohchr.org/Documents/Issues/ClimateChange/InfoNoteHRBA.pdf accessed 2 February 2012.

201 Shelton, D.L. (2011). Human rights and the environment: substantive rights. In: Fitzmaurice, M., Ong, D.M. & Merkouris, P. (Eds.). *Research Handbook on International Environmental Law.* Cheltenham (UK) and Northampton (USA): Edward Elgar Publishing, pp. 265–283.

202 OHCHR. Applying a human rights-based approach to climate change negotiations, policies and measures, www.ohchr.org/Documents/Issues/ClimateChange/InfoNoteHRBA.pdf accessed 2 February 2012.

203 Hesselink, F.J. *et al.* (2007). *Communication, Education and Public Awareness: a Toolkit for the Convention on Biological Convention.* Montreal: Secretariat of the Convention on Biological Diversity, www.cbd.int/cepa/toolkit/2008/doc/CBD-Toolkit-Complete.pdf accessed 3 March 2012.

PART II

ANALYSIS OF THE RELATIONSHIP BETWEEN HUMAN RIGHTS AND PROTECTED AREAS CONSERVATION IN CHINA AND IN EUROPE

CHAPTER 3

PROTECTED AREAS CONSERVATION IN CHINA AND IN EUROPE

Protected areas are widely recognised as a cornerstone of biodiversity management and sustainable development.[1] A large number of global and regional treaties and other instruments promote the establishment of protected areas. Among these, the CBD,[2] with 193 countries as members, is a particularly important endorsement of protected areas. It states that, as far as possible and appropriate, parties shall "*establish a system of protected areas or areas where special measures need to be taken to conserve biological diversity*".[3] Other agreements and actions[4] in the international arena also support protected areas.[5]

Under this global framework on protected areas, this idea was actively supported by some NGOs, for instance IUCN's WCPA (World Commission on Protected Areas). The WCPA is the major global network of protected areas specialists; its mission is "*to promote the establishment and effective management of a representative world-wide network of terrestrial and marine protected areas*".[6] Besides this, the fifth IUCN World Parks Congress, which

---

1 UNDP. Ecosystems and biodiversity. http://web.undp.org/biodiversity/protected_areas.shtml accessed 5 March 2012.

2 For detailed information see www.cbd.int/ accessed 4 December 2011.

3 Convention on Biological Diversity (CBD), opened for signature on 5 June 1992 and entered into force on 29 December 1993, [1993] ATS 32/1760 UNTS 79/31 ILM 818 (1992), www.cbd.int/ accessed 8 June 2012.

4 For instance the United Nations Convention on Law of the Sea; the Convention on Wetlands of International Importance Especially as Waterfowl Habitat; Convention Concerning the Protection of the World Cultural and Natural Heritage; United Nations Educational, Scientific and Cultural Organization's Man and the Biosphere Programme and so on.

5 Task Force on Economic Benefits of Protected Areas of the World Commission on Protected Areas (WCPA) of IUCN, in collaboration with the Economics Service Unit of IUCN (1998). *Economic Values of Protected Areas: Guidelines for Protected Areas Managers.* Gland (Switzerland): IUCN, https://portals.iucn.org/library/efiles/edocs/PAG-002.pdf accessed 26 January 2014, p. 5.

6 Task Force on Economic Benefits of Protected Areas of the World Commission on Protected Areas (WCPA) of IUCN, in collaboration with the Economics Service Unit of IUCN (1998). *Economic Values of Protected Areas: Guidelines for Protected Areas Managers.* Gland (Switzerland): IUCN, https://portals.iucn.org/library/efiles/edocs/PAG-002.pdf accessed 26 January 2014, p. 6.

is regarded as a landmark global forum on protected areas, held in Durban in 2003 under the title "Benefits Beyond Boundaries", aimed to consolidate the role of protected areas in conserving biodiversity, as well as encouraging debate on their role in human development, in the fight against poverty and in moderating the effects of global change.[7] This led to the more formalised process of the CBD's Programme of Work on Protected Areas, adopted in 2004, and still relevant to policy today.[8] It triggered the launch of regional and national protected areas initiatives, and facilitated the documentation of social, economic, cultural, ecological and legal benefits of protected areas. As a result, protected areas have become a major instrument to reduce the rate of worldwide biodiversity loss. This calls for the effectiveness in protected areas management.

The CBD's Programme of Work on Protected Areas aimed to help countries meet specific targets on biodiversity. The CBD 2010 Biodiversity Target, which was agreed in April 2002, was the first set of targets. This target was subsequently endorsed by the World Summit on Sustainable Development and the United Nations General Assembly, and was incorporated as a new target under the Millennium Development Goals; however, this target was not met, leading to a reformulation of the Biodiversity Target.[9] In 2010, a revised and updated Strategic Plan for Biodiversity 2011–2020, including the Aichi Biodiversity Targets, was adopted by the CBD in Nagoya, Japan. Under these targets, countries must ensure that by 2020 at least 17% of their terrestrial and inland water areas, 10% of their coastal and marine areas are conserved through a system of protected areas.[10] Obviously, it is not an easy task for most countries, especially the developing countries with a large population who had to make good use of land and natural resources to promote economic development.

The legal and policy framework on protected areas conservation in China and in Europe and some problems both in theory and in practice will be analysed in the following sections.

---

7 EEA (European Environment Agency) (2012). Protected areas in Europe – an overview. Published on 22 October 2012, www.eea.europa.eu/publications/protected-areas-in-europe-2012 accessed 1 March 2013, p. 15.

8 EEA (European Environment Agency) (2012). Protected areas in Europe – an overview. Published on 22 October 2012, www.eea.europa.eu/publications/protected-areas-in-europe-2012 accessed 1 March 2013, p. 15.

9 EEA (European Environment Agency) (2012). Protected areas in Europe – an overview. Published on 22 October 2012, www.eea.europa.eu/publications/protected-areas-in-europe-2012 accessed 1 March 2013, p. 15.

10 EEA (European Environment Agency) (2012). Protected areas in Europe – an overview. Published on 22 October 2012, www.eea.europa.eu/publications/protected-areas-in-europe-2012 accessed 1 March 2013, p. 16.

3.1. PROTECTED AREAS CONSERVATION IN CHINA

3.1.1. GENERAL INTRODUCTION

Environmental protection in China dates back at least to the Qin Dynasty (221–207 BC) when mountain areas were preserved as imperial hunting reserves and temple grounds were protected.[11] Tracing back to the history of protecting areas, Guan Zhong, the prime minister of the State of Qi, around the time of Confucius (551–479 BC), placed great emphasis on the management of mountains, rivers, and forests, promoting the principle of "prohibition of exploitation at the proper time".[12] Confucianism teaches people to "live in harmony" with the universe and hence live in harmony with nature, holding that all things should be "loved" and "respected", and resources should be managed in a sustainable way.[13]

As a consequence of its size, varying nature and complex geological history, China has a wide range of habitats and large numbers of species. The country is also recognised by Conservation International (CI) as a mega-diversity country because of its rich vertebrate and other zoological wealth.[14] Thus, the status quo of protected areas and the relevant law and policy in China have received worldwide attention. China has seen a rapid increase in both number and areal coverage of protected areas over the past couple decades, and improving the effectiveness of existing reserves is currently the management focus.[15] In 2010, the different kinds of protected areas reached a total surface of 1,562,257 km^2 in China, among which there are 1,557,431 km^2 terrestrial protected areas, and 4,826 km^2 marine protected areas,[16] which play a vital role in various aspects. Generally, based on their relative importance, each type of protected area can be further graded into three levels (national, provincial and prefectural/country

---

11 Edmonds, R.L. (1994). *Patterns of China's Lost Harmony: a Survey of the Country's Environmental Degradation and Protection*. London: Routledge, p. 16.

12 Zhou, S.X. (2006). *Forestry in China: Historical Transitions and Industry Developments*. Singapore: Thomson Learning.

13 Zhou, S.X. (2006). *Forestry in China: Historical Transitions and Industry Developments*. Singapore: Thomson Learning.

14 Mackinnon, J. & Xie, Y. (2008). *Regional Action Plan for the Protected Areas of East Asia*. Bangkok (Thailand): IUCN, http://cmsdata.iucn.org/downloads/east_asia_action_plan_english_final.pdf accessed 18 May 2011, p. 12.

15 Hull, V., Xu, W., Liu, W., Zhou, S., Vina, A., Zhang, J., *et al.* (2011). Evaluating the efficacy of zoning designations for protected area management. *Biological Conservation*, 144, pp. 3028–3037; Wu, R.D., Ma, G.Z., Long, Y.C., Yu, J.H., Li, S.N. & Jiang, H.S. (2011). The performance of nature reserves in capturing the biological diversity on Hainan Island, China. *Environmental Science and Pollution Research*, 18, pp. 800–810; Wu, R.D., Zhang, S., Yu, D.W., Zhao, P., Li, X.H., Wang, L.Z., *et al.* (2011). Effective-ness of China's nature reserves in representing ecological diversity. *Frontiers in Ecology and the Environment*, 9, pp. 383–389.

16 World Database on Protected Areas (WDPA). Statistics, www.wdpa.org/Statistics.aspx accessed 19 September 2011.

level), such as national, provincial, and prefectural nature reserves, national parks, geo-parks, wetland parks, and so on.

Once demarcated, all areas are appropriated by the State (if they are not government-owned already), formally becoming public property.[17] In China, there is an old saying: "Mountaineers rely on the mountains, just like those by the waterside profit from water". Local people's access to natural resources, territory, and land-use practices, moreover, are regarded increasingly as an inextricable part of their cultural diversity or even human rights.[18] Many protected areas are established in areas that include well-established rural communities who depend on the resources that have been put under protection; however, China's strict nature reserve[19] regulations greatly limit human activities in protected areas, and it thus creates direct conflicts regarding protected areas and people.[20] In recognition of these problems and to help mitigate conflicts, the Chinese government mandated that all protected areas be divided into three zones, a core zone where strict nature conservation is enforced, and buffer and experimental zones where more intensive human presence and activities are allowed.[21] However, it is still necessary to develop a better legal system to protect the rights of local people to establish harmony in Chinese society.

Although China has a philosophy of harmony with nature, frequent deforestation occurred throughout various periods in Chinese history,

---

17 Xu, J.C. & Melick, D. (2007). Towards community-driven conservation in southwest china: reconciling state and local perceptions. ICRAF (International Center for Research in AgroForestry) Working Paper No. 52, www.worldagroforestry.org/downloads/publications/PDFs/WP15421.PDF accessed 17 October 2012, p. 1.

18 Xu, J.C. & Melick, D. (2007). Towards community-driven conservation in southwest china: reconciling state and local perceptions. ICRAF (International Center for Research in AgroForestry) Working Paper No. 52, www.worldagroforestry.org/downloads/publications/PDFs/WP15421.PDF accessed 17 October 2012, p. 1.

19 The phrase of "nature reserve" was adopted by most of the relevant regulations; however, at present, more people and NGOs think that the phrase of "protected areas" is more formal and meaningful. For instance, the Nature Conservation Legislation Research Group has argued to replace the phrase of "nature reserve" with "protected areas". This group was organised by Yan Xie (解焱) from the Institute of Zoology in Chinese Academy of Sciences (中国科学院动物研究所) and consisted of more than fifty experts in law, biology and other relevant aspects from universities, NGOs, local governments and so on. This book adopts the more popular phrase "protected areas", but when it refers to legal documents, it adopts "nature reserve" to keep consistent with their translation.

20 Xu, L. (2002). Current situation and development of Nature Reserves in Yunnan Province, China. *Forest Inventory and Planning*, 27(4), pp. 56–459 (in Chinese).

21 Hull, V., Xu, W., Liu, W., Zhou, S., Vina, A., Zhang, J., *et al.* (2011). Evaluating the efficacy of zoning designations for protected area management. *Biological Conservation*, 144, pp. 3028–3037; McNeely, J.A. (1994). Protected areas for the 21st century: working to provide benefits to society. *Biodiversity and Conservation*, 3, pp. 95–100; SFA (State Forestry Administration) (1999). National focal protected wild plant list of China. (in Chinese); Yu, G.Z. & Jiang, Z.-G. (2003). Buffer zones: Pattern, function and design principles. *Biodiversity Science*, 11, pp. 256–261.

transforming the environment significantly.[22] China's legal framework is rather young and started almost from scratch in the early 1970s after the country's attendance at the Stockholm Conference on the Human Environment.[23] In the subsequent era of China's open policy and reform, initiated by Deng Xiaoping, the environmental legal regime began to develop, coinciding with a growing awareness of environmental issues.[24] The basic target of conserving protected areas in China is not only to preserve natural ecosystems and biodiversity but also to guarantee the economic development of the surrounding areas.[25] It specifically aims to protect the basic biological processes and ecological system, to save the genetic diversity, namely by maintaining the biodiversity types of genetic material and to ensure the sustainable utilisation of species and biological system, especially fisheries, wildlife, forest and pasture. The government at different levels has issued numerous laws and regulations in China.[26] Separate laws and regulations cover wildlife protection, forest, marine and wetlands conservation.[27] The model of the existing legal system in table 2 below provides useful insights.

22 Elvin, M. (1998). The environmental legacy of imperial China. *The China Quarterly*, 156, pp. 733–756.

23 Beyer, S. (2006). Environmental law and policy in the people's republic of China. *Chinese Journal of International Law*, 5(1), p. 185.

24 Beyer, S. (2006). Environmental law and policy in the people's republic of China. *Chinese Journal of International Law*, 5(1), p. 185.

25 He, M. & Cliquet, A. (2013). Sustainable development through a rights-based approach to conserve protected areas in China. *China-EU Law Journal*. DOI 10.1007/s 12689-013-0031-7. http://link.springer.com/article/10.1007%2Fs12689-013-0031-7 accessed 4 November 2013.

26 He, M. & Cliquet, A. (2013). Sustainable development through a rights-based approach to conserve protected areas in China. *China-EU Law Journal*. DOI 10.1007/s 12689-013-0031-7. http://link.springer.com/article/10.1007%2Fs12689-013-0031-7 accessed 4 November 2013.

27 Mackinnon, J. & Xie, Y. (2008). *Regional Action Plan for the Protected Areas of East Asia*. Bangkok (Thailand): IUCN, http://cmsdata.iucn.org/downloads/east_asia_action_plan_english_final.pdf accessed 18 May 2011, p. 12.

Table 2

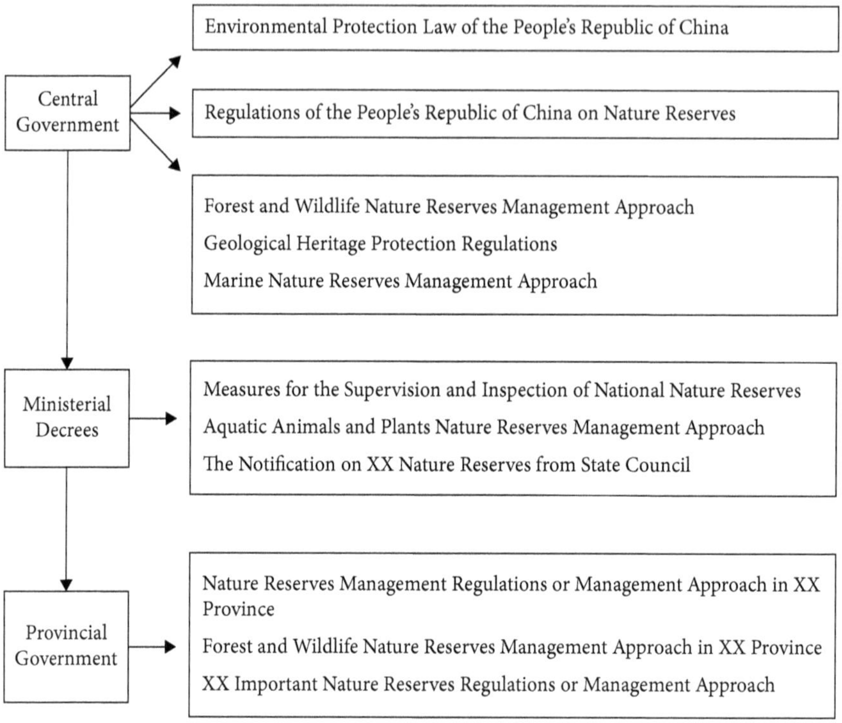

Generally, environmental management in China has been government centralised and community participation has been low.[28] The public is not well informed about the function and performance of protected areas in China.[29] Important decisions are usually driven by local socio-economic interests rather than by strategic objectives. As indicated in the introduction (see 1.1.4.1), it is often the economically poor provinces and counties that contain the best natural areas for biodiversity in China.[30] In this situation, the occurrences of conflicts regarding conserving protected areas and protecting human rights consequently appear to be inevitable. The conflicts have become a major challenge in the conservation of protected areas and have threatened the further development of management of protected areas in recent years. How

28 Liang, Q., Wang, X.H. & Lees, B. (2011). Community participation in the management of marine protected areas in China. *Labour and Management in Development Journal*, 11, www.nla.gov.au/openpublish/index.php/lmd/%20article/viewFile/2135/2654 accessed 2 January 2011.

29 Qiu, W., Wang, B., Jones, P.J.S. & Axmacher, J.C. (2009). Challenges in developing China's marine protected areas system. *Marine Policy*, 33(4), www.homepages.ucl.ac.uk/~ucfwpej/pdf/MPAsChinaMarinePolicyPaperCopy.pdf accessed 5 May 2012, pp. 599–605.

30 PATF (Protected Area Task Force) (2004). *Evaluation and policy recommendations to the protected area system of China*. Protected Area Task Force report to the China Council for International Cooperation on Environment and Development (CCICED). Beijing: State Environmental Protection Administration.

to prevent or solve the conflicts becomes an urgent problem by improving or implementing relevant laws and regulations. As explored in the introduction, the main drive for and benefit of decentralised management of protected areas is the empowerment of local communities.[31] Internationally, legislation proves effective in promoting public participation.[32] Local involvement is crucial for conservation and management of biodiversity and ecosystems to meet people's needs.[33] In most countries protected areas conservation will only be sustainable if local communities become an integral part of conservation efforts and benefit economically from those efforts.[34] Undoubtedly, management and monitoring of natural resources by local stakeholders is a long-term and sustainable approach to conservation.[35] However, the relevant legislation or regulation is vague in China. The history of the existing legal system for protected areas and the existing administrative and legal system concerning protected areas in China will be introduced in the next two sections.

3.1.2. HISTORY OF THE LEGAL AND POLICY FRAMEWORK FOR PROTECTED AREAS IN CHINA

The first period is the initial stage (1956–1966). The recognition of the characteristics, motivation, and influence on protected areas is still in the initial stage. China has been actively establishing protected areas since it created the first such an area in Dinghushan in the Guangdong province in 1956.[36] Up to the end of 1965, there were 20 protected areas in 8 different provinces; the total surface was 1,005,283 km^2, which was 1% of the total land area.[37] During this period, the Forest Ministry not only brought forth the criterion basis for setting up protected areas, but also established some typical protected areas in different bio-climatic zones. The "Instruction on Positive Development of Hunting"

[31] Ribot, J.C. (2002). *Democratic Decentralization of Natural Resources: Institutionalizing Popular Participation*. Washington, D.C.: World Resource Institute.

[32] Pirk, S. (2002). Expanding public participation in environmental justice: methods, legislation, litigation and beyond. *Journal of Environmental Law and Litigation*, 17(1), pp. 207–240.

[33] IUCN (2012). Nature + people and governance – key messages from the IUCN congress forum. Posted on 12 September 2012, www.iucnworldconservationcongress.org/about/theme_and_slogan/people/?11038/Nature-people-and-governance---Key-messages accessed 18 October 2012.

[34] MacKinnon, K. (2001). Editorial. *Parks*, 11(2). Gland (Switzerland): IUCN.

[35] IUCN (2012). Nature + people and governance – key messages from the IUCN congress forum. Posted on 12 September 2012, www.iucnworldconservationcongress.org/about/theme_and_slogan/people/?11038/Nature-people-and-governance---Key-messages accessed 18 October 2012.

[36] Mackinnon, J. & Xie, Y. (2008). *Regional Action Plan for the Protected Areas of East Asia*. Bangkok (Thailand): IUCN, http://cmsdata.iucn.org/downloads/east_asia_action_plan_english_final.pdf accessed 18 May 2011, p. 12.

[37] www.nre.cn/htm/04/bhq/2004-03-24-10682.htm accessed 2 September 2011, in Chinese.

formulated by the Forest Ministry in 1959, states "*it can be conditionally chosen to be a protected area to forbid hunting. Setting up some scientific research agencies to do some research on birds and animals as well as hunting.*"[38] The State Council issued "Instruction on Positive Protecting and Reasonable Utilizing Wild Animal Resources" in 1962. It explicitly requires that all level of governments should establish protected areas in the habitats of special, rare birds and animals. The Forest Department would be in charge of all these issues. This instruction was the legal basis for the establishment of the first protected area in China during this period. At the same year, the State Council publicly announced a name list for national protected animals. Article 13 and Article 14 of the "Regulation for Forest Protection" issued by the State Council in 1963 states that it needs to protect rare forests and the forests in forbidden hunting areas and nature reserves.[39] Although the instructions and regulation expired, they are a strong basis for the further development of protected areas designation and management.

The second period is the lag phase (1967–1972). Rather than implementation of conservation, this period saw extensive environmental degradation resulting from the creation of enormous – often ill-conceived – water control and industrial and agricultural projects.[40] During this period, no protected areas were established, and some existing protected areas were even destroyed.

The third period is the recovery period (1973–1979). In 1973, the formal Forest Ministry held a conference named "National Environmental Protection" and issued "Provisional Regulations on Management of Nature Reserves (draft)"[41] which is the foundation for the legislation of protected areas. It proposed that it should regard typical natural complexes, rare species and special areas with a significant value as the criteria for establishing protected areas. The State Council transmitted the "Report on the Protection and Management for Rare Animals Written by the Ministry of Agriculture and Forest and Revolution Committee in Sichuan Province" in 1975. The report states that "*it is necessary to establish some protected areas in the main habitats for rare animals and to enrich the management agency for protected areas with the principle of simplification. All the required funding, materials, equipment and so on should be brought into the national plan. It is forbidden to illegally hack trees and to destroy protected areas.*"[42] Then, the Ministry of Agriculture and Forest issued "the Notification on Protection, Development and Rational Utilization of the Rare Forest Species".

38 www.cnwyj.com/guojijiaoliu/270.htm accessed 3 December 2011, in Chinese.

39 www.cnwyj.com/guojijiaoliu/270.htm accessed 3 December 2011, in Chinese.

40 Xu, J.C. & Melick, D. (2007). Towards community-driven conservation in southwest china: reconciling state and local perceptions. ICRAF (International Center for Research in AgroForestry) Working Paper No. 52, www.worldagroforestry.org/downloads/publications/PDFs/WP15421.PDF accessed 17 October 2012, p. 2.

41 The "Provisional Regulations on Management of Nature Reserves (draft)" [自然保护区暂行条例（草案）] was only a draft in 1973 and it expired later, but it could be regarded as the first model for the relevant regulations on protected areas in China.

42 www.nre.cn/htm/04/bhq/2004-03-24-10682-2.htm accessed 3 December 2011, in Chinese.

The National Committee of the People's Republic of China for Man and Biosphere was established by the Chinese Academy of Science in 1978.[43]

The fourth period is the rapid growth of protected areas conservation period (1980–1990). Prior to 1979, protected areas were designated centrally with minimum participation from lower-level governments in a straightforward process that aimed to reduce logging and hunting in high-value natural areas. The formal Forest Ministry conveyed the "Notification for Managing, Planning and Scientific Investigation for Protected Areas" in April 1980.[44] Special planning teams for protected areas were established in provincial governments and city governments. The "Grassland Law of the People's Republic of China"[45] was born in 1985. In 1986, the State Council distributed document No. 75 to notify 20 protected areas, such as Chang bai shan protected areas, as the first group of national forest and wildlife protected areas. The "Chinese Programme for Nature Conservation" was issued in 1987.[46] Several Articles of the "Environmental Protection Law of the People's Republic of China" (1989 version)[47] approved by the National People's Congress (NPC) refer to the issues of protected areas, and especially, Article 2 points out that protected areas should be regarded as "*one of the natural factors that influence human beings existence and development*".[48]

The fifth period is the rescue construction period (1991–2000). In 1991, the General Office of the State Council promulgated document no. 17 that pointed out that the application and ratification of national protected areas should follow the provided process. Regulations of the People's Republic of China on Natural Resources,[49] promulgated in 1994, as the first specific regulation on

43 For detailed information see www.china-mab.cas.cn/ accessed 3 December 2011, in Chinese.

44 www.cnwyj.com/guojijiaoliu/270.htm accessed 3 December 2011, in Chinese.

45 The "Grassland Law of the Peoples Republic of China" [中华人民共和国草原法] was issued on 18 June 1985, and it was revised on 28 December 2002. The revised version went into effect on 1 March 2003, www.eduzhai.net/yingyu/615/763/yingyu_247335.html accessed 3 December 2011.

46 www.cnwyj.com/guojijiaoliu/270.htm accessed 3 December 2011, in Chinese.

47 Articles 2, 17, 18, 20, 23 and 44, the "Environmental Protection Law of the People's Republic of China" (1989 version) [中华人民共和国环境保护法] was promulgated by Order No. 22 of the President of the People's Republic of China on 26 December 1989, and was effective on the date of promulgation, www.law-lib.com/law/law_view.asp?id=6229 accessed 3 December 2011. It will be discussed in detail later.

48 Article 2 of the "Environmental Protection Law of the People's Republic of China" (1989 version) is the same with Article 2 of the "Environmental Protection Law of the People's Republic of China" (2014 version). The "Environmental Protection Law of the People's Republic of China" (2014 version) [中华人民共和国环境保护法] was newly modified based on the "Environmental Protection Law of the People's Republic of China" (1989 version) on 24 April 2014 and entered into force on 1 January 2015, http://edu.sina.com.cn/en/2014-05-20/144680376.shtml accessed 30 June 2014.

49 The "Regulations of the People's Republic of China on Nature Reserves" [中华人民共和国自然保护区条例] was entered into effective on 1 December 1994, http://english.mep.gov.cn/Policies_Regulations/regulations/Natural_Conservation_Biosafety/200711/t20071123_113364.htm accessed 3 December 2011.

natural resources, provides the strong legal basis for constructing and managing protected areas. Based on this law, some regulations and acts, such as the "Marine Protected Areas Management Measures" (1995),[50] "Land Management Approach in Nature Reserve" (1995),[51] "Aquatic Animals and Plants Nature Reserve Management Approach" (1997),[52] and "Regulations on the Protection of Wild Plants" (1997)[53] were issued by relevant governmental departments. The "Forest Law of the People's Republic of China"[54] was amended in 1998. In addition, a Chinese Nature Reserve Development Planning Outline (1996–2010)[55] was issued by the State Bureau of Environmental Protection in 1997, and it called for different levels of government to establish their own nature reserve development outlines and add them to the national economic and social development plan.

The sixth period is the construction and management period (2001–present). In December 2001, the State Forestry Administration (SFA) implemented the Wildlife Conservation and Nature Reserve Construction Project, which aims to establish 2500 nature reserves covering 172.8 million ha (18% of China's land area) by 2050.[56] A national Nature Reserve Development Plan was issued by the State Bureau of Environmental Protection in 2005. It provides the development plan and main task for conserving protected areas in the future. Generally speaking, the Constitution of the People's Republic of China[57]

---

50 The "Marine Protected Areas Management Measures" [海洋自然保护区管理办法] were issued on 24 July 1995, www.mep.gov.cn/gkml/hbb/gwy/200910/t20091030_180677.htm accessed 3 December 2011.

51 The "Land Management Approach in Nature Reserve" [自然保护区土地管理办法] was issued by the State Land Administration and the State Environment Protection Bureau on 24 July 1995 as Order No. 117, on the basis of the Land Management Law, Environmental Protection Law, and Nature Reserve ordinance in order to improve land management in nature reserves, www.mlr.gov.cn/zwgk/flfg/tdglflfg/200406/t20040625_585545.htm accessed 3 December 2011.

52 The "Aquatic Animals and Plants Nature Reserve Management Approach" [中华人民共和国水生动植物自然保护区管理办法] was issued on 17 October 1997, http://zfs.mep. gov.cn/gz/bmgz/qtgz/199710/t19971017_81935.htm accessed 3 December 2011.

53 The "Regulations of the People's Republic of China on the Protection of Wild Plants" [中华人民共和国野生植物保护条例] was effective on 1 January 1997, www.xj.xinhuanet.com/shengtai/2004-04/23/content_2026071.htm accessed 3 December 2011.

54 The "Forest Law of the People's Republic of China" [中华人民共和国森林法] was adopted in 1984 and amended on 29 April 1998, www.china.org.cn/english/environment/207457.htm accessed 3 December 2011.

55 The "Chinese Nature Reserve Development Planning Outline" (1996–2010) [中国自然保护区发展规划纲要] was issued on 24 November 1997, www.zhb.gov.cn/ztbd/rdzl/2010sdn/bhcj/201001/t20100113_184243.htm accessed 3 December 2011, in Chinese. Although it was a planning outline, it was regarded as a general principle to establish protected areas and solve the relevant issues.

56 Xu, J.C. & Melick, D. (2007). Towards community-driven conservation in southwest China: reconciling state and local perceptions. ICRAF (International Center for Research in AgroForestry) Working Paper No. 52, www.worldagroforestry.org/downloads/publications/PDFs/WP15421.PDF accessed 17 October 2012, p. 3.

57 The "Constitution of the People's Republic of China" [中华人民共和国宪法] was adopted in 1982 and newly amended on 14 March 2004, www.for68.com/new/201007/he60492159127010212383.shtml accessed 3 December 2010, in both Chinese and English.

establishes a basic principle for conserving protected areas. The "Environmental Protection Law of the People's Republic of China" is regarded as an important criterion for conserving protected areas. In addition, the "Regulations on Comprehensive Scientific Survey for Protected Areas (Trial)"[58] were issued in 2010. The central government organised the application and evaluation for the "Special Funding Programme on Improving Management Ability of National Protected Areas" in 2010. The programme supported 48 national protected areas to improve the management ability with 0.15 billion Yuan (about 17.85 million EUR).[59] The Environmental Protection Department has issued the "Notification on Further to Strengthen Hydropower Construction and Environmental Protection" on 6 January 2012.[60] It points out it is forbidden to establish any hydropower construction in protected areas or other areas with special environmental value.[61] Furthermore, in order to strengthen wetland protection and to implement the Ramsar Convention on Wetlands,[62] the SFA adopted the "Management Rules on Wetland Protection"[63] on 28 March 2013.

Other non-regulatory policy documents, such as the "Conservation Action Plan for Wetlands in China",[64] the "Strategy and Action Plan for Biodiversity Preservation in China (2011–2030)"[65] and the "National Wildlife Conservation

58 http://wenku.baidu.com/view/844713da5022aaea998f0ff8.html accessed 4 December 2011, in Chinese.

59 Bulletin on Environment in China in 2010 (2010年中国环境状况公报) (2011). The establishment and management on protected areas in China in 2010 (2010年自然保护区建设与管理情况). Published on 3 June 2011, http://sts.mep.gov.cn/zrbhq/zrbhqgzjb/201106/t20110603_211638.htm, in Chinese accessed 20 October 2011.

60 The "Notification on Further to Strengthen Hydropower Construction and Environmental Protection" [关于进一步加强水电建设环境保护的通知] was issued on 6 January 2012 by the Ministry of Environmental Protection of the People's Republic of China, www.mep.gov.cn/gkml/hbb/bgt/201201/t20120117_222665.htm accessed 11 January 2012. This notification can be regarded as a policy, but it helps to forbid some economic activities in protected areas in China.

61 China Youth Daily (中国青年报) (2012). The Ministry of Environmental Protection: forbid to explore hydropower. Posted on 20 January 2012, http://env.people.com.cn/GB/16928251.html accessed 12 January 2012, in Chinese.

62 Convention on Wetlands of International Importance (Ramsar Convention), adopted on 2 February 1971 and entered into force on 21 December 1975, amended by the Paris Protocol on 3 December 1982, 11 ILM (1972) 963, www.ramsar.org/cda/en/ramsar-documents-texts/main/ramsar/1-31-38_4000_0__ accessed 8 June 2012.

63 The "Management Rules on Wetland Protection" [湿地保护管理规定] was issued by the State Forestry Administration on 28 March 2013 and entered into force on 1 May 2013, www.forestry.gov.cn/portal/main/s/72/content-594660.html accessed 29 May 2014.

64 The "Conservation Action Plan for Wetlands in China" [中国湿地保护行动计划] was issued on 8 November 2000, http://lianghui.china.com.cn/chinese/2000/Nov/10342.htm accessed 4 December 2011.

65 The "Strategy and Action Plan for Biodiversity Preservation in China (2011–2030)" [中国生物多样性保护战略与行动计划(2011–2030)] was issued on 17 September 2010, www.mep.gov.cn/gkml/hbb/bwj/201009/t20100921_194841.htm accessed 3 December 2011.

and Natural Reserve Construction General Plan"[66] also provide guidance for constructing and managing protected areas.

Furthermore, regarding the relevant connection with the international level for protected areas conservation, China acceded to many relevant international treaties, such as the World Heritage Convention[67] in 1985, the Ramsar Convention on Wetlands[68] and the Convention on Biological Diversity[69] in 1992. China concluded many bilateral and regional agreements with different countries, such as the "Protection of Migratory Birds and Their Habitat Agreement" with Japan on 3 March 1981,[70] the "Cooperation Agreement on Natural Environment" with Mongolia on 6 May 1990 and the "Agreement on the Establishment of a Natural Reserve with Mongolia and Russia" on 29 March 1994.[71]

3.1.3. ADMINISTRATIVE AND LEGAL SYSTEM FOR PROTECTED AREAS CONSERVATION IN CHINA

3.1.3.1. Administrative System for Protected Areas Conservation in China

As for the Chinese environmental administration system, there are ten different ministries or administrations now managing protected areas (see table 3), and during the turbulence of decades, the roles and responsibilities of government departments have been constantly defined and redefined.[72] In 2008 the State Environmental Protection Administration (SEPA) was upgraded to ministerial level under the name Ministry of Environmental Protection (MEP) emphasising

66 The "National Wildlife Conservation and Natural Reserve Construction General Plan" [全国野生动植物保护及自然保护区建设工程总体规划] was issued in 2001, www.beinet.net.cn/zcfg/gh/qggh/200802/P020080423597945791148.pdf accessed 4 December 2011.

67 Convention Concerning the Protection of the World Cultural and Natural Heritage (World Heritage Convention), adopted on 16 November 1972 and entered into force on 17 December 1975, 11 ILM (1972) 1358, http://portal.unesco.org/en/ev.php-URL_ID=13055&URL_DO=DO_TOPIC&URL_SECTION=201.htm accessed 8 June 2012.

68 Convention on Wetlands of International Importance (Ramsar Convention), adopted on 2 February 1971 and entered into force on 21 December 1975, amended by the Paris Protocol on 3 December 1982, 11 ILM (1972) 963, www.ramsar.org/cda/en/ramsar-documents-texts/main/ramsar/1-31-38_4000_0__ accessed 8 June 2012.

69 Convention on Biological Diversity (CBD), opened for signature on 5 June 1992 and entered into force on 29 December 1993, [1993] ATS 32/1760 UNTS 79/31 ILM 818 (1992), www.cbd.int/ accessed 8 June 2012.

70 www.pressdisplay.com/pressdisplay/viewer.aspx accessed 4 December 2011.

71 http://amur-heilong.net/http/09_int_argeements/0902chinamongolianagreements.html accessed 4 December 2011.

72 Xu, J.C. & Melick, D. (2007). Towards community-driven conservation in southwest China: reconciling state and local perceptions. ICRAF (International Center for Research in AgroForestry) Working Paper No. 52, www.worldagroforestry.org/downloads/publications/PDFs/WP15421.PDF accessed 17 October 2012, p. 24.

the increased prioritisation of the environment as issued by the central government.[73]

Table 3. Chinese environmental administration system (2008 version)[74]

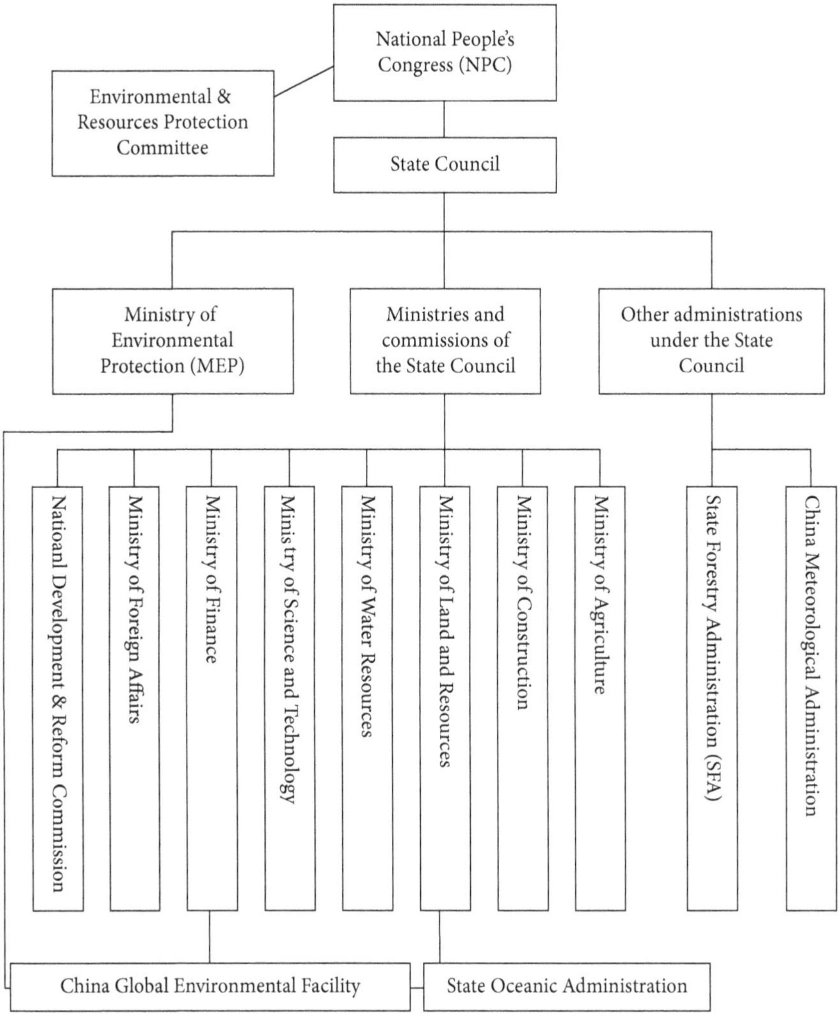

73 Economy, E.C. (2007). The great leap backward? *Foreign Affairs*, 86 (5), pp. 38–59.

74 The table 3 was updated from 2007 version; see Xu, J.C. & David, R.M. (2007). Rethinking the Effectiveness of Public Protected Areas in Southwestern China. *Conservation Biology*, 21(2), p. 320.

3.1.3.2. Legal and Policy Framework for Protected Areas Conservation in China

The "Constitution of the People's Republic of China",[75] which is regarded as the fundamental law in China, points out the protection for natural resources and the general ownership of natural resources in China (see 4.2.2). The "Environmental Protection Law of the People's Republic of China" (1989 version)[76] is widely accepted as the fundamental environmental law in China. Article 17 points out the duty of the governments for environmental protection.[77] Specifically concerning the nature reserves and other zones, Article 18 states: "*Within the scenic spots or historic sites, nature reserves and other zones that need special protection, as designated by the State Council, the relevant competent department under the State Council, and the people's governments of provinces, autonomous regions and municipalities directly under the Central Government, no industrial production installations that cause environmental pollution shall be built; other installations to be built in these areas must not exceed the prescribed standards for the discharge of pollutants. If the installations that have been built discharge more pollutants than are specified by the prescribed discharge standards, such pollution shall be eliminated or controlled within a prescribed period of time.*"[78] The relationship between utilisation and protection for natural resources

---

75 The "Constitution of the People's Republic of China" [中华人民共和国宪法] was adopted in 1982 and newly amended on 14 March 2004, www.for68.com/new/201007/he6049215912701021 2383.shtml accessed 3 December 2010, in both Chinese and English.

76 The "Environmental Protection Law of the People's Republic of China" [中华人民共和国环境保护法] was promulgated by Order No. 22 of the President of the People's Republic of China on 26 December 1989, and was effective on the date of promulgation, www.law-lib.com/law/law_view.asp?id=6229 accessed 3 December 2011.

77 Article 17 states: "The people's governments at various levels shall take measures to conserve areas representing various types of natural ecological systems, areas with a natural distribution of rare and endangered wild animals and plants, areas where major sources of water are conserved, geological structures of major scientific and cultural value, famous areas where karst caves and fossil deposits are distributed, traces of glaciers, volcanos and hot springs, traces of human history, and ancient and precious trees. Damage to the mention-above shall be strictly forbidden", www.law-lib.com/law/law_view.asp?id=6229 accessed 3 December 2011. Article 17 of the "Environmental Protection Law of the People's Republic of China" (1989 version) is the same as Article 29 of the "Environmental Protection Law of the People's Republic of China" (2014 version). The "Environmental Protection Law of the People's Republic of China" (2014 version) [中华人民共和国环境保护法] was newly modified based on the "Environmental Protection Law of the People's Republic of China" (1989 version) on 24 April 2014 and entered into force on 1 January 2015, http://edu.sina.com.cn/en/2014-05-20/144680376.shtml accessed 30 June 2014.

78 Article 18 of the "Environmental Protection Law of the People's Republic of China" (1989 version) does not exist in the "Environmental Protection Law of the People's Republic of China" (2014 version). The "Environmental Protection Law of the People's Republic of China" (2014 version) [中华人民共和国环境保护法] was newly modified based on the "Environmental Protection Law of the People's Republic of China" (1989 version) on 24 April 2014 and entered into force on 1 January 2015, http://edu.sina.com.cn/en/2014-05-20/144680376.shtml accessed 30 June 2014.

is briefly discussed in Article 19. It states: "*Measures must be taken to protect the ecological environment while natural resources are being developed or utilized.*"[79]

Although there are several general provisions in the Constitution, the Environmental Protection Law and other laws in particular areas of natural resources, it is disappointing to find that "protected areas conservation" was not safeguarded at the level of "Law".[80] The "Regulations of the People's Republic of China on Nature Reserves"[81] is the most important regulation for protected areas protection under Chinese jurisdiction. It emphasises that "*[t]he local economic construction, the production activities and everyday life of local residents shall be properly considered when the nature reserves are established and managed.*"[82] The direct goal of the effective conservation of protected areas is to conserve natural resources and the environment and achieve sustainable management of ecosystems and biodiversity. The interests of local people and the local economy shall thereby be properly considered to realise the direct goal. Article 26 and 27 point out the forbidden activities in protected areas, and Article 26 states: "*In nature reserves, such activities as felling, grazing, hunting, fishing, gathering medicinal herbs, reclaiming, burning, mining, stone quarrying and sand dredging etc., shall be prohibited unless it is otherwise provided by relevant laws and regulations*", while Article 27 states: "*Nobody shall be allowed to enter the core area of nature reserves (...). For residents living in the core area of the nature reserve who are necessitated to move out, the local people's government shall arrange the proper settlement for them.*" The visiting and sightseeing tourist

79 Article 19 of the "Environmental Protection Law of the People's Republic of China" (1989 version) is the similar to Article 30 of the "Environmental Protection Law of the People's Republic of China" (2014 version). Article 30 says: "Exploitation and utilization of natural resources shall be developed in a rational way that conserves biological diversity and safeguards ecological security. Ecological protection and restoration programmes shall be developed in accordance with laws and be implemented. For introduction of exotic species as well as the research, development and utilization of biotechnology, effective measures shall be taken to prevent destruction of biodiversity." The "Environmental Protection Law of the People's Republic of China" (2014 version) [中华人民共和国环境保护法] was newly modified based on the "Environmental Protection Law of the People's Republic of China" (1989 version) on 24 April 2014 and entered into force on 1 January 2015, http://edu.sina.com.cn/en/2014-05-20/144680376.shtml accessed 30 June 2014.

80 Regarding the hierarchy of legislative documents, generally speaking, there are five categories, namely law (法律), administrative regulation (行政法规), local regulation (地方性法规), autonomous regulation and separate regulation (自治条例和单行条例), department rule (部门规章) and local government rule (地方政府规章). The "Law" refers to the one enacted by the National People's Congress (NPC) or its standing Committee.

81 The "Regulations of the People's Republic of China on Nature Reserves" [中华人民共和国自然保护区条例] entered into force on 1 December 1994, http://english.mep. gov.cn/Policies_Regulations/regulations/Natural_Conservation_Biosafety/200711/t20071123_113364.htm accessed 3 December 2011.

82 Article 5, the "Regulations of the People's Republic of China on Nature Reserves" [中华人民共和国自然保护区条例] was entered into effective on 1 December 1994, http://english.mep.gov.cn/Policies_Regulations/regulations/Natural_Conservation_Biosafety/200711/t20071123_113364.htm accessed 3 December 2011.

activities in the nature reserves are discussed in Articles 28 and 29. Articles 32 and 33 explain the general punitive measures for forbidden activities within protected areas. Based on what is mentioned above, it should be noted that this law points out that it should properly consider the interests of local residents,[83] but it does not mention how to consider the interests when conflicts occur. This law states that the governments shall arrange for the proper settlement for local people, but it does not point out what kind of settlement it is. It also prescribes punitive measures for the forbidden activities,[84] but it does not mention how and who examines the accident. However, other laws and regulations below have specifically supplemented some aspects.

The "Forest Law of the People's Republic of China"[85] also points out some issues concerning protected areas. Article 24 states that: "*Serious protection should be given to rare and precious trees outside nature reserves and plant resources with special value in forest regions; it is forbidden to cut or collect any plants resources without the approval of the competent department of forestry of the provinces, autonomous regions and municipalities directly under the Central Government.*" Article 20 of the "Mineral Resources Law of the People's Republic of China"[86] states: "*Unless approved by the competent departments authorized by the State Council, no one may mine mineral resources in the following places: (...) (5) nature reserves and important scenic spots designated by the State, major sites of immovable historical relics and places of historical interest and scenic beauty that are under State protection; and (6) other areas where mineral mining is prohibited by the State.*"

The "Regulations of the People's Republic of China on the Prevention of Pollution Damage to the Marine Environment by Land-sourced Pollutions"[87] also points out forbidden activities in protected areas. Article 8 states: "*No organization or individual may establish outlets for discharging sewage within*

83 Articles 32 and 33, the "Regulations of the People's Republic of China on Nature Reserves" [中华人民共和国自然保护区条例] entered into effect on 1 December 1994, http://english.mep.gov.cn/Policies_Regulations/regulations/Natural_Conservation_Biosafety/200711/t20071123_113364.htm accessed 3 December 2011.

84 Articles 32 and 33, the "Regulations of the People's Republic of China on Nature Reserves" [中华人民共和国自然保护区条例] entered into effect on 1 December 1994, http://english.mep.gov.cn/Policies_Regulations/regulations/Natural_Conservation_Biosafety/200711/t20071123_113364.htm accessed 3 December 2011.

85 The "Forest Law of the People's Republic of China" [中华人民共和国森林法] was adopted in 1984 and amended on 29 April 1998, www.china.org.cn/english/environment/207457.htm accessed 3 December 2011.

86 The "Mineral Resources Law of the People's Republic of China" [中华人民共和国矿产资源保护法] was adopted in 1989 and amended on 29 August 1996, www.china.org.cn/environment/2007-08/20/content_1034342.htm accessed 5 December 2011.

87 The "Regulations of the People's Republic of China on the Prevention of Pollution Damage to the Marine Environment by Land-sourced Pollution" [中华人民共和国防治陆源污染物污染损害海洋环境管理条例] was effective on 1 August 1990, http://dinrac.nowpap.org/documents/law/China/Regulations_on_Prevention_of_Pollution_Damage_to_Marine_Environment_by_Land-Based_Pollutants_China.pdf accessed 5 December 2011.

special marine reserves, marine nature reserves, seashore scenic and tourist areas, salt works reserves, bathing beaches, important fishing areas and other areas which need special protection. Those outlets already established within these areas stipulated in the preceding paragraph, where the discharge of pollutants is in excess of the national or local discharge standards, shall be improved within a prescribed period of time."

The "Law of the People's Republic of China on Prevention of Environmental Pollution Caused by Solid Waste"[88] also points out forbidden activities in the nature reserves. Article 22 states: "*It shall be forbidden to construct facilities or sites for the centralized storage and disposal of industrial solid waste or burial site for residential refuse in nature reserves, scenic spots, historic sites, drinking water sources, and other places of special protection designated by the State Council and the people's governments at the provincial, municipal or autonomous regional levels.*"

Article 22 from the "Law of the People's Republic of China on Prevention and Control of Desertification"[89] points out: "*The local people's government at or above the county level shall make plans to help the farmers and herdsmen living in the enclosed and forbidden reserves of desertified land move out of the areas and settle down appropriately. With regards to production and everyday life of the farmers and herdsmen still living in the enclosed and forbidden reserves of desertified land, the authority there shall make proper arrangements for them. Without approval of the State Council or the authority designated by the State Council, no railways, highways, etc. may be constructed in enclosed and forbidden reserves of desertified land.*"

The "Interim Management Measures on the Special Marine Protected Areas"[90] is a relative new regulation for the special marine protected areas in China. Article 13 states that before the designation of marine protected areas, the authority shall inform the public and let the public give some suggestions and comments. As for the information issue, Article 17 points out that after establishing special marine protected areas, the authority shall build some landmarks and signs in some appropriate places according to their boundaries,

88 The "Law of the People's Republic of China on Prevention of Environmental Pollution Caused by Solid Waste" [中华人民共和国固体废物污染环境防治法] was issued in 1995, amended on 29 December 2004 and effective on 1 April 2005, www.lawinfochina.com/display.aspx?lib=law&id=119 accessed 3 December 2011.

89 The "Law of the People's Republic of China on Prevention and Control of Desertification" [中华人民共和国防沙治沙法] entered into effect on 31 August 2001, www.china.org.cn/china/LegislationsForm2001-2010/2011-02/14/content_21915867.htm accessed 6 December 2011.

90 The "Interim Management Measures on the Special Marine Protected Areas" [海洋特别保护区管理暂行办法] was issued by the State Oceanic Administration of the People's Republic of China on 31 August 2010, www.shanghaiwater.gov.cn/xwzx!view.action?fan.fileId=20091759&sdh.code=004015001 accessed 4 December 2011. Although it is called and translated as "management measures", it is a regulation for special marine protected areas in China.

the authority also shall publish management rules, measures and other relevant information on special marine protected areas. Article 28 states that the authority and local community shall co-manage special marine protected areas, and design a cooperation project plan, a community development plan, a management plan and so on. Article 46 refers to the interests of right-holders. It states that "*the authority and the enterprises who explore the special marine protected areas shall sign a franchise agreement that the income should be devoted to conserve protected areas and give the compensation to rights holders*".

Besides these laws and regulations, some important recent policy instruments are regarded as guidelines for solving the protected areas relevant issues in China. For instance, the "Strategy and Action Plan for Biodiversity Preservation in China (2011–2030)"[91] pointed out four basic principles for biodiversity conservation, namely: conservation priority; sustainable utilisation; public participation; and benefit-sharing. It also clarified ten pioneer fields and actions. The first pioneer field is to improve the policy and legal system for biodiversity conservation and sustainable utilisation, including completely reviewing the laws and regulations to solve the conflicts regarding them, researching on the laws and regulations on protected areas management, and strengthening the implementation system for laws and regulations. Action 4 is to formally manage protected areas and to improve the quality of management, including drawing up an all-aspects plan for designation and management, regularly evaluating the implementation, exploring the different co-management models for different protected areas, and experimenting in the selected areas and popularising the experimentation. Action 29 indicates that it should establish a broad public participation mechanism, including improving the effective public participation system, concerning hearings, seminars; establishing a public and media supervision mechanism to guarantee the implementation of relevant policy.[92]

In addition, the "Notification on Well Managing Protected Areas" was issued by the General Office of the State Council in December 2010.[93] Ganjie Li, the deputy Minister of the Environmental Protection Department, said that the State Council proposed the Notification for several reasons. Among

---

91 The "Strategy and Action Plan for Biodiversity Preservation in China (2011–2030)" [中国生物多样性保护战略与行动计划 (2011–2030)] was issued by the Chinese Environmental Protection Bureau on 17 September 2010, www.mep.gov.cn/gkml/hbb/bwj/201009/t20100921_194841.htm accessed 3 December 2011. Although it is only a legal document from the Chinese Environmental Protection Bureau, it is regarded as guidelines for solving the relevant issues in China.

92 He, M. & Cliquet, A. (2013). Sustainable development through a rights-based approach to conserve protected areas in China. *China-EU Law Journal.* DOI 10.1007/s 12689-013-0031-7. http://link.springer.com/article/10.1007%2Fs12689-013-0031-7 accessed 4 November 2013.

93 The "Notification on Well Managing Protected Areas from the General Office of the State Council" [国务院办公厅关于做好自然保护区管理有关工作的通知] was issued in December 2010, www.gzhjbh.gov.cn/hjpj/tzwj/45214.shtml, in Chinese accessed 8 October 2012. Although it is called and translated as "Notification", it is regarded as guidelines for implementing the relevant regulation and solving the relevant issues on protected areas in China.

these reasons are the facts that tougher protection implementation is needed, the production and life of local population have been affected, the conflicts regarding protected areas management and the local communities are becoming serious. He pointed out that in order to solve the conflicts, firstly, it is necessary to establish a reasonable compensation system for local people, considering the function, ownership and other characters of different protected areas, to increase financial transfer payments to gradually increase the level of basic public service for local people. If the local residents have damage from wild animals within protected areas, they should be given compensation. Secondly, there is a need to establish a co-management mechanism with local people. The participation of local people in protected areas management not only can strengthen the power of the protection, but also can increase their income.[94]

Based on what was mentioned above, it can be seen that the Chinese government and different departments have issued various laws and regulations that provide for the establishment and management of protected areas and forbidden activities in or near the protected areas. The laws and regulations, such as the "Regulations of the People's Republic of China on Nature Reserves" (1994) (Articles 14, 27), the "Law of the Peoples of Republic of China on Prevention and Control of Desertification" (2001) (Article 35);[95] and the "Land Management Law of the People's Republic of China" (2004)[96] (Article 34), also point out that the interests of local people shall be taken into consideration. However, there are few Articles specifically addressing how to solve the conflicts mentioned in the introduction (see 1.1.4.1). Unfortunately, those problems, though absolutely necessary for the achievement of the protection goals, have largely been ignored.

Due to the ancient Confucian concept of social harmony, law in general is not seen as an adequate mechanism to shape human behaviour.[97] According to this philosophy, the ultimate goal of social harmony is not attained by harmonising subjective rights of persons intended to defend their own interest.[98] Moreover,

94 China Environmental Newspaper (中国环境报) (2010). Strengthen protected areas management and promote ecological civilization (加强自然保护区管理，促进生态文明建设). www.clapv.org/weiquanwenxian_content.asp?id=175 accessed 8 October 2012.

95 The "Law of the People's Republic of China on Prevention and Control of Desertification" [中华人民共和国防沙治沙法] entered into effect on 31 August 2001, www.china.org.cn/china/LegislationsForm2001-2010/2011-02/14/content_21915867.htm accessed 6 December 2011.

96 The "Land Management Law of the People's Republic of China" [中华人民共和国土地管理法] was issued in 1986 and amended in 1998 and later amended on 28 August 2004, detailed information see (1998 version) www.zhb.gov.cn/ztbd/rdzl/2010sdn/zcfg/201001/t20100113_184226.htm, and (2004 version) www.china.com.cn/chinese/law/647616.htm accessed 3 January 2012.

97 Beyer, S. (2006). Environmental law and policy in the people's republic of China. *Chinese Journal of International Law*, 5(1), p. 185.

98 Beyer, S. (2006). Environmental law and policy in the people's republic of China. *Chinese Journal of International Law*, 5(1), p. 185.

individual rights are considered to disturb the social order.[99] Consequently, the focus lies on preventing disputes from happening rather than on finding out whose rights have been infringed.[100] When ownership of a particular resource is vested in the state, as happens in domestic regimes, the rights of other entities are usually limited to the rights to use, manage, control, or enjoy benefits as derived from the resources.[101] The right to property and protected areas in China will be explored in the substantive rights part (see Chapter 4).

In a developing country like China, the accountability and capacity of local governments are typically low.[102] The degree to which local governments adhere to the principles of nature conservation is also questionable.[103] Local governments in China often perceive the development of protected areas as a symbol of administrative achievement and a potential source of tourism income.[104] As a result, important decisions such as the zoning and configuration of protected areas are regularly driven by local socio-economic interests rather than by strategic objectives.[105] In addition, local communities in developing countries often have limited experiences in public decision-making,[106] this being particularly true in a country like China with a long standing tradition of top-down governance. The present legal system for protected areas in China arguably has the disadvantages of decentralisation, i.e. design, enforcement and monitoring of the forbidden activities are all left to the government, mainly to the local government which focuses more on economic development than on strategic protected areas conservation objectives, without the advantages of bottom-up approaches, i.e. promotion of stakeholder participation, cooperation, and innovation.[107] China's experience demonstrates

99 Beyer, S. (2006). Environmental law and policy in the people's republic of China. *Chinese Journal of International Law*, 5(1), p. 185.

100 Wong, B. (2000). Traditional Chinese philosophy and dispute resolution. *Hong Kong Law Journal*, 30, p. 304.

101 Clerk, A. & Kohler, P. (2005). *Property Law: Commentary and Materials.* Cambridge: Cambridge University Press, p. 40.

102 Bardhan, P. (2002). Decentralization of governance and development. *Journal of Economic Perspectives*, 16(4), pp. 185–206.

103 Ribot, J.C. (2002). *Democratic decentralization of natural resources: institutionalizing popular participation.* Washington, D.C.: World Resource Institute.

104 Qiu, W., Wang, B., Jones, P.J.S. & Axmacher, J.C. (2009). Challenges in developing China's marine protected areas system. *Marine Policy*, 33(4), pp. 599–605, www.homepages.ucl.ac.uk/~ucfwpej/pdf/MPAsChinaMarinePolicyPaperCopy.pdf accessed 5 May 2012.

105 Jim, C.Y. & Xu, S.S.W. (2004). Recent protected-area designation in China: an evaluation of administrative and statutory procedures. *The Geographical Journal*, 170, pp. 39–50.

106 Ribot, J.C. (2002). *Democratic decentralization of natural resources: institutionalizing popular participation.* Washington, D.C.: World Resource Institute.

107 Qiu, W., Wang, B., Jones, P.J.S. & Axmacher, J.C. (2009). Challenges in developing China's marine protected areas system. *Marine Policy*, 33(4), www.homepages.ucl.ac.uk/~ucfwpej/pdf/MPAsChinaMarinePolicyPaperCopy.pdf accessed 5 May 2012, pp. 599–605.

the need for a balance between top-down and bottom-up approaches.[108] While methods and procedures for public participation have been established in some new environmental regulations in China, such as the Law on Environmental Impact Assessment of the People's Republic of China,[109] they have yet to be incorporated into protected area regulations.[110] Although there are some Articles that refer to the interests of rights holders in protected areas, for instance the "Interim Management Measures on the Special Marine Protected Areas"[111] (Article 46), they do not clearly mention the specific definition of rights and rights holders, how to judge the loss of rights holders and the procedures to deal with possible compensation. Furthermore, insufficient public consultation in protection areas decision-making may potentially escalate into conflicts regarding people and protected areas. In such a context, seeking better solutions to solve the conflicts regarding protected areas and human rights, such as using the right to participation, is not about weakening the role of the State. On the contrary, the State needs to play an active role in certain areas, such as building competent and accountable local institutions, ensuring quality standards, and establishing statutory procedures for public participation in decision-making.[112]

China is in the process of drafting a new protected area law, with one of the objectives being to provide an overarching legal framework for different types of managed areas (e.g. national reserves, national parks, heritage areas, and sustainable resource use areas),[113] which may present opportunities to review the main problem in legislation, which is the harmonious development of protected areas conservation and people's rights, especially for local residents.

---

108 Qiu, W., Wang, B., Jones, P.J.S. & Axmacher, J.C. (2009). Challenges in developing China's marine protected areas system. *Marine Policy* 33(4), www.homepages.ucl.ac.uk/~ucfwpej/pdf/MPAsChinaMarinePolicyPaperCopy.pdf accessed 5 May 2012, pp. 599–605.

109 The "Law on Environmental Impact Assessment of the People's Republic of China" [中华人民共和国环境影响评价法] was adopted in 2012 and entered into effective on 1 September 2003, www.people.com.cn/GB/shehui/212/3572/3574/20021029/853043.html accessed 4 May 2012.

110 Qiu, W., Wang, B., Jones, P.J.S. & Axmacher, J.C. (2009). Challenges in developing China's marine protected areas system. *Marine Policy* 33(4), www.homepages.ucl.ac.uk/~ucfwpej/pdf/MPAsChinaMarinePolicyPaperCopy.pdf accessed 5 May 2012, pp. 599–605.

111 The "Interim Management Measures on the Special Marine Protected Areas" [海洋特别保护区管理暂行办法] was issued by the State Oceanic Administration of the People's Republic of China on 31 August 2010, www.shanghaiwater.gov.cn/xwzx!view.action?fan.fileId=20091759&sdh.code=004015001 accessed 4 December 2011. Although it is called and translated as "management measures", it is a regulation for special marine protected areas in China.

112 Bardhan, P. (2002). Decentralization of governance and development. *Journal of Economic Perspectives*, 16(4), pp. 185–206; Pomeroy, R.S. & Berkes, F. (1997). Two to tango: the role of government in fisheries co-management. *Marine Policy,* 21(5), pp. 465–80.

113 Sun, Y.H. & Chen, S.Y. (2004). Arguments for the new Law of protected areas. *Environmental Protection*, 3, pp. 7–12.

3.2. PROTECTED AREAS CONSERVATION IN EUROPE

Protected areas are important havens for biodiversity and vital to preserving some of Europe' most threatened species.[114] There are 105,000 nationally designated protected sites, which occupy almost 21% of the territory of European Environment Agency (EEA) members and cooperating countries,[115] Europe has more protected areas in number than any other region.[116] Protected areas have increased to cover one fifth of Europe's land,[117] across eleven distinct biogeographic regions, from the Arctic polar deserts and the boreal forests in the North to the arid or dense mattoral shrubland in the south.[118] These areas can place very different limits on human activity, for instance it is forbidden to plant, build, fish and so on within some areas. To some extent this reflects the high pressure on land use arising from agriculture, transport and urban development in Europe.[119]

The current rationale for designating protected areas in Europe combines two main motivations. Firstly, there has been a growing recognition that protected areas play an irreplaceable role in safeguarding biodiversity. Secondly, as indicated in the introduction, there has been a wide acknowledgment that protected areas are vital parts of the European economy. Jacqueline McGlade, EEA Executive Director, said: "*Europe's protected areas are vital for maintaining and restoring biodiversity. Even more important are the direct benefits these areas provide for people, in terms of health, clean water and air, economic benefits such as tourism and fisheries, and for education. Observing nature inside the confines*

---

114 EEA (European Environment Agency) (2012). Protected areas have increased to cover one fifth of Europe's land. Published on 23 October 2012, www.eea.europa.eu/highlights/protected-areas-have-increased-to accessed 23 October 2012.

115 The EEA now has 32 member counties and seven cooperating countries. The 32 member countries include the 28 European Union Member States together with Iceland, Liechtenstein, Norway, Switzerland and Turkey. The seven West Balkan countries are cooperating countries: Albania, Bosnia and Herzegovina, the former Yugoslav Republic of Macedonia, Montenegro, Serbia as well as Kosovo under the UN Security Council Resolution 1244/99. These cooperation activities are integrated into European Environment Information and Observation Network (Eionet) and are supported by the European Union under the Instrument for Pre-Accession Assistance, more information see www.eea.europa.eu/highlights/about-us/countries-and-eionet accessed 5 April 2013.

116 Biodiversity International System for Europe. Protected areas. http://biodiversity.europa.eu/topics/protected-areas accessed 1 March 2013.

117 EEA (European Environment Agency) (2012). Protected areas have increased to cover one fifth of Europe's land. Published on 23 October 2012, www.eea.europa.eu/highlights/protected-areas-have-increased-to accessed 23 October 2012.

118 EEA (European Environment Agency) (2012). Protected areas have increased to cover one fifth of Europe's land. Published on 23 October 2012, www.eea.europa.eu/highlights/protected-areas-have-increased-to accessed 23 October 2012.

119 EEA (European Environment Agency) (2012). Protected areas have increased to cover one fifth of Europe's land. Published on 23 October 2012, www.eea.europa.eu/highlights/protected-areas-have-increased-to accessed 23 October 2012.

of protected areas can help to give us early warnings of changes that will be critical to our future wellbeing."[120]

3.2.1. THE EUROPEAN CONTEXT

In Europe, both the number of nationally designated protected areas as well as their total size has been growing ever since.[121] The primary instrument in this region is the Convention on the Conservation of European Wildlife and Natural Habitats, better known as the Bern Convention.[122] It was established as a binding international legal instrument adopted by the Council of Europe (CoE) in 1979 to foster the conservation and sustainable use of biological diversity in the European continent.[123]

In the framework of the Bern Convention, the Emerald Network is an ecological network made up of "areas of special conserving interest", set up by the Council of Europe (CoE) in 1989 and launched in 1996.[124] It is to be set up in each Contracting Party or observer State to the Bern Convention.[125] In 2013, these include all the European Union states, twenty other European countries, four African States and the European Community.[126] Algeria, Cape Verde, and Mauritania have been invited to accede.[127] The Emerald Network contributes to the setting-up of the Pan-European Ecological Network (PEEN)[128] and promotes the establishment of national protected areas.

120 EEA (European Environment Agency) (2013). Is there a protected area near you? find out on UN Biodiversity Day. Published on 22 May 2013, www.eea.europa.eu/highlights/is-there-a-protected-area accessed 23 May 2013.

121 Jones-Walters, L. & Civic, K. (2013). European protected areas: past, present and future. *Journal for Nature Conservation*, 21, p. 123.

122 Convention on the Conservation of European Wildlife and Natural Habitats (Bern Convention), issued in 1979 and entered into effective on 1 June 1982, BH756.txt;1284 UNTS 209, http://conventions.coe.int/Treaty/Commun/QueVoulezVous.asp?NT=104&CM=8&DF=&CL=ENG accessed 3 December 2012.

123 Jones-Walters, L. & Civic, K. (2013). European protected areas: past, present and future. *Journal for Nature Conservation*, 21, p. 123.

124 Council of Europe. Nature ecological networks and emerald network, www.coe.int/t/dg4/cultureheritage/nature/econetworks/default_en.asp accessed 23 June 2014. More information see Resolution No. 3. Concerning the Setting Up of a Pan-European Ecological Network. CoE (1996). Report of the fifth Meeting of the Bern Convention. T-PVS (96) 23. Appendix 7. Also, the Recommendation to the Parliamentary Assembly. CoE (1997). Report of the sixteenth Meeting of the Bern Convention. T-PVS (97) 63. Appendix 3.

125 Jones-Walters, L. & Civic, K. (2013). European protected areas: past, present and future. *Journal for Nature Conservation*, 21, p. 123.

126 www.coe.int/t/dg4/cultureheritage/nature/EcoNetworks/Documents/Plaquette_en.pdf accessed 17 February 2014.

127 Council of Europe. Nature ecological networks and emerald network, www.coe.int/t/dg4/cultureheritage/nature/econetworks/default_en.asp accessed 23 June 2014.

128 The Pan-European Ecological Network (PEEN) aims to ensure that a full range of ecosystems, habitats, species and landscapes of European importance is conserved; habitats are large

3.2.2. THE CONTEXT OF THE EUROPEAN UNION

The European Union's first response to the Bern Convention was the Council Directive 79/409/EEC on the conservation of wild birds (more recently updated as 2009/147/EC), the Birds Directive;[129] and Council Directive 92/43/EEC on the conservation of natural habitats and of wild fauna and flora, the Habitats Directive.[130, 131] The Special Protection Areas (SPAs) classified under the Birds Directive and Special Areas of Conservation (SACs) designated under the Habitats Directive form the Natura 2000 network and are intended to support the provision of a coherent EU-wide ecological network of sites.[132] The establishment of the EU's Natura 2000 network has been an important milestone and a turning point in the history of European protected areas.[133] Together with the Emerald Network mentioned above, they contribute to develop a coherent approach to the protection of natural habitats in the European continent. The Natura 2000 network is the most extensive protected areas system worldwide, at the moment comprising more than 26,400 sites, which covers about 18% of the EU's territory.[134]

However, as also indicated in the introduction (see 1.1.4.3), the majority of Natura 2000 sites were privately owned and their use was not primarily nature conservation. As the European Community edges closer to the establishment of the Natura 2000 network provided for in the Habitats Directive, key issues

---

enough to place species in a favourable conservation status; there are sufficient opportunities for the dispersal and migration of species; damage parts of the key environmental systems are restored; and the key environmental systems are buffered from potential threats. The originality of this network is that it intends to link core areas physically through the restoration or preservation of corridors. www.coe.int/t/dg4/cultureheritage/nature/econetworks/default_en.asp accessed 20 March 2013.

129 Directive 79/409/EEC of 2 April 1979 on the Convention of Wild Birds, OJ L 103, 25 April 1979 (Birds Directive) was replaced by the 2009 Birds Directive, http://euro-lex.europa.eu/LexUriServ/site/nl/consleg/1979/L/01979L0409-20070101-nl.pdf accessed 20 October 2012.

130 Directive 92/43/EEC of 21 May 1992 on the Conservation of Natural Habitats and of Wild Fauna and Flora, OJ L 206, 22 July 1992 (Habitats Directive); text of the Directive, with later amendments, see http://ec.europa.eu/environment/nature.legislation.habitatsdirective.index_en.htm accessed 20 October 2012.

131 Jones-Walters, L. & Civic, K. (2013). European protected areas: past, present and future. Journal for Nature Conservation, 21, p. 123.

132 Jones-Walters, L. & Civic, K. (2013). European protected areas: past, present and future. *Journal for Nature Conservation*, 21, p. 123.

133 Jones-Walters, L. & Civic, K. (2013). European protected areas: past, present and future. *Journal for Nature Conservation*, 21, p. 123.

134 European Commission (2010). Communication from the Commission to the European Parliament, the Council, the European Economic and Social Committee and the committee of the regions: options for an EU vision and target for biodiversity beyond 2010. Issued on 19 January 2010, http://ec.europa.eu/environment/nature/biodiversity/policy/pdf/communication_2010_0004.pdf accessed 17 April 2013.

have begun to emerge about the Community's role.[135] One important issue was the high cost of managing the sites protected under the Wild Birds and Habitats Directives, together with the role that the Community should play in helping Member States to pay for this management.[136] The European Commission estimated that the cost of managing these sites would be between 3.4 billion EUR and 6.1 billion EUR per year over the period from 2003 to 2013.[137] If these sites could be managed well, their multiple benefits, particularly including environmental (e.g. biodiversity, water regulation and purification), social (e.g. employment, rural development) and economic (e.g., provision of food and raw material) perspectives, would be worth much more than the cost[138] (see 1.1.4.3)

The attractive point is that the European Commission stated that for the Natura 2000 network to be a success, the active involvement of those who live in or depend on these sites is needed.[139] What's more, as also introduced above (see 1.1.4.3), by involving a huge number of stakeholders – owners and occupiers of land, local, national and European authorities – across all sectors, the Natura 2000 network aims to ensure biodiversity conservation beyond national boundaries, while maintaining dynamic rural areas.[140] Some of protected areas allow building, fishing and industry, while other areas are closed to most human intervention.

As part of its commitments to the CBD, the European Commission in 2011 also adopted a new Biodiversity Strategy, "Our life insurance, our natural capital: an EU biodiversity strategy to 2020".[141] The strategy also provides a framework

135 Jack, B. (2006). The European Community and biodiversity loss: missing the target? *Review of European Community and International Environmental Law*, 15(3), p. 304.

136 Jack, B. (2006). The European Community and biodiversity loss: missing the target? *Review of European Community and International Environmental Law*, 15(3), p. 304.

137 Commission Communication of 15 July 2004 on Financing Natura 2000, COM (2004) 431, 5.

138 e.g. see Gantionler, S., Rayment, M., Bassi, S., Kettunen, M., McConville A., Landgrebe, R., Gerdes, H. & ten Brink, P. (2010). *Costs and Socio-Economic Benefits Associated with the Natura 2000 Network*. Final report to the European Commission, DG Environment on Contract ENV.B.2/SER/2008/0038. Brussels: Institute for European Environmental Policy/GHK/Ecologic, http://ec.europa.eu/environment/nature/natura2000/financing/docs/natura2000_costs_benefits.pdf accessed 23 June 2014; European Union. (2013). *The Economic Benefits of the Natura 2000 Network*. Luxembourg: Publications Office of the European Union. http://ec.europa.eu/environment/nature/natura2000/financing/docs/ENV-12-018_LR_Final1.pdf accessed 23 June 2014.

139 European Commission (2000). Managing Natura 2000 sites, the provisions of Article 6 of the Habitats Directive 92/43/CEE. http://ec.europa.eu/environment/nature/natura2000/management/docs/art6/provision_of_art6_en.pdf accessed 11 March 2013. Also see European Union (2013). *The Economic Benefits of the Natura 2000 Network*. Luxembourg: Publications Office of the European Union. http://ec.europa.eu/environment/nature/natura2000/financing/docs/ENV-12-018_LR_Final1.pdf accessed 23 June 2014, p. 46.

140 EEA (European Environment Agency) (2010). 10 messages for 2010 protected areas. Published on 16 March 2010, www.eea.europa.eu/publications/10-messages-for-2010-2014 accessed 11 March 2013.

141 http://ec.europa.eu/environment/nature/biodiversity/common2006/2020.htm accessed 1 March 2013.

for the EU to meet its own independent biodiversity objectives, and it sets out both a long-term vision and a short-term target.[142] The long-term vision (also known as the "2050 vision") is that, by 2050, the European Union biodiversity and the ecosystem services provides – its natural capital – are protected, valued and appropriately restored for biodiversity's intrinsic value, and for their essential contribution to human well-being and economic prosperity, and so that catastrophic changes caused by the loss of biodiversity are avoided.[143] The short-term target (also known as the "2020 headline target") aims to halt the loss of biodiversity and the degradation of ecosystem services in the EU by 2020, and restoring them in so far as feasible, while stepping up the EU contribution to averting global biodiversity loss. Target 1 is specifically important for protected areas. The target is "*to fully implement the Birds and Habitats Directives: to halt the deterioration in the status of all species and habitats covered by EU nature legislation and achieve a significant and measurable improvement in their status so that, by 2020, compared to current assessments: (i) 100% more habitat assessments and 50% more species assessments under the Habitats Directive show an improved conservation status; and (ii) 50% more species assessments under the Birds Directive show a secure or improved status.*"[144]

142 EEA (European Environment Agency) (2012). Protected areas in Europe – an overview. Published on 22 October 2012, www.eea.europa.eu/publications/protected-areas-in-europe-2012 accessed 1 March 2013, pp. 16–17.

143 EEA (European Environment Agency) (2012). Protected areas in Europe – an overview. Published on 22 October 2012, www.eea.europa.eu/publications/protected-areas-in-europe-2012 accessed 1 March 2013, pp. 16–17.

144 For detailed information see www.cbd.int/nbsap/about/targets/eu/ accessed 7 July 2014.

CHAPTER 4

SUBSTANTIVE RIGHT (RIGHT TO PROPERTY) AND PROTECTED AREAS CONSERVATION

As we have seen in the introduction (see 1.1.4), there can be strong linkages between halting the ongoing loss of biodiversity through protected areas, improving human livelihoods, and ensuring peoples' rights. The right to property is among the human rights most prone to be affected by nature conservation.[1] In most cases, property rights have played a decisive role in determining whether communities would be involved in proposed conservation and environmental projects.[2] Indeed, to secure the right to property is a precondition to the effective enjoyment of core human rights,[3] for instance the right to life and the right to respect private and family life, home, and correspondence. A system of land tenure that acknowledges different layers of use, access, control, and ownership and accommodates both traditional indigenous system of land tenure alongside modern property rights is the starting point in the process of recognition and inclusion of stakeholders in decisions pertaining to land and related resources.[4] As for the local people and communities, the essence of property to land is not the possession of a physical piece of land per se, but the right to live off the land,[5] and enjoy the benefit stream it provides.[6]

---

1 Desmet, E. (2011). *Indigenous Rights Entwined with Nature Conservation*. Antwerp: Intersentia, p. 211.

2 Razzaque, J. & Blanco, E. (2009). Ecosystem services and human well-being in a globalized world: assessing the role of law. *Human Rights Quarterly*, 31, p. 714.

3 United States: Congressional-Executive Commission on China (2004). *Access to Justice in China: Roundtable before the Congressional-Executive Commission on China*. In: One Hundred Eighth Congress, second session, 12 July 2004. Washington D.C.: United States Government Printing Office, http://babel.hathitrust.org/cgi/pt?id=umn.31951d024064594;view=1up;seq=11 accessed 18 November 2013, p. 7.

4 Razzaque, J. & Blanco, E. (2009). Ecosystem services and human well-being in a globalized world: assessing the role of law. *Human Rights Quarterly*, 31, p. 715.

5 Soupajärvi, L. (2003). Competing industries and contested nature in Finnish Lapland after World War II. In: Möller, S. & Pehkonen, S. (Eds.). *Encountering the North. Cultural Geography, International Relations and Northern Landscapes*. Farnham (UK): Ashgate Publishing, pp. 203–220.

6 Vatn, A. (2005). *Institutions and the Environment*, Cheltenham (UK) and Northampton (USA): Edward Elgar Publishing.

4.1. RELATIONSHIP BETWEEN THE RIGHT TO PROPERTY AND PROTECTED AREAS

Man may possess such things as are appropriate to preserve himself and satisfy his needs; it is over these things that his right to liberty is exercised in all its fullness, this is called property. At a more fundamental level, the property laws raise issues of what can be "owned" and what "ownership" entails. More specifically, property laws are the legal concepts that most strongly enshrine the view that economic wealth, freely pursued through the free use and enjoyment of natural resources, will provide for both individual and the so-called net social benefit, or common good.[7]

4.1.1. GENERAL RIGHT TO PROPERTY IN INTERNATIONAL AND REGIONAL HUMAN RIGHTS INSTRUMENTS

The Universal Declaration of Human Rights includes the right of everyone to own property alone as well as in association with others, and in Article 17, it adds that "*no one shall be arbitrarily deprived of his property.*"[8] The Universal Declaration is not a binding instrument for States. Both the International Covenant on Civil and Political Rights (ICCPR)[9] and the International Covenant on Economic, Social and Cultural Rights (ICESCR)[10] do not include the right to property. The reason for this can be found in the lack of consensus at the time of drafting between the West and East on issues such as the exact formulation of the right and the possible limitations, the role of domestic law and the extent of compensation in cases of property deprivation.[11] The

---

7 Grinlinton, D. (2011). Evolution, adaptation and invention: property rights in natural resources in a changing world. In: Grinlinton D. & Taylor, P. (Eds.). *Property Rights and Sustainability – the Evolution of Property Rights to Meet Ecological Challenges*. Leiden: Martinus Nijhoff Publishers, p. 275.

8 Universal Declaration of Human Rights, adopted on 10 December 1948, UN Doc. A/810 AT 71, UNGA Res. 217 A (III), www.un.org/en/documents/udhr/ accessed 4 November 2011.

9 International Covenant on Civil and Political Rights (ICCPR), adopted by the United Nations General Assembly on 16 December 1966 and entered into force from 23 March 1976, 999 UNTS 171. It commits its parties to respect the civil and political rights of individuals, including the right to life, freedom of region, freedom of speech, freedom of assembly, electoral rights and rights to due process and a fair trial, http://treaties.un.org/doc/Publication/UNTS/Volume%20999/volume-999-I-14668-English.pdf accessed 9 March 2011.

10 International Covenant on Economic, Social and Cultural Rights, adopted and opened for signature, ratification and accession by General Assembly resolution 2200 A (XXI) of 16 December 1966, and went into force 3 January 1976, 993 UNTS 3, www.ohchr.org/EN/ProfessionalInterest/Pages/CESCR.aspx accessed 8 April 2012.

11 Pechota, V. (1981). The development of the Covenant on Civil and Political Rights. In: Henkin, L. (Ed.). *The International Bill of Rights: the Covenant on Civil and Political Rights*. New York: Columbia University Press, p. 44; Rosas, A. (1992). Property rights. In: Rosas, A. &

right to property is indirectly touched in Article 16 of the Convention on the Elimination of Discrimination Against Women (CEDAW),[12] which sets out equal rights of spouses to enjoyment and disposition of property. It is also approved by Article 15 of the UN Convention on the Protection of the Rights of Migrant Workers and Members of their Families[13] that recognises the right to property and the right to adequate compensation in case of expropriation with regards to migrant workers and their families.[14] The right to property is guaranteed, however, by regional human rights instruments. For instance, the ECHR's Protocol 1, Article 1, as set forth earlier, will be discussed in detail in the section of "right to property protection and protected areas conservation in Europe" (see 4.3). Besides, Article 21 of the American Convention[15] similarly guarantees everyone the right to the use and enjoyment of his property, which may be subordinated to the "interest of society".

4.1.2. ROLE OF THE RIGHT TO PROPERTY IN ENVIRONMENTAL PROTECTION

Some recognise that property rights (properly understood) have the potential to be a valuable and powerful tool for responding to ecological problems. Ronald Bryant, writing in the early 1970s, recognised the need to re-establish the social responsibility element in property ownership: "*In respect of land, we hold that there is very good reason for radical reappraisal and very particular reasons for holding to the view that property rights in land exist only so far as they are delegated to individuals by law, implicitly or explicitly. Such rights may endure to the extent that the individuals concerned are able and willing to exercise them according to the public interest, but ought to be withdrawn where they are not so willing or capable.*"[16] As another scholar observed, "*[t]oday the individual*

Helgesen, J. (Eds.). *The Strength of Diversity: Human Rights and Pluralist Democracy*. Leiden: Martinus Nijhoff Publishers, p. 138.

12 Convention on the Elimination of Discrimination Against Women (CEDAW), adopted and opened for signature on 18 December 1979 and entry into force 3 September 1981, 1249 UNTS 14, www.ohchr.org/Documents/ProfessionalInterest/cedaw.pdf accessed 17 July 2014.

13 Convention on the Protection of the Rights of All Migrant Workers and Members of their Families (Migrant Workers Convention), signed on 18 December 1990 and entered into force on 1 July 2003, 2220 UNTS 3, It is an international agreement governing the protection of migrant workers and families, www2.ohchr.org/english/bodies/cmw/cmw.htm accessed 17 July 2014.

14 Sepúlveda, M., van Banning, T., Gudmundsdóttir, G.D., Chamoun, C. & van Genugten, W. (2010). *Human Rights Reference Handbook*. Iceland: The Icelandic Human Rights Centre, p. 239.

15 American Convention on Human Rights (ACHR), adopted in the Western Hemisphere San José, Costa Rica, on 22 November 1969, entered into force on 18 July 1978, 1144 UNTS 123, www.hrcr.org/docs/American_Convention/oashr5.html accessed 23 June 2014.

16 Bryant, R.W.G. (1972). *Land Private Property, Public Control*. Montreal: Harvest House, p. 147.

creativity and moral self-governance, which private property fairly distributed potentially encourages, is necessary to preserve the planet."[17]

Property has played and continues to play a constitutive role in current environmental crises.[18] Property rights are something of a two-edged sword in the context of environmental and natural resources management.[19] On the one hand, we abuse land because we regard it as a commodity belonging to us;[20] on the other hand, if exercised and utilised appropriately, and in accordance with natural limitations the assignment of ownership to a natural resource can be an effective tool to achieve a win-win goal of the sustainable use of the resource and the interests of people. In addition, mainstream economics suggests that a set of property rights, which is comprehensive, exclusive, enforceable, and transferable, is necessary for efficient outcomes.[21] Yet many of the problems in the economics of the environment can be understood in terms of the failure of system of property rights to meet this ideal.[22] The failures range from the overexploitation of open access resources to the creation of nuisance or enjoyment to others without compensation (called externalities in the language of economics).[23]

Specifically, most conflicts regarding human rights protection and protected areas conservation nowadays are essentially about the exercise of property rights over land and resources. While governance involves authority for decision-making with respect to a protected area, tenure relates to who holds land ownership rights or use rights to resources on the site, along with the benefits and responsibilities that come with the exercise of those rights.[24] As land-use change occurs outside the administrative boundaries of existing protected

17 Engel, J.R. (2009). Faustian Pact or New Covenant with Earth? In: the conference Property Rights and Sustainability, University of Auckland, Auckland, New Zealand, 16–18 April 2009.

18 Graham, N. (2012). Dephysicalisation and entitlement: legal and cultural discourses of place as property. In: Jessup, B. & Rubenstein, K. (Ed.), *Environmental Discourses in Public and International Law.* Cambridge: Cambridge University Press, p. 97.

19 Grinlinton, D. (2011). Evolution, adaptation and invention: property rights in natural resources in a changing world. In: Grinlinton D. & Taylor, P. (Eds.). *Property Rights and Sustainability – the Evolution of Property Rights to Meet Ecological Challenges.* Leiden: Martinus Nijhoff Publishers, p. 277.

20 Leopold, A. (1968). *A Sand County Almanac and Sketches Here and There.* Oxford: Oxford University Press, pp. viii–ix.

21 Millennium Ecosystem Assessment (2005). *Ecosystems and Human Well-being: Biodiversity Synthesis.* Washington D.C.: World Resources Institute, www.maweb.org/documents/document.354.aspx.pdf accessed 22 January 2014, p. 184.

22 Millennium Ecosystem Assessment (2005). *Ecosystems and Human Well-being: Biodiversity Synthesis.* Washington D.C.: World Resources Institute, www.maweb.org/documents/document.354.aspx.pdf accessed 22 January 2014, p. 184.

23 Millennium Ecosystem Assessment (2005). *Ecosystems and Human Well-being: Biodiversity Synthesis.* Washington D.C.: World Resources Institute, www.maweb.org/documents/document.354.aspx.pdf accessed 22 January 2014, p. 184.

24 IUCN (2008). Governance of natural resources, equality and human rights, www.iucn.org/about/work/initiatives/sp_cprihome/sp_cpri_themes_/sp_cpri_natural_resources accessed 3 September 2012.

areas, with potential negative consequences for the ecological functioning of the protected areas themselves,[25] the trade-offs between human use and longer term conservation of ecosystem services become complex.[26] To employ the discourse of property in attempting to solve the problems is neither rational nor viable.[27] The rights restrictions responsibilities that go along with the boundaries must be recorded.[28] For example, marine protected areas have defined boundaries for the purpose of excluding or restricting the opportunities and rights of the marine stakeholders.[29] The restrictions are only effective if this information is attached to the boundaries available to stakeholders and the public.[30] These will be specifically discussed in Chapter 5 on procedural rights protection and protected areas conservation of this book.

4.1.3. RELATIONSHIP BETWEEN THE RIGHT TO PROPERTY OF INDIGENOUS PEOPLES AND PROTECTED AREAS CONSERVATION

4.1.3.1. General Right to Property of Indigenous Peoples

The binding legal instruments recognising indigenous land rights are the International Labor Organization (ILO) No. 107[31] and No. 169.[32] Article 11 of the ILO Convention No. 107 says that: "*The right of ownership, collective or*

25 Hansen, A.J. & DeFries, R. (2007). Ecological mechanisms linking protected areas to surrounding lands. *Ecological Applications*, 17, pp. 974–988.

26 Defries, R., Hansen, A., Turner, B.L., Reid, R. & Liu, J.G. (2007). Land use change around protected areas: management to balance human needs and ecological function. *Ecological Applications*, 17(4), www.jstor.org/stable/40061895 accessed 2 August 2012, pp. 1031–1038.

27 Graham, N. (2012). Dephysicalisation and entitlement: legal and cultural discourses of place as property. In: Jessup, B. & Rubenstein, K. (Ed.), *Environmental Discourses in Public and International Law*. Cambridge: Cambridge University Press, p. 97.

28 Dumashie, D. (2010). The marine cadastre: a rights based approach to marine conservation in England. In: Falque, M. & Lamotte, H. (Eds.). *Biodiversity, Property Rights, Economics and Environment*. Brussels: Bruylant Publisher, p. 85.

29 Dumashie, D. (2010). The marine cadastre: a rights based approach to marine conservation in England. In: Falque, M. & Lamotte, H. (Eds.). *Biodiversity, Property Rights, Economics and Environment*. Brussels: Bruylant Publisher, p. 85.

30 Williams, I., Enemark, S., Wallace, J. & Rajabifard, A. (2010). *Land Administration for Sustainable Development*. ESRI Press Academic.

31 International Labor Organization Convention No. 107 was a first attempt to codify international obligations of States in respect indigenous and tribal populations and was the first international convention on the subject, and was adopted by the ILO at the request of the UN system on 26 June 1957 and entered into force on 2 June 1959, www.ilo.org/indigenous/Conventions/no107/lang--en/index.htm accessed 1 October 2012.

32 International Labor Organization Convention No. 169: Indigenous and Tribal Peoples Convention, adopted on 27 June 1989 and entered into force on 5 September 1991, 28 ILM 1382, www.ilo.org/indigenous/Conventions/no169/lang--en/index.htm accessed 1 October 2012.

individual, of the members of the populations concerned over the lands which these populations traditionally occupy shall be recognized."[33] The land rights of indigenous peoples are specified in Article 14 (1) of the ILO Convention No. 169 as: "*The rights of ownership and possession of the peoples concerned over the lands which they traditionally occupy shall be recognized.*"[34] Article 13 (2) of the ILO Convention No. 169 recognises rights of indigenous peoples to "*the total areas which the peoples concerned occupy or otherwise use*". Article 15 specifically refers to rights to natural resources. It is interesting to note that the ILO Convention No. 169 "*distinguishes between the right of ownership to the lands and the right to use natural resources.*"[35]

Furthermore, the land rights of indigenous peoples were confirmed by the recommendations and concluding observations of international treaty monitoring bodies. Among these, the Committee on the Elimination of Racial Discrimination (CERD), which supervises the International Convention on the Elimination of All Forms of Racial Discrimination,[36] has called in particular upon States parties "*to recognize and protect the rights of indigenous peoples to own, develop, control and use their communal lands, territories and resources.*"[37] In addition, the rights of indigenous peoples were also approved by Article 26 of the UN Declaration on the Rights of Indigenous Peoples.[38] It says: "*Indigenous peoples have the right to the lands, territories and resources which they have traditionally owned, occupied or otherwise used or acquired. Indigenous peoples have the right to own, use, develop and control the lands, territories and resources.*"[39]

---

33 Articles 11–14, International Labor Organization Convention No. 107 was a first attempt to codify international obligations of States in respect indigenous and tribal populations and was the first international convention on the subject, and was adopted by the ILO at the request of the UN system on 26 June 1957 and entered into force on 2 June 1959, www.ilo.org/indigenous/Conventions/no107/lang--en/index.htm accessed 1 October 2012.

34 Article 14(1), International Labor Organization Convention No. 169: Indigenous and Tribal Peoples Convention, adopted on 27 June 1989 and entered into force on 5 September 1991, 28 ILM 1382, www.ilo.org/indigenous/Conventions/no169/lang--en/index.htm accessed 1 October 2012.

35 Gilbert, J. (2006). *Indigenous Peoples' Land Rights under International Law: from Victims to Actors*. New York: Transnational Publisher, p. 105.

36 International Convention on the Elimination of All Forms of Racial Discrimination, signed on 21 December 1965 and entered into force on 4 January 1969, 660 UNTS 195, www.ohchr.org/EN/ProfessionalInterest/Pages/CERD.aspx accessed 6 December 2013.

37 CERD (The Committee on the Elimination of Racial Discrimination), Office of the High Commissioner for Human Rights, "General Recommendation No. 23: Indigenous Peoples". Issued on 18 August 1997, §5, detailed information see www.unhchr.ch/tbs/doc.nsf/0/739842 90dfea022b802565160056fe1c accessed 29 October 2012.

38 United Nations Declaration on the Rights of Indigenous Peoples (UNDRIP), issued on 13 September 2007, UN Doc. A/RES/61/295, www.un.org/esa/socdev/unpfii/documents/DRIPS_en.pdf accessed 30 October 2012.

39 Article 26, United Nations Declaration on the Rights of Indigenous Peoples (UNDRIP), issued on 13 September 2007, UN Doc. A/RES/61/295, www.un.org/esa/socdev/unpfii/documents/DRIPS_en.pdf accessed 30 October 2012.

Apart from these legal instruments, the interests of indigenous peoples in nature conservation were approved by the Kari-Oca Declaration[40] and the Indigenous Peoples' Earth Charter[41] in 1992. In the same year, the "Charter of the Indigenous and Tribal Peoples of the Tropical Forest" was adopted by the International Alliance of the Indigenous and Tribal Peoples of the Tropical Forests in Malaysia.[42] Article 42 points out that "*[c]onservation programmes must respect our rights to the use and ownership of the territories and resources we depend on.*

4.1.3.2. Right to Property of Indigenous Peoples and Protected Areas Conservation

Some large nature conservation non-governmental organisations pay more attention to the right to property of indigenous peoples. For instance, the IUCN, as an important player on the international environmental scene, pays particular attention to the relationship between rights and interests of indigenous peoples and protected areas conservation.

Among several IUCN's resolutions and recommendations, it is noted that governments were recommended to develop means by which indigenous peoples could bring their lands into conservation areas "*without relinquishing their ownership, use and tenure rights.*"[43] It also states that the creation of protected areas should not normally cause the displacement of indigenous peoples from their ancestral territories. In the review of IUCN's resolutions and recommendations, particular attention is also paid to the relationship between the procedural rights of indigenous peoples and protected areas conservation. These will be discussed in Chapter 5 on procedural rights protection and protected areas conservation of this book.

As indicated above, Article 41 of the Indigenous Peoples' Earth Charter states that: "*Parks must not be created at the expense of indigenous peoples. There is no way to separate indigenous peoples from their lands.*"[44] Besides these, in 1996, the

40 Kari-Oca Declaration, signed during the World Conference of Indigenous Peoples on Territory, Environment and Development at Kari-Oca, Brazil on 30 May 1992 and reaffirmed at Bali, Indonesia on 4 June 2002, www.dialoguebetweennations.com/ir/english/kariocakimberley/KODeclaration.html accessed 22 March 2013.

41 Indigenous Peoples Earth Charter, signed at Kari-Oca (Brazil) Conference on 25–30 May 1992, www.dialoguebetweennations.com/ir/english/kariocakimberley/KOCharter.html accessed 22 March 2013.

42 Charter of the Indigenous and Tribal Peoples of the Tropical Forest, adopted by the IAITPTF (International Alliance of the Indigenous and Tribal Peoples of the Tropical Forests on 15 February 1992 and revised on 22 November 2002, www.forestpeoples.org/partners/international-alliance-indigenous-and-tribal-peoples-tropical-forests-iaitptf accessed 22 March 2013.

43 IUCN (1979). Recommendation GA 12.05, Protection of Traditional Ways of Life, principle 1.

44 Indigenous Peoples Earth Charter, signed at Kari-Oca (Brazil) Conference on 25–30 May 1992, www.dialoguebetweennations.com/ir/english/kariocakimberley/KOCharter.html accessed 22 March 2013.

"Statement of Principles on Indigenous Peoples and Conservation", adopted by World Wide Fund for Nature (WWF), recognises that "*without recognition of the rights of indigenous peoples, no constructive agreements can be drawn up between conservation organizations and indigenous peoples groups.*"[45] It led WWF to be "*the first major conservation organization to formally adopt a policy recognizing the indigenous peoples' rights.*"[46] Furthermore, a set of "Principles and Guidelines on Protected Areas and Indigenous/Traditional Peoples" was adopted by WWF and IUCN in 1999.[47]

In addition, the "Indigenous Peoples' Plan of Implementation on Sustainable Development"[48] was adopted at the World Summit on Sustainable Development in Johannesburg in 2002. Article 38 of this plan states: "*We demand that all legislation, policies or work programs on forests and protected areas guarantee and rigorously respect our lands and territories, rights, needs and benefits and recognize our full rights to control and manage our forests.*"[49]

All these reflect that the relationship between the right to property of indigenous peoples and protected areas conservation was widely recognised at the international level. It is also noted that the right to property should be respected in environmental protection, especially in protected areas conservation. However, there are different forms of property rights, such as "*the right to own, use, develop and control*" in the UN Declaration on the Rights of Indigenous Peoples. It is necessary to analyse different forms of property rights for the reason that they might be treated in different ways in practice.

4.1.4. DIFFERENT FORMS OF PROPERTY RIGHTS

Many gradations and different forms of property rights are conceivable: from private property, to State-vested property, to common property and any number of "quasi proprietary" rights. A.M. Honore helped to popularise the bundle of rights metaphor with his list of the "categories" of property ownership: ownership comprises the right to possess, the right to use, the right to manage,

---

45 International Alliance of Indigenous – Tribal Peoples of the Tropical Forest (1996). *Indigenous Peoples, Forests, and Biodiversity.* Copenhagen: IWGIA, pp. 147–156.

46 WWF (World Wide Fund for Nature) International (2008). *Indigenous Peoples and Conservation: WWF Statement of Principles.* Gland (Switzerland): WWF International, p. iii.

47 IUCN & WWF (1999). Principles and guidelines on indigenous and traditional peoples and protected areas: joint policy statement, www.wwf.fi/wwf/www/uploads/pdf/indigenous_people_policy.pdf accessed 22 March 2013.

48 Indigenous Peoples' Plan of Implementation on Sustainable Development (2002). www.dialoguebetweennations.com/ir/english/kariocakimberley/IndigenousPeoplesPlan.htm accessed 22 March 2013.

49 Article 38, Indigenous Peoples' Plan of Implementation on Sustainable Development (2002), www.dialoguebetweennations.com/ir/english/kariocakimberley/IndigenousPeoplesPlan.htm accessed 22 March 2013.

the right to the income of the thing, the right to the capital, the right to security, the prohibition of harmful use, liability to execution, and so on.[50] Different rights (strands of the bundle) may be distributed in various combinations among natural and legal persons, groups, and several publics, including the many units of government.[51] Generally speaking, property characterised by rights of exclusion is often called private property, while property which is characterised by rights of inclusion is termed public or common property. The public or common property in a State normally refers to State property. If public property only belongs to "a certain group of people", it would be called collective property.

The advent of neo-liberal or market-based forms of environmental and natural resource management over the last few decades obscures the fact that property rights have long formed the basis for law and regulation of the natural world over much of the globe.[52] The environmental dimension of property can be traced to the Roman concepts of *iura* and *dominium* as the essence of political culture.[53] The two concepts are different. A person's *dominium* over his property could include his land, his slaves, or his money, but it was not constituted by *iura* (rights), that is, by an agreement or other transaction between individuals.[54] *Dominium* originated in social status, either gained or inherited, and for this reason included the element of protection and care.[55] Some legal systems have a legal or normative framework that defines the relationship between individuals and/or groups, and the lands, forest, water and resources that are occupied and used. Such assumptions about the nature of the environment and human relationship to the environment are typically legally conceptualised in terms of various gradations of access and control which are seen as the hallmarks of "property".[56] While some theorists emphasise the right to exclude and others the right to use, many environmentalists emphasise the

50 Honore, A.H. (1961). Ownership. *Oxford Estates in Jurisprudence*, 107, p. 113.

51 Ciriacy-Wantrup, S.V. & Bishop, R.C. (2003). 'Common property' as a concept in natural resources policy. In: Larson, B.A. (Ed.), *Property Rights and Environmental Problems*. Farnham (UK): Ashgate Publishing, p. 68.

52 Godden, L. (2010). Governing common resources: environmental markets and property in water. In Mcharg, A. *et al.* (Eds.). *Property and the Law in Energy and Natural Resources*. Oxford: Oxford University Press, p. 414.

53 Bosselmann, K. (2011). Property rights and sustainability: can they be reconciled? In: Grinlinton D. & Taylor, P. (Eds.). *Property Rights and Sustainability – the Evolution of Property Rights to Meet Ecological Challenges*. Leiden: Martinus Nijhoff Publishers, p. 29.

54 Bosselmann, K. (2011). Property rights and sustainability: can they be reconciled? In: Grinlinton D. & Taylor, P. (Eds.). *Property Rights and Sustainability – the Evolution of Property Rights to Meet Ecological Challenges*. Leiden: Martinus Nijhoff Publishers, p. 29.

55 Bosselmann, K. (2011). Property rights and sustainability: can they be reconciled? In: Grinlinton D. & Taylor, P. (Eds.). *Property Rights and Sustainability – the Evolution of Property Rights to Meet Ecological Challenges*. Leiden: Martinus Nijhoff Publishers, p. 29.

56 Godden, L. (2010). Governing common resources: environmental markets and property in water. In Mcharg, A. *et al.* (Eds.). *Property and the Law in Energy and Natural Resources*. Oxford: Oxford University Press, p. 414.

opposite of rights, that is, the duties in the bundle of entitlements that make up the notion of property.[57]

Furthermore, with the advent of the Cold War, the right to property became a contentious East–West issue.[58] According to Marxism–Leninism the production in society takes place in certain forms of ownership which are depending from the particular stage of development in society.[59] In the light of the communist ideology, the property relations are described as the most important social relations, as they determine all the other social relations; this is because the basis of the development of the socialist society was found in the socialist ownership of the means of production.[60] The collective property in the socialist countries derived from the private property of the citizens unified in cooperatives after its socialisation.[61] This process usually is called collectivisation. This is also the situation in China, as a socialist society in the world (see 4.2). The juridical form of the socialist collective property is a form in which property already could exist before the Marxist-Leninists took over the rule in Eastern Europe.[62] The right to property will be discussed in detail later (see 4.3).

4.1.5. DISCUSSION

Nevertheless, the essence of property rights to land is not the possession of a physical piece of land *per se*, but the right to live off the land[63] and enjoy the

---

57 e.g., Singer, J.W. (2000). *Entitlement: the Paradoxes of Property.* New Haven: Yale University Press; Underkuffler, L.S. (Ed.) (2003). *The Idea of Property: Its Meaning and Power.* Oxford: Oxford University Press.

58 Anton, D.K. & Shelton, D.L. (2011). *Environmental Protection and Human Rights.* Cambridge: Cambridge University Press, p. 513.

59 Sagel-Grande, H.I. (2000). Property rights and ownership in eastern and western Europe and Article 1 Protocol No. 1 European Convention on Human Rights. In: Loof, J.P., Ploeger, H. & van der Steur, A. (Eds.). *The Right to Property: the Influence of Article 1 Protocol No. 1 ECHR on Several Fields of Domestic Law.* Maastricht: Shaker Publishing, p. 54.

60 Sagel-Grande, H.I. (2000). Property rights and ownership in eastern and western Europe and Article 1 Protocol No. 1 European Convention on Human Rights. In: Loof, J.P., Ploeger, H. & van der Steur, A. (Eds.). *The Right to Property: the Influence of Article 1 Protocol No. 1 ECHR on Several Fields of Domestic Law.* Maastricht: Shaker Publishing, p. 55.

61 Sagel-Grande, H.I. (2000). Property rights and ownership in eastern and western Europe and Article 1 Protocol No. 1 European Convention on Human Rights. In: Loof, J.P., Ploeger, H. & van der Steur, A. (Eds.). *The Right to Property: the Influence of Article 1 Protocol No. 1 ECHR on Several Fields of Domestic Law.* Maastricht: Shaker Publishing, p. 56.

62 Sagel-Grande, H.I. (2000). Property rights and ownership in eastern and western Europe and Article 1 Protocol No. 1 European Convention on Human Rights. In: Loof, J.P., Ploeger, H. & van der Steur, A. (Eds.). *The Right to Property: the Influence of Article 1 Protocol No. 1 ECHR on Several Fields of Domestic Law.* Maastricht: Shaker Publishing, p. 56.

63 Soupajärvi, L. (2003). Competing industries and contested nature in Finnish Lapland after World War II. In: Möller, S. & Pehkonen, S. (Eds.). *Encountering the North. Cultural Geography, International Relations and Northern Landscapes.* Farnham (UK): Ashgate Publishing, pp. 203–220.

benefit stream it provides.[64] This is also the similar meaning for property rights on other natural resources. Land ownership or resource use rights may be established through written law (for example, constitutions, statutes, regulations) or judicial decisions, or through customary law where certain rights of use and practice are widely accepted by the communities involved even though they are not set out in written law.[65] In the developed world, protection of property is, despite its complexity and controversial nature, considered an important element in the market economy, and a prerequisite for security of the individual.[66] The rules and legislation historically revolve around the protection of private property rights. In the developing world, property and, more specifically, land issues are frequently sources of controversy.[67] Much attention was given to the protection of the collective property rights or the State ownership in the eastern countries, for instance China. Essentially, questions remain about whether and to what extent property rights should rest with the individual (private property) or a group of people (collective property) as opposed to the State or the government or some forms of developed authorities. The balance between individual freedom and community responsibility, the tension between legal rules and local practice on the ground, and the mechanics of control over land use and development are strategic responsibilities.[68]

Based on the different social, political, cultural and legal circumstances, it seems that it is impossible to reach an agreement on what property is. Anthropological insights illuminate the interrelationships between laws, normative ground and institutional practices that mediate between property and system of allocation, distribution and use, whereby individuals and groups negotiate for strategic advantage or to gain status.[69] In this sense, property concepts are "thick" language with cultural, social, legal and even political constructs resonance. The description and discussion in the following sections about the property rights related to environmental protection in general, and

---

64 Vatn, A. (2005). *Institutions and the Environment*, Cheltenham (UK) and Northampton (USA): Edward Elgar Publishing.

65 Lausche, B. (2011). *Guidelines for Protected Area Legislation*, Gland (Switzerland): IUCN, http://data.iucn.org/dbtw-wpd/edocs/EPLP-081.pdf accessed 8 July 2012, p. 99.

66 Sepúlveda, M., van Banning, T., Gudmundsdóttir, G.D., Chamoun, C. & van Genugten, W. (2010). *Human Rights Reference Handbook*. Iceland: The Icelandic Human Rights Centre, p. 239.

67 Sepúlveda, M., van Banning, T., Gudmundsdóttir, G.D., Chamoun, C. & van Genugten, W. (2010). *Human Rights Reference Handbook*. Iceland: The Icelandic Human Rights Centre, p. 239.

68 Dumashie, D. (2010). The marine cadastre: a rights based approach to marine conservation in England. In: Falque, M. & Lamotte, H. (Eds.). *Biodiversity, Property Rights, Economics and Environment*. Brussels: Bruylant, p. 96.

69 Godden, L. (2010). Governing common resources: environmental markets and property in water. In: Mcharg, A. *et al.* (Eds.). *Property and the Law in Energy and Natural Resources*. Oxford: Oxford University Press, p. 414; Singer, J.W. (2000). *Entitlement: The Paradoxes of Property*. New Haven: Yale University Press; Underkuffler, L.S. (Ed.) (2003). *The Idea of Property: Its Meaning and Power*. Oxford: Oxford University Press.

protected areas in specific, will show the different understandings of the right to property in China and in Europe.

4.2. RIGHT TO PROPERTY AND PROTECTED AREAS CONSERVATION IN CHINA

4.2.1. RIGHT TO PROPERTY AND PROTECTED AREAS CONSERVATION IN GENERAL

As already mentioned protected areas in China occupy more than 15% of land areas, for instance ⅛ of the land in Shenzhen city will be protected areas,[70] and the land of protected areas in Yunnan Province will occupy more than 8% of provincial land in the next five or ten years.[71] Ownership of land and resources is vital for responsible land management because it strengthens a community's long-term, cultural attachment to such areas.[72] Any talk of conservation management in China invariably returns to the thorny question of collective forests – they are a fundamentally important part of the diverse landscapes (accounting for 58.4% of the nation's total forested lands) and illustrate ongoing uncertainty over land tenure and resource access.[73] Take the forest protected areas in Guangdong Province for instance, as of 2010, there are 5,154 km^2 forest protected areas, of which 62.03% of the land belongs to the collective. It is a similar situation in the whole country that most land in protected areas is collectively owned. The management of protected areas will be affected by some complex social factors for the reason that a large number of the areas are collective.[74] In the "Chinese Protected Areas Strategy and Plan Seminar" organised by The Nature Conservancy (TNC) on 28 March 2011, Jianwei Chen said: "*Most of the land in protected areas in Fujian, Shandong, Hunan, Zhejiang province belongs to the collective. The collective forest tenure*

70 Nanfang Newspaper, posted on 21 February 2012, http://epaper.nfdaily.cn/html/2012-02/21/content_7058782.htm accessed 2 February 2012.

71 Kunming Daily (昆明日报) (2011). The land of protected areas in yunnan province will occupy more than 8% of provincial land in next five or ten years (云南自然保护区在5至10年内将达土地面积的8%). Posted on 23 December 2011, http://trip. house.sina.com.cn/News/2011-12-23/12655.html accessed 1 January 2012, in Chinese.

72 Xu, J.C. & David, R.M. (2007). Rethinking the Effectiveness of Public Protected Areas in Southwestern China. *Conservation Biology*, 21(2), pp. 318–328.

73 Xu, J.C. & David, R.M. (2007). Rethinking the Effectiveness of Public Protected Areas in Southwestern China. *Conservation Biology*, 21(2), pp. 318–328.

74 Wang, D.Q. & He, K.J. (王权典，何克军) (Eds.) (2012). *The Innovation for Rule of Law on Protected Areas and the Methods for the Reformation on Forest – Based on Field Work on the Construction for a Protected Areas Model Province in Guangdong* (自然保护区法制创新与"林改"方略 – 基于广东自然保护区示范省建设实施探索). Beijing: China Legal Publishing House (中国法制出版社), p. 47.

reform being implemented gives a great deal of pressure on the management for protected areas. The local people have their own interests; it is unreasonable if you want to establish a protected area on the land, which they are using, without giving them the appropriate compensation".[75] Collective ownership in China is still poorly defined, and it is not clear who represents local communities and how decisions are made.[76] Higher levels of governments still intervene in community decisions and forest resource management. For instance, timber collection for personal use or marketing from contracted collective forests requires a quota permit from the ownership and final approval from the county Forestry Bureau.[77]

As mentioned above (see 4.1.2), most environmental conflicts are essentially about the exercise of property rights over land and resources, and most would agree with the necessity of balancing those rights against the right of other property owners, and the public interest in the protection and sustainable management of the environmental at large.[78] Property is recognised as a bundle of rights, and common property systems can be highly complex.[79] With regard to natural resources, this bundle is usually broken down along a continuum from access, to withdrawal, management, exclusion and alienation.[80] There is a similar situation concerning the collective property system. Local people's organisations and activists are calling on governments to fully implement their commitments to uphold human rights, including rights to lands and resources as an essential cornerstone for achieving socially just and ecologically sustainable development.[81]

---

75 First Financial Daily (第一财经报) (2011). Chinese protected areas: closed or open? (中国自然保护区：封闭还是开发). Posted on 13 April 2011, www.forestry.gov.cn/portal/bhxh/s/651/content-472781.html accessed 13 May 2011, in Chinese.

76 Miao, G.P. & West, R.A. (2004). Chinese collective forestlands: contributions and constraints. *International Forestry Review*, 6, pp. 282–298.

77 Xu, J.C. & Ribot, J.C. (2004). Decentralization and accountability in forest management: case from Yunnan, southwest China. *European Journal of Development Research*, 16(1).

78 Grinlinton, D. (2011). Evolution, adaptation and invention: property rights in natural resources in a changing world. In: Grinlinton D. & Taylor, P. (Eds.). *Property Rights and Sustainability – the Evolution of Property Rights to Meet Ecological Challenges*. Leiden: Martinus Nijhoff Publishers, p. 275.

79 Larson, A.M., Cronkleton, P., Barry, D. & Pacheco, P. (2008). *Tenure Rights and Beyond: Community Access to Forest Resources in Latin America*. Occasional Paper No. 50, Bogor (Indonesia): CIFOR, www.pefc.org/images/stories/documents/external/OP-50.pdf accessed 4 August 2012.

80 Schlager, E. & Ostrom, E. (1992). Property rights regimes and natural resources: a conceptual analysis. *Land Economics*, 68(3), pp. 249–262.

81 Forest Peoples Programme. (2012). Press release: indigenous peoples insist on human rights-based approaches and respect for traditional knowledge and practices in Rio+20 outcomes. Published on 20 June 2012, www.forestpeoples.org/topics/sustainable-livelihoods/news/2012/06/press-release-indigenous-peoples-insist-rights-based-app accessed 21 June 2012.

There is a fundamental distinction in China between "rights of ownership of land" and "rights to use land".[82] Most of the land is owned by the State or by a rural collective. Under the Household Responsibility System (HRS), which gave China's rural households a thirty-year land-use right,[83] China's rural land remains collectively owned, but the use right is allocated to households.[84] Rights of ownership of land are not transferrable. By contrast, the right to use State-owned land is transferrable and such land-use rights can be leased or mortgaged.[85] The timing and extent of land protection has been very uneven among and within countries.[86] Although ownership rights in regard to other forms of immovable property such as buildings and other improvements are regulated separately from land-use rights, Chinese law recognised the principle of unity of title.[87] Under the "Law of the People's Republic of China on Property Rights"[88] (see 4.2.2), the creation, modification, transfer or termination of property rights in regard to immovable property, including land-use rights and buildings, is effective only upon registration.[89] It is a universal

82 Herrold, B. & Beijing, L. (2008). An Overview of Property Development in China. *SGLA (Sino-Global Legal Alliance) Law Journal*, 1(2), http://sglalaw.com/uploads/news/id217/REAL%20ESTATE%20AND%20CONSTRUCTION%20-%20AN%20OVERVIEW%20OF%20PROPERTY%20DEVELOPMENT%20IN%20CHINA%20-%20BRAD%20HERROLD.pdf accessed 13 October 2012.

83 Since 1998, the revised Land Management Law (Article 14.1) formalised and lengthened the HRS policy into a legally recognised 30-years land use right, www.jlp.bham.ac.uk/volumes/55/vanrooij-art.pdf accessed 13 October 2012, p. 213.

84 Van Rooij, B. (2007). The return of the landlord: Chinese land acquisition conflicts as illustrated by peri-urban Kunming, www.jlp.bham.ac.uk/volumes/55/vanrooij-art.pdf accessed 12 September 2012, p. 213.

85 Herrold, B. & Beijing, L. (2008). An Overview of Property Development in China. *SGLA (Sino-Global Legal Alliance) Law Journal*, 1(2), http://sglalaw.com/uploads/news/id217/REAL%20ESTATE%20AND%20CONSTRUCTION%20-%20AN%20OVERVIEW%20OF%20PROPERTY%20DEVELOPMENT%20IN%20CHINA%20-%20BRAD%20HERROLD.pdf accessed 13 October 2012.

86 Coad, L. *et al.* (2009). Progress towards the convention on biological diversity terrestrial 2010 and marine 2012 targets for protected area coverage. *Parks* 17, pp. 35–42; Hoekstra, J.M., Boucher, T.M., Ricketts, T.H. & Roberts, C. (2005). Confronting a biome crisis: global disparities of habitat loss and protection. *Ecology Letters*, 8, pp. 23–29; Soutullo, A., De Castro, M. & Urios, V. (2008). Linking political and scientifically derived targets for global biodiversity conservation: implications for the expansion of the global network of protected areas. *Diversity and Distributions*, 14, pp. 604–613.

87 Herrold, B. & Beijing, L. (2008). An Overview of Property Development in China. *SGLA (Sino-Global Legal Alliance) Law Journal*, 1(2), http://sglalaw.com/uploads/news/id217/REAL%20ESTATE%20AND%20CONSTRUCTION%20-%20AN%20OVERVIEW%20OF%20PROPERTY%20DEVELOPMENT%20IN%20CHINA%20-%20BRAD%20HERROLD.pdf accessed 13 October 2012.

88 The "Law of the People's Republic of China on Property Rights" [中华人民共和国物权法] was adopted on 16 March 2007 and entered into effect on 1 October 2007, www.lehmanlaw.com/fileadmin/lehmanlaw_com/laws___regulations/Propoerty_Rights_Law_of_the_PRC__LLX__03162007.pdf accessed 9 December 2011.

89 Herrold, B. & Beijing, L. (2008). An Overview of Property Development in China. *SGLA (Sino-Global Legal Alliance) Law Journal*, 1(2), http://sglalaw.com/uploads/news/id217/

phenomenon that farmers who lost their land did not turn to the courts, but instead resorted to extra-legal factual measures to address their grievances,[90] which will be further discussed in the section of access to justice (see 5.3). This observation is supported by nationwide data on legal address for land takings which demonstrated that only 0.9% of the aggrieved farmers filed a lawsuit for more compensation.[91] One important reason for this phenomenon is a lack of awareness of law and rights, especially in some poor villages.

4.2.2. LEGAL AND POLICY FRAMEWORK CONCERNING PROPERTY RIGHTS IN CHINA

The "Constitution of the People's Republic of China"[92] points out the protection for natural resources and the general ownership of the natural resources in China. Article 9 states that: "*All mineral resources, waters, forests, mountains, grassland, unclaimed land, beaches and other natural resources are owned by the State, that is, by the whole people, with the exception of the forests, mountains, grasslands, unclaimed land and beaches that are owned by the collective in accordance with the law. The State ensures the rational use of natural resources and protects rare animals and plants, Appropriation or damaging of natural resources by any organization or individual by whatever means is prohibited.*" Article 10 specifically highlights the ownership of land in China.[93] Besides the collective property concerning natural resources and land, Article 13 of

REAL%20ESTATE%20AND%20CONSTRUCTION%20-%20AN%20OVERVIEW%20OF%20PROPERTY%20DEVELOPMENT%20IN%20CHINA%20-%20BRAD%20HERROLD.pdf accessed 13 October 2012.

90 Of course there have been some instances where citizens have made use of courts. Examples can be found in Phan (2005) who details urban acquisition cases from Liaoning in which neighbourhood organisations have made use of legal aid support to get their rights asserted. Phan, P.N. (2005) Enriching the Land or the Political Elite? Lessons from China on Democratization of the Urban Renewal Process. *Pacific Rim Law and Policy Journal*, 14, pp. 607–657.

91 Zhu, K.L. *et al.* (2006). The rural land question in China: analysis and recommendations based on a 17-Province in 2003 Survey. *Journal of International Law & Politics*, 38, p. 783.

92 The "Constitution of the People's Republic of China" [中华人民共和国宪法] was adopted in 1982 and newly amended on 14 March 2004, www.for68.com/new/201007/he60492159127010212383.shtml in both Chinese and English accessed 3 December 2010.

93 It states: "land in the cities is owned by the state. Land in the rural and suburban areas is owned by collectives except for those portions which belong to the state in accordance with the law; house sites and privately farmed plots of cropland and hilly land are also owned by collectives. The state may, for the public interest, expropriate or take over land for public use, and pay compensation in accordance with the law. No organisation or individual may appropriate, buy, sell or otherwise engage in the transfer of land by unlawful means. The rights to the use of land may be transferred according to law. All organisations and individuals using land must ensure its rational use". For detailed information see www.for68.com/new/201007/he60492159127010212383.shtml in both Chinese and English accessed 3 December 2010.

the Constitution also states: "*Citizens' lawful private property is inviolable (...). The State may, in the public interest and in accordance with law, expropriate or requisition private property for its use and provide compensation for the private property expropriated or requisitioned*". As introduced above, most natural resources and land belong to the collective; however, for instance, some buildings or agricultural plants on land belong to the private property of local people. This is confirmed and emphasised by Article 5 of the "Regulations of the People's Republic of China on Nature Reserves" which states that: "*The local economic construction, the production activities and everyday life of local residents shall be properly considered when the nature reserves are established and managed.*"[94]

According to the "Land Management Law of the People's Republic of China (modified in 2004)"[95] and the "Land Management Approach in Nature Reserve (1995)",[96] the land in protected areas is national or collective ownership. Besides the protected areas that are established based on national ownership of forest or farm, most of the protected areas occupy the collective land. Some protected areas are even established on land that totally belongs to the collective. The local people and communities rely on the land to make a living. It also means that there is not enough right to use land to guarantee the core and buffer area not to be disturbed. Article 2 of "the Land Management Law of the People's Republic of China (modified in 2004)"[97] states: "*The State may make expropriation or requisition on land according to law for public interests, but shall give compensations accordingly. The State introduces the system of compensated use of land owned by the State except the land has been allocated for use by the State according to laws.*" It does not give a clear definition of what are "the public interests" and who would take responsibility to give compensation accordingly. Besides these, Articles 15 and 16 respectively point out that land owned by the

94 Article 5 of the "Regulations of the People's Republic of China on Nature Reserves" [中华人民共和国自然保护区条例] was entered into effective on 1 December 1994, http://english.mep.gov.cn/Policies_Regulations/regulations/Natural_Conservation_Biosafety/200711/t20071123_113364.htm accessed 3 December 2011.

95 The "Land Management Law of the People's Republic of China" [中华人民共和国土地管理法] was issued in 1986 and amended in 1998, and later amended on 28 August 2004, for detailed information see (1998 version) www.zhb.gov.cn/ztbd/rdzl/2010sdn/zcfg/201001/t20100113_184226.htm, and (2004 version) www.china.com.cn/chinese/law/647616.htmaccessed 3 January 2012.

96 The "Land Management Approach in Nature Reserve" [自然保护区土地管理办法] was issued by the State Land Administration and the State Environment Protection Bureau on 24 July 1995 as Order No. 117, on the basis of the Land Management Law, Environmental Protection Law, and Nature Reserve ordinance in order to improve land management in nature reserves, www.mlr.gov.cn/zwgk/flfg/tdglflfg/200406/t20040625_585545.htm accessed 3 December 2011.

97 The "Land Management Law of the People's Republic of China" [中华人民共和国土地管理法] was issued in 1986 and amended in 1998, and later amended on 28 August 2004, for detailed information see (1998 version) www.zhb.gov.cn/ztbd/rdzl/2010sdn/zcfg/201001/t20100113_184226.htm, and (2004 version) www.china.com.cn/chinese/law/647616.htmaccessed 3 January 2012.

State may be contracted out to be run by someone else for certain reasons[98] and how to solve the disputes arising from the ownership or use right of land.[99]

As for the land in the protected areas, Article 7 of "Land Management Approach in Nature Reserve (1995)"[100] states: *"The State land-user and collective land owner in protected areas shall apply for land registration and land certification from the local people's government above the village level according to the national land management laws and regulations. The right to ownership of land and right to use land determined by the laws cannot be changed because of establishing the protected areas. If it is necessary to change the right to ownership of land or right to use land, it must apply for the registration on land ownership alternation from the administrative authority in local government above the village level to change the land certification."* Article 15 points out that the unity or individual who use the land in protected areas according to the law should strictly follow the land registration and land certification. Article 18 states: *"It forbids to reclaiming, mining, quarrying, sand-digging and other activities in the protected areas, except for the situation provided by the laws and administrative regulations (...) the local people can have a normal life in the surrounding zone of protected areas, but they cannot do any harm to the protected areas. If any land in the nature reserve have been destroyed but can be recovered, the relevant parties or individual shall take responsibility to reclaim."*

After more than a decade of deliberation, China adopted the Property Law in 2007.[101] The "Law of the People's Republic of China on Property

---

98 Article 15 points out: "Land owned by the State may be contracted out to run by units or individuals for farming, forestry, animal husbandry and fisheries (...). Whereas land collectively owned by farmers is contracted out for operation to those not belonging to the corresponding collective organizations, a consent shall be got from over two-thirds majority vote of the villagers' congress or over two-thirds of the villagers' representatives with the resulted contract being submitted to the township (town) people's government for approval." Detailed information see www.china.org.cn/china/LegislationsForm2001–2010/2011–02/14/content_21917380.htm.

99 Article 16 states that: "Disputes arising from the ownership or use right of land shall be settled through negotiation among parties concerned; if negotiation fails, the disputes shall be handled by people's governments (...). No party shall change the status quo of the land before the disputes over ownership and use right are settled." Detailed information see www.china.org.cn/china/LegislationsForm2001–2010/2011–02/14/content_21917380.htm.

100 The "Land Management Approach in Nature Reserve" [自然保护区土地管理办法] was issued by the State Land Administration and the State Environment Protection Bureau on 24 July 1995 as Order No. 117, on the basis of the Land Management Law, Environmental Protection Law, and Nature Reserve ordinance in order to improve land management in nature reserves, www.mlr.gov.cn/zwgk/flfg/tdglflfg/200406/t20040625_585545.htm accessed 3 December 2011.

101 In recent discussions, Chinese officials state that the Peoples' Court will refuse to consider any farmer's complaint about the non-payment of compensation in takings of land for non-agricultural purposes if the farmer cannot produce one of these documents showing that the farmer holds rights to the land in question. Detailed information see Li, P., Prosterman, R., Ye, J.P., Wu, J. & van Rooij, B. (2010). Land reform and tenure security in China: history and current challenges. In: Ubink, J.M., Hoekema, A.J. & Assies, W.J. (Eds.). *Legalizing*

Rights",[102] enacted by the National People's Congress (NPC) and effective on 1 October 2007, is heralded by some as a major watershed in China's development and seen as a major step towards better protection of land rights.[103] In the context of the Property Rights Law, the creation, modification, transfer or termination of property rights with regards to immovable property, including land-use rights and buildings, is effective only upon registration,[104] while "*as regards the ownership of the natural resources owned by the State in accordance with law, the registration is not required*".[105] The conflict regarding protected area conservation and property right protection mainly focuses on the dispute of immovable property. "*In light of the different registration items, an applicant shall, when applying for the registration of an immovable property, provide the certificate of ownership, the location, the dimension and other necessary documents.*"[106] What is a certificate of ownership? Article 17 explains that: "*The reality ownership certificate shall be the evidence for the holder's ownership of a reality*". With respect to compensation for land takings, Article 42 reiterates that: "*for expropriation of collectively-owned land, such fees shall be paid as compensations for the land expropriated, subsides for resettlement, compensations for the fixtures and the young crops on land, and the premiums for social security of the farmers whose land is expropriated shall be allocated in full, in order to guarantee their normal lives and safeguard their lawful rights and interests (...) where houses and other real properties of institutes and individuals are expropriated, compensations for demolition and resettlement shall be paid according to law in order to maintain the legal rights and interests of the expropriated; where an individual residential house is*

Land Rights – Local Practices, State Responses and Tenure Security in Africa, Asia and Latin America. Leiden: Leiden University Press, p. 426.

102 The "Law of the People's Republic of China on Property Rights" [中华人民共和国物权法] was adopted on 16 March 2007 and entered into effect on 1 October 2007, www.lehmanlaw.com/fileadmin/lehmanlaw_com/laws___regulations/Propoerty_Rights_Law_of_the_PRC__LLX__03162007.pdf accessed 9 December 2011.

103 Ubink, J.M., Hoekema, A.J. & Assies, W.J. (2010). *Legalizing Land Rights – Local Practices, State Responses and Tenure Security in Africa, Asia and Latin America.* Leiden: Leiden University Press.

104 Herrold, B. & Beijing, L. (2008). An Overview of Property Development in China. *SGLA (Sino-Global Legal Alliance) Law Journal*, 1(2), http://sglalaw.com/uploads/news/id217/REAL%20ESTATE%20AND%20CONSTRUCTION%20-%20AN%20OVERVIEW%20OF%20PROPERTY%20DEVELOPMENT%20IN%20CHINA%20-%20BRAD%20HERROLD.pdf accessed 13 October 2012.

105 Article 9 of the "Law of the People's Republic of China on Property Rights" [中华人民共和国物权法] was adopted on 16 March 2007 and entered into effect on 1 October 2007, www.lehmanlaw.com/fileadmin/lehmanlaw_com/laws___regulations/Propoerty_Rights_Law_of_the_PRC__LLX__03162007.pdf accessed 9 December 2011.

106 Article 11 of the "Law of the People's Republic of China on Property Rights" [中华人民共和国物权法] was adopted on 16 March 2007 and entered into effect on 1 October 2007, www.lehmanlaw.com/fileadmin/lehmanlaw_com/laws___regulations/Propoerty_Rights_Law_of_the_PRC__LLX__03162007.pdf accessed 9 December 2011.

expropriated, the residential conditions of the expropriated shall be guaranteed. No institution or individual shall withhold, misappropriate, embezzle or privately divide the compensation for expropriation." The added measures and principles are certainly an improvement on existing compensation laws.[107] Regarding the specific natural resources, the law contains clear Articles to explain the ownership.[108] Articles 58, 59 and 60 point out the contents of the collective ownership and who determines the different important issues according to the statutory procedures.[109] Articles 99 and 105 are regarded as a big improvement on existing laws governing rural women's land rights that are silent on the partition ability, for the reason that these stipulations open a door for rural women to partition their land shares from household landholdings when they

---

107 Li, P., Prosterman, R., Ye, J.P., Wu, J. & van Rooij, B. (2010). Land reform and tenure security in China: history and current challenges. In: Ubink, J.M., Hoekema, A.J. & Assies, W.J. (Eds.). *Legalizing Land Rights – Local Practices, State Responses and Tenure Security in Africa, Asia and Latin America*. Leiden: Leiden University Press, p. 426.

108 For instance Article 46 points out that "mineral deposits, water and sea areas shall be in the ownership of the State." Article 47 states that: "Urban land shall be in the ownership of the State. The land in the rural areas and suburban areas that shall be owned by the State as prescribed by law, they shall be in the ownership of the State." Article 48 states: "Forests, mountains, grasslands, waste lands and other natural resources belongs to the State, except for those that shall be in the ownership of collective as provided for law." Article 49 adds: "the wildlife resources that shall be owned by the State as provisioned by law, they shall be in the ownership of the State." Detailed information see www.lehmanlaw.com/fileadmin/lehmanlaw_com/laws___regulations/Propoerty_Rights_Law_of_the_PRC__LLX__03162007.pdf accessed 9 December 2011.

109 The "Law of the People's Republic of China on Property Rights" [中华人民共和国物权法], Articles 58, 59 and 60 (Article 58 points out that the collectively owned real and movable properties shall contain: (1) lands, forests, mountains, grasslands, wastelands and tidal flats; (2) buildings, production devices, cultivate land and water power facilities owned collectively; (3) facilities with regards to education, science, culture, health and gymnasium collectively owned; and (4) other real and movable properties owned collectively. Article 59 states: "The real and movable properties which are collectively-owned by the urban collective shall be collectively owned by members of such collective. Things stated below shall be decided collectively by the members of the respective collective in accordance with relevant legal procedure: (1) The land contract scheme and subcontracting of the lands to institutions or individuals outside of this collective; (2) The adjustment of the contracted lands among contractor of the right to land contractual management; (3) The utilisation and distribution ways in respect of such fees as land compensations; (4) Such matters as changes of ownership of the enterprise whose capital is contributed by the collective; and (5) Other matters required by law." Article 60 specifically explains: "The exercise of the ownership of the collectively-owned lands, forests, mountains, grasslands, unclaimed land, beaches shall be in accordance with provisions as follows: (1) As to those owned collectively by peasants of a village, the village's collective economic organisation or villager's Committee shall, on behalf of the collective, exercise the ownership; (2) As to those owned collectively by two or more peasants of a village, the collective economic organisations or groups of villagers shall, on behalf of the collective, exercise the ownership; (3) As to those owned collectively by peasants of the townships (town), the collective economic organisations of the townships (town) shall, on behalf of the collective, exercise the ownership." For more information see www.lehmanlaw.com/fileadmin/lehmanlaw_com/laws___regulations/Propoerty_Rights_Law_of_the_PRC__LLX__03162007.pdf accessed 9 December 2011.

move out of the household as a result of marriage and divorce.[110] Article 126 explains the contractual term for land; it states that: "*The contractual term of cultivated land shall be 30 years. The contractual term of grassland shall be 30 up to 50 years. The contractual term of wood land shall be 30 up to 70 years. The contractual term of special forest land may, upon approval of the forestry administrative department under the State Council, be extended. After the contractual term as referred to in the preceding paragraph expires, the holder of the right to the contracted management of land may, according to the relevant provisions of the State, contract continuously.*" This is the first time that Chinese law has clarified the uncertainties with respect to farmers' present thirty-year land rights when they expire.[111] It shows that the central government wants to clearly favour long-term security for farmers' land rights. Under this context, even if farmers do not have private ownership on the land, they certainly have a right to use the land for thirty years, for instance the cultivated land. If the establishment and management of protected areas infringe on their rights within these thirty years, they could expect to get compensation according to the relevant law or regulation. Article 132 explicitly provides for the first time that the holder of rural land rights, when such rights are taken through State expropriations, are entitled to the compensation package as provided under Article 42. The new property law clearly strikes down the exclusive right of the collective owner to compensation for loss of land.[112] In October 2008, the government issued new measures allowing farmers to lease and sell rights to use the property allocated to them by the State.[113]

From these, it can be seen that great progress is made to protect property rights, but some problems still remain. Firstly, the existing prohibition of mortgage of rural land rights still exists. Secondly, as mentioned above, Article 42 does not clarify whether the social security costs are a supplemental compensation or merely a replacement of all or part of the three traditional categories. If there is no further legal interpretation from the central authority to explain it, the local government might reduce its financial obligations

---

110 Li, P., Prosterman, R., Ye, J.P., Wu, J. & van Rooij, B. (2010). Land reform and tenure security in China: history and current challenges. In: Ubink, J.M., Hoekema, A.J. & Assies, W.J. (Eds.). *Legalizing Land Rights – Local Practices, State Responses and Tenure Security in Africa, Asia and Latin America*. Leiden: Leiden University Press, p. 426.

111 Li, P., Prosterman, R., Ye, J.P., Wu, J. & van Rooij, B. (2010). Land reform and tenure security in China: history and current challenges. In: Ubink, J.M., Hoekema, A.J. & Assies, W.J. (Eds.). *Legalizing Land Rights – Local Practices, State Responses and Tenure Security in Africa, Asia and Latin America*. Leiden: Leiden University Press, p. 427.

112 Li, P., Prosterman, R., Ye, J.P., Wu, J. & van Rooij, B. (2010). Land reform and tenure security in China: history and current challenges. In: Ubink, J.M., Hoekema, A.J. & Assies, W.J. (Eds.). *Legalizing Land Rights – Local Practices, State Responses and Tenure Security in Africa, Asia and Latin America*. Leiden: Leiden University Press, p. 427.

113 While the state owns all land in China, farmers are granted rights of use via long-term (thirty-year) contracts with the state. Washington Post. (2008). China to all land leasing, transfer. Published on 20 October 2008.

to restore the dispossessed farmers' livelihoods. Thirdly, Article 132 keeps silent on the eligibility of unaffected villagers whose contracted land is not taken. This may at least arguably be interpreted as avoiding an egalitarian distribution of the compensation among all villagers followed by a village-wide land readjustment that will substantially reduce tenure security for all villagers.[114] Fourth, Article 245 provides that when a plaintiff seeks the remedy of restitution on the ground of wrongful possession, the claim must be filed within one year of when the wrong possession starts.[115] Compared with international practice, a one year limitation seems too short to claim property rights. Fifth, similar to the problem with the "Land Management Law of the People's Republic of China" mentioned above, it fails to define "the needs for public interests". It is an important omission, if there is no clear definition, anyone can violate other peoples' property right in the name of "public interests".

In addition, Article 28 from the "Interim Management Measures on the Special Marine Protected Areas"[116] states that the authority and local community shall co-manage special marine protected areas, and design a cooperation project plan, community development plans, a management plan and so on. Article 46 refers to the interests of rights holders, it states that: *"the authority and the enterprises who explore the special marine protected areas shall sign a franchise agreement that the income should be devoted to conserve protected areas and give the compensation to right-holders"*.

What is more, the "Notification on the National Major Functional Zonation Plan of China",[117] which was newly issued by the State Council in 2010, points out the basic situation of non-development zones (see table 4 below).

---

114 Li, P., Prosterman, R., Ye, J.P., Wu, J. & van Rooij, B. (2010). Land reform and tenure security in China: history and current challenges. In: Ubink, J.M., Hoekema, A.J. & Assies, W.J. (Eds.). *Legalizing Land Rights – Local Practices, State Responses and Tenure Security in Africa, Asia and Latin America*. Leiden: Leiden University Press, p. 427.

115 Li, P., Prosterman, R., Ye, J.P., Wu, J. & van Rooij, B. (2010). Land reform and tenure security in China: history and current challenges. In: Ubink, J.M., Hoekema, A.J. & Assies, W.J. (Eds.). *Legalizing Land Rights – Local Practices, State Responses and Tenure Security in Africa, Asia and Latin America*. Leiden: Leiden University Press, p. 426.

116 The "Interim Management Measures on the Special Marine Protected Areas" [海洋特别保护区管理暂行办法] was issued by the State Oceanic Administration of the People's Republic of China on 31 August 2010, www.shanghaiwater.gov.cn/xwzx!view.action?fan.fileId=20091759&sdh.code=004015001 accessed 4 December 2011. Although it is called and translated as "management measures", it is a regulation for special marine protected areas in China.

117 The "Notification on the National Major Functional Zonation Plan of China" [国务院关于印发全国主体功能区规划的通知] was issued by the State Council on 21 December 2010, www.gov.cn/zwgk/2011-06/08/content_1879180.htm accessed 9 October 2012, in Chinese. Although it is called and translated as "notification", it is a basis guideline to solve the relevant issues in China.

Table 4. The basic situation of non-development zones

Styles	Number	Dimension (ten thousand square kilometers)	Proportion of land area
National Protected Areas	319	92.85	9.67
World Cultural and Natural Heritage	40	3.72	0.39
World-class Scenic Area	208	10.17	1.06
National Forest Park	738	10.07	1.05
National Geological Park	138	8.56	0.89
Total	1443	120	12.5

Note: The statistical results of the table were updated on 31 October 2010. The total area does not include double calculations of the overlapping areas.

Besides the basic situation of non-development zones, the "Notification on the National Major Functional Zonation Plan of China" also emphasises that regarding a large nature reserve with a large population in the core area, if this group of people does not affect the main function of the nature reserve, they could maintain modest agriculture and animal husbandry activities and steadily improve their living standard. The fourth section named "Land Policy" of the "Notification on the National Major Functional Zonation Plan of China" states that it should properly handle the relationship between ownership of agricultural and pastoral land in a nature reserve, which will help people who are living in the core area and buffer area of nature reserves to gradually migrate.[118] It reflects that the central government really wants to solve the potential conflicts regarding protected areas conservation and the interests of local people and communities. It is indeed a big step forward; however, much more needs to be done to solve the conflicts in practice.

4.2.3. CONFLICTS REGARDING PROPERTY RIGHTS AND PROTECTED AREAS CONSERVATION IN PRACTICE

In practice, there are four main kinds of conflict situations for property rights and protected areas. Firstly, a clear ownership was changed by the establishment of protected areas. Land ownership in protected areas is clear,

118 The "Notification on the National Major Functional Zonation Plan of China" [国务院关于印发全国主体功能区规划的通知] was issued by the State Council on 21 December 2010, www.gov.cn/zwgk/2011-06/08/content_1879180.htm accessed 9 October 2012, in Chinese. Although it is called and translated as "notification", it is a basis guideline to solve the relevant issues in China.

but the ownership is a mixed type,[119] including State ownership, collective ownership and even farmers' plots (hill). The establishment of protected areas broke part of the ownership of the original collective forest land and hilly land allotted for private use, and such areas were removed from the land or forest land ownership (especially the right to use and the right to benefit from) of the local people and communities. For instance, the Sanjiangyuan protected area and Yancheng protected area occupied some land which is the collective property of local peasants. This leads to some conflicts regarding protected areas conservation and the development of local communities.[120] Secondly, there is a vague ownership. Some ownership of land or forest is vague; the authority over the land belongs to the State when establishing protected areas. It leads the local people and community to have some disagreement about it, even to take rivalries to fight for continually using the existing resources, thus affecting the normal management work on protected areas. Thirdly, ownership is clear, but the right to use is changed or the right to management is vague.[121] According to what has been introduced above, there is an obvious distinction in China between "rights of ownership in land" and "rights to use land". Rights of ownership in land are not transferrable, while the right to use State-owned land is transferrable and it can be leased or mortgaged. The land in protected areas belongs to the State, but there is a phenomenon that the real management areas in protected areas are larger than the legally recognised part.[122] Accordingly, the conflicts regarding protected areas conservation and land ownership negatively affect more than 80% of protected areas in China.[123] At the same time, the establishment of protected areas changed the original hidden ownership of some cultural resources (such as the endemic cultural heritage, customs, etc.). It also causes conflicts regarding protected areas and local communities. Fourth, ownership is clear, but the border of protected areas is unstable. The protected areas lack permanent boundary signs. In the beginning of establishing some protected areas, the boundary (especially the areas to be expanded) was unstable, which

---

119 Guo, C.R. (郭昌荣) (2012). *Research on Protected Areas Management from the Perspective of the Theory of Property Rights* (产权理论视野下自然保护区管理体制研究). Master dissertation in Kunming Technology University (昆明理工大学硕士学位论文), pp. 27–42.

120 State Forestry Administration (国家林业局) (2007). *Research on the Legislation for Protected Areas in China* (《中国自然保护区立法研究》). China Forestry Publishing House (中国林业出版社), p. 21.

121 Guo, C.R. (郭昌荣) (2012). *Research on Protected Areas Management from the Perspective of the Theory of Property Rights* (产权理论视野下自然保护区管理体制研究). Master dissertation in Kunming Technology University (昆明理工大学硕士学位论文), pp. 27–42.

122 Fu, Y.F. (付延芳) (2012). *Discussion on the Legal Guarantee of Harmonious Development between Natural Reserve and Local Communities* (论自然保护区与当地社区和谐发展的法律保障). Master Dissertation in China University of Political Science and Law (中国政法大学硕士论文), p. 4.

123 State Forestry Administration (国家林业局) (2007). *Research on the Legislation for Protected Areas in China* (《中国自然保护区立法研究》). China Forestry Publishing House (中国林业出版社), pp. 196–197.

also led to the natural resources in protected areas being eroded and to disputes between protected areas and local communities.

Regarding the problem for land management in protected areas, there are also some problems that need to be mentioned: (1) owing to a vague ownership of the land in some protected areas, the local peoples and communities cannot use the land, the authorities have not signed any agreement or contract with the local people and communities; (2) before expropriating the land as a part of protected areas, the authority sometimes has not consulted with the local people and communities, the conflicts occur at the very beginning; (3) because the compensation in some provinces is limited, the interests of local people and communities cannot be guaranteed. In addition, relying on the compensation, such as letting the local people completely move out of protected areas, the authority cannot provide enough funding and land to them; (4) the attitude of the local government also will affect the implementation of the land management in protected areas. Considering the local interests, some local governments may not cooperate with the requirements of relevant laws and regulations mentioned in the previous section. The local people cannot get certification for land or forest from the local government.

4.2.4. UNDERLYING CAUSES FOR THE CONFLICTS

There are several underlying causes for the conflict regarding property rights and protected areas conservation. Firstly, from a historical perspective, as has been introduced above (see 3.1), China began to establish protected areas from the 1950s on, while the Chinese government only began to really pay attention to land ownership and management in protected areas from the 1980s on. There is not enough law or regulation or policy to give clear guidelines on how to solve the problems, such as the right to ownership of land and the right to use land in protected areas. In addition, when establishing protected areas without enough social investigation and full consultation, the authority did not determine a reasonable scope of protected areas, which resulted in an unclear ownership.

Secondly, from a legislative perspective: (a) the existing legal instruments lack a clear regulation on some important issues, such as how to get the right to use land if the local people's land has been expropriated, how to get access to a legal remedy if the compensation is unreasonable.[124] (b) The existing legal instruments, neglecting the interests of local people and communities, pay most attention to the conservation of protected areas. The local people and communities are forbidden by laws or regulations to use some natural resources that they could use before the protected areas were established, but they cannot

124 WFFPDSFA (Wild Fauna and Flora Protection Division of the State Forestry Administration) (2003). *Chinese Nature Reserve Policy Research*. Beijing: China Forestry Publishing House.

get enough compensation. (c) The responsibilities of the authorities are unclear. For instance, who shall take responsibility to take the interests of local people and communities into consideration? Who has the obligation to provide compensation when the conflicts occur? Thus, the local people and communities think their rights and interests are not respected by the relevant authorities. Some of them might undertake some illegal activities to realise their rights and interests, for instance cutting down the trees that have been sustainably managed. They would be punished by laws or regulations if they have been caught; if not, they would continue to perform these illegal activities and harm the natural resources in protected areas. Obviously, this is not the intention of legislators and policy-makers. It is noted that the newly-issued "Overall Plan for the Reform of Ecological Civilization System"[125] provides overall guidelines for clarifying the boundary of protected areas and improving property rights system for natural resources. However, these overall guidelines could be merely regarded as a basis to issue the relevant law and regulation, much detailed and further work needs to be done for solving these specific problems.

Thirdly, from a social development perspective, in the early years of constructing protected areas in China, due to the planned economic system and the public ownership, it was not necessary to care about ownership. With the establishment of a market economic system, vague ownership obviously becomes a challenge for the development of economic activities. In addition, owing to the increasing need of the population and production activities, land has become a serious scarce resource. The right to the ownership of land or forest or other natural resources or the right to use the natural resources becomes an extremely important issue for various parties. Thus, conflicts in practice seem inevitable.

There are some other reasons for the conflicts, such as political and cultural ones, but this book mainly focuses on the legal perspective and the relevant points.

There is a claim that China increasingly needs clearer property rights because much of the argument for the virtues of ambiguous or informal property rights is an argument about what works in a transitional system, and an economic system cannot be in transition forever.[126] China has made great progress in clarifying the property rights and solving the conflicts regarding human rights

125 The "Overall Plan for the Reform of Ecological Civilization System" [生态文明体制改革总体方案] was issued by the State Council on 21 September 2015, http://news.xinhuanet.com/politics/2015-09/21/c_1116632281.htm accessed 25 September 2015.

126 United States' Congressional-Executive Commission on China (2004). *Property seizure in China: round-table before the Congressional-Executive Commission on China*. In: One Hundred Eighth Congress, second session, 12 July 2004. Washington D.C.: United States Government Printing Office, http://hdl.handle.net/2027/umn.31951d02406427h accessed 8 August 2012.

protection and protected areas conservation these years, but some problems are still waiting to be solved in a better way.

4.3. RIGHT TO PROPERTY IN ENVIRONMENTAL PROTECTION IN EUROPE

Despite unsolved problems in China, it would be interesting to look at what the baselines and general principles for the potential conflicts regarding property rights protection and protected areas conservation are in Europe. Is there any lesson that China could learn from Europe, taking into account the different historical, cultural, political, economic and legal circumstances?

4.3.1. RIGHT TO PROPERTY UNDER THE EUROPEAN CONVENTION ON HUMAN RIGHTS

4.3.1.1. Article 1 of Protocol No. 1 to the Convention

Protection of property is part of the "inheritance" of human rights development and many see private property as a cornerstone of the western concept of freedom.[127] This notion of freedom and protection of property rights is also found in Emmanuel Kant's writing.[128] For Edmund Burke protection of private property is at the heart of a moral society governed by the rule of law.[129] However, the right to property has been characterised as "the problem child of the European family of rights and freedoms".[130] When drafting the European Convention on Human Rights, the Member States of the Council of Europe were unable to agree on the inclusion or the character of the right to property, which was specifically controversial to the (at that time) socialist governments of the United Kingdom and Sweden.[131] It is probably one of the main reasons why the

---

127 Loof, J.P., Ploeger, H. & van der Steur, A. (2000). The right to property in European human rights and its influence on several fields of domestic law. In: Loof, J.P., Ploeger, H. & van der Steur, A. (Eds.). *The Right to Property: the Influence of Article 1 Protocol No. 1 ECHR on Several Fields of Domestic Law*. Maastricht: Shaker Publishing, p. 1.

128 Habermas, J. (1996). *Between Facts and Norms; Contributions to a Discourse Theory of Law and Democracy*. (Trans: Regh, W.). The MIT (Massachusetts Institute of Technology) Press, p. 100.

129 Burke, E. (1791). *Reflections on the Revolution in France*, www.constitution.org/eb/rev_fran.htm and www.fordham.edu/halsall/mod/1791burke.asp accessed 1 January 2012.

130 Anderson, D. (1999). Compensation for interference with property. *European Human Rights Law Review*, 9, p. 545.

131 See the Collected Edition of the travaux préparatoires to the ECHR, vols 1 to VIII, The Hague/Boston/London: Martinus Nijhoff 1985. Also see *Trav. Prep., II, 60–86* (Ungoed-Thomas and Edberg). It is not likely that the vision of the British and the Swedes, who feared a too broad interpretation of a property clause by the future European Court (showing a form

ECHR (in 1951) did not originally include an Article on the protection of the right to property. Robertson and Merrills give a good insight into the problems during the drafting process: "*The key issue, which the formulation in the Universal Declaration emphasizes, is the meaning of the word 'arbitrarily', for these points to all the problems of international and municipal law which are raised when property is confiscated. The right to nationalize private property had to be recognized in the Protocol, particularly when one remembers that nationalization was a major element in the programme of the Labor Government which was in power in Britain when the protocol was being drafted. It was, however, a task of some difficulty to draft a provision which would both recognize the right to private property as a basic principle, and at the same time permit a socialist Government to nationalize property in the general interest.*"[132]

Nevertheless, the right to property was contained in an additional Protocol to the Convention[133] in 1952 as follows: "*Every natural or legal person is entitled to the peaceful enjoyment of his possessions. No one shall be deprived of his possessions except in the public interest and subject to the conditions provided for by law and by the general principles of international law. The preceding provisions shall not, however, in any way impair the right of a State to enforce such laws as it deems necessary to control the use of property in accordance with the general interest or to secure the payment of taxes or other contributions or penalties.*"[134]

Although some scholars[135] criticise this Article, we cannot deny that this Article, as an important part of the European system of human rights protection, has influenced the legal system of the Member States of the Council of Europe.

---

of "judicial activism"), was inspired by the earlier experience (and collision) that US president Roosevelt had had at the start of the 20th century with the (then conservative) US Supreme Court on the Bill of Rights, whereby the US Supreme Court had interpreted the constitutional rights on the protection of property, contractual freedom and the freedom of commerce in a way that strongly restricted the possibilities of the executive to interfere in economic matters (Cf. US Supreme Court, Lochner v. New York 198 US 45, 25 S.Ct. 539, 49 L.Ed., 937 (1905), www.tourolaw.edu/PATCH/). On this: Ely, Y.W. (1997). *The Guardian of Every Other Rights. a Constitutional History of Property Rights*. Oxford: Oxford University Press, pp. 100–110.

132 Robertson, A.H. & Merrills, J.G. (1993). *Human Rights in Europe: a Study of the European Convention on Human Rights* (third edition). Manchester: Manchester University Press, p. 212.

133 Protocol to the Convention for the Protection of Human Rights and Fundamental Freedoms as amended by Protocol No. 11 in 1952, http://conventions.coe.int/Treaty/en/Treaties/Html/009.htm accessed 20 May 2013.

134 Protocol to the Convention for the Protection of Human Rights and Fundamental Freedoms as amended by Protocol No. 1 in 1952, http://conventions.coe.int/Treaty/en/Treaties/Html/009.htm accessed 20 May 2013.

135 For instance, Schermers points to the strange fact that the Article acknowledges a right to enjoy what one owns without acknowledging the right to own it. See for detailed information in Schermers, H.G. (1988). The international protection of the right of property. In: Matscher, F. & Petzold, H. (Eds.). *Protecting Human Rights: the European Dimension* (Studies in honour of Gerard J. Wiarda). Koln/Berlin/Bonn/Munchen: Carl Heymanns, pp. 565–580.

4.3.1.2. *Three "Rules" for the Right to Property under the European Convention on Human Rights*

As is well known, the concept of property is not dependent on the definition in domestic law but has an autonomous content in the case law of the European Commission on Human Rights[136] and the European Court.[137] Although Article 1 of the Protocol refers to the "enjoyment of possessions", the Court stated that, "*by recognizing that everyone has the right to peaceful enjoyment of his possessions, Article 1 is in substance guaranteeing the right of property.*"[138] The Court has also emphasised that the concept of "possessions" contains the ownership of physical goods, certain other rights and interests constituting assets,[139] and a "legitimate expectation" of obtaining effective enjoyment of a property right.[140] This broad understanding of property is illustrated by the fact that the ECtHR and the former Commission have considered hunting and fishing rights to fall within the ambit of the right to property.[141] Besides these, it

136 European Commission of Human Rights. From 1954 to the entry into force of Protocol No. 11 of the European Convention on Human Rights, individuals did not have direct access to the European Court of Human Rights; they had to apply to the Commission, which if it found the case to be well-founded would launch a case in the Court on the individual's behalf. Protocol No. 11 which came into force in 1998 abolished the Commission, enlarged the Court, and allowed individuals to take cases directly to it. http://migrationeducation.de/28.2.html?&rid=32&cHash=e1406ce90478dac99328adbd62782641 accessed 22 April 2013.

137 Alkema, E.A. (2000). The concept of property – in particular in the European Convention on Human Rights. In: Loof, J.P., Ploeger, H. & van der Steur, A. (Eds.). *The Right to Property: the Influence of Article 1 Protocol No. 1 ECHR on Several Fields of Domestic Law.* Maastricht: Shaker Publishing, p. 20.

138 ECtHR, Marckx v. Belgium (1979), App. No. 6833/74, Judgment of 13 June 1979, §31, http://hudoc.echr.coe.int/sites/eng/pages/search.aspx?i=001-57534#{%22itemid%22:[%22001-57534%22]} accessed 1 March 2013; ECtHR, Airey v. Ireland (1979), App. No. 6289/73, Judgment of 9 October 1979, §63, http://hudoc.echr.coe.int/sites/fra/pages/search.aspx?i=001-57420#{%22itemid%22:[%22001-57420%22]} accessed 1 March 2013. In the case law, ownership is defined in the extensive sense of general international law, that is, as "an acquired/vested rights". The Commission has considered as "possessions" within the meaning of Article 1 not only rights in rem, but also intangible rights, corporation shares, commercial goodwill, etc. Peukert, W. (1981). Protection of ownership under Article 1 of First Protocol to the European Convention on Human Rights. *Human Rights Law Journal*, 3, 37(43).

139 See, e.g., ECtHR, Gasus Dosier-und Fordertechnik GmbH v. the Netherlands (1995), App. No. 15375/89, Judgment of 23 February 1995, §53, http://hudoc.echr.coe.int/sites/eng/pages/search.aspx?i=001-57918#{%22itemid%22:[%22001-57918%22]} accessed 1 March 2013; ECtHR, Iatridis v. Greece (1999), App. No. 31107/96, Judgment of 25 March 1999,§54,http://hudoc.echr.coe.int/sites/eng/pages/search.aspx?i=001-58227#{%22itemid%22:[%22001-58227%22]} accessed 2 March 2013.

140 ECtHR, Pine Valley Developments Ltd and Others v. Ireland (1991), App. No. 1274/87, Judgment of 29 November 1991, §51, http://echr.ketse.com/doc/12742.87-en-19930209/, www.javier-leon-diaz.com/property/Pine%20Valley.pdf accessed 2 March 2013.

141 For hunting rights, see, e.g., ECtHR, Chassagnou and Others v. France (1999), App. Nos. 25088/94, 28331/95 and 28443/95, Judgment of 29 April 1999, §74, http://hudoc.echr.coe.int/sites/eng/pages/search.aspx?i=001-58288#{%22itemid%22:[%22001-58288%22]} accessed 2 March 2013. Regarding fishing rights, see, e.g., ECtHR, Gunther v.

is interesting to note that, while Article 1 Protocol No. 1 ECHR does not include explicit procedural requirements, the ECtHR is of the opinion that the provision does imply a number of procedural guarantees, the violation of which may result in the breach of the right to property.[142]

A central feature of the criterion in Article 1 is the need for "*a fair balance between the demands of the general interest of the community and the requirements of the protection of the individual's fundamental rights*".[143] According to the constant jurisprudence of the European Court of Human Rights, Article 1 of Protocol No. 1 consists of "three distinct rules".[144] The first rule, enshrined in the first sentence of the first paragraph, is of a general nature and enunciates the principle of the peaceful enjoyment of property. The second rule, set out in the second sentence of the first paragraph, allows the deprivation of possessions subject to certain conditions. The second paragraph indicates the third rule that allows the States are entitled to enact laws to control the use of property in accordance with the general interest.[145] The Court has emphasised the interconnection of these three rules: "the second and third rules are concerned with particular instances of interference with the right to peaceful enjoyment of property and should therefore be construed in the light of the general principle enunciated in the first rule."[146] Briefly, the three rules can be summarised as "enjoy (the peaceful enjoyment of property)", "deprivation (the deprivation of possessions subject to certain conditions)" and "control (to control the use of property in accordance with the general interest)". That is to say, on the one hand, States have the duties to respect, protect and fulfil the

---

Sweden (1996), App. No. 26265/92, Commission decision of 27 November 1996, http://echr.ketse.com/doc/26265.92-en-19961127/ accessed 2 March 2013; ECtHR, Posti and Rahko v. Finland (2002), App. No. 27824/95, Judgment of 24 September 2002, §76, http://sim.law.uu.nl/sim/caselaw/Hof.nsf/1d4d0dd240bfee7ec12568490035df05/bb445d6738ec3a2d41256c3f002f588e?OpenDocument accessed 2 March 2013.

142 See, e.g., ECtHR, Agosi v. the United Kingdom (1986), App. No. 9118/80, Judgment of 24 October 1986, §55, http://echr.ketse.com/doc/9118.80-en-19861024/ accessed 3 March 2013; ECtHR, Jokela v. Finland (2002), App. No. 28856/95, Judgment of 21 May 2002, §45 and §62–65, http://echr.ketse.com/doc/28856.95-en-20020521/ accessed 3 March 2013; ECtHR, Tsironis v. Greece (2001), App. No. 44584/98, Judgment of 6 December 2001, §41, http://echr.ketse.com/doc/44584.98-en-20011206/ accessed 3 March 2013.

143 Ploeger, H.D. & Stolker, C.J.J.M. (2000). In search of the importance of Article 1 Protocol No. 1 ECHR to private law. In: Loof, J.P., Ploeger, H. & van der Steur, A. (Eds.). *The Right to Property: the Influence of Article 1 Protocol No. 1 ECHR on Several Fields of Domestic Law.* Maastricht: Shaker Publishing, p. 79.

144 ECtHR, James and Others v. the United Kingdom (1986), App. No. 8793/79, Judgment of 21 February 1986, §37, http://sim.law.uu.nl/SIM/CaseLaw/Hof.nsf/1d4d0dd240bfee7ec12568490035df05/0ef9f8927a96c5a5c1256640004c2410?OpenDocument accessed 1 June 2013.

145 ECtHR, Sporrong and Lönnroth v. Sweden (1982), App. Nos. 7151/75, 7152/75, Judgment of 23 September 1982, §52, http://hudoc.echr.coe.int/sites/eng/pages/search.aspx?i=001-57580#{%22itemid%22:[%22001-57580%22]} accessed 1 June 2013.

146 ECtHR, James and Others v. the United Kingdom (1986), App. No. 8793/79, Judgment of 21 February 1986, http://sim.law.uu.nl/SIM/CaseLaw/Hof.nsf/1d4d0dd240bfee7ec12568490035df05/0ef9f8927a96c5a5c1256640004c2410?OpenDocument accessed 1 June 2013.

right to property of any person, including aliens and Stateless persons, who are able to prove their legal title;[147] on the other hand, property may be taken by the State under the first paragraph of Article 1, if the public interest requires this and compensation is paid; and under the second paragraph of Article 1, the use of property may be restricted if the public interest requires.[148] The main problems do not arise from the State intervention which leads to loss of property, but arise from restricting the use of property.[149]

4.3.1.3. *Three Criteria for Restricting the Right to Property under the European Convention on Human Rights*

To determine the acceptability of an interference, a three-fold test is consistently used: lawfulness, public or general interest, and proportionality.[150] The first criterion is lawfulness, that is to say, the interference must be provided in a domestic law that is adequately accessible and sufficiently precise, as to enable a citizen to foresee the consequences of his or her actions.[151] This condition of lawfulness has hardly ever been an issue in the conservation-related cases examined.[152] The second criterion is that an interference by public authorities with the enjoyment of private property must pursue a public or general interest goal. The protection of the natural environment has been accepted by both the

---

147 Vande Lanotte, J. & Haeck Y. (Eds.) (2004). *Handboek EVRM*. Volume 2, Antwerp: Intersentia, p. 310.

148 Last, K. (2005). Property Rights and Natura 2000 in Great Britain. In: Paques, M. (Ed.). *Natura 2000 and Property Rights: International and National Reports*. Brussels: Etablissements Emile Bruylant, p. 123.

149 George, R. (2007). Reflections on the protection of property under the European Convention on Human Rights. In: Breitenmoser, S. et al (Eds.). *Human Rights, Democracy and the Rule of Law: Liber Amicorum Luzius Wildhaber*. Berlin: Nomos Publishers, pp. 625–645.

150 Desmet, E. (2010). Balancing conflicting goods: the European human rights jurisprudence on environmental protection. *Journal for European Environmental & Planning Law*, 7(3), https://biblio.ugent.be/input/download?func=downloadFile&recordOId=3095650&fileOId=3095651 accessed 17 January 2013, pp. 303–323.

151 ECtHR, Sunday Times v. the United Kingdom (1979), App. No. 6538/74, Judgment of 26 April 1979, §49, http://hudoc.echr.coe.int/sites/eng/pages/search.aspx?i=001-57584#{%22itemid%22:[%22001-57584%22]} accessed 4 October 2013. For the application of these criteria in case of Article 1 of Protocol No. 1 see, e.g., on the rule deprivation: ECtHR, Lithgow and Others v. the United Kingdom (1986), App. Nos. 9006/80, 9262/81, 9263/81, 9265/81, 9266/81, 9313/81, 9405/81, Judgment of 8 July 1986, http://hudoc.echr.coe.int/sites/eng/pages/search.aspx?i=001-57526#{%22itemid%22:[%22001-57526%22]} accessed 4 October 2013; and on the rule on control of the use of property: ECtHR, Spacek, s.r.o. v. the Czech Republic (1999), App. No. 26449/95, Judgment of 9 November 1999, §54, http://sim.law.uu.nl/SIM/CaseLaw/hof.nsf/2422ec00f1ace923c1256681002b47f1/c8e2de4aaec806f4c12568470053ca73?OpenDocument accessed 4 October 2013.

152 See, ECtHR, Saliba v. Malta (2005), App. No. 4251/02, Judgment of 8 November 2005, http://echr.ketse.com/doc/4251.02-en-20051108/ accessed 5 October 2013, with dissenting opinion as regards the issue of lawfulness of Judge Bonello joined by Judge Borrego.

former Commission and the Court as a legitimate public or general interest.[153] The ECtHR will only intervene when the judgment of the legislator is "manifestly without reasonable foundation".[154] This wide margin of appreciation has also been applied in cases concerning nature conservation.[155] The third and central feature of the criterion in Article 1 is the need for "*a fair balance between the demands of the general interest of the community and the requirements of the protection of the individual's fundamental rights*".[156] Accordingly, in order to decide that a fair balance has been struck, a general interest is presupposed, which clearly shows that both tests are interlinked.[157] In the Greek case of 9 December 1994, the Court applies the fair balance test: "*the Court must therefore determine whether a fair balance was struck between the demands of the general interest of the community and the requirements of the protection of the individual's fundamental rights.*"[158] Thus, not only must a measure depriving a person of his property pursue, on the facts as well as in principle, a legitimate aim "in the public interest", but there must also be a reasonable relationship

153 See, e.g., ECtHR, Herrick v. the United Kingdom (1985), App. No. 11185/84, Commission decision of 11 March 1985, http://echr.ketse.com/doc/11185.84-en-19850311/ accessed 5 October 2013; ECtHR, Oerlemans v. the Netherlands (1991), App. No. 12565/86, Judgment of 27 November 1991, http://echr.ketse.com/doc/12565.86-en-19911127/view/ accessed 4 November 2013. Also see ECtHR, Fredin v. Sweden (1991), App. No. 12033/86, Judgment of 18 February 1991, §48, http://sim.law.uu.nl/sim/caselaw/Hof.nsf/2422ec00f1ace923c12566810 02b47f1/a3f2e913fcf974fec1256640004c18e0?OpenDocument accessed 11 October 2013, the Court addressed that "in today's society the protection of the environment is an increasingly important consideration."

154 ECtHR, James and Others v. the United Kingdom (1986), App. No. 8793/79, Judgment of 21 February 1986, §46, http://sim.law.uu.nl/SIM/CaseLaw/Hof.nsf/1d4d0dd240bfee7ec12568 490035df05/0ef9f8927a96c5a5c1256640004c2410?OpenDocument accessed 1 June 2013.

155 See, e.g. ECtHR, Lazaridi v. Greece (2006), App. No. 31282/04, Judgment of 13 July 2006, http://sim.law.uu.nl/sim/caselaw/Hof.nsf/1d4d0dd240bfee7ec12568490035df05/47 ce77ee58527b39c12571b0003ebca4?OpenDocument accessed 2 June 2013; ECtHR, Nikas and Nika v. Greece (2006), App. No. 31273/04, Judgment of 13 July 2006, §33, http://echr.ketse.com/doc/31273.04-en-20060713/ accessed 3 June 2013.

156 Ploeger, H.D. & Stolker, C.J.J.M. (2000). In search of the importance of Article 1 Protocol No. 1 ECHR to private law. In: Loof, J.P., Ploeger, H. & van der Steur, A. (Eds.). *The Right to Property: the Influence of Article 1 Protocol No. 1 ECHR on Several Fields of Domestic Law.* Maastricht: Shaker Publishing, p. 79.

157 See ECtHR, Hutten-Czapska v. Poland (2006), App. No. 35014/97, Judgment of 19 June 2006, §119, §§147–150, http://hudoc.echr.coe.int/sites/eng/pages/search.aspx?i=001-75882#{%22ite mid%22:[%22001-75882%22]} accessed 3 June 2013.

158 See ECtHR, Stran Greek Refineries and Andreadis Stratis v. Greece (1994), App. No. 13427/87, Judgment of 9 December 1994, §69, http://hudoc.echr.coe.int/sites/eng/pages/ search.aspx?i=001-57913#{%22itemid%22:[%22001-57913%22]} accessed 1 June 2013; ECtHR, Wiesinger v. Austria (1991), App. No. 11796/85, Judgment of 30 October 1991, §73, http://sim.law.uu.nl/sim/caselaw/Hof.nsf/e4ca7ef017f8c045c1256849004787f5/e682c df930183cd3c1256640004c1b27?OpenDocument accessed 1 June 2013; ECtHR, Sporrong and Lönnroth v. Sweden (1982), App. No. 7151/75; 7152/75, Judgment of 23 September 1982, §69, http://hudoc.echr.coe.int/sites/eng/pages/search.aspx?i=001-57580#{%22itemid %22:[%22001-57580%22]} accessed 1 June 2013.

of proportionality between the means employed and the aim sought to be realised.[159]

Proportionality is characterised by an exercise of striking a balance between the general and the individual interests.[160] Such a balance is absent if a person has to bear "an individual and excessive burden".[161] Whether this burden has been mitigated by procedures or forms of relief will be relevant to whether the State has struck the right balance.[162] The proportionality principle or test usually contains the following three elements[163]:

- there must be a causal connection between the national measures and the aim pursued; the measures are relevant or pertinent;
- there is no alternative measure available, which is less restrictive concerning trade or free movement generally; and
- there must be a relationship of proportionality between the obstacle introduced, on the one hand, and on the other, the objective thereby pursued and its actual attainment. Reference is made to proportionality *stricto sensu*; meaning that the measures will be disproportionate if the resulting restriction is out of proportion to the aim sought by or the result brought about by the national rule.

The test of proportionality aims to verify whether two requirements have been accomplished: firstly, the means chosen by the national authorities must be proportionate to the legitimate aim pursued; and secondly, the respect of a fair balance between the different competing interests at stake should be assured.[164] In practice, this second requirement implies two things: on the one hand, the requirement of not imposing restrictions (in those articles which permit them) other than those which are strictly necessary; on the other hand, there must not be other means, involving less severe threats to applicants' rights, to achieve the

159 ECtHR, James and Others v. the United Kingdom (1986), App. No. 8793/79, Judgment of 21 February 1986, §54, http://sim.law.uu.nl/SIM/CaseLaw/Hof.nsf/1d4d0dd240bfee7ec12568490035df05/0ef9f8927a96c5a5c1256640004c2410?OpenDocument accessed 1 June 2013.

160 Alkema, E.A. (2000). The concept of property – in particular in the European Convention on Human Rights. In: Loof, J.P., Ploeger, H. & van der Steur, A. (Eds.). *The Right to Property: the Influence of Article 1 Protocol No. 1 ECHR on Several Fields of Domestic Law.* Maastricht: Shaker Publishing, p. 20.

161 ECtHR, Sporrong and Lönnroth v. Sweden (1982), App. Nos. 7151/75; 7152/75, Judgment of 23 September 1982, §69, http://hudoc.echr.coe.int/sites/eng/pages/search.aspx?i=001-57580#{%22itemid%22:[%22001-57580%22]} accessed 1 June 2013.

162 Reid, K. (2004). *A Practitioner's Guide to the European Convention on Human Rights* (second edition). London: Sweet & Maxwell, p. 45.

163 Jans, J.H. (2000). Proportionality revisited. *Legal Issues of Economic Integration*, 27, p. 239.

164 Garcia San José, D. (2005). *Environmental Protection and the European Convention on Human Rights.* Council of Europe Publishing, p. 50.

legitimate aims pursued by means of the interference.[165] The proportionality assessment takes place in the designing of substantial measures such as the measures which allow encroachments and compensations.[166] A lack of proportionality would occur in the case of expropriation if a person is deprived of a right without payment of a reasonable compensation. Although Article 1 does not directly confer a full compensation:

> *the taking of property without payment of an amount reasonably related to its value would normally constitute a disproportionate interference which could not be considered justifiable under Article 1. Article 1 does not, however guarantee a right to full compensation in all circumstances. Legitimate objectives of "public interest", such as pursued in measures of economic reform or measures designed to achieve greater social justice, may call for less than reimbursement of the full market value.*[167]

On the one hand Article 1 does not contain an absolute right to claim compensation. On the other hand, the protection afforded by this stipulation may be undermined if property were taken without compensation and without any consideration of the public interest justifying this deprivation.[168] It was confirmed[169] later:

> *compensation terms under the relevant legislation are material to the assessment whether the contested measure respects the requisite fair balance and, notably, whether it does not impose a disproportionate burden on the applicants. In this connection, the taking of property without payment of an amount reasonably related to its value will normally constitute a disproportionate interference and a total lack of compensation can be considered justifiable under Article 1 only in exceptional circumstances. Article 1 does not, however, guarantee a right to full compensation in all circumstances,*

165 Garcia San José, D. (2005). *Environmental Protection and the European Convention on Human Rights.* Council of Europe Publishing, p. 50.

166 Paques, M. (2005) (Ed.). *Natura 2000 and Property Rights: International and National Reports.* Brussels: Etablissements Emile Bruylant, p. 40.

167 ECtHR, James and Others v. the United Kingdom (1986), App. No. 8793/79, Judgment of 21 February 1986, §54, http://sim.law.uu.nl/SIM/CaseLaw/Hof.nsf/1d4d0dd240bfee7ec12568490035df05/0ef9f8927a96c5a5c1256640004c2410?OpenDocument accessed 1 June 2013.

168 ECtHR, James and Others v. the United Kingdom (1986), App. No. 8793/79, Judgment of 21 February 1986, §54, http://sim.law.uu.nl/SIM/CaseLaw/Hof.nsf/1d4d0dd240bfee7ec12568490035df05/0ef9f8927a96c5a5c1256640004c2410?OpenDocument accessed 1 June 2013; ECtHR, Lithgow and Others v. the United Kingdom (1986), App. Nos. 9006/80, 9262/81, 9263/81, 9265/81, 9266/81, 9313/81, 9405/81, Judgment of 8 July 1986, §120, http://hudoc.echr.coe.int/sites/eng/pages/search.aspx?i=001-57526#{%22itemid%22:[%22001-57526%22]} accessed 4 October 2013.

169 ECtHR, The Holy Monasteries v. Greece (1994), App. No. 13092/87; 13984/88, Judgment of 9 December, §71, http://hudoc.echr.coe.int/sites/fra/pages/search.aspx?i=001-57906#{%22itemid%22:[%22001-57906%22]} accessed 5 October 2013.

since legitimate objectives of "public interest" may call for less than reimbursement of the full market value.[170]

Nevertheless, in determining the amount of adequate compensation, which does not necessarily have to reflect the full value of the property, the Court must base itself on the criteria laid down in its judgments regarding Article 1 of Protocol No. 1 and according to which, without payment of an amount reasonably related to its value, a deprivation of property would normally constitute a disproportionate interference which could not be considered justifiable under Article 1 of Protocol No. 1.[171] This Article will be analysed in detail later (see 4.3.2.3).

4.3.2. CASE LAW IN THE EUROPEAN COURT OF HUMAN RIGHTS

The interpretation of the property rights clause included in the framework of the European Convention for the Protection of Human Rights and Fundamental Freedoms, by the European Court of Human Rights is very important to respond to environmental concerns within the context of human rights. In this section, the Court's approach to environmental protection, especially concerning protected areas conservation, is analysed through judgments related to interference in individual's property rights in order to protect the general interest.

The two concepts of proportionality and a fair balance between the interests have been used by the ECtHR in many judgments as a means of assessing the margin of appreciation which Contracting States have, to deal with Convention obligations and to determine whether or not there has been a breach of one or more of the rights set out in the Convention.[172] The key seems to be how to

170 See ECtHR, Lithgow and Others v. the United Kingdom (1986), App. Nos. 9006/80, 9262/81, 9263/81, 9265/81, 9266/81, 9313/81, 9405/81, Judgment of 8 July 1986, §121, http://hudoc.echr.coe.int/sites/eng/pages/search.aspx?i=001-57526#{%22itemid%22:[%22001-57526%22]} accessed 4 October 2013; ECtHR, Tsomtsos and Others v. Greece (1996), App. No. 20680/92, Judgment of 15 November 1996, §§40–42, http://echr.ketse.com/doc/20680.92-en-19961115/ accessed 5 October 2013, in this case, the Court rejected a compensation scheme which was too standardised, therefore not flexible enough, and which left insufficient opportunity to claim punitive damages. Similarly, ECtHR, Katikaridis and Others v. Greece (1996), App. No. 31423/96, Judgment of 15 November 1996, §§49–51, http://echr.ketse.com/doc/19385.92-en-19961115/ accessed 5 October 2013; ECtHR, Papachelas v. Greece (1999), App. No. 31423/96, Judgment of 25 March 1999, §53, http://hudoc.echr.coe.int/sites/fra/pages/search.aspx?i=001-58291#{%22itemid%22:[%22001-58291%22]} accessed 6 October 2013.

171 ECtHR, James and Others v. the United Kingdom (1986), App. No. 8793/79, Judgment of 21 February 1986, §54, http://sim.law.uu.nl/SIM/CaseLaw/Hof.nsf/1d4d0dd240bfee7ec12568490035df05/0ef9f8927a96c5a5c1256640004c2410?OpenDocument accessed 1 June 2013.

172 Garcia San José, D. (2005). *Environmental Protection and the European Convention on Human Rights*. Council of Europe Publishing, p. 50.

predict in a consistent way that the reasons provided by national authorities should be "relevant" or "sufficient". According to the ECtHR's environmental case law, whenever an intimate aspect of individuals' rights is at stake (for example, intimacy within private life), the reasons must be particularly convincing and a very narrow margin of appreciation is left to Contracting States. In this way, the ECtHR can easily develop at the same time, both a "harmonising" and "standardising" logic according to its own judicial policy options in managing the obligations assumed by 47 States as dissimilar as San Marino and Russia.[173] Sometimes, it is not easy to find out a "harmonising" and "standardising" logic to get a satisfying result for all the relevant parties. When applying the principle of proportionality,[174] the ECtHR usually asks itself about the extent of the margin of appreciation that, in the concrete circumstances of the case, should be permitted to the state concerned in order to merit the necessity of a restriction in the exercise of European Convention rights.[175]

Several parameters may be considered as the indicators which influence the assessment of the ECtHR and the former Commission of whether the principle of proportionality and a fair balance have been respected. Only some very important parameters will be discussed below.

4.3.2.1. The Bottom Line: Whether the Livelihood is Really Affected or Not

In *Claesson and Others v. Sweden* (1992),[176] the applicants owned properties on the Swedish east coast which included private waters located in areas where, before 1985, fishing was the exclusive right of the property owner. Between 1965 and 1973 the County Administrative Board of the County of Kalmar declared ten land and water areas as nature conservation areas under the 1964 Nature Conservation Act (the 1964 Act).[177] In 1973 the Board issued, under section 8 of the 1964 Act, regulations restricting the use of the land within these areas, *inter alia* regarding the right to build, to excavate and to undertake other similar activities. At the same time the Board also issued, under section 10 of the 1964 Act, a prohibition for the general public to hunt, catch, kill or in any way hurt

---

173 Garcia San José, D. (2005). *Environmental Protection and the European Convention on Human Rights*. Council of Europe Publishing, p. 51.

174 For a general approach to the application of this principle in the reasoning of the European Bodies, for instance see, Eissen, M.-A. (1993). The principle of proportionality in the case-law of the European Court of Human Rights. In: Macdonald, R.S.J., Matscher, F. & Petzold, H. (Eds.). *The European System for the Protection of Human Rights*. Leiden: Martinus Nijhoff Publishers.

175 Garcia San José, D. (2005). *Environmental Protection and the European Convention on Human Rights*. Council of Europe Publishing, pp. 51–52.

176 ECtHR, Claesson and Others v. Sweden (1992), App. No. 13903/88, Commission decision of 1 July 1992, http://echr.ketse.com/doc/13903.88-en-19920701/view/ accessed 8 May 2013.

177 ECtHR, Claesson and Others v. Sweden (1992), App. No. 13903/88, Commission decision of 1 July 1992, http://echr.ketse.com/doc/13903.88-en-19920701/view/ accessed 8 May 2013.

wild animals – including, according to the applicants, fish – within the nature conservation areas.

The applicants maintained that the property owners would keep the exclusive right to fish in their water forever even if laws were to be introduced granting the general public a right to fish in private waters. The applicants also claimed that this guarantee was at the basis of certain agreements reached at the time regarding compensation for the restrictions imposed on the use of their properties.

Concerning the proportionality of the interference, the applicants complained about the fact that they were deprived of any right to compensation: they could not allege any loss of income under the Fishing Rights Compensation Act 1985[178] as their entitlement to grant fishing rights to the general public had been taken away by the 1973 regulations; furthermore, the Government had, through their above-mentioned decision, taken away any right to compensation on the basis of the 1964 Act since it had concluded that the impugned amendment to these regulations was to be based on section 10, and not on section 8 of the Act.

The Commission recalled that the only loss which could be taken into account in the present case was the possible loss of catch occasioned by the general public's right to fish freely with hand-held tackle in the applicants' waters. To the extent that such a loss did not cause a direct loss of income the European Commission of Human Rights accepted that no compensation was available under Swedish law. What is more and notably, considering the limited scope of this interference and the fact that none of the applicants had alleged to be dependent on fishing for his or her livelihood, the Commission could not find any indication that any of the applicants was made to bear an excessive burden or that there had otherwise been a lack of proportionality between the means used and the undoubtedly legitimate aims sought to be achieved, for instance, the preservation of nature and making fishing with hand-held tackled available to the general public. Finally, the Commission declared the application inadmissible.

Another case illustrates that the main source of income to support the applicants' family cannot be easily deprived. In the case of *Devecioĝlu v. Turkey*,[179] the applicants had been deprived of their property, which was classified as forest land. The Court noted that "*the applicants did not receive any compensation for the transfer of their property to the Treasury; (...) the Government did not cite any exceptional circumstances to justify the total lack*

178 A special law, the Fishing Rights Compensation Act 1985 regulated the question of economic compensation. According to section 1 of this Act only losses of income could be compensated. According to the Government, compensation could be paid where the owner of the fishing rights had had a financial gain from these rights and could prove this.

179 ECtHR, Devecioĝlu v. Turkey (2009), App. No. 17203/03, Judgment of 4 May 2009, http://echr.ketse.com/doc/17203.03-en-20081113/view/ accessed 23 March 2014.

of compensation for that deprivation, the land being the main source of income to sustain the applicants' family."[180] Finally, the Court concluded that there had been a breach of Article 1 of Protocol No. 1.

It is obvious to see that whether the livelihood is really affected or not is the bottom line for the decision. People will not usually object to conserving biodiversity, providing it does not clash with personal or institutional goals.[181] When conservation activities directly affect the livelihood of stakeholders, a solution can be to conserve biodiversity while encouraging individual stakeholders' economic growth.[182] Conservation efforts thus not only have to address questions on biodiversity conservation in a protected area but also on local livelihoods which depend on these resources in a protected area. This is a particular important bottom line for protected areas conservation. To avoid any possible conflict, China may adopt this bottom line according to the local standards.

4.3.2.2. The Legitimate Aim: The General Interest

The European Court of Human Rights has found that environmental protection is a legitimate aim and restrictions maybe reasonable. This was confirmed by the decision in *Pine Valley Developments Ltd and Others v. Ireland*.[183] The Court upheld the government's interference with property rights in order to protect the environment. The case deals with the purchase of land for possible development purposes in the County of Dublin. Whether the land can or cannot be developed may make it more or less valuable in the hands of its purchasers. In November 1978 private developer Pine Valley purchased 21.5 acres of land for 550,000 Irish pounds. Pine Valley relied on the outline planning permission[184] for industrial

180 ECtHR, Devecioğlu v. Turkey (2009), App. No. 17203/03, Judgment of 4 May 2009, §40, http://echr.ketse.com/doc/17203.03-en-20081113/view/ accessed 23 March 2014.

181 Young, J. *et al.* (2005). Towards sustainable land use: identifying and managing the conflicts between human activities and biodiversity conservation in Europe. *Biodiversity and Conservation*, 14, p. 1652. Doi.10.1007/s10531-004-0536-z.

182 Young, J. *et al.* (2005). Towards sustainable land use: identifying and managing the conflicts between human activities and biodiversity conservation in Europe. *Biodiversity and Conservation*, 14, p. 1652. Doi.10.1007/s10531-004-0536-z.

183 The Court did find a violation of Article 14 taken in conjunction with the right to peaceful enjoyment of possessions. ECtHR, Pine Valley Developments Ltd and Others v. Ireland (1991), App. No. 1274/87, Judgment of 29 November 1991, http://echr.ketse.com/doc/12742.87-en-19930209/, www.javier-leon-diaz.com/property/Pine%20Valley.pdf accessed 2 March 2013.

184 An outline planning permission (based on the Local Government Planning and Development Act 1963) allows the applicant in principle to build on the land, but without approval of a detailed plan the work cannot be commenced. This permission is not a prerequisite before submitting detailed proposals. However, it is important for land owners to have assurance that a proposal is acceptable in principle before deciding to buy land. Detailed information see ECtHR, Pine Valley Developments Ltd and Others v. Ireland (1991), App. No. 1274/87, Judgment of 29 November 1991, http://echr.ketse.com/doc/12742.87-en-19930209/, www.javier-leon-diaz.com/property/Pine%20Valley.pdf accessed 2 March 2013.

and office development that was granted by the Minister for Local Government in 1977. However, in the development plans of the Dublin County Council the site was located in an area zoned for agricultural and green purposes ("green belt").

The High Court and the Supreme Court in Ireland ruled against the applicants, because there was no injustice done by the State. This caused the applicants' appeal to the ECtHR: the applicants submitted that, as a result of the Supreme Court's decision holding the outline planning permission to be invalid, coupled with the respondent State's alleged failure to validate that permission retrospectively or its failure to provide compensation for the reduction in value of their property, they had been victims of a breach of Article 1 of Protocol No. 1 to the Convention.[185]

Apart from other relevant Articles of the Convention, the most notable issue in this case is that the ECtHR had to decide whether there was an interference with a right of the applicants. The main question was whether the applicants ever enjoyed a right to develop the land. The Court ruled that there was at least a "legitimate expectation" of being able to develop the land. The Court recognised that an interference with the right to peaceful enjoyment of property which was in conformity with planning legislation and was "designed to protect the environment" was clearly a legitimate aim "in accordance with the general interest" for the purposes of the second paragraph of Article 1 of the First Protocol to the ECHR.[186] Therefore, the Court held that the applicants cannot claim a violation of Article 1 of Protocol No. 1.

Another interesting case is *Posti and Rahko v. Finland*.[187] The applicants were fishermen operating in State-owned waters in the coastal region of the Gulf of Bothnia on the basis of leases contracted with the State in 1989 and renewed in 1995 (for a further period ending in 1999) as well as in 2000 (for the period 2000–2004). According to the relevant law, the Ministry of Agriculture

---

185 ECtHR, Pine Valley Developments Ltd and Others v. Ireland (1991), App. No. 1274/87, Judgment of 29 November 1991, §51, http://echr.ketse.com/doc/12742.87-en-19930209/, www.javier-leon-diaz.com/property/Pine%20Valley.pdf accessed 2 March 2013.

186 ECtHR, Pine Valley Developments Ltd and Others v. Ireland (1991), App. No. 1274/87, Judgment of 29 November 1991, §§54–57, http://echr.ketse.com/doc/12742.87-en-19930209/, www.javier-leon-diaz.com/property/Pine%20Valley.pdf accessed 2 March 2013. Also see ECtHR, Mateos e Silva, Lda. and Others v. Portugal (1996), App. No. 15777/89, Judgment of 16 September 1996, http://echr.ketse.com/doc/15777.89-en-19960916/ accessed 2 March 2013 (finding a violation of Article 1 of Protocol 1 where there had been no formal or *de facto* expropriation, since the measures to create a nature reserve for animals had serious and harmful effects that hindered the applicants' enjoyment of their property right for more than thirteen years, creating uncertainty as to what would become of the possessions and as other question of compensation, and upsetting the balance between the requirements of the general interest and the protection of property rights).

187 ECtHR, Posti and Rahko v. Finland (2002), App. No. 27824/95, Judgment of 24 September 2002, http://sim.law.uu.nl/sim/caselaw/Hof.nsf/1d4d0dd240bfee7ec12568490035df05/bb445d6738ec3a2d41256c3f002f588e?OpenDocument accessed 2 March 2013.

and Forestry might restrict fishing, *inter alia*, if this was deemed necessary in order to safeguard future fish stocks. The applicants complained, in particular, that fishing restrictions imposed and maintained by government decree had violated their right to the peaceful enjoyment of their possessions.[188] The European Court of Human Rights observed that the applicants' right to fish in State-owned waters on the basis of their 1995 leases constituted a "possession" and the limitation of that right through the 1996 and 1998 decrees amounted to a control of the use of those possessions.[189] What is more, the interference did not totally prohibit the applicants' right to fish in the relevant waters. The applicants also got some compensation for losses because of the fishing prohibition. The Court considered that this interference with the applicants' property rights was justified, being lawful and pursuing, by means proportionate to that aim, the legitimate general interest of protecting the fish stocks. Accordingly, the Court decided there was no appearance of any violation of Article 1 of Protocol No. 1.

From these, it can be seen that there are also some conflicts regarding environmental protection and property rights in Europe. The ECtHR rigorously points out that the national authorities shall take measures to continuously guarantee environmental protection, even if these measures may interfere with the enjoyment of certain fundamental rights, such as the right to property.[190] However, the Court also focuses on the proportionality that do not affect the people's livelihood. The legitimate aim is for the general interest. In considering the issue of proportionality, although there is no presumption in favour of compensation, its availability is one of the factors relevant to whether a fair balance has been struck between the public interest and an individual's rights.[191] Moreover, as introduced in Chapter 3, most of the land and natural resources in China belong to the State or the collective; the local people signed a contract with the State or the collective committee to have a right to use it. If there is any prohibition in the name of the legitimate public interest within the contract term, this prohibition is reasonable and lawful. However, some reasonable compensation should be arranged for the local people.

---

188 ECtHR, Posti and Rahko v. Finland (2002), App. No. 27824/95, Judgment of 24 September 2002, http://sim.law.uu.nl/sim/caselaw/Hof.nsf/1d4d0dd240bfee7ec12568490035df05/bb445d6738ec3a2d41256c3f002f588e?OpenDocument accessed 2 March 2013.

189 ECtHR, Posti and Rahko v. Finland (2002), App. No. 27824/95, Judgment of 24 September 2002, http://sim.law.uu.nl/sim/caselaw/Hof.nsf/1d4d0dd240bfee7ec12568490035df05/bb445d6738ec3a2d41256c3f002f588e?OpenDocument accessed 2 March 2013.

190 ECtHR, Fredin v. Sweden (1991), App. No. 12033/86, Judgment of 18 February 1991, §48, http://sim.law.uu.nl/sim/caselaw/Hof.nsf/2422ec00f1ace923c1256681002b47f1/a3f2e913fcf974fec1256640004c18e0?OpenDocument accessed 11 October 2013.

191 ECtHR, James and Others v. the United Kingdom (1986), App. No. 8793/79, Judgment of 21 February 1986, http://sim.law.uu.nl/SIM/CaseLaw/Hof.nsf/1d4d0dd240bfee7ec12568490035df05/0ef9f8927a96c5a5c1256640004c2410?OpenDocument accessed 1 June 2013.

4.3.2.3. *A Better Solution for a Fair Balance: Reasonable Compensation*

Article 17 of the International Covenant on Civil and Political Rights has indicated that "interference with one's home" can only take place "in cases envisaged by the law." It is not enough, however, that such interference is addressed in the law, but it must (particularly when involving the complete removal of ownership or tenancy rights without relocation, re-housing or compensation) "be in accordance with the provisions, aims and objectives of the Covenant and should be, in any event, reasonable in particular circumstances."[192]

Whether compensation has been paid by the State is a crucial element in the evaluation of whether the applicant bore a disproportionate burden as a consequence of the interference.[193] At the European level, although Article 1 of Protocol No. 11 ("the right to the peaceful enjoyment of possessions") to the European Convention on Human Rights does not directly confer full compensation (see 4.3.1), the jurisprudence provides a valuable source of case law supporting restitution rights. For instance, *Lithgow and others v. the United Kingdom*,[194] originated in the seven applications against the United Kingdom. The applicants had certain of their interests nationalised under the Aircraft and Shipbuilding Industries Act 1977.[195] They claimed that the compensation which they received was grossly inadequate and discriminatory and alleged that they had been victims of breaches of Article 1 of Protocol No. 1 to the Convention.

The Court observed that under the legal system of the Contracting States, the taking of property in the public interest without payment of compensation was treated as justifiable only in exceptional circumstances not relevant for present

---

192 Human Rights Committee (1988) General Comment No. 16 of Human Rights Committee on Article 17 of the Covenant on Civil and Political Rights (1988) (The right to respect of privacy, family, home and correspondence, and protection of honour and reputation (Article 17)). The Human Rights Committee has interpreted Article 17 to mean that: "1. (...) The obligations imposed by this Article require the State to adopt legislative and other measures to give effect to the prohibition against such interferences and attacks as well as the protection of this right (...) 4. The expression 'arbitrary inference' is also relevant to the protection of the right provided for in Article 17. In the Committee's view the expression 'arbitrary interference' can also extend to interference provided for under the law. The introduction of the concept of arbitrariness is intended to guarantee that even interference provided for by a law should be in accordance with the provisions, aims and objectives of the Covenant and should be, in any event, reasonable in particular circumstances".

193 Desmet, E. (2011). *Indigenous Rights Entwined with Nature Conservation*. Antwerp: Intersentia, p. 247.

194 ECtHR, Lithgow and Others v. The United Kingdom (1986), App. Nos. 9006/80, 9262/81, 9263/81, 9265/81, 9266/81, 9313/81, 9405/81, Judgment of 8 July 1986, http://hudoc.echr.coe.int/sites/eng/pages/search.aspx?i=001-57526#{%22itemid%22:[%22001-57526%22]} accessed 4 October 2013.

195 ECtHR, Lithgow and Others v. The United Kingdom (1986), App. Nos. 9006/80, 9262/81, 9263/81, 9265/81, 9266/81, 9313/81, 9405/81, Judgment of 8 July 1986, http://hudoc.echr.coe.int/sites/eng/pages/search.aspx?i=001-57526#{%22itemid%22:[%22001-57526%22]} accessed 4 October 2013.

purposes.[196] The requisite balance would not be found "*if the person concerned had had to bear an individual excessive burden (...) clearly, compensation terms were material to the assessment when a fair balance had been struck between the various interests at stake and, notably, whether or not a disproportionate burden had been imposed on the person who had been deprived of his possessions.*"[197] Finally, the Court concluded that there had been no violation of the Convention.

It is obvious to see how important the role of compensation played when the Court analysed and assessed the case.

However, if there were no exceptional circumstances, the Court would conclude that there was a breach of Article 1 of Protocol No. 1 in all the cases that conservation activities caused the deprivation of property and the applicants did not get a reasonable compensation. For instance, in *Turgut and Others v. Turkey*,[198] the applicants' property has been taken away in the name of nature and forest protection. The applicants did not get any form of compensation. And more importantly, the government did not invoke any exceptional circumstance to justify this total lack of compensation. The Court was unanimous in finding a breach of the right to the peaceful enjoyment of one's possessions.[199]

Another interesting case is *Loizidou v. Turkey*.[200] The applicant, who grew up in Northern Cyprus and owned many plots of land, lived elsewhere in Cyprus. Since 1974, she had been prevented from gaining access to her properties and as a result of the presence of Turkish forces in Cyprus who exercised an overall control in the relevant areas.[201] The European Court of Human Rights noted that: "*Because of the continuous denial of access the applicant had effectively lost all control, as well as all possibilities to use, to sell, to bequeath, to mortgage, to*

196 ECtHR, Lithgow and Others v. the United Kingdom (1986), App. Nos. 9006/80, 9262/81, 9263/81, 9265/81, 9266/81, 9313/81, 9405/81, Judgment of 8 July 1986, http://hudoc.echr.coe.int/sites/eng/pages/search.aspx?i=001-57526#{%22itemid%22:[%22001-57526%22]} accessed 4 October 2013. Also see Lechie, S. (Ed.) (2007). *Housing, Land and Property Restitution Rights of Refugees and Displaced Persons: Laws, Cases And Materials*. Cambridge: Cambridge University Press, p. 397.

197 ECtHR, Lithgow and Others v. the United Kingdom (1986), App. Nos. 9006/80, 9262/81, 9263/81, 9265/81, 9266/81, 9313/81, 9405/81, Judgment of 8 July 1986, §120, http://hudoc.echr.coe.int/sites/eng/pages/search.aspx?i=001-57526#{%22itemid%22:[%22001-57526%22]} accessed 4 October 2013.

198 ECtHR, Turgut and Others v. Turkey (2008), App. No. 1411/03, Judgment of 8 July 2008, §§91–92, http://echr.ketse.com/doc/1411.03-en-20080708/ accessed 22 March 2014.

199 ECtHR, Turgut and Others v. Turkey (2008), App. No. 1411/03, Judgment of 8 July 2008, §§91–92, http://echr.ketse.com/doc/1411.03-en-20080708/ accessed 22 March 2014. The text of this judgment is available in French only. The case analysis is based on the summary from Desmet, E. (2011). *Indigenous Rights Entwined with Nature Conservation*. Antwerp: Intersentia, p. 248.

200 ECtHR, Loizidou v. Turkey (1995), App. No. 15318/89, Judgment of 23 March 1995, http://hudoc.echr.coe.int/sites/eng/pages/search.aspx?i=001-57920 accessed 5 June 2013.

201 ECtHR, Loizidou v. Turkey (1995), App. No. 15318/89, Judgment of 23 March 1995, http://hudoc.echr.coe.int/sites/eng/pages/search.aspx?i=001-57920 accessed 5 June 2013.

develop and to enjoy her land (...) the continuous denial of access must therefore be regarded as an interference with her rights under Article 1 of Protocol No. 1".[202]

The applicant stated that she did not claim compensation for any purported expropriation of her property. In the light of the Court's finding that she was still the legal owner of the property no issue of expropriation arises.[203] With reference to a valuation report assessing the value of her property and the return that could be expected from it, the method in the valuation report involved calculating the market price of the property as in 1974 and increasing it by 12% per year to calculate the value that the property would have had if the northern part of Cyprus had not been occupied by the Turkish army. The occupation of the properties had deprived the owner of her right to lease and thus resulted in as substantial loss of rent.[204] Making an equitable assessment, the Court awarded CYP 20,000 (about 11,696 EUR)[205] under this head.

Despite other issues in this case, it is interesting to note how "reasonable compensation" is defined – "calculating the market price of the property as in 1974 and increasing it by 12% per year to calculate the value that the property would have had". This "reasonable and dynamic" compensation with the development of the market price would be an important guideline for solving the conflicts regarding protected areas conservation and property rights protection. It could also provide an economic basis for further development of local people and communities if they lost their property for their livelihoods.

Based on what has been discussed, it can be seen how important the role of compensation played and how to give "the reasonable compensation" a clear definition according to the local standards. What is more, implementation has to happen within a reasonable time in order to secure respect for property rights. These are quite important elements for China, with a huge population and large differences among different regions, to handle with the potential conflicts regarding protected areas conservation and property rights protection.

---

202 ECtHR, Loizidou v. Turkey (1995), App. No. 15318/89, Judgment of 23 March 1995, http://hudoc.echr.coe.int/sites/eng/pages/search.aspx?i=001-57920 accessed 5 June 2013.

203 ECtHR, Loizidou v. Turkey (1995), App. No. 15318/89, Judgment of 23 March 1995, http://hudoc.echr.coe.int/sites/eng/pages/search.aspx?i=001-57920 accessed 5 June 2013, and Damages (1998). Also see Lechie, S. (Ed.) (2007). *Housing, Land and Property Restitution Rights of Refugees and Displaced Persons: Laws, Cases And Materials.* Cambridge: Cambridge University Press, p. 421.

204 ECtHR, Loizidou v. Turkey (1995), App. No. 15318/89, Judgment of 23 March 1995, http://hudoc.echr.coe.int/sites/eng/pages/search.aspx?i=001-57920 accessed 5 June 2013 and Damages (1998). Also see Lechie, S. (Ed.) (2007). *Housing, Land and Property Restitution Rights of Refugees and Displaced Persons: Laws, Cases And Materials.* Cambridge: Cambridge University Press, p. 421.

205 According to the exchange rate on 15 July 2014, 1 CYP equal to 1.71 EUR, www.forexticket.com/zh/currency/converter-CYP-EUR accessed 15 July 2014. The following statistics all follow this exchange rate.

4.3.3. RIGHT TO PROPERTY UNDER EUROPEAN UNION LAW

Since the ECHR and ECtHR set the minimum standards for national law on the right to property, it is not necessary to further examine the relevant cases on the right to property at the EU level for the reason that the baseline would be similar with what has been discussed on the ECHR and the ECtHR.

4.3.4. RIGHT TO PROPERTY IN PROTECTED AREAS CONSERVATION LAW IN EUROPE

Based on what has been explored from the perspective of human rights, in order to better balance the potential conflicts regarding human rights protection and protected areas conservation, it is necessary to specifically examine the relevant issues in protected areas conservation law in Europe.

4.3.4.1. The Bern Convention

As indicated above (see 3.2.1), there is no specific provision on the right to property of local people and communities in the Bern Convention. The Secretariat examines all letters sent to the Standing Committee of the Convention itself, or to its Chairman or Secretariat, by a Contracting Party, individual(s) or NGO(s) containing a complaint about the failure of one or more Contracting Parties to comply with the provisions of the Convention. The majority of complaints that reach the Secretariat are based on specific plans or projects that affect a natural protected area and whose potential effects may be negative to the habitats of species protected by the Convention.[206] These types of projects or programmes are mostly related to economic development, such as constructing a road or building a dam. In addition, in recent decades, landscape and habitat fragmentation throughout Europe has been generally recognised as a core problem of conservation.[207]

There is also no explicit mentioning of social, economic or cultural value in the criteria or management regime of Emerald sites and the States implementing the Emerald Network have the flexibility to liaise in any way with local

206 Directorate of Culture and Cultural and Natural Heritage (2011). Improving the case-file system of the Bern Convention. Convention on the Conservation of European Wildlife and Natural Habitats Standing Committee. In: thirty-first meeting, Strasbourg, 29 November – 2 December 2011, https://wcd.coe.int/com.instranet.InstraServlet?command=com.instranet.CmdBlobGet&InstranetImage=1956319&SecMode=1&DocId=1811880&Usage=2 accessed 8 April 2014.

207 Council of Europe (2004). Naturaopa: the 25 years of the Bern Convention. No. 101, http://128.121.10.98/coe/pdfopener?smd=1&md=1&did=594649 accessed 8 April 2014, p. 30.

communities.[208] Nonetheless, as many of these areas in the Emerald Network are located in human dominated landscapes, human activities and social-cultural values can be expected.[209]

However, there is no doubt that the Emerald Network stands the test of proportionality for property rights protection and meets the minimum standards for property rights protection from the ECHR and the ECtHR. If there is any infringement on the right to property in these areas in Europe, the relevant provision(s) from the ECHR will be applied.

4.3.4.2. The Birds Directive and the Habitats Directive

Although the EU is a Party to the Bern Convention, the majority of the parties to the Bern Convention are now under the more strict obligations of the Habitats Directive and the Birds Directive. These Directives represent the most ambitious and large-scale initiative undertaken to conserve protected areas in the EU.

As for the Habitats Directive, only Articles 14(2)[210] and 16(1)(b)[211] address "property", but these provisions do not explicitly refer to the right to property. Concerning the Birds Directive, it does not provide any Article referring to "property", let alone referring to the right to property. Similar to the Emerald Network, one can assure that the Natura 2000 stands the test of proportionality for property rights protection and meets the minimum standards for property rights protection from the ECHR and the ECtHR. Nevertheless, if there is any infringement of the right to property of local people and communities, some relevant provisions from the ECHR will be applied.

---

208 Emerald Network Sites. Published on Areas of Biodiversity Importance, www.biodiversitya-z.org/areas/5#areaReferences accessed 28 March 2014.

209 Emerald Network Sites. Published on Areas of Biodiversity Importance, www.biodiversitya-z.org/areas/5#areaReferences accessed 28 March 2014.

210 Article 14(2): "where such measures are deemed necessary, they shall include continuation of the surveillance provided for in Article 11. Such measures may also include in particular: regulations regarding access to certain *property*; temporary or local prohibition of the taking of specimens in the wild and exploitation of certain populations". Directive 92/43/EEC of 21 May 1992 on the Conservation of Natural Habitats and of Wild Fauna and Flora, OJ L 206, 22 July 1992 (Habitats Directive); text of the Directive, with later amendments, see http://ec.europa.eu/environment/nature.legislation.habitatsdirective.index_en.htm accessed 20 October 2012.

211 Article 16(1)(b) "provided that there is no satisfactory alternative and the derogation is not detrimental to the maintenance of the populations of the species concerned at a favourable conservation status in their natural range, Member States may derogate from the provisions of Article 12,13,14 and 15(a) and (b) (…) to prevent serious damage, in particular to crops, livestock, forests, fisheries and water and other types of *property*". Directive 92/43/EEC of 21 May 1992 on the Conservation of Natural Habitats and of Wild Fauna and Flora, OJ L 206, 22 July 1992 (Habitats Directive); text of the Directive, with later amendments, see http://ec.europa.eu/environment/nature.legislation.habitatsdirective.index_en.htm accessed 20 October 2012.

4.3.4.3. *Case Law in the Court of Justice of the European Union According to Protected Areas Conservation Law*

There are not many cases relevant for human rights protection and protected areas conservation following the provisions of protected areas conservation law in the Court of Justice of the European Union.

A quite new case of *Cascina Tre Pini S.s. v. Ministero dell' Ambiente e della Tutela del Territorio e del Mare and Others*[212] concerns the rights to which the owners of the land in question are entitled. The answer is quite important for the reason that "*it will depend on the provisions of general European Union law on the implementation of the Habitats Directive by national administrations, with particular reference to the fundamental right to property and the right to be heard.*"[213] Cascina Tre Pini S.s. is a partnership which owns an area of about 22 hectares in the Commune di Somma Lombardo, near the Milan-Malpensa airport. The Commission has included this area in the list of Sites of Community Importance (SCI) for the continental biogeographical region. Cascina Tre Pini S.s. found that the steady increase in air traffic at the airport had led to serious environmental damage on its land, but no measure had been taken upon its request to prevent the environmental degradation. Then, Cascina Tre Pini S.s. called on the Italian Environment Ministry to withdraw its land from the protected area, but it was refused. Cascina Tre Pini S.s. therefore appealed to the Court of Justice of the European Union.[214] The Court noted that: "*the classification of land as part of an SCI limits the ways in which it may be used and so restricts the right to property of the owners of the land concerned. As long as the site protection requirements apply, such restrictions of the right to property are, as a rule, justified by the objective of protecting the environment. However, where those requirements no longer apply, continuing to restrict the use of land might be an infringement of the right to property. In the European Union, no measures may be accepted as lawful if they are incompatible with the observance of recognised and guaranteed human rights.*" That is to say, the owners' right to property shall be respected.

---

212 Cascina Tre Pini S.s. v. Ministero dell' Ambiente e della Tutela del Territorio e del Mare and Others, Case C-301/12, Judgment of the Court (Second Chamber) of 3 April 2014, http://curia.europa.eu/juris/liste.jsf?language=en&jur=C,T,F&num=C-301/12&td=ALL accessed 7 April 2014.

213 Cascina Tre Pini S.s. v. Ministero dell' Ambiente e della Tutela del Territorio e del Mare and Others, Case C-301/12, Judgment of the Court (Second Chamber) of 3 April 2014, §2, http://curia.europa.eu/juris/liste.jsf?language=en&jur=C,T,F&num=C-301/12&td=ALL accessed 7 April 2014.

214 With the entry into force of the Treaty of Lisbon in 2009, the court's name was changed from the Court of Justice of the European Communities to the Court of Justice of the European Union. More information see European sources online, www.cardiff.ac.uk/insrv/resources/edc/Court%20of%20Justice.pdf accessed 12 April 2014.

The Court then concluded that: "*If the request is based on substantiated reasoning that, despite compliance with Articles in the Habitats Directive, the land cannot contribute towards the conservation of natural habitats and wild fauna and flora or to the setting up of the Natura 2000 network.*"[215] Furthermore, the Court also held that: "*the Member States must give the owners of land concerned an opportunity to submit observations when considering whether to propose to the Commission, in relation to that land, the adaptation of the list of Sites of Community Interest pursuant to the fourth sentence of Article 4 (1) of the Directive.*"[216]

This case reflects that Cascina Tre Pini S.s., as a relevant party to the land, can ask the government to take appropriate steps to avoid the deterioration of natural habitats and the habitats of species. The States has the obligation to take the measures necessary to safeguard the site, and the relevant party to the land works as a "watchdog" in this case. It also indicates that if empowering some reasonable rights to the relevant party(ies), for instance the right to property and the right to be heard in this case, the relevant party(ies) would play their potential roles in helping to conserve protected areas.

4.4. ANALYSIS AND INTERIM CONCLUSION

4.4.1. GENERAL ANALYSIS

According to what has been discussed above, some similar conflicts can be found in both China and Europe. The relevant laws from both China and Europe allow the competent authorities to expropriate or restrict the use of property on behalf of the public interest.

Comparing the property rights protection between China and Europe, there are several differences. The important points are summarised below. Firstly and most importantly, there is mainly collective ownership in China, whereas there is much more private ownership in Europe. As has been introduced (see 4.3.1), it was difficult to reach an agreement when drafting the ECHR on the right to property among the European countries because of different social and economic reasons. Owing to the different cultural understanding of property

215 Cascina Tre Pini S.s. v. Ministero dell' Ambiente e della Tutela del Territorio e del Mare and Others, Case C-301/12, Judgment of the Court (Second Chamber) of 3 April 2014, §81(1), http://curia.europa.eu/juris/liste.jsf?language=en&jur=C,T,F&num=C-301/12&td=ALL accessed 7 April 2014.

216 Cascina Tre Pini S.s. v. Ministero dell' Ambiente e della Tutela del Territorio e del Mare and Others, Case C-301/12, Judgment of the Court (Second Chamber) of 3 April 2014, §81(3), http://curia.europa.eu/juris/liste.jsf?language=en&jur=C,T,F&num=C-301/12&td=ALL accessed 7 April 2014.

rights, unsurprisingly, there are different forms of property rights in China and in Europe.

Secondly, based on the different ownership, China focuses on the collective interest while Europe countries pay relatively more attention to the private interest when there is any conflict. Collective property represents a social right rather than a personal or individual right and as a consequence is not a right connected with the human rights of a person, aiming to offer individuals the way to a life of freedom and to her or his personal development.[217] China pays much more attention to the collective interests for the reason that the collective organisations can easily unite together to achieve a common goal. This is very important for China as a developing country, which has a huge population, limited natural resources and big differences among different regions. From a biodiversity conservation standpoint, the collective right to land and natural resources is the basis for maintaining the integrity of a territory, avoiding ecological fragmentation and fostering long-term objectives – a key requirement for biodiversity conservation.[218] Collective rights also provide a strong basis for the building and functioning of community institutions, which are quite important for sound long-term land and resource management.[219] These may reflect some of the reasons why China could establish so many protected areas covering a vast area within such a short time, especially since the year 2000. However, it does not mean that China does not need to consider private interests, especially with respect to the interests of local people and communities, when establishing and managing protected areas. Handling these issues with reasonable proportionality is a common concern. Conversely, European countries pay more attention to the private interests and proportionality is a general principle of law which examines whether the relevant parties place too much of a burden on certain individuals (see 4.3).

Thirdly, because of a different cultural background, if there is any conflict, Chinese prefer negotiations, rather than litigations, which will be further discussed in the section of "access to justice" (see 5.3). There are few cases from People's Courts concerning environmental protection or human rights protection. However, the right to a clean and healthy environment became a common phrase for the public in China. There are some cases in Europe, for instance the cases mentioned above, regarding environmental protection and human rights protection. The case law has concentrated on questions of

---

217 Sagel-Grande, H.I. (2000). Property rights and ownership in eastern and western Europe and Article 1 Protocol No. 1 European Convention on Human Rights. In: Loof, J.P., Ploeger, H. & van der Steur, A. (Eds.). *The Right to Property: the Influence of Article 1 Protocol No. 1 ECHR on Several Fields of Domestic Law.* Maastricht: Shaker Publishing, p. 57.

218 Lockwood, M., Kothari, A. & Worboys, G. (Eds.) (2006). *Managing Protected Areas: a Global Guide.* London: Earthscan, p. 132.

219 Lockwood, M., Kothari, A. & Worboys, G. (Eds.) (2006). *Managing Protected Areas: a Global Guide.* London: Earthscan, p. 132.

balance, necessity, and the degree of interference.[220] Therefore, the guidelines and some possible solutions to better balance environmental protection and human rights protection could be drawn from these cases. These guidelines and possible solutions are particularly important for guaranteeing procedural rights and a right of reasonable compensation of local people and communities. Just as what has been discussed in the section of "right to property concerning environmental protection in Europe" (see 4.3), "*it is interesting to note that, while Article 1 Protocol No. 1 ECHR does not include explicit procedural requirements (...)*" and "*(...) Article 1 does not contain an absolute right to claim compensation (...)*", however, some key answers for these missing points can be found in the jurisprudence from the ECtHR.

Fourthly, it is interesting to note that there is no independent human rights law in China, however, besides the "Law of the People's Republic of China on Property Rights" (see 4.2.2), some relevant protected areas conservation laws discussed above (see 4.2.2), for instance the "Regulations of the People's Republic of China on Nature Reserves" (Article 5) and the "Land Management Approach in Nature Reserve" (Article 7), address some issues related to property rights. Conversely, the Bern Convention, the Birds Directive and the Habitats Directive, as the important protected areas conservation law in Europe, do not contain any provision on property rights. But the ECHR and the ECtHR fill this gap to solve the human rights infringement issues in Europe, while the CJEU works as an important player at the EU level.

Last but not least, as for future development, the coverage of protected areas in China is significantly increasing, a better balanced approach for conserving protected areas and protecting human rights is worth pursuing. China began to pay more attention to human rights protection, not only to the substantial rights but also to the procedural rights. For instance, the Information Office of the State Council in China issued a White Paper on "Progress in China's Human Rights in 2012" on 14 May 2013.[221] This White Paper, with a lot of facts and statistics, introduces the new development of human rights protection in China. For the first time an independent chapter is concluded on the "Protection of Human Rights in Ecological Improvement". This chapter can be regarded as a milestone to combine human rights protection and environmental conservation in China. "Protection of Human Rights in Ecological Progress" covers three main parts, namely "the legal and policy framework has been established to protect citizens' environmental rights", "the right to live in a clean and healthy environment has been further protected", and "the guarantee standards for the right to live

---

220 Boyle, A. (2013). Relationship between international environmental law and other branches of international law. In: Bodansky, D., Brunnee, J. & Hey, E. (Eds.). *The Oxford Handbook of International Environmental Law*. Oxford: Oxford University Press, p. 142.

221 Xinhua Net (新华网) (2013). The Progress in China's Human Rights in 2012 (2012 年中国人权事业的进展) Posted on 14 May 2013, http://news.xinhuanet.com/politics/2013-05/14/c_115758619.htm accessed 16 May 2013.

in a clean and healthy environment have been greatly improved". Conversely, European countries have a long history to protect human rights, as at least the ECHR was born in 1950s. Since 1985, there has been a steady increase in conservation-related cases brought before the European human rights organs.[222] In the majority of these cases the applicant complained that conservation measures had disproportionately interfered with his or her right to the peaceful enjoyment of possessions.[223] Only in 1996, the Court found for the first time a violation of Article 1 of Protocol No. 1 in a conservation-related case, namely in *Matos e Silva, Lda. and Others v. Portugal.*[224] This developmental tendency implies that China needs more time to learn some lessons from abroad to solve the conflicts regarding property rights protection and environmental protection in general, and protected areas conservation in particular. Regarding protected areas in Europe, the number of protected areas in Europe is continuously increasing, and better approaches for protected areas conservation have attracted more attention.

Unfortunately, there is no one-size-fits-all solution to solve these kinds of issues to achieve ecological justice in different countries or regions with different social, economic, political and cultural circumstances. The only way is to try to learn from some experiences from the other on the road to pursuing the final goal. Some possible suggestions for China will be explored below.

4.4.2. FROM CONFLICTS TO COOPERATION

Conflicts can be transferred into cooperation if some requirements can be met. Limitations to the right to property need to serve the "general interests" based on respecting the "private interests". Land owners and land users need to be involved in decision-making processes for management planning, as well as in the management itself. It is important to acknowledge their shared responsibilities by setting clear objectives for conservation, but ensure flexibility in agreed

---

222 Desmet, E. (2011). *Indigenous Rights Entwined with Nature Conservation.* Antwerp: Intersentia, p. 254.

223 Desmet, E. (2011). *Indigenous Rights Entwined with Nature Conservation.* Antwerp: Intersentia, p. 254.

224 ECtHR, Mateos e Silva, Lda. and Others v. Portugal (1996), App. No. 15777/89, Judgment of 16 September 1996, http://echr.ketse.com/doc/15777.89-en-19960916/ accessed 2 March 2013. In this case, the Portuguese government sought to create a nature reserve out of land on the Algarve coast, containing parcel owned by the applicants. As for the right to property, the Court accepted that measures pursued through town and country planning for the purposes of protecting the environment serve a legitimate public purpose justifying restrictions on property rights, but found that in this case the restriction was not "necessary" because the government had never implemented the proposed plan for the nature reserve. However, the Court recognised the right to property in this conservation-related case. See Picolotti, R. & Taillant, J.D. (Eds.) (2010). Linking human rights and the environment, www.uapress.arizona.edu/Books/bid1492.htm accessed 2 February 2012.

management measures.[225] Besides these, local knowledge and experience should be used to fill knowledge gaps and to develop site-specific management measures tested over time. This has the added advantage of increasing support and sense of ownership of the process among land owners and land users.[226] What is more, on the one hand, clear outreach, communication, information and education strategies are needed, especially in rural areas in China. Such strategies should, for instance, highlight that a balance can be achieved between (perceived) socio-economic constraints, and benefits and opportunities from protected areas, where clear rights–duties arrangements are developed in collaboration with stakeholders, no matter whether they are individuals or collectives. On the other hand, a differentiated communication approach according to the target groups is essential. For example, land owners and Natura 2000 site users need short, clear and brief factual explanations about rules and (land use or business) opportunities at local level, whereas policy-makers and the general public would rather require reports outlining the wider benefits to society in terms of ecosystem services provided by the Natura 2000 network.[227] This is also a good experience that China could learn from according to the different target groups in the different areas.

As indicated above (see 3.2), the success of the management of Natura 2000 sites is fully dependent on a positive attitude and cooperation from a range of land owners and land users, who have personal ambitions, feelings, emotions and cultural backgrounds. The local people and communities, as the most relevant groups, care more about the environmental situation in the area where they have previously lived in or benefited from (see 4.3.4.3). This should be better reflected in the processes and sufficient time should be allowed for involvement of land owners and land users, who often have a strong emotional bond to the land.[228] This is what China needs to widely adopt for the whole country, although some progress has been made in some protected areas, for instance, in the Wuyishan protected areas in Fujian Province.[229]

---

225 Natura 2000 (2010). Natura 2000 – addressing conflicts and promoting benefits, http://ec.europa.eu/environment/nature/natura2000/management/docs/conflict_solving2010.pdf accessed 20 April 2013.

226 Natura 2000 (2010). Natura 2000 – addressing conflicts and promoting benefits, http://ec.europa.eu/environment/nature/natura2000/management/docs/conflict_solving2010.pdf accessed 20 April 2013.

227 Natura 2000 (2010). Natura 2000 – addressing conflicts and promoting benefits, http://ec.europa.eu/environment/nature/natura2000/management/docs/conflict_solving2010.pdf accessed 20 April 2013.

228 Natura 2000 (2010). Natura 2000 – addressing conflicts and promoting benefits, http://ec.europa.eu/environment/nature/natura2000/management/docs/conflict_solving2010.pdf accessed 20 April 2013.

229 The government in Fujian Province issued a series of policies to improve local people's daily life; at the same time, the government established a formal management mechanism by signing a management contract, establishing a common management authority and so on. For detailed information see Wang, D.Q. & He, K.J. (王权典，何克军) (Ed.) (2012). *The*

4.4.3. FROM PRINCIPLES TO PRACTICE

Environment-related property law at the national level can play an irreplaceable role in the progressive development and implementation of economic, social and cultural rights. The local people and communities cannot achieve real equality without political and territorial rights. Local people's organisations and activists are calling on governments to fully implement their commitments to uphold human rights, including rights to lands and resources as an essential cornerstone for achieving socially just and ecologically sustainable development.[230] These rights cannot play real roles without guarantees from the relevant legislation and regulations. As has been mentioned above, there are some bottom lines and principles that urgently need to be paid attention to. In practice, when determining the property content by law, the legislator has wide discretion to shape what the content limits of property shall be.[231] In other words, he must respect the proportionality principle, i.e. when imposing burdens on private property the goal must be important enough to justify the measure.[232] If there are many measures suited to reach the legitimate goal, only the least burdensome measures can be taken. If the burden resulting from the least intrusive measures is still significant, the legislator or the relevant authority has the duty to provide reasonable compensation. The possible right to compensation of the relevant parties shall be guaranteed by the legislation and regulations. It is reasonable that the protected areas laws provide compensation for every burdensome restrictions of land use in nature protection areas. What is more, the awareness of asking reasonable compensation and legal remedy from local people and communities are also very important in practice.

Even though China has taken significant steps forward in improving human rights protection, for instance "Progress in China's Human Rights in 2012" mentioned above (see 4.4), much more detailed progress on the right to property still needs to be implemented in practice.

Innovation for Rule of Law on Protected Areas and the Methods for the Reformation on Forest – Based on Field Work on the Construction for a Protected Areas Model Province in Guangdong (自然保护区法制创新与"林改"方略 – 基于广东自然保护区示范省建设实施探索). Beijing: China Legal Publishing House (中国法制出版社), pp. 221–224.

230 Forest Peoples Programme (2012). Press release: indigenous peoples insist on human rights-based approaches and respect for traditional knowledge and practices in Rio+20 outcomes. Published on 20 June 2012, www.forestpeoples.org/topics/sustainable-livelihoods/news/2012/06/press-release-indigenous-peoples-insist-rights-based-app accessed 21 June 2012.

231 Wang, D.Q. & He, K.J. (王权典，何克军) (Ed.) (2012). *The Innovation for Rule of Law on Protected Areas and the Methods for the Reformation on Forest – Based on Field Work on the Construction for a Protected Areas Model Province in Guangdong* (自然保护区法制创新与"林改"方略 – 基于广东自然保护区示范省建设实施探索). Beijing: China Legal Publishing House (中国法制出版社), pp. 84–85.

232 This doctrinal construction is somewhat paradoxical: on the one hand the legislator has the power to define and shape property, on the other hand he is bound by some "pre-legal" characteristics of property.

As for the procedural human rights perspective, an open and transparent participation process should be based on a stakeholder analysis, identifying groups which each require their own approach. For example, a small number of key stakeholders should be involved from the start and throughout the process, whereas other groups may only need to be informed and or to be consulted at key stages.[233] Besides the right to information and the right to participation, the right to access to justice (court) cannot be ignored, especially in China where people do not have enough awareness to ask for a legal remedy. These will be discussed in the procedural rights part (see Chapter 5).

When comparing Chinese property rights and property rights in Europe, it is impossible to conclude which one is better. However, it is reasonable to conclude that both these methods (collective ownership and private ownership) are social experiments with a goal of achieving a better balance between property rights protection and protected areas conservation.

233 Natura 2000 (2010). Natura 2000 – addressing conflicts and promoting benefits, http://ec.europa.eu/environment/nature/natura2000/management/docs/conflict_solving2010.pdf accessed 20 April 2013.

CHAPTER 5

PROCEDURAL RIGHTS AND PROTECTED AREAS CONSERVATION

Procedural rights are generally regarded as an aspect of the rule of law and detached from substantive rights.[1] Procedural rights, as entry points for supporting substantive rights,[2] play an irreplaceable role in helping substantive rights come into practice, when an interference occurs. For instance, broad access to information promotes better decisions by mobilising a demand for sustainable solutions to problems.[3] However, procedural guarantees of information and participation can prove insufficient to protect the environment if a fully informed society decides to sacrifice environmental quality in order to advance economic or cultural considerations. Nevertheless, people should be involved in decisions that potentially affect them. To empower people with procedural rights could be a better guarantee for their involvement.

Historically, after the 1972 Stockholm Conference on the Human Environment, environmental scholars and activists began to consider human rights in a more instrumental fashion, identifying those rights whose enjoyment could be considered a prerequisite to effective environmental protection.[4] They focused in particular on the procedural rights of access to environmental information, public participation in decision-making, and access to justice and remedies in the event of environmental harm.[5]

---

1 ECtHR, Al-Nashif v. Bulgaria (2002), App. No. 50963/99, Judgment of 20 June 2002, §§119–129, http://hudoc.echr.coe.int/sites/eng/Pages/search.aspx#{%22fulltext%22:[%22Al-Nashif%20v.%20Bulgaria%22],%22documentcollectionid2%22:[%22GRANDCHAMBER%22,%22CHAMBER%22],%22itemid%22:[%22001-60522%22]} accessed 20 April 2013.

2 Conservation, human rights & protected areas governance: a field-based workshop in the Baviaanskloof Mega-Reserve. (2007). South Africa, 6–7 July 2007, http://cmsdata.iucn.org/downloads/bav_workshop. pdf accessed 10 October 2012, p. 10.

3 Robinson, J R *et al.* (1996). Public access to environmental information: a means to what end? *Journal of Environmental Law*, 8 (1), pp. 19–42.

4 Anton, D.K. & Shelton, D.L. (2011). *Environmental Protection and Human Rights*. Cambridge: Cambridge University Press, p. 356.

5 See, e.g., Kiss, A. (1992). An introductory note on a human right to environment. In: Weiss, E.B. (Ed.), *Environmental Change and International Law*. Tokyo (Japan): United Nations University Press, http://archive.unu.edu/unupress/unupbooks/uu25ee/uu25ee00.htm accessed 8 September 2013, p. 551.

This was confirmed by "Our Common Future" (the Brundtland report) published in 1987. And then, the World Commission on Environment and Development (WCED) adopted a list of proposed legal principles for environmental protection and sustainable development, the first of which reads "*all human beings have the fundamental right to an environment adequate for their health and wellbeing*". Principle 6 specifically concerns the right to information and equal access and due process in administrative and judicial proceedings.[6]

After these, the Convention on Trans-boundary Effects of Industrial Accidents[7] was the first international treaty to contain the three procedural environmental rights, which are the right to information, the right to participation and the right to access to remedies (Article 9). Three months later, these three procedural environmental rights were approved in Principle 10 of the Rio Declaration on Environment and Development.[8] It says that: "*Environmental issues are best handled with the participation of all concerned citizens, at the relevant level. At the national level, each individual shall have appropriate access to information concerning the environment that is held by public authorities; (...) States shall facilitate and encourage public awareness and participation by making information widely available. Effective access to judicial and administrative proceedings, including redress and remedy, shall be provided.*" In order to catalyse and to accelerate action in terms of implementing Principle 10, States adopted the Bali Guidelines[9] in February 2010. The main elements of these voluntary guidelines respectively include that: (1) States should make environmental information available and accessible to any person in an affordable, effective and timely manner; (2) States should provide opportunities for early and effective public participation in decision-making; (3) States should ensure that any natural or legal person has access to a review procedure before a court of law or another independent and impartial body to challenge a decision, act or

6 Dejeant-Pons, M. (2002). Human rights to environmental procedural rights. In: Dejeant-Pons, M. & Pallemaerts, M. (Eds.). *Human Rights and the Environment*. Strasbourg (France): Council of Europe Publishing, p. 23.

7 Convention on the Trans-boundary Effects of Industrial Accident, adopted in Helsinki on 17 March 1992 and entered into force on 19 April 2000, ECE/CP. TEIA/15/Add.1. It is designed to protect people and the environment against industrial accidents, www.unece.org/env/teia/ accessed 1 December 2012.

8 Rio Declaration on Environment and Development (United Nations Conference on Environment and Development, UNCED), adopted in June 1992, A/CONF.151/26, www.unep.org/Documents.Multilingual/Default.asp?documentid=78&articleid=1163 accessed 22 June 2012.

9 UNEP (2011). Guidelines for the Development of National Legislation on Access to Information, Public Participation and Access to Justice in Environmental Matters was adopted at the eleventh Special Session of United Nations Environment Programme Governing Council/Global Ministerial Environmental Forum in Bali, Indonesia, www.unep. org/civil-society/Portals/24105/documents/Guidelines/GUIDELINES_TO_ACCESS_TO_ENV_INFO_2.pdf accessed 18 February 2014.

omission by the public authority; and (4) States should clearly define in their law the specific grounds on which a request for environmental information can be refused.

Besides the international recognition of the importance of procedural rights in environmental issues, in practice, the evaluation of stakeholder involvement is not only important for accountability and auditing purposes but, in line with the more normative and substantive arguments for stakeholder involvement, can help ensure fair representation and involvement and increases our knowledge of human behaviour in some contexts.[10]

The president of the International Union for Conservation of Nature at the time concluded that: "*If local people do not support protected areas then protected areas cannot last*".[11] This understanding, together with the recognition of local stakeholder rights and democratisation of policy processes, has resulted in a move from State-centred to multi-level governance of protected areas,[12] which has been accompanied by the development of mechanisms and management of protected areas. Protected areas therefore represent an appropriate setting in which to evaluate stakeholder involvement.[13]

Under the above-mentioned contexts, a rights-based approach from a procedural rights perspective to conserve protected areas has received great attention the past decades. Indeed, anthropogenic pressures on ecosystem goods and services, combined with the current global financial crisis, are increasingly leading to the devolution of biodiversity governance through stakeholder involvement.[14] However, this approach is not always interpreted and implemented well.

The following sections will respectively introduce the status quo of the legal system of three important procedural rights, namely the right to information, right to participation and right to access to justice in China and in Europe, and then discuss the relationship and potential conflicts regarding three procedural rights and protected areas conservation in China. After that, some baselines and good experience in Europe will be explored for China. Finally, a conclusion

---

10 Rowe, G. & Frewer, L.J. (2004). Evaluating public-participation exercises: a research agenda. *Science, Technology & Human Values*, 29, pp. 512–557.

11 Warren, C. (2002). *Managing Scotland's Environment.* Edinburgh: Edinburgh University Press, p. 196.

12 Lockwood, M. (2010). Good governance for terrestrial protected areas: a framework, principles and performance outcomes. *Journal of Environmental Management*, 91, pp. 754–766.

13 Young, J.C. *et al.* (2013). Does stakeholder involvement really benefit biodiversity conservation? *Biological Conservation*, p. 158, http://ac.els-cdn.com/S0006320712003734/1-s2.0-S0006320712003734-main.pdf?_tid=b4f07e64-a75a-11e2-8ec0-00000aab0f27&acdnat=1366202060_f9f1bfb289f96e75b326b5675d02595d accessed 17 April 2013, pp. 359–370.

14 Young, J., Butler, J.R.A., Jordan, A. & Watt, A.D. (2012). Less government intervention in biodiversity management: risks and opportunities. *Biological Conservation*, 21(4), pp. 1095–1100.

with some possible suggestions for protected areas conservation in China will be made.

5.1. RIGHT TO INFORMATION AND PROTECTED AREAS CONSERVATION

As indicated above, access to environmental information is a prerequisite to public participation in decision-making and to monitoring governmental and private-sector activities.[15] The right to information, as the first and key procedural human right, plays an irreplaceable role in environmental protection in general, and protected areas conservation in specific.

5.1.1. RELATIONSHIP BETWEEN THE RIGHT TO INFORMATION AND PROTECTED AREAS

This section will describe the relationship between the right to information and protected areas in the perspective of international human rights instruments and international environmental instruments. The situations of the general right to information and the right to information of indigenous peoples will be introduced respectively from these two perspectives.

5.1.1.1. Right to Information in International Human Rights Instruments

5.1.1.1.1. General Right to Information in International Human Rights Instruments

The right to information is contained in various human rights texts. Article 19 of the Universal Declaration of Human Rights says that: "*Everyone has the right to freedom of opinion and expression; this right includes freedom to hold opinions without interference and to seek, receive and impart information and ideas through any media and regardless of frontiers.*"[16] Article 19 of the International Covenant on Civil and Political Rights deals with the "*freedom to seek, receive and impart information.*"[17] Besides these, for instance, Article 5(d)(viii) of

15 Anton, D.K. & Shelton, D.L. (2011). *Environmental Protection and Human Rights*. Cambridge: Cambridge University Press, p. 357.

16 Universal Declaration of Human Rights, adopted on 10 December 1948, UN Doc. A/810 AT 71, UNGA Res. 217 A (III), www.un.org/en/documents/udhr/ accessed 4 November 2011.

17 International Covenant on Civil and Political Rights (ICCPR), adopted by the United Nations General Assembly on 16 December 1966 and entered into force from 23 March 1976, 999 UNTS 171. It commits its parties to respect the civil and political rights of individuals, including the right to life, freedom of region, freedom of speech, freedom of

the International Convention on the Elimination of All Forms of Racial Discrimination (ICERD)[18] and Articles 12(1) and 13(1) of the Convention on the Rights of the Child (CRC)[19] also embody the right to information. In addition, international human rights bodies such as the UN Human Rights Committee, the European Court of Human Rights, the Inter-American Court of Human Rights and the European Committee on Social Rights have today accepted the existence of a right to information in certain circumstances.[20]

5.1.1.1.2. Right to Information of Indigenous Peoples in International Human Rights Instruments

In the above context, the right to information of indigenous peoples is also widely recognised in international human rights instruments. For instance, ILO Convention No. 169,[21] as the most comprehensive binding standard in international human rights law on the rights of indigenous peoples, recognises the principle of free and informed consent in the context of relocation. Although this principle aims to reach "consent", the "free and informed" is the vital important premise. "Consent" refers to a freely given decision from the rights-holders based on full, prior and objective information; a decision made by the people or community in question, through their designated representatives and in accordance with their traditions, customs and norms.[22] "Consent" is a type of participation; however, it is regarded as two-way flow of information and the exchange of ideas. This principle can be also found in soft law, for instance, the United Nations Declaration on the Rights of Indigenous Peoples (UNDRIP).[23] Furthermore, the Committee on the Elimination of Racial Discrimination (CERD) addresses in its General Recommendation No. 23 that States parties

---

assembly, electoral rights and rights to due process and a fair trial. http://treaties.un.org/doc/Publication/UNTS/Volume%20999/volume-999-I-14668-English.pdf accessed 9 March 2011.

18 International Convention on the Elimination of All Forms of Racial Discrimination, signed on 21 December 1965 and entered into force on 4 January 1969, 660 UNTS 195, www.ohchr.org/EN/ProfessionalInterest/Pages/CERD.aspx accessed 6 December 2013.

19 Convention on the Rights of the Child, signed on 20 November 1989 and entered into effective on 2 September 1990, 1577 UNTS 3, www.unicef.org/crc/ accessed 7 December 2013.

20 McDonagh, M. (2013). The right to information in international human rights law. *Human Rights Law Review*, http://hrlr.oxfordjournals.org/content/early/2013/02/20/hrlr.ngs045.full.pdf+html accessed 24 March 2014.

21 Articles 15(2) and 16(2), International Labor Organization Convention No. 169: Indigenous and Tribal Peoples Convention, adopted on 27 June 1989 and entered into force on 5 September 1991, 28 ILM 1382, www.ilo.org/indigenous/Conventions/no169/lang--en/index.htm accessed 1 October 2012.

22 UN – REDD (2013). Guidelines on free, prior and informed consent. Geneva: UN – REDD Programme Secretariat, www.unredd.net/index.php?option=com_docman&task=doc_download&gid=8717&Itemid=53 accessed 11 July 2014, p. 36.

23 Article 10, United Nations Declaration on the Rights of Indigenous Peoples (UNDRIP), issued on 13 September 2007, UN Doc. A/RES/61/295, www.un.org/esa/socdev/unpfii/documents/DRIPS_en.pdf accessed 30 October 2012.

should ensure that "*no decisions directly relating to the rights and interests (of indigenous peoples) are taken without their informed consent.*"[24] Remarkably, the CERD has adopted the principle of free, prior and informed consent (FPIC) in nature conservation. As a component of a rights-based approach to address the conflict about the resettlement of the Basarwa/San outside the Central Kalahari Game Reserve,[25] the Committee recommended that the State should "*seek the prior free and informed consent of the persons and groups concerned*".[26]

Recently, the free, prior and informed consent (FPIC) of indigenous peoples was further clarified. The UN Expert Mechanism on the Rights of Indigenous Peoples, particularly its final report of the 2011 study on indigenous peoples and the right to participate in decision-making (A/HRC/18/42),[27] states that "*the duty to obtain the free, prior and informed consent of indigenous peoples is not only a procedural process but a substantive mechanism to ensure the respect of indigenous peoples' rights*". In 2012, the Human Rights Council adopted the "Guiding Principles on extreme poverty and human rights", which states at paragraph 40 that: "*States must ensure that indigenous peoples, who are particularly susceptible to extreme poverty, enjoy the right to free, prior and informed consent through their own representative institutions regarding all decisions concerning the use of their lands, territories and resources by State and non-State actors*".[28] The UN Expert Mechanism on the Rights of Indigenous Peoples said: "*Free, Prior and Informed Consent is one of the most important principles that indigenous peoples believe can protect their right to participation. It is embedded in the right to self-determination. The duty of States to obtain indigenous peoples' free prior informed consent*[29] *entitles indigenous people to effectively determine the outcome of decision-making that affects them, not merely a right to be involved.*"[30]

---

24 CERD (The Committee on the Elimination of Racial Discrimination) (1997). Office of the High Commissioner for Human Rights, "General Recommendation No. 23: Indigenous Peoples", issued on 18 August 1997, §4(d), www.unhchr.ch/tbs/doc.nsf/0/73984290dfea022b802565160056fe1c accessed 29 October 2012.

25 Desmet, E. (2011). *Indigenous Rights Entwined with Nature Conservation*. Antwerp: Intersentia, p. 319.

26 CERD (The Committee on the Elimination of Racial Discrimination) (2006). Conclusions and Recommendation of the Committee on the Elimination of Racial Discrimination, Botswana, UN Doc. CERD/C/BWA/CO/16, §12.

27 UN (2011). United Nations final report of the study on indigenous peoples and the right to participate in decision-making: report of the expert mechanism on the rights of indigenous peoples. Issued on 17 August 2011, www2.ohchr.org/english/bodies/hrcouncil/docs/18session/A-HRC-18–42_en.pdf accessed 11 December 2012.

28 UN (2012). United Nations final draft of the guiding principles on extreme poverty and human rights. Issued on 18 July 2012, www.ohchr.org/Documents/Issues/Poverty/A-HRC-21-39_en.pdf accessed 12 December 2012.

29 Report of the Special Rapporteur on the situation of human rights and fundamental freedoms of indigenous peoples, UN Doc A/HRC/12/34, 2009, §48 and §53, www.refworld.org/docid/4ae5b9f02.html accessed 24 December 2012.

30 Portalewska, A. (2012). Free, prior and informed consent: protecting indigenous peoples' rights to self-determination, participation and decision-making. Published on

5.1.1.1.3. Discussion

It is noted that international human rights instruments have devoted more attention to the principle of free, prior and informed consent of indigenous peoples in the context of natural conservation rather than the general right to information of indigenous peoples. The understanding of "prior informed consent" proposed by the UN Special Rapporteur on indigenous peoples' rights is that prior informed consent does not provide indigenous people with a veto power when the State acts legitimately and faithfully in the public interest, but rather "*establishes the need to frame consultation procedures in order to make every effort to build consensus on the part of all concerned*" and that consensus-driven consultation processes should not only address measures to mitigate or compensate for adverse impacts of projects, but also explore and arrive at means of equitable benefit-sharing in a spirit of true partnership.[31] This understanding clarifies why the principle provides more requirements than the general right to information. Furthermore, although "consent" is a type of participation, the realisation of this principle largely depends on the general right to information (see 5.1.1.1.2). All these might explain why the principle of free, prior and informed consent is so important for indigenous peoples, especially when establishing and managing a protected area on their lands or on the lands they were/are using. Only recently, the CERD explicitly applied the principle of free prior informed consent to the establishment of protected areas on indigenous lands and territories.[32] Although the ILO Convention No. 169 and the UNDRIP have not specifically adopted this principle to the protected areas establishment and management, it could not be said that they would not apply it in this field later. At least, they strongly indicate the importance of the principle for indigenous peoples.

5.1.1.2. Right to Information in International Environmental Instruments

5.1.1.2.1. General Right to Information in International Environmental Instruments

Reliable, relevant, targeted and timely environmental information is an essential element in implementing environmental policy and management

27 November 2012, www.culturalsurvival.org/publications/cultural-survival-quarterly/free-prior-and-informed-consent-protecting-indigenous accessed 14 October 2013.

31 Report of the Special Rapporteur on the situation of human rights and fundamental freedoms of indigenous peoples, UN Doc. A/HRC/12/34, 2009, §48 and §53, www.refworld.org/docid/4ae5b9f02.html accessed 24 December 2012.

32 Desmet, E. (2011). *Indigenous Rights Entwined with Nature Conservation.* Antwerp: Intersentia, p. 322.

processes.[33] Accordingly, the right to information is usually invoked in relation to information about environmental hazards or (potentially) harmful activities for the environment and for human well-being.[34] No conservation-related cases brought before international human rights judicial bodies were found where a violation of the right to information was explicitly alleged.[35] However, access to information is considered to be at the heart of sound environmental protection and sustainable development.[36] It enables citizens to obtain information about the environment and human health, factors affecting or potentially affecting the environment such as pollution, proposed projects that could impact on the environment, laws, policies and international agreements potentially affecting the environment as well as learning about threats to the environment and how to respond to them.[37]

Historically, the right to information was first established by the United Nations Conference on Human Environment in 1972. More specifically, its final Declaration and the following action plan addressed the need for the improvement of access to environmental information on an international level.[38] More than a decade later, the right of an individual to access to environmental information in the sense of sustainable development was mentioned in the Brundtland Report.[39] Based on these, principle 10 of the 1992 Rio Declaration on Environment and Development states: "*at the national level, each individual shall have appropriate access to information concerning the environment that is held by public authorities (...) States shall facilitate and*

33 EEA (European Environment Agency) (2012). *Environmental Indicator report 2012 – Ecosystem Resilience and Resource Efficiency in a Green Economy in Europe*. Luxembourg: Publications Office of the European Union, www.eea.europa.eu/publications/environmental-indicator-report-2012 accessed 9 September 2012, p. 7.

34 Desmet, E. (2011). *Indigenous Rights Entwined with Nature Conservation*. Antwerp: Intersentia, p. 306.

35 Desmet, E. (2011). *Indigenous Rights Entwined with Nature Conservation*. Antwerp: Intersentia, p. 306.

36 Kostic, M. (2006). *The Right of Access to Environmental Information in the Sense of the Aarhus Convention: European Streams and Legal Framework in Serbia and Montenegro*. CPRINT Beograd, p. 20.

37 Bruch, C. (2000). Regional opportunities for improving environmental governance through access to information, public participation and access to justice. In: the Eighth Session of the African Ministerial Conference on Environment (AMCE), Abuja, Nigeria, 3–6 April 2000, www.eli.org/pdf/africa/csamcen00.pdf accessed 14 September 2013.

38 Article 7(a), UNEP (1972). Action Plan for the Human Environment, 11 ILM (1972), 1416, www.unep.org/Documents.multilingual/Default.asp?DocumentID=97&ArticleID=1505&l=en accessed 13 October 2013; Article 7(a) says "It is recommended that Governments and the Secretary General provide equal possibilities for everybody, both by training and by ensuring access to relevant means and information to influence their own environment by themselves".

39 United Nations Report of the World Commission on Environment and Development: Our Common Future (Brundtland Report), adopted on 4 August 1987, A/42/427, http://conspect.nl/pdf/Our_Common_Future-Brundtland_Report_1987.pdf accessed 21 June 2012.

encourage public awareness and participation by making information widely available".[40]

Since then, several environmental instruments have included obligations of State Parties to make information held by the government accessible to members of the public.[41] For example, Article 9 of the Convention on the Trans-boundary Effects of Industrial Accidents requires Parties to "*ensure that adequate information is given to the public in areas capable of being affected by an industrial accident arising out of a hazardous activity.*"[42] Article 6(a)(ii) of the United Nations Framework Convention on Climate Change requires State Parties to "*promote and facilitate (...) public access to information on climate change and its effects.*"[43] The United Nations Convention on Biological Diversity does not oblige State Parties to provide public information. However, Article 15(5) of the CBD specifically refers to the Free Prior and Informed Consent (FPIC). Article 15(2) of the Rotterdam Convention on the Prior Informed Consent Procedure for Certain Hazardous Chemicals and Pesticides in International Trade requires State Parties to ensure "*to the extent practicable*" that the public has appropriate access to certain information on chemical handling, accident management and alternatives.[44] Article 10(1) of the Convention on Persistent Organic Pollutants requires each Party to ensure that the public has access to public information.[45] Remarkably, the Aarhus Convention is a landmark international convention for procedural human rights relating to environmental protection. The Convention establishes some minimum standards to be achieved in a democratic context. The right to information is one of the important pillars in this Convention. It will be discussed in detail in the European part (see 5.1.3).

---

40 Principle 10, Rio Declaration on Environment and Development (The United Nations Conference on Environment and Development, UNCED), adopted in June 1992, A/CONF. 151/26, www.unep.org/Documents.Multilingual/Default.asp?documentid=78&articleid=1163 accessed 22 June 2012.

41 Kravchenko, S. (2009). Is access to environmental information a fundamental human right? *Oregon Review of International Law*, 11, http://law.uoregon.edu/org/oril/docs/11-2/Kravchenko.pdf accessed 23 September 2013, pp. 228–266.

42 Article 9(1), Convention on the Trans-boundary Effects of Industrial Accident, adopted in Helsinki on 17 March 1992 and entered into force on 19 April 2000, ECE/CP. TEIA/15/Add.1. It is designed to protect people and the environment against industrial accidents, www.unece.org/env/teia/ accessed 1 December 2012.

43 Article 6(a)(ii), United Nations Framework Convention on Climate Change (UNFCCC), adopted on 9 May 1992 and entered into force 21 March 1994, 1771 UNTS 107; 31 ILM 849, http://unfccc.int/2860.php accessed 8 June 2012.

44 Article 15(2), Rotterdam Convention on the Prior Informed Consent Procedure for Certain Hazardous Chemicals and Pesticides in International Trade, adopted on 10 September 1998 and revised in 2011, www.pic.int/TheConvention/Overview/TextoftheConvention/tabid/1048/language/en-US/Default.aspx accessed 8 June 2012.

45 Article 10(1), Stockholm Convention on Persistent Organic Pollutants, signed on 22 May 2001 and entered into effect from May 2004, www.pops.int/documents/convtext/convtext_en.pdf accessed 18 September 2013.

Broader guarantees of public information can be found in other multilateral treaties, such as the Espoo Convention on Environmental Impact Assessment in a Trans-boundary Context (Article 3(8));[46] the Helsinki Convention on Protection and Use of Trans-boundary Watercourses and International Lakes (Article 16);[47] the Convention for the Protection of the Marine Environment of the North-East Atlantic (Article 9).[48] These Conventions require the contracting parties to ensure that their competent authorities are required to make available relevant information to any natural or legal person, in response to any reasonable request, without the person having to prove an interest, without unreasonable charges, and within two months of the request. Other treaties require State parties to inform the public of specific environmental hazards. For instance, the preamble of the International Atomic Energy Agency (IAEA) Joint Convention on the Safety of Spent Fuel Management and on the Safety of Radioactive Waste Management[49] recognises the importance of informing the public on issues regarding the safety of spent fuel and radioactive waste management. This is reinforced in Articles 6 and 13, on the siting of proposed facilities, which require each State party to take the appropriate steps to ensure that procedures are established and implemented to make information available to members of the public on the safety of any proposed spent-fuel management facility or radioactive waste management facility. Similarly, Article 10(1) of the Stockholm Convention on Persistent Organic Pollutants[50] specifies that each party shall, within its capabilities, promote and facilitate provision to the public of all available information on persistent organic pollutants and ensure that the public has access to public information and that the information is kept up to date (Article 10(1)(b) and (2)). The provisions of these treaties reflect that there is an obligation to make information held by government accessible to the public.

46 Convention on Environmental Impact Assessment in a Trans-boundary Context (Espoo Convention), adopted on 25 February 1991, www.unece.org/fileadmin/DAM/env/eia/documents/legaltexts/conventiontextenglish.pdf accessed 1 October 2013.

47 Helsinki Convention on Protection and Use of Trans-boundary Watercourses and International Lakes, adopted on 17 March 1992, www.unece.org/fileadmin/DAM/env/water/pdf/watercon.pdf accessed 1 October 2013.

48 Convention for the Protection of the Marine Environment of the North-East Atlantic (the OSPAR Convention), adopted on 22 September 1992, www.ospar.org/content/content.asp?menu=00340108070000_000000_000000 accessed 1 October 2013.

49 International Atomic Energy Agency (IAEA) Joint Convention on the Safety of Spent Fuel Management and on the Safety of Radioactive Waste Management, opened for signature on 29 September 1997 and entered into force on 18 June 2001, www.iaea.org/Publications/Documents/Conventions/jointconv.html accessed 1 October 2013.

50 Stockholm Convention on Persistent Organic Pollutants, signed on 22 May 2001 and effective from May 2004, www.pops.int/documents/convtext/convtext_en.pdf accessed 18 September 2013.

5.1.1.2.2. Right to Information of Indigenous Peoples in International Environmental Instruments

It is widely accepted that indigenous peoples are particularly affected by environmental harm and sometimes by environmental protection. Their right to information is mentioned specifically in a number of binding and voluntary international instruments with respect to lands, waters and natural resource use, genetic resources and traditional knowledge, innovations and practices. Binding provisions include for instance Articles 6(2), 7, 12(1), 15(1) and 16(1) from the Nagoya Protocol to the Convention on Biological Diversity.[51] Voluntary guidelines include for instance numbers 37 and 38 of the Akwé: Kon[52] Guidelines for the Conduct of Cultural, Environmental and Social Impact Assessment regarding Developments Proposed to Take Place on, or which are Likely to Impact on, Sacred Sites and on Lands and Waters Traditionally Occupied or Used by Indigenous and Local Communities;[53] sections 1(4) and 2(8), (10) and (11) of the Tkarihwaié:Ri[54] Code of Ethical Conduct to Ensure Respect for the Cultural and Intellectual Heritage of Indigenous and Local Communities;[55] number 9(9) of the Food and Agriculture Organization Voluntary Guidelines on the Responsible Governance of Tenure Guidelines.[56]

5.1.1.3. Right to Information in Protected Areas Conservation Law

Since the linkages of the right to information and environmental protection were widely acknowledged as discussed above, the indigenous peoples' right to information in protected areas conservation was approved by Activity 2.2.5 of the CBD Programme of Work on Protected Areas.[57]

---

51 Nagoya Protocol to the Convention on Biological Diversity, adopted on 29 October 2010, www.cbd.int/abs/doc/protocol/nagoya-protocol-en.pdf accessed 1 October 2012.

52 The word "Akwé: Kon" is a holistic Mohawk term meaning "everything in creation" provided by the Kahnawake community located near Montreal, where the guidelines were negotiated.

53 Akwé: Kon Guidelines for the Conduct of Cultural, Environmental and Social Impact Assessment regarding Developments Proposed to Take Place on, or which are Likely to Impact on, Sacred Sites and on Lands and Waters Traditionally Occupied or Used by Indigenous and Local Communities was issued in 2004, https://www.cbd.int/doc/publications/akwe-brochure-en.pdf accessed 1 October 2012.

54 The word "Tkarihwaié:Ri" is a Mohawk term meaning "the proper way". The term was provided by the Elders of the Mohawk Community of Kahnawake. The Mohawk are the traditional custodians of the area of Montreal where the code was negotiated.

55 Tkarihwaié:ri Code of Ethical Conduct to Ensure Respect for the Cultural and Intellectual Heritage of Indigenous and Local Communities was adopted in 2011, www.cbd.int/traditional/code/ethicalconduct-brochure-en.pdf accessed 1 October 2012.

56 Food and Agriculture Organization Voluntary Guidelines on the Responsible Governance of Tenure Guidelines. Issued in 2012, www.fao.org/docrep/016/i2801e/i2801e.pdf accessed 2 December 2012.

57 The CBD Programme of Work on Protected Areas, issued in 2004, www.cbd.int/doc/publications/pa-text-en.pdf accessed 1 October 2012.

Besides, some important conventions concerning protected areas also explicitly point out the importance of access to information. For example, Article 27 of the Convention Concerning the Protection of the World Cultural and Nature Heritage[58] pointed out that: "*The State Parties to this Convention shall endeavor by all appropriate means, and in particular by educational channel and information programmes, to strengthen appreciation and respect by their peoples of the cultural and natural heritage (...) they shall undertake to keep the public broadly informed of the dangers threatening this heritage and of the activities carried on in pursuance of this Convention.*"

Indigenous peoples are the most relevant parties for protected areas conservation. The principle of free, prior and informed consent is of great significance to guarantee their rights and interests. For instance, the Charter of the Indigenous and Tribal Peoples of the Tropical Forest points out that: "*Control of our territories and the resources that we depend on: all development in our areas should only go ahead with the free, prior and informed consent of the indigenous people involved or affected.*"[59] The IUCN and WPC approved that "*to ensure the establishment of protected areas is based on the free, prior informed consent of indigenous peoples.*"

Not only indigenous peoples mentioned above, but also local communities, NGOs and the broader public could have a right to access the relevant information. What's more, the right to information refers to, but is not limited to a legal requirement to have key protected area information (e.g. designation, roles, responsibilities, vision and key objectives, boundaries and zones, management plans, budgets, progress, achievements) made available in a transparent way (on a website, via public reports, newsletters or other) to the public or to some rights-holders and stakeholders in particular.[60] The essential feature is that local people and communities can get enough information on the planning of establishing a protected area. By this way they could be really involved in the designation and management of protected areas, as well as get some reasonable benefit-sharing from the protected areas management. It must surely be accepted by now that, unless people have been informed about the way

---

58 Convention Concerning the Protection of the World Cultural and Natural Heritage (World Heritage Convention) was adopted on 16 November 1972 and entered into force on 17 December 1975, 11 ILM (1972) 1358, http://portal.unesco.org/en/ev.php-URL_ID=13055&URL_DO=DO_TOPIC&URL_SECTION=201.htm accessed 8 June 2012.

59 Article 21, Charter of the Indigenous and Tribal Peoples of the Tropical Forest was adopted by the IAITPTF (International Alliance of the Indigenous and Tribal Peoples of the Tropical Forests) on 15 February 1992 and revised on 22 November 2002, www.forestpeoples.org/partners/international-alliance-indigenous-and-tribal-peoples-tropical-forests-iaitptf accessed 22 March 2013.

60 Borrini-Feyerabend, G., Dudley, N., Jaeger, T., Lassen, B., Broome, N.P., Phillips, A. & Sandwith, T. (2013). *Governance of Protected Areas: from Understanding to Action.* Best Practice Protected Area Guidelines Series No. 20. Gland (Switzerland): IUCN, https://cmsdata.iucn.org/downloads/iucn_governance_1109_1.pdf accessed 26 September 2013, p. 91.

a project is designed and managed, they will not feel that it is "theirs", whatever (often temporary) benefits they derive from it.[61] In addition, some information on a project in or near protected areas should be accessible for the public, especially for the local people and communities, for the reason that this project could destroy or damage protected areas. For instance, information about building a dam or mining in or near protected areas should be made accessible. If local people and communities feel protected areas are "theirs", they would certainly help the relevant conservation authorities to play an irreplaceable role in protected areas conservation.

The status quo of the right to information concerning nature conservation, especially protected areas conservation, in China and in Europe will be respectively discussed in the next two sections.

5.1.2. RIGHT TO INFORMATION AND PROTECTED AREAS CONSERVATION IN CHINA

Among the procedural rights, the right to information, the right to participation and the right to access to justice are very important, but they are not always fully taken into account in China. For example, in the Binzhou Shellfish Bank Wetland Marine Nature Reserve, local enterprise owners have appealed to the National People's Congress for a more open and transparent designation and management process, in order to safeguard the rights of the affected communities and reduce the conflicts regarding conservation and local development needs.[62]

Early transparency experiments in China were conducted by the collective work of villagers, enterprises, public organisations, the governing political party, and government agencies.[63] In many cases farmers are informed of their rights by local governments and local leaders who may not always tell them the full content of such rights.[64] However, although farmers are increasingly well informed about their rights nowadays, it is still insufficient for them to access the

61 Turton, D. (2002). The mursi and the elephant question. In: Chatty, D. & Colchester, M. (Eds.). *Conservation and Mobile Indigenous Peoples: Displacement, Forced Settlement and Sustainable Development*. Oxford: Berghahn Books, p. 110.

62 Li, L. (2006). Topics about environment at the National People's Congress. China Environment News No. 8. Published on 6 March 2006 (in Chinese).

63 Liu, W.J. (2011). Approaching democracy through transparency: a comparative law study on Chinese open government information. *American University International Law Review*, 26(4), www.law.yale.edu/documents/pdf/Intellectual_Life/CLC_Liu_Wenjing-Approaching_democracy_through_transparency_2010.pdf accessed 23 October 2012, p. 98.

64 Van Rooij, B. (2010). Land loss and conflict in China: illustrated by cases from Yunnan province. In: Ubink, J.M., Hoekema, A.J. & Assies, W.J. (Eds.). *Legalizing Land Rights – Local Practices, State Responses and Tenure Security in Africa, Asia and Latin America*. Leiden: Leiden University Press, p 451.

legal system. This developmental process of right to information for farmers is a typical example for local people in or near a protected area in China.

Nevertheless, the right to information is a key tool to show that government actions are all fulfilling their public responsibilities according to the law. With economic development being the overwhelming motivation behind almost every institutional construction including transparency in mid-1980s China, the inherent tension between public power and the right to information was almost not touched either by the general public, or by immature lawyers and academics.[65] What is the legal system and policy for the right to information in environmental protection, especially protected areas conservation in China? What are the conflicts regarding the right to information and protected areas conservation and their possible cooperation in China? These two questions will be discussed in the sections below.

5.1.2.1. *Legal and Policy Framework Concerning the Right to Information*

5.1.2.1.1. Legal and Policy Framework Concerning the Right to Information in General

China's Constitution does not specifically address information rights,[66] nor does Chinese environmental law. The first official statement on government transparency appeared in 1988, when the Secretariat of the CPC (Communist Party of China) Central Committee proposed the disclosure of all administrative regulations, procedures, and decisions in preparation for democracy.[67] Some principles of openness were contained in some laws and regulations by the late 1990s.[68] Since the 1997 report to the Fifteenth National Congress of the CPC

65 Liu, W.J. (2011). Approaching democracy through transparency: a comparative law study on Chinese open government information. *American University International Law Review*, 26(4), www.law.yale.edu/documents/pdf/Intellectual_Life/CLC_Liu_Wenjing-Approaching_democracy_through_transparency_2010.pdf accessed 23 October 2012, p. 98.

66 Horsley, J.P. (2007). Toward a more open China. In: Florini, A. (Ed.). *The Right to Know: Transparency for an Open World*. New York: Columbia University Press, www.law.yale.edu/documents/pdf/Intellectual_Life/CL-OGI-Toward_More_Open-English.pdf accessed 24 October 2012.

67 See Liu, J. (刘杰) (2005). *The Right to Know and Laws on Information Disclosure* (知情权与信息公开法). Beijing: Qinghua University Press (北京：清华大学出版社有限公司), p. 246.

68 Article 4, the "Law on Administrative Penalty" [中华人民共和国行政处罚法], promulgated by National People's Congress on 17 March 1996, and entered into effective on 1 October 1996, www.npc.gov.cn/englishnpc/Law/2007–12/11/content_1383613.htm accessed 18 April 2013. ("An administrative Penalty shall be imposed in adherence to the principles of fairness and openness (…) Regulations on administrative penalty to be imposed for violations of law must be published; those which are not published shall not be taken as the basis for administrative penalty"). Article 31 requires parties to be notified of both "the facts, grounds and basis on which the administrative penalties are to be decided" and the rights of remedy which are required before a decision of penalty is imposed. In addition, Articles 42 and 43 of the Law provide a right to and prescribe a procedure for public hearings.

Central Committee, in which then-General Secretary Zemin Jiang stressed the "principles of fairness, justice and openness",[69] the practice of open government started to blossom throughout the country, almost simultaneously with the assistance of "government".[70]

It is noted that, with several years of experimental practice, the Guangzhou Municipal government was well prepared to take the leap to the "Rules on open government information of Guangzhou Municipality" (Guangzhou OGI Rules).[71] The Rules are generally credited as the first official legislation on open government information (OGI). For the first time in China's history, the "right to know" was provided formally by statute.[72] After this, the Shanghai Municipal government adopted China's first provincial-level OGI legislation (Shanghai OGI Rules) in January 2004.[73] It is interesting to point out that the Guangzhou Rules define individuals and organisations as "persons with the right to access", and government agencies and their functionaries as "persons with the obligation to make public". The Shanghai OGI Rules similarly provide that citizens, legal persons, and other organisations have the "right to request information" from government agencies, and conversely impose "a legal obligation" on the agencies to disclose all information not covered by a specified exemption.[74] It is a good sign that local regulations clarify "right" and "obligation". In addition, in February 2004, the business centre of Shenzhen in Guangdong province

69 Jiang, Z.M. (江泽民) (1997). Hold high the great banner of Deng Xiaoping theory, for an all-around advancement of the cause of building socialism with Chinese characteristics in the 21st Century (高举邓小平理论伟大旗帜，把建设有中国特色社会主义事业全面推向二十一世纪). In: The Fifteenth National Congress of the Communist Party of China (中国共产党第十五次全国代表大会), http://www.fas.org/news/china/1997/970912-prc.htm, http://news.xinhuanet.com/zilia/2003-01/20content_697189.htm accessed 23 October 2012.

70 See Liu, J. (刘杰) (2005). *The Right to Know and Laws on Information Disclosure* (知情权与信息公开法). Beijing: Qinghua University Press (北京：清华大学出版社有限公司). pp. 247–248.

71 The "Rules on Open Government Information of Guangzhou Municipality" [广州市政府信息公开规定] (2003 Guangzhou Rules) was promulgated on 6 November 2002 and entered into effective on 1 January 2003, www.people.com.cn/item/flfgk/dffg/1992/D442053199204.html accessed 23 October 2012. It is a statute issued by the local government.

72 The "Rules on Open Government Information of Guangzhou Municipality" [广州市政府信息公开规定] (2003 Guangzhou Rules) was promulgated on 6 November 2002 and entered into effective on 1 January 2003, www.people.com.cn/item/flfgk/dffg/1992/D442053199204.html accessed 23 October 2012.

73 The "Rules on Open Government Information of Shanghai Municipality" [上海市政府信息公开规定], www.chinacourt.org/flwk/show1.php?file_id=91244. See also Jamie Horsley, "Shanghai Advances the Cause of Open Government Information in China" (2004), www.freedominfo.org/news/shanghai/index.htm (with an English translation by The China Law Center, Yale Law School).

74 The Guangzhou OGI Provisions specifically apply to foreigners requesting information, but other local OGI provisions are typically limited to Chinese citizens and organisations. Nonetheless, some localities such as Shanghai have announced that foreign individuals, legal persons, organisations, and news media will in practice be given equal access to government information.

passed China's first "online OGI" provisions.[75] By the end of the year, more than 24 provincial and municipal-level governments had adopted OGI legislation, and the spread of local legislation continued throughout the country until an announcement in September 2006 that national Open Government Information Regulations might be issued by the end of that year.[76] They aim to protect the "right to know" of individuals and organisations – a right that does not appear in China's Constitution and is not defined specifically as such in any national law to date – and establish two fundamental and, for China, novel ideas: that Chinese government agencies have an "obligation" to disseminate on their own initiative and disclose upon request most of the information that they hold, and that Chinese citizens have a "right" to access such information.[77]

In fact, the concept of a "right to know" first appeared in scholarly literature in the early 1990s, and is now frequently cited in scholarly articles, media reports and even policy documents.[78] For instance, it was mentioned in an important party document issued by the Fourth Plenum of the sixteenth Party Congress Central Committee in September 2004 as one of the Chinese people's "democratic rights" that need to be protected, as well as in the March 2005 Joint Opinions.[79] The right to know was also listed as one of the civil and political rights in China's White Paper on Human Rights Progress in China in 2003,[80] released by the State Council Information Office on 30 March 2004.[81]

---

75 The "Measures of Shenzhen Municipality for Online Open Government Information" [深圳市政府信息网上公开办法] (2004), went into effect 1 April 2004, www.chinacourt.org/flwk/show1.php?file_id=92369 accessed 8 October 2013. It requires government agencies to disseminate and post online, on their own initiative, some 35 categories of information, but do not provide a mechanism for requesting information that is not disseminated.

76 Horsley, J.P. (2007). Toward a more open China. In: Florini, A. (Ed.). *The Right to Know: Transparency for an Open World.* New York: Columbia University Press, www.law.yale.edu/documents/pdf/Intellectual_Life/CL-OGI-Toward_More_Open-English.pdf accessed 24 October 2012.

77 Horsley, J.P. (2007). Toward a more open China. In: Florini, A. (Ed.). *The Right to Know: Transparency for an Open World.* New York: Columbia University Press, www.law.yale.edu/documents/pdf/Intellectual_Life/CL-OGI-Toward_More_Open-English.pdf accessed 24 October 2012.

78 Horsley, J.P. (2007). Toward a more open China. In: Florini, A. (Ed.). *The Right to Know: Transparency for an Open World.* New York: Columbia University Press, www.law.yale.edu/documents/pdf/Intellectual_Life/CL-OGI-Toward_More_Open-English.pdf accessed 24 October 2012.

79 Wen, J.B. (温家宝) (2004). Report on the work of the government (政府工作报告). Section III, www.peopledaily.com.cn/GB/shizheng/1024/2394441.html accessed 24 October 2012; Opinions of the General Office of the Central Committee of the Chinese Communist Party and of the State Council on Further Promoting Open Government Affairs (中国中央报告厅, 国务院办公厅关于进一步推行政务公开的意见). Published on 24 March 2005, http://news.xinhuanet.com/newscenter/2005-04/26/content_2877607.htm accessed 25 October 2012.

80 People's Daily (人民日报) (2003). Human rights progress in China in 2003 (2003 中国人权事业的进展). www.people.com.cn/GB/shizheng/1026/2418866.html and http://english.peopledaily.com.cn/whitepaper/hr2004/hr2004(2).html accessed 25 October 2012.

81 Horsley, J.P. (2007). Toward a more open China. In: Florini, A. (Ed.). *The Right to Know: Transparency for an Open World.* New York: Columbia University Press,

Under these contexts, the "Regulation of the People's Republic of China on Open Government Information" (OGI Regulations)[82] was issued by the State Council in 2007. This regulation has provided the principles, guidelines, scopes, procedures and other important aspects for information openness. Under China's unitary legal system, the OGI Regulations, as a milestone of citizens' right to know, would apply not only to central government agencies but also extend the disclosure obligation downward through the Chinese government hierarchy to the provinces, villages and townships, the lowest level of the government in China.[83] Comparatively speaking, the OGI regulations are more conservative than many of the local predecessors. By not establishing a clear presumption of disclosure or purporting to grant information "rights" per se, they follow the basic structure of and utilise many of the mechanisms adapted in China's local information regimes and found in information access system around the world.[84] With this legislation taking effect, "*China officially started its own process of developing an effective, enforceable nationwide information access regime.*"[85] Article 8 of the OGI Regulations states that the government information disclosed by administrative agencies may not endanger State security, public security, economic security and social stability.[86] Article 14 states "*administrative agencies may not disclose government information that involves national secrets, commercial secrets or individual privacy*".[87] There is no clear definition about "national secret" and "commercial secret", which will be further explained in the "Law on Guarding State Secrets" below. Even if the relevant authorities have the obligation to provide information, they can refuse to publish information if that information would infringe upon a "national

www.law.yale.edu/documents/pdf/Intellectual_Life/CL-OGI-Toward_More_Open-English.pdf accessed 24 October 2012.

82 The "Regulations of the People's Republic of China on Open Government Information" [中华人民共和国政府信息公开条例] was adopted on 17 January 2007 and entered into effective on 1 May 2008, www.law.yale.edu/documents/pdf/Intellectual_Life/Ch_OGI_Regualtions_Eng_Final_051607.pdf accessed 25 October 2012.

83 Horsley, J.P. (2007). China adopts first nationwide open government information regulations. Published on 9 May 2007, www.law.yale.edu/documents/pdf/Intellectual_Life/Ch_China_Adopts_1st_OGI_Regulations.pdf accessed 12 October 2012.

84 Horsley, J.P. (2007). China adopts first nationwide open government information regulations. Published on 9 May 2007, www.law.yale.edu/documents/pdf/Intellectual_Life/Ch_China_Adopts_1st_OGI_Regulations.pdf accessed 12 October 2012.

85 Horsley, J.P. (2007). China adopts first nationwide open government information regulations. Published on 9 May 2007, www.law.yale.edu/documents/pdf/Intellectual_Life/Ch_China_Adopts_1st_OGI_Regulations.pdf accessed 12 October 2012.

86 He, M. & Cliquet, A. (2013). Sustainable development through a rights-based approach to conserve protected areas in China. *China-EU Law Journal*. DOI 10.1007/s 12689-013-0031-7. http://link.springer.com/article/10.1007%2Fs12689-013-0031-7 accessed 4 November 2013.

87 Article 4, the "Measures on Open Environmental Information (for trial implementation)" [环境信息公开办法（试行）] was adopted on 8 February 2007 and entered into effective on 1 May 2008, www.epa.gov/ogc/china/open_environmental.pdf accessed 24 October 2012.

secret" or "business secret". It could lead to the abuse of "national secret" and "commercial secret".[88]

Nevertheless, in order to better implement the OGI Regulations, the local government also published the related regulation, for instance "Measures of Hunan Province to Implement the Regulations of the People's Republic of China on Open Government Information".[89] The State Council General Office recently released additional guidance on handling OGI requests that appears to endorse a restrictive interpretation of the "special needs" language of Article 13 of the Regulations, although it also urges government agencies to more proactively disseminate information that is the subject of a request but is something the general public should or might want to know about, both so as to reduce the number of requests and to increase the efficiency of OGI work.[90]

Similarly with China's inaugural OGI Regulations, it is clear that much work remains to be done on the government side in terms of additional clarification, updating the Regulations, making revisions of conflicting legislation like the State Secrets and Archives Laws, and the eventual adoption of a more authoritative access to information law, as well as providing necessary resources, training and guidance to improve government performance and understanding of its OGI obligations.[91]

Besides these, some restrictions on access to information were approved by the "Law on Guarding State Secrets".[92] The law defined "State secrets" broadly, to encompass "*matters that affect the security and interests of the State and, as*

---

88 Wang, C. (王超) (2013). *Study on Legal System for Public Participation in Promoting Ecological Progress* (公众参与生态文明建设法制制度研究). Master dissertation in Environment and Resources Protection Law of Central South University of Forestry and Technology (中南林业科技大学环境资源保护法硕士学位论文), pp. 20–22.

89 The "Measures of Hunan Province to Implement the Regulations of the People's Republic of China on Open Government Information" [湖南省关于执行中华人民共和国政府信息公开条例的办法], adopted on 27 October 2009 and entered into Effective on 1 January 2010, www.law.yale.edu/documents/pdf/Intellectual_Life/CL-OGI_Hunan_OGI_Measures_%28Eng_FINAL%29.pdf accessed 23 October 2012.

90 The "State Council General Office Opinions on Doing a Good Job of Disclosing Government Information on Request" [国务院办公厅关于做好政府信息依申请公开工作的意见], Document Guobanfa [2010] No. 5, 12 January 2010, www.hubei.gov.cn/zwgk/zfxxgk/zfxxgkgd/201002/t20100201_112443.shtml accessed 5 October 2012.

91 Horsley, J.P. (2010). Update on China's open government information regulations: surprising public demand yielding some positive results. Posted 23 April 2010, www.freedominfo.org/2010/04/update-on-china-open-government-information-regulations accessed 5 September 2012.

92 The first statute on government information in China after 1949 was the "Provisional Regulations on Safeguarding State Secrets" [保守国家机密暂行条例], which was promulgated by the State Council in 1951. The Regulations remained in effect until 1989, when the "Law on Guarding State Secrets" was enacted. The "Law on Guarding State Secrets" [保守国家秘密法], promulgated by Standing Committee of National People's Congress on 5 September 1988, entered into effective on 1 May 1989, and then revised on 29 April 2010, entered into effective on 1 October 2010, www.lawinfochina.com/law/display.asp?id=1191 accessed 23 October 2012.

specified by legal procedure, are entrusted to a limited number of people for a given period of time."[93] This definition is illustrated by general categories of information such as secrets "*concerning major policy decisions on State affairs*", "*secrets in national economic and social development*", and "*secrets of political parties that conform with the provisions of the preceding clause of this Article.*"[94] The amendments to the Law in 2010 made the procedure of defining State secrets (classification) and safeguarding them more practical and clearer. The general definition of "State secrets", however, remains almost untouched from the 1989 version.[95] Later, the "Implementation Regulations of the People's Republic of China on Guarding State Secrets", which is effective since 1 March 2014, emphasise that the scope of guarding State secrets should be updated accordingly.[96]

In practice, the legislation and regulations[97] require government to disclose on its own initiative a broad range of information about its operations and that is deemed to be of particular interest to the public, using a variety of channels ranging from public libraries, government offices and the Internet.[98] Even prior

---

93 The first statute on government information in China after 1949 was the "Provisional Regulations on Safeguarding State Secrets" [保守国家机密暂行条例], which was promulgated by the State Council in 1951. The Regulations remained in effect until 1989, when the Law on Guarding State Secrets was enacted. See Article 2, "Law on Guarding State Secrets" [保守国家秘密法], promulgated by Standing Committee of National People's Congress on 5 September 1988, entered into effective on 1 May 1989, and then revised on 29 April 2010, entered into effective on 1 October 2010, www.lawinfochina.com/law/display.asp?id=1191 accessed 23 October 2012.

94 The first statute on government information in China after 1949 was the "Provisional Regulations on Safeguarding State Secrets" [保守国家机密暂行条例], which was promulgated by the State Council in 1951. The Regulations remained in effect until 1989, when the Law on Guarding State Secrets was enacted. See Article 8(1)(4)–(5), "Law on Guarding State Secrets" [保守国家秘密法], promulgated by Standing Committee of National People's Congress on 5 September 1988, entered into effective on 1 May 1989, and then revised on 29 April 2010, entered into effective on 1 October 2010, www.lawinfochina.com/law/display.asp?id=1191 accessed 23 October 2012.

95 Liu, W.J. (2011). Approaching democracy through transparency: a comparative law study on Chinese open government information. *American University International Law Review*, 26(4), www.law.yale.edu/documents/pdf/Intellectual_Life/CLC_Liu_Wenjing-Approaching_democracy_through_transparency_2010.pdf accessed 23 October 2012, p. 98.

96 The "Implementation Regulations of the People's Republic of China on Guarding State Secrets" [中华人民共和国保守国家秘密法实施条例] was issued in February 2014 and went to effective on 1 March 2014, http://news.163.com/14/0203/02/9K4HVN5800014AED.html accessed 9 February 2014.

97 For instance, Article 4, the " Opinions of the General Office of the State Council on Various Issues of Implementing the Open Government Information Regulations of the People's Republic of China" [国务院办公厅关于贯彻落实中华人民共和国政府信息公开条例的各种问题的意见] was issued on 29 April 2008, www.law.yale.edu/documents/pdf/Intellectual_Life/CL-OGI-State_Council_Opinions-English.pdf accessed 22 October 2012.

98 Horsley, J.P. (2010). Update on China's open government information regulations: surprising public demand yielding some positive results. Posted 23 April 2010, www.freedominfo.org/2010/04/update-on-china-open-government-information-regulations accessed 5 September 2012.

to the Regulations, government agencies were releasing and posting on their websites an ever increasing amount of information, although they recognise that texts of regulations and speeches by leaders are not necessarily what the people most want to know about.[99] Now many government websites have special OGI columns, leaders' mailboxes and chat-room capability, although a study conducted by the Chinese Academy of Social Sciences of government websites toward the end of 2009 found that many websites are not well organised and operable.[100]

More broadly, information disclosure is spreading to institutions not technically covered by the Regulations, including the courts and the Party.[101] The Supreme People's Court (SPC)[102] has announced, referring to the Regulations, that the courts should start making judicial proceedings, their decisions and enforcement information more open to the public.[103] Mandatory information disclosure and disclosure upon request are two main types of administrative action. This is confirmed by the "Supreme People's Court's Judicial Interpretation on Several Issues of Adjudicating Open Government Information Administrative Litigation",[104] which listed four types of specific administrative actions, including both mandatory information disclosure and information disclosure upon request, which shall be accepted by a court. Some citizens also began to seek information through administrative appeals. For example, on 26 May 2008, 68 villagers asked Yuyao City government in Zhejiang province to provide more information on expropriating more than 200 mu (about 0.133 km^2) land in the village for an unclear reason. On 4 July 2008, they

99 Horsley, J.P. (2010). Update on China's open government information regulations: surprising public demand yielding some positive results. Posted 23 April 2010, www.freedominfo.org/2010/04/update-on-china-open-government-information-regulations accessed 5 September 2012.

100 Clem, W. (2010). Half of websites miss the mark. Published in South China Morning. Post on 23 February 2010, www.scmp.com/portal/site/SCMP/menuitem.2af62ecb329d3d7733492d9253a0a0a0/?vgnextoid=12f549df716f6210VgnVCM100000360a0a0aRCRD accessed 5 September 2012.

101 Horsley, J.P. (2010). Update on China's open government information regulations: surprising public demand yielding some positive results. Posted 23 April 2010, www.freedominfo.org/2010/04/update-on-china-open-government-information-regulations accessed 5 September 2012.

102 The People's Court is translated from "人民法院" in Chinese. The different levels of the People's Court will be discussed further in section 5.3.1.2.

103 The "Supreme People's Court Issues Notice of Six Provisions on Judicial Transparency and Certain Provisions on Acceptance by the People's Courts of Supervision by the Media and Public Opinion" [最高人民法院印发《关于司法公开的六项规定》和《关于人民法院接受新闻媒体舆论监督的若干规定》的通知》] was issued on 8 December 2009, www.chinacourt.org/flwk/show.php?file_id=140270 accessed September 2012.

104 The "Supreme People's Court, Rules on Several Issues of Adjudicating Open Government Information Administrative Litigation" [最高人民法院关于审理政府信息公开行政案件若干问题的规定] was passed by the Judicial Committee of the Supreme People's Court on 29 July 2011 and entered into force on 13 August 2011, fashi [2011] No. 17, for detailed information see http://lvshi.sz.bendibao.com/news/2011817/315374.shtm accessed 8 May 2012.

applied the administrative review from Ningbo City government for replying their request because they had not received any reply from the Yuyao City government. Although the lower level government (Yuyao City government) said it had already contacted the group's representative by phone to request an additional identification and tell them to seek the information from the land resources bureau, the Ningbo government ordered it to properly handle the information request within thirty days.[105]

For sure, substantial challenges continue to frustrate the realisation of the Chinese people's "right to know" in practice.[106] As also indicated above, these include restrictions in the language of the Regulations themselves,[107] conflicts with prevailing legislation like the State Secrets Law, bureaucratic unease with and confusion over how to carry them out, and lack of adequate resources to meet records management and information request demands.[108]

Nevertheless, empirical research has demonstrated that, although full implementation is still an ideal, great progress has been made.[109] An example of this progress is the right to information for farmers. In practice, farmers are increasingly well informed about their rights. For instance, the central State has initiated nationwide legal education campaigns in which special attention has been paid to the 1998 Land Management Law[110] and the 2003 Rural Land Contract Law,[111] giving local governments little opportunity to

---

105 China News (中国新闻网) (2008). 68 Villagers of Yu Yao, Zhejiang Successfully Sue Municipal Government Over Open Information Case (浙江余姚68名村民信息公开案告赢市政府). Issued on 10 October 2008, www.chinanews.com.cn/sh/news/2008/10-10/1407244.shtml accessed 5 September 2012.

106 Horsley, J.P. (2010). Update on China's open government information regulations: surprising public demand yielding some positive results. Posted 23 April 2010, www.freedominfo.org/2010/04/update-on-china-open-government-information-regulations accessed 5 September 2012.

107 Horsley, J.P. (2007). China adopts first nationwide open government information regulations. Published on 9 May 2007, www.law.yale.edu/documents/pdf/Intellectual_Life/Ch_China_Adopts_1st_OGI_Regulations.pdf accessed 12 October 2012.

108 Horsley, J.P. (2010). Update on China's open government information regulations: surprising public demand yielding some positive results. Posted 23 April 2010, www.freedominfo.org/2010/04/update-on-china-open-government-information-regulations accessed 5 September 2012.

109 Prosterman, R., Schwarzwalder, B. & Y, J.P. (2000). Implementation of 30-year land use rights for farmers under China's 1998 land management law: an analysis and recommendations based on a 17-province survey. *Pacific Rim Law & Policy Journal*, 9, pp. 507–568; Schwarzwalder, B. *et al.* (2002). An update on China's rural land tenure reforms: analysis and recommendations based upon a seventeen-province survey. *Columbia Journal of Asian Law*, 16, pp. 142–225.

110 Article 47(1), the "Land Management Law of the People's Republic of China" [中华人民共和国土地管理法] was issued in 1986 and amended in 1998, and later amended on 28 August 2004, for detailed information see (1998 version) www.zhb.gov.cn/ztbd/rdzl/2010sdn/zcfg/201001/t20100113_184226.htm, and (2004 version) www.china.com.cn/chinese/law/647616.htm accessed 3 January 2012.

111 The "Law of the People's Republic of China on Land Contract in Rural Areas" [中华人民共和国农村土地承包法] was entered into effect on 1 March 2003, http://english.gov.cn/laws/2005-10/09/content_75300.htm accessed 11 December 2012.

distort the flow of information.[112] An important and logical change would be to grant farmers rights of negotiation about compensation prior to the land acquisition approval.[113] In local Beijing municipal regulations farmers have gotten a stronger voice in the compensation negotiation process as the local rules require that a written agreement between the requisitioning unit and the rural collective economic institutions or village committees is required which governs the compensation amount and procedures.[114] Research has also demonstrated that farmers have increased knowledge of their land rights and know about the thirty-year land-use right regulations and the fact that these cannot be violated at will.[115] In the Yunnan province, a district government initially forced a village to provide 100 mu (0.066 km^2) of arable land for a landscape theme park. When this land was not duly compensated and another 100 mu (0.066 km^2) was to be requisitioned, one of the local farmers went to the local city bookshop to get books about the existing land laws.[116] Through self-study, he learned about their rights, which eventually led to extra-legal protest.[117]

5.1.2.1.2. Legal and Policy Framework Concerning Environmental Information

As for environmental information, a relatively new regulation referring to environmental information, the "Measures on Open Environmental Information (for Trial Implementation)" (OEI Measures)[118] was issued in 2007. It specifically

112 Van Rooij, B. (2010). Land loss and conflict in China: illustrated by cases from Yunnan province. In: Ubink, J.M., Hoekema, A.J. & Assies, W.J. (Eds.). *Legalizing Land Rights – Local Practices, State Responses and Tenure Security in Africa, Asia and Latin America*. Leiden: Leiden University Press, p. 450.

113 Van Rooij, B. (2007). The return of the landlord: Chinese land acquisition conflicts as illustrated by peri-urban Kunming, www.jlp.bham.ac.uk/volumes/55/vanrooij-art.pdf accessed 12 September 2012, p. 213.

114 Subrahmanyan, A. (2004). Land use in China: the impact of the economic revolution. *China Law & Practice*, 18(9), pp. 24–31.

115 Schwarzwalder, B. *et al.* (2002). An update on China's rural land tenure reforms: analysis and recommendations based upon a seventeen-province survey. *Columbia Journal of Asian Law*, 16, pp. 142–225.

116 Van Rooij, B. (2010). Land loss and conflict in China: illustrated by cases from Yunnan province. In: Ubink, J.M., Hoekema, A.J. & Assies, W.J. (Eds.). *Legalizing Land Rights – Local Practices, State Responses and Tenure Security in Africa, Asia and Latin America*. Leiden: Leiden University Press, p. 451.

117 Based on an interview with a local Yunnan researcher, April 2006, see van Rooij, B. (2010). Land loss and conflict in China: illustrated by cases from Yunnan province. In Ubink, J.M., Hoekema, A.J. & Assies, W.J. (Eds.). *Legalizing Land Rights – Local Practices, State Responses and Tenure Security in Africa, Asia and Latin America*. Leiden: Leiden University Press, p. 451.

118 The "Measures on Open Environmental Information (for trial implementation)" [环境信息公开办法(试行)] was adopted on 8 February 2007 and entered into effective on 1 May 2008 by the States Environmental Protection Administration (SEPA, which was subsequently elevated to ministry status in 2008), www.epa.gov/ogc/china/open_environmental.pdf accessed 24 October 2012. This regulation is still on the stage of the trial implementation since 1 May 2008.

requires environmental protection departments to disclose environmental information "*that is compiled or obtained during environmental protection departments' exercising their environmental protection responsibilities and recorded and stored in a given form*".[119]

In the 18th National People's Congress of the Chinese Communist Party in 2012, the Ministry of Environmental Protection said concerning environmental issues that four measures were needed. One of the measures was to improve information openness; all the information related to environmental impact assessment would be provided, including the promises made by the government to the public.[120]

The newly modified "Environmental Protection Law of the People's Republic of China" (2014 version)[121] provides an independent chapter on "information disclosure and public participation". Notably, Article 53 says that: "*Citizens, legal persons and other organizations shall have the right to obtain environmental information, participation and supervise the activities of environment protection in accordance with the law. The competent environmental protection administrations of the people's governments at various levels and other departments with environmental supervision responsibilities shall disclose environmental information pursuant to the law, improve public participation procedures, and facilitate citizens, legal persons and other organizations to participate in, and supervise, environmental protection work.*" Article 54 points out the governments from different levels have some different obligations on information disclosure. Although the newly modified environmental law (2014 version) would only be entered into effective on 1 January 2015, it is a big step forward for environmental information.

More recently, in order to safeguard right to information and right to participation in environmental matters for citizens, units and other organisations, the "Measures on Right to Participation in Environmental Protection"[122] was issued by the department of environmental protection on 2 July 2015. Article 5 points out that when the environmental protection agencies

---

119 Article 2, the "Measures on Open Environmental Information (for trial implementation)" [环境信息公开办法(试行)] was adopted on 8 February 2007 and entered into effective on 1 May 2008, www.epa.gov/ogc/china/open_environmental.pdf accessed 24 October 2012.

120 Xinhua Net (2012). The department of environmental protection response to environmental groups events: it is rule of development. Posted on 12 November 2012, http://news.163.com/12/1112/19/8G4PDG5L0001124J.html accessed 12 November 2012.

121 The "Environmental Protection Law of the People's Republic of China" [中华人民共和国环境保护法] was promulgated by Order No. 22 of the President of the People's Republic of China on 26 December 1989, and was effective on the date of promulgation; it was newly modified on 24 April 2014 and entered into force on 1 January 2015, http://edu.sina.com.cn/en/2014-05-20/144680376.shtml accessed 30 June 2014.

122 The "Measures on Right to Participation in Environmental Protection" [环境保护公众参与办法] was issued by the department of environmental protection on 2 July 2015 and it entered into force on 1 September 2015, www.zhb.gov.cn/gkml/hbb/bl/201507/t20150720_306928.htm accessed 1 October 2015.

consult with citizens, units or other organisations, the agencies shall publish the information as follows: (1) the background information on the relevant events or activities; (2) the begging and ending time for the consultation; (3) the methods for submitting the suggestions or advices from the public and (4) the department to contact and the means of contacting it. Article 8 also says that environmental protection agencies shall announce that some matters should be hearing according to law and regulations, and the agencies shall hold the hearing for the public. Furthermore, the point 38 of the newly-issued "Overall Plan for the Reform of Ecological Civilization System"[123] points out it is necessary to improve the current environmental information disclosure system. This provides an overall guideline for improving the existing legal system and further issuing the relevant law and regulation later on.

In practice, it is fair to say that as China is only at the start of an environmental transparency system, standards are low and the public still struggles to get some basic environmental information.[124] This was confirmed by the survey of 113 cities made by the Institute of Public and Environmental Affairs (IPE) and the American NGO the Natural Resources Defense Council (NRDC). The survey gave each a mark for environmental information disclosure. Both organisations behind the report point out that environmental transparency is still in its infancy.[125]

However, there was also some progress in practice. In January 2012, the first landmark case of environmental information disclosure administrative litigation was decided by the Intermediate People's Court in Qingzhen City of Guizhou Province.[126] The judgment ordered the Xiuwen City EPB (Environmental Protection Bureau), as the defendant to provide the requested information to the Plaintiff, the All-China Environmental Federation (ACEF).[127] The ACEF

---

123 The "Overall Plan for the Reform of Ecological Civilization System" [生态文明体制改革总体方案] was issued by the State Council on 21 September 2015, http://news.xinhuanet.com/politics/2015-09/21/c_1116632281.htm accessed 25 September 2015.

124 China Dialogue (中外对话) (2012). The environmental information disclosure in most regions of China cannot get a satisfied result (中国大部分地区环境信息公开不及格). Posted on 18 January 2012, www.chinadialogue.net/weblogs/4/weblog_posts/436?lang=en accessed 8 May 2012.

125 China Dialogue (中外对话) (2012). The environmental information disclosure in most regions of China cannot get a satisfied result (中国大部分地区环境信息公开不及格). Posted on 18 January 2012, www.chinadialogue.net/weblogs/4/weblog_posts/436?lang=en accessed 8 May, 2012.

126 "The First Successful Environmental Information Disclosure Public Interest Litigation in China", www.acef.com.cn/html/xwdt/11057.html accessed 16 October 2012; All-China Environment Federation (ACEF) v. The Land Resources Bureau in Qingzhen City (中华环保联合会诉贵州省清镇市国土资源管理局), The Intermediate People's Court in Qingzhen City of Guizhou Province (贵州省清镇市国土资源管理局), 29 July 2009, for detailed information see www.jcrb.com/zhuanti/fzzt/lpsh/gyss/201001/t20100112_300833.html accessed 22 October 2013.

127 The All-China Environmental Federation (ACEF (中华环保联合会)), established in 2005, is a nationwide non-profit civil society organisation in the field of the environment, and is

sued a milk company for causing water pollution in October 2011. In order to seek evidence, it requested Xiuwen City EPB to disclose related information concerning the milk company but failed.[128] Thus the ACEF sued the EPB before the court.[129] The court affirmed that to obtain environmental information was an important right for citizens, legal persons and other organisations, and it was an important approach for the public to participate in environmental protection and monitor the implementation of environmental protection laws.[130] Another point that needs to be mentioned is that it is the first public interest administrative litigation relating to open government information brought up by an environmental NGO. Although this case is a good starting point in improving the right to information, much more detailed work needs to be done, especially for local people and communities and NGOs in and around protected areas.

5.1.2.1.3. Right to Information in Protected Areas Conservation in China

Among the regulations concerning protected areas conservation (see 3.1.3.2), only the "Land Management Approach in Nature Reserve" (1995)[131] provides some specific Articles for public information on protected areas. Article 13 states that the scope and boundaries of protected areas are determined by the People's government which approves the establishment of protected areas. The establishment of a protected area should clearly be indicated and announced to the public. Article 14 points out that any dispute because of unclear scope or boundaries of protected areas is determined by the people's government which

---

supported by the government. www.un.org/democracyfund/sites/dr7.un.org.democracyfund/files/UDF-CPR-09-320_ER.pdf accessed 10 October 2012, p. 2.

128 "The First Successful Environmental Information Disclosure Public Interest Litigation in China", www.acef.com.cn/html/xwdt/11057.html accessed 16 October 2012; All-China Environment Federation (ACEF) v. The Land Resources Bureau in Qingzhen City (中华环保联合会诉贵州省清镇市国土资源管理局), The Intermediate People's Court in Qingzhen City of Guizhou Province (贵州省清镇市国土资源管理局), 29 July 2009, www.jcrb.com/zhuanti/fzzt/lpsh/gyss/201001/t20100112_300833.html accessed 22 October 2013.

129 Guizhou Qingzhen People's Court Administrative Litigation Judgment (2010) Qinghuanbaochuzi No. 1, 10 January 2012; All-China Environment Federation (ACEF) v. The Land Resources Bureau in Qingzhen City (中华环保联合会诉贵州省清镇市国土资源管理局), The Intermediate People's Court in Qingzhen City of Guizhou Province (贵州省清镇市国土资源管理局), 29 July 2009, www.jcrb.com/zhuanti/fzzt/lpsh/gyss/201001/t20100112_300833.html accessed 22 October 2013.

130 Guizhou Qingzhen People's Court Administrative Litigation Judgment (2010) Qinghuanbaochuzi No. 1, 10 January 2012; All-China Environment Federation (ACEF) v. The Land Resources Bureau in Qingzhen City (中华环保联合会诉贵州省清镇市国土资源管理局), The Intermediate People's Court in Qingzhen City of Guizhou Province (贵州省清镇市国土资源管理局), 29 July 2009, www.jcrb.com/zhuanti/fzzt/lpsh/gyss/201001/t20100112_300833.html accessed 22 October 2013.

131 For detailed information see www.hbepb.gov.cn/hbdt/rdzt/zrbhqzl/bhqzlzcwj/201108/t20110831_47204.html accessed 22 October 2013, in Chinese.

approves the establishment of protected areas. The environmental protection authority can cooperate with the department in charge of protected areas and other relevant authorities to submit their advice to the People's government. In addition, Article 7 of the "Regulation on the Adjustment for Boundaries and Functional Areas of National Nature Reserves and Changing their Name"[132] indirectly approves that the public can view some important documents on protected areas, if protected areas are changed or adjusted.

In practice, a remarkable case concerning the right to information and protected areas happened in 2011. In order to get more information about the national protected areas for rare and special fish in the upper reaches of the Yangtze River, "Friends of Nature",[133] one of the famous environmental NGOs in China, asked the Ministry of Environmental Protection to release some important information.[134] Friends of Nature was of the opinion that, according to Article 7 from the "Regulation on the Adjustment for Boundaries and Functional Areas of National Nature Reserves and Changing Their Name",[135] if the national protected areas needed to be changed or adjusted, some important documents should be accessible, including the application report for adjustment of the protected area (the reason for the application, the report on the environmental impact assessment), the comprehensive research report on the adjustment part in the protected area, the review comments for this protected area by the Evaluation Committee of the National Nature Reserve in the 2010 annual meeting and the general planning map for adjustment. Only the general planning map for adjustment was available on the website of the Ministry of Environmental Protection. Friends of Nature asked the Ministry of Environmental Protection to provide the missing documents mentioned above and the 2010 annual meeting cahier

132 The "Regulation on the Adjustment for Boundaries and Functional Areas of National Nature Reserves and Changing Their Name" [国家级自然保护区范围调整和功能区调整及更改名称管理规定] was issued on 29 January 2002, www.gov.cn/gongbao/content/2002/content_61943.htm accessed 6 August 2011. This regulation was expired and replaced by "Regulation on the Adjustment for National Nature Reserves" on 2 December 2013. http://vip. chinalawinfo.com/newlaw2002/slc/slc.asp?db=chl&gid=214332 accessed 8 March 2014.

133 "Friends of Nature" is the first Chinese environmental NGO approved by Chinese government in 1994, more information see www.fon.org.cn/ accessed 22 October 2013.

134 China Youth Daily (中国青年报) (2011). Friends of Nature, an environmental NGOs in China, asked the Ministry of Environmental Protection to release some important information (民间环保组织"自然之友"就长江上游珍稀特有鱼类国家级自然保护区调整向环境保护部申请信息公开). Published on 13 May 2011, http://env.people.com.cn/GB/14625045.html accessed 4 August 2011.

135 The "Regulation on the Adjustment for Boundaries and Functional Areas of National Nature Reserves and Changing Their Name" [国家级自然保护区范围调整和功能区调整及更改名称管理规定] was issued on 29 January 2002, www.gov.cn/gongbao/content/2002/content_61943.htm accessed 6 August 2011. This regulation was expired and replaced by "Regulation on the Adjustment for National Nature Reserves" on 2 December 2013, http://vip. chinalawinfo.com/newlaw2002/slc/slc.asp?db=chl&gid=214332 accessed 8 March 2014.

to the public. The Ministry of Environmental Protection accepted all the requirements.[136]

Although what has been discussed is only a step forward, they do reflect the prospect of a fully developed right to information in protected areas conservation in China in the future.

5.1.2.2. Analysis on the Right to Information in China

From the discussion above, some important points need to be pointed out. First, Chinese legislation, regulations and policies emphasise that government agencies and relevant parties "open" information by using their administrative powers, which is regarded as their obligations, rather than responding to the right of "anyone" to access government information. Although some local regulations, for instance, the Guangzhou OGI Rules and the Shanghai OGI Rules (see 5.1.2.1.1), reflect a sign to clarify the "right" and" obligation", they do not have countrywide effect. Second, due to the shorter history of open information in a legal perspective in China, where the long journey towards democracy and the rule of law began merely thirty years ago,[137] the right to information cannot be truly realised in practice within a short period of time. The international trend of environmental information disclosure was triggered by the 1984 Bhopal gas tragedy. The US first launched the Toxic Release Inventory (TRI) in 1986.[138] The situation in Europe as to the evolving right to information in environmental issues will be discussed in detail below (see 5.1.3). However, China did not have a widely accepted environmental information disclosure until the OEI Measures issued in 2007. Although the Guangzhou OGI Rules stated that disclosure of government information is a basic principle in 2003, it is only a local regulation in China. Third, domestic factors are crucial for the development of transparency in China.[139] Local governments have played (and are still playing) an important

---

136 Rule of Law Internet (2011). NGOs asks the information discourse on protected area adjustment. Posted by on 20 January 2011, www.chinatransparency.org/newsinfo.asp?newsid=9667 accessed 10 October 2012.

137 Liu, W.J. (2011). Approaching democracy through transparency: a comparative law study on Chinese open government information. *American University International Law Review*, 26(4), www.law.yale.edu/documents/pdf/Intellectual_Life/CLC_Liu_Wenjing-Approaching_democracy_through_transparency_2010.pdf accessed 23 October 2012, p. 124.

138 Hu, Y.Q. (2009). One year of openness: environmental information disclosure laws in China and Pollution Information Transparency Index (PITI). In: the IUCN Colloquium, Wuhan, China, www.greenlawchina.org/2009/05/one-year-of-openness-greenlaw-and-the-first-anniversary-of-chinas-open-information-regulations/ accessed 23 October 2012.

139 Liu, W.J. (2011). Approaching democracy through transparency: a comparative law study on Chinese open government information. *American University International Law Review*, 26(4), www.law.yale.edu/documents/pdf/Intellectual_Life/CLC_Liu_Wenjing-Approaching_democracy_through_transparency_2010.pdf accessed 23 October 2012, p. 123.

role in building the institutions of government transparency.[140] Fourth, under the existing right to information context in China, the right to information in the protected areas construction, management, adjustment and benefit-sharing is limited, although some improvements have been made since the last decade. Fifth, without a well-informed citizenry, public participation is impossible.

5.1.3. RIGHT TO INFORMATION IN ENVIRONMENTAL PROTECTION IN EUROPE

Based on what has been discussed about China, let us explore some issues in Europe. What are the baselines and general principles for the potential conflicts regarding right to information protection and environmental protection in general, and protected areas conservation in specific, in Europe?

5.1.3.1. Right to Information under the European Convention on Human Rights

In the framework of the Council of Europe neither the European Convention for the Protection of Human Rights and Fundamental Freedoms (1950), adopted in Rome on 4 November 1950, nor the protocols thereto explicitly acknowledge any human right relating to environmental information.[141] However, Article 10 in the European Convention for the Protection of Human Rights and Fundamental Freedoms (1950) provides: "*Everyone has the right to freedom of expression. This right shall include freedom to hold opinions and to receive and impart information and ideas without interference by public authority and regardless of frontiers. The (...) formalities, conditions, restrictions or penalties as are prescribed by law and are necessary in a democratic society, in the interests of national security, territorial integrity or public safety, for the prevention of disorder or crime, for the protection of health or morals, for the protection of the reputation or rights of others, for preventing the disclosure of information received in confidence, or for maintaining the authority and impartiality of the judiciary.*"[142] It establishes a general right to information in Europe. This provision has been interpreted by the European Court of Human Rights, in the

---

140 Liu, W.J. (2011). Approaching democracy through transparency: a comparative law study on Chinese open government information. *American University International Law Review*, 26(4), www.law.yale.edu/documents/pdf/Intellectual_Life/CLC_Liu_Wenjing-Approaching_democracy_through_transparency_2010.pdf accessed 23 October 2012, p. 124.

141 Dejeant-Pons, M. (2002). Human rights to environmental procedural rights. In: Dejeant-Pons, M & Pallemaerts, M. (Eds.). *Human Rights and the Environment*. Strasbourg (France): Council of Europe Publishing, p. 24.

142 Article 10, European Convention on Human Rights (formally the Convention for the Protection of Human Rights and Fundamental Freedoms), drafted in 1950 and entered into force on 3 September 1953, 213 UNTS, www.echr.coe.int/Documents/Convention_ENG.

sense that a government may not restrict a person from receiving information that others wish to impart[143] (see 5.1.3.2.1.1 on the case of *Anna Marina Guerra and 39 Others v. Italy*).[144]

5.1.3.2. Case Law in the European Court of Human Rights

As has been discussed above, besides respecting substantive rights, the Convention for the Protection of Human Rights and Fundamental Freedoms generally establishes the right to information (Article 10 on the freedom of expression includes the freedom to hold opinions and to receive and impart information and ideas). European States are bound by this Article. Article 10 does not confer on an individual a right of access to register information on his personal position, nor does it embody an obligation on the government to impart such information to the individual.[145] The case law of the ECHR concerning the right of access to public information is a bit controversial, since there are different interpretations of Article 10 of the European Convention on Human Rights regarding access to public information possible.[146] In order to fully understand its real meaning, it is necessary to see how to interpret the relevant provisions in the case law from the European Court, which will supplement what is not explicitly pointed out in the existing provisions.

5.1.3.2.1. Public Access to Clear and Full Information is a Basic Human Right

5.1.3.2.1.1. Right to Information Was Indirectly Approved by the ECHR

In a democracy, the people have the right to gain access to information, including environmental information.[147] In the case of *Anna Marina Guerra*

pdf accessed 12 April 2013. For detailed information see www.echr.coe.int/Pages/home.aspx?p=home accessed 12 April 2013.

143 Desmet, E. (2011). *Indigenous Rights Entwined with Nature Conservation*. Antwerp: Intersentia, p. 308.

144 ECtHR, Anna Marina Guerra and 39 Others v. Italy (1998), App. No. 14967/89, Judgment of 19 February 1998, http://hudoc.echr.coe.int/sites/eng/pages/search.aspx?i=001-58135 accessed 12 October 2013.

145 ECtHR, Leander v. Sweden (1987), App. No. 9248/81, Judgment of 26 March 1987, http://hudoc.echr.coe.int/sites/eng/pages/search.aspx?i=001-57519#{%22itemid%22:[%22001-57519%22]} accessed 24 October 2013.

146 Tsukhishvili, N. The case law of the European Court of Human Rights (ECHR): the right of access to public information. Institute for Development of Freedom of Information (IDFI). Published on February 2013, www.idfi.ge/uploadedFiles/files/ECHR%20Case%20Laws%20Analysis%281%29.pdf accessed 12 February 2014.

147 UNECE (United Nations Economic Commission for Europe) and UNEP (United Nations Environment Programme) (2006). Your right to a healthy environment: a simplified guide to the Aarhus convention on access to information, public participation in decision-making and access to justice in environmental matters, www.unece.org/fileadmin/DAM/env/documents/2006/pp/ece%20mp%20pp%205_E.pdf accessed 10 October 2013, p. 5.

and 39 Others v. Italy,[148] residents of Manfredonia, brought an action against the Italian government for failing to provide them with information about the health risks posed by a nearby chemical factory. The applicants alleged that the Italian authorities violated Articles 2, 8 and 10 of the ECHR[149] by failing to mitigate the risk of a major accident at a nearby chemical factory and by withholding information from local residents about the risks and emergency procedures. With regards to Article 10 of the European Convention on Human Rights, the applicants asserted in particular the government's failure to inform the public of the risks and the measures to be taken in case of a major accident, prescribed by the domestic law transposing the EC "Seveso" Directive.[150] As for Article 10, "*the Court reiterates that freedom to receive information, referred to in paragraph 2 of Article 10 of the Convention, 'basically prohibits a government from restricting a person from receiving information that others wish or may be willing to impart to him.' That freedom cannot be construed as imposing on a State, in circumstances such as those of the present case, positive obligations to collect and disseminate information of its own motion.*"[151] The "right to information" claim was dismissed, because the ECHR does not require the collection and dissemination of information about the environment, but the ECtHR effectively incorporates this requirement into the applicant's Article 8 claim as the "procedural dimension" of the obligation of States to secure effective respect for the applicants' right to family and home life.[152] Eight of the twenty judges suggested in separate opinions that positive obligations to collect and disseminate information might exist in some circumstances. In conclusion, Article 10 was not applicable in the instant case.

The conclusion reached by the ECtHR, as expressed in paragraph 53 in fine of its judgment, was that "*the freedom to receive information referred to in*

148 ECtHR, Anna Marina Guerra and 39 Others v. Italy (1998), App. No. 14967/89, Judgment of 19 February 1998, http://hudoc.echr.coe.int/sites/eng/pages/search.aspx?i=001-58135 accessed 12 October 2013.

149 Article 2 right to life; Article 8 right to respect for one's private and family life; and Article 10 right to freedom of expression.

150 Council Directive of 24 June 1982 on the Major-Accident Hazards of Certain Industrial Activities (82/501/EEC) was issued on 24 June 1982 and replaced by 87/216/EEC which was signed on 19 March 1987 (1982 Directive http://eur-lex.europa.eu/LexUriServ/LexUriServ.do?uri=CELEX:31982L0501:EN:HTML; 1987 Directive www.safety-s2s.eu/modules.php?name=s2s_wp7&op=v&idp=40) The Seveso law required disclosure of the production process; the substances present and their quantities; possible risks for employees, workers, the population and the environment; security measures, and rules to follow in case of accident. Other laws supplemented the right to environmental information.

151 ECtHR, Anna Marina Guerra and 39 Others v. Italy (1998), App. No. 14967/89, Judgment of 19 February 1998, §53, http://hudoc.echr.coe.int/sites/eng/pages/search.aspx?i=001-58135 accessed 12 October 2013.

152 Shelton, D.L. (2012). Using law and equity for the poor and the environment. In: Bouthillier, Y.L., Cohen, M.A., Marquez, J.J.G., Mumma, A. & Smith, S. (Eds.). *Poverty Alleviation and Environmental Law*. The IUCN Academy of Environmental Law Series. Cheltenham (UK) and Northampton (USA): Edward Elgar Publishing, p. 31.

paragraph 2 of Article 10 of the Convention basically prohibits a government from restricting a person from receiving information that other wishor may be willing to impart to him."[153] The ECtHR concluded there had been a breach of Article 8 of the ECHR because the applicants did not receive environmental information in their interest.[154] Rather than the creation of a "new" right by way of jurisprudence (namely the right to ask for environmental information retained by local authorities),[155] it seems that an example of the environmental cross-dimension of the European Convention on Human Rights is obvious. The right to receive environmental information from the State, which is not protected as such under Article 10, is, in addition to its connection with Article 8 (which sometimes implies a procedural connotation), also linked to Article 2 by way of a positive duty on States to inform people on environmental risks to their lives.[156] Thus, under Article 8 there is a positive duty on States whose Governments engage in hazardous activities to respect private and family life by establishing an effective and accessible procedure which enables interested parties to seek (and obviously obtain) any relevant and appropriate information, including on the environment.[157]

5.1.3.2.1.2. Right to Information Was Recently Contained in Article 10 of the ECHR

Recently, in the case of *Társaság a Szabadságjogokért v. Hungary*,[158] Társaság a Szabadságjogokért, the Hungarian Civil Liberties Union, made a complaint against the Hungarian government over a submission to the Hungarian Constitutional Court filed by a member of parliament concerning drug policy. The ECtHR stated that access to original documentary sources for legitimate historical research was an essential element of the exercise of the applicant's right to freedom of expression.[159] The landmark decision of this case shows that

---

153 Garcia San José, D. (2005). *Environmental Protection and the European Convention on Human Rights*. Council of Europe Publishing, p. 62.

154 In such a modern way as provided in the Aarhus Convention and its recent follows-up in the European Union and in the Council of Europe. For detailed information see Garcia San José, D. (2005). *Environmental Protection and the European Convention on Human Rights*. Council of Europe Publishing, p. 62.

155 ECtHR, Anna Marina Guerra and 39 Others v. Italy (1998), App. No. 14967/89, Judgment of 19 February 1998, §99, http://hudoc.echr.coe.int/sites/eng/pages/search.aspx?i=001-58135 accessed 12 October 2013.

156 Garcia San José, D. (2005). *Environmental Protection and the European Convention on Human Rights*. Council of Europe Publishing, p. 65.

157 Garcia San José, D. (2005). *Environmental Protection and the European Convention on Human Rights*. Council of Europe Publishing, pp. 63–64.

158 ECtHR, Társaság a Szabadságjogokért v. Hungary (2009), App. No. 37374/05, Judgment of 14 July 2009, http://hudoc.echr.coe.int/sites/eng/pages/search.aspx?i=001-92171#{%22itemid%22:[%22001-92171%22]} accessed 15 March 2014.

159 ECtHR, Társaság a Szabadságjogokért v. Hungary (2009), App. No. 37374/05, Judgment of 14 July 2009, §§35–39, http://hudoc.echr.coe.int/sites/eng/pages/search.aspx?i=001-92171#{%22itemid%22:[%22001-92171%22]} accessed 15 March 2014.

it is the first time that the ECtHR has unanimously recognised that freedom of expression, as amended by Article 10 of the ECHR, also includes the right to information from public bodies.[160] It is noted that the Court has consistently recognised that the public has a right to receive information of general interest.[161]

Besides this direct confirmation that the right of access to information is a human right, more recently, NGO's right of access to official documents was established in the case of *Österreichische Vereinigung zur Erhaltung, Stärkung und Schaffung eines wirtschaftlich gesunden land- und forstwirtschaftlichen Grundbesitzes v. Austria*.[162] The Austrian Association for the Preservation, Strengthening and Creation of an Economically Sound Agricultural and Forestry Land Ownership, as the applicant, aims to examine the impact of transfers of ownership of agricultural and forest land on society and to give opinions on draft laws. In 2005 the association twice requested the Tyrol Real Property Transaction Commission, which is responsible for approving agricultural and forest land transactions under the Tyrol Real Property Transactions Act,[163] to provide the association with the decisions it had issued over a certain period of time (since January 2005 and since January 2000, respectively).[164] The requests were refused on the ground that they did not fall within the scope of the Tyrol Access to Information Act. Moreover, even if the request did fall within its scope, pursuant to the Act, an authority did not have the duty to provide the requested information. If doing so would require so many resources that its functioning would be affected and would jeopardise the fulfilment of the Commission's

160 freedominfo.org (2009). European Court of Human Rights: right to information essential to free expression. Posted on 14 April 2009, www.freedominfo.org/2009/04/european-court-of-human-rights-right-to-information-essential-to-free-expression/ accessed 15 March 2014.

161 ECtHR, Társaság a Szabadságjogokért v. Hungary (2009), App. No. 37374/05, Judgment of 14 July 2009, §26, http://hudoc.echr.coe.int/sites/eng/pages/search.aspx?i=001-92171#{%22itemid%22:[%22001-92171%22]} accessed 15 March 2014.

162 ECtHR, Österreichische Vereinigung zur Erhaltung, Stärkung und Schaffung eines wirtschaftlich gesunden land- und forstwirtschaftlichen Grundbesitzes v. Austria (2013), App. No. 39534/07, Judgment of 28 November 2013, http://hudoc.echr.coe.int/sites/eng/pages/search.aspx?i=001-139084#{%22itemid%22:[%22001-139084%22]} accessed 16 March 2014.

163 The aim of the Tyrol Real Property Transactions Act as in force at the material time (Regional Law Gazette 61/1996 as amended by Regional Law Gazette 75/1999), was to preserve land for agricultural and forestry use and to avoid the proliferation of second homes. ECtHR, Österreichische Vereinigung zur Erhaltung, Stärkung und Schaffung eines wirtschaftlich gesunden land- und forstwirtschaftlichen Grundbesitzes v. Austria (2013), App. No. 39534/07, Judgement of 28 November 2013, §20, http://hudoc.echr.coe.int/sites/eng/pages/search.aspx?i=001-139084#{%22itemid%22:[%22001-139084%22]} accessed 16 March 2014.

164 Voorhoof, D. & Fathaigh, R.Ó. (2013). The press and NGOs' right of access to official documents under strict scrutiny of the European Court of Human Rights. Strasbourg Observers. Published on 3 December 2013, http://strasbourgobservers.com/2013/12/03/the-press-and-ngos-right-of-access-to-official-documents-under-strict-scrutiny-of-the-european-court-of-human-rights-2/ accessed 16 March 2014.

other tasks.[165] The applicant's complaints to the Administrative Court and the Constitutional Court were rejected. Therefore, the applicant complained in Strasbourg that its right to receive information, guaranteed by Article 10 of the Convention, had been violated as it was refused access to the decisions of the Tyrol Real Property Transactions Commission. In conclusion, the European Court found that a complete refusal had been disproportionate to the legitimate aim pursued. There had accordingly been a violation of Article 10.

The judgment above continues in the post-2005 direction of the Court's case law towards recognising a right of access to information under Article 10, building upon cases such as *Matky v. Czech Republic*[166] and *Kenedi v. Hungary*,[167] which all concerned contributions on issues of public/social interest, and media or NGOs as public watchdog.[168] Furthermore, the Court's judgment and recognition of the right of access to official documents is to be considered itself as a new incentive for the European States to sign and ratify the Council of European Convention on Access to Official Documents.[169]

5.1.3.2.1.3. Discussion

There is no doubt that the right to information has been increasingly recognised as a basic human right. This was indirectly confirmed in the case of *Anna Marina Guerra and 39 Others v. Italy*, and then the landmark decision of *Társaság a Szabadságjogokért v. Hungary* explicitly addressed that the right to information is contained in Article 10 of the ECHR. What is more, besides the individuals' right to information, the NGOs' right to information has also been recognised by the post-2005 direction of the Court's case law, such as *Társaság a Szabadságjogokért v. Hungary* mentioned above.

This interesting tendency reflects that the recognition of the right to information has increasingly been recognised as part of Article 10 in the ECHR

165 Voorhoof, D. & Fathaigh, R.Ó. (2013). The press and NGOs' right of access to official documents under strict scrutiny of the European Court of Human Rights. Strasbourg Observers. Published on 3 December 2013, http://strasbourgobservers.com/2013/12/03/the-press-and-ngos-right-of-access-to-official-documents-under-strict-scrutiny-of-the-european-court-of-human-rights-2/ accessed 16 March 2014.

166 ECtHR, Matky v. Czech Republic (2006), App. No. 19101/03, Judgment of 10 July 2006, http://hudoc.echr.coe.int/sites/eng/pages/search.aspx?i=001-76707#{%22itemid%22:[%22001-76707%22]} accessed 13 March 2014.

167 ECtHR, Kenedi v. Hungary (2009), App. No. 31475/05, Judgment of 26 August 2009, http://hudoc.echr.coe.int/sites/eng/pages/search.aspx?i=001-92663#{%22itemid%22:[%22001-92663%22]} accessed 13 March 2014.

168 Voorhoof, D. & Fathaigh, R.Ó. (2013). The press and NGOs' right of access to official documents under strict scrutiny of the European Court of Human Rights. Strasbourg Observers. Published on 3 December 2013, http://strasbourgobservers.com/2013/12/03/the-press-and-ngos-right-of-access-to-official-documents-under-strict-scrutiny-of-the-european-court-of-human-rights-2/ accessed 16 March 2014.

169 Council of European Convention on Access to Official Documents, CETS No. 205, 18 June 2009, http://conventions.coe.int/Treaty/EN/Treaties/Html/205.htm accessed 16 March 2014.

step by step. At present, the scope of the right to information is broader than it was first recognised by the ECHR. In addition, on the basis of an analysis of the case law of the ECtHR, we can conclude that the ECHR imposes a positive obligation upon the States to provide relevant information regarding the public interest.

There is no reason to doubt that, with the increasing recognition of the right to information, this right can contribute more and more to environmental protection in general and the protection of protected areas specifically.

5.1.3.2.2. Restrictions on the Right to Information Must "Be Prescribed by Law", "Be Necessary in a Democratic Society" and "Follow a Legitimate Aim"

Although the role of the right to information in environmental protection is widely acknowledged, as indicated by Article 10 of the ECHR, restrictions are possible. The three main conditions of the right to information must (1) "be prescribed by law"; (2) "be necessary in a democratic society"; and (3) "follow a legitimate aim".

The case of *Vides Aizsardzibas Klubs v. Latvia*[170] refers to the sentencing of an NGO criticising the behaviour of a municipal councillor favouring illegal building projects in protected areas. The applicant, Vides Aizsardzibas Klubs (the Environmental Protection Club – known as the "VAK"), is a non-governmental organisation based in Riga. The applicant organisation alleged that a local mayor had not halted building works which were causing damage to the coastline and complained that the order against it had infringed its right to freedom of expression, and in particular its right to impart information, as guaranteed by Article 10 of the Convention. The Court noted that the main aim of the resolution had drawn the public authorities' attention to a sensitive issue of public interest. As a non-governmental organisation specialised in the relevant area, the applicant organisation had been exercising its role of a public "watchdog".[171] That kind of participation by an association was essential in a democratic society.[172] In the Court's view, measures interfering with this right must be proportionate to the legitimate aim pursued and a fair balance must therefore be struck between the interest of the individual and the interest of the community as a whole.[173] Consequently, despite the discretion afforded to

170 ECtHR, Vides Aizsardzibas Klubs v. Latvia (2004), App. No. 57829/00, Judgment of 27 May 2004, http://echr.ketse.com/doc/57829.00-en-20040527/ and https://wcd.coe.int/ViewDoc.jsp?id=1025311&Site=COE accessed 12 October 2013.

171 Manual on Human Rights and the Environment, Council of Europe Publishing (2012), http://echr.coe.int/Documents/Pub_coe_Environment_2012_ENG.pdf accessed 3 October 2013, p. 79.

172 For detailed information see https://wcd.coe.int/ViewDoc.jsp?id=1025311&Site=COE accessed 12 October 2013.

173 ECtHR, Vides Aizsardzibas Klubs v. Latvia (2004), App. No. 57829/00, Judgment of 27 May 2004, §40, http://echr.ketse.com/doc/57829.00-en-20040527/ and https://wcd.coe.int/ViewDoc.jsp?id=1025311&Site=COE accessed 12 October 2013.

the national authorities, the Court held that there had not been a reasonable relationship of proportionality between the restrictions imposed on the applicant organisation's freedom of expression and the legitimate aim pursued.[174] The Court therefore concluded that there had been a violation of Article 10.

In addition, in the case of *Leander v. Sweden*,[175] the applicant was denied a public position with important national security implications because of information provided to the employer by a secret police register. He alleged a violation of Article 10 since he was denied access to the file. However, the ECtHR unanimously stated that: "*the right to receive information basically prohibited a Government from restricting a person from receiving information that others wish or may be willing to impart to him. Article 10 does not, in circumstances such as those of the present case, confer on the individual a right to access to a register containing information on his personal position, nor does it embody an obligation on the Government to impart such information to the individual*".[176]

Besides the main restrictions, such as a legitimate aim and national security mentioned above, the Court went further in the case of *Thoma v. Luxembourg*.[177] The applicant was at the time a journalist on a national radio station, in Luxembourg entitled "Oekomagazin" dealing with nature and the environment. He considered that his right to freedom of expression had been violated by the Luxembourg authorities. The ECtHR held that when criticising public officials, as opposed to private individuals, a degree of exaggeration or even provocation is allowed when it is first, proportionate to the legitimate aim pursued; second with sufficient reason provided for its necessity to the functioning of a democratic society; and third, is in the general interest.[178] Then, the Court concludes there has been a violation of Article 10 of the Convention.

These cases may indicate merely that, in the given circumstances, the applicants did not really enjoy a right to information and the public authorities were not obliged to provide the relevant information. However, restrictions on the right to information could be justified under the second paragraph of Article 10. Obviously, how to handle a reasonable proportionality is the key issue in identifying these restrictions on the right to information. How to judge

174 For detailed information see https://wcd.coe.int/ViewDoc.jsp?id=1025311&Site=COE accessed 12 October 2013.

175 ECtHR, Leander v. Sweden (1987), App. No. 9248/81, Judgment of 26 March 1987, http://hudoc.echr.coe.int/sites/eng/pages/search.aspx?i=001-57519#{%22itemid%22:[%22001-57519%22]} accessed 24 October 2013.

176 ECtHR, Leander v. Sweden (1987), App. No. 9248/81, Judgment of 26 March 1987, §74, http://hudoc.echr.coe.int/sites/eng/pages/search.aspx?i=001-57519#{%22itemid%22:[%22001-57519%22]} accessed 24 October 2013.

177 ECtHR, Thoma v. Luxembourg (2001), App. No. 38432/97, Judgment of 29 June 2001, http://hudoc.echr.coe.int/sites/eng/pages/search.aspx?i=001-59363#{%22itemid%22:[%22001-59363%22]} accessed 12 October 2013.

178 Yusuf, S. (2012). Pursuing the right for today, securing the environment for tomorrow. UNISCI (Research Unit on International Security and Cooperation) Discussion Paper No. 29, www.redalyc.org/pdf/767/76724487011.pdf accessed 12 December 2013, p. 183.

the reasonable proportionality will depend on different cases. Nevertheless, these restrictions on such a right are necessary and important to improve the realisation of the right to information in practice.

5.1.3.3. Right to Environmental Information in the Aarhus Convention

The Aarhus Convention, a landmark international convention for procedural human rights relating to environmental protection, became open for signature at Aarhus, Denmark in June 1998. The Convention was sponsored by the UNECE and was open for signature by the 55 members of the UNECE, which includes all of Western Europe as well as the United States, Canada and former states of the former Soviet Union.[179] Under the Convention, meaningful involvement in environmental decision-making of the government is facilitated by greater transparency and accountability among government bodies. The subject of the Aarhus Convention goes to the heart of the relationship between people and governments.[180] The Convention's objectives are clustered into three main guarantees to the public, called the pillars of the Convention. These are: (1) reasonable access to information on the environment; (2) public participation in decision-making; and (3) access to justice in environmental matters (Article 1). Each Party is required to take the necessary legislative, regulatory and other measures to implement the objectives, achieve compatibility between them, and provide proper enforcement (Article 3).[181] The preamble to the Aarhus Convention sets out the aspirations and goals that show its origins as well as guide its future path.[182] In particular, the preamble emphasises two main concepts: environmental rights as human rights and the importance of access to information, public participation and access to justice for sustainable and environmentally sound development.[183] The Convention links environmental protection to human rights norms, raises environmental rights to the level of other human rights and acknowledges the existence of an obligation to protect

---

179 Alexandre, K. & Shelton, D.L. (2004). *International Environmental Law* (third edition). New York (USA): Transnational Publishers.

180 Lavrysen, L. (2010). The Aarhus Convention between environmental protection and human rights. *Liège, Strasbourg, Brussels: parcours des droits de l'homme.* Limal: Anthemis, pp. 647–671.

181 Lausche, B. (2011). *Guidelines for Protected Areas Legislation.* Gland (Switzerland): IUCN, http://data.iucn.org/dbtw-wpd/edocs/EPLP-081.pdf accessed 8 July 2012, pp. 43–44.

182 Ewing, M., Hough, A. & Amajirionwu, M. (2007). Environmental RTDI programme 2000–2006: assessing access to information, participation, and justice in environmental decision-making in Ireland. Prepared for the Environmental Protection Agency by Centre for Sustainability, Institute of Technology, Sligo in Partnership with Department of Law, University College Cork COMHAR, the Sustainable Development Council, www.environmentaldemocracy.ie/pdf/finalreport.pdf accessed 23 September 2013, p. 10.

183 Stec, S. & Casey-Lefkowitz, S. (2000). *The Aarhus Convention: an Implementation Guide.* United Nations Publication, www.unece.org/fileadmin/DAM/env/pp/acig.pdf accessed 23 March 2014, p. 16.

the environment for future generations.[184] It also establishes that sustainable development can be achieved only through the involvement of all stakeholders, and links government accountability, transparency, and responsiveness to environmental protection.[185]

The Aarhus Convention therefore expresses a particular blend of human environmental rights, making procedural entitlements necessary for the successful exercise of substantive environmental rights.[186] As the first pillar, access to information may be interpreted as an indispensable prerequisite for the other environmental rights in the Convention.[187] Effective public participation in decision-making depends on full, accurate, up-to-date information.[188] The Convention prescribes a general time limit for public authorities to make information available.[189] The requested information must be provided "as soon as possible and at the latest within one month". Numerous reforms have put this Convention on the top of the development chart for the right to information, giving this right its, at least until now, the most perfect, classic form.[190] Firstly, among the various information related to the environmental activities that public authorities conduct, a thorough list of documents in whose form these activities can appear is shown (environmental agreements, policies, plans, programmes,

---

184 Preamble paragraphs 1–2 and Article 1, the UNECE Convention on Access to Information, Public Participation in Decision-making and Access to Justice in Environmental Matters (Aarhus Convention), adopted on 25 June 1998 in the Danish city of Aarhus at the Fourth Ministerial Conference in the "Environment for Europe" process, 2161 UNTS 447, www.unece.org/env/pp/introduction.html accessed 10 March 2012.

185 Giorgetta, S. (2002). The right to a healthy environment, human rights and sustainable development, *International Environmental Agreements: Politics, Law and Economics*, 2, p. 184.

186 Mason, M. (2010). Information disclosure and environmental rights: the Aarhus Convention, global environmental politics, 10(3), http://eprints.lse.ac.uk/29135/1/information%20disclosure%20and%20environmental%20rights%20%28LSERO%29.pdf accessed 6 October 2013, p. 16.

187 Hayward, T. (2005). *Constitutional Environmental Rights*. Oxford: Oxford University Press, p. 178.

188 Ewing, M., Hough, A. & Amajirionwu, M. (2007). Environmental RTDI programme 2000–2006: assessing access to information, participation, and justice in environmental decision-making in Ireland. Prepared for the Environmental Protection Agency by Centre for Sustainability, Institute of Technology, Sligo in Partnership with Department of Law, University College Cork COMHAR, the Sustainable Development Council, www.environmentaldemocracy.ie/pdf/finalreport.pdf accessed 23 September 2013, p. 49.

189 Article 4(2), the UNECE Convention on Access to Information, Public Participation in Decision-making and Access to Justice in Environmental Matters (Aarhus Convention) was adopted on 25 June 1998 in the Danish city of Aarhus at the Fourth Ministerial Conference in the "Environment for Europe" process, 2161 UNTS 447, www.unece.org/env/pp/introduction.html accessed 10 March 2012.

190 Vucic, M. (2011). The right to environmental information as a techniques for the protection of the environment, www.doiserbia.nb.rs/img/doi/0025-8555/2011/0025-85551103449V.pdf accessed 9 October 2013, p. 455.

cost-benefit and other economic analyses).[191] Secondly, the provision in the Convention states that all the exceptions must be interpreted restrictively.[192] Thirdly, an obligation is introduced for the public authority which has received the request, if it does not possess the information, to direct the requesting person to another organ which might, by its knowledge be able to issue the given information.[193] Fourth, in order that the "free flow" of information to public authorities about proposed and existing activities could seriously influence the environment, mandatory system need to be established.[194]

Notably, this information pillar has two components. The first "passive" part is covered by Article 4[195] and consists of the right of the public to seek information from public authorities and the duty of public authorities to place

---

191 Article 2(3), the UNECE Convention on Access to Information, Public Participation in Decision-making and Access to Justice in Environmental Matters (Aarhus Convention) was adopted on 25 June 1998 in the Danish city of Aarhus at the Fourth Ministerial Conference in the "Environment for Europe" process, 2161 UNTS 447, www.unece.org/env/pp/introduction.html accessed 10 March 2012.

192 Article 4, the UNECE Convention on Access to Information, Public Participation in Decision-making and Access to Justice in Environmental Matters (Aarhus Convention) was adopted on 25 June 1998 in the Danish city of Aarhus at the Fourth Ministerial Conference in the "Environment for Europe" process, 2161 UNTS 447, www.unece.org/env/pp/introduction.html accessed 10 March 2012.

193 Article 4(5), the UNECE Convention on Access to Information, Public Participation in Decision-making and Access to Justice in Environmental Matters (Aarhus Convention) was adopted on 25 June 1998 in the Danish city of Aarhus at the Fourth Ministerial Conference in the "Environment for Europe" process, 2161 UNTS 447, www.unece.org/env/pp/introduction.html accessed 10 March 2012.

194 Article 5(1)(a) and (b), the UNECE Convention on Access to Information, Public Participation in Decision-making and Access to Justice in Environmental Matters (Aarhus Convention) was adopted on 25 June 1998 in the Danish city of Aarhus at the Fourth Ministerial Conference in the "Environment for Europe" process, 2161 UNTS 447, www.unece.org/env/pp/introduction.html accessed 10 March 2012.

195 Article 4.1, the UNECE Convention on Access to Information, Public Participation in Decision-making and Access to Justice in Environmental Matters (Aarhus Convention) was adopted on 25 June 1998 in the Danish city of Aarhus at the Fourth Ministerial Conference in the "Environment for Europe" process, 2161 UNTS 447, www.unece.org/env/pp/introduction.html accessed 10 March 2012. Article 4.1 points out: "Each party shall ensure that, subject to the following paragraphs of this article, public authorities, in response to a request for environmental information, make such information available to the public, within the framework of national legislation, including, where requested and subject to subparagraph (b) below, copies of the actual documentation containing or comprising such information: (a) Without an interest having to be stated; (b) In the form requested unless: (i) It is reasonable for the public authority to make it available in another form, in which case reasons shall be given for making it available in that form; or (ii) The information is already publicly available in another form." The UNECE Convention on Access to Information, Public Participation in Decision-making and Access to Justice in Environmental Matters (Aarhus Convention), adopted on 25 June 1998 in the Danish city of Aarhus at the Fourth Ministerial Conference in the "Environment for Europe" process, 2161 UNTS 447, www.unece.org/env/pp/introduction.html accessed 10 March 2012.

the information at the public's disposal in reply to an inquiry.[196] This Article requires the parties to (1) create an access-to-environmental-information law or regulation; (2) let the public know which public authority holds which type of information; (3) have a system to help the public formulate properly directed requests; (4) set clear standards for time limits; (5) create a schedule for charges; and (6) clearly define any exemptions.[197] In contrast to the "passive" (request-based) disclosure obligations on public authorities contained in Article 4, Article 5 covers the forms and categories of environmental information which public authorities are actively required to collect and disseminate.[198] This Article requires the Parties to (1) require record-keeping and reporting by public authorities and from operators to public authorities; (2) make lists, registers and files publicly accessible free of charge; (3) develop environmental information offices and identify individual points of contact; (4) use electronic databases and the Internet; and (5) create incentives for operators to give information directly to the public.[199] Both Article 4 and Article 5 include the provision that obligations are enacted "within the framework of national legislation," which allows Parties a significant discretion in disclosing information, including conditions for refusing information requests (e.g. for reasons of national defence and security, commercial confidentiality and personal data protection).[200] Article 5(1)(c) of the Aarhus Convention imposes a positive obligation on States to provide information in situations where individuals are exposed or are likely to be exposed to accidents linked to the presence of

196 United Nations Economic Commission for Europe (UNECE) (2013). The Aarhus Convention: an Implementation Guide, www.unece.org/fileadmin/DAM/env/pp/ppdm/Aarhus_Implementation_Guide_second_edition_-_text_only.pdf accessed 14 March 2014, pp. 90–95.

197 Ewing, M., Hough, A. & Amajirionwu, M. (2007). Environmental RTDI programme 2000–2006: assessing access to information, participation, and justice in environmental decision-making in Ireland. Prepared for the Environmental Protection Agency by Centre for Sustainability, Institute of Technology, Sligo in Partnership with Department of Law, University College Cork COMHAR, the Sustainable Development Council, www.environmentaldemocracy.ie/pdf/finalreport.pdf accessed 23 September 2013, p. 49.

198 Mason, M. (2010). Information disclosure and environmental rights: the Aarhus Convention, global environmental politics, 10(3), http://eprints.lse.ac.uk/29135/1/information%20disclosure%20and%20environmental%20rights%20%28LSERO%29.pdf accessed 6 October 2013, p. 15.

199 Ewing, M., Hough, A. & Amajirionwu, M. (2007). Environmental RTDI programme 2000–2006: assessing access to information, participation, and justice in environmental decision-making in Ireland. Prepared for the Environmental Protection Agency by Centre for Sustainability, Institute of Technology, Sligo in Partnership with Department of Law, University College Cork COMHAR, the Sustainable Development Council, www.environmentaldemocracy.ie/pdf/finalreport.pdf accessed 23 September 2013, p. 50.

200 Mason, M. (2010). Information disclosure and environmental rights: the Aarhus Convention, global environmental politics, 10(3), http://eprints.lse.ac.uk/29135/1/information%20disclosure%20and%20environmental%20rights%20%28LSERO%29.pdf accessed 6 October 2013, p. 15.

hazardous substances.[201] Article 5(3) of the Aarhus Convention requires Parties to ensure that environmental information progressively becomes available in electronic databases that are publicly accessible, and a majority of Parties are now reportedly using electronic communications tools.[202] Thus, it is becoming more feasible for these Parties to advance "targeted transparency" in which the holders of Aarhus rights are able to make reasoned judgments on specific policy choices.[203] Such moves would complement rather than supplant the general information disclosure provisions of the Convention, and are in keeping with its aspirations to environmental democracy.[204]

However, some previously existing constraints have survived in the Aarhus Convention, and since they are again vaguely defined, they are liable to discretionary interpretation by the public authorities which apply them.[205] These restrictions will be clarified below (see 5.1.3.4.3).

5.1.3.4. Case Law of the Aarhus Convention Compliance Committee

The Aarhus Convention Compliance Committee (ACCC) has now a long history of remarkable and sometimes ground-breaking recommendations (in the environmental activist jargon often mistakenly called "decisions").[206] It is interesting to discuss how the case law of the ACCC interprets the Aarhus Convention.

---

201 Right to information and participation in environmental decision-making, https://community.iucn.org/rba1/Pages/Rights%20to%20information%20and%20participation.aspx accessed 6 October 2013.

202 Economic Commission for Europe. (2008). Meeting of the parties to the convention on access to information, public participation in decision-making and access to justice in environmental matters. Third meeting Riga, 11–13 June 2008. Item 6(a) of the provisional agenda procedures and mechanisms facilitating the implementation of the Convention: reports on implementation. ECE/MP.PP/2008/4, 21 May 2008, www.unece.org/fileadmin/DAM/env/documents/2008/pp/mop3/ece_mp_pp_2008_4_e.pdf accessed 28 November 2013.

203 "Targeted transparency" means transparency measures tailored to the decision requirements of users and decision-makers. For detailed information see Fung, A., Graham, M. & Weil, D. (2007). *Full Disclosure: the Perils and Promise of Transparency.* New York: Cambridge University Press.

204 Mason, M. (2010). Information disclosure and environmental rights: the Aarhus Convention, global environmental politics, 10(3), http://eprints.lse.ac.uk/29135/1/information%20disclosure%20and%20environmental%20rights%20%28LSERO%29.pdf accessed 6 October 2013, p. 26.

205 Vucic, M. (2011). The right to environmental information as a techniques for the protection of the environment, www.doiserbia.nb.rs/img/doi/0025-8555/2011/0025-85551103449V.pdf accessed 9 October 2013, p. 457.

206 Justice and Environment (2011). The most recent (2008–2011) case law of the Aarhus Convention Compliance Committee, www.justiceandenvironment.org/_files/file/2011%20ACCC%281%29.pdf accessed 26 March 2014.

5.1.3.4.1. Providing Environmental Information upon a Request is an Obligation of a Relevant Authority

In the communication of *ACCC/C/2004/03 (Ukraine)*,[207] the Ukrainian non-governmental organisation Ecopravo – Lviv submitted a communication to the Committee alleging non-compliance by Ukraine with its obligations under the Aarhus Convention.[208] This communication concerned a plan to build a navigation canal in the Danube Delta passing through a protected area (wetland) with national and international importance. The Communicant provided some examples where it was refused access to documentation on the project either as a whole or in part. The Committee noted that the volume of information requested does not justify a refusal to provide the requested information. The Committee stated: "*In case where the volume is large, the public authority has several practical options: it can provide such information in an electronic form or inform the applicant of the place where such information can be examined and facilitate such examination, or indicate the charge for supplying such information, in accordance with Article 4, paragraph 8, of the Convention.*"[209] The Committee then found that, by failing to ensure that information was provided by the responsible public authorities upon request, Ukraine was not incompliance with Article 4(1) of the Convention.[210]

It could be concluded that providing environmental information upon a request is an obligation of a relevant authority. As for protected area conservation, the relevant information not only refers to the information about protected areas conservation and management, but any information that would potentially affect a protected area should also be provided for the public.

---

207 ACCC/C/2004/03 (Ukraine), ECE/MP.PP/C.1/2005/2/Add.3, 14 March 2005, www.unece.org/fileadmin/DAM/env/documents/2005/pp/c.1/ece.mp.pp.c1.2005.2.Add.3.e.pdf accessed 26 March 2014. Although this case also links to right to participation, this section only discusses right to information part in this case.

208 Economic Commission for Europe (2005). Findings and Recommendations with regards to compliance by Ukraine with the obligations under the Aarhus Convention in the case of Bystre deep-water navigation canal construction (submission ACCC/S/2004/01 by Romania and communication ACCC/C/2004/03 by Ecopravo-Lviv (Ukraine)). Adopted by the Aarhus Convention's Compliance Committee on 18 February 2005, ECE/MP.PP/C.1/2005/2/Add.3, 14 March 2005, www.unece.org/fileadmin/DAM/env/pp/compliance/C2004-03/S01C03findings.pdf accessed 28 March 2014.

209 ACCC/C/2004/03 (Ukraine), ECE/MP.PP/C.1/2005/2/Add.3, 14 March 2005, §33, www.unece.org/fileadmin/DAM/env/documents/2005/pp/c.1/ece.mp.pp.c1.2005.2.Add.3.e.pdf accessed 26 March 2014.

210 Economic Commission for Europe (2005). Findings and Recommendations with regards to compliance by Ukraine with the obligations under the Aarhus Convention in the case of Bystre deep-water navigation canal construction (submission ACCC/S/2004/01 by Romania and communication ACCC/C/2004/03 by Ecopravo-Lviv (Ukraine)). Adopted by the Aarhus Convention's Compliance Committee on 18 February 2005, ECE/MP.PP/C.1/2005/2/Add.3, 14 March 2005, www.unece.org/fileadmin/DAM/env/pp/compliance/C2004-03/S01C03findings.pdf accessed 28 March 2014.

In the communication of *ACCC/C/2008/24 (Spain)*,[211] the Spanish non-governmental organisation Association for Environmental Justice submitted a communication to the Compliance Committee. One of the arguments from the Communicant is that the Party imposed a fee for environmental information related to decision-making on a residential development project in the city of Murcia, Spain. The Party failed to comply with Articles 4(8) and 6(6) of the Convention. The Committee found that authorities provided paper copies of the information instead of an electronic version on a CD-ROM, as requested. The paper copies were 100 times more expensive than a CD-ROM. The requester found that it could not pay 1,200 EUR for the whole documents (600 pages). The requester decided to take only 34 pages, and also gave up its request for copies of certain relevant plans, as it would mean that it had to pay.

Therefore, the failure to provide information in the manner requested greatly limited the public's access to environmental information. The Committee concluded that Spain failed to comply with Article 4(1)(b), (2) and (8) of the Convention. The Committee held that providing environmental information upon a request is an obligation of a relevant authority. It also recommended the Party that only reasonable costs can be charged for providing environmental information to the public.

We can conclude from these two communications that providing environmental information on request is an obligation of a relevant authority and a relevant authority could only ask for a reasonable fee from the public for providing environmental information.

5.1.3.4.2. Access to Environmental Information Shall Be Readily Available to Support Public Participation in Environmental Matters

According to the introduction on the communication of *ACCC/C/2008/24 (Spain)*[212] above, the Communicant also alleged that the Party's responses to information requests were excessively delayed. Article 4(2) of the Convention requires that the environmental information be made available within one month after the request has been submitted. The total time of all extensions on the volume and complexity of the information provided cannot exceed two months after the submission of the request for environmental information.

The Committee noted that information itself was provided only three to seven months after the request for information had been submitted. Thus, the Party concerned failed to comply with Article 4(2) of the Convention. The

211 ACCC/C/2008/24 (Spain), ECE/MP.PP/C.1/2009/8/Add.1, 8 February 2011, www.unece.org/fileadmin/DAM/env/pp/compliance/CC-26/ece_mp.pp_c.1_2009_8_add.1_e.pdf accessed 21 March 2014.

212 ACCC/C/2008/24 (Spain), ECE/MP.PP/C.1/2009/8/Add.1, 8 February 2011, www.unece.org/fileadmin/DAM/env/pp/compliance/CC-26/ece_mp.pp_c.1_2009_8_add.1_e.pdf accessed 21 March 2014.

Committee recommended the Party concerned that information requests shall be answered as soon as possible and at least within two months from the date of the request for the volume and the complexity of the information. The related national legislation should be reviewed to provide for an easy and specific procedure to be followed.

The dispute in the communication of *ACCC/C/2009/37 (Belarus)*[213] concerns the access to information and public participation in relation to the proposed construction of a hydroelectric power plant on the Neman River in Belarus, which provides habitat to an array of imperilled bird species.[214] The Communicant claimed that the developer violated Article 4 and Article 6 of the Aarhus Convention for the reasons that firstly, the public was not sufficiently informed about how to acquire the Statement on the "assessment of impact upon the environment"; secondly, the information provided was often too vague to answer specific requests; thirdly, the national law did not guarantee public participation to be considered. The Committee then concluded that the developer indeed violated Articles 4 and 6 of the Aarhus Convention.

This communication shows that besides the relevant authorities indicated in the previous communications, a private developer also has the obligation to provide sufficient and timely information for the public to promote wide public participation.

We can conclude from these two communications that, as also indicated above, the realisation of the right to environmental information is a premise and an essential element for achieving the right to participation in environmental matters. However, if the realisation of the right to environmental information is excessively delayed, it will definitely obstruct the meaningful right to participation. Thus, access to information shall be readily available to support public participation.

5.1.3.4.3. Restrictions for a Request for Environmental Information

A request for environmental information may be refused if the disclosure would adversely affect: (1) various kinds of confidentiality under national law; (2) national security; (3) the ability of a public authority to conduct a criminal or disciplinary investigation; (4) intellectual property rights; (5) the interests of a third party who voluntarily gives the information to the government and who

213 ACCC/C/2009/37 (Belarus), ECE/MP.PP/2011/11/Add.2, 12 May 2011, www.unece.org/fileadmin/DAM/env/pp/compliance/C2009-37/Findings/ece_mp.pp_2011_11_eng_add2.pdf accessed 26 March 2014.

214 Justice and Environment. (2011). The Most Recent (2008–2011) Case Law of the Aarhus Convention Compliance Committee, www.justiceandenvironment.org/_files/file/2011%20ACCC%281%29.pdf accessed 26 March 2014, pp. 25–26.

does not consent to its release; or (6) the environment to which the information relates, such as the breeding sites of rare species and so on.[215]

For instance, the communication *ACCC/C/2007/21 (European Community)*[216] submitted by the Albanian non-governmental organisation Civic Alliance for the Protection of the Bay of Vlora deal with compliance by the European Union with its obligations under the Convention in relation to the actions of the European Investment Bank with respect to access to information and public participation in the decision-making on the financing and construction of a thermal power plant in Vlora (Albania).

The Committee rejected the position of the Party concerned that the identification of any harm to one of the protected interests would be sufficient to keep the information from being disclosed. According to Article 4(4)(d) of the Convention, a request for information may be refused if the disclosure would adversely affect "*the confidentiality of commercial and industrial information, where such confidentiality is protected by law in order to protect a legitimate economic interest*". As the Committee states, "*in situations where there is a significant public interest in disclosure of certain environmental information and a relatively small amount of harm to the interests involved, the Convention would require disclosure.*"[217]

Although this communication does not reach any conclusion as to what extent any "environmental information" contained in the documentation could have been considered as falling within an exempt category, the situation discussed above reflects that there should be some restrictions for a request for environmental information. How to judge the restrictions for a request for environmental information or to what extent environmental information could be disclosed largely depends on the different cases.

5.1.3.5. Influence of the Aarhus Convention on EU Law on Access to Environmental Information

At the European Union level, the Aarhus Convention has triggered the introduction of a new Directive 2003/4/EC. Directive 2003/4/EC on Public Access to Environmental Information[218] entered into force and replaced

---

215 United Nations Economic Commission for Europe (UNECE) (2013). The Aarhus Convention: an Implementation Guide, www.unece.org/fileadmin/DAM/env/pp/ppdm/Aarhus_Implementation_Guide_second_edition_-_text_only.pdf accessed 14 March 2014, pp. 90–95.

216 ACCC/C/2007/21 (European Community), ECE/MP.PP/C.1/2009/2/Add.1, 8 February 2011, www.unece.org/fileadmin/DAM/env/pp/compliance/CC-23/ece_mp.pp_c.1_2009_2_add.1_eng.pdf accessed 23 March 2014.

217 ACCC/C/2007/21 (European Community), ECE/MP.PP/C.1/2009/2/Add.1, 8 February 2011, §30 (c), www.unece.org/fileadmin/DAM/env/pp/compliance/CC-23/ece_mp.pp_c.1_2009_2_add.1_eng.pdf accessed 23 March 2014.

218 Directive 2003/4/EC of the European Parliament and of the Council of 28 January 2003 on Public Access to Environmental Information and Repealing Council Directive 90/313/EEC,

Directive 90/313/EEC[219] and expanded citizens' active rights of access to environmental information held by public authorities in the Member States, based on ideas and decrees of the Aarhus Convention.

As well as the Aarhus Convention, the Directive guarantees to every natural and legal person free access to environmental information, which is known to authorities or other subjects of private law, and that right may be exercised without any legal claim.[220] Directive 2003/4/EC states its aims in Article 1, namely the right of access to environmental information and its legal character[221] as well as the novelty that the right of access to environmental information applies to information held by or for public authorities. This means a significant broadening of the existing framework of this right, because it relates now even to environmental information, which the authorities do not in fact hold, but are in the possessions of some other authority.[222] In practice, "some other authority" could refer to the authority in private projects or NGOs that hold the relevant information. According to the regulations of the Aarhus Convention and of Directive 2003/4/EC, texts of all legal documents, politics, plans and programmes that are related to environmental protection[223] should be publicly available in the form of electronic databases, which means on the web pages of the relevant Ministries.

Since the Aarhus Convention sets the minimum standards for the EU law on access to environmental information, it is not necessary to further examine the relevant cases on access to environmental information in EU law for the reason that the baseline would be similar with what has been discussed in the ECtHR and the ACCC.

OJ L41/26, http://eur-lex.europa.eu/LexUriServ/LexUriServ.do?uri=OJ:L:2003:041:0026:0032:EN:PDF accessed 9 October 2013.

219 European Council Directive 90/313/EEC of 7 June 1990 on freedom of access to information on the environment, OJ L158, 23/06/1990 P, http://eur-lex.europa.eu/LexUriServ/LexUriServ.do?uri=CELEX:31990L0313:EN:HTML accessed 9 October 2013.

220 Kostic, M. (2006). *The Right of Access to Environmental Information in the Sense of the Aarhus Convention: European Streams and Legal Framework in Serbia and Montenegro*. CPRINT Beograd, p. 21.

221 Whereas the objective of Directive 90/313/EEC was to ensure freedom of access to environmental information (Article 1), the objective of Directive 2003/4/EC is to grant a right of access. This underlines that access to information for the public is a legal right and is in line with Article 1 of the Aarhus Convention; for more details see Henrike, M. (2000). *Access to Environmental Information in EU: the Revision of Directive 90/313/EEC*. Environmental Network Law International (ELNI). No. 2, p. 17.

222 Kostic, M. (2006). *The Right of Access to Environmental Information in the Sense of the Aarhus Convention: European Streams and Legal Framework in Serbia and Montenegro*. CPRINT Beograd, p. 46.

223 The quotations of the Aarhus Convention concerning dissemination of policies, programmes and plans relating to the environment, contain subsequently the expression "as appropriate" which means that the contracting parties of the Convention have right to decide which policies, programmes and plans are the most useful for the public and therefor should be publicly distributed. Regarding the legal acts contracting states do not have this right on the selection. See also: Stec, S. & Casey-Lefkowitz, S. (2000). *The Aarhus Convention: an Implementation Guide*. United Nations Publication, www.unece.org/fileadmin/DAM/env/pp/acig.pdf accessed 23 March 2014, p. 76.

5.1.3.6. *Right to Information in Protected Areas Conservation Law in Europe*

Based on what has been explored from the perspective of human rights, in order to better balance the potential conflicts regarding human rights protection and protected areas conservation, it is necessary to specifically examine the relevant provisions in the protected areas conservation law in Europe.

5.1.3.6.1. The Bern Convention

There is no specific provision on the right to information in the Bern Convention. Only Article 3 of the Bern Convention points out that: "*Each Contracting Party shall promote education and disseminate general information on the need to conserve species of wild flora and fauna and their habitats.*"[224] As indicated in the "Right to property concerning protected areas in Europe" section (see 4.3.4.1), if there is any infringement on the right to information in Europe, the relevant provision(s) from the European Convention on Human Rights can be applied.

5.1.3.6.2. The Birds Directive and the Habitats Directive

Concerning the Birds Directive, Articles 4(3),[225] 7(4),[226] 9(3)[227] and 10(2)[228] specifically say that the Member States shall send some relevant information

224 Convention on the Conservation of European Wildlife and Natural Habitats (Bern Convention) was issued in 1979 and entered into effective on 1 June 1982, BH756.txt;1284 UNTS 209, http://conventions.coe.int/Treaty/Commun/QueVoulezVous.asp?NT=104&CM=8&DF=&CL=ENG accessed 3 December 2012.

225 Article 4(3), Directive 79/409/EEC of 2 April 1979 on the Convention of Wild Birds, OJ L 103, 25 April 1979 (Birds Directive) was replaced by 2009 Birds Directive, http://euro-lex.europa.eu/LexUriServ/site/nl/consleg/1979/L/01979L0409-20070101-nl.pdf accessed 20 October 2012. Article 4(3) says: "Member States shall send the Commission all relevant information so that it may take appropriate initiatives with a view to the coordination necessary to ensure that the areas provided for in paragraphs 1 and 2 from a coherent whole which meets the protection requirements of these species in the geographical sea and land area where this Directive applies."

226 Article 7(4), Directive 79/409/EEC of 2 April 1979 on the Convention of Wild Birds, OJ L 103, 25 April 1979 (Birds Directive) was replaced by 2009 Birds Directive, http://euro-lex.europa.eu/LexUriServ/site/nl/consleg/1979/L/01979L0409-20070101-nl.pdf accessed 20 October 2012. Article 7(4) says: "Member States shall send the Commission all relevant information on the practical application of their hunting regulations."

227 Article 9(3), Directive 79/409/EEC of 2 April 1979 on the Convention of Wild Birds, OJ L 103, 25 April 1979 (Birds Directive) was replaced by 2009 Birds Directive, http://euro-lex.europa.eu/LexUriServ/site/nl/consleg/1979/L/01979L0409-20070101-nl.pdf accessed 20 October 2012, Article 9(3) says: "Each year the Member States shall send a report to the Commission on the implementation of paragraphs 1 and 2."

228 Article 10(2), Directive 79/409/EEC of 2 April 1979 on the Convention of Wild Birds, OJ L 103, 25 April 1979 (Birds Directive) was replaced by 2009 Birds Directive, http://euro-lex.europa.eu/LexUriServ/site/nl/consleg/1979/L/01979L0409-20070101-nl.pdf accessed 20 October 2012, Article 10(2) says: "Member States shall send the Commission any information required to

required by the Directive to the Commission. Article 12(2)[229] states that the Commission shall prepare a report as a feedback to the Member States.

As for the Habitats Directive, Article 17[230] refers to "information". It specifically points out that "*Member States shall draw up a report on the implementation of the measures taken under this Directive. This report shall include in particular information concerning the conservation measures (...) as well as evaluation of the impact of those measures on the conservation status of the natural habitats (...) and this report shall be forwarded to the Commission and made accessible to the public.*" Article 17 also says that "*the Commission shall prepare a composite report based on the reports referred to above. This report shall include an appropriate evaluation of the progress achieved and, in particular, of the contribution of Natura 2000 to the achievement of the objectives set out in Article 3. (...) This report shall be published by the Commission.*"

Furthermore, Article 18[231] says that the Member States and the Commission shall provide the relevant information for the purposes of proper coordination of research, especially for trans-boundary cooperative research between Member States.

These provisions indicate that although the Birds Directive and the Habitats Directive do not directly refer to the right to information of any individual(s) or NGO(s), the obligations of Member States and the Commission on providing the relevant information are addressed in these Directives. If anyone's right to access to the relevant information is infringed in Europe, the relevant provisions from the ECHR, the Aarhus Convention and EU Directive 2003/34/EC can be applied.

---

enable it to take appropriate measures for the coordination of the research and work referred to in paragraph 1."

229 Article 12(2), Directive 79/409/EEC of 2 April 1979 on the Convention of Wild Birds, OJ L 103, 25 April 1979 (Birds Directive) was replaced by 2009 Birds Directive, http://euro-lex.europa.eu/LexUriServ/site/nl/consleg/1979/L/01979L0409-20070101-nl.pdf accessed 20 October 2012, Article 12(2) says: "The Commission shall prepare every three years a composite report based on the information referred to in paragraph 1. That part of the draft report covering the information supplied by a Member State shall be forwarded to the authorities of the Member State in question for verification. The final version of the report shall be forwarded to the Member States."

230 Directive 92/43/EEC of 21 May 1992 on the Conservation of Natural Habitats and of Wild Fauna and Flora, OJ L 206, 22 July 1992 (Habitats Directive); text of the Directive, with later amendments, http://ec.europa.eu/environment/nature.legislation.habitatsdirective.index_en.htm accessed 20 October 2012.

231 Directive 92/43/EEC of 21 May 1992 on the Conservation of Natural Habitats and of Wild Fauna and Flora, OJ L 206,22 July 1992 (Habitats Directive); text of the Directive, with later amendments, see http://ec.europa.eu/environment/nature.legislation.habitatsdirective.index_en.htm accessed 20 October 2012.

5.1.3.6.3. Case Law in the Court of Justice of the European Union According to Protected Areas Conservation Law

One interesting case on protected areas conservation in the Court of Justice of the European Union[232] is *Commission v. Belgium*.[233] The Commission of the European Union was seeking a declaration that the Kingdom of Belgium has failed to fulfil its obligations under Article 4(1), (2) and (4) of Council Directive 79/409/EEC of 2 April 1979 on the conservation of wild birds.[234] The Commission explained that according to Belgian law, measures to ensure the complete transposition of Article 4 of the Directive, adopted by the regional authorities, must be published in the official journal of the Kingdom of Belgium in order to have binding force. Only such publication can make sure that citizens are aware of the measures and therefore could ensure that the measures are enforceable against third parties.

The Commission notes that although the maps demarcating the Special Protection Areas were simply to be found in the municipal offices, this cannot meet the requirements from Article 4 of the Directive. Then the Court declared that Belgium had failed to fulfil its obligation under Article 4 of the Directive.

This case reflects that in order to meet the requirements of the Directive, Member States shall fulfil their obligations to provide the relevant information in a certain way to the public. It means that the Directives indirectly guarantee the right to information of any individual(s) or NGO(s).

5.1.4. ANALYSIS AND INTERIM CONCLUSION

A right to information can mean, narrowly, freedom to seek information or, more broadly, a right to access information or a right to receive information.[235]

---

232 With the entry into force of the Treaty of Lisbon in 2009, the court's name was changed from the Court of Justice of the European Communities to the Court of Justice of the European Union. More information see European sources online, www.cardiff.ac.uk/insrv/resources/edc/Court%20of%20Justice.pdf accessed 12 April 2014.

233 Commission of the European Communities v. Kingdom of Belgium, Case C-415/01, Judgment of the Court (Sixth Chamber) of 27 February 2003, http://curia.europa.eu/juris/liste.jsf?language=en&num=C-415/01 accessed 10 April 2014.

234 Although the Birds Directive has been modified in 2009, the Article 4 from the 1979 version is consistent with the Article 4 from the 2009 version. Article 4 of the directive concerns measures of special protection and similar measures. Article 4(1) requires Member States to determine the most suitable territories for the conservation of the species listed in Annex I and to classify them as special protection areas. Article 4(2) requires Member States to take similar measures for regularly occurring migratory species not listed in Annex I. Article 4(4) requires *inter alia* that Member States take appropriate steps to avoid deterioration of natural habitats and the habitats of species as well as disturbance of the species for which the areas haven been designated.

235 Anton, D.K. & Shelton, D.L. (2011). *Environmental Protection and Human Rights*. Cambridge: Cambridge University Press, p. 357.

Governments increasingly recognise that environmental legislation will only be effective if individuals have a formal right to obtain environmental information, are empowered to participate fully in environmental decision-making and have redress to the courts when necessary.[236] Access to information about environmental conditions and proposed activities that might affect conservation as well as human rights is a prerequisite to public participation in decision-making and to monitoring governmental and private-sector activities.[237] This is explicitly approved by the case law of the ACCC in the section of "access to information shall be readily available to support public participation" (see 5.1.3.4.2). Therefore, there is no doubt on the importance of the right to information in environmental conservation in general, and protected areas conservation in specific. To empower local people and communities, to have the right to information is the first guarantee towards involving them in protected areas conservation.

5.1.4.1. Differences in the Right to Environmental Information in China and in Europe

Compared with the right to environmental information in China and in Europe, some differences as to the right to information in China and in Europe will be analysed below.

5.1.4.1.1. Different Historical Stages of the Right to Environmental Information

China did not have a widely accepted environmental information disclosure until the OEI Measures issued in 2007 (see 5.1.2.2). However, there is a long history and a vast amount of legislation and regulations on access to information in Europe. Although the right to information was recognised step by step under Article 10 of the ECHR, according to the case analysis above (see 5.1.3.2.1), the gap in the ECHR on the access to State information has recently been formally filled by a new convention, the Council of Europe Convention on Access to Official Documents, which was adopted by the Committee of Ministers on 27 November 2008.[238] Public access to clear and full information is widely accepted as a basic human right, although some restrictions exist. The right to

---

236 UNECE (United Nations Economic Commission for Europe) and UNEP (United Nations Environment Programme) (2006). Your right to a healthy environment: a simplified guide to the Aarhus Convention on access to information, public participation in decision-making and access to justice in environmental matters, www.unece.org/fileadmin/DAM/env/documents/2006/pp/ece%20mp%20pp%205_E.pdf accessed 10 October 2013, p. 2.

237 Greiber, T. *et al.* (2009). Conservation with justice – a human rights based approach. Gland (Switzerland): IUCN Environmental Law Centre, http://data.iucn.org/dbtw-wpd/edocs/eplp-071.pdf accessed 28 October 2011, p. 28.

238 Council of Europe Convention on Access to Official Documents, https://wcd.coe.int/ViewDoc.jsp?id=1377737 accessed 22 March 2013.

environmental information was also guaranteed in the Aarhus Convention as an important pillar in 1998. The case law of the ACCC and the Directive at the EU level further reflect some baselines for the right to environmental information.

5.1.4.1.2. Different Levels of the Right to Environmental Information

The right to environmental information contains a passive part, which focuses on the duty of the relevant authorities to disseminate information; and an active part, that is individuals or NGOs or the public have an active right to access to environmental information.

On the one hand, the authorities have duties or obligations to provide information which is requested by an individual, NGOs or the public. Corresponding obligations of the State can be limited to abstention from interfering with individual efforts to obtain information from public or private entities, or it can require the State to obtain and disseminate all relevant information concerning both public and private projects that might affect the environment.[239] The obligation on the part of public authorities to inform citizens about all the information related to the environment is correlative to the right to request the information, and thus raises in power above the simple obligation to inform and educate the public.[240] On the other hand, individuals or NGOs or the public have an active right to access the relevant information. It is fair to say that the relevant law and policy in China pay more attention to the obligations of the authorities, and pay less attention to the right to information of an individual or NGOs or the public (see 5.1.2). It is obvious to see that both of these issues (human rights and the obligations of the authorities) are addressed in Europe (see 5.1.3).

5.1.4.1.3. Different "Supporters" of the Right to Environmental Information

There is no independent human rights law in China at present; however some recent policy and environmental laws address the obligations of the authority to provide the relevant information (see 5.1.2). These recent policy and environmental laws also indirectly point out the right to information, but these cannot meet the requirements for practice. If there is any infringement on human rights, individuals or NGOs may appeal to the People's Court. This will be further discussed in the section of access to justice (see 5.3.1).

Conversely, on the one hand, the right to information is contained in the ECHR, although it was only indirectly approved by the ECHR at first

239 Anton, D.K. & Shelton, D.L. (2011). *Environmental Protection and Human Rights*. Cambridge: Cambridge University Press, p. 357.

240 Vucic, M. (2011). The right to environmental information as a techniques for the protection of the environment, www.doiserbia.nb.rs/img/doi/0025-8555/2011/0025-85551103449V.pdf accessed 9 October 2013, p. 461.

(see 5.1.3.2.1.1). The Aarhus Convention explicitly addresses the right to environmental information. On the other hand, protected areas conservation law in Europe focuses more on the obligations of the States to provide the relevant information on protected areas. If there is any infringement on human rights, individuals or NGOs can appeal to the specific human rights court (the ECtHR). The important role of the right to information can also be found in the CJEU case law with regards to protected areas conservation law.

We can conclude that the "supporters" for the right to environmental information in China are some recent policy and environmental laws in theory, and the People's Court in practice. However, there are various methods to solve the relevant issues in practice in China, which are not limited to going to a court (see 5.3.1). In Europe, the ECHR and the Aarhus Convention address the right to information, and the protected areas conservation law focuses more on the obligation to provide information. The ECtHR, the case law from the ACCC and the CJEU further provide some guidelines to solve the relevant issues in practice. These various "supporters" could effectively deal with the potential conflicts regarding the right to information protection and protected areas conservation in Europe.

5.1.4.2. Similarities in the Right to Environmental Information Between China and Europe

Apart from these differences, there are also some similarities between China and Europe. Firstly, the obligations on providing the relevant information can be restricted for some reasons. For instance, "national secret" or "business secret" are the normal reasons to restrict the obligations in China. According to Article 10 on freedom of expression of the ECHR, when public authorities take steps which may interfere with freedom of expression, their actions must fulfil three requirements.[241] These three requirements are: (1) their action must have a legal basis and its effects must be foreseeable, and the relevant action and the relevant domestic law must be accessible; (2) their action must pursue one of the interests set out in Article 10 paragraph 2; and (3) the means used by the authorities must be proportionate to the interest pursued. These are cumulative, meaning all three must be present for the restriction to be permitted under Article 10.[242] The Court has frequently stated that the adjective

241 Manual on Human Rights and the Environment, Council of Europe Publishing (2012), http://echr.coe.int/Documents/Pub_coe_Environment_2012_ENG.pdf accessed 3 October 2013, p. 78.

242 Article 10, European Convention on Human Rights (formally the Convention for the Protection of Human Rights and Fundamental Freedoms), drafted in 1950 and entered into force on 3 September 1953, 213 UNTS, www.echr.coe.int/Documents/Convention_ENG.pdf accessed 12 April 2013. For detailed information see www.echr.coe.int/Pages/home.aspx?p=home accessed 12 April 2013, Article 10 says: "The exercise of these freedoms, since it carries with it duties and responsibilities, may be subject to such formalities, conditions, restrictions or penalties as are prescribed by law and are necessary in a democratic society,

"necessary" in paragraph 2 implies the existence of a "pressing social need".[243] The Aarhus Convention and the case law from the ACCC also provide the detailed restrictions (see 5.1.3.4). Nevertheless, these restrictions also need to be necessary in a democratic society.

Secondly, although the development stages are different, the developmental tendencies in China and in Europe are similar. The status quo of the public access to environmental information has significantly improved in recent decades in China (see 5.1.2). The scope of the right holders is broader than before. For instance, besides an individual, NGOs can also ask for more environmental information in China (see 5.1.2.1.2). Similarly, an NGO in Europe was regarded as a public "watchdog" in the case of *Vides Aizsardzibas Klubs v. Latvia*. Notably, the right to environmental information has been improved both in Europe and in China. There is a similar situation for the right to information in protected areas conservation. Because of the different historical stages of the right to environmental information in China and in Europe as indicated above, we cannot expect the right to information in environmental protection, especially concerning protected areas conservation in China reach the same protection level as in Europe within such a short time. But China could make a great progress and learn some lessons from Europe in this regard.

5.1.4.3. *Some Lessons for China*

Besides the differences and similarities, some important lessons could be drawn for China. A governmental obligation to release information shall contain: (1) the information about its own projects that can affect human rights and the environment; (2) the information on numerous private-sector activities that can affect human rights and the environment;[244] (3) the information on some environmental protection activities that would potentially affect human rights; and (4) the information on the restrictions for the right to access information. The second point is difficult, but it may be obtained by the government through licensing or environmental impact requirements.[245] The third and fourth points are not always taken into consideration, but it cannot be missed. From the passive perspective, imposing on the State an obligation to disseminate this

in the interests of national security, territorial integrity or public safety, for the prevention of disorder or crime, for the protection of health or morals, for the protection of the reputation or rights of others, for preventing the disclosure of information received in confidence, or for maintaining the authority and impartiality of the judiciary."

243 e.g. ECtHR, Observer and Guardian v. the United Kingdom (1991), App. No. 13585/88, Judgment of 26 November 1991, §59, http://hudoc.echr.coe.int/sites/eng/pages/search.aspx?i=001-57705#{%22itemid%22:[%22001-57705%22]} accessed 4 November 2013.

244 Anton, D.K. & Shelton, D.L. (2011). *Environmental Protection and Human Rights*. Cambridge: Cambridge University Press, p. 357.

245 Anton, D.K. & Shelton, D.L. (2011). *Environmental Protection and Human Rights*. Cambridge: Cambridge University Press, p. 357.

information could help the public to participate in these activities. From the active perspective, the right to access to information shall also be addressed. This right could promote the realisation of the right to participation. In these two ways, local interests and concerns might be taken into account at an early stage, and then it would lead to fewer disputes and promote the process of the projects. Ideally, realising the public access to information requires governments to set up two systems. One system is to allow the public to request and receive information. The other system is needed for record-keeping and dissemination mechanisms. In this way the relevant authorities could collect and actively distribute information without request.

Furthermore, to address the difficulties and barriers encountered by the public when requesting for information in China, the Ministry of Environmental Protection (MEP) should draw from the best practices at the local Environmental Protection Bureaus (EPBs) as well as the experiences of environmental agencies overseas, and establish a set of standard operating procedures to provide environmental information.[246] It should also help local bureaus put the system in place and provide relevant training and assistance in applying the system. For instance, the inclusion of a column on "open government information" on the websites of the Gansu and Beijing EPBs is a practice that should be encouraged and rolled out across the country.[247] The MEP should also conduct regular assessments on the performance of local bureaus in environmental information disclosure – commending and rewarding those that have performed well and promoting best practices.[248] This will motivate the poorer performers to increase their level of responsiveness, and help build momentum for the implementation of the OGI Regulations and OEI Measures.[249]

What is more, to empower individuals or NGOs to have the "right" to information in China, both in theory and in practice, it is necessary to have further improvement. Some baselines and guidelines from Europe could serve

[246] CLAPV (Center for Legal Assistance to Pollution Victims) (2010). Access to environmental information in China: evaluation of local compliance, www.article19.org/data/files/pdfs/reports/access-to-environmental-information-in-china-evaluation-of-local-compliance.pdf accessed 23 September 2012, p. 28.

[247] CLAPV (Center for Legal Assistance to Pollution Victims) (2010). Access to environmental information in China: evaluation of local compliance, www.article19.org/data/files/pdfs/reports/access-to-environmental-information-in-china-evaluation-of-local-compliance.pdf accessed 23 September 2012, p. 28.

[248] CLAPV (Center for Legal Assistance to Pollution Victims) (2010). Access to environmental information in China: evaluation of local compliance, www.article19.org/data/files/pdfs/reports/access-to-environmental-information-in-china-evaluation-of-local-compliance.pdf accessed 23 September 2012, p. 29.

[249] CLAPV (Center for Legal Assistance to Pollution Victims) (2010). Access to environmental information in China: evaluation of local compliance, www.article19.org/data/files/pdfs/reports/access-to-environmental-information-in-china-evaluation-of-local-compliance.pdf accessed 23 September 2012, p. 29.

as good examples for China. This will be further clarified in the implementation part (see Chapter 7).

Specifically, in protected areas legislation, access to information is activated through two main approaches. First, the legislation should identify specific documents to be made publicly available for review, comment and information in the draft and final form.[250] These documents could include who is in charge of providing information, what type of information is needed, how and where to distribute information, when this information will expire, where and when the response or comment from the public could be submitted if this is necessary, and what the exemptions for the information are if necessary. As reflected in the general elements for protected areas legislation, public access should be provided by protected areas authorities to such key documents as draft and final protected areas system plans, proposals to declare an area as a protected area, draft and final management plans, and monitoring, evaluation and financial reports where public money is involved.[251] The second approach is to provide public access to certain government documents upon request, outside of any review and comment process.[252] The documents could contain some establishment and management plans for a protected area, scientific reports and detailed situation analyses for a protected area by the relevant authorities, assessment of the living standards of local people and communities before and after the establishment of a protected area, comments received by the relevant authorities as part of a review process for a draft plan. What is more, the detailed information on human activities, particularly some activities such as mining or building a road/dam that might destroy protected areas should be provided for the public, especially for the local people and communities. The local people and communities and some environmental NGOs could work as a "watchdog" to help the relevant authorities conserve protected areas. This is addressed in the case of *ACCC/C/2004/03* (see 5.1.3.4.1).

In many jurisdictions, access to information in general is governed by legislation of its own, which lays out the procedures for requests and for government response.[253] If separate legislation does not exist or is insufficient for the purpose of protected areas, protected areas legislation should contain some basic provisions on how the public can access the relevant document regarding the establishment and management of a protected area as was discussed above.

Nevertheless, the right to information is the lowest level of the right to participation. Groups and individuals can have access to information about

---

250 Lausche, B. (2011). *Guidelines for Protected Area Legislation*, Gland (Switzerland): IUCN, http://data.iucn.org/dbtw-wpd/edocs/EPLP-081.pdf accessed 8 July 2012, p. 44.

251 Lausche, B. (2011). *Guidelines for Protected Area Legislation*, Gland (Switzerland): IUCN, http://data.iucn.org/dbtw-wpd/edocs/EPLP-081.pdf accessed 8 July 2012, p. 44.

252 Lausche, B. (2011). *Guidelines for Protected Area Legislation*, Gland (Switzerland): IUCN, http://data.iucn.org/dbtw-wpd/edocs/EPLP-081.pdf accessed 8 July 2012, pp. 44–45.

253 Lausche, B. (2011). *Guidelines for Protected Area Legislation*, Gland (Switzerland): IUCN, http://data.iucn.org/dbtw-wpd/edocs/EPLP-081.pdf accessed 8 July 2012, pp. 44–45.

proposed actions or the information they want to search; however, they do not have a real opportunity to voice their opinions about the information or change the information if there is no right to participation.

5.2. RIGHT TO PARTICIPATION AND PROTECTED AREAS CONSERVATION

5.2.1. RELATIONSHIP BETWEEN THE RIGHT TO PARTICIPATION AND PROTECTED AREAS

While access to information is indispensable for an effective participation, the information itself is useless without having access to a forum for public participation. In other words, these two rights are interdependent and go hand in hand.[254]

5.2.1.1. Right to Participation in International Human Rights Instruments

This section will describe the relationship between the right to participation and protected areas in the light of international (regional) human rights instruments and international environmental instruments. The situation of the general right to participation and the right to participation of indigenous peoples will be introduced respectively from these two perspectives.

5.2.1.1.1. General Right to Participation in International Human Rights Instruments

The general right to participation is widely expressed in both international and regional human rights texts. Article 21 of the 1948 Universal Declaration of Human Rights affirms the right of everyone to take part in governance of his or her country,[255] so does the American Declaration of the Rights and Duties of Man (Article 20),[256] the African Charter on Human and Peoples' Rights (Article 13)[257] and Protocol No. 1 of the European Convention on Human

---

254 Atapattu, S.A. (2006). *Emerging Principles of International Environmental Law*. Leiden: Martinus Nijhoff Publishers, p. 360.

255 Universal Declaration of Human Rights, adopted on 10 December 1948, UN Doc. A/810 AT 71, UNGA Res. 217 A (III), www.un.org/en/documents/udhr/ accessed 4 November 2011.

256 The American Declaration of the Rights and Duties of Man was adopted in 1948, detailed information see www1.umn.edu/humanrts/oasinstr/zoas2dec.htm accessed 20 October 2012.

257 African Charter on Human and Peoples' Rights (also known as the Banjul Charter), adopted on 27 June 1981, OAU Doc. CAB/LEG/67/3/Rev.5 (1981), reprinted in 21 ILM 58 (1982), www.achpr.org/files/instruments/achpr/banjul_charter.pdf accessed 12 December 2013.

Rights.[258] Article 25 of the 1966 International Convention on Civil and Political Rights (ICCPR) provides that citizens have the right, without unreasonable restrictions, "*to take part in the conduct of public affairs, directly or through freely chosen representatives.*"[259]

5.2.1.1.2. Right to Participation of Indigenous Peoples in International Human Rights Instruments

Specifically, the right to participation of indigenous peoples was approved in some soft law. For instance, the General Recommendation No. 23: Indigenous Peoples[260] of the Committee on the Elimination of Racial Discrimination (CERD) called in particular upon States parties to "*ensure that members of indigenous peoples have equal rights in respect of effective participation in public life and that no decisions directly relating to their rights and interests are taken without their informed consent*".[261] In addition, the United Nations Declaration on the Rights of Indigenous Peoples also states that "*indigenous people have the right to participate in decision-making in matters which would affect their rights, through representatives chosen by themselves in accordance with their own procedures, as well as to maintain and develop their own indigenous decision-making institutions.*"[262]

Also, there are some provisions on participation in the ILO Convention No. 169.[263] Notably, among these, Article 6(b) points out that governments shall "*establish means by which indigenous and tribal peoples can freely participate, in all levels of decision-making (...) which concern them.*"[264] Participation is done through the indigenous and tribal people's own traditional or representative

258 Article 3: right to free elections. Protocol No. 1 of European Convention on Human Rights, www.echr.coe.int/Documents/Convention_ENG.pdf accessed 20 October 2012.

259 For detailed information see www.ohchr.org/en/professionalinterest/pages/ccpr.aspx accessed 25 October 2012.

260 For detailed information see www.unhchr.ch/tbs/doc.nsf/0/73984290dfea022b802565160056fe1c accessed 29 October 2012.

261 CERD (The Committee on the Elimination of Racial Discrimination), Office of the High Commissioner for Human Rights, "General Recommendation No. 23: Indigenous Peoples" was issued on 18 August 1997, §4(d), www.unhchr.ch/tbs/doc.nsf/0/73984290dfea022b802565160056fe1c accessed 29 October 2012.

262 Article 18, United Nations Declaration on the Rights of Indigenous Peoples (UNDRIP) was issued on 13 September 2007, UN Doc. A/RES/61/295, www.un.org/esa/socdev/unpfii/documents/DRIPS_en.pdf accessed 30 October 2012.

263 See also Articles 2, 5(c), 6(b), 7(1)(2)(4), 15(1), 22, 23, 29, International Labor Organization Convention No. 169: Indigenous and Tribal Peoples Convention, adopted on 27 June 1989 and entered into force on 5 September 1991, 28 ILM 1382, www.ilo.org/indigenous/Conventions/no169/lang--en/index.htm accessed 1 October 2012.

264 International Labor Organization Convention No. 169: Indigenous and Tribal Peoples Convention was adopted on 27 June 1989 and entered into force on 5 September 1991, 28 ILM 1382, www.ilo.org/indigenous/Conventions/no169/lang--en/index.htm accessed 1 October 2012.

institutions, "*and not through structures imposed from outside the community, unless the people have accepted them.*"[265] Article 13 adds that governments shall respect the special importance of indigenous peoples' relationship with their lands, particularly the collective aspects of this relationship.

The ILO Committee of Experts on the Application of Conventions and Recommendations (CEACR) commenced its discussion of ILO (International Labor Organization) Convention No. 169 in its General Report of 2009 with the following observation:

> *On the eve of the 20th anniversary of the adoption of the Convention, the Committee notes that the establishment of appropriate and effective mechanisms for the consultation and participation of indigenous and tribal peoples regarding matters that concern them is the cornerstone of the Convention, yet remains one of the main challenges in fully implementing the Convention in a number of countries.*[266]

5.2.1.2. Right to Participation in International Environmental Instruments

5.2.1.2.1. General Right to Participation in International Environmental Instruments

In the environmental sphere, public participation in environmental decision-making is an essential part of sustainable development. Although the basic human rights instruments (which do not focus specifically on the environment) sweep broadly enough to touch environmental issues, they are supplemented by many international legal instruments that specifically address the right to political participation in the context of the environment.[267]

From a historical perspective, public participation is indirectly but more formally emphasised in the 1972 Stockholm Declaration, which talks about equitable sharing of common efforts of citizens, communities, governments and private sectors in order to "defend and improve the human environment".[268]

---

265 Article 7(1), International Labor Organization Convention No. 169: Indigenous and Tribal Peoples Convention was adopted on 27 June 1989 and entered into force on 5 September 1991, 28 ILM 1382, www.ilo.org/indigenous/Conventions/no169/lang--en/index.htm accessed 1 October 2012.

266 International Labor Office (2009). Report of the Committee of experts on the application of conventions and recommendations", www.ilo.org/wcmsp5/groups/public/---ed_norm/---relconf/documents/meetingdocument/wcms_103484.pdf accessed 11 October 2013, p. 672.

267 Popovic, N.A.F. (1993). The right to participate in decisions that affect the environment. *Pace Environmental Law Review*, 10(2), http://digitalcommons.pace.edu/cgi/viewcontent.cgi?article=1572&context=pelr accessed 25 October 2011, p. 687.

268 Declaration of the United Nations Conference on the Human Environment (Stockholm Declaration), adopted on 16 June 1972, UN Doc. A/CONF.48/14/Rev.1 www.unep.org/Documents.Multilingual/Default.asp?documentid=97&articleid=1503 accessed 23 December 2012, Preamble, §7.

Apart from the 1972 Stockholm Declaration, some other non-binding[269] instruments refer to public participation. Notably, Principle 23 of the World Charter for Nature[270] and section III of Agenda 21[271] also refer to public participation. Agenda 21 also indirectly mentioned organisational capacities in the context of developing countries. There is one specific reference in Agenda 21 to environmental NGOs.[272] The Rio Declaration recognises the crucial role of public participation, not only in Principle 10,[273] but also in reference to different groups: women (Principle 20), youths (Principle 21), and indigenous peoples and local communities (Principle 22).

What is more, recent multilateral and many bilateral agreements contain references to or guarantees of public participation.[274] For instance, Article 16

---

269 e.g. Draft Principles of Conduct in the Field of Environment for Guidance of States in the Conservation and Harmonious Utilization of Natural Resources Shared by Two or More States (1978); WCED (World Commission on Environment and Development) Experts Group on Environmental Law for Environmental Protection and Sustainable Development (1986); UNEP (United Nations Environment Programme) Goals and Principles of Environmental Impact Assessment (1987); IUCN (International Union for Conservation of Nature) Draft Covenant on Environmental Conservation and Sustainable Use of Natural Resources (1991).

270 UN General Assembly. World Charter for Nature, adopted on 28 October 1982, A/RES/37/7, www.refworld.org/docid/3b00f22a10.html accessed 31 January 2014: "All persons, in accordance with their national legislation, shall have the opportunity to participate, individually or with others, in the formulation of decisions of direct concern to their environment, and shall have access to means of redress when their environment has suffered damage or degradation".

271 Agenda 21, adopted at United Nations Conference on Environment & Development in Rio de Janeiro in June 1992, http://sustainabledevelopment.un.org/content/documents/Agenda21.pdf accessed 8 June 2012, Section III identifies major groups whose participation is needed: women (chapter 24), children and youths (chapter 25), indigenous and local populations (chapter 26), nongovernmental organisations (chapter 27), workers and trade unions (chapter 29), business and industry (chapter 30), farmers (chapter 31), and the scientific and technological community (chapter 32).

272 Agenda 21, adopted at United Nations Conference on Environment & Development in Rio de Janeiro in June 1992, http://sustainabledevelopment.un.org/content/documents/Agenda21.pdf accessed 8 June 2012, Chapter 36, Activities 36.10(k): "Countries, the United Nations and non-governmental organizations should encourage mobilization of both men and women in awareness campaigns, stressing the role of the family in environmental activities", http://sustainabledevelopment.un.org/content/documents/Agenda21.pdf accessed 24 October 2011.

273 Rio Declaration on Environment and Development (The United Nations Conference on Environment and Development, UNCED), adopted in June 1992, A/CONF.151/26, www.unep.org/Documents.Multilingual/Default.asp?documentid=78&articleid=1163 accessed 22 June 2012.

274 In addition to the treaties discussed in the text, other agreements referring to public participation are, for instance Geneva Protocol Concerning the Control of Emission of Volatile Organic Compounds or Their Trans-boundary Fluxes entered into effective on 18 November 1991 at Geneva, Article 2(3)(a)(4), www.unece.org/env/lrtap/vola_h1.html accessed 8 October 2013; North American Convention on Environmental Cooperation came into effective on 1 January 1994, Articles 2(1)(a), 14, www.cec.org/Page.asp?PageID=1226&SiteNodeID=567&AA_SiteLanguageID=1 accessed 8 October 2013; Convention on Cooperation and Sustainable Development of the Waters of the Danube entered into effective on 29 June 1994 at Sofia, Article 14, www.icpdr.org/main/icpdr/danube-river-protection-convention accessed 8 October 2013; Protocol Concerning Specially

of the Helsinki Convention on Protection and Use of Trans-boundary Watercourses and International Lakes;[275] Article 9 of the Convention on the Trans-boundary Effects of Industrial Accidents;[276] Article 17 of the Convention for the Protection of the Marine Environment of the Baltic Sea;[277] Article 9 of the Convention for the Prevention of Marine Pollution of the North-East Atlantic;[278] Articles 13–16 of the Convention on Civil Responsibility for Damage resulting from Activities Dangerous to the Environment;[279] Articles 4.1(i) and 6(3) of the Kyoto Protocol to the United Nations Framework Convention on Climate Change;[280] and Article 14(1)(a) of the CBD.[281] Furthermore, the Stockholm Convention on Persistent Organic Pollutants[282] is more specific on public participation than most environmental agreements of global reach, in obliging the parties to promote and facilitate: "*Public participation in addressing persistent organic pollutants and their health and environmental effects and in developing adequate responses, including opportunities for providing input at the national level regarding implementation of this Convention.*"

Despite the softer form of "promote and facilitate", rather than "ensure" public participation, the Stockholm Convention sets out that participation must also include an opportunity for members of the public to address responses concerning persistent organic compounds as well as in considering the implementation of the Convention as such.[283]

Protected Zones and Biological Diversity in the Mediterranean was signed on 10 June 1995 in Barcelona and entered into force on 12 December 1999, Article 19, http://ec.europa.eu/world/agreements/prepareCreateTreatiesWorkspace/treatiesGeneralData.do?step=0&redirect=true&treatyId=598 accessed 8 October 2013.

275 Helsinki Convention on Protection and Use of Trans-boundary Watercourses and International Lakes, adopted on 17 March 1992, www.unece.org/fileadmin/DAM/env/water/pdf/watercon.pdf accessed 1 October 2013.

276 Convention on the Trans-boundary Effects of Industrial Accident, adopted in Helsinki on 17 March 1992 and entered into force on 19 April 2000, ECE/CP.TEIA/15/Add.1. It is designed to protect people and the environment against industrial accidents, www.unece.org/env/teia/ accessed 1 December 2012.

277 For detailed information see http://helcom.fi/Recommendations/Rec%2015-3.pdf accessed 26 October 2011.

278 For detailed information see http://eur-lex.europa.eu/Notice.do?val=225381:cs&lang=en&list=225381:cs,&pos=1&page=1&nbl=1&pgs=10&hwords=&checktexte=checkbox&visu= accessed 26 October 2011.

279 For detailed information see http://conventions.coe.int/Treaty/Commun/QueVoulezVous.asp?CL=ENG&CM=4&NT=150 accessed 27 October 2011.

280 United Nations Framework Convention on Climate Change (UNFCCC), adopted on 9 May 1992 and entered into force 21 March 1994, 1771 UNTS 107; 31 ILM 849, http://unfccc.int/2860.php accessed 8 June 2012.

281 For detailed information see www.cbd.int/convention/ accessed 26 October 2011.

282 Stockholm Convention on Persistent Organic Pollutants, signed on 22 May 2001 and entered into effective from May 2004, www.pops.int/documents/convtext/convtext_en.pdf accessed 18 September 2013.

283 Ebbesson, J. (2009). Draft paper on: Participatory and procedural rights in environmental matters: state of play. In: High Level Expert Meeting on the New Future of Human Rights and Environment: Moving the Global Agenda Forward Co-organized by UNEP and OHCHR,

5.2.1.2.2. Right to Participation of Indigenous Peoples in International Environmental Instruments

With regard to the right to participation of indigenous peoples, the UN Special Rapporteur on Human Rights and the Environment found that: "*Indigenous peoples have a special relationship with the land and the environment in which they live. (...) the notion of sustainability is the essence of both indigenous economies and their cultures.*"[284]

The CBD, as a typical international environmental instrument, affirms the need for the full participation of women at all levels of policy-making and implementation. It also calls for the participation of indigenous people and local communities in decision-making about sharing their knowledge, innovations and practices concerning conservation and sustainable use of biological diversity (Article 8(j)).

Among international environmental instruments, the most innovative with regard to indigenous rights and responsibilities is the Declaration on the Establishment of the Arctic Council.[285] A major feature of the Council is the involvement of indigenous peoples as "Permanent Participants", based on "*recognition of the special relationship and unique contributions to the Arctic of indigenous peoples and their communities*" (Preamble). Three organisations – the Inuit Circumpolar Conference, the Sami Council and the Association of Indigenous Minorities of the North, Siberia and the Far East of the Russian Federation – are specifically included in the Declaration.[286] The Declaration also proposes to "*provide for active participation and full consultation with the Arctic indigenous representatives within the Arctic Council.*"

Based on what has been discussed, we can conclude that the legal instruments from both the human rights perspective and the environmental perspective provide valuable insight into the elements of an operational public participation (or formal "right to participation") regarding environmental protection. They also reflect that the relationship between the right to participation

Nairobi, 30 November – 1 December 2009, www.unep.org/environmentalgovernance/LinkClick.aspx?fileticket=vZU4Z-_S4Vo%3d&tabid=2046&language=en-US accessed 28 October 2012.

284 Commission on Human Rights (1991). Human Rights and the Environment, Preliminary Report Prepared by Mrs. Fatma Zhora Ksentini, Special Rapporteur, pursuant to Sub-Commission on the Prevention of Discrimination and Protection of Minorities Resolutions 1900/7 and 1900/27 (E/CN.4/Sub.2/1991/8), 2 August 1991, §25.

285 Joint Communique (Canada-Demark-Finland-Iceland-Norway-the Russian Federation-Sweden-United States) and Declaration on the Establishment of the Arctic Council, adopted on 19 September 1996 at Ottawa, reprinted in 35 ILM 1382. Preamble and Articles 1(a), 2 and 3(c), for detailed information see http://1997–2001.state.gov/www/global/oes/oceans/arctic_council.html accessed 9 October 2013.

286 Shelton, D.L. A rights-based approach to public participation and local management of natural resources. http://pub.iges.or.jp/modules/envirolib/upload/1503/attach/3ws-26-dinah.pdf accessed 17 February 2014.

and environmental protection was recognised at the international level. In addition, Shelton notes that "*international human rights law limits the right to participation to citizens, whereas international environmental law extends the right to participation to all affected persons, irrespective of their nationality. International environmental law also provides more specific procedures as to how to exercise this right to participation.*"[287] Furthermore, the right to participation of the indigenous peoples attracts more attention.

5.2.1.3. The Value of the Right to Participation

"Public participation" is a generic term covering several mechanisms and practices that are different in mode, degree of formality, and timing in the decision-making process.[288] A government that involves the public in decision-making processes would first equip the public with the necessary information on the issues of their concern, then provide venues for the public to express views and deliberate on alternatives, and empower them to make decisions to advance their individual as well as collective interests.[289] In many situations multiple purposes are listed without differentiation between them or without discussion of how they relate to each other, or of whether certain potential benefits are omitted because they are not considered significantly. For instance Momtaz and Gladstone[290] include in the objectives of public participation "sharing information, involving the community at an early stage of decision-making, taking community aspirations into considerations and giving the community the ability to influence the outcome of decision-making". Stewart and Sinclair[291] envisage an even wider range of benefits, including access to local knowledge, broadening the range of solutions considered, avoiding costly litigation, strengthening the democratic

---

287 Shelton, D.L. (2001). Environmental rights. In: Alston, P. (Ed.). *Peoples' Rights*. Oxford: Oxford University Press, pp. 185–258.

288 Gauthier, M., Simard, L. & Waaub, J.P. (2011). Public participation in strategic environmental assessment: critical review and the Quebec (Canada) approach. *Environmental Impact Assessment Review*, 31, http://ac.els-cdn.com/S019592551000020X/1-s2.0-S019592551000020X-main.pdf?_tid=a3f8df34-3bc5-11e3-816d-00000aacb361&acdnat=1382520759_2a38087ba004286a7fcae70f901767e0 accessed 22 October 2013, p. 49.

289 Li, W.X., Liu, J.Y. & Li, D.D. (2012). Getting their voices heard: Three cases of public participation in environmental protection in China. *Journal of Environmental Management*, 98, http://ac.els-cdn.com/S0301479711004725/1-s2.0-S0301479711004725-main.pdf?_tid=12d7f9d0-3a22-11e3-a525-00000aacb35f&acdnat=1382340557_79eddc3b2a0974e6422e81879662b4e5 accessed 20 October 2013, p. 66.

290 Momtaz, S. & Gladstone, W. (2008). Ban on commercial fishing in the estuarine waters of New South Wales, Australia: community consultation and social impacts. *Environmental Impact Assessment Review*, 28(2–3), www.sciencedirect.com/science/article/pii/S0195925507000285 accessed 20 October 2013, p. 223.

291 Stewart, J.M.P. & Sinclair, A.J. (2007). Meaningful public participation in environmental assessment: perspectives from Canadian participants, proponents and government. *Journal of Environmental Assessment Policy and Management*, 9(2), www.worldscientific.com/doi/abs/10.1142/S1464333207002743 accessed 20 October 2013, p. 162.

fabric of society, acting as a vehicle for individual and community empowerment, and promoting broadly-based individual and social learning, so enabling the transition to sustainability.[292] Public participation cannot guarantee that every relevant party will be satisfied with a decision for the reason that different groups of peoples would have different priorities and concerns. However, involving all the relevant parties at an early stage in the decision-making process, and seeking methods for their ideas to be heard and taken into consideration, helps to allay concerns. It means that concerns can often be met early in a planning process, when changes may be easier to make, rather than late in the process when even small changes may cost both time and money.[293] Indeed, greater citizen input may promote environmental justice and help integrate ecological and social considerations in governmental decisions.[294] Furthermore, if the public is exposed to the whole range of factors which may influence a decision, even though people do not agree with the final decision, they are more likely to understand why it was made.[295] This may lead to less litigation, fewer delays and generally better implementation of decisions.[296]

Broadly evaluating whether stakeholder participation had improved the quality of local plans for the long-term management of ecological systems on the basis of theoretically-derived criteria, it was found that the presence of specific stakeholders significantly increased their quality.[297] It is claimed that stakeholder

---

292 André, P., Enserink, B., Connor, D. & Croal, P. (2006). *Public Participation International Best Practice Principles.* (Special publication series no. 4). Fargo (USA): International Association for Impact Assessment, www.iaia.org/publicdocuments/special-publications/SP4%20web.pdf?AspxAutoDetectCookieSupport=1 accessed 20 October 2013; Chávez, B.V. & Bernal, A.S. (2008). Planning hydroelectric power plants with the public: a case of organizational and social learning in Mexico. *Impact Assessment and Project Appraisal*, 26(3), pp. 168–160; Del Furia, L. & Wallace-Jones, J. (2000). The effectiveness of provisions and quality of practices concerning public participation in EIA in Italy. *Environmental Impact Assessment Review*, 20(4), pp. 460–461; Lockie, S., Franetovich, M., Sharma, S. & Rolfe, J. (2008). Democratization versus engagement? social and economic impact assessment and community participation in the coal mining industry of the Bowen Basin, Australia. *Impact Assessment and Project Appraisal*, 26(3), pp. 178–180; Peterlin, M., Kross B.C. & Kontic, B. (2006). Information in an EIA process and the influence thereof on public opinion. *Journal of Environmental Assessment Policy and Management*, 8(2), pp. 184–186.

293 DETR (Department of Environment Transport Regions) (2000). Public participation in making local environmental decisions: the Aarhus Convention Newcastle workshop, www.unece.org/fileadmin/DAM/env/pp/ecases/handbook.pdf accessed 18 March 2013.

294 Lee, M. & Abbot, C. (2003). The usual suspects? public participation under the Aarhus Convention. *The Modern Law Review*, 66(1), pp. 82–85.

295 DETR (Department of Environment Transport Regions) (2000). Public participation in making local environmental decisions: the Aarhus Convention Newcastle workshop, www.unece.org/fileadmin/DAM/env/pp/ecases/handbook.pdf accessed 18 March 2013.

296 Wirth, D.A. (1996). Public participation in international processes: environmental case studies at the national and international levels. *Colorado Journal of International Law and Policy*, 7, pp. 1–38.

297 Brody, S.D. (2003). Measuring the effects of stakeholder participation on the quality of local plans based on the principles of collaborative ecosystem management. *Journal of Planning Education and Research*, 22, pp. 407–419.

participation may increase the likelihood that environmental decisions are perceived to be holistic and fair, accounting for a diversity of values and needs and recognising the complexity of human-environmental interactions.[298] Some scholars also argue that participatory processes should lead to higher quality decisions, as they can be based on more complete information, anticipating and ameliorating unexpected negative outcomes before they occur.[299] By establishing common ground and trust between participants and learning to appreciate the legitimacy of others' viewpoints, participatory processes have the capacity to transform adversarial relationships and find new ways for participants to work together.[300] This may lead to a sense of ownership over the process and outcomes.[301] If this is shared by a broad coalition of stakeholders, long-term support and active implementation of decisions may be enhanced.[302] Depending on the nature of the initiative, this may significantly reduce implementation costs.[303]

However, there is a growing concern that stakeholder participation is not easily implemented well in practice. Stakeholder participation does not take place in a power vacuum: the empowerment of marginalised groups may have unexpected and potentially negative interactions with existing power structures.[304] The right to participation of local people and communities who live in or near protected areas could be regarded as a typical example.

---

298 Richards, C., Blackstock, K. & Carter, C. (2004). *Practical Approaches to Participation.* SERG (Socio-Economic Research Group) Policy Brief No. 1. Macauley Land Use Research Institute, www.macaulay.ac.uk/socioeconomics/research/SERPpb1.pdf accessed 17 March 2013.

299 Beierle, T.C. (2002). The quality of stakeholder-based decisions. *Risk Analysis*, 22(4), pp. 739–749. Fischer, F. (2000). *Citizens, Experts and the Environment: the Politics of Local Knowledge.* London: Duke University Press; Newig, J. (2007). Does public participation in environmental decisions lead to improved environmental quality? Towards an analytical framework. *Communication, Cooperation, Participation (International Journal of Sustainability Communication)*, 1, pp. 51–71; Koontz, T.M. & Thomas, C.W. (2006). What do we know and need to know about the environmental outcomes of collaborative management? *Public Administration Review*, 66, pp. 111–121.

300 Stringer, L., Dougill, A., Fraser, E.D.G., Hubacek, K., Prell, C. & Reed, M. (2006). Unpacking 'participation' in the adaptive management of socio-ecological systems: a critical review. *Ecology and Society*, 11, pp. 1–39.

301 Reed, M.S. (2008). Stakeholder participation for environmental management: a literature review. *Biological Conservation*, 141, http://ac.els-cdn.com/S0006320708002693/1-s2.0-S0006320708002693-main.pdf?_tid=ed10c162-3a82-11e3-9b8a-00000aacb361&acdnat=1382382155_c3a981c760012795fcaf6e6477e24e0d accessed 21 October 201, p. 2421.

302 Richards, C., Blackstock, K. & Carter, C. (2004). *Practical Approaches to Participation.* SERG (Socio-Economic Research Group) Policy Brief No. 1. Macauley Land Use Research Institute, www.macaulay.ac.uk/socioeconomics/research/SERPpb1.pdf accessed 17 March 2013.

303 Reed, M.S. (2008). Stakeholder participation for environmental management: a literature review. *Biological Conservation*, 141, http://ac.els-cdn.com/S0006320708002693/1-s2.0-S0006320708002693-main.pdf?_tid=ed10c162-3a82-11e3-9b8a-00000aacb361&acdnat=1382382155_c3a981c760012795fcaf6e6477e24e0d accessed 21 October 2011, p. 2421.

304 Kothari, U. (2001). Power, knowledge and social control in participatory development. In: Cooke, B. & Kothari, U. (Eds.). *Participation: the New Tyranny?* London: Zed Books, pp. 139–152.

5.2.1.4. Right to Participation in Protected Areas Conservation

Although the linkages between local people, biodiversity and protected areas are multifarious, the core idea is that protected areas created in isolation of local populations, in terms of their values, participation, or sharing of benefits, risk failure.[305] As the Director General of UNESCO states, "*without the understanding and support of the public at large, without the respect and daily care of the local communities, which are the true custodians of World Heritage, no amount of funds or army of experts will suffice in protecting the sites*".[306]

Notably, in 2004, the signatories to the Programme of Work on Protected Areas (PoWPA) in the CBD adopted and formalised a framework for the development of ecologically representative and effectively managed systems of protected areas in which a participatory approach is an essential element.[307] This CBD's 2004 Programme of Work on Protected Areas contains four programmes, 16 goals and associated targets and 92 activities for Parties. It emphasises the equitable sharing of costs and benefits, recognises various governance types and gives prominence to management effectiveness and multiple benefits.[308] By 2008, the public awareness, understanding and appreciation of the importance and benefits of protected areas is significantly increased (goal 3.5);[309] there should be full and effective participation of indigenous and local communities, in full respect of their rights and recognition of their responsibilities, consistent with national law and applicable international obligations, and the participation of relevant stakeholders in the management of the existing protected areas, or in the establishment and management of new protected areas (goal 2.2).[310] All protected areas should have effective management in existence by 2020, using participatory and science-based site planning processes that incorporate clear biodiversity objectives, targets, management strategies and monitoring programmes, drawing upon existing methodologies and a long-term

305 Gillespie, A. (2007). *Protected Areas and International Environmental Law.* Leiden (Netherland): Martinus Nijhoff Publishers, p. 168.

306 UNESCO (1999). The Twelfth General Assembly of the World Heritage Convention. WHC -99/COF.206/7, 8 November 1999, 4. Also see further comments on this point in UNESCO. (1998). The Twenty-second Session of the WHC. WHC-98/CONF.203/16, 31 January 1996, 63. UNESCO (1993). UNESCO. (1999). Second World Heritage Global Strategy Meeting for the Pacific Islands Region. August 2000.

307 Jones-Walters, L. & Civic, K. (2013). European protected areas: past, present and future. *Journal for Nature Conservation*, 21, p. 123.

308 Jones-Walters, L. & Civic, K. (2013). European protected areas: past, present and future. *Journal for Nature Conservation*, 21, p. 123.

309 For detailed information see www.cbd.int/programmes/pa/pow-goal-35.pdf accessed 9 March 2012.

310 For detailed information see www.cbd.int/programmes/pa/pow-goal-22.pdf accessed 9 March 2012.

management plan with active stakeholder involvement (goal 1.4).[311] Particularly, to review of implementation of goals 2 and 3 of the Strategic Plan, at the ninth meeting of the Conference of the Parties (COP) to the CBD, participants were therefore encouraged "*to ensure that conservation and development activities in the context of protected areas contribute to the eradication of poverty and sustainable development and ensure that benefits arising from the establishment and management of protected areas are fairly and equitably shared in accordance with national legislation and circumstances, and do so with the full and effective participation of indigenous and local communities and where applicable taking into account indigenous and local communities' own management systems and customary use.*"[312]

Moreover, the UNESCO's Man and the Biosphere (MAB) Programme,[313] the Ramsar Convention[314] and the World Heritage Convention (WHC)[315] stand out their detailed work on the local participation.[316] Among these, it is interesting to point out that the Ramsar Parties place a premium on the involvement of local communities, through what it currently identified as "Participatory Environmental Management".[317] The Guidelines for management planning for Ramsar Sites have called upon all Parties "*to make specific efforts to encourage active and informed participation of local and indigenous people (...) and their direct involvement, through appropriate mechanisms, in wetland management (...)*

---

311 For detailed information see www.cbd.int/programmes/pa/pow-goal-14.pdf accessed 9 March 2012.

312 Ninth meeting of the Conference of the Parties to the Convention on Biological Diversity, 19–30 May 2008, Bonn (Germany). Decision IX/8. https://www.cbd.int/decisions/cop/?m=cop-09 accessed 19 February 2014.

313 e.g. UNESCO (1968). Use and Conservation of the Biosphere. Paris: UNESCO, 223; UNESCO (1998). Biosphere Reserves: Myth or Reality? Paris: UNESCO, 48; Sumaco Biosphere Reserve in Ecuador, and Mulanje in Malawi. MAB (2000). The sixteenth Session of the ICC Bureau. SC-00/CONF.208/13.21; UNESCO (2002), Biosphere Reserves: Special Places for People and Nature. Paris: UNESCO, 48–55.

314 e.g. Resolution 5.6. Wise Use of Wetlands (1993, Kushiro); Resolution 8.14. New Guidelines for Management Planning for Ramsar Sites and Other Wetlands. (2002, San Jose). Annex; Resolution 8.25. The Ramsar Strategic Plan. (2002, Valencia). Annex. Operational Objective 6; Resolution 8.39. High Andean Wetlands as Strategic Resources. (2002, Valencia); Resolution VI:14. The Ramsar twenty-fifth Anniversary Statement and the Strategic Plan. (1996, Brisbane); Resolution 8.14. New Guidelines for Management Planning for Ramsar Sites and Other Wetlands. (2002, San Jose). Annex; Resolution 7.8. Local Communities and Indigenous People. (1999, San Jose).

315 e.g. Article 5, Convention Concerning the Protection of the World Cultural and Natural Heritage (WHC), http://whc.unesco.org/en/conventiontext/ accessed 18 February 2014; UNESCO (1995). The eighteenth session of the WHC. WHC -94/CONF.003/16, 31 January 1995, 42; UNESCO (2003). The sixth Extra-ordinary Session of the WHC. WHC – 03/6.EXT. COM/8. Paris, 27 May 2003, 9; UNESCO. (2005). Assessment and Conclusion of the Kazan Meeting. WHC -05/29.COM/9, Sections 19(g) and 20(c).

316 Gillespie, A. (2007). *Protected Areas and International Environmental Law.* Leiden (Netherland): Martinus Nijhoff Publishers, p. 172.

317 See Resolution 8.36. Participatory Environmental Management (PEM) as a Tool for Management and Wise Use of Wetland. (2002, Valencia).

with a view to reflecting their needs and values, traditional and other knowledge and practices in national wetland policies and programmes".[318] With regards to World Heritage Convention (WHC), the WHC Committee emphasised that meaningful dialogue and continuing participation and negotiation, between the interested groups, especially the traditional aboriginal owners of the area, who had serious cultural concerns about the project, was essential.[319] The UNESCO's Man and the Biosphere (MAB) Programme, the Ramsar Convention[320] and the World Heritage Convention (WHC)[321] also approved the NGOs' participatory roles in protected areas conservation.

Furthermore, the importance of active participation of local people and communities in protected areas management is repeated in some important regional instruments, for instance, in the framework of the OSPAR Convention.[322] In addition, the public participation of local people in protected areas conservation and management has long been advocated by the IUCN[323] and the World Parks Congress.[324]

---

318 Recommendation 6.3. Involving Local and Indigenous People. (1996, Brisbane).

319 UNESCO (1998). The twenty-second Session of the WHC. WHC -98/CONF.208/18, 29 January 1998, 43; UNESCO (2001). The twenty-fourth Session of the WHC. WHC -2000/CONF.204/21, 16 February 2001, 45; UNESCO (2002). The twenty-sixth Session of the WHC. WHC -02/CONF.202/25. 1 August 2002, 39; UNESCO (2003). The twenty-seventh Session of the WHC. WHC -03/27. COM/24. 10 December 2003, 45–46.

320 e.g. Recommendation 5.6. The Role of Non Governmental Organizations in the Ramsar Convention. (1993, Kushiro); Recommendation 6.12. Private and Public Funded Activities. (1996, Brisbane); Resolution 6.21. Assessment and Reporting on the Status of Wetlands. (1996, Brisbane).

321 e.g. UNESCO (1996). The nineteenth Session of the WHC. WHC -95/CONF.203/16. 31 January 1996, 35; UNESCO (1996). The Twenty Session of the WH. WHC -96/CONF.201/21. 10 March 1997, 15 and 17; UNESCO (1997). The Twenty-first Session of the WHC. WHC -97/CONF.208/17. 27 February 1998, 11 and 13; UNESCO (1998). The Twenty-second Session of the WHC. WHC -98/CONF. 208/18. 29 January 1998, 60; UNESCO (2001). The Twenty-fifth Session of the WHC. WHC -01/CONF.208/24. 8 February 2002, 36; UNESCO (2002). The Twenty-sixth Session of the WHC. WHC -02/CONF.202/25. 1 August 2002, 19.

322 The Convention for the Protection of the marine Environment of the North-East Atlantic (OSPAR Convention) was open for signature at the Ministerial Meeting of the Oslo and Paris Commission in Pairs on 22 September 1992. www.ospar.org/content/content.asp?menu=01481200000000_000000_000000 accessed 21 July 2013. The OSPAR Recommendation 2003/3 on a Network of Marine Protected Areas. Section 3. Management of the MPAs of the OSPAR Network. Appendix 2 Practical criteria/considerations. Section 3. Degree of acceptance. See http://rod.eionet.europa.eu/obligations/493 accessed 18 February 2014.

323 e.g. IUCN (1994). Indigenous Peoples' Resolution 22; IUCN (1996). Indigenous Peoples and Marine and Coastal Areas' Resolution 52, the first World Conservation Congress (Montreal); IUCN (1996). Indigenous Peoples and Protected Areas' Resolution 53, the first World Conservation Congress (Montreal); IUCN (2008). Indigenous Peoples, Protected Areas and the Implementation of the Durban Accord' Resolution 4.048; IUCN (2008). Supporting Indigenous Conservation Territories' Resolution 4.049; IUCN (2008). Recognition of Indigenous Conservation Territories' Resolution 4.050; IUCN (2008). Mobile Indigenous Peoples and Biodiversity Conservation' Resolution 4.053.

324 The third WPC (1982): "Parks for Development". WPC (2003). Mobile Indigenous Peoples and Conservation's Recommendation 5.27; WPC (2003). Cultural and Spiritual Values

Besides these, in practice, the Global Environment Facility (GEF) has actively facilitated the involvement of local communities. For example, by 2005, 6 million USD had been invested in participatory planning processes involving local and national stakeholders in more than 100 community based protected areas initiatives.[325] It also has 137 projects, focused on engaging the public (and NGO involvement in particular), covering 751 protected areas,[326] as well as supporting the involvement of local communities in protected areas, from traditional knowledge, to modern management initiatives.[327]

Based on what has been discussed, where necessary, all these should include removing barriers to participation by introducing regional and national legislation, policies, capacities and resources so that all rights-holders and stake-holders can participate effectively, if they wish.[328] In this way, greater involvement would occur. Allowing greater involvement by local people and communities is prudent for reasons of both pragmatism and social fairness. From the pragmatic viewpoint, it is better to establish good cooperation and collaboration with local people than to alienate and exclude them.[329] Local people and communities could contribute to the protection work, boundary maintenance and so on; they could be also given privilege of access to certain resources or jobs or some benefit-sharing which would stimulate their enthusiasm to conserve the areas and prevent encroachment. From the viewpoint of social fairness, protected areas are in most cases lands that local communities have protected and respected for centuries.[330] They have more emotional feelings for protected areas than any other person. Normally, if a person is attached to a place by owning property, having a family, or having a career, he/she may be

---

of Protected Areas' Recommendation 5.13; WPC (2003). Recognizing and Supporting a Diversity of Governance Types for Protected Areas' Recommendation 5.17; WPC (2003). Indigenous Peoples and Protected Areas' Recommendation 5.24; Brosius, P. (2004). Indigenous Peoples and Protected Areas. *Conservation Biology.* 18(3), pp. 609–612.

325 GEF (Global Environment Facility) (2005). Making a Visible Difference in Our World. Washington D.C.: GEF. p. 7; GEF (Global Environment Facility) (2005). People and Protected Areas. Washington D.C.: GEF. p. 1.

326 GEF (Global Environment Facility) (2005). People and Protected Areas. Washington D.C.: GEF. p. 17.

327 GEF (Global Environment Facility) (2005). People and Protected Areas. Washington D.C.: GEF. p. 18.

328 Borrini-Feyerabend, G., Dudley, N., Jaeger, T., Lassen, B., Broome, N.P., Phillips, A. & Sandwith, T. (2013). *Governance of Protected Areas: from Understanding to Action.* Best Practice Protected Area Guidelines Series No. 20. Gland (Switzerland): IUCN, https://cmsdata.iucn.org/downloads/iucn_governance_1109_1.pdf accessed 26 September 2013, p. 4.

329 Mackinnon, J. & Xie, Y. (2008). *Regional Action Plan for the Protected Areas of East Asia.* Bangkok (Thailand): IUCN, http://cmsdata.iucn.org/downloads/east_asia_action_plan_english_final.pdf accessed 18 May 2011, p. 46.

330 Mackinnon, J. & Xie, Y. (2008). *Regional Action Plan for the Protected Areas of East Asia.* Bangkok (Thailand): IUCN, http://cmsdata.iucn.org/downloads/east_asia_action_plan_english_final.pdf accessed 18 May 2011, p. 46.

more concerned about the environmental and health impacts of a project and participate more actively than those who do not have a sense of residence.[331]

Thus, public participation in the planning, establishment, management and enforcement strategies of protected areas could generate an increased sentiment of local ownership over protected areas, ensure that the needs of the local people and communities are incorporated into the decision-making process, provide a positive forum for conflict negotiation and settlement, and increase local compliance with the legislation, regulations or rules about protected areas.

It is necessary and important to evaluate the potential conflicts regarding the right to participation of local people and communities and protected areas conservation and their possible cooperation. The existing legal system and some cases regarding these issues in China and in Europe will be discussed respectively below.

5.2.2. RIGHT TO PARTICIPATION AND PROTECTED AREAS CONSERVATION IN CHINA

The right to information is the premise of the right to participation, and the right to participation is the effective way to access to the legal system. When the collective forests of Yuhu village were incorporated into the Yu Long Xue Shan protected areas in northwest China, without full consultation and meaningful involvement of local farmers, the farmers responded by cutting down the trees they had previously managed sustainably.[332] The right to participation not only means that you can participate in the decision-making, to some degree, but also means that you are esteemed.

5.2.2.1. The Development of "Public Participation" in China from a Historical Perspective

Before discussing the existing legal instruments, it would be interesting to explore the development of "public participation" in China from a historical perspective. The concept of "public participation" can be traced to the legacy of farmer participation in the rural collectivisation and commune programmes of

---

331 Li, W.X., Liu, J.Y. & Li, D.D. (2012). Getting their voices heard: Three cases of public participation in environmental protection in China. *Journal of Environmental Management*, 98, http://ac.els-cdn.com/S0301479711004725/1-s2.0-S0301479711004725-main.pdf?_tid=12d7f9d0-3a22-11e3-a525-00000aacb35f&acdnat=1382340557_79eddc3b2a0974e6422e81879662b4e5 accessed 20 October 2013, p. 67.

332 Fritz, K. (2009). National parks in China: a new model for nature conservation. http://digitalcollections.sit.edu/cgi/viewcontent.cgi?article=1708&context=isp_collection accessed 20 October 2012.

the 1950s, especially in overseeing local finances.[333] Later, in the 1970s, when Chinese environmental protection emerged, the government emphasised that environmental protection "depended on the public"; "everyone work" embodied the government's simple recognition on public participation.[334]

Notably, the first instrument evidencing a political will to provide for public participation appeared in a 1973 document entitled "Several Opinions on the Protection and Improvement of the Environment".[335] This was regarded as the most important outcome of the first National Conference on Environmental Protection of the State Council, for the reason that there was no previous public participation of any kind until 1996. It called on "the masses" to be involved in environmental protection.[336] Along with the emergence of various market players in post-reform China, political restructuring and democratisation have laid a foundation for public participation.[337] In 1996, the central government definitely pointed out to "*establish a public participation mechanism, develop social group function, and encourage the public to participate in environmental protection, impeach and reveal all kinds of behaviour against the environmental laws*" in the "Decision of the State Council on Several Issues Concerning Environmental Protection".[338] Then, the term "public participation" was used by the Chinese leadership in a decision of the third Plenum of the sixteenth Communist Party Congress in October 2003 (Central Committee 2003).[339]

From then on, the use of the term "public participation" is of relatively recent in China, although the concept itself is not. In its loose sense, "public participation" is used by Chinese observers to refer to a variety of participatory

---

333 Zhou, H.H. (2003). *Our Country's Experience with and Consideration of Open Government Affairs*. Beijing: China Law Press, Chapter 4.

334 Zhao, H.X., Qu, F.T., Zhu, P. & Shi, X.P. (2010). Resource and environmental issues in transitional China: a perspective from the interaction among market, government and society. *Chinese Journal of Population Resources and Environment*, 8(2), www.tandfonline.com/doi/abs/10.1080/10042857.2010.10684972#.UmvBdFJ-ghM accessed 20 October 2012, p. 20.

335 Du, Q. (2009). Public participation and the challenges of environmental justice in China. In: Ebbesson, J. & Okowa, P. (Eds.). *Environmental Law and Justice in Context*. Cambridge (UK): Cambridge University Press, p. 145.

336 Jin, R.L. (1990). *Environmental Law Science*. Beijing: Peking University Press, p. 8.

337 Zhao, H.X., Qu, F.T., Zhu, P. & Shi, X.P. (2010). Resource and environmental issues in transitional China: a perspective from the interaction among market, government and society. *Chinese Journal of Population Resources and Environment*, 8(2), www.tandfonline.com/doi/abs/10.1080/10042857.2010.10684972#.UmvBdFJ-ghM accessed 20 October 2012, p. 20.

338 Zhao, H.X., Qu, F.T., Zhu, P. & Shi, X.P. (2010). Resource and environmental issues in transitional China: a perspective from the interaction among market, government and society. *Chinese Journal of Population Resources and Environment*, 8(2), www.tandfonline.com/doi/abs/10.1080/10042857.2010.10684972#.UmvBdFJ-ghM accessed 20 October 2012, p. 20.

339 Horsley, J.P. (2009). Public participation in the People's Republic: developing a more participatory governance model in China, www.law.yale.edu/documents/pdf/Intellectual_Life/CL-PP-PP_in_the__PRC_FINAL_91609.pdf accessed 27 October 2012.

mechanisms, ranging from innovative deliberative democracy experiments at the local level,[340] to lawsuits against or complaints and petitions to the State, to request information from government agencies pursuant to China's recently promulgated government information disclosure regulations, to online activism by China's "citizens", to various kinds of protest.[341]

5.2.2.2. Legal and Policy Framework Concerning the Right to Participation

With regards to the existing legal instruments, Article 2 of the "Constitution of the People's Republic of China"[342] points out that: "*All power in the People's Republic of China belongs to the people. The National People's Congress and the local people's congresses at various levels are the organs through which the people exercise State power. The people administer State affairs and manage economic and cultural undertakings and social affairs through various channels and in various ways in accordance with the provisions of law.*" It provides, at least in theory, a principal legal basis for public participation in environmental protection.[343] In addition, in order to meet the requirements of the Rio Declaration and Agenda 21, the "Chinese Agenda 21" (1994)[344] was adopted by the State Council as an important guidance document for environmental protection and sustainable development in China. It points out that the methods and degree of participation for the public, communities and organisations will determine the process of achieving sustainable development. Since then, the modified "Law on the Protection of Women's Interest and Rights of the People's Republic of China" (2005 version)[345] and the political document "Programme for the Development of Chinese Women (2001–2010)"[346] aim to protect Chinese women's rights and

340 Leib, E.J. & He, B. (Eds.) (2006). *The Search for Deliberative Democracy in China*. New York: Palgrave Macmillan.

341 Horsley, J.P. (2009). Public participation in the People's Republic: developing a more participatory governance model in China, www.law.yale.edu/documents/pdf/Intellectual_Life/CL-PP-PP_in_the__PRC_FINAL_91609.pdf accessed 27 October 2012.

342 The "Constitution of the People's Republic of China" [中华人民共和国宪法] was adopted in 1982 and newly amended on 14 March 2004, www.for68.com/new/201007/he6049215912701021238З.shtml in both Chinese and English accessed 3 December 2010.

343 Article 2, the "Constitution of the People's Republic of China" [中华人民共和国宪法], www.for68.com/new/201007/he60492159127010212383.shtml in both Chinese and English accessed 3 December 2010.

344 Chinese Agenda 21 [中国21世纪进程] (1994), for detailed information see www.unescap. org/drpad/vc/conference/ex_cn_1_ca21.htm and www.acca21.org.cn/english/index.html accessed 4 October 2011.

345 The "Law of the People's Republic of China on the Protection of Rights and Interests of Women" [中华人民共和国妇女权益保障法] was adopted on 3 April 1992 and amended on 28 August 2005, www.china.org.cn/english/government/207405.htm accessed 2 December 2011.

346 The Programme for the Development of Chinese Women (2001–2010) [中国妇女发展纲要(2001–2010)] was published on 22 May 2001, www.china.org.cn/english/features/cw/140979.htm accessed 3 December 2011.

ensure their participation in national management and environmental decision-making. In addition, some law concerning environmental issues, such as the "Law of Land Management of the People's Republic of China"[347] and the "Water Pollution Prevention and Control Law of the People's Republic of China",[348] have included public participation, but they do not give a clear explanation about it, let alone establishing an integrated system for public participation.[349] The "Legislation Law of the People's Republic of China"[350] has stipulated that it should widely listen to the opinion from the relevant organs, organisations and citizens when the State Council formulates an administrative law and the different departments and local governments draft different regulations and the Chinese people should "*participate in legislation through various channels*".[351] Although these laws and implementing regulations issued thereunder do not use the term "public participation" *per se*, they enumerate a variety of mechanisms that could be used to obtain public input, with slightly different formulations depending on which drafting institution is involved.[352]

Article 11 of the "Regulations on procedures for the Formulation of Administrative Regulations"[353] points out that: "*the drafting of administrative regulations shall comply with the principles established by the legislation law and conform to the provisions of the Constitution and laws and meet the following requirements*". One of the requirements is "*safeguarding the lawful rights and interests of citizens, legal persons and other organizations in real earnest, and while prescribing the obligations they ought to perform, providing their*

347 The "Land Management Law of the People's Republic of China" [中华人民共和国土地管理法] was issued in 1986 and amended in 1998, and later amended on 28 August 2004, for detailed information see (1998 version) www.zhb.gov.cn/ztbd/rdzl/2010sdn/zcfg/201001/t20100113_184226.htm, and (2004 version) www.china.com.cn/chinese/law/647616.htmaccessed 3 January 2012.

348 The "Water Pollution Prevention and Control Law of the People's Republic of China" [中华人民共和国水污染防治法] was issued on 11 May 1984 and amended on 28 February 2008 and entered into force on 1 June 2008, www.lawinfochina.com/display.aspx?lib=law&id=6722 accessed 11 August 2011.

349 He, M. & Cliquet, A. (2013). Sustainable development through a rights-based approach to conserve protected areas in China. *China-EU Law Journal*. DOI 10.1007/s 12689-013-0031-7. http://link.springer.com/article/10.1007%2Fs12689-013-0031-7 accessed 4 November 2013.

350 The "Legislation Law of the People's Republic of China" [中华人民共和国立法法] was issued on 15 March 2000, http://english.gov.cn/laws/2005-08/20/content_29724.htm accessed 15 October 2011.

351 Article 5, the "Legislation Law of the People's Republic of China" [中华人民共和国立法法] was issued on 15 March 2000, http://english.gov.cn/laws/2005-08/20/content_29724.htm accessed 15 October 2011.

352 Horsley, J.P. (2009). Public participation in the People's Republic: developing a more participatory governance model in China, www.law.yale.edu/documents/pdf/Intellectual_Life/CL-PP-PP_in_the__PRC_FINAL_91609.pdf accessed 27 October 2012.

353 The "Regulations of the State Council on the Procedures for Formulating Rules" [行政法规制定程序条例] was promulgated by Decree No. 321 of the State Council of the People's Republic of China on 16 November 2001 and entered into force on 1 January 2001, www.gov.cn/english/laws/2005-08/24/content_25827.htm accessed 25 October 2012.

corresponding rights and the means by which the realization of these rights are guaranteed."[354]

Article 6 from the "Cleaner Production Promotion Law of the People's Republic of China"[355] states that the nation is committed to encouraging social groups and citizens to participate in the dissemination of public awareness with respect to cleaner production through education, popularisation, implementation and supervision.

A Chinese environmental journalist explains the historic importance of the "Law of the People's Republic of China on Environmental Impact Assessment" (EIA Law):[356] "*this was the first time in 2000 years that a law had been passed to give people the right to participate*".[357] Actually, this law is regarded as a great progress in the history of environmental legislation in China, for the reason that it makes a meaningful contribution to implement the basic national policy of environmental protection and the sustainable development strategy. The EIA Law emphasises that: "*The organ of formulation shall seriously think about the comments of related units, experts and the public on the draft environmental impact report, and enclose an explanation on whether to adopt the comments or not within the environmental impact report when submitting them for review.*"[358] It also points out that, with the exception of confidential circumstances specified by the State, for construction projects that might cause significant impact on the environment and need an environmental impact report, the construction unit shall hold a feasibility study meeting or hearing, or solicit relevant units, experts and the public by other means for comments before submitting the project environmental impact report for approval.[359] The "Regulation of the People's Republic of China on Environmental Impact Assessment of Planning"

354 The "Regulations of the State Council on the Procedures for Formulating Rules" [行政法规制定程序条例] was promulgated by Decree No. 321 of the State Council of the People's Republic of China on 16 November 2001 and entered into force on 1 January 2001, www.gov.cn/english/laws/2005-08/24/content_25827.htm accessed 25 October 2012.

355 The "Cleaner Production Promotion Law of the People's Republic of China" [中华人民共和国清洁生产促进法] was entered into effective on 1 January 2003 and amended on 29 February 2012, www.chinacp. org.cn/eng/cppolicystrategy/cp_law2002.html accessed 13 October 2012.

356 The "Law on Environmental Impact Assessment of the People's Republic of China" [中华人民共和国环境影响评价法] was adopted in 2002 and entered into effective on 1 September 2003, www.people.com.cn/GB/shehui/212/3572/3574/20021029/853043.html accessed 4 May 2012.

357 Cited in the film of "Walking the Green Tiger", further information see http://thetyee.ca/ArtsAndCulture/2011/10/07/Waking-The-Green-Tiger/.

358 Article 11, the "Law on Environmental Impact Assessment of the People's Republic of China" [中华人民共和国环境影响评价法] was adopted in 2012 and entered into effective on 1 September 2003, www.people.com.cn/GB/shehui/212/3572/3574/20021029/853043.html accessed 4 May 2012.

359 Article 21, the "Law on Environmental Impact Assessment of the People's Republic of China" [中华人民共和国环境影响评价法] was adopted in 2012 and entered into effective on 1 September 2003, www.people.com.cn/GB/shehui/212/3572/3574/20021029/853043.html accessed 4 May 2012.

(EIA Planning)[360] points out that the follow-up assessment of the environmental impacts of planning shall include public opinions of environmental impacts while the planning is implemented.[361]

The Ministry of Land and Resources promulgated provisions in 2004 that require hearings on the formulation of rules and regulatory documents relating to land use, compensation for land takings and development projects, all extremely sensitive issues in recent years.[362] Continued experiments in this area led to the revised 2008 "Urban and Rural Planning Law",[363] which requires that draft urban and rural land-use plans must be published for comment for not less than thirty days, the opinions of both experts and the general public must be sought through hearings, expert meetings and other channels, and those opinions must be considered and set forth in a report accompanying the draft plan submitted for approval.[364]

Besides these, in order to further promote the public participation in legislation, on 19 December 2006, the State Environmental Protection Administration, Chinese Communist Party's Propaganda Department and the Ministry of Education jointly issued an "instruction" on environmental communication and education in the eleventh five year period, which requires to build a better mechanism and provide broader channels for public participation in environmental protection, protect the public's rights to know, to participate, to express and to monitor, and ensure social stability.[365] According to the "Notification on Further Intensifying the Degree of Public Participation in Matters Related to Government Legislative Work from the

360 The "Regulation of the People's Republic of China on Environmental Impact Assessment of Planning" [规划环境影响评价条例] was adopted by the State Council on 12 August 2009 and came into force on 1 October 2009 (EIA Planning), www.lawinfochina.com/ProductsServices/index.shtm accessed 8 August 2011.

361 Article 25(3), the "Law on Environmental Impact Assessment of the People's Republic of China" [中华人民共和国环境影响评价法] was adopted in 2012 and entered into effect on 1 September 2003, www.people.com.cn/GB/shehui/212/3572/3574/20021029/853043.html accessed 4 May 2012.

362 Horsley, J.P. (2009). Public participation in the People's Republic: developing a more participatory governance model in China, www.law.yale.edu/documents/pdf/Intellectual_Life/CL-PP-PP_in_the__PRC_FINAL_91609.pdf accessed 27 October 2012.

363 The "Urban and Rural Planning Law of the People's Republic of China" [中华人民共和国城乡规划法] was issued on 28 October 2007 and entered into effect on 1 January 2008, www.lawinfochina.com/display.aspx?lib=law&id=6495 accessed 28 October 2012.

364 Article 26, the "Urban and Rural Planning Law of the People's Republic of China" [中华人民共和国城乡规划法] was issued on 28 October 2007 and entered into effect on 1 January 2008, www.lawinfochina.com/display.aspx?lib=law&id=6495 accessed 28 October 2012.

365 Wang, H. (2011). Stakeholder dialogue as an institutional strategy for sustainable development in China: the case of community environmental round-tables. The World Bank Development Research Group Environment and Energy Team, www-wds.worldbank.org/external/default/WDSContentServer/IW3P/IB/2011/08/15/000158349_20110815113133/Rendered/PDF/WPS5759.pdf accessed 21 October 2013, p. 7.

Legislative Affairs Office of the State Council",[366] local governments also published the related detailed regulations. For instance, the 2005 "Provisions on Public Participation in Environmental Protection of the Shenyang Municipality (Decree No. 42 of the People's Government of Shenyang City)" was the first legal document defining the rights of the public to participate in all aspects of environmental protection; it took effect on 1 January 2006.[367] It creates better defined legal concepts and jurisprudence on environmental rights, although its jurisdiction is limited to Shanyang City.[368] It also defines some key legal concepts such as: the public, rights of public participation in environmental protection, environmental information, and the responsibility to publish public environmental information, procedures to attain environmental information, and penalties for violation. All these stipulations significantly fill the vacuum in national legislation and provide a consolidated foundation for public participation.[369] In order to promote and standardise the work of public participation in the course of formulating rules and ensure that the formulation of rules is scientific, democratic and lawful, the "Guangzhou Municipal Measures on Public Participation in Formulating Rules"[370] was adopted. It sets out the requirements for the opinions raised by the public,[371] the principles of

366 The "Notification on Further Intensifying the Degree of Public Participation in Matters Related to Government Legislative Work from the Legislative Affairs Office of the State Council" [国务院法制办关于进一步提高政府立法工作公众参与程度有关事项的通知] was issued on 31 March 2007, www.chinabaike.com/law/zy/bw/bs/fzb/1376475.html accessed 25 October 2012. Although it is only a notification from the States Council, but it works as an important guidance document for local governments in China.

367 Du, Q. (2009). Public participation and the challenges of environmental justice in China. In: Ebbesson, J. & Okowa, P. (Eds.). *Environmental Law and Justice in Context.* Cambridge (UK): Cambridge University Press, p. 148.

368 Du, Q. (2009). Public participation and the challenges of environmental justice in China. In: Ebbesson, J. & Okowa, P. (Eds.). *Environmental Law and Justice in Context.* Cambridge (UK): Cambridge University Press, p. 148.

369 Du, Q. (2009). Public participation and the challenges of environmental justice in China. In: Ebbesson, J. & Okowa, P. (Eds.). *Environmental Law and Justice in Context.* Cambridge (UK): Cambridge University Press, p. 149.

370 The "Guangzhou Municipal Measures on Public Participation in Formulating Rules" [广州市规章制定公众参与办法] was adopted by the Guangzhou Municipal Government Standing Committee on 27 June 2006 and entered into effect on 1 January 2007, www.law.yale.edu/documents/pdf/Intellectual_Life/CL-PP-Final_GZ_PP_MeasuresFinal__tr9-4-09_%28Eng%29.pdf accessed 13 October 2013.

371 Article 4, the "Guangzhou Municipal Measures on Public Participation in Formulating Rules" [广州市规章制定公众参与办法] was adopted by the Guangzhou Municipal Government Standing Committee on 27 June 2006 and entered into effect on 1 January 2007, www.law.yale.edu/documents/pdf/Intellectual_Life/CL-PP-Final_GZ_PP_MeasuresFinal__tr9-4-09_%28Eng%29.pdf accessed 13 October 2013. Article 4 says: "When the public states their opinions, they should observe the country's laws, regulations and policies, may not violate good customs and may not maliciously attack the country, the government, organizations or individuals".

public participation[372] and the exceptions to the principle of openness.[373] It also emphasises the right to propose rules, handling opinions on the formulation of rules, making public the public's opinions and forms of soliciting the public's opinions and other detailed clauses for public participation.

In spite of the progress made on public participation, there is still a long way to go. According to Kezhu Xu, the deputy director of the Center for Legal Assistance to Pollution Victims of China University of Political Science and Law, "*the existing legal system for environmental issues in China emphasizes national environmental management rights, but it neglects the public participation. For instance, in Chinese environmental legislation, only environmental emergency treatment, pollutant emissions management and environmental impact assessment have provided some clear provisions for public participation*".[374]

Recently, the "National Human Rights Action Plan of China" (2012–2015)[375] points out the environmental rights, and it states that: "*China will strengthen its environmental protection work to guarantee the public's environmental rights, focusing on serious environmental pollution affecting the people's life, like heavy metal pollution, drinking water pollution, and air, soil and marine contamination, including improving environmental monitoring and supervision mechanisms establishing a trans-regional and inter-departmental cooperative mechanism for the enforcement of environmental laws, and improving the accountability system for major environmental and pollution accidents.*"

---

372 Article 5, the "Guangzhou Municipal Measures on Public Participation in Formulating Rules" [广州市规章制定公众参与办法] was adopted by the Guangzhou Municipal Government Standing Committee on 27 June 2006 and entered into effect on 1 January 2007, www.law.yale.edu/documents/pdf/Intellectual_Life/CL-PP-Final_GZ_PP_MeasuresFinal__tr9-4-09_%28Eng%29.pdf accessed 13 October 2013, Article 5 says "Public participation shall carry out the principles of openness, equality, inclusiveness and convenience".

373 Article 6, the "Guangzhou Municipal Measures on Public Participation in Formulating Rules" [广州市规章制定公众参与办法] was adopted by the Guangzhou Municipal Government Standing Committee on 27 June 2006 and entered into effect on 1 January 2007, www.law.yale.edu/documents/pdf/Intellectual_Life/CL-PP-Final_GZ_PP_MeasuresFinal__tr9-4-09_%28Eng%29.pdf accessed 13 October 2013. Article 6 says: "The opinions raised in the course of public participation should be made public, except for the following opinions: (1) opinions involving state secrets, commercial secrets or personal privacy; (2) opinions that violate the norms of morality; (3) where the public, at the time of submitting opinions, requests the administrative agency not to make the opinions public; (4) opinions that the administrative agency has reasonable grounds to believe are not suitable to made public."

374 www.taizhou.name/biz6/06930233102562447294.htm accessed 20 May 2012.

375 The "National Human Rights Action Plan of China (2012–2015)" [国家人权行动计划 (2012–2015)] was issued by Information Office of the State Council of the People's Republic of China in June 2012, www.hrol.org/Documents/ChinaDocs/Reports/2012-12/2982.html accessed 22 November 2013, in Chinese and English. It is only an action plan issued by the State Council, but it works as a guidance document for solving the relevant issues. It is also a remarkable step to show the progress that Chinese government has been made.

More recently, Article 5 of the newly modified "Environmental Protection Law of the People's Republic of China" (2014 version)[376] states that: "*Activities concerning environmental protection shall adhere to the following principles: (...) public participation (...).*" Article 9 says that "*The people's governments at various levels shall strengthen environmental protection publicity and dissemination, encourage self-governing grassroot organizations, social organizations and environmental protection volunteers to carry out the publicity of environmental protection laws, regulations and knowledge, so as to facilitate a favorable atmosphere for environmental protection*". Article 11 points out the government shall give awards to anyone who makes a great contribution in protecting and improving the environment. It remains to be seen how these Articles will be put into practice later on. Article 14 states that: "*When developing economic and technical policies, relevant departments of the State Council and people's governments of provinces, autonomous regions and municipalities directly under the Central Government shall take into full account their environmental impacts, and opinions from experts and relevant stakeholders.*"[377] This is indeed an exciting step forward for the reason that this Article specifically mentions the important roles of the opinions from relevant stakeholders.

Furthermore, as introduced above (see 5.1.2.1.2), the newly modified "Environmental Protection Law of the People's Republic of China" (2014 version)[378] provides an independent chapter on "information disclosure and public participation". Article 56 addresses that the opinions from the public shall be taken into account by the project owner and the competent department that is responsible for the examination and approval of environmental impact assessment documents for the construction project.

What is more, as introduced above (see 5.1.2.1.2), the "Measures on Right to Participation in Environmental Protection"[379] provide further information

376 The "Environmental Protection Law of the People's Republic of China" [中华人民共和国环境保护法] was promulgated by Order No. 22 of the President of the People's Republic of China on 26 December 1989, and was entered into effective on the date of promulgation; it was newly modified on 24 April 2014 and entered into force on 1 January 2015, http://edu.sina.com.cn/en/2014-05-20/144680376.shtml accessed 30 June 2014.

377 Article 14, the "Environmental Protection Law of the People's Republic of China" [中华人民共和国环境保护法] was promulgated by Order No. 22 of the President of the People's Republic of China on 26 December 1989, and was entered into effective on the date of promulgation; it was newly modified on 24 April 2014 and entered into force on 1 January 2015. http://edu.sina.com.cn/en/2014-05-20/144680376.shtml accessed 30 June 2014.

378 The "Environmental Protection Law of the People's Republic of China" [中华人民共和国环境保护法] was promulgated by Order No. 22 of the President of the People's Republic of China on 26 December 1989, and was entered into effective on the date of promulgation; it was newly modified on 24 April 2014 and entered into force on 1 January 2015. http://edu.sina.com.cn/en/2014-05-20/144680376.shtml accessed 30 June 2014.

379 The "Measures on Right to Participation in Environmental Protection" [环境保护公众参与办法] was issued by the department of environmental protection on 2 July 2015 and entered into force on 1 September 2015, www.zhb.gov.cn/gkml/hbb/bl/201507/t20150720_306928.htm accessed 1 October 2015.

on right to participation in environmental protection. For instance, Article 3 states that the public participate in environmental protection shall follow some principles, including according to law and regulation, orderly, voluntary and convenient. Article 4 says that environmental protection agencies shall take various measures, such as consultation, questionnaire survey, seminars, expert discussion meeting, hearing, to ask for suggestions and comments on environmental protection events or activities from citizens, units and other organisations. Citizens, units and other organisations could provide their suggestions or comments by phone, email, fax internet and other methods. Article 9 points out: "*Environmental protection agencies shall analyze and sum up the suggestions and comments from citizens, units and other organizations, give some feedback to them in an appropriate way and take these suggestions and comments fully into account when making a decision.*" Besides these, to some degree, right to participation also contain the public could have a right to monitor other citizens or units who would damage the environment and the public could have a right to report government or supervisory institutions if they find that local government or environmental protection agencies above the county level do not fulfil their duties in accordance with law or regulation. Articles 11 and 12 of the "Measures on Right to Participation in Environmental Protection" support these and Article 15 states that we shall reward any unit or individual who have a significant contribution in protecting and improving the environment. Furthermore, Article 18 says that the environmental protection agencies could support and guide social organisations to participate in environmental protection activities by various methods, including providing project funding and buying service. All these provide a more detailed legal basis for right to participation in environmental matters.

Similarly, as introduced above (see 5.1.2.1.2), the newly-issued "Overall Plan for the Reform of Ecological Civilization System"[380] points out the first principle for the reform of ecological civilisation system is to stimulate the role of social organisations and the public in participation and supervision. Point 38 states that it is necessary to improve the public participation system and to safeguard the public's right to supervise the environment. Although these are some general guidelines for public participation, these are helpful to improve the existing legal system for the right to participation in environmental matters.

5.2.2.3. The Right to Participation in Protected Areas Conservation

There are few clear Articles that mention any right to information or right to participation in the laws and regulations concerning protected areas. Only

380 The "Overall Plan for the Reform of Ecological Civilization System" [生态文明体制改革总体方案] was issued by the State Council on 21 September 2015, http://news.xinhuanet.com/politics/2015-09/21/c_1116632281.htm accessed 25 September 2015.

Article 7 from the "Regulations of the People's Republic of China on Nature Reserves" states that: "*People's governments above the country level shall strengthen the power to lead the development of protected areas. Every unit or individual has the obligation to protect the natural environment and natural resources and the right to report or accuse any unit or individual who destroys protected areas.*"

However, in order to stimulate the public's power in environmental protection, the Chinese State Environmental Protection Administration entrusted the Center for Legal Assistance to Pollution Victims of China University of Political Science and Law to write the "Measures on Public Participation in Environmental Protection" as an administrative rule. Participants from all over the world[381] have given different valuable suggestions on it, some of them suggested that the scope of public participation in environmental issues is mainly limited within the environmental impact assessment and construction projects, whereas the scope of public participation in environmental issues should be broader, especially for protected areas construction, resource exploration and so on.[382] Although this administrative rule has some limitations, it is a remarkable step to show that public participation in environmental issues in general and protected areas in specific is recognised by the central government. Canfa Wang, the director of the Center for Legal Assistance to Pollution Victims of the China University of Political Science and Law, further explained that: "*when the government is in a dilemma of developing the economy and protecting the environment, if there is another power to balance it, the government will certainly prefer developing the economy. The essential reason why we formulate 'the Measures on Public Participation in Environmental Protection' is to promote the power from the public to protect our environment*".[383]

Nevertheless, it is necessary to bring environmental democracy into the legislation, especially ensuring the right to information and the right to participation for any parties, including NGOs, in protected areas management.[384] The real public participation should include pre-planning participation (the public can get the opportunity to participate in the discussions

---

381 The participants include the representatives from National People's Congress, the State Council, local Courts, local Environmental Protection Bureau, United Nations Economic Commission for Europe, the Secretariat of Aarhus Convention, United Sates Natural Resources Defense Council.

382 Xian, P. (2006). Experts discussing the public participation in environmental protection legislation – the scope of participation should be broader and the participants should be pluralism, www.clapv.org/NewsContent.asp?id=532 accessed 9 May 2012.

383 Xian, P. (2006). Experts discussing the public participation in environmental protection legislation – the scope of participation should be broader and the participants should be pluralism, www.clapv.org/NewsContent.asp?id=532 accessed 9 May 2012.

384 He, M. & Cliquet, A. (2013). Sustainable development through a rights-based approach to conserve protected areas in China. *China-EU Law Journal*. DOI 10.1007/s 12689-013-0031-7. http://link.springer.com/article/10.1007%2Fs12689-013-0031-7 accessed 4 November 2013.

or negotiations before drafting environmental policy or legislation, or preparing construction projects), process participation (the public can participate in the process of implementing the environmental law, regulation or policy or constructing programmes), action participation (the public has an awareness of "protecting environment by ourselves" and put the awareness into real behaviour), final participation (the public can access the legal system and get a legal remedy). Only through these four kinds of participation, can the public have a holistic and real participation to achieve the final environmental goal. Simply, it is better to change "passive participation"[385] to "self-mobilisation participation"[386] or "active participation".

Fortunately, some improvements have been made in new regulations and policy since 2010. For instance, Article 13 of the "Interim Management Measures on the Special Marine Protected Areas"[387] states that before establishing marine protected areas, the authority shall inform the public and let the public give some suggestions and comments. Article 17 points out to the information issue: it states that after establishing special marine protected areas, the authority shall build some landmarks and signs in some appropriate places according to their boundaries, the authority also shall publish management rules, measures and other relevant information on special marine protected areas.

The "Strategy and Action Plan for Biodiversity Preservation in China" (2011–2030)[388] pointed out four basic principles for biodiversity conservation,

---

385 The "passive participation" means people participate by being told what is going to happen or what has already happened, but they have no opportunity to change them. Detailed information see Pimber, M.L. & Pretty, J.N. (1997). Parks people and professionals: putting "participation" into protected area management. In: Ghimire, K.B. & Pimber, M.P. (Eds.). *Social Change and Conservation: Environmental Politics and Impacts of National Parks and Protected Areas*. London: Earthscan, pp. 297–330.

386 The "self-mobilization participation" means people participate by taking initiatives independent of external institutions to change systems. For detailed information see Pimber, M.L. & Pretty, J.N. (1997). Parks people and professionals: putting "participation" into protected area management. In: Ghimire, K.B. & Pimber, M.P. (Eds.). *Social Change and Conservation: Environmental Politics and Impacts of National Parks and Protected Areas*. London: Earthscan, pp. 297–330. The "self-mobilization participation" also means all the relevant parties actively participate in the whole process and take their possible reasonable responsibilities. Detailed information see Zhao, L.L. (赵丽丽) (2009). *The Community-based Management on Fishery in China* (中国基于社区的渔业管理研究). Doctoral Dissertation in Ocean University of China(中国海洋大学博士论文).

387 The "Interim Management Measures on the Special Marine Protected Areas" [海洋特别保护区管理暂行办法] was issued by the State Oceanic Administration of the People's Republic of China on 31 August 2010, www.shanghaiwater.gov.cn/xwzx!view.action?fan.fileId=20091759&sdh.code=004015001 accessed 4 December 2011. Although it is called and translated as "management measures", it is a regulation for special marine protected areas in China.

388 The "Strategy and Action Plan for Biodiversity Preservation in China (2011–2030)" [中国生物多样性保护战略与行动计划(2011–2030)] was issued on 17 September 2010, www.mep. gov.cn/gkml/hbb/bwj/201009/t20100921_194841.htm accessed 3 December 2011. Although it is only a legal document from the Chinese Environmental Protection Bureau, it is regarded as guidelines for solving the relevant issues in China.

namely conservation priority, sustainable utilisation, public participation, and benefit-sharing. It also clarified ten pioneer fields and actions. The first pioneer field is to improve the policy and legal system for biodiversity conservation and sustainable utilisation, including completely reviewing the law and regulations to solve the conflicts regarding them, researching the law and regulations on protected areas management, and strengthening the implementation system for the law and regulations. The fourth action is to formally manage protected areas and to improve the quality of management, including drawing up an all-aspects plan for designation and management, regularly evaluating the implementation, exploring the different co-management models for different protected areas, experimenting in the selected areas, and popularising the experimentation. Action 29 indicates that it should establish a broad public participation mechanism, including improving the effective public participation system, such as hearings, seminars and establishing a public and media supervision mechanism to guarantee the implementation of the relevant policy.

Besides these, the Ministry of Environmental Protection issued a "Notification on Further Strengthening the Hydropower Construction for Environmental Protection" on 6 January 2012.[389] It points out that it is forbidden to explore any hydropower resource in any protected area, scenic spot and other areas with special conservation values. When building hydroelectric dams, the right to information and right to participation of the public must be guaranteed.[390] Furthermore, in the 18th National People's Congress of the Chinese Communist Party in 2012, the Ministry of Environmental Protection commented on environmental issues, stating that four measures are needed; one of them being to further expand the degree of public participation[391]

In addition, the provincial governments also make some progress in ensuring the public's rights. For instance, in order to further clarify the boundaries of protected areas and to guarantee the public's right to information and right to participation, the Ethnic and Religious Overseas Foreign Affairs Committee of the Hubei Provincial People's Congress proposed some

389 The "Notification on Further to Strengthen Hydropower Construction and Environmental Protection" [关于进一步加强水电建设环境保护的通知] was issued on 6 January 2012 by the Ministry of Environmental Protection of the People's Republic of China, www.mep.gov.cn/gkml/hbb/bgt/201201/t20120117_222665.htm accessed 11 January 2012. This notification can be regarded as a policy, but it helps to forbidden some economic activities in protected areas in China.

390 He, M. & Cliquet, A. (2013). Sustainable development through a rights-based approach to conserve protected areas in China. *China-EU Law Journal.* DOI 10.1007/s 12689-013-0031-7. http://link.springer.com/article/10.1007%2Fs12689-013-0031-7 accessed 4 November 2013.

391 Xinhua Net (2012). The department of environmental protection response to environmental groups events: it is rule of development. Posted on 12 November 2012, http://news.163.com/12/1112/19/8G4PDG5L0001124J.html accessed 12 November 2012.

suggestions to modify the "Hubei Xingdoushan National Nature Reserve Management Regulation in Enshi Tujia and Miao autonomous prefecture".[392] This regulation also indicates a step forward for the public's right in protected areas conservation.

5.2.2.4. Public Participation in Practice

In practice, public participation contains legislative hearings, development of other kinds of meetings and workshops, notice and comment procedures, and extending public participation to policy decision-making.[393] The first public hearing ever convened by the State Environmental Protection Administration (SEPA) did not take place until April 2005 in response to a public outcry over a water conservation project to line lakes with plastic tubes in Beijing's historic Yuanmingyuan Park.[394] The project had not obtained the required environmental impact assessment approval, and academics and conservationists argued it would negatively impact Beijing's underground water systems.[395] There were 120 participants that raised different views in the hearing. An assessment was conducted and the plastic lining was largely replaced with clay. The SEPA then issued interim measures specifically on public participation in environmental impact assessment, which were effective on 18 March 2006, to attempt to ensure greater disclosure of environment-relevant information and provide more details on different mechanisms that should be used to obtain public input into the EIA process.

Another notable case is the Nujiang[396] hydroelectric power station planning campaign of 2003, in which the public used an environmental impact assessment to correct governmental planning proceedings.[397] Since Yunnan provincial government approved the Nujiang hydroelectric power station in 2003,

---

392 The "Hubei Xingdoushan National Nature Reserve Management Regulation in Enshi Tujia and Miao autonomous prefecture" [湖北省人民代表大会民族宗教侨务外事委员会关于《恩施土家族苗族自治州湖北星斗山国家级自然保护区管理条例》] was issued on 30 July 2010, www.hppc.gov.cn/list-hyzl.asp?id=164 accessed 10 February 2012.

393 Horsley, J.P. (2009). Public participation in the People's Republic: developing a more participatory governance model in China, www.law.yale.edu/documents/pdf/Intellectual_Life/CL-PP-PP_in_the__PRC_FINAL_91609.pdf accessed 27 October 2012.

394 Gong, Y.D. (2006). Public hearings: driving the engine of democracy in China. Posted in China Daily, www.chinadaily.com.cn/china/2006-10/05/content_701880.htm accessed 20 July 2011. Horsley, J.P. (2009). Public participation in the People's Republic: developing a more participatory governance model in China, www.law.yale.edu/documents/pdf/Intellectual_Life/CL-PP-PP_in_the__PRC_FINAL_91609.pdf accessed 27 October 2012.

395 Horsley, J.P. (2009). Public participation in the People's Republic: developing a more participatory governance model in China, www.law.yale.edu/documents/pdf/Intellectual_Life/CL-PP-PP_in_the__PRC_FINAL_91609.pdf accessed 27 October 2012.

396 Nujiang River is located in Yunnan Province and has considerable biodiversity.

397 Du, Q. (2009). Public participation and the challenges of environmental justice in China. In: Ebbesson, J. & Okowa, P. (Eds.). *Environmental Law and Justice in Context*. Cambridge (UK): Cambridge University Press, p. 153.

NGOs and the public nationwide have been protesting against this planning permission by arguing that the governmental planning in 2003 did not follow the environmental impact assessment, in particular the procedure for collecting public opinions on the project.[398] The public and NGO's campaign had the consequence that in 2006 the National Development and Reform Commission announced that it would reconsider the project. Although this "reconsideration" does not improve any specific solution referring to dam construction, the roles of the public and environmental NGOs was accepted by the relevant authority. Public participation in environmental decision-making is still by no means regularised, but public interest and involvement in that sector continue to increase.[399]

5.2.2.5. Some Limitations for Public Participation in China

In spite of the progress on public participation in China, compared to some developed counties, there are still large limitations for public participation. Firstly, the organisational form of participation is limited in scale,[400] Chinese environmental protection associations, especially environmental NGOs, have limited impact on governments' decision-making.[401] Currently, although the environmental protection associations in China number more than 3,000, many NGOs have official governmental sponsors who guide them through the registration processes and provide political cover and support for their work.[402]

---

398 Detailed information see www.china5e.com/focus/focus.php?type=nujiang, cited in Du, Q. (2009). Public participation and the challenges of environmental justice in China. In: Ebbesson, J. & Okowa, P. (Eds.). *Environmental Law and Justice in Context*. Cambridge (UK): Cambridge University Press, p. 153.

399 Horsley, J.P. (2009). Public participation in the People's Republic: developing a more participatory governance model in China, www.law.yale.edu/documents/pdf/Intellectual_Life/CL-PP-PP_in_the__PRC_FINAL_91609.pdf accessed 27 October 2012.

400 Wang, C. (王超) (2013). *Study on Legal System for Public Participation in Promoting Ecological Progress* (公众参与生态文明建设法制制度研究). Master dissertation in Environment and Resources Protection Law of Central South University of Forestry and Technology (中南林业科技大学环境资源保护法硕士学位论文), pp. 20–22.

401 Wu, Y. & Tian, B. (吴勇，田犇) (2012). Improvement of public participation system in the east dongting lake nature reserve (论东洞庭湖自然保护区公众参与机制的完善), *Journal of Wuling* (武陵学刊), 37(3), p. 12. Wang, C. (王超) (2013). *Study on Legal System for Public Participation in Promoting Ecological Progress* (公众参与生态文明建设法制制度研究). Master dissertation in Environment and Resources Protection Law of Central South University of Forestry and Technology (中南林业科技大学环境资源保护法硕士学位论文), p. 21. Zhou, G.J. (卓光俊) (2012). *Public Participation System for Environmental Protection in China* (我国环境保护中的公众参与制度研究). Doctoral Dissertation of Chongqing University (重庆大学博士论文), p. 40.

402 Zhang, K.M. & Wen, Z.G. (2008). Review and challenges of politicizes of environmental protection and sustainable development in China. *Journal of Environmental Management*, 88, http://ac.els-cdn.com/S0301479707002435/1-s2.0-S0301479707002435-main.pdf?_tid=ad5ac5ac-3a6b-11e3-a56f-00000aab0f01&acdnat=1382372169_5295209c6da3c1e15714ddb01ae84eb3 accessed 21 October 2013, p. 1259.

Very few of them are initiated by civil environmentalists.[403] Environmental NGOs in China can be divided into two general categories: those affiliated with government agencies, namely government organised NGOs (GONGOs), and other private NGOs. Their limited funding and acceptance determine their participation status.[404] In fact, China needs to develop a rich collection of citizens' groups to respond to the growing environmental crisis, and strongly encourage NGOs to embrace the diversity of citizens groups that care about the environment, thereby allowing them to find their collective voice.[405]

Secondly, the process of participation is not comprehensive,[406] as public participation is mainly post-supervision. There is little pre-supervision and process supervision.[407] For instance, Article 6 of the "Environmental Protection Law of the People's Republic of China" (1989 version)[408] states: "*All units and individuals shall have the obligation to protect the environment, and have the right to report on or file charges against any units or individuals that cause pollution or environmental destruction*".[409] The "Decision by the State Council on

---

403 He, M. & Cliquet, A. (2013). Sustainable development through a rights-based approach to conserve protected areas in China. *China-EU Law Journal.* DOI 10.1007/s 12689-013-0031-7. http://link.springer.com/article/10.1007%2Fs12689-013-0031-7 accessed 4 November 2013.

404 He, M. & Cliquet, A. (2013). Sustainable development through a rights-based approach to conserve protected areas in China. *China-EU Law Journal.* DOI 10.1007/s 12689-013-0031-7. http://link.springer.com/article/10.1007%2Fs12689-013-0031-7 accessed 4 November 2013.

405 Zhang, K.M. & Wen, Z.G. (2008). Review and challenges of politicizes of environmental protection and sustainable development in China. *Journal of Environmental Management*, 88, http://ac.els-cdn.com/S0301479707002435/1-s2.0-S0301479707002435-main.pdf?_tid=ad5ac5ac-3a6b-11e3-a56f-00000aab0f01&acdnat=1382372169_5295209c6da3c1e15714ddb01ae84eb3 accessed 21 October 2013, pp. 1259–1260.

406 Zeng, C.L. (曾彩琳) (2012). Research on legal system of right protection of residents of nature reserves in China (我国自然保护区地居民权利保障法律制度研究). *Journal of Dalian University of Technology (Social Sciences)* (大连理工大学学报（社会科学版）), 33(3), p. 124. Wu, Y. & Tian, B. (吴勇，田犇) (2012). Improvement of public participation system in the east Dongting lake nature reserve (论东洞庭湖自然保护区公众参与机制的完善), *Journal of Wuling* (武陵学刊), 37(3), p. 12.

407 He, M. & Cliquet, A. (2013). Sustainable development through a rights-based approach to conserve protected areas in China. *China-EU Law Journal.* DOI 10.1007/s 12689-013-0031-7. http://link.springer.com/article/10.1007%2Fs12689-013-0031-7 accessed 4 November 2013.

408 The "Environmental Protection Law of the People's Republic of China" (1989 version) [中华人民共和国环境保护法] was promulgated by Order No. 22 of the President of the People's Republic of China on 26 December 1989, and was effective on the date of promulgation, www.law-lib.com/law/law_view.asp?id=6229 accessed 3 December 2011.

409 Article 6 of the "Environmental Protection Law of the People's Republic of China" (1989 version) is the similar with Article 6 of the "Environmental Protection Law of the People's Republic of China" (2014 version). The Article 6 says: "All units and individuals shall have the obligation to protect the environment. Local people's governments at various levels shall be responsible for the environmental quality within areas under their jurisdiction. Enterprises, public institutions and any other producers/business operators shall prevent and reduce environmental pollution and ecological destruction, and shall bear the liability for their damage caused by them in accordance with the law. Citizens shall enhance environmental protection awareness, adopt low-carbon and energy-saving lifestyle, and conscientiously fulfill the obligation of environmental protection." The "Environmental

Several Environmental Protection Issues"[410] also emphasises that: "*It should (...) encourage the public to participate in environmental protection, and inform and disclose the various illegal actions against environmental laws and regulations.*" It can be seen from these examples that the laws in China concerning public participation emphasise the post-supervision on illegal action to the environment, neglecting the pre-supervision and process supervision.[411] In practice, after the pollution or environmental destruction has already happened, the public would inform the relevant parties and rely on the government to solve the problems.

Thirdly, from the perspective of the contents of participation, the current public participation is feeble, mainly limited to consciousness's participation, such as asking for comments from the public, while there is little participation in the actual behaviour.[412] The public and environmental NGOs involved in environmental protection activities mainly focus on publicity and education.[413] They support environmental protection from the perspectives of consciousness and public opinion, rather than the actual behaviour, especially referring to the participation in government's decision-making.

Fourth, from the perspective of a guarantee of participation, public participation is mainly organised by the government, while the system for public participation is insufficient in China.[414] To a great extent, the scope and effect of participation is decided by the main administrative department, and the people fail to really recognise that environmental protection is also their obligation.[415] For instance, Article 13 from the "Law of the People's Republic

---

Protection Law of the People's Republic of China" (2014 version) [中华人民共和国环境保护法] was newly modified based on the "Environmental Protection Law of the People's Republic of China" (1989 version) on 24 April 2014 and entered into force on 1 January 2015, http://edu.sina.com.cn/en/2014-05-20/144680376.shtml accessed 30 June 2014.

410 The "Decision of the State Council on Several Issues Concerning Environmental Protection" [国务院关于环境保护若干问题的决定] was issued on 3 August 1996, www.lawinfochina.com/display.aspx?lib=law&id=6372 accessed 3 December 2011. Although it is named as the "decision", it is regarded as an important guideline for legislation and policy on environmental protection issues.

411 Li, Y.F. (2004) The legal system for the public participation and environmental protection. *Zhejiang Social Science*, 2.

412 Zeng, C.L. (曾彩琳) (2012). Research on legal system of right protection of residents of nature reserves in China (我国自然保护区地居民权利保障法律制度研究). *Journal of Dalian University of Technology (Social Sciences)* (大连理工大学学报（社会科学版）), 33(3), p. 124.

413 He, M. & Cliquet, A. (2013). Sustainable development through a rights-based approach to conserve protected areas in China. *China-EU Law Journal*. DOI 10.1007/s 12689-013-0031-7. http://link.springer.com/article/10.1007%2Fs12689-013-0031-7 accessed 4 November 2013.

414 He, M. & Cliquet, A. (2013). Sustainable development through a rights-based approach to conserve protected areas in China. *China-EU Law Journal*. DOI 10.1007/s 12689-013-0031-7. http://link.springer.com/article/10.1007%2Fs12689-013-0031-7 accessed 4 November 2013.

415 Wang, H. (2009). Public participation in environmental management from the perspective of China. Discussion Papers in Social Responsibility, www.socialresponsibility.biz accessed 8 August 2012.

of China on Prevention and Control of Pollution from Environmental Noise" (1996)[416] states "*the environmental impact statement shall include the comments and suggestions of the units and residents in the place where the construction project is located.*" However, these provisions are too theoretical, they do not point out when the public can participate, in which way the public can participate and how to guarantee public participation. What is more, even though the EIA Law explicitly requires public participation in environmental impact assessment, questionnaire surveys and public meetings are two most popularly adopted means and have been criticised as insufficient.[417] There are no explicit procedures or guidelines for holding consultation meetings or environmental hearings for the formulation of public opinion.[418] Yue Pan, the deputy director of the Ministry of Environmental Protection of the People's Republic of China, pointed out that according to the first public environmental people's livelihood index, released by the China Environmental Culture Promotion Association, only 6.3% of the public has participated in environmental activities in the last three months in 2006; less than 20% of the public recognise "12369", which is the free phone call for environmental issues.[419] The essential reason for this is not the low level of public environmental awareness, but the lack of effective mechanisms for the public to access to environmental information and to participate in environmental issues.[420] Public opinions, although procedurally significant, remain legally non-binding.[421]

416 The "Law of the People's Republic of China on Prevention and Control of Pollution from Environmental Noise" [中华人民共和国噪声污染防治法] was issued on 29 October 1996 and entered into effective on 1 March 1997, www.lawinfochina.com/display.aspx?lib=law&id=544 accessed 9 August 2012.

417 Wu, G. (2011). China in 2010: dilemmas of "scientific development". *Asian Survey*, 51(1), pp. 18–32.

418 Du, Q. (2009). Public participation and the challenges of environmental justice in China. In: Ebbesson, J. & Okowa, P. (Eds.). *Environmental Law and Justice in Context*. Cambridge (UK): Cambridge University Press, p. 147.

419 People's Net (人民网), The first "measures on public participation in environmental issues was issued, it strengthens democracy in decision-making" （第一部环境问题中的公共参与措施颁布，加强决策民主）. Posted on 22 February 2006, http://env.people.com.cn/GB/1072/4130691.html accessed 10 October 2012.

420 People's Net (人民网), The first "measures on public participation in environmental issues was issued, it strengthens democracy in decision-making" （第一部环境问题中的公共参与措施颁布，加强决策民主）. Posted on 22 February 2006, http://env.people.com.cn/GB/1072/4130691.html accessed 10 October 2012.

421 Du, Q. (2009). Public participation and the challenges of environmental justice in China. In: Ebbesson, J. & Okowa, P. (Eds.). *Environmental Law and Justice in Context*. Cambridge (UK): Cambridge University Press, p. 147.

5.2.2.6. *Analysis on the Right to Participation in China*

From the discussion above, it can be seen that although public participation has a short history in China, the Chinese government and different departments have realised the vital importance of public participation and have made some progress in theory.[422] For instance, the relatively new laws and regulations all contain provisions on public participation and even the Ministry of Environmental Protection also pointed out to further expand the degree of public participation as one of the useful measures to solve the existing environmental issues in China.[423] As for public participation in protected areas' construction and management, the highest priority should be given to ensuring that engagement with local actors is an empowering process and ensuring that representation is effective and just.[424] A human rights-based approach can be a good way to help to achieve the goals. A comparative analysis on the right to participation in China and in Europe will be discussed later (see 5.2.4).

5.2.3. RIGHT TO PARTICIPATION IN ENVIRONMENTAL PROTECTION IN EUROPE

In this section we will examine the right to participation and environmental protection, especially protected areas conservation in Europe. The following questions will be explored: what are the general principles for the potential conflicts regarding right to participation protection and protected areas conservation in Europe? Specifically, how could China promote both the features of "early" and "effective" for the right to participation concerning environmental protection, especially for protected areas conservation?

5.2.3.1. *Right to Participation under the European Convention on Human Rights*

There is no specific provision directly referring to the right to participation in the European Convention on Human Rights. However, some relevant cases in the European Court of Human Rights have indirectly addressed the importance of the right to participation.

---

422 He, M. & Cliquet, A. (2013). Sustainable development through a rights-based approach to conserve protected areas in China. *China-EU Law Journal*. DOI 10.1007/s 12689-013-0031-7. http://link.springer.com/article/10.1007%2Fs12689-013-0031-7 accessed 4 November 2013.

423 He, M. & Cliquet, A. (2013). Sustainable development through a rights-based approach to conserve protected areas in China. *China-EU Law Journal*. DOI 10.1007/s 12689-013-0031-7. http://link.springer.com/article/10.1007%2Fs12689-013-0031-7 accessed 4 November 2013.

424 Conservation, human rights & protected areas governance: a field-based workshop in the Baviaanskloof Mega-Reserve. (2007). South Africa, 6–7 July 2007, http://cmsdata.iucn.org/downloads/bav_workshop. pdf accessed 10 October 2012, p. 15.

5.2.3.2. Case Law in the European Court of Human Rights

Although the ECHR did not explicitly provide any provisions on the right to participation, it is interesting to find that some cases from the ECtHR provide some baselines about the right to participation.

5.2.3.2.1. The Public Authorities Need to Take into Account the Interests of Individuals or Groups who May be Affected

In the process of making decisions related to environmental issues, public authorities need to take into account the interests of individuals who may be affected, especially as to ethnic minorities or vulnerable groups.

In the case of *Chapman v. the United Kingdom,*[425] Chapman, a gypsy, alleged a violation of her right to private life as she was refused a planning permission to station caravans on her land, and in respect of enforcement measures implemented as a consequence of the occupation of her land.[426] The Court applied the exception of Article 8 (2) that the interference was "necessary in a democratic society", since the land inhabited by the gypsy family was the subject of environmental protection and therefore a wide margin of discretion was to be accepted to national authorities in planning issues.[427]

Notably, "*the procedural safeguards available to the individual will be especially material in determining whether the respondent State has, when fixing the regulatory framework, remained within its margin of appreciation.*"[428] "*In particular, the Court must examine whether the decision-making process leading to measures of interference was fair such as to afford due respect to the interests safeguarded to the individual by Article 8*".[429]

Moreover, "*although the fact of belonging to a minority with a traditional lifestyle different from that of the majority does not confer immunity from general laws intended to safeguard the assets of the community as a whole, such as the environment, it may have an incidence on the manner in which such laws are*

---

425 ECtHR, Chapman v. the United Kingdom (2001), App. No. 27238/95, Judgment of 18 January 2001, http://hudoc.echr.coe.int/sites/eng/pages/search.aspx?i=001-59154#{%22itemid%22:[%22001-59154%22]} accessed 4 November 2013.

426 For detailed information see www.minorityrights.org/1291/minority-rights-jurisprudence/chapman-v-uk.html accessed 4 November 2013.

427 For detailed information see www.escr-net.org/docs/i/673056 accessed 4 November 2013.

428 ECtHR, Chapman v. the United Kingdom (2001), App. No. 27238/95, Judgment of 18 January 2001, §92, http://hudoc.echr.coe.int/sites/eng/pages/search.aspx?i=001-59154#{%22itemid%22:[%22001-59154%22]} accessed 4 November 2013.

429 ECtHR, Chapman v. the United Kingdom (2001), App. No. 27238/95, Judgment of 18 January 2001, §94, http://hudoc.echr.coe.int/sites/eng/pages/search.aspx?i=001-59154#{%22itemid%22:[%22001-59154%22]} accessed 4 November 2013; ECtHR, Buckley v. the United Kingdom (1996), App. No. 20348/92, Judgment of 29 September 1996, §76, http://hudoc.echr.coe.int/sites/eng/pages/search.aspx?i=001-58076#{%22itemid%22:[%22001-58076%22]} accessed 4 November 2013.

to be implemented."[430] Furthermore, "*as intimated in the Buckley case,*[431] *the vulnerable position of Gypsies as a minority means that some special consideration should be given to their needs and their different lifestyle.*"[432] Obviously, the Court recognised a possible future consensus among the Member States of the Council of Europe regarding the special needs of minorities and an obligation to protect their security, identity and lifestyle, which may lead to a different outcome in a similar case.[433]

The conclusion in this case is not directly relevant for our study, but what was discussed above reflects that the public authorities need to take into account the interests of individuals or groups who may be affected, especially the minorities.

5.2.3.2.2. The Decision-Making Process Must Involve Appropriate Investigations and Studies

The case of *Dubetska and Others v. Ukraine*[434] concerns Ukrainian families living in the neighbourhood of a mine and a mine spoil heap. The applicants alleged that the State authorities had failed to protect their home, private and family life from excessive pollution generated by two State-owned industrial facilities. The Court stressed that it examined whether the authorities did sufficient investigations to evaluate the risks of a potentially hazardous activities.[435] The Court stated that whether the authorities conducted sufficient studies to evaluate the risks of a potential hazardous activity, and on the basis of the information available, whether they developed an adequate policy vis-à-vis the polluter.[436] The Court was particularly interested in the extent to which the individuals affected by the policy at issue were able to voice their opinions to the decision-making, which contained the individuals having access to the relevant

---

430 ECtHR, Chapman v. the United Kingdom (2001), App. No. 27238/95, Judgment of 18 January 2001, §96, http://hudoc.echr.coe.int/sites/eng/pages/search.aspx?i=001-59154#{%22itemid%22:[%22001-59154%22]} accessed 4 November 2013.

431 ECtHR, Buckley v. the United Kingdom (1996), App. No. 20348/92, Judgment of 29 September 1996, http://hudoc.echr.coe.int/sites/eng/pages/search.aspx?i=001-58076#{%22itemid%22:[%22001-58076%22]} accessed 4 November 2013.

432 ECtHR, Chapman v. the United Kingdom (2001), App. No. 27238/95, Judgment of 18 January 2001, §96, http://hudoc.echr.coe.int/sites/eng/pages/search.aspx?i=001-59154#{%22itemid%22:[%22001-59154%22]} accessed 4 November 2013.

433 For detailed information see www.escr-net.org/docs/i/673056 accessed 4 November 2013.

434 ECtHR, Dubetska and Others v. Ukraine (2011), App. No. 30499/03, Judgment of 10 February 2011, 10 May 2011 (Final), http://hudoc.echr.coe.int/sites/eng/pages/search.aspx?i=001-103273#{%22itemid%22:[%22001-103273%22]} accessed 5 November 2013.

435 ECtHR, Dubetska and Others v. Ukraine (2011), App. No. 30499/03, Judgment of 10 February 2011, 10 May 2011 (Final), §21, http://hudoc.echr.coe.int/sites/eng/pages/search.aspx?i=001-103273#{%22itemid%22:[%22001-103273%22]} accessed 5 November 2013.

436 ECtHR, Dubetska and Others v. Ukraine (2011), App. No. 30499/03, Judgment of 10 February 2011, 10 May 2011 (Final), §143, http://hudoc.echr.coe.int/sites/eng/pages/search.aspx?i=001-103273#{%22itemid%22:[%22001-103273%22]} accessed 5 November 2013.

information and the capability to challenge the decisions in an effective way.[437] The Court also addressed that as the Convention is intended to protect effective rights, not illusory ones, a fair balance between the various interests at stake may be upset not only where the regulations to protect the guaranteed rights are lacking, but also where they are not duly complied with.[438]

After the assessment above, the Court concluded that there had been a violation of Article 8 of the Convention. This case reflects that some appropriate investigations and studies could reduce the potential conflicts at the early stage of the project or conservation activities. In this way, the relevant rights could be effectively guaranteed and various interests could also be balanced well.

5.2.3.2.3. The Affected Groups Have a Right to Participate in the Decision-Making

The case of *Taşkın and Others v. Turkey*[439] concerned the granting of permits to operate a gold mine in Ovacik, in the district of Bergama. The applicants lived in Bergama and the villages nearby. The applicants alleged that, because of the Ovacik gold mine's development and operation, they had suffered and continued to suffer the effects of environmental damage. The Court reiterated that it was necessary to consider all the procedural aspects, including the type of policy or decision involved, the extent to which the views of individuals were taken into account throughout the decision-making process, and the procedural safeguards available.[440] This case also envisaged an informed process: "*Where a State must determine complex issues of environmental and economic policy, the decision-making process must firstly involve appropriate investigations and studies in order to allow them to predict and evaluate in advance the effects of those activities which might damage the environment and infringe individuals' rights and to enable them to strike a fair balance between the various conflicting interests at stake.*"[441] The Court then concluded that there had been a violation of Article 8 of the Convention. This aspect in this case approves the previous section.

---

437 ECtHR, Dubetska and Others v. Ukraine (2011), App. No. 30499/03, Judgment of 10 February 2011, 10 May 2011 (Final), §143, http://hudoc.echr.coe.int/sites/eng/pages/search.aspx?i=001-103273#{%22itemid%22:[%22001-103273%22]} accessed 5 November 2013.

438 ECtHR, Dubetska and Others v. Ukraine (2011), App. No. 30499/03, Judgment of 10 February 2011, 10 May 2011 (Final), §144, http://hudoc.echr.coe.int/sites/eng/pages/search.aspx?i=001-103273#{%22itemid%22:[%22001-103273%22]} accessed 5 November 2013.

439 ECtHR, Taşkın and Others v. Turkey (2004), App. No. 46117/99, Judgment of 10 November 2004, 30 March 2005 (Final), http://hudoc.echr.coe.int/sites/eng/pages/search.aspx?i=001-67401#{%22itemid%22:[%22001-67401%22]} accessed 5 November 2013.

440 ECtHR, Taşkın and Others v. Turkey (2004), App. No. 46117/99, Judgment of 10 November 2004, 30 March 2005 (Final), §118, http://hudoc.echr.coe.int/sites/eng/pages/search.aspx?i=001-67401#{%22itemid%22:[%22001-67401%22]} accessed 5 November 2013.

441 ECtHR, Taşkın and Others v. Turkey (2004), App. No. 46117/99, Judgment of 10 November 2004, 30 March 2005 (Final), §119, http://hudoc.echr.coe.int/sites/eng/pages/search.aspx?i=001-67401#{%22itemid%22:[%22001-67401%22]} accessed 5 November 2013.

More importantly and notably, this case suggests that the most important contribution existing human rights law has to offer with regard to environmental protection and sustainable development is the empowerment of individuals and groups affected by "environmental problems", and for whom the opportunity to participate in decisions is the most useful and direct means of influencing the balance of environmental, social, and economic interests.[442] Similarly, to empower individuals and groups affected by nature conservation measures to have an opportunity to participate in the decision-making could also help to balance environmental, social and economic interests. That is to say, besides environmental impact assessment, a human rights assessment should also be taken into account. This will be discussed in detail in Chapter 7 (see 7.3).

What's more, the individuals concerned must also be able to appeal to the courts against any decision, act or omission where they consider that their interests or their comments have not been given sufficient weight in the decision-making process.[443] The right to access to justice will be discussed in detail in the section "right to access to justice in environmental matters" (see 5.3).

5.2.3.3. *Public Participation in Environmental Decision-Making in the Aarhus Convention*

The right to public participation in the Aarhus Convention in Europe is a major step forward. The Aarhus Convention is the first international environmental treaty that lays the foundation and prescribes legally binding obligations on states so as for the latter to provide the public with the opportunity to express its concerns and enable public authorities to take due account of such concerns.[444] Unlike previous international initiatives of a soft law character, such as Principle 10 of the Rio Declaration, this multilateral agreement recognises for the first time the importance of public involvement in environmental decision-making also at the international level.[445]

---

442 A point recognised by the OHCHR (Office of the High Commissioner for Human Rights): see UN (2008). *Claiming the Millennium Development Goals: A Human Rights Approach* (New York and Geneva), at VIII, Goal 7: "a human rights approach to sustainable development emphasizes improving and implementing accountability systems, [and] access to information on environmental issues". www.ohchr.org/Documents/Publications/Claiming_MDGs_en.pdf and www.ohchr.org/Documents/Publications/HRAndMDGsInPractice.pdf accessed 6 November 2013.

443 ECtHR, Taşkın and Others v. Turkey (2004), App. No. 46117/99, Judgment of 10 November 2004, 30 March 2005 (Final), §119, http://hudoc.echr.coe.int/sites/eng/pages/search.aspx?i=001-67401#{%22itemid%22:[%22001-67401%22]} accessed 5 November 2013.

444 Kritikos, M. (2011). Shaping transnational public participation norms in the field of modern biotechnology: time for a global good governance approach? In: Pallemaerts, M. (Ed.). *The Aarhus Convention at Ten: Interactions and Tensions between Conventional International Law and EU Environmental Law*. Groningen: Europa Law Publishing, p. 226.

445 Article 3(7), the UNECE Convention on Access to Information, Public Participation in Decision-making and Access to Justice in Environmental Matters (Aarhus Convention),

The former UN Secretary-General Kofi Annan has described the significance of the Convention as follows: "*Although regional in scope, the significance of the Aarhus Convention is global. It is by far the most impressive elaboration of principle 10 of the Rio Declaration, which stresses the need for citizen's participation in environmental issues and for access to information on the environment held by public authorities. As such, it is the most ambitious venture in the area of environmental democracy so far undertaken under the auspices of the United Nations.*"[446] Where democracy may not be attainable at the international level, the Aarhus Convention may also provide significant assistance to "*enhanced transparency, participation, more balanced voting procedures and effectiveness of decisions as possible ways of making decisions more legitimate*".[447] It has also served to link the environment and human rights in international law.[448]

Regarding participation, what are the provisions in the Convention? The first thing to note is that it refers only to participation and not to consultation, the former being an active process, the latter a more passive one.[449] The Convention recognises that the public are the holders of a wealth of wisdom and information, and that these resources should be included in the thinking processes for any decision-making.[450] The Convention provides that public participation should

adopted on 25 June 1998 in the Danish city of Aarhus at the Fourth Ministerial Conference in the "Environment for Europe" process, 2161 UNTS 447, www.unece.org/env/pp/introduction.html accessed 10 March 2012. Article 3(7) says: "each Party shall promote the application of the principles of this Convention in international environmental decision-making processes and within the framework of international organizations in matters relating to the environment."

446 Annan, K. (2010). The Aarhus Convention, an Implementation Guide, http://live.unece.org/environmentalpolicy/treaties/publicparticipation/publications/guidance/2000/aarhus-convention implementation-guide/aarhus convention-implementation-guide.html accessed 10 March 2012, forward, p. v.

447 Andresen, S. & Hey, E. (2005). The effectiveness and legitimacy of international environmental institutions. *International Environmental Agreements: Politics, Law and Economics*, 5 (3), p. 211.

448 Morgera, E. (2005). An update on the Aarhus Convention and its continued global relevance. *Review of European Community and International Environmental Law*, 14(2), p. 138; McAllister, S.T. (1998). Human rights and the environment: the Convention on access to information, public participation in decision-making, and access to justice in environmental matters. *Colorado Journal of International Environmental Law Yearbook*, 9, p. 187.

449 Ewing, M., Hough, A. & Amajirionwu, M. (2007). Environmental RTDI programme 2000–2006: assessing access to information, participation, and justice in environmental decision-making in Ireland. Prepared for the Environmental Protection Agency by Centre for Sustainability, Institute of Technology, Sligo in Partnership with Department of Law, University College Cork COMHAR, the Sustainable Development Council, www.environmentaldemocracy.ie/pdf/finalreport.pdf accessed 23 September 2013, p. 89.

450 Ewing, M., Hough, A. & Amajirionwu, M. (2007). Environmental RTDI programme 2000–2006: assessing access to information, participation, and justice in environmental decision-making in Ireland. Prepared for the Environmental Protection Agency by Centre for Sustainability, Institute of Technology, Sligo in Partnership with Department

be timely, effective, adequate and formal, and contain information, notification, dialogue, consideration, and response.[451]

In the Aarhus Convention, public participation is guaranteed in Articles 6–8. The Aarhus Convention provides for public participation in decision-making at three stages: "decisions on specific activities",[452] "plans, programs and policies relating to the environment",[453] and "the preparation of executive regulations and/or generally applicable legally binding normative instruments".[454] Article 6 provides the most specified form of participation in the Convention. Its purposes are to increase "real" participation with the potential to exert a genuine influence on decisions and to encourage "prospective applicants to identify the public concerned, to enter into discussions" before they apply for a permit, again "where appropriate".[455] Concerning the subjects of participation, the Aarhus Convention defines the public as "*natural or legal persons, and, in accordance with national legislation or practice, their associations, organizations or groups.*"[456] The "public concerned", which features in most of the Article 6 rights, is "*the public affected or likely to be affected by or having an interest in, the environmental decision-*

---

of Law, University College Cork COMHAR, the Sustainable Development Council, www.environmentaldemocracy.ie/pdf/finalreport.pdf accessed 23 September 2013, p. 89.

451 Ewing, M., Hough, A. & Amajirionwu, M. (2007). Environmental RTDI programme 2000–2006: assessing access to information, participation, and justice in environmental decision-making in Ireland. Prepared for the Environmental Protection Agency by Centre for Sustainability, Institute of Technology, Sligo in Partnership with Department of Law, University College Cork COMHAR, the Sustainable Development Council, www.environmentaldemocracy.ie/pdf/finalreport.pdf accessed 23 September 2013, p. 90.

452 Article 6, UNECE Convention on Access to Information, Public Participation in Decision-making and Access to Justice in Environmental Matters (Aarhus Convention) was adopted on 25 June 1998 in the Danish city of Aarhus at the Fourth Ministerial Conference in the "Environment for Europe" process, 2161 UNTS 447, www.unece.org/env/pp/introduction.html accessed 10 March 2012.

453 Article 7, UNECE Convention on Access to Information, Public Participation in Decision-making and Access to Justice in Environmental Matters (Aarhus Convention) was adopted on 25 June 1998 in the Danish city of Aarhus at the Fourth Ministerial Conference in the "Environment for Europe" process, 2161 UNTS 447, www.unece.org/env/pp/introduction.html accessed 10 March 2012.

454 Article 8, UNECE Convention on Access to Information, Public Participation in Decision-making and Access to Justice in Environmental Matters (Aarhus Convention) was adopted on 25 June 1998 in the Danish city of Aarhus at the Fourth Ministerial Conference in the "Environment for Europe" process, 2161 UNTS 447, www.unece.org/env/pp/introduction.html accessed 10 March 2012.

455 Article 6(5), UNECE Convention on Access to Information, Public Participation in Decision-making and Access to Justice in Environmental Matters (Aarhus Convention) was adopted on 25 June 1998 in the Danish city of Aarhus at the Fourth Ministerial Conference in the "Environment for Europe" process, 2161 UNTS 447, www.unece.org/env/pp/introduction.html accessed 10 March 2012.

456 Article 2(4), UNECE Convention on Access to Information, Public Participation in Decision-making and Access to Justice in Environmental Matters (Aarhus Convention) was adopted on 25 June 1998 in the Danish city of Aarhus at the Fourth Ministerial Conference in the "Environment for Europe" process, 2161 UNTS 447, www.unece.org/env/pp/introduction.html accessed 10 March 2012.

making (...) non-governmental organizations promoting environmental protection and meeting any requirements under national law shall be deemed to have an interest."[457] Article 7 requires Parties to make "*appropriate practical and/or other provisions for the public to participate during the preparation of plans and programs relating the environment*". It can be argued that the term "relating to the environment" is quite broad, covering not just plans or programmes prepared by an environment ministry, but also sectorial plans (transport, energy, tourism, etc.) where these have significant environmental implications.[458] Although the Convention does not apply to bodies acting in a legislative capacity, Article 8 clearly would apply to the executive stage of preparing rules and regulations even if they are later to be adopted by parliament.[459]

The key public participation requirements of the Aarhus Convention emphasise the need to[460]:

- time participation programmes to achieve "early" participation;
- provide the public with access to all documentation relevant to the decision-making process;
- enter into discussions with the public concerned;
- allow the public to submit their opinions at public inquiries;
- consider the outcome of public participation in the decision-making process; and
- achieve "effective" participation.

Certain barriers need to be overcome before "early" and "effective" participation can be achieved and the ideals of the Aarhus Convention fulfilled. These include[461]:

---

457 Article 2(5), UNECE Convention on Access to Information, Public Participation in Decision-making and Access to Justice in Environmental Matters (Aarhus Convention) was adopted on 25 June 1998 in the Danish city of Aarhus at the Fourth Ministerial Conference in the "Environment for Europe" process, 2161 UNTS 447, www.unece.org/env/pp/introduction.html accessed 10 March 2012.

458 Lavrysen, L. (2010). The Aarhus Convention between environmental protection and human rights. *Liège, Strasbourg, Brussels: parcours des droits de l'homme.* Limal: Anthemis, pp. 647–671.

459 Stec, S. & Casey-Lefkowitz, S. (2000). *The Aarhus Convention: an Implementation Guide.* United Nations Publication, www.unece.org/fileadmin/DAM/env/pp/acig.pdf accessed 23 March 2014, p. 119.

460 Hartley, N. & Wood, C. (2005). Public participation in environmental impact assessment – implementing the Aarhus Convention. *Environmental Impact Assessment Review,* 25, http://ac.els-cdn.com/S019592550400160X/1-s2.0-S019592550400160X-main.pdf?_tid=a326ed60-3a32-11e3-9c79-00000aab0f26&acdnat=1382347671_4ab9b00f888b2d73caf36042b1ff8428 accessed 20 October 2013, pp. 325–327.

461 Hartley, N. & Wood, C. (2005). Public participation in environmental impact assessment – implementing the Aarhus Convention. *Environmental Impact Assessment Review,* 25, http://ac.els-cdn.com/S019592550400160X/1-s2.0-S019592550400160X-main.pdf?_

- current legislative participation time provisions;
- technical complexity of project proposals;
- developer and public attitudes;
- poor provision of legal and procedural information; and
- financial constraints.

Although achieving "effective" participation is of vital importance, this phrase remains undefined in the Convention. It could be found that achieving effective public participation is very difficult and that the extent to which public participation is "effective" appears to be determined by two key factors[462]:

- stakeholder attitudes: a variety of differing opinions prevail about what constitutes "effective" public participation. Consequently, when designing a participation programme it is very difficult to "please everyone"; and
- operation of the participation process: the literature[463] suggests that a number of benefits can be secured by using particular methods. However, as this research has demonstrated, unless properly operated and planned, any chosen participation method will not achieve its aim and will not be entirely "effective".

5.2.3.4. Case Law of the Aarhus Convention Compliance Committee

Based on what have been discussed above, the case law of the ACCC will further explain the baselines of the right to participation in environmental matters.

5.2.3.4.1. Meaningful Public Participation Shall be at an Early Stage

The dispute in the communication of *ACCC/C/2007/22 (France)*[464] concerned the process that cumulated in the construction of a waste incinerator in Fos-sur-Mer, France.

---

tid=a326ed60-3a32-11e3-9c79-00000aab0f26&acdnat=1382347671_4ab9b00f888b2d73caf36042b1ff8428 accessed 20 October 2013, p. 338.

462 Hartley, N. & Wood, C. (2005). Public participation in environmental impact assessment – implementing the Aarhus Convention. *Environmental Impact Assessment Review*, 25, http://ac.els-cdn.com/S019592550400160X/1-s2.0-S019592550400160X-main.pdf?_tid=a326ed60-3a32-11e3-9c79-00000aab0f26&acdnat=1382347671_4ab9b00f888b2d73caf36042b1ff8428 accessed 20 October 2013, p. 338.

463 Petts, J. (1999). Public participation and environmental impact assessment. In: Petts, J. (Ed.). *Handbook of Environmental Impact Assessment*. London: Blackwell Science, pp. 145–173.

464 ACCC/C/2007/22 (France), ECE/MP.PP/C.1/2009/4/Add.1, 8 February 2011, www.unece.org/fileadmin/DAM/env/pp/compliance/C2008-22/Findings/ece_mp.pp_c.1_2009_4_add.1_eng.pdf accessed 27 March 2013.

The Communicant, FARE Sud,[465] alleged that France was in violation of Articles 3, 6 and 9 of the Aarhus Convention because the Communauté Urbaine Marseille Provence Métropole (CUMPM) and the Prefect did not allow for sufficient public participation or access to justice.[466] France claimed that the CUMPM resolutions are non-binding, and they do not exclude consideration of other options. Thus they are not subject to the Aarhus Convention.

The Compliance Committee concluded that the CUMPM resolutions are not within the scope of Articles 6 and 7 of the Aarhus Convention because the resolutions do not have the effect of precluding the Prefect from considering other options, at which point meaningful public participation does occur.[467] The Committee found that the determinative question was whether all waste management facility options were still open and meaningful participation could take place at the early stage. It was found that the CUMPM resolutions failed to do so.

It is noted that if a decision about a plan, programme, or project has the effect of reducing available options or the chance for meaningful public participation at a later stage, and there is no participation guaranteed in this earlier stage, this may be in non-compliance with Articles 6 or 7.[468] On the contrary, if it shows that the decision makers allow for meaningful public participation and a sufficient amount of options are provided, then it means that it does not violate Articles 6 and 7.

Another notably communication is *ACCC/C/2005/12 (Albania),*[469] which was submitted by the Albanian non-governmental organisation Alliance for the Protection of the Vlora Gulf (also translated as Civil Alliance for the Protection of the Vlora Bay) on 7 April 2005 with regards to a lack of compliance by Albania with its obligations under Articles 3(2), 6(2), and 7 of the Convention in connection with decision-making on the planning of an industrial park comprising, *inter alia*, oil and gas pipelines, installations for the storage of petroleum, a three-unit thermal power plant and a refinery near the lagoon of

465 L'Association de Défense et de Protection du Littoral du Golfe de Fosse-sur-Mer and Le Collectif Citoyen Santé Environment de Port-Saint – Louis-du-Rhône and Fédération d'Action Régionale pour l'Environnement (FARE Sud).

466 Justice and Environment (2011). The Most Recent (2008–2011) Case Law of the Aarhus Convention Compliance Committee, www.justiceandenvironment.org/_files/file/2011%20ACCC%281%29.pdf accessed 26 March 2014, pp. 5–6.

467 Justice and Environment (2011). The Most Recent (2008–2011) Case Law of the Aarhus Convention Compliance Committee, www.justiceandenvironment.org/_files/file/2011%20ACCC%281%29.pdf accessed 26 March 2014, pp. 5–6.

468 Justice and Environment (2011). The Most Recent (2008–2011) Case Law of the Aarhus Convention Compliance Committee, www.justiceandenvironment.org/_files/file/2011%20ACCC%281%29.pdf accessed 26 March 2014, pp. 5–6.

469 ACCC/C/2005/12 (Albania), ECE/MP.PP/C.1/2007/4/Add.1, 31 July 2007, www.unece.org/env/pp/compliance/Compliancecommittee/12TableAlbania.html accessed 28 March 2014.

Narta.[470] The Communicant held that the Albanian authorities failed to make appropriate provisions for public participation in accordance with Article 7 of the Convention.

The Committee found that, although some efforts were made to provide for public participation, these largely took place after the crucial decision on siting and they were subject to some qualitative deficiencies, leading the Committee to find that the Albanian authorities concerned failed to comply fully with the requirements in question.[471] Thus, one of the important recommendations made by the Committee is that the Albanian authorities concerned take the necessary legislative, regulatory, administrative and other measures to ensure that practical and/or other provisions for the public to participate during the preparation of plans and programmes relating to the environment are in place, not only during preparation of individual projects, including through development of detailed procedures,[472] but also at the early stage.

We could conclude from the two communications above that it is required that public participation shall be meaningful. The meaningful public participation shall be in the early stage. In this way, the public can actively and effectively participate in the decision-making process, especially in a complex decision-making with several stages and parallel processes.

5.2.3.4.2. Public Participation Procedures Shall Include Reasonable Time-Frames for Different Phases

Similar to the section on "access to information shall be readily available to support public participation" in the right to information section (see 5.1.3.4.2), this section discusses the need to allow the public adequate time to prepare their participation in the decision-making.

---

470 Economic Commission for Europe (ECE) (2008). Meeting of the parties to the Convention on access to information, public participation in decision-making and access to justice in environmental matters. Third meeting, Riga, 11–13 June 2008. Item 6(b) of the provisional agenda, www.unece.org/fileadmin/DAM/env/documents/2008/pp/mop3/ece_mp_pp_2008_5_add_1_e.pdf accessed 28 March 2014.

471 Economic Commission for Europe (ECE) (2007). Meeting of the parties to the Convention on access to information, public participation in decision-making and access to justice in environmental matters. Sixteenth meeting, Geneva, 13–15 June 2007, www.unece.org/fileadmin/DAM/env/documents/2008/pp/mop3/ece_mp_pp_2008_5_add_1_e.pdf accessed 28 March 2014, p. 22.

472 Economic Commission for Europe (ECE) (2007). Meeting of the parties to the Convention on access to information, public participation in decision-making and access to justice in environmental matters. Sixteenth meeting, Geneva, 13–15 June 2007, www.unece.org/fileadmin/DAM/env/documents/2008/pp/mop3/ece_mp_pp_2008_5_add_1_e.pdf accessed 28 March 2014, p. 22.

As discussed in the previous section (see 5.2.3.4.1), in the communication of *ACCC/C/2007/22 (France),*[473] the Committee noted that the public inquiry provided 45 days for public participation and for the public to submit information, comments, opinions which is related to the proposed activity. The Committee also holds that it was "*convinced that the provision of approximately six weeks for the public concerned to exercise its rights under Article 6, paragraph 6, of the Convention and approximately the same time relating to the requirements of Article 6, paragraph 7, in this case meet the requirements of these provisions in connection with Article 6, paragraph 3, of the Convention.*"[474]

The time-frames in this communication refer not only to a reasonable time frame, but also a clear indication of the period for inspecting the documents and the period for submitting comments or opinions.

Besides these, certain periods which are traditionally considered as holidays should also be taken into account for the reasonable time frames for public participation. According to the introduction on the communication of *ACCC/C/2008/24 (Spain)*[475] in the right to information section (see 5.1.3.4), the Committee found that "*a period of 20 days for the public to prepare and participate effectively cannot be considered reasonable, in particular if such period includes days of general celebration in the country. (...) the time span between the initial proposal and the public notice was 10 days, it indicates that the authority was in an extraordinary rush to initiate the commenting period; this can indeed give reason to suspect that making the notice so fast was not a routine procedure.*" The Committee therefore found that Spain was not complying with Articles 6(3) of the Convention.

It is obvious that the reasonable time-frames are an important guarantee for the realisation of the meaningful public participation.

5.2.3.4.3. NGOs' Roles in Public Participation

In the communication of *ACCC/C/2004/04 (Hungary),*[476] the Hungarian NGO Clean Air Action Group submitted a communication to the Committee alleging non-compliance by Hungary with its obligations under Articles 6 and 9(2)–(4) of the Aarhus Convention.

---

473 ACCC/C/2007/22 (France), ECE/MP.PP/C.1/2009/4/Add.1, 8 February 2011, www.unece.org/fileadmin/DAM/env/pp/compliance/C2008-22/Findings/ece_mp.pp_c.1_2009_4_add.1_eng.pdf accessed 27 March 2013,.

474 ACCC/C/2007/22 (France), ECE/MP.PP/C.1/2009/4/Add.1, 8 February 2011, §44, www.unece.org/fileadmin/DAM/env/pp/compliance/C2008-22/Findings/ece_mp.pp_c.1_2009_4_add.1_eng.pdf accessed 27 March 2013,.

475 ACCC/C/ 2008/24 (Spain), ECE/MP.PP/C.1/2009/8/Add.1, www.unece.org/fileadmin/DAM/env/pp/compliance/CC-26/ece_mp.pp_c.1_2009_8_add.1_e.pdf accessed 21 March 2014.

476 ACCC/C/2004/04 (Hungary), ECE/MP.PP/C.1/2005/2/Add.4, 14 March 2005, www.unece.org/fileadmin/DAM/env/pp/compliance/C2004-04/C04findings.pdf accessed 28 March 2014.

The communication referred to the alleged incompatibility of the new Hungarian Act on Public Interest and Development of the Expressway Network with the provisions of the Aarhus Convention. According to the Communicant, the procedure established by the new Act is different from some procedures for decision-making on other specific activities with potential adverse effects of the same significance, *inter alia* with regard to decision-making authority, the practicalities of ensuring public participation procedures, the status of the decision, time frames, and procedures for appeal.[477]

> *Exclusion of environmental authorities from the decision-making on construction permits for expressways, can potentially have a negative effect on the environmental quality of the final decision and various aspects of the construction, moreover as this exclusion also entail a de – facto exclusion of the rights of NGOs under the Hungarian Environmental Protection Act to represent the public concerned vis – á- vis environmental authorities.*[478]

The Committee concluded that the new Hungarian legislation on the development of the expressway network reduced the opportunities for public participation in decision-making on this type of specific activity. It did not meet the minimum level of public participation required by the Convention.

The final conclusion made by the Committee is not relevant for this study, the notable point in this communication is the important role played by the environmental NGOs. It is fair to say that environmental NGOs play an irreplaceable role in environmental protection. Public participation in the decision-making process on environmental protection cannot miss the contribution from environmental NGOs.

5.2.3.4.4. Each Party Shall Ensure that the Decision-Maker Takes Due Account of the Outcome of the Public Participation

The Aarhus Convention obliges Parties to ensure that the decision maker takes due account of the outcome of the public participation.[479] The communication

---

477 ACCC/C/2004/04 (Hungary), ECE/MP.PP/C.1/2005/2/Add.4, 14 March 2005, www.unece.org/fileadmin/DAM/env/pp/compliance/C2004-04/C04findings.pdf accessed 28 March 2014.

478 Andrusevych, A., Alge, T. & Clemens, C. (Eds.) (2008). Case Law of the Aarhus Convention Compliance Committee (2004–2008), http://doku.cac.at/case_law_accc.pdf accessed 28 March 2014, p. 22.

479 Article 6, UNECE Convention on Access to Information, Public Participation in Decision-making and Access to Justice in Environmental Matters (Aarhus Convention), adopted on 25 June 1998 in the Danish city of Aarhus at the Fourth Ministerial Conference in the "Environment for Europe" process, 2161 UNTS 447, www.unece.org/env/pp/introduction.html accessed 10 March 2012.

ACCC/C/2008/29 (Poland)[480] was submitted by Zabinaka Housing Cooperative and Ms Maria Cholewińska, president of the Protest Committee, regarding the alleged non-compliance by Poland with its obligation under the Aarhus Convention in relation to access to information and the decision-making process for the construction of a multifunctional sports hall in the city of Gdansk.

As for the public participation, the Compliance Committee observed that: "*The requirement of Article 6, paragraph 8, that public authorities take due account of the outcome of public participation, does not amount to the right of the public to veto the decision. In particular, this provision should not be read as requiring that the final say about the fate and design of the project rests with the local community living near the project, or that their acceptance is always needed.*"[481] Due to lack of sufficient information made available to the Committee, the Committee was not able to reach a conclusion concerning the alleged failure by Poland to comply with the obligations under the Convention. However, what the Committee observed addresses the important position of the outcome of public participation in the decision-making.

Furthermore, in the communication of *ACCC/C/2008/24 (Spain)*[482] (see 5.1.3.4), the Spanish NGO Association for Environmental Justice submitted a communication to the Compliance Committee. One of the arguments from the Communicant was that proper public participation was not provided for the decision-making processes concerning the land-use planning and the implementation of the urbanisation project in a residential area, and also concerning the decision of the City of Murcia to allocate special land for that purpose. These failed to meet the requirements of Article 6(1)(a), (2)(a) and (b), and (4) of the Convention.

The Compliance Committee found that: "*It is quite clear to the Committee that the obligation to take due account in the decision of the outcome of the public participation cannot be considered as a requirement to accept all comments, reservations or opinions submitted. However, while it is impossible to accept in substance all the comments submitted, which may often be conflicting, the relevant authority must still seriously consider all the comments received. The Committee recalls that the obligation to take 'due account' under Article 6, paragraph 9, to 'make accessible to the public the text of the decision along with the reasons and*

---

480 ACCC/C/2008/29 (Poland), ECE/MP.PP/C.1/2009/6/Add.2, 25 September 2009, www.unece.org/fileadmin/DAM/env/pp/compliance/CC-25/ece_mp.pp_c.1_2009_6_add.2_e.pdf accessed 6 April 2014.

481 ACCC/C/2007/22 (France), ECE/MP.PP/C.1/2009/4/Add.1, 8 February 2011, §29, www.unece.org/fileadmin/DAM/env/pp/compliance/C2008-22/Findings/ece_mp.pp_c.1_2009_4_add.1_eng.pdf accessed 27 March 2013; ACCC/C/2008/24 (Spain), ECE/MP.PP/C.1/2009/8/Add.1, 8 February 2011, §98, www.unece.org/fileadmin/DAM/env/pp/compliance/CC-26/ece_mp.pp_c.1_2009_8_add.1_e.pdf accessed 21 March 2014.

482 ACCC/C/2008/24 (Spain), ECE/MP.PP/C.1/2009/8/Add.1, 8 February 2011, www.unece.org/fileadmin/DAM/env/pp/compliance/CC-26/ece_mp.pp_c.1_2009_8_add.1_e.pdf accessed 21 March 2014.

considerations on which the decision is based.' Therefore the obligation to take due account of the outcome of the public participation should be interpreted as the obligation that the written reasoned decision includes a discussion of how the public participation was taken into account (...) The Committee notes that a system where, as a routine, comments of the public were disregarded or not accepted on their merits, without any explanation, would not comply with the Convention."[483]

The necessity for the authorities to seriously take into account the outcome of public participation and to address it in policy-making, law-making and decision-making is a vital point of the Convention. This aspect decides whether the public participation is really meaningful or not. This communication further explains how to deal with the potential conflicts among all the comments from the process of public participation. However, the baseline is that "*the relevant authority must still seriously consider all the comments received.*"[484]

If some opinions from a member of the public are not taken into account in the decision-making process, he/she will be able to challenge the decision in an administrative or judicial proceeding under Article 9(2) of the Convention. This will be discussed in detail in the access to justice part. Because of Article 9 of the Convention, decision-maker(s) will seriously think about all the comments or opinions from the public and devote serious attention to the requirement that due account shall be taken of the outcome of public participation.

5.2.3.5. The Influence of the Aarhus Convention on EU Law on the Right to Participation

The main vehicles for implementing the relevant Aarhus obligations are considered to be the SEA Directive[485] and Water Framework Directive.[486] Notably, Article 7 of the SEA Directive asks Member States to consult with individuals of other Member States if the proposed development activity

483 ACCC/C/2008/24 (Spain), ECE/MP.PP/C.1/2009/8/Add.1, 8 February 2011, §§99–100, www.unece.org/fileadmin/DAM/env/pp/compliance/CC-26/ece_mp.pp_c.1_2009_8_add.1_e.pdf accessed 21 March 2014.

484 ACCC/C/2008/24 (Spain), ECE/MP.PP/C.1/2009/8/Add.1, 8 February 2011, §§99–100, www.unece.org/fileadmin/DAM/env/pp/compliance/CC-26/ece_mp.pp_c.1_2009_8_add.1_e.pdf accessed 21 March 2014.

485 Directive 2001/42/EC of the European Parliament and of the Council of 27 June 2001 on the Assessment of the Effects of Certain Plans and Programs on the Environment [2001] OJ L197/30 (SEA Directive), issued on 27 June 2001 and entered into effect 21 July 2001, www.ecolex.org/ecolex/ledge/view/RecordDetails;jsessionid=05602270319C24F8AA6403BAB3123F46?id=LEX-FAOC034996&index=documents accessed 12 October 2013.

486 Directive 2000/60/EC of the European Parliament and of the Council of 23 October 2000 Establishing a Framework for Community Action in the Field of Water Policy [2000] OJ L327/1 (Water Framework Directive), issued on 23 October 2000, http://eur-lex.europa.eu/LexUriServ/LexUriServ.do?uri=OJ:L:2000:327:0001:0072:en:PDF accessed 12 October 2013.

(project, plan or programme) is likely to have a "significant effect" on these people.[487]

The two Directives above have been singled out as performing such functions by Directive 2003/35/EC,[488] which is meant to supplement them by providing for a set of public participation requirements in relation to plans and programmes considered to be "relating to the environment" within the meaning of the Aarhus Convention but introduced by environmental directives adopted before it.[489]

The Directive 2003/35/EC is one of the important legal initiatives to implement the second pillar of the Aarhus Convention in the European Union. It provides for public participation in respect of the drawing up of certain plans and programmes relating to the environment in the Member States and strengthens the provisions on public participation in the 1985 EIA Directive[490] and in Directive 96/61/EC on integrated pollution prevention and control (IPPC),[491] which was recently recast as Directive 2010/75/EU on Industrial Emissions.[492]

The overall aim of Directive 2003/35/EC and the role of public participation in environmental decision-making are clearly outlined in the preamble which states: "*Effective public participation in the taking of decisions enables the public to express, and the decision-maker to take account of, opinions and concerns which may be relevant to those decisions, thereby increasing the accountability and*

---

487 Razzaque, J. (2013). Information, public participation and access to justice in environmental matters. In Alam, S. *et al.* (Eds.). *Routledge Handbook of International Environmental Law.* London and New York: Routledge, p. 145.

488 Directive 2003/35/EC of the European Parliament and of the Council of 26 May 2003 Providing for Public Participation in Respect of the Drawing up of Certain Plans and Programs Relating to the Environment and Amending with regards to Public Participation and Access to Justice Council Directive 85/337/EEC and 96/61/EC [2003] OJ L 156/17, issued on 26 May 2003, http://eur-lex.europa.eu/LexUriServ/LexUriServ.do?uri=OJ:L:2003:156:0017:0024:EN:PDF accessed 28 October 2013.

489 Jendroska, J. (2011). Public participation in environmental decision-making: interactions between the Convention and EU Law and other key legal issues in its implementation in the light of the opinions of the Aarhus Convention Compliance Committee. In: Pallemaerts, M. (Ed.). *The Aarhus Convention at Ten: Interactions and Tensions between Conventional International Law and EU Environmental Law.* Groningen: Europa Law Publishing, p. 103.

490 Council Directive 85/337/EEC of 27 June 1985 on the Assessment of Certain Public and Private Projects on the Environment [1985] OJ L175/40, Articles 6, 8 and 9, issued on 27 June 1985, http://ec.europa.eu/environment/eia/full-legal-text/85337.htm accessed 12 October 2013.

491 Council Directive 96/61/EC of 24 September 1996 Concerning Integrated Pollution Prevention and Control [1996] OJ L257/26, issued on 24 September 1996, http://eur-lex.europa.eu/LexUriServ/LexUriServ.do?uri=CELEX:31996L0061:en:HTML accessed 12 October 2013.

492 Directive 2010/75/EU of the European Parliament and of the Council of 24 November 2010 on Industrial Emissions (Integrated Pollution Prevention and Control) [2010] OJ L334/17, issued on 24 November 2010, www.energy-community.org/pls/portal/docs/2394177.PDF accessed 12 October 2013.

transparency of the decision-making process and contributing to public awareness of environmental issues and support for the decisions taken".[493]

Directive 2003/35/EC expressly states that the Member States reserve the competence to identify the stakeholders to be consulted in accordance with nationally stipulated requirements and that they are also entitled to develop detailed arrangements for conducting those consultations.[494] Article 3(4) of Directive 2003/35/EC has the potential to ensure that participation commences "earlier". Besides this, the Directive instructs the Member States to develop detailed arrangements for both informing and consulting the public concerned for the purpose of fulfilling the Aarhus requirements.[495] It stipulates that those arrangements can, for example, take the form of written submissions or public inquiries.[496]

Moreover, Directive 2003/35/EC addresses that all organisations have a possibility or an opportunity to participate in the consultation process to challenge before national courts non-compliance of national authorities with the requirements of the Aarhus consultation.[497] It regards the breach of the Member State duty to consult the public prior to taking decisions on issues falling with the area of application of the Aarhus Convention as constituting an infringement of an essential procedural requirement for adopting such measures and consequently a basis for challenging their legality.[498]

In fact, the Aarhus Convention and Directive 2003/35/EC restrict the Aarhus public participation requirements to the duty of national and EU authorities to provide a timely opportunity for civil interest groups to express their opinion

---

493 European Commission. Directive 2003/35/EC of the European Parliament and of the Council of May 2003 providing for Public Participation in respect of the drawing up of Certain Plans and Programs relating to the Environment and amending with regards to Public Participation and Access to Justice Council Directives 85/337/EEC and 96/61/EC [2003] OJ L156/17–24, §3, http://eur-lex.europa.eu/LexUriServ/LexUriServ.do?uri=OJ:L:2003:156:0017:0024:EN:PDF accessed 12 October 2013.

494 Article 2(3), Directive 2003/35/EC of the European Parliament and of the Council of 26 May 2003 providing for public participation in respect of the drawing up of certain plans and programs relating to the environment and amending with regards to public participation and access to justice Council Directive 85/337/EEC and 96/61/EC [2003] OJ L156/17, http://eur-lex.europa.eu/LexUriServ/LexUriServ.do?uri=OJ:L:2003:156:0017:0024:EN:PDF accessed 28 October 2013.

495 Obradovic, D. (2011). EU rules on public participation in environmental decision-making operating at the European and National Levels. In: Pallemaerts, M. (Ed.). *The Aarhus Convention at Ten: Interactions and Tensions between Conventional International Law and EU Environmental Law.* Groningen: Europa Law Publishing, p. 163.

496 Articles 3 and 5 of the Annex V, http://eur-lex.europa.eu/LexUriServ/LexUriServ.do?uri=OJ:L:2003:156:0017:0024:EN:PDF accessed 28 October 2013.

497 Article 10(a) of Directive 85/337/EEC as amended by Directive 2003/35/EC and Article 15(a) of Directive 96/61/EC as amended by Directive 2003/35/EC.

498 Obradovic, D. (2011). EU rules on public participation in environmental decision-making operating at the European and National Levels. In: Pallemaerts, M. (Ed.). *The Aarhus Convention at Ten: Interactions and Tensions between Conventional International Law and EU Environmental Law.* Groningen: Europa Law Publishing, p. 178.

on particular administrative decisions and/or regulatory proposals, and grant them no decision-making rights. The obligations placed upon the Member States are stricter than those expected to be complied with by the Community institutions.[499] The reason for this is as follows: while national participation practice must be aligned with the requirements of Aarhus Articles 6, 7 and 8, EU consultations are to fulfil only Article 7 and 8 requirements because EU institutions do not take decisions listed in Article 6.[500]

Since the Aarhus Convention sets the minimum standards for EU law on the right to participation, it is not necessary to further examine the relevant cases on the right to participation within EU law for the reason that the baseline would be similar to what has been discussed in the ECtHR and the ACCC.

5.2.3.6. Right to Participation in Protected Areas Conservation Law in Europe

5.2.3.6.1. The Bern Convention

There is no explicit reference to the right to participation in the Bern Convention. If there is any infringement on the right to participation in Europe, the mechanisms under the ECHR or the Aarhus Convention can be applied.

5.2.3.6.2. The Birds Directive and the Habitats Directive

The Birds Directive and the Habitats Directive do not make any explicit reference to the right to participation. However, there is a limited form of participation in Article 6, §3 of the Habitats Directive: "*Any plan or project not directly connected with or necessary to the management of the site but likely to have a significant effect thereon, either individually or in combination with other plans or projects, shall be subject to appropriate assessment of its implications for the site in view of the site's conservation objectives. In the light of the conclusions of the assessment of the implications for the site and subject to the provisions of paragraph 4, the competent national authorities shall agree to the plan or project only after having ascertained that it will not adversely affect the integrity of the site concerned and, if appropriate, after having obtained the opinion of the general public.*" It is noted that even though the Habitats Directive does not mention a participatory rights, the Aarhus Convention imposes obligations compelling the public authorities

499 Obradovic, D. (2011). EU rules on public participation in environmental decision-making operating at the European and National Levels. In: Pallemaerts, M. (Ed.). *The Aarhus Convention at Ten: Interactions and Tensions between Conventional International Law and EU Environmental Law.* Groningen: Europa Law Publishing, p. 163.

500 Obradovic, D. (2011). EU rules on public participation in environmental decision-making operating at the European and National Levels. In: Pallemaerts, M. (Ed.). *The Aarhus Convention at Ten: Interactions and Tensions between Conventional International Law and EU Environmental Law.* Groningen: Europa Law Publishing, p. 163.

in the Member States to inform and consult the people concerned, particularly because management plans would normally contain general rules.[501]

However, some cases from the Court of Justice of the European Union, which will be discussed in the next section, shows that the right to participation plays an important role in protected areas conservation. Nevertheless, if there is any infringement on the right to participation of local people and communities, some relevant provisions from the ECHR, the Aarhus Convention and Directive 2003/35/EC[502] can be applied.

5.2.3.6.3. Case Law in the Court of Justice of the European Union According to Protected Areas Conservation Law

If the right to be heard could be regarded as an indirect way of public participation, the situation in the case of *Cascina Tre Pini S.s. v. Ministero dell' Ambiente e della Tutela del Territorio e del Mare and Others*[503] (see 4.3.4.3) reflects that the public participation of the relevant party could make a great contribution to protected areas conservation.

This reflection was also shown in the opinion of the advocate general on the case of *Peter Sweetman and Others v. An Bord Pleanala.*[504] In this case an Bord Pleanala (the Irish Planning Board), which is the competent national authority in Ireland for the purposes of Article 6 of the Directive, had adopted a decision to grant development consent to build a proposed road through part of the Lough Corrib Natura 2000 site. The planned road would lead to the permanent

---

501 García-Ureta, A. & Lazkano, Í. (2014). Instruments for sites active management of Natura 2000: balancing between stakeholders and nature conservation? In: Born, C.-H., Cliquet, A., Schoukens, H., Misonne, D. & Van Hoorick, G. (Eds.), *The Habitats Directive in its EU Environmental Law Context: European Nature's Best Hope?* Oxford: Routledge, pp. 79–97.

502 For instance, Terre Wallonne ASBL v. Région Wallonne, Case C-105/09; Inter-Environment Wallonie ASBL v. Région Wallonne, Case C-110/09; Joined Case Judgment of the Court (Fourth Chamber) of 17 June 2010, http://curia.europa.eu/juris/document/document.jsf?text=&docid=83020&pageIndex=0&doclang=EN&mode=lst&dir=&occ=first&part=1&cid=135853 accessed 10 April 2014. These two cases adopted some provisions on public participation in Directive 2003/35/EC. http://curia.europa.eu/juris/document/document.jsf?text=%2522natura%2B2000%2522%2B%2522participation%2522&docid=79351&pageIndex=0&doclang=EN&mode=req&dir=&occ=first&part=1&cid=890743#ctx1 accessed 10 April 2014.

503 Cascina Tre Pini S.s. v. Ministero dell' Ambiente e della Tutela del Territorio e del Mare and Others, Case C-301/12. Judgment of the Court (Second Chamber) of 3 April 2014, http://curia.europa.eu/juris/liste.jsf?language=en&jur=C,T,F&num=C-301/12&td=ALL accessed 7 April 2014.

504 Peter Sweetman and others v. An Bord Pleanala, Case C-258/11, Judgment of the Court (Third Chamber) of 11 April 2013, http://curia.europa.eu/juris/liste.jsf?pro=&nat=or&oqp=&dates=&lg=&language=en&jur=C%2CT%2CF&cit=none%252CC%252CCJ%252CR%252C2008E%252C%252C%252C%252C%252C%252C%252C%252C%252C%252Ctrue%252Cfalse%252Cfalse&num=258%252F11&td=%3BALL&pcs=Oor&avg=&page=1&mat=or&jge=&for=&cid=383224 accessed 10 July 2014.

loss of about 1.47 hectares of limestone pavement, a protected priority habitat type. Mr Sweetman challenged the decision at issue before the High Court (Ireland), arguing in particular that the Board had been wrong to conclude the road would not adversely affect the Lough Corrib site. It was noted that: "*The threshold at the first stage of Article 6(3) is thus a very low one. It operates merely as a trigger, in order to determine whether an appropriate assessment must be undertaken of the implications of the plan or project for the conservation objectives of the site. The purpose of that assessment is that the plan or project in question should be considered thoroughly, on the basis of what the Court has termed 'the best scientific knowledge in the field'.*[505] *Members of the general public may also be invited to give their opinion. Their views may often provide valuable practical insights based on their local knowledge of the site in question and other relevant background information that might otherwise be unavailable to those conducting the assessment.*"[506]

The result of this case is not relevant to this book, but the opinion of the Advocate General addressed the important role of the opinion from the general public in protected areas conservation.

5.2.4. ANALYSIS AND INTERIM CONCLUSION

To a large extent, legitimacy is a matter of participation: the governed must have and perceive that they have a voice in governance through representation, deliberation or some other form of action.[507] A considerable variety of reasons are commonly given for pursuing the participation agenda, and these are inextricably linked to some of the most fundamental elements of modern governance. They commonly include: democratic values (participation is thought to promote public "ownership" of decisions that often affect not only the immediate parties to the process in question, but also the broader public interest); accountability (participation can be viewed as endorsing transparent

---

505 Waddenvereniging and Vogelbeschermingsvereniging, Case C-127/02, Judgment of the Court (Grand Chamber) of 7 September 2004, §54, http://curia.europa.eu/juris/liste.jsf?pro=&nat=or&oqp=&dates=&lg=&language=en&jur=C%2CT%2CF&cit=none%252CC%252CCJ%252CR%252C2008E%252C%252C%252C%252C%252C%252C%252C%252C%252C%252Ctrue%252Cfalse%252Cfalse&num=127%252F02&td=%3BALL&pcs=Oor&avg=&page=1&mat=or&jge=&for=&cid=420788 accessed 10 July 2014.

506 Peter Sweetman and Others v. An Bord Pleanala, Case C-258/11, Judgment of the Court (Third Chamber) of 11 April 2013, §49, http://curia.europa.eu/juris/liste.jsf?pro=&nat=or&oqp=&dates=&lg=&language=en&jur=C%2CT%2CF&cit=none%252CC%252CCJ%252CR%252C2008E%252C%252C%252C%252C%252C%252C%252C%252C%252C%252Ctrue%252Cfalse%252Cfalse&num=258%252F11&td=%3BALL&pcs=Oor&avg=&page=1&mat=or&jge=&for=&cid=383224 accessed 10 July 2014.

507 Shelton, D.L. (2010). Linkages between human rights and environmental protection, www.ttenvironmentalcommission.org/lectureseries/2010/dinah_shelton.pdf accessed 10 October 2013, p. 17.

and open decision-making processes and requiring that decisions be adequately justified); improved decision-making (given the complexity of the issues involved in environmental decision-making, methodologies which gather information from a broad range of sources are viewed as likely to be more robust); and education (awareness of salient issues generated on the part of the decision-maker, the applicant, statutory consultants and the public).[508]

5.2.4.1. Differences in Public Participation in China and in Europe

What is appropriate in one country will not necessarily work elsewhere. Appropriate forms of public participation and consultation need to reflect the different situations, capabilities, and stages of development of each country.[509] Some differences of public participation in China and in Europe will be analysed below.

5.2.4.1.1. Different Theories of Public Participation

Public participation is regarded as a method and an end to democracy. Whilst there are dozens, perhaps hundreds of theories as to what democracy means, two particular theories are dominant.[510] These are "elite democracy" on the one hand and "participatory democracy" on the other. The elite theory has also been described as "bureaucratic" or "technical" and the "participatory" theory as the "pluralist" or "social democratic" approach.[511] In between these two theories lie a range of compromise theories seeking to reconcile some of the inherent inconsistencies in our aspirations such as a desire for increased public participation and a desire for greater expertise and efficiency in decision-making.[512]

These two theories might respectively represent what democracy means in China and in Europe. As for "elite democracy", one outcome of elite or bureaucratic theories of democracy in relation to environmental decision-

508 Morrow, K. (2011). The Courts and public participation in environmental decision-making. In: Benidickson, J., Boer, B., Benjamin, A.H. & Morrow, K. (Eds.) *Environmental Law and Sustainability after Rio*. The IUCN Academy of Environmental Law Series. Cheltenham (UK) and Northampton (USA): Edward Elgar Publishing, p. 139.

509 Kritikos, M. (2011). Shaping transnational public participation norms in the field of modern biotechnology: time for a global good governance approach? In: Pallemaerts, M. (Ed.). *The Aarhus Convention at Ten: Interactions and Tensions between Conventional International Law and EU Environmental Law*. Groningen: Europa Law Publishing, p. 242.

510 Parnell, M., Public participation in environmental decision-making, www.edo.org.au/edosa/research/aialpaper.htm accessed 5 November 2013.

511 Parnell, M., Public participation in environmental decision-making, www.edo.org.au/edosa/research/aialpaper.htm accessed 5 November 2013.

512 Parnell, M., Public participation in environmental decision-making, www.edo.org.au/edosa/research/aialpaper.htm accessed 5 November 2013.

making is that public participation is discouraged or denied.[513] The assumption is that governments know best and that public participation would simply lead to inefficiencies in the decision-making process and not add substantially to the quality of the decisions that are made.[514] Similarly, owing to the greater pressure of the urgent need for economic development and the educational level of the public in China, it is obvious why there is less public participation than in the developed countries. The government at different levels in China had to pay more attention to the efficiency than to the relative fairness. However, with the rapid development of the economy and the increasing growth of the education level of the public, it is the right time to learn how to stimulate the potential roles of the public. "Participatory democracy" does provide an institutional and legal framework that allows the poor to fight for their rights and defend the natural resources on which their livelihoods depend.[515]

Conversely, public participation is a popular term in Europe. Except the ECHR (see 5.2.3.1), the cases from the ECtHR, the Aarhus Convention and the cases from the ACCC explicitly address public participation in environmental matters.

5.2.4.1.2. Different Historical Stages of Public Participation

According to what has been introduced (see 5.2.2.1), "public participation" was not adopted until it was definitely pointed out in an official document in China in 1996. In 2002 when the "Law of the People's Republic of China on Environmental Impact Assessment" was adopted, the right to participation in environmental matters was granted to the public in China (see 5.2.2.2). In this context, the right to participation in protected areas conservation cannot be earlier than these.

Although the ECHR did not provide any provision on public participation (see 5.2.3.1), the cases from the ECtHR have indirectly addressed the importance of the right to participation (see 5.2.3.2). The Aarhus Convention and the case law from the ACCC explicitly addressed the right to participation in environmental matters. All these reflect that public participation in Europe was formally established earlier than in China. At present, the historical stages of public participation are quite different. Therefore, it is not surprising to see that the right to participation in Europe is more advanced than it is in China.

---

513 Parnell, M., Public participation in environmental decision-making, www.edo.org.au/edosa/research/aialpaper.htm accessed 5 November 2013.

514 Parnell, M., Public participation in environmental decision-making, www.edo.org.au/edosa/research/aialpaper.htm accessed 5 November 2013.

515 Narain, S. & Agarwal, A. (2007). Harvesting the rain: fighting ecological poverty through participatory democracy. In: Boyce, J.K., Narain, S. & Stanton, E.A. (Eds.). *Reclaiming Nature: Environmental Justice and Ecological Restoration*. London: Anthem Press, p. 107.

5.2.4.1.3. Different Scopes of Public Participation

The participation rights should be as broad as possible, and should include the right to be informed, the right to be involved at an early stage and the right to be heard.[516] At a minimum, this broad standing should include interested environmental NGOs and the affected/interested public.[517] The "scopes" of public participation not only include participating as early as possible, but also contain stimulating the affected/interested public as much as possible. An important improvement for public participation in law-making would be to have legally guaranteed rights allowing interested NGOs to participate at an early stage (i.e. when options are still open and NGOs can still influence the outcome of the decision).[518] NGOs are known to play a vital role in forging supranational protected areas agreements and initiatives and holding governmental agencies accountable for their action or lack of action on protected areas.[519] In addition, NGOs can also powerfully influence protected areas through policy since many play advisory roles in national and international policy-making, acting as advocates for specific provisions within national legislation and international protected areas agreements, such as the CBD, the World Heritage Convention or the Ramsar Convention.[520] Undoubtedly, the roles of NGOs in various aspects cannot be ignored.

Moreover, when implementing a participatory process, stakeholder participation should be considered right from the outset, from concept development and planning, through implementation, to monitoring and evaluation of outcomes.[521] Engagement with stakeholders as early as possible in

516 Bolshakova, M. Dusik, J. & Toth Nagy, M. (1998). Chapter 2: public participation in environmental decision-making. In: *Doors to Democracy: a Pan-European Assessment of Current Trends and Practices in Public Participation in: Environmental Matters.* Szentendre (Hungary): The Regional Environmental Center for Central and Eastern Europe, http://archive.rec.org/REC/Publications/PPDoors/EUROPE/PP. html accessed 30 October 2013.

517 Bolshakova, M. Dusik, J. & Toth Nagy, M. (1998). Chapter 2: public participation in environmental decision-making. In: *Doors to Democracy: a Pan-European Assessment of Current Trends and Practices in Public Participation in Environmental Matters.* Szentendre (Hungary): The Regional Environmental Center for Central and Eastern Europe, http://archive.rec.org/REC/Publications/PPDoors/EUROPE/PP.html accessed 30 October 2013.

518 Bolshakova, M. Dusik, J. & Toth Nagy, M. (1998). Chapter 2: public participation in environmental decision-making. In *Doors to Democracy: a Pan-European Assessment of Current Trends and Practices in Public Participation in Environmental Matters.* Szentendre (Hungary): The Regional Environmental Center for Central and Eastern Europe, http://archive.rec.org/REC/Publications/PPDoors/EUROPE/PP.html accessed 30 October 2013.

519 Lockwood, M., Kothari, A. & Worboys, G. (Eds.) (2006). *Managing Protected Areas: a Global Guide.* London: Earthscan, p. 127.

520 Lockwood, M., Kothari, A. & Worboys, G. (Eds.) (2006). *Managing Protected Areas: a Global Guide.* London: Earthscan, p. 127.

521 Reed, M.S. (2008). Stakeholder participation for environmental management: a literature review. *Biological Conservation*, 141, http://ac.els-cdn.com/S0006320708002693/1-s2.0-S0006320708002693-main.pdf?_tid=ed10c162-3a82-11e3-9b8a-00000aacb361&acdnat=1382382155_c3a981c760012795fcaf6e6477e24e0d accessed 21 October 2011, p. 2423.

decision-making has been frequently cited as essential if participatory processes are to lead to high quality and durable decisions.[522] Typically, stakeholders only get involved in decision-making at the implementation phase of the project cycle, and not in earlier project identification and preparation phases.[523] This is the main challenge concerning public participation in practice. Comparatively speaking, European countries have broadened the scopes of public participation both on paper and in jurisprudence. While China has made some progress, however, it is still on the road of broadening the scopes of public participation. How to stimulate the affected groups' roles as much as possible to let them participate in the programme or action as early as possible is a challenging question both in theory and in practice. When the right to participation of the public, especially the right to participation of local people and communities and NGOs, is recognised by laws and regulations from different levels of governments in China, their potential roles in environmental protection or protected areas conservation will at least have a legal guarantee to be stimulated and realised.

However, unless flexibility can be built into the project design, this can mean that stakeholders are invited to get involved in a project that is at variance with their own needs and priorities.[524] This may make it a challenge to motivate stakeholders to engage with the decision-making process, and those who are engaged may be placed in a reactive position, where they are asked to respond to proposals that they perceive to have already been finalised.[525] These may refer to the levels of public participation: the first one is passive; the next one is active (see 5.2.2.3 and 5.2.3.3). To be successful, it is absolutely necessary

---

522 Reed, M.S., Fraser, E.D.G. & Dougill, A.J. (2006). An adaptive learning process for developing and applying sustainability indicators with local communities. *Ecological Economics*, 59, pp. 406–418; Chess, C. & Purcell, K. (1999). Public participation and the environment – do we know what works. *Environmental Science and Technology*, 33, pp. 2685–2692; Garie'py, M. (1991). Toward a dual-influence system: assessing the effects of public participation in environmental impact assessment for hydro-Quebec projects. *Environmental Impact Assessment Review*, 11, pp. 353–374; Blahna, D.J. & Yonts-Shepard, S. (1989). Public involvement in resource planning: toward bridging the gap between policy and implementation. *Society and Natural Resources*, 2, pp. 209– 227; Stewart, T.R., Dennis, R.L. & Ely, D.W. (1984). Citizen participation and judgment in policy analysis – a case-study of urban air quality policy. *Policy Science*, 17, pp. 67–87.

523 Reed, M.S. (2008). Stakeholder participation for environmental management: a literature review. *Biological Conservation*, 141, http://ac.els-cdn.com/S0006320708002693/1-s2.0-S0006320708002693-main.pdf?_tid=ed10c162-3a82-11e3-9b8a-00000aacb361&acdnat=1382382155_c3a981c760012795fcaf6e6477e24e0d accessed 21 October 2013, p. 2424.

524 Reed, M.S. (2008). Stakeholder participation for environmental management: a literature review. *Biological Conservation*, 141, http://ac.els-cdn.com/S0006320708002693/1-s2.0-S0006320708002693-main.pdf?_tid=ed10c162-3a82-11e3-9b8a-00000aacb361&acdnat=1382382155_c3a981c760012795fcaf6e6477e24e0d accessed 21 October 2011, p. 2424.

525 Chess, C. & Purcell, K. (1999). Public participation and the environment – do we know what works. *Environmental Science and Technology*, 33, pp. 2685–2692.

to make people active participants, not simply integrate and validate local knowledge.[526]

5.2.4.1.4. Different Levels of Public Participation

Generally speaking, in developed countries, the public has an active role in all social events including environmental matters, while in the countries that are still in the process of integration into wider regional economic and political frameworks, this is just a tendency.[527]

As what has been mentioned before, the level of participation in the stakeholder analysis can also vary considerably.[528] This may consist of passive consultation, where stakeholders simply provide information for the analysis.[529] It may extend to active engagement, where there is a two-way exchange of information between stakeholders and analysts as equal partners, in a process which is designed to allow stakeholders to influence who is included in the analysis.[530] However, people in many developing and developed countries lack information on their participatory rights and fail to actively participate in decision-making processes.[531] In many developed countries (e.g. in Europe), the participation agenda is generally integrated in the public consultation and review mechanisms and has tended to take a more legal form than in many developing countries where it has, to some extent, been confined to policy mechanisms.[532] All these largely depend upon the development of the existing political, economic, cultural circumstances, specifically the educational levels of the public.

---

526 Carvalho, A.M. & Frazao-Moreira, A. (2011). Importance of local knowledge in plant resources management and conservation in two protected areas from Tras-os-Montes, Portugal. *Journal of Ethnobiology and Ethnomedicine*, 7(36), p. 11.

527 Marija Kostic. (2006). *The Right of Access to Environmental Information in the Sense of the Aarhus Convention – European Streams and Legal Framework in Serbia and Montenegro.* CPRINT: Beograd. Dissertation zur Erlangung der Würde des akademischen Grades eines Doktors der Rechte. Europa-Universität Viadrina Frankfurt, p. 1.

528 Reed, M.S. (2008). Stakeholder participation for environmental management: a literature review. *Biological Conservation*, 141, http://ac.els-cdn.com/S0006320708002693/1-s2.0-S0006320708002693-main.pdf?_tid=ed10c162-3a82-11e3-9b8a-00000aacb361&acdnat=1382382155_c3a981c760012795fcaf6e6477e24e0d accessed 21 October 2011, p. 2424.

529 Reed, M.S. (2008). Stakeholder participation for environmental management: a literature review. *Biological Conservation*, 141, http://ac.els-cdn.com/S0006320708002693/1-s2.0-S0006320708002693-main.pdf?_tid=ed10c162-3a82-11e3-9b8a-00000aacb361&acdnat=1382382155_c3a981c760012795fcaf6e6477e24e0d accessed 21 October 2011, p. 2424.

530 Reed, M.S. (2008). Stakeholder participation for environmental management: a literature review. *Biological Conservation*, 141, http://ac.els-cdn.com/S0006320708002693/1-s2.0-S0006320708002693-main.pdf?_tid=ed10c162-3a82-11e3-9b8a-00000aacb361&acdnat=1382382155_c3a981c760012795fcaf6e6477e24e0d accessed 21 October 2011, p. 2424.

531 Razzaque, J. (2013). Information, public participation and access to justice in environmental matters. In Alam, S. *et al.* (Eds.). *Routledge Handbook of International Environmental Law.* London and New York: Routledge, p. 152.

532 Renn, O., Webler, T. & Wiedemann, P. (Eds.) (1995). *Fairness and Competence in Citizen Participation: Evaluating Models for Environmental Discourse.* Dordrecht: Kluwer, pp. 17–33.

According to what has been discussed (see 5.2.3), at least in theory, the public can participate in all the phases of an environmental project in Europe, in both passive and active ways. The public participation in China is mainly post-supervision, and there is little pre-supervision and process supervision (see 5.2.2.5). At present, some "early" and "active" participation barriers need to be overcome in China.

5.2.4.1.5. Different "Supporters" of Public Participation

There is no independent human rights law in China at present; however, the right to participation in environmental matters was addressed in the relevant policy and environmental law in China (see 5.2.2). If there is any infringement on human rights, individuals or NGOs may appeal to the People's Court. This will be further clarified in the section of access to justice (see 5.3.1).

Conversely, the right to participation in environmental matters was approved by the ECtHR (see 5.2.3.2), the Aarhus Convention (see 5.2.3.3) and the ACCC (see 5.2.3.4). Protected areas conservation law in Europe contains only very limited reference to public participation (see 5.2.3.6). However, it is widely accepted that the protected areas management plans in national countries shall be compliant with the Aarhus Convention. Furthermore, if there is any infringement on human rights, individuals or NGOs can appeal to the specific human rights Court (the ECtHR). The important role of the right to participation can also be found in the CJEU with regards to the protected areas conservation law.

We can conclude that the "supporters" of the right to participation in China are some recent policies and environmental law in theory, and the People's Court in practice. However, there are various methods to solve the relevant issues in practice in China, which is not limited to appeal to a court (see 5.3.1). In Europe, the ECtHR, the case law from the ACCC and the CJEU further provide some guidelines to solve the relevant issues in practice. These various "supporters" could be effectively dealing with the potential conflicts regarding the right to participation and protected areas conservation in Europe.

5.2.4.2. Similarities in Public Participation Between China and Europe

Besides these differences, the developmental tendencies of the right to participation are similar in China and Europe. At the beginning, public participation was unknown in Chinese policy and law, let alone realising right to participation. However, at present, public participation is a popular term in Chinese policy and law, and the right to participation is also recognised in recent Chinese policy and law. As indicated above (see 5.2.3.1), the ECHR did not provide any provision on public participation, but the recent cases from the ECtHR have indirectly addressed the importance of the right to participation. More importantly, the Aarhus Convention, the case law from the ACCC and

Directive 2003/35/EC have approved the right to participation in environmental matters. From these developmental trends, we can see that the right to participation was recognised step by step.

5.2.4.3. *Some Lessons for China*

Concerning public participation and protected areas conservation, it still remains a challenge for Europe and China how to stimulate the role of the local people and communities and NGOs as much as possible and let them participate in the protected areas establishment and management. Based on the different theories of public participation and different development stages of policy, economy, culture and law, Europe began to solve this challenging question earlier than China and made more progress than China. It is impossible to copy what European countries have done to China; however, there are some baselines or principles that need to be mentioned, viz:

(1) the public authorities need to take into account the interests of individuals who may be affected. It is especially necessary for minorities or vulnerable groups. More than half of the local people near or within protected areas in China are the ethnic minorities. Fully guaranteeing their interests is a good method to solve the potential conflicts to achieve the stability for the whole country;
(2) the decision-making process must involve appropriate investigation and studies;
(3) the affected groups have a right to participate in the decision-making;
(4) broadening the scopes of participation and deepening the levels of participation. The realisation of consultation in environmental legislation or regulation depends on various reasons, however, consultation is an irreplaceable method to prevent potential conflicts from happening in advance;
(5) participation requires time, resources and preferably skills to achieve the realisation;
(6) the NGOs' vital role cannot be underestimated. Many NGOs tend to assume that any level of interaction and dialogue with local people will give the project or action legitimacy and accountability.

Although there were a lot of conflicts in the initial stage of protected areas conservation, some conflicts have been effectively solved. Some conflicts are still waiting to be solved; however, the tendency undoubtedly reflects procedural human rights play an irreplaceable role in protected areas conservation.

How these baselines or principles can be put into practice in China needs further research. More specifically, how to further stimulate all the possible parties to actively participate in protected areas conservation as earlier as possible in practice in China needs to be deeply explored for different situations at the local levels.

5.3. RIGHT TO ACCESS TO JUSTICE IN ENVIRONMENTAL MATTERS

If rights are to be effective, the public must have a way of seeking justice when those rights are accidentally, or deliberately, denied.[533] Access to justice is an irreplaceable complementary right; it shows itself as an inevitable legal remedy. From the environmental perspective, without enforcement, environmental law would be "toothless" in practice.[534] From the perspective of environmental decision-making, access to justice refers to the right for members of the public to have access to review procedures where they can challenge decisions, acts and omissions by public authorities, and by private persons.[535]

There are not too many international instruments explicitly pointing out the right to access to justice. However, various universal legal instruments contain some provisions on the right to an effective remedy. For instance, from the angle of human rights instruments, Article 8 of the Universal Declaration of Human Rights (UDHR),[536] Article 6 of the International Convention on the Elimination of All Forms of Racial Discrimination (ICERD),[537] Article 2(3) of the International Covenant on Civil and Political Rights (ICCPR).[538] From

---

533 AEETC (Asia-Europe Environmental Technology Centre) (2002). Public Involvement in Environmental Issues in the ASEM (Asia-Europe Meeting) – Background and Overview, published by Asia-Europe Environmental Technology Centre, Helsinki: Edita Prima, http://bch.cbd.int/protocol/outreach/ASEM.pdf accessed 25 November 2013, p. 60.

534 Kostic, M. (2006). *The Right of Access to Environmental Information in the Sense of the Aarhus Convention: European Streams and Legal Framework in Serbia and Montenegro.* CPRINT Beograd, p. 129.

535 Ebbesson, J. (2011). Access to justice at the national level: impact of the Aarhus Convention and European Union law. In: Pallemaerts, M. (Ed.). *The Aarhus Convention at Ten: Interactions and Tensions between Conventional International Law and EU Environmental Law.* Groningen: Europa Law Publishing, p. 247.

536 Article 8, Universal Declaration of Human Rights, adopted on 10 December 1948, UN Doc. A/810 AT 71, UNGA Res. 217 A (III), www.un.org/en/documents/udhr/ accessed 4 November 2011. Article 8: "Everyone has the right to an effective remedy by the competent national tribunals for acts violating the fundamental rights granted him by the constitution or by law".

537 Article 6, International Convention on the Elimination of All Forms of Racial Discrimination, signed on 21 December 1965 and entered into force on 4 January 1969, 660 UNTS 195, www.ohchr.org/EN/ProfessionalInterest/Pages/CERD.aspx accessed 6 December 2013, Article 6: "States Parties shall assure to everyone within their jurisdiction effective protection and remedies, through the competent national tribunals and other State institutions, against any acts of racial discrimination which violate his human rights and fundamental freedoms contrary to this Convention".

538 Article 2(3), International Covenant on Civil and Political Rights (ICCPR), adopted by the United Nations General Assembly on 16 December 1966 and entered into force from 23 March 1976, 999 UNTS 171. It commits its parties to respect the civil and political rights of individuals, including the right to life, freedom of region, freedom of speech, freedom of assembly, electoral rights and rights to due process and a fair trial. http://treaties.un.org/doc/Publication/UNTS/Volume%20999/volume-999-I-14668-English.pdf accessed 9 March 2011. Article 2(3) states: "Every state party to the Convention undertakes: (a) To ensure that any person whose rights or freedoms as herein recognized are violated shall have an effective

the angle of environmental protection instruments, the right to an effective remedy can be found in chapter 8 of Agenda 21,[539] Article 235(2) of United Nations Convention on the Law of the Sea (UNCLOS),[540] point 7 of title B in the OECD Recommendation on Equal Right of Access in Relation to Trans-frontier Pollution.[541] Furthermore, Article 2(6) and (8) of the Espoo Convention[542] and the 1992 Helsinki Convention on the Trans-boundary Effects of Industrial Accidents[543] also provide similar provisions on the right to an effective remedy. All these legal instruments concern either human rights protection or environmental protection. Access to justice and effective legal remedies are crucial elements in both environmental protection and human rights protection. Although these only refer to the right to an effective remedy, the term "remedy" is used to refer to the procedural side of access to justice.[544] What is more, the right to a fair trial is also enshrined in universal human rights documents.[545]

remedy, notwithstanding that the violation has been committed by persons acting in an official capacity; (b) To ensure that any person claiming such a remedy shall have his right thereto determined by competent judicial, administrative or legislative authorities, or by any other competent authority provided for by the legal system of the State, and to develop the possibilities of judicial remedy; (c) To ensure that the competent authorities shall enforce such remedies when granted".

539 It stresses the involvement of the public in devising the relevant policies and grant individuals, groups and organisations having recognised legal interest access to the courts in order to vindicate violations of the law or encroachments on legally guaranteed rights, www.unep.org/Documents.Multilingual/Default.asp?DocumentID=52&ArticleID=56 accessed 6 December 2013.

540 It claims that States shall ensure that recourse is available in accordance with their legal systems for prompt and adequate compensation or other relief in respect of damage caused by pollution of the marine environment by natural or juridical persons under their jurisdiction. United Nations Convention on the Law of the Sea was adopted on 10 December 1982, www.un.org/Depts/los/convention_agreements/texts/unclos/unclos_e.pdf accessed 3 December 2012.

541 OECD (Organization for Economic Cooperation and Development) (1976). Recommendation of equal right of access in relation to trans-frontier pollution. Posted on 11 May 1976, www.dipublico.com.ar/english accessed 3 May 2013.

542 Convention on Environmental Impact Assessment in a Trans-boundary Context (Espoo Convention) was adopted on 25 February 1991 and entered into force in 1997, www.unece.org/env/eia/eia.htm accessed 2 December 2013.

543 Convention on the Trans-boundary Effects of Industrial Accident was adopted in Helsinki on 17 March 1992 and entered into force on 19 April 2000, ECE/CP.TEIA/15/Add.1. It is designed to protect people and the environment against industrial accidents, www.unece.org/env/teia/ accessed 1 December 2012.

544 Desmet, E. (2011). *Indigenous Rights Entwined with Nature Conservation.* Antwerp: Intersentia, p. 324.

545 Article 8, Universal Declaration of Human Rights, adopted on 10 December 1948, UN Doc. A/810 AT 71, UNGA Res. 217 A (III), www.un.org/en/documents/udhr/ accessed 4 November 2011. Article 8: "Everyone has the right to an effective remedy by the competent national tribunals for acts violating the fundamental rights granted him by the constitution or by law", www.un.org/en/documents/udhr/ accessed 6 December 2013. Article 14(1), International Covenant on Civil and Political Rights (ICCPR), adopted by the United Nations General Assembly on 16 December 1966 and entered into force from 23 March

For instance, the ILO Convention No. 169 emphasises that guaranteeing the right to a fair trial may require additional measures in the case of indigenous peoples.[546] Article 12 points out that measures must ensure that "*members of these peoples (indigenous peoples) can understand and be understood in legal proceedings, where necessary through the provision of interpretation or by other effective means.*" According to Article 40 of the UN Declaration on the Rights of Indigenous Peoples, "*indigenous peoples have the right to access to and prompt decision through just and fair procedures for the resolution of conflicts and disputes with States or other parties.*"

Some scholars[547] addressed that the right to access to justice contains both substantial and procedural aspects. Briefly, the substantial aspect of the right to access to justice means getting justice, while the procedural aspect of the right to access to justice means the process to get justice. The right to access to justice in this book only refers to the procedural aspect.

From the perspective of its ingredient, access to justice contains several factors, for instance, criteria for legal standing, review procedure, scope of the case, cost, available remedy and so on. From its external point of view, it is even difficult to reach agreement on what justice really is.[548] Justice is a dynamic concept with a complex of merits; it ought to fluctuate with the changes of cultural, social and historic conditions.[549] Therefore, the process to get justice largely depends on these conditions. These are the main reasons that there are great differences for the right to access to justice between developing countries and developed countries.

Within this context, with regards to protected areas conservation, the third World Conservation Congress in Bangkok in 2004 held that State members should analyse their legislation in the field of human rights and the environment

---

1976, 999 UNTS 171. It commits its parties to respect the civil and political rights of individuals, including the right to life, freedom of region, freedom of speech, freedom of assembly, electoral rights and rights to due process and a fair trial, http://treaties.un.org/doc/Publication/UNTS/Volume%20999/volume-999-I-14668-English.pdf accessed 9 March 2011.

546 Desmet, E. (2011). *Indigenous Rights Entwined with Nature Conservation.* Antwerp: Intersentia, p. 330.

547 e.g. Brunnee, J. (2009). Climate change, global environmental justice and international environmental law. In Ebbesson, J. & Okowa, P. (Eds.). *Environmental Law and Justice in Context.* Cambridge: Cambridge University Press; Desmet, E. (2011). *Indigenous Rights Entwined with Nature Conservation.* Antwerp: Intersentia, p. 324.

548 Stec, S. (1998). Chapter 3: Access to Justice in Environmental Matters. In: *Doors to Democracy: a Pan-European Assessment of Current Trends and Practices in Public Participation in Environmental Matters.* Szentendre (Hungary): The Regional Environmental Center for Central and Eastern Europe, http://archive.rec.org/REC/Publications/PPDoors/EUROPE/Justice.html accessed 25 November 2013.

549 Du, Q. (2009). Public participation and the challenges of environmental justice in China. In: Ebbesson, J. & Okowa, P. (Eds.). *Environmental Law and Justice in Context.* Cambridge (UK): Cambridge University Press, p. 139.

"with the aim of providing effective access to justice in the event of violations of those human rights."[550]

Specifically, there are several inhibiting conditions for access to justice, for instance, standing, the scope of review, costs, length of proceedings and so on. Nevertheless, the key obstacle to realising access to justice from both national and international perspectives is the doctrine of *locus standi* (standing).[551] The key factor for access to justice in the environmental realm is the question of who has legal standing.[552] Legal standing is the ability of a person to show a sufficient legal interest in a matter to allow him or her to bring a case to court.[553] The challenges of legal standing are also linked to the economic, social, cultural, legal and political conditions prevalent in China and in Europe.

The following two sections will introduce and discuss access to justice in environmental matters in China both in theory and in practice. It will also point out some important obstacles for the realisation of access to justice concerning the conflicts regarding human rights protection and environmental protection. The first and essential obstacle among them is that individuals and NGOs do not have enough legal standing to challenge a decision. The access to justice in environmental matters in Europe will be discussed both in theory and in practice.

5.3.1. ACCESS TO JUSTICE IN CHINA

Compared with the human rights discussed in the previous sections, the linkage between the right to access to justice and traditional Chinese culture is even closer. Law really cannot be understood without understanding the culture on which it sits.[554] Chinese traditional ideas have a negative view on litigation.

---

550 IUCN (2004). Resolution WCC 3.015, Conserving Nature and Reducing Poverty by Linking Human Rights and the Environment. Also see IUCN (2005). *Resolutions and Recommendations*. Gland and Cambridge: IUCN, pp. 17–19.

551 Tava, I.V. (2013). The role of non-governmental organizations, peoples and courts in implementing international environmental laws. In: Alam, S., Hossain Bhuiyan, M.J., Chowdhury, T.M.R. & Techera, E.J. (Ed.). *Routledge Handbook of International Environmental Law*. London and New York: Routledge, p. 132.

552 Public participation and sustainable development on-line module, www.docstoc.com/docs/44508222/Public-Participation-and-Sustainable-Development-On-Line-Module accessed 25 October 2013, p. 12.

553 Public participation and sustainable development on-line module, www.docstoc.com/docs/44508222/Public-Participation-and-Sustainable-Development-On-Line-Module accessed 25 October 2013, p. 12.

554 Eberle, J.E. (2009). The method and role of comparative law. *Washington University Global Studies Law Review*, 8(3), http://law.wustl.edu/WUGSLR/Issues/Volume8_3/Eberle.pdf accessed 7 May 2014, p. 452.

Confucianism,[555] Legalism[556] and Taoism,[557] as three main different schools of traditional ideas that strongly influenced future generations in China, all pursue no litigation.[558] Under these contexts, it is interesting to see what the right to access to justice in environmental matters in China means.

5.3.1.1. *Legal and Policy Framework Concerning the Right to Access to Justice in Environmental Matters in China*

There is no provision explicitly referring to the right to access to justice in environmental matters in the Chinese Constitution. However, Article 41 of the Constitution[559] points out that: "*Citizens of the People's Republic of China have the right to criticize and make suggestions on any State organ or functionary. Citizens have the right to appeal or sue or report the actions that violate the law or neglect the duty from any State authority or any official staff*".

Based on this Article in the Constitution, Article 6 of the "Environmental Protection Law of the People's Republic of China" is regarded as the basic provision on access to justice in environmental matters in the existing legal system.[560] It points out that: "*All units and individuals shall have the obligation to protect the environment and shall have the right to report on or sue units*

555 Confucianism is an ethical and philosophical system developed from the teachings of the Chinese philosopher Confucius (551–479 BC). "Li (礼)" is one of the basic virtues promoted by Confucius; "Li (礼)" means to achieve "the preservation of natural harmony (achieved through mediation)", some typical ideas such as "[i]t is better to keep a friend than to win a lawsuit". Detailed information see www.mrrena.com/misc/gier__dancing_ru.php accessed 21 November 2013.

556 Legalism that had arisen during the early Warring State period (475–221 BC) advocated strict obedience to the legal system, which was in direct conflict with Confucian ideals. In the legalistic view, human beings are naturally greedy and selfish. Detailed information see www.oocities.org/stenrose_och_teg/Kinas_dyn.htm accessed 21 November 2013.

557 Taoism that had arisen during the Han Dynasty (206–220 BC) is a philosophical and religious tradition that emphasises living in harmony. The ambiguous term "wu-wei" constitutes the leading ethical concept in Taoism. "Wu-wei (无为)" means "action without action", that is to say, the universe works harmoniously according to its own ways, a potentially harmful interference is to be avoided, and in this way, goals can be achieved effortlessly. Detailed information see http://enlight.lib.ntu.edu.tw/FULLTEXT/JR-PHIL/ew27139.htm and http://home.wlu.edu/~lubint/Touchstone/Acupuncture-Valeri.htm accessed 21 November 2013.

558 Wu, J.K. (吴进科) (2007). Chinese traditional no litigation ideas and harmony society construction (我国传统无讼思想与构建和谐社会). *Enterprise Civilization* (企业文明), 10, p. 69.

559 The "Constitution of the People's Republic of China" [中华人民共和国宪法] was adopted in 1982 and newly amended on 14 March 2004, www.for68.com/new/201007/he60492159127010212383.shtml in both Chinese and English accessed 3 December 2010.

560 Zhang, S.J. & Lu, L. (张式军　卢磊) (2006). On legal guarantee for realization of access to justice in environmental matters: some ideas on improving Article 6 in 'Environmental Protection Law of the People's Republic of China' (论环境诉权实现的法律保障 – 对完善《环境保护法》第六条的思考). Published on 4 May 2006, www.procedurallaw.cn/msss/zdwz/200807/t20080724_49656.html accessed 22 November 2013.

or individuals that cause pollution or damage to the environment."[561] Further, Article 41 says that: "*A unit that has caused an environmental pollution hazard shall have the obligation to eliminate it and make compensation to the unit or individual that suffered direct losses. A dispute over the liability to make compensation or the amount of compensation may, at the request of the parties, be settled by the competent department of environmental protection administration or another department invested by law with power to conduct environmental supervision and management. If a party refuses to accept the decision on the settlement, it may bring a lawsuit in a People's Court. The party may also directly bring a lawsuit in a People's Court*".[562] Article 42 states that: "*The limitation period for prosecution with respect to compensation for environmental pollution shall be three years, counted from the time when the party becomes aware of or should become aware of the pollution losses.*"[563]

The "Marine Environmental Protection Law of the People's Republic of China (the 1999 version)"[564] states that: "*All units and individuals shall have the*

561 Article 6 of the "Environmental Protection Law of the People's Republic of China" (1989 version) is the similar with Article 6 of the "Environmental Protection Law of the People's Republic of China" (2014 version). Article 6 says: "All units and individuals shall have the obligation to protect the environment. Local people's governments at various levels shall be responsible for the environmental quality within areas under their jurisdiction. Enterprises, public institutions and any other producers/business operators shall prevent and reduce environmental pollution and ecological destruction, and shall bear the liability for their damage caused by them in accordance with the law. Citizens shall enhance environmental protection awareness, adopt low-carbon and energy-saving lifestyle, and conscientiously fulfill the obligation of environmental protection." The "Environmental Protection Law of the People's Republic of China" (2014 version) [中华人民共和国环境保护法] was newly modified based on the "Environmental Protection Law of the People's Republic of China" (1989 version) on 24 April 2014 and entered into force on 1 January 2015, http://edu.sina.com.cn/en/2014-05-20/144680376.shtml accessed 30 June 2014.

562 Article 41 of the "Environmental Protection Law of the People's Republic of China" (1989 version) is the similar with Article 64 of the "Environmental Protection Law of the People's Republic of China" (2014 version). Article 64 says: "Those who cause damages due to environmental pollution and ecological destruction shall bear tort liability in accordance with provisions of Tort Liability Law of the People's Republic of China." The "Environmental Protection Law of the People's Republic of China" (2014 version) [中华人民共和国环境保护法] was newly modified based on the "Environmental Protection Law of the People's Republic of China" (1989 version) on 24 April 2014 and entered into force on 1 January 2015, http://edu.sina.com.cn/en/2014-05-20/144680376.shtml accessed 30 June 2014.

563 Article 42 of the "Environmental Protection Law of the People's Republic of China" (1989 version) is the same with Article 66 of the "Environmental Protection Law of the People's Republic of China" (2014 version). The "Environmental Protection Law of the People's Republic of China" (2014 version) [中华人民共和国环境保护法] was newly modified based on the "Environmental Protection Law of the People's Republic of China" (1989 version) on 24 April 2014 and entered into force on 1 January 2015, http://edu.sina.com.cn/en/2014-05-20/144680376.shtml accessed 30 June 2014.

564 The "Marine Environmental Protection Law of the People's Republic of China" [中华人民共和国海洋环境保护法] was adopted on 23 August 1982 and revised on 25 December 1999, Article 3 of the 1982 version and Article 4 of the 1999 version have the similar provision on environmental citizen suits, www.novexcn.com/marine_environemental_prot.html and

obligation to protect the marine environment and have the right to watch for and report on actions causing pollution damages to the marine environment by any unit and individual, as well as on the act of transgression of the law and neglect of duty by marine environment supervision and administration personnel."

The "Water Pollution Prevention and Control Law of the People's Republic of China"[565] also provides similar provisions. For instance, Article 85 advocates that: "*The party whose rights and interests are damaged by a water pollution accident is entitled to ask the party discharging pollutants to eliminate the damage and make compensation for their losses.*"[566] Article 86 continues: "*For a dispute over liability for damage or amount of compensation in a water pollution accident, the administrative department of environmental protection, the marine governing authority or the administrative department of fishery may, according to the division of functions and duties among them and in light of the request of the parties concerned, settle it through mediation; if no agreement can be reached upon mediation, the parties concerned may file a lawsuit with the People's Court. The parties concerned may also file a lawsuit with the People's Court directly without going through the mediation procedure.*"[567] Besides these, Articles 87, 88 and 89 provide some detailed information on the burden of proof, the number of parties, liability for damage or the amount of compensation if litigation happens.

Similarly, Article 62 of the "Law of the People's Republic of China on the Prevention and Control of Atmospheric Pollution"[568] points out that: "*Any unit has caused an atmospheric pollution hazard shall have the responsibility of removing the hazard and of making compensation to the units or individuals that have suffered direct losses. Any dispute over the liability to make compensation or the amount of compensation may, at the request of the parties, be settled by the administrative department of environmental protection. If a party refuses to*

---

www.mlr.gov.cn/mlrenglish/laws/200710/t20071012_656329.htm accessed 25 November 2013.

565 The "Water Pollution Prevention and Control Law of the People's Republic of China" [中华人民共和国水污染防治法] was issued on 11 May 1984 and amended on 28 February 2008 and entered into force on 1 June 2008, www.lawinfochina.com/display.aspx?lib=law&id=6722 accessed 11 August 2011.

566 Article 85, the "Water Pollution Prevention and Control Law of the People's Republic of China" [中华人民共和国水污染防治法] was issued on 11 May 1984 and amended on 28 February 2008 and entered into force on 1 June 2008, www.lawinfochina.com/display.aspx?lib=law&id=6722 accessed 11 August 2011.

567 Article 86, the "Water Pollution Prevention and Control Law of the People's Republic of China" [中华人民共和国水污染防治法] was issued on 11 May 1984 and amended on 28 February 2008 and entered into force on 1 June 2008, www.lawinfochina.com/display.aspx?lib=law&id=6722 accessed 11 August 2011.

568 The "Law of the People's Republic of China on the Prevention and Control of Atmospheric Pollution" [中国人民共和国大气污染防治法] was issued in 1987 and revised on 29 April 2000, www.lawinfochina.com/display.aspx?lib=law&id=6722 accessed 21 November 2013.

accept the decision, it may bring a lawsuit to a People's Court. The party may also bring a lawsuit to a People's Court directly."[569]

Article 84 of the "Law of People's Republic of China on Prevention and Control of Environmental Pollution by Solid Waste Law"[570] says that: "*Units and individuals that have suffered damage from solid waste pollution shall have the right to claim compensation according to law. A dispute over the liability for damage and amount of compensation may, at the request of the parties, be settled through mediation by the administrative department for environmental protection or the administrative department for supervision over prevention and control of environmental pollution by solid waste; if mediation fails, the parties may bring a lawsuit to a People's Court. The parties may also directly bring a lawsuit to a People's Court.*" Further, Article 61 of the "Law of the People's Republic of China on Prevention and Control of Pollution from Environmental Noise"[571] states that: "*Any unit or individual suffering from the hazards of environmental noise pollution shall have the right to demand the polluter to eliminate the hazards; if a loss has been caused, it shall be compensated according to law. Any dispute over the liability for losses or over the amount of compensation may, at the request of the parties concerned, be mediated by the competent administrative department for environmental protection or any other supervisory and administrative department or institution in charge of prevention and control of environmental noise pollution; if such mediation fails, the parties may bring a lawsuit to a People's Court. They may also directly bring a lawsuit in a People's Court.*" What is more, Article 59 of the People's Republic of China Law on the Prevention and Control of Radioactive Pollution[572] pointed out that: "*where radioactive pollution causes harm to people, civil liability shall be borne in accordance with law.*"[573]

---

569 Article 62, the "Law of the People's Republic of China on the Prevention and Control of Atmospheric Pollution" [中国人民共和国大气污染防治法] was issued in 1987 and revised on 29 April 2000, www.lawinfochina.com/display.aspx?lib=law&id=6722 accessed 21 November 2013.

570 The "Law of the People's Republic of China on Prevention of Environmental Pollution Caused by Solid Waste" [中华人民共和国固体废物污染环境防治法] was issued in 1995, amended on 29 December 2004 and entered into effect on 1 April 2005, www.lawinfochina.com/display.aspx?lib=law&id=119 accessed 3 December 2011.

571 The "Law of the People's Republic of China on Prevention and Control of Pollution from Environmental Noise" [中华人民共和国噪声污染防治法] was issued on 29 October 1996 and entered into effect on 1 March 1997, www.lawinfochina.com/display.aspx?lib=law&id=544 accessed 9 August 2012.

572 The "People's Republic of China Law on the Prevention and Control of Radioactive Pollution" [中华人民共和国放射性污染防治法] was adopted on 28 June 2003 and entered into effect on 1 October 2003, www.china.org.cn/china/LegislationsForm2001-2010/2011-02/14/content_21915263.htm accessed 21 November 2013.

573 Article 59, the "People's Republic of China Law on the Prevention and Control of Radioactive Pollution" [中华人民共和国放射性污染防治法] was adopted on 28 June 2003 and entered into effect on 1 October 2003, www.china.org.cn/china/Legislations Form2001-2010/2011-02/14/content_21915263.htm accessed 21 November 2013.

As also indicated above (see 5.1.2.1.2 and 5.2.2.2), the newly modified "Environmental Protection Law of the People's Republic of China" (2014 version)[574] also make a remarkable progress on access to justice in environmental matters in China. For instance, Article 57 points out that: "*Citizens, legal persons and other organizations shall be entitled to report and complain environmental pollution and ecological damage activities of any units and individuals to competent environmental protection administrations or other departments with environmental supervision responsibilities. In the event the local people's government and its environmental protection administrations or any other relevant departments fail to fulfil their responsibilities in accordance with the law, any citizen, legal person or other organizations have the right to report it to the competent higher level governments or the supervisory department according to law*". Article 58 states that: "*For activities that cause environmental pollution, ecological damage and public interest harm, social organizations that meet the following conditions may file litigation to the people's Courts: (1) having been registered at the civil affair department of people's governments at or above municipal level with sub-districts in accordance with the law; (2) specializing in environmental protection public interest activities for five consecutive years or more without any law-breaching records. Courts shall accept the litigation filed by social organizations that meet the above criterion. The social organizations that file the litigation shall not seek economic benefits from the litigation.*"[575]

Furthermore, as introduced above (see 5.1.2.1.2), Article 16 of the "Measures on Right to Participation in Environmental Protection"[576] states that environmental protection agencies can support environmental social organisations who have a legal standing to go to a court by various methods, including providing legal consultation, submitting suggestion and cooperatively investigation.

Based on what has been introduced, it is obvious to see that concerning the right to access to justice in environmental matters, Articles 41 and 42 of the "Environmental Protection Law of the People's Republic of China" (1989 version), the "Law of People's Republic of China on Prevention and Control

574 The "Environmental Protection Law of the People's Republic of China" [中华人民共和国环境保护法] was promulgated by Order No. 22 of the President of the People's Republic of China on 26 December 1989, and was effective on the date of promulgation; it was newly modified on 24 April 2014 and entered into force on 1 January 2015, http://edu.sina.com.cn/en/2014-05-20/144680376.shtml accessed 30 June 2014.

575 Article 58, the "Environmental Protection Law of the People's Republic of China" [中华人民共和国环境保护法] was promulgated by Order No. 22 of the President of the People's Republic of China on 26 December 1989, and was effective on the date of promulgation; it was newly modified on 24 April 2014 and entered into force on 1 January 2015, http://edu.sina.com.cn/en/2014-05-20/144680376.shtml accessed 30 June 2014.

576 The "Measures on Right to Participation in Environmental Protection" [环境保护公众参与办法] was issued by the department of environmental protection on 2 July 2015 and it entered into force on 1 September 2015, www.zhb.gov.cn/gkml/hbb/bl/201507/t20150720_306928.htm accessed 1 October 2015.

of Environmental Pollution by Solid Waste Law" revised in 2004 and the "Water Pollution Prevention and Control Law of the People's Republic of China" revised in 2008, made a bigger step forward in clarifying some detailed information on environmental civil litigation, such as the burden of proof, the parties of litigation, legal assistance and so on. According to Article 58 of the "Environmental Protection Law of the People's Republic of China" (2014 version) mentioned above, the legal standing for public interest litigation would be expanded for NGOs on 1 January 2015. It is a good sign to reflect the developmental tendency of the legal standing for public interest litigation in China.

A local progress concerning access to justice is that, on 5 September 2008, "Some Practical Suggestions on Establishing for the Environmental Enforcement Coordination Mechanism" (Practical Suggestions) was issued by the Kunming Intermediate People's Court, the Kunming[577] People's procuratorate, the Kuming Policy department and the Environmental Protection Bureau in Yunnan Province. The "Practical Suggestions" support that environmental groups may, in some cases, have the right to access to justice in their own name in order to protect the public environmental interests.[578] Another local example is that the "Regulation for Promoting Ecological Civilization Construction in Guiyang" was issued on 18 January 2010 and entered into force on 1 March 2010.[579] It is regarded as the first local legislative document on environmental public interest litigation in China.[580] These tendencies reflect that Chinese governments from different levels began to realise the important role of environmental litigation in dealing with environmental matters. However, owing to the traditional ideas and the previously existing legal system concerning access to justice, this step mainly focused on environmental pollution. Another point that needs to be mentioned is that all these environmental law lack some specific provisions on the qualification of the plaintiff, the scope of cases, the burden of proof and legal liability and other practical issues for access to justice in environmental

577 Kunming City is a Capital city in Yunnan Province.

578 The guidelines for the judgment in environmental issues in Yunnan Province (云南出台环保案"审判指南"). Posted on 18 May 2009, http://fiance.ifeng.com/huanbao/fgbz/20090518/673278.shtml accessed 2 April 2012. Qi, D. (齐玎) (2012). *Access to Environmental Justice: Environmental Groups Participating in Environmental Public Interest Litigation* (接近环境正义：环保团体参与环境公益诉讼问题研究). Master Dissertation in Fudan University, p. 23.

579 Xinhua Net (新华网) (2010). Guiyang: environmental organization can sue the administrative omission concerning environmental resources" (《贵阳：环保组织可对涉及环境资源行政不作为提起诉讼》). Posted on 15 January 2010, www.gz.xinhuanet.com/2008htm/xwzx/2010-01/15/content_18774216.htm accessed 2 April 2012.

580 Qi, D. (齐玎) (2012). *Access to Environmental Justice: Environmental Groups Participating in Environmental Public Interest Litigation* (接近环境正义：环保团体参与环境公益诉讼问题研究). Master Dissertation in Fudan University, p. 24.

matters.[581] There are few cases in practice. Furthermore, most of these forms of environmental litigations will result in civil liability, criminal liability and administrative liability.

Some relevant provisions on access to justice in environmental matters in civil law, administrative law and criminal law will be discussed in the following paragraphs. Article 98 of the "General Principles of the Civil Law of the People's Republic of China"[582] states that: "*Citizens shall enjoy the right of life and health.*"[583] Article 124 points out that: "*Any person who pollutes the environment and causes damage to others in violation of State provisions for environmental protection and the prevention of pollution shall bear civil liability in accordance with the law.*"[584] This Article corresponds with the previous Articles mentioned in environmental protection laws. However, Article 119 of the "Civil Procedural Law of the People's Republic of China"[585] explicitly points out that when a lawsuit is brought, the first condition which must be met is that the plaintiff must be a citizen, legal person or any other organisation that has a direct interest in the case. The second condition is that there must be a definite defendant. As for civil law litigation, these restrictions might be useful, but regarding civil law litigation concerning environmental matters, these restrictions would not always be equal for the plaintiff and the defendant. In some cases, a victim who suffers from environmental pollution or environmental project is indirect. What he has lost may be intangible. Instead of a specific person, normally a group of people would have suffered from environmental damage or an environmental project.[586] It is

---

581 Cao, M.D. & Wang, F.Y. (曹明德，王凤远) (2009). The theoretical basis of environmental public interest litigation – the necessity and obstacles of the environmental public interest litigation by ENGO in China (《ENGO环境公益诉讼的理论依据 – 兼论中国ENGO环境公益诉讼的必要性及主要困境》). In: Ecological Civilization and Environmental Protection Law – National Environmental and Resources Law Symposium in 2009 (生态文明与环境资源法 – 2009年全国环境资源法学研讨会论文集), Kunming (昆明), 3–6 August 2009, p. 856.

582 The "General Principles of the Civil Law of the People's Republic of China" [中华人民共和国民法通则] was adopted in 1986 and entered into force on 1 January 1987, www.china.com.cn/policy/txt/2012-01/14/content_24405953.htm accessed 22 November 2013.

583 Article 98, the "General Principles of the Civil Law of the People's Republic of China" [中华人民共和国民法通则] was adopted in 1986 and entered into force on 1 January 1987, www.china.com.cn/policy/txt/2012-01/14/content_24405953.htm accessed 22 November 2013.

584 Article 124, the "General Principles of the Civil Law of the People's Republic of China" [中华人民共和国民法通则] was adopted in 1986 and entered into force on 1 January 1987, www.china.com.cn/policy/txt/2012-01/14/content_24405953.htm accessed 22 November 2013.

585 The "Civil Procedural Law of the People's Republic of China" [中华人民共和国民事诉讼法] was adopted on 9 April 1991 and amended on 31 August 2012, www.kd325.com/ShowArticle.shtml?ID=201051016355390786.htm accessed 22 November 2013.

586 Zhang, S.J. & Lu, L. (张式军　卢磊) (2006). On legal guarantee for realization of access to justice in environmental matters: some ideas on improving Article 6 in "Environmental Protection Law of the People's Republic of China" (论环境诉权实现的法律保障 – 对完善《环境保护法》第六条的思考). Published on 4 May 2006, www.procedurallaw.cn/msss/zdwz/200807/t20080724_49656.html accessed 22 November 2013; Qi, D. (齐玎) (2012). *Access to Environmental Justice: Environmental Groups Participating in Environmental*

not always easy to find out the direct linkages between environmental damage or an environmental project and what victims really suffer from. In this sense, this would be one of the big obstacles for the realisation of access to justice in environmental matters in reality. Notably, the draft Amendment of the Civil Procedural Law was submitted to the Standing Committee of the National People's Conference on 24 October 2011. It proposed that "*the relevant agency, social groups can sue against the actions which harm social public interests, such as environmental pollution*".[587] The only fly in the ointment is that "the relevant agency and social groups" in this amendment do not contain an individual, in other words, it does not provide an explicit legal support for an individual in the Civil Procedural Law.[588] Just like the above-mentioned environmental legislation and regulation, the scope of environmental cases in the amendment only focuses on environmental pollution.

Broadly speaking, environmental public interest litigation contains environmental civil public interest litigation and environmental administrative public interest litigation. The former one aims to prevent or stop any harmful activities from enterprises and the latter one intends to urge administrative agencies to take effective measures to protect the environment.[589]

Concerning the administrative procedural law, Article 2 of the "Administrative Procedural Law of the People's Republic of China"[590] points out that: "*If a citizen, a legal person or any other organization considers that his or its lawful rights and interests have been infringed upon by a specific administrative act of an administrative organ or its personnel, he or it shall have the right to bring a suit to a People's Court in accordance with this law.*"[591] According to this provision, some obstacles for access to justice in environmental matters need to be pointed out. Firstly, the "lawful rights

---

Public Interest Litigation (接近环境正义：环保团体参与环境公益诉讼问题研究). Master Dissertation in Fudan University, pp. 20–21.

587 Article 55, the "Civil Procedural Law of the People's Republic of China" [中华人民共和国民事诉讼法] was adopted on 9 April 1991 and amended on 31 August 2012, www.kd325.com/ShowArticle.shtml?ID=201051016355390786.htm accessed 22 November 2013.

588 Qi, S.J. & Zhou, Y.Y. (齐树洁，周一颜) (2013). Judicial reforms and access to justice: after civil procedural law amended (《司法改革与接近正义 – 写在民事诉讼法修改之后》), *Journal of Heilongjiang Administrative Cadre College of Politics and Law* (黑龙江省政法管理干部学院学报), 1, p. 4.

589 Zhang, Y. R. (张艳蕊). Promoting Environmental Protection through Environmental Civil Public Interest Litigation (通过环境民事公益诉讼促进环境保护). Published on 25 January 2013, http://theory.people.com.cn/n/2013/0125/c40531-20326493.html accessed 13 November 2013.

590 The "Administrative Procedural Law of the People's Republic of China" [中华人民共和国行政诉讼法] was adopted on 4 April 1989 and entered into effect on 1 October 1990, www.law-lib.com/law/law_view.asp?id=5641 accessed 22 November 2013.

591 Article 2, the "Administrative Procedural Law of the People's Republic of China" [中华人民共和国行政诉讼法] was adopted on 4 April 1989 and entered into effect on 1 October 1990, www.law-lib.com/law/law_view.asp?id=5641 accessed 22 November 2013.

and interest" in this provision would be infringed upon by a "specific"[592] administrative act. It means that a citizen, a legal person or any other organisation would not have the right to bring a case to a People's Court if an administrative act is not specific.[593] Secondly, similar to the civil law, this restriction on the qualification of the plaintiff also hinders a person or a unit to have real access to justice. Thirdly, besides the restriction for the plaintiff, it is not very clear who the defendant in some environmental administrative disputes is. These environmental administrative disputes would be excluded from a People's Court if there is an uncertain defendant. Last but not least, the administrative act or decision from an administrative unit, could lead to environmental harm, which would be serious and irreversible.[594] From this perspective, it also reflects the important role of public participation in environmental matters; the potential environmental harm could be eliminated or reduced through public participation from various parties.

Besides access to justice in environmental matters in civil and administrative law, criminal law could also be applied to punish anyone or any unit that seriously harms the environment. The "National Human Rights Action Plan of China" (2012–2015)[595] says that "*China will improve the legal stipulations regarding judicial proceedings to guarantee the litigants' right to a fair trial.*" Although it mainly refers to the criminal procedural litigation, it can be regarded as a sign for a broad entrance for access to court and a big step forward for access to justice as well.

---

592 A "specific" administrative act is that administrative authority makes a unilateral act for a "specific" citizen, legal person and other organisation on their rights and obligations. The "specific" administrative act could be categorised as "the act to create a right or obligation, including empowering a right or ability", "the act to deprive or limit right or the act to revoke obligation", "the act to change right or obligation" and "omission (dereliction of duty)." More information see www.chinabaike.com/law/zhishi/1008/1506894.html accessed 27 December 2013.

593 Zhang, S.J. & Lu, L. (张式军 卢磊) (2006). On legal guarantee for realization of access to justice in environmental matters: some ideas on improving Article 6 in "Environmental Protection Law of the People's Republic of China" (论环境诉权实现的法律保障 – 对完善《环境保护法》第六条的思考). Published on 4 May 2006, www.procedurallaw.cn/msss/zdwz/200807/t20080724_49656.html accessed 22 November 2013.

594 Zhang, S.J. & Lu, L. (张式军 卢磊) (2006). On legal guarantee for realization of access to justice in environmental matters: some ideas on improving Article 6 in "Environmental Protection Law of the People's Republic of China" (论环境诉权实现的法律保障 – 对完善《环境保护法》第六条的思考). Published on 4 May 2006, www.procedurallaw.cn/msss/zdwz/200807/t20080724_49656.html accessed 22 November 2013.

595 The "National Human Rights Action Plan of China (2012–2015)" [国家人权行动计划(2012–2015)] was issued by Information Office of the State Council of the People's Republic of China in June 2012, www.hrol.org/Documents/ChinaDocs/Reports/2012-12/2982.html accessed 22 November 2013, in Chinese and English. It is only an action plan issued by the State Council, but it works as a guidance document for solving the relevant issues. It is also a remarkable step to show the progress that Chinese government has been made.

Remarkably, the "Guiyang Regulations on Promoting Ecological Progress",[596] which was regarded as the first local regulation on promoting ecological progress, was implemented on 1 March 2010. The regulation points out that in order to protect environmental public interests, an individual or an environmental protection and management agency has the right to sue the related party (parties) who has (have) polluted the environment or destroyed natural resources. The plaintiff can ask the related party (parties) to stop the intervention, remove the obstruction, eliminate the dangers, and restore its original situation for the environment or natural resources.[597] At present, there is no case relevant to this regulation, but it would be interesting to see how it works in practice.

5.3.1.2. Right to Access to Justice in Environmental Matters in Practice in China

In practice, there are four levels of People's Courts in China: the basic level; the intermediate level; the high level and the supreme level. Each level of court is essentially responsible to political operatives at that level.[598] Local governments are responsible for their budgets and salaries.[599] This allows for strong local protectionism and in the event of politically sensitive cases, courts often refuse to hear them or leave them unresolved.[600]

The People's Courts at different levels normally contain a civil tribunal, a criminal tribunal and an administrative tribunal and other agencies. Concerning an environmental tribunal, since the first environmental tribunal in China was established at Qiaokou Area of Wuhan city in 1989, according to the statistics in 2013, there are 134 environmental tribunals in different courts in China.[601] It is noted that the environment and resource tribunal was newly established at the supreme level.[602] However, the scope of cases in environmental tribunals is limited to "four pests" (wastewater, waste-gas, industrial residue,

---

596 The "Guiyang Regulations on Promoting Ecological Civilization Construction" [贵阳市促进生态文明建设条例] was issued on 8 January 2010, www.ghb.gov.cn/doc/201029/52054307.shtml accessed 8 February 2012, in Chinese.

597 Xinhuang net (2010). Guiyang: environmental NGOs may bring cases for inaction of the government concerning the environmental and resources. Posted on 15 January 2010, www3.xinhuanet.com/chinanews/2010-01/15/content_18777895.htm accessed 6 September 2012.

598 Legal Blog: Judicial Studies (2008). Access to justice in China. Published on 7 November 2008, http://seiya.fyfz.cn/b/659795 accessed 18 November 2013.

599 Legal Blog: Judicial Studies (2008). Access to justice in China. Published on 7 November 2008, http://seiya.fyfz.cn/b/659795 accessed 18 November 2013.

600 Legal Blog: Judicial Studies (2008). Access to justice in China. Published on 7 November 2008, http://seiya.fyfz.cn/b/659795 accessed 18 November 2013.

601 Why is there no case in environmental Court in China? Published on 14 August 2013, http://toutiao.baike.com/article-1264543.html accessed 18 September 2013.

602 Wangyi News (网易新闻). The environment and resource tribunal was newly established at the supreme of People's Court: its name has been changed for several times (最高法院成立环境资源审判庭："名字曾经改了好几次"). Published on 30 June 2014, http://news.163.com/14/0630/09/9VVQHKB600014AED.html accessed 30 June 2014.

noise) and "four pollution" types (air pollution, water pollution, marine pollution and soil pollution). This means that other forms of environmental pollution, ecological damage and disputes about natural resources are excluded from environmental tribunals.[603] In fact, according to the statistics from the Ministry of Environmental Protection of the People's Republic of China, there were 51,000 environmental disputes in 2005, increasing by 30% every year.[604] Other statistics show that there were more than 100,000 environmental disputes in 2007, but only less than 1% of these environmental disputes were brought before in tribunals at different levels in China.[605]

Besides these, there are also other factors limiting the right to access to justice in China, for instance the traditional cultural background, the capacity of the plaintiff and the judges and so on, which will be discussed in this section.

Based on the traditional idea of "no litigation", the lack of independence by the judiciary has led Chinese citizens to use some of the following ways to seek justice:[606]

- *Petitioning for justice.* One of the most common methods used by Chinese citizens is to lodge their grievances with government authorities through a system known as "*xinfang*" ("letters and visits") petitioning. The roots of the *xinfang* system can be traced back centuries to Imperial China, when central authorities employed such petitions as a means of ensuring justice in individual cases, but also as an information channel on grassroots conditions and a performance review of local magistrates. According to the news reports, there are 10 million to 13 million petitions filed every year as compared to 90,000 to 100,000 administrative lawsuits in Chinese courts. An increase in the number of petitions or collective petitions by large numbers of people may result in central government sanctions against local officials. As a result, these authorities often block individuals from traveling to Beijing to present their complaints. Central authorities also do not want these petitioners on Beijing's streets during important national events.
- *Mediation.* Given the traditional Chinese preference for mediation, a huge number of civil disputes are dealt with through the use of this method. For

603 Cai, Shouqiu (蔡守秋) (2012). On strengthening the construction for environmental court (《论加强环境法庭的建设》). *Research on Front Issues in Environmental Law* (《环境法前沿问题研究》), p. 26.

604 Pan, Y. (2006). Reflections on Chinese Environmental Problems (《中国环境问题的思考》). Posted on the website of the Ministry of Environmental Protection of the People's Republic of China (中华人民共和国环境保护部) on 12 December 2006, www.sepa.gov.cn/info/ldjh/200701/t20070118_99754.htm accessed 22 November 2013, in Chinese.

605 Wu, W.Z. (武卫政) (2008). Safeguarding a right in environmental issues urgently needs to find away out (环境维权亟待走出困境). Posted in People's Daily (《人民日报》) on 22 January 2008.

606 Legal Blog: Judicial Studies (2008). Access to justice in China. Published on 7 November 2008, http://seiya.fyfz.cn/b/659795 accessed 18 November 2013.

small-scale disputes this is an important mechanism for resolution. Often at the local level, disputes may be mediated by village officials or the local police.
- *Protests.* In recent years, China has witnessed a sharp increase in social protests. Between 1994 and 2004, the number of protests annually rose from 10,000 to 74,000. Some official statistics place the number as high as 87,000 for 2005. Chinese experts say that local courts usually push out or block politically sensitive issues. Lawyers may not accept such cases, inducing citizens to resort to protests to express their displeasure and call for attention to their grievances. For example, in early 2008 farmers intensified protests against forced land seizures and called for land reform.

Nevertheless, according to the experience from both international and national theory and practice, litigation is an important method to solve environmental conflicts. It is encouraging to note that Chinese citizens are more frequently heading to court with the gravest pollution problems,[607] but people must be willing to challenge less obvious, but nonetheless serious, pollution and natural resource destruction.[608] These are consistent with what the environmental laws in China focus on. It is noteworthy that China, with its growing population, has acted in the past five years to establish and expand the system of environmental courts and tribunals.[609] Over the coming years, tribunals and courts will become increasingly more valuable to societies worldwide for resolving environmental conflicts and enforcing environmental safeguards.[610] It is particularly true in China where the citizens have a growing awareness of access to justice since the last decade.

However, without proper legal assistance, Chinese citizens may remain without adequate access to the judicial system.[611] The number of government lawyers providing legal aid remains insufficient to meet the demand.[612] In

607 Wang, A. (2006). The role of law in environmental protection in China: recent developments. *Vermont Journal of Environmental Law*, 195, p. 204.

608 Goelz, J.D. (2009). China's environmental problems: is a specialized court the solution? *Pacific Rim Law & Policy Journal Association*, 10(1), http://digital.law.washington.edu/dspace-law/bitstream/handle/1773.1/522/18PacRimLPolyJ155.pdf accessed 16 November 2013, p. 173.

609 The Washington Times (2009). China resolves pollution case, avoids suit. Posted on 2 September 2009, www.washingtontimes.com/news/2009/sep/02/china-resolves-pollution-case-avoids-suit accessed 14 November 2013. It discussed that the Qingzhen Municipal People's Court was established to face "growing public concern about the health effects of widespread pollution stemming from China's rapid economic growth".

610 Robinson, N.A. (2012). Ensuring access to justice through environmental courts. *Pace Environmental Law Review*, 29, http://digitalcommons.pace.edu/cgi/viewcontent.cgi?article=1691&context=pelr accessed 16 November 2013, p. 369.

611 Goelz, J.D. (2009). China's environmental problems: is a specialized court the solution? *Pacific Rim Law & Policy Journal Association*, 10(1), http://digital.law.washington.edu/dspace-law/bitstream/handle/1773.1/522/18PacRimLPolyJ155.pdf accessed 16 November 2013, p. 173.

612 Legal Blog: Judicial Studies (2008). Access to justice in China. Published on 7 November 2008, http://seiya.fyfz.cn/b/659795 accessed 18 November 2013.

many rural areas, unlicensed, self-trained individuals are the only available legal advisers.[613] Public interest law firms, usually based within universities or law schools, also offer legal services, but these services are limited.[614] In most cases, the vulnerable groups are too poor to pay lawyers to ask for environmental litigation. In this sense, non-profit legal assistance will be an important contributor to the effective operation and legitimacy of an environmental court system.[615] China has embraced legal assistance to a dramatic degree since the last decade. There were virtually no government supported legal aid centres in 1994. By the end of 2002, China had more than 2,400 legal aid offices, the overwhelming majority of which were State-funded.[616] Official statistics state that legal aid lawyers handled some 180,000 cases in 2002, a 28% increase on the prior year.[617] Furthermore, some relevant institutes were increasingly set up these years, for instance, the Centre for Legal Assistance to Pollution Victims mentioned in the previous section. Out of a total of 135 cases in which aid was provided by the Centre for Legal Assistance to Pollution Victims (CLAPV) between November 1999 and October 2009, 70 cases have been resolved.[618] Of these 70 cases, the CLAPV won 32 cases and lost 26 cases.[619] Just to illustrate, in the case of *1721 People v. Rongping Chemical Plant*,[620] the High People's Court in Fujian Province awarded plaintiffs 684,000 Yuan (81,400 EUR)[621] for damage

613 Legal Blog: Judicial Studies (2008). Access to justice in China. Published on 7 November 2008, http://seiya.fyfz.cn/b/659795 accessed 18 November 2013.

614 Legal Blog: Judicial Studies (2008). Access to justice in China. Published on 7 November 2008, http://seiya.fyfz.cn/b/659795 accessed 18 November 2013.

615 Wang, A. (2006). The role of law in environmental protection in China: recent developments. *Vermont Journal of Environmental Law*, 195, pp. 204–205. Many argue for NGO standing to sue in environmental pollution cases.

616 United States' Congressional-Executive Commission on China (2004). *Access to Justice in China: Round-table before the Congressional-Executive Commission on China*. In: One Hundred Eighth Congress, second session, 12 July 2004. Washington D.C.: United States Government Printing Office, http://babel.hathitrust.org/cgi/pt?id=umn.31951d024064594;view=1up;seq=11 accessed 18 November 2013, p. 7.

617 United States' Congressional-Executive Commission on China (2004). *Access to Justice in China: Round-table before the Congressional-Executive Commission on China*. In: One Hundred Eighth Congress, second session, 12 July 2004. Washington D.C.: United States Government Printing Office, http://babel.hathitrust.org/cgi/pt?id=umn.31951d024064594;view=1up;seq=11 accessed 18 November 2013, p. 7.

618 Wang, C.F. (2010). The role of environmental litigation in protecting environmental rights and improving environment. In: the Workshop on Business, Human Rights and Access to Justice in China, Hong Kong, 5–6 March 2010.

619 ICJ (International Commission of Jurists) (2010). *Access to Justice: Human Rights Abuses Involving Corporations – People's Republic of China*, Geneva: ICJ, http://icj.wpengine.netdna-cdn.com/wp-content/uploads/2012/06/China-access-justice-publication-2010.pdf accessed 14 November 2013, pp. 23–24.

620 1721 People v. Rongping Chemical Plant (屏南县溪坪村张长建等1721人诉容屏联营化工厂环境污染损害赔偿纠纷案), Fujian Provincial High People's Court, 2003, www.fsou.com/html/text/fnl/1175258/117525863.html accessed 12 December 2013.

621 According to the exchange rate on 20 June 2014, 1 EUR is equal to 8.4 Yuan. http://huilv.911cha.com/EURCNY.html accessed 20 June 2014. The following statistics all follow this exchange rate.

caused to their crops by the chemicals emanating from the plant.[622] What is more, in the 1980s, China developed a network of paraprofessionals known as basic level legal workers.[623] Such workers are not lawyers, but have received some legal training. There are approximately 100,000 such workers in China, only somewhat fewer than the 130,000 registered lawyers. They operate out of some 27,000 legal services offices, ten times the total number of legal aid offices, and handle hundreds of thousands of civil cases a year.[624] These tendencies reflect that Chinese governments at different levels began to steer disputes into the courts. These developments also demonstrate both the significant progress over the past decade in making the courts more accessible, and also some of the continuing barriers to those seeking redress through law.[625]

Another problem is whether judges have enough capacity. Judicial capacity-building is best undertaken by judges and for judges.[626] Courts supervise their own continuing judicial education, and thereby ensure their independence, autonomy, and credibility with all parties that appear before the courts.[627] In theory, citizens can sue a company which is in violation of environmental regulations.[628] However, with an emphasis on economic growth on the part of local governments, it is very difficult for the suits to succeed. Even if a polluting

---

622 Wang, C.F. (2010). The role of environmental litigation in protecting environmental rights and improving environment. In: the Workshop on Business, Human Rights and Access to Justice in China, Hong Kong, 5–6 March 2010; Wang, A. (2006). The role of law in environmental protection in China: recent developments. *Vermont Journal of Environmental Law*, 195, pp. 212–214.

623 United States' Congressional-Executive Commission on China (2004). *Access to Justice in China: Round-table before the Congressional-Executive Commission on China*. In: One Hundred Eighth Congress, second session, 12 July 2004. Washington D.C.: United States Government Printing Office, http://babel.hathitrust.org/cgi/pt?id=umn.31951d024064594;view=1up;seq=11 accessed 18 November 2013, p. 7.

624 United States' Congressional-Executive Commission on China (2004). *Access to Justice in China: Round-table before the Congressional-Executive Commission on China*. In: One Hundred Eighth Congress, second session, 12 July 2004. Washington D.C.: United States Government Printing Office, http://babel.hathitrust.org/cgi/pt?id=umn.31951d024064594;view=1up;seq=11 accessed 18 November 2013, p. 7.

625 United States' Congressional-Executive Commission on China (2004). *Access to Justice in China: Round-table before the Congressional-Executive Commission on China*. In: One Hundred Eighth Congress, second session, 12 July 2004. Washington D.C.: United States Government Printing Office, http://babel.hathitrust.org/cgi/pt?id=umn.31951d024064594;view=1up;seq=11 accessed 18 November 2013, p. 7.

626 Robinson, N.A. (2012). Ensuring access to justice through environmental courts. *Pace Environmental Law Review*, 29, http://digitalcommons.pace.edu/cgi/viewcontent.cgi?article=1691&context=pelr accessed 16 November 2013, p. 374.

627 Robinson, N.A. (2012). Ensuring access to justice through environmental courts. *Pace Environmental Law Review*, 29, http://digitalcommons.pace.edu/cgi/viewcontent.cgi?article=1691&context=pelr accessed 16 November 2013, p. 374.

628 Wang, H. (2011). Stakeholder dialogue as an institutional strategy for sustainable development in China: the case of community environmental round-tables. The World Bank Development Research Group Environment and Energy Team, www-wds.worldbank.org/external/default/WDSContentServer/IW3P/IB/2011/08/15/000158349_20110815113133/Rendered/PDF/WPS5759.pdf accessed 21 October 2013, p. 7.

company loses a law suit, it can still escape legal punishment, as a large number of court orders have not been enforced in China.[629] Thus, the capacity for judges refers not only to their professional improvement but also to their independence from outside factors.

Within this context, environmental NGOs are playing an increasingly important role in environmental public interest litigation. The plaintiff in two notable cases was the ACEF.[630] In 2009, the ACEF respectively sued the Jiangyin Container Ltd in Jiangsu Province[631] and the Land Resources Bureau[632] in Qingzhen city in Guizhou province.[633] These two cases were accepted by the People's Courts in two provinces. It shows that environmental NGOs were accepted as a plaintiff in environmental litigation in practice. Compared with an individual, environmental NGOs have their own advantages, especially in environmental litigation cases where there is a large group of victims that cannot choose a representative or that lacks the ability to go to court.[634]

However, the NGOs lack official acceptance in the relevant laws and regulations. In order to promote public participation and access to justice in China, the People's Court in the supreme level is drafting the judicial interpretations on the environmental public interest litigation.[635] This reflects that the People's Court

---

629 Wang, H. (2011). Stakeholder dialogue as an institutional strategy for sustainable development in China: the case of community environmental round-tables. The World Bank Development Research Group Environment and Energy Team, www-wds.worldbank.org/external/default/WDSContentServer/IW3P/IB/2011/08/15/000158349_20110815113133/Rendered/PDF/WPS5759.pdf accessed 21 October 2013, p. 7.

630 All-China Environment Federation is an official environmental organization with a goal to guaranteeing public environmental rights and interests. Detailed information see www.baike.com/wiki/%E7%8E%AF%E4%BF%9D%E4%B8%AD%E5%9B%BD accessed 22 November 2013.

631 All-China Environment Federation (ACEF) v. Jiangyin Container Ltd. (中华环保联合会诉江苏省江阴港集装箱有限公司环境污染侵权案), The Intermediate People's Court in Wuxi City of Jiangsu Province (江苏省无锡市中级人民法院), 6 July 2009, detailed information see http://blog.voc.com.cn/blog.php?do=showone&type=blog&itemid=726395 accessed 22 October 2013.

632 All-China Environment Federation (ACEF) v. The Land Resources Bureau in Qingzhen City (中华环保联合会诉贵州省清镇市国土资源管理局), The Intermediate People's Court in Qingzhen City of Guizhou Province (贵州省清镇市国土资源管理局), 29 July 2009, detailed information see www.jcrb.com/zhuanti/fzzt/lpsh/gyss/201001/t20100112_300833.html accessed 22 October 2013.

633 Gao, X.Y. (高筱妤) (2012). The obstacles and strategies for Chinese environmental NGOs participating environmental public interest litigation (我国环保NGO参与环境公益诉讼的障碍及方略). Published on 12 December 2012, www.hicourt.gov.cn/theory/artilce_list.asp?id=7578&l_class=4 accessed 23 November 2013.

634 Zhang, X. (张鑫) (2005). Who should hold the key for an environmental litigation (《环境诉讼启动钥匙该谁拿》). Posted in Legal Daily (《法制日报》) on 3 November 2005; Qi, D. (齐玎) (2012). *Access to Environmental Justice: Environmental Groups Participating in Environmental Public Interest Litigation* (接近环境正义：环保团体参与环境公益诉讼问题研究). Master Dissertation in Fudan University, p. 6.

635 Li, Y. (李莹) (2014). Environmental trial must go in a professional way (环境审判必须走专业化道路). Published in China Environment News (中国环境报) on 14 July 2014, p. 2.

at the supreme level has a positive attitude towards the environmental public interest litigation. It is worth seeing how it would work in practice in China.

5.3.1.3. Right to Access to Justice Concerning Protected Areas Conservation in China

In the context of the historic, cultural, social and legal conditions, the right to access to justice concerning protected areas conservation seems very difficult to be achieved for the following reasons. Firstly, the traditional idea of "no litigation" steers people to pursue other channels to solve conflicts. Secondly, the defendant in this kind of case is sometimes unclear. No matter the cases are related to property rights, right to information or right to participation, they normally refer to environmental administrative litigation. This can include private interests against public power or private interest against public interests. The defendant can for instance be the local government or the management committee of a protected area. If a decision on a protected area is issued by several authorities, the defendant would be more than one. If this happens, whether the case would be accepted by a People's Court is unknown. Thirdly and more essentially, the legislative constraints for the plaintiff's standing would form an obstacle for cases, not only on the potential conflicts regarding human rights protection and protected areas conservation, but also on citizens' potential roles in conserving protected areas. For instance, if the case is related to the collective property right, whether the collective would have a legal standing or not is uncertain at present. One possible solution is to choose one or more representative(s) from the group. Another important problem is how to choose one or more representative(s) in a reasonable way. After this, whether the representative(s) has(ve) a legal standing is still unknown. As for citizens' potential role in conserving protected areas, the court would reject the suit for fighting against some activities that would destroy protected areas in case the plaintiff lacks a legal standing. For instance, in 2005, two citizens sued the Planning Bureau to build a viewing tower in a protected area; the Court rejected this suit because the applicants lacked standing to bring the suit.[636] This marked reticence by the courts in practice is an important reason why citizens normally prefer to solve environmental disputes by mediation rather than litigation from a court. Fourth, the situation of the local people and communities would even be more difficult for the reason that they are vulnerable groups. Even if they want to sue the relevant authority to guarantee their interests, they do not have enough money to pay lawyers to litigate their cases. Fifthly, it will take a long time to sue an environmental litigation if all the above-mentioned obstacles have been overcome. Compared with litigation, negotiation and mediation will

[636] Xinhua Net (2006). Viewing tower construction in zjingshan mount – state-invested capital in vain. Posted on 25 January 2006, www.xinhua.net accessed 10 September 2013.

be more efficient. It is noted that as at the end of 2011, there are 0.811 million environmental mediation organisations and 4.336 million mediators in China.[637] 8.935 million environmental disputes were mediated, of which 96.9% were successfully mediated.[638]

Therefore, instead of pursuing the right to access to justice in environmental matters, citizens prefer to solve disputes through a more efficient channel. As vulnerable groups, local people and communities would like to find an easier and more efficient way to solve conflicts regarding protected areas conservation and protection of their interests. In this sense, efficiency is more important than anything else in China; the right to access to justice is only one of the channels to achieve efficiency.

5.3.2. ACCESS TO JUSTICE IN ENVIRONMENTAL PROTECTION IN EUROPE

The question of access to justice in Europe is a highly complex one due to the diversity of current conditions.[639] The following sections will discuss the right to access to justice in environmental matters at the European level. The legal standing of access to justice in environmental matters is the main concern.

5.3.2.1. Access to Justice under the European Convention on Human Rights

Article 6(1) of the European Convention on Human Rights[640] guarantees the right to a fair trial, which the Court has found to include the right of access to

637 Qi, S.J. & Zhou, Y.Y. (齐树洁，周一颜) (2013). Judicial reforms and access to justice: after civil procedural law amended (《司法改革与接近正义 – 写在民事诉讼法修改之后》), *Journal of Heilongjiang Administrative Cadre College of Politics and Law* (黑龙江省政法管理干部学院学报), 1, p. 4.

638 Qi, S.J. & Zhou, Y.Y. (齐树洁，周一颜) (2013). Judicial reforms and access to justice: after civil procedural law amended (《司法改革与接近正义 – 写在民事诉讼法修改之后》), *Journal of Heilongjiang Administrative Cadre College of Politics and Law* (黑龙江省政法管理干部学院学报), 1, p. 4.

639 De Sadeleer, N. (2002). Access to justice in environmental matters. ENV.A.3/ETU/2002/0030. Final Report, www.ucastverejnosti.cz/dokumenty/studie-aarhus-zeme-eu.pdf accessed 25 February 2014.

640 Article 6(1) of the European Convention on Human Rights says that: "In the determination of his civil rights and obligations or of any criminal charge against him, everyone is entitled to a fair and public hearing within a reasonable time by an independent and impartial tribunal established by law. Judgment shall be pronounced by publicly but the press and public may be excluded from all or part of the trial in the interests of morals, public order or national security in a democratic society, where the interests of juveniles or the protection of the private life of the parties so require, or to the extent strictly necessary in the opinion of the court in special circumstances where publicity would prejudice the interests of justice." Detailed information see www.echr.coe.int/Documents/Convention_ENG.pdf accessed 6 December 2013.

court.[641] The right to access to a court is not an absolute right.[642] Restrictions may be compatible with the Convention if they have a legitimate purpose and are proportionate to their aim. From the other perspective, legal or factual restrictions on this right may be in violation of the Convention if they impede the applicant's effective right of access to a court. Article 13[643] of the European Convention on Human Rights guarantees that persons, who have an arguable claim that their rights and freedoms as set forth in the Convention have been violated, have an effective remedy before a national authority. The objective of this Article is to provide a way whereby individuals can get appropriate relief at the domestic level for violations of their rights to avoid bringing a suit before the European Court of Human Rights. States enjoy a certain margin of appreciation as to how they provide remedies within their own legal systems.[644]

5.3.2.2. Case Law in the European Court of Human Rights

The European Convention on Human Rights empowers the Court to receive applications from any person, NGO or group of individuals claiming to be the victim of a violation by a State party of the rights set forth in the Convention.[645] Although this represents a unique opportunity for individuals to seek protection of their rights, the jurisdiction of the Court extends only to matters concerning

---

641 e.g. ECtHR, Airey v. Ireland (1979), App. No. 6289/73, Judgment of 9 October 1979, §20, http://hudoc.echr.coe.int/sites/eng/Pages/search.aspx#{%22fulltext%22:[%22Airey%20v.%20Ireland%22],%22documentcollectionid2%22:[%22GRANDCHAMBER%22,%22CHAMBER%22],%22itemid%22:[%22001-57420%22]} accessed 16 July 2014; Also see Manual on Human Rights and the Environment, Council of Europe Publishing (2012), http://echr.coe.int/Documents/Pub_coe_Environment_2012_ENG.pdf accessed 3 October 2013, p. 94.

642 e.g. ECtHR, Sace Elektrik Ticaret Ve Sanayi A.Ş. v. Turkey (2014), App. No. 20577/05, Judgment of 22 January 2014 (Final), §26, http://hudoc.echr.coe.int/sites/eng/Pages/search.aspx#{%22fulltext%22:[%22\%22effective%20right%20of%20access%20to%20a%20court\%22%22],%22documentcollectionid2%22:[%22GRANDCHAMBER%22,%22CHAMBER%22],%22itemid%22:[%22001-127105%22]} accessed 16 July 2014. Also see Manual on Human Rights and the Environment, Council of Europe Publishing (2012), http://echr.coe.int/Documents/Pub_coe_Environment_2012_ENG.pdf accessed 3 October 2013, p. 97.

643 Article 13, European Convention on Human Rights (formally the Convention for the Protection of Human Rights and Fundamental Freedoms), drafted in 1950 and entered into force on 3 September 1953, 213 UNTS, www.echr.coe.int/Documents/Convention_ENG.pdf accessed 12 April 2013. Detailed information see www.echr.coe.int/Pages/home.aspx?p=home accessed 12 April 2013, Article 13 says that: "Everyone whose rights and freedoms as set forth in this Convention are violated shall have an effective remedy before a national authority notwithstanding that the violation has been committed by persons acting in an official capacity."

644 e.g. ECtHR, Kudla v. Poland (2000), App. No. 20577/05, Judgment of 26 October 2000, §152, http://hudoc.echr.coe.int/sites/eng/Pages/search.aspx#{%22appno%22:[%2230210/96%22],%22itemid%22:[%22001-58920%22]} accessed 16 July 2014. Also see Manual on Human Rights and the Environment, Council of Europe Publishing (2012), http://echr.coe.int/Documents/Pub_coe_Environment_2012_ENG.pdf accessed 3 October 2013, p. 103.

645 Andrusevych, A. (2013). Environmental human rights protection in the European Court of Human Rights. In: Stec, S. (Ed.). *Handbook on Access to Justice under the Aarhus Convention.* Szentendre (Hungary): The Regional Environmental Center for Central and Eastern Europe, p. 71.

the interpretation and application of the Convention and its protocols.[646] Thus, access to the Court is quite limited, especially with regard to environmental matters, as the text of the Convention does not contain an explicit reference to the environment.[647]

5.3.2.2.1. Whether Individuals Have an Opportunity to Appeal to the Courts against Any Decision

As discussed above, the key factor for the right to access to justice is whether people have an opportunity to challenge a decision from an authority.

In the case of *Oerlemans v. the Netherlands,*[648] the government designated as a protected natural site an area of land, including land belonging to applicant. According to the applicant's submission he was not able to challenge the lawfulness of the designation order before a court, and the appeal procedure to the Crown did not involve an independent and impartial tribunal within the meaning of Article 6(1) of the ECHR.[649] In fact, he did not consider that an action before the civil courts was open to him. The Court then concluded that, under well-established principles of Netherlands law which existed at the time of the Royal Decree in the present case (14 March 1986), the applicant could submit his dispute to the civil courts for examination.[650] Accordingly, there was no violation of Article 6(1).[651]

According to what has been introduced, we know that Articles 6 and 13 specifically refer to access to justice. The case of *Ivan Atanasov v. Bulgaria*[652] shows how these two Articles are implemented in practice. The applicant alleged that a reclamation scheme for the tailings pond of a former copper mine had had an adverse impact on his private and family life and his home, and had impinged on the peaceful enjoyment of his possessions. The applicant complained that the Supreme Administrative Court had refused to consider the merits of his

646 Andrusevych, A. (2013). Environmental human rights protection in the European Court of Human Rights. In: Stec, S. (Ed.). *Handbook on Access to Justice under the Aarhus Convention.* Szentendre (Hungary): The Regional Environmental Center for Central and Eastern Europe, p. 71.

647 Andrusevych, A. (2013). Environmental human rights protection in the European Court of Human Rights. In: Stec, S. (Ed.). *Handbook on Access to Justice under the Aarhus Convention.* Szentendre (Hungary): The Regional Environmental Center for Central and Eastern Europe, p. 71.

648 ECtHR, Oerlemans v. Netherlands (1991), App. No. 12565/86, Judgment of 27 November 1991, http://echr.ketse.com/doc/12565.86-en-19911127/view/ accessed 4 November 2013.

649 ECtHR, Oerlemans v. Netherlands (1991), App. No. 12565/86, Judgment of 27 November 1991, §50, http://echr.ketse.com/doc/12565.86-en-19911127/view/ accessed 4 November 2013.

650 ECtHR, Oerlemans v. Netherlands (1991), App. No. 12565/86, Judgment of 27 November 1991, §57, http://echr.ketse.com/doc/12565.86-en-19911127/view/ accessed 4 November 2013.

651 ECtHR, Oerlemans v. Netherlands (1991), App. No. 12565/86, Judgment of 27 November 1991, §58, http://echr.ketse.com/doc/12565.86-en-19911127/view/ accessed 4 November 2013.

652 ECtHR, Ivan Atanasov v. Bulgaria (2010), App. No. 12853/03, Judgment of 2 December 2010, 11 April 2011 (Final), http://hudoc.echr.coe.int/sites/eng/Pages/search.aspx#{%22fulltext%22:[%22\%22right%20to%20participation\%22%22],%22documentcollectionid2%22:[%22GRANDCHAMBER%22,%22CHAMBER%22],%22itemid%22:[%22001-101958%22]} accessed 9 November 2013.

application for judicial review, and had failed to address a number of decisive arguments raised by him and to rule properly and in good time on the request to implement the impugned decision.

Concerning Article 6 of the Convention, "*he relied on paragraph 1 in Article 6 of the Convention, which provides, in so far as relevant: 'in the determination of his civil rights and obligations (...), everyone is entitled to a fair and public hearing within a reasonable time by a (...) tribunal'*".[653] As for Article 13, in this case, the applicant complained that he had not had an effective remedy for his complaints under Article 8 of the Convention and Article 1 of Protocol No. 1: "*he relied on Article 13 of the Convention, which provides as follows: 'Everyone whose rights and freedoms as set forth in the Convention are violated shall have an effective remedy before a national authority notwithstanding that the violation has been committed by persons acting in an official capacity.'*"[654]

The ECtHR found that "*the outcome of the proceedings before the Supreme Administrative Court was decisive for the question whether the license granted to ET Marin Blagiev was valid, but not for the 'determination' of any 'civil right' which Bulgarian law conferred on the applicant as a private individual.*" The Court also held that there had been no breach of Article 1 of Protocol No. 1 for the reason that there was no clear evidence that the reclamation scheme had had a negative effect on the applicant's possessions. The applicant asked for an effective remedy (Article 13) on the condition that the peaceful enjoyment of his possessions was infringed. Therefore, Article 13 did not apply in this case. The ECtHR concluded that there had been no violation of Article 1 of Protocol No. 1 or Articles 6 and 13 of the Convention.

Furthermore, according to the discussion in the case of *Leander v. Sweden*[655] (see 5.1.3.4.3), it clearly interprets the meaning of Article 13 of the ECHR Convention. The following general principles are of relevance:

(a) where an individual has an arguable claim to be the victim of a violation of the rights set forth in the Convention, he should have a remedy before a national authority in order both to have his claim decided and, if appropriate, to obtain redress;

653 ECtHR, Ivan Atanasov v. Bulgaria (2010), App. No. 12853/03, Judgment of 2 December 2010, 11 April 2011 (Final), §85, http://hudoc.echr.coe.int/sites/eng/Pages/search.aspx#{%22fulltext%22:[%22\%22right%20to%20participation\%22%22],%22documentcollectionid2%22:[%22GRANDCHAMBER%22,%22CHAMBER%22],%22itemid%22:[%22001-101958%22]} accessed 9 November 2013.

654 ECtHR, Ivan Atanasov v. Bulgaria (2010), App. No. 12853/03, Judgment of 2 December 2010, 11 April 2011 (Final), §97, http://hudoc.echr.coe.int/sites/eng/Pages/search.aspx#{%22fulltext%22:[%22\%22right%20to%20participation\%22%22],%22documentcollectionid2%22:[%22GRANDCHAMBER%22,%22CHAMBER%22],%22itemid%22:[%22001-101958%22]} accessed 9 November 2013.

655 ECtHR, Leander v. Sweden (1987), App. No. 9248/81, Judgment of 26 March 1987, http://hudoc.echr.coe.int/sites/eng/pages/search.aspx?i=001-57519#{%22itemid%22:[%22001-57519%22]} accessed 24 October 2013.

(b) *the authority referred to in Article 13 need not be a judicial authority but, if it is not, the powers and the guarantees which it affords are relevant in determining whether the remedy before it is effective;*
(c) *although no single remedy may itself entirely satisfy the requirements of Article 13, the aggregate of remedies provided for under domestic law may do so;*
(d) *Article 13 does not guarantee a remedy allowing a Contracting State's laws as such to be challenged before a national authority on the ground of being contrary to the Convention or equivalent domestic norms.*[656]

Based on what has been introduced and discussed, it can be concluded that the realisation of access to justice largely depends on different national situations.

5.3.2.2.2. Whether NGOs Have an Opportunity to Appeal to the Courts against Any Decision

NGOs play an irreplaceable role in environmental protection. Environmental litigation by NGOs can be a service towards raising public awareness and understanding of citizens of their rights. In fact NGOs can protect the citizens' rights in the case as the people's representative.[657]

However, whether NGOs have an opportunity to appeal to the courts against any decision cannot be easily explored at the European level, because it also largely depends on different legal traditions, systems and circumstances in different countries in Europe. At the level of the European Union, given the different legal systems and traditions in the Member States, NGOs' standing generally differs according to which court is exercising jurisdiction.[658] Broadly speaking, in the countries where administrative courts are established as a separate court, the main venue for environmental NGOs is the administrative courts. All countries that have instituted an administrative court system grant NGOs standing in environmental matters.[659] In addition, standing could also be conferred on environmental NGOs before civil and criminal courts. Owing to the fact that there are some differences as to the criteria for "access", the standing for NGOs in civil and criminal courts will be different in different countries.

---

656 ECtHR, Leander v. Sweden (1987), App. No. 9248/81, Judgment of 26 March 1987, §77, http://hudoc.echr.coe.int/sites/eng/pages/search.aspx?i=001-57519#{%22itemid%22:[%22001-57519%22]} accessed 24 October 2013.

657 Khalesi, A.M. (2013). Principles and content of right to environment (in the light of international documents and conventions). *Advances in Applied Science Research*, 4(4), http://pelagiaresearchlibrary.com/advances-in-applied-science/vol4-iss4/AASR-2013-4-4-371-380.pdf accessed 10 October 2013, p. 379.

658 De Sadeleer, N., Roller, G. & Dross, M. (2005). *Access to Justice in Environmental Matters and the Role of NGOs: Empirical Findings and Legal Appraisal.* Groningen: Europa Law Publishing, p. 179.

659 De Sadeleer, N., Roller, G. & Dross, M. (2005). *Access to Justice in Environmental Matters and the Role of NGOs: Empirical Findings and Legal Appraisal.* Groningen: Europa Law Publishing, p. 180.

In some countries, civil courts do not recognise standing for NGOs. In others, NGOs may bring cases before the civil courts. The situation is even more complex concerning NGOs' standing in criminal trials.[660]

Comparatively speaking, as for the NGOs' legal standing concerning environmental matters, the Aarhus Convention goes deeper than the ECHR and the jurisprudence from the ECtHR. Therefore, this issue will be discussed further below.

5.3.2.3. Access to Justice in Environmental Matters in the Aarhus Convention

Although the Aarhus Convention is autonomous from other international human rights instruments, it is clear that its provisions on access to justice draw on and develop established notions from international human rights law, especially Article 9 of the Aarhus Convention.[661] However, the access to justice provisions of the Aarhus Convention directly governs environmental matters; they are not covered by the European Convention on Human Rights.[662] Either "procedural" rights provisions (such as Article 6 of the European Convention on Human Rights – right to a fair trial) must be used, while giving access to the court regardless of the substantial matter of the suit, or specific rights must be interpreted so that environmental concerns are taken into account (such as Article 8 – right to respect for private and family life, Article 10 – freedom of expression, and Article 2 – right to life).[663] Compared with the ECHR, the Aarhus Convention provides a clearer provision on the right to access to justice in environmental matters.

Basically, access to justice, as defined by the Aarhus Convention, is a means for having erroneous administrative decision on environmental issues corrected by a court or another independent and impartial body established by law.[664] Specifically, as the third pillar of the Convention, access to justice contains three different contexts: (a) review procedures with respect to information requests, (b) review procedures with respect to specific (project-type) decisions which are subject to public participation requirements, and (c) challenges to breaches

---

660 De Sadeleer, N., Roller, G. & Dross, M. (2005). *Access to Justice in Environmental Matters and the Role of NGOs: Empirical Findings and Legal Appraisal.* Groningen: Europa Law Publishing, p. 169.

661 United Nations Economic Commission for Europe (UNECE) (2013). The Aarhus Convention: an Implementation Guide, www.unece.org/fileadmin/DAM/env/pp/ppdm/Aarhus_Implementation_Guide_second_edition_-_text_only.pdf accessed 14 March 2014, p. 194.

662 Andrusevych, A. (2013). Environmental human rights protection in the European Court of Human Rights. In: Stec, S. (Ed.). *Handbook on Access to Justice under the Aarhus Convention.* Szentendre (Hungary): The Regional Environmental Center for Central and Eastern Europe, p. 71.

663 Andrusevych, A. (2013). Environmental human rights protection in the European Court of Human Rights. In: Stec, S. (Ed.). *Handbook on Access to Justice under the Aarhus Convention.* Szentendre (Hungary): The Regional Environmental Center for Central and Eastern Europe, p. 71.

664 Ebbesson, J. (2002). Comparative introduction. In: Ebbesson, J. (Ed.). *Access to Justice in Environmental Matters in the EU.* Leiden: Kluwer Law International, p. 13.

of environmental law in general.[665] That is to say, the "access to justice" in the Convention contains not only the first two pillars but is also addressing the way to empower individuals and NGOs to promote the enforcement of the law. Table 5 below shows the structure and provisions of Article 9.

Table 5[666]

Provision	Obligation	Implementation elements
Article 9(1)	Provides review procedures relating to information requests under Article 4	– Judicial or other independent and impartial review – Additional expeditious and inexpensive reconsideration or review procedure – Standing requirements – Binding final decisions – Reasons for decision in writing
Article 9(2)	Provides review procedures relating to public participation under Article 6 and other relevant provisions of the Convention	– Judicial or other independent and impartial review – Possibility for preliminary administrative review procedure – Standing requirements
Article 9(3)	Provides review procedures for public review of acts and omissions of private persons or public authorities concerning national law relating to the environment	– Administrative review procedures – Judicial review procedures
Article 9(4)	Minimum standards applicable to access-to-justice procedures, decisions and remedies	– Adequate and effective remedies, including injunctive relief – Fairness – Equity – Timeliness – Not prohibitively expensive – Record decisions in writing – Publicly accessible decisions
Article 9(5)	Requires parties to facilitate effective access to justice	– Information on access to administrative and judicial review procedures – Appropriate assistance mechanisms to remove or reduce financial and other barriers to access to justice

665 Lavrysen, L. (2010). The Aarhus Convention between environmental protection and human rights. *Liège, Strasbourg, Brussels: parcours des droits de l'homme.* Limal: Anthemis, pp. 647–671.

666 Ewing, M., Hough, A. & Amajirionwu, M. (2007). Environmental RTDI programme 2000–2006: assessing access to information, participation, and justice in environmental decision-making in Ireland. Prepared for the Environmental Protection Agency by Centre for Sustainability, Institute of Technology, Sligo in Partnership with Department of Law, University College Cork COMHAR, the Sustainable Development Council, www.environmentaldemocracy.ie/pdf/finalreport.pdf accessed 23 September 2013, p. 121.

Article 9(1) of the Aarhus Convention deals with access to justice concerning information appeals.[667] Article 9(2) states that what constitutes a sufficient interest and impairment of a right shall be determined "*in accordance with the requirements of national law and consistently with the objective of giving the public concerned wide access to justice within the scope of this Convention.*"[668] More importantly, standing depends on the question of "sufficient interest" or "impairment of a right", depending on domestic law. Environmental interest groups that comply with the Convention definition of "the public concerned"[669] are explicitly deemed to have a "sufficient interest" or "rights capable of being impaired".[670] Article 9(3) provides for access to administrative or judicial procedures to challenge acts and omissions by private and public bodies that contravene domestic law relating to the environment; it is for national (or EC) law to lay down the criteria for standing.[671] It should be pointed out that Article 9(3) does not require the Aarhus contracting parties to provide access to justice to any and all members of the public without distinction.[672] One scholarly analysis concluded: "This provision allows the public to enforce a broad range of environmental laws".[673]

Furthermore, Article 9(4) and (5) set minimum requirements concerning access to justice which should be provided for under Article 9(1), (2) and (3) of the Aarhus Convention.[674] Particularly important is Article 9(4) which provides

---

667 Lavrysen, L. (2010). The Aarhus Convention between environmental protection and human rights. *Liège, Strasbourg, Brussels: parcours des droits de l'homme.* Limal: Anthemis, pp. 647–671.

668 Černý, P. (2010). Practical application of Article 9 of the Aarhus Convention in 10 EU countries – comparative remarks. In: ENELO (European Network of Environmental Law Organizations). *Access to Justice in Environmental Matters.* Co-sponsored by the European Commission – LIFE+programme and the Ministry of Housing, Spatial Planning and the Environment of the Netherlands, www.justiceandenvironment.org/_files/old-uploads-wordpress/2010/05/JE-Aarhus-AtJ_Report_10-05-24.pdf accessed 25 November 2013, p. 2.

669 The "public concerned" is "the public affected or likely to be affected by or having an interest in, the environmental decision-making (...) non-governmental organizations promoting environmental protection and meeting any requirements under national law shall be deemed to have an interest", Aarhus Convention, Article 2.5. The "public" is more broadly defined as "national or legal persons, and, in accordance with national legislation or practice, their associations, organizations or groups", Aarhus Convention, Article 2.4.

670 Lee, M. (2005). *EU Environmental Law: Challenges, Change and Decision-making.* Oxford: Hart Publishing, p. 160.

671 Lee, M. (2005). *EU Environmental Law: Challenges, Change and Decision-making.* Oxford: Hart Publishing, p. 160.

672 Pallemaerts, M. (2011). Access to environmental justice at EU Level: has the 'Aarhus Regulation' improved the situation? In: Pallemaerts, M. (Ed.), *The Aarhus Convention at Ten: Interactions and Tensions between Conventional International Law and EU Environmental Law.* Groningen: Europa Law Publishing, p. 275.

673 Bruch, E.C. & Czebiniak, R. (2002). Globalizing environmental governance: making the leap from regional initiatives on transparency, participation, and accountability in environmental matters. *Environmental Law Reporter*, 32.

674 Lavrysen, L. (2010). The Aarhus Convention between environmental protection and human rights. *Liège, Strasbourg, Brussels: parcours des droits de l'homme.* Limal: Anthemis, pp. 647–671.

that the procedures for the right to access to justice shall provide "adequate and effective" remedies, including injunctive relief as appropriate, and be "fair, equitable, timely and not prohibitively expensive".[675] Access to justice is not limited to cases where the participatory or informational rights of the Aarhus Convention are infringed, but must also be granted in order to challenge the substantive legality of a decision.[676]

Specifically, similar to the ECHR, the essential factor for access to justice in environmental matters is the legal standing of an individual or an NGO. It is noted that the Aarhus Convention prevents the Parties from granting standing to any person without distinction. However, the Convention requires – as a minimum – that members of the "public concerned", either having a sufficient interest or maintaining impairment of a right, have standing to review the substantive and procedural legality of any decision, act or omission subject to the provisions of Article 6.[677] As for NGOs, the Convention states clearly that NGOs meeting the requirements of Article 2(5), are deemed to have a "sufficient interest" or a right capable of being impaired.

As pointed out above, various countries grant different degrees of legal standing and possess a wide range of interpretation of legal standing.[678] In Switzerland, which was the first European country to legislate a right of action (or standing to sue) for environmental NGOs,[679] NGOs must be in existence for ten years before they are granted an unconditional right to challenge certain projects.[680] While open standing for NGOs may indeed be a stepping-stone towards broader standing rights in Western Europe (and therefore ought to be encouraged in that context), this situation in Central and Eastern Europe is quite

675 Access to Environmental Justice, www.commonlawreview.cz/access-to-environmental-justice accessed 5 December 2013.

676 Ebbesson, J. (2002). Comparative introduction. In: Ebbesson, J. (Ed.). *Access to Justice in Environmental Matters in the EU.* Leiden: Kluwer Law International, p. 13.

677 United Nations Economic Commission for Europe (UNECE) (2013). The Aarhus Convention: an Implementation Guide, www.unece.org/fileadmin/DAM/env/pp/ppdm/Aarhus_Implementation_Guide_second_edition_-_text_only.pdf accessed 14 March 2014, p. 218.

678 Obradovic, D. (2011). EU rules on public participation in environmental decision-making operating at the European and National Levels. In: Pallemaerts, M. (Ed.). *The Aarhus Convention at Ten: Interactions and Tensions between Conventional International Law and EU Environmental Law.* Groningen: Europa Law Publishing, p. 179.

679 Führ, M., Gebers, B., Ormond, T. & Roller, G. (1995). Access to justice: legal standing for environmental associations in the European Union. In: Robinson, D. & Dunkeley, J. (Eds.). *Public Interest Perspectives in Environmental Law.* London: Wiley Chancery, p. 89.

680 Stec, S. (1998). Chapter 3: Access to Justice in Environmental Matters. In: *Doors to Democracy: a Pan-European Assessment of Current Trends and Practices in Public Participation in Environmental Matters.* Szentendre (Hungary): The Regional Environmental Center for Central and Eastern Europe, http://archive.rec.org/REC/Publications/PPDoors/EUROPE/Justice.html accessed 25 November 2013.

different.[681] Besides this, NGOs' legal standing would be treated differently in different kinds of courts. For instance, in some countries, such as Germany, according to the literature in 2011, civil courts do not recognise standing for NGOs, and the administrative courts are the only venue possible for public interest actions.[682] In other countries, NGOs may bring cases before the civil courts. In the majority of states, NGOs are allowed to bring proceedings in environmental matters before administrative courts. The general trends are towards more open standing in certain administrative proceedings, especially those relating to access to information, and special standing for NGOs in specific procedures.[683]

Nevertheless, the interest of any NGO promoting environmental protection and meeting any requirements under national law shall be deemed sufficient.[684] In some European countries, the NGOs cannot generally gain standing in cases going beyond the scope of Article 9(2) of the Aarhus Convention (e.g. Austria and with some exceptions Slovakia).[685] This will be discussed in detail in the section on the national limited legal standing for NGOs shall meet the minimum standards of Aarhus Convention (see 5.3.2.4.2).

5.3.2.4. *Case Law of the Aarhus Convention Compliance Committee*

5.3.2.4.1. EU Law Shall Follow the Aarhus Convention on Access to Justice

The communication of *ACCC/C/2006/18 (Denmark)*[686] concerns access to justice for individuals in Denmark. In 2006, the municipality of Hillerod acting

681 Stec, S. (1998). Chapter 3: Access to Justice in Environmental Matters. In: *Doors to Democracy: a Pan-European Assessment of Current Trends and Practices in Public Participation in Environmental Matters*. Szentendre (Hungary): The Regional Environmental Center for Central and Eastern Europe, http://archive.rec.org/REC/Publications/PPDoors/EUROPE/Justice.html accessed 25 November 2013.

682 Obradovic, D. (2011). EU rules on public participation in environmental decision-making operating at the European and National Levels. In: Pallemaerts, M. (Ed.). *The Aarhus Convention at Ten: Interactions and Tensions between Conventional International Law and EU Environmental Law*. Groningen: Europa Law Publishing, p. 180.

683 Stec, S. (1998). Chapter 3: Access to Justice in Environmental Matters. In: *Doors to Democracy: a Pan-European Assessment of Current Trends and Practices in Public Participation in Environmental Matters*. Szentendre (Hungary): The Regional Environmental Center for Central and Eastern Europe, http://archive.rec.org/REC/Publications/PPDoors/EUROPE/Justice.html accessed 25 November 2013.

684 Obradovic, D. (2011). EU rules on public participation in environmental decision-making operating at the European and National Levels. In: Pallemaerts, M. (Ed.). *The Aarhus Convention at Ten: Interactions and Tensions between Conventional International Law and EU Environmental Law*. Groningen: Europa Law Publishing, p. 179.

685 Lavrysen, L. (2010). The Aarhus Convention between environmental protection and human rights. *Liège, Strasbourg, Brussels: parcours des droits de l'homme*. Limal: Anthemis, pp. 647–671.

686 ACCC/C/2006/18 (Denmark), ECE/MP.PP/2008/5/Add.4, 29 April 2008, www.unece.org/fileadmin/DAM/env/documents/2008/pp/mop3/ece_mp_pp_2008_5_add_4_e.pdf accessed 29 March 2014.

as the landowner (and not as public authority) implemented a decision on extensive culling of juvenile rooks in order to reduce vocal noise resulting from the breeding behaviour of the birds.[687] The Communicant claims that Danish law does not provide him with any mcans to challenge the alleged failure of Denmark to correctly implement the European Community Directive 79/409/ EEC on the Conservation of Wild Birds (Birds Directive).[688]

The Committee finds that the right of the public to challenge acts and omissions regarding wildlife as far as these contravene national law regarding the environment is covered by Article 9(3) of the Convention. The EC Directive can be also considered as national law of the Member States. Thus, it was possible to consider the Birds Directive in the light of Article 9(3) of the Convention.

The Committee also finds that on the one hand, the Communicant has not tried all means on a national level to prevent the culling. On the other hand, according to available case law, this possibility would most likely have existed for certain NGOs.[689] The Committee then declared that the standards for access to justice for NGOs as determined in the case law would have to be considered a minimum standard for the compliance of Denmark.[690]

Finally, "*[o]n the basis of the information provided in the case, the Committee can not conclude that Danish law effectively bars all or almost all members of the public, in particular all or almost all non-governmental organizations devoted to wildlife and nature conservation, from challenging the culling of wild birds, as covered by Article 9, paragraph 3.*"[691]

The conclusion in this communication is less relevant here. The notable point in this communication is that it stresses the importance of a minimum standard of access to justice in cases relating to the protection of wildlife. Furthermore,

---

687 Andrusevych, A., Alge, T. & Clemens, C. (Eds.) (2011). Case law of the Aarhus Convention Compliance Committee (2004–2011), http://rac.org.ua/fileadmin/user_upload/publications/ACCC_Case_Law_Electronic_Advanced_Version.pdf accessed 28 March 2014, p. 149.

688 Economic Commission for Europe (ECE). Meeting of the parties to the Convention on access to information, public participation in decision-making and access to justice in environmental matters. Third meeting, Riga, 11–13 June 2008. Item 6(b) of the provisional agenda. Procedures and mechanisms facilitating the implementation of the Convention: Compliance mechanism, www.unece.org/fileadmin/DAM/env/documents/2008/pp/mop3/ece_mp_pp_2008_5_add_4_e.pdf accessed 29 March 2014.

689 Andrusevych, A., Alge, T. & Clemens, C. (Eds.) (2011). Case law of the Aarhus Convention Compliance Committee (2004–2011), http://rac.org.ua/fileadmin/user_upload/publications/ACCC_Case_Law_Electronic_Advanced_Version.pdf accessed 28 March 2014, p. 149.

690 Andrusevych, A., Alge, T. & Clemens, C. (Eds.) (2011). Case law of the Aarhus Convention Compliance Committee (2004–2011), http://rac.org.ua/fileadmin/user_upload/publications/ACCC_Case_Law_Electronic_Advanced_Version.pdf accessed 28 March 2014, p. 149.

691 Economic Commission for Europe (ECE). Meeting of the parties to the Convention on access to information, public participation in decision-making and access to justice in environmental matters. Third meeting, Riga, 11–13 June 2008. Item 6(b) of the provisional agenda. Procedures and mechanisms facilitating the implementation of the Convention: Compliance mechanism, www.unece.org/fileadmin/DAM/env/documents/2008/pp/mop3/ece_mp_pp_2008_5_add_4_e.pdf accessed 29 March 2014.

acts and omissions that may contravene EU regulations and EU directives relating to the environment and applicable by national courts and authorities in the Member States may be challenged under Article 9(3) of the Convention.[692]

5.3.2.4.2. National Limited Legal Standing for NGOs Shall Meet the Minimum Standards of the Aarhus Convention

In the communication of *ACCC/C/2008/31 (Germany),*[693] the Communicant, the NGO ClientEarth, alleged that by restricting the rights of environmental organisations as regards the review of decisions, acts and omissions by public authorities as well as the review of provisions, Germany had failed to implement Article 9(2) of the Convention.[694] It in particular alleged that German legislation established criteria for the standing for environmental NGOs which were narrower in scope than those set out in Article 9(2) of the Convention (e.g. linking standing requirements to an NGO's statutory objectives, restricting review to decisions contradicting legislative provisions promoting environmental protection and to provisions establishing personal rights for individuals).

The Committee found that "*by imposing a requirement that an environmental NGO, to be able to file an appeal (...), must assert that the challenged decision contravenes a legal provision 'serving the environment' the Party concerned fails to comply with Article 9, paragraph 2 of the Convention in this respect. By not ensuring the standing of environmental NGOs in many of its sectoral laws to challenge acts or omissions of public authorities or private persons which contravene provisions of national law relating to the environment, the Party concerned fails to comply with Article 9, paragraph 3 of the Convention.*"[695]

From this communication, we can see to what extent NGOs could have a legal standing largely depends on the national level; however, it needs to meet the minimum standards of the Aarhus Convention.

Another interesting communication, *ACCC/C/2005/11 (Belgium),*[696] was made by "*the Belgian non-governmental organization Bond Beter Leefmilieu*

---

692 United Nations Economic Commission for Europe (UNECE) (2013). The Aarhus Convention: an Implementation Guide, www.unece.org/fileadmin/DAM/env/pp/ppdm/Aarhus_Implementation_Guide_second_edition_-_text_only.pdf accessed 14 March 2014, p. 207.

693 ACCC/C/2008/31 (Germany), more information see www.unece.org/env/pp/compliance/Compliancecommittee/31TableGermany.html accessed 29 March 2014.

694 Andrusevych, A., Alge, T. & Clemens, C. (Eds.) (2011). Case law of the Aarhus Convention Compliance Committee (2004–2011), http://rac.org.ua/fileadmin/user_upload/publications/ACCC_Case_Law_Electronic_Advanced_Version.pdf accessed 28 March 2014, p. 149.

695 Findings and recommendations with regards to communication ACCC/C/2008/31 concerning compliance by Germany was adopted by the Compliance Committee on 20 December 2013, www.unece.org/fileadmin/DAM/env/pp/compliance/C2008-31/Findings/C31Germany_findings_advancedunedited.pdf accessed 28 March 2014.

696 ACCC/C/2005/11 (Belgium), more information see www.unece.org/env/pp/compliance/Compliancecommittee/11TableBelgium.html accessed 28 March 2014.

Vlaanderen VZW on 3 January 2005 with regards to compliance by Belgium with its obligations under Article 2, paragraph 5, Article 3, paragraph 1 and Article 9, paragraphs 1 to 4, of the Convention in connection with requirements for standing for environmental non-governmental organizations (NGOs) before the Belgian judicial bodies in a case concerning construction permits and planning decisions."[697] The Belgian judiciary had applied the general criteria for standing under Belgian law to NGOs, meaning that NGO applicants had to show a direct, personal and legitimate interest as well as a "required quality".

The Convention asks for the Parties to ensure access to justice for three generic categories of acts and omissions by public authorities. Leaving aside decisions concerning access to information, the distinction is made between, on the one hand, acts and omissions related to permits for specific activities by a public authority for which public participation is required under Article 9(2) and, on other hand, all other acts and omissions by private persons and public authorities which contravene national law relating to the environment is required under Article 9(3). It is also noted that "*although what constitutes a sufficient interest and impairment of a right shall be determined in accordance with national law, it must be decided 'with the objective of giving the public concerned wide access to justice*'"[698] within the scope of the Convention.

The Committee finds that if the jurisprudence of the relevant courts was not altered, Belgium would fail to comply with Article 9(2)–(4), of the Convention. The Committee concludes that even if the wording of the relevant Belgian laws did not as such imply a lack of compliance, the jurisprudence of the Belgian courts, as developed before the entry into force of the Convention for Belgium, implied a too restrictive access to justice for environmental organisations, and thus did not meet the requirements of the Convention.[699] The Committee recommends the Party to "*undertake practical and legislative measures to overcome the previous shortcomings reflected in the jurisprudence of the Council in providing environmental organizations with access to justice in a case concerning town planning permits as well as in case concerning area plans;*

---

697 Economic Commission for Europe (ECE) (2008). Meeting of the parties to the Convention on access to information, public participation in decision-making and access to justice in environmental matters. Third meeting, Riga, 11–13 June 2008. Item 6(b) of the provisional agenda. Procedures and mechanisms facilitating the implementation of the Convention: Compliance mechanism. ECE/MP.PP/2008/5/Add.3, 2 April 2008, www.unece.org/fileadmin/DAM/env/pp/compliance/C2005-11/Update/ece_mp_pp_2008_5_add_3_e.pdf accessed 29 March 2014.

698 ACCC/C/2005/11 (Belgium), §27, more information see www.unece.org/env/pp/compliance/Compliancecommittee/11TableBelgium.html accessed 28 March 2014.

699 Economic Commission for Europe (ECE) (2006). Meeting of the parties to the Convention on access to information, public participation in decision-making and access to justice in environmental matters. Twelfth meeting, Geneva, 14–16 June 2006. ECE/MP.PP/C.1/2006/4/Add.2. 28 July 2006, §40, www.unece.org/fileadmin/DAM/env/documents/2006/pp/ece.mp.pp.c.1.2006.4.add.2.e.pdf accessed 28 March 2014.

and promote awareness of the Convention, in particular the provision concerning access to justice, among the Belgian judiciary."[700]

This case also approves that the minimum standards on access to justice from the Aarhus Convention should be respected at the national level. Furthermore, the awareness of the Convention at national level plays an important role in promoting access to justice.

5.3.2.4.3. Access to Justice is Affordable for the Public

A practical obstacle for access to justice is the lack of enough financial means for individuals or NGOs. There is a clear link between the requirement in Article 9(4) that access to justice procedures cannot be prohibitively expensive and the obligation on Parties in Article 9(5) to consider the establishment of appropriate assistance mechanisms to remove or reduce financial barriers.[701]

Based on the analysis of communication *ACCC/C/2008/24 (Spain)*[702] in the right to participation part (see 5.2.3.4.4), the Communicant firstly filed an administrative lawsuit to the Administrative Proceedings Court challenging the Urbanization Project UA1, and then the Administrative Proceedings Court took a separate decision on the suspension request, rejecting the application. After that, the Communicant lodged an appeal, which was rejected by the Murcia High Court, and the High Court decided to impose all costs (2,148 EUR) on the Communicant. The Communicant argued that the costs were equal to the average monthly budget of a local family in Murcia for three months at that moment. It was a heavy financial burden on the Communicant. The Committee holds that: "*Article 9, paragraph 4 of the Convention, applies also to situations where a member of the public seeks to appeal an unfavorable court decision that involves a public authority and matters covered by the Aarhus Convention. Thus the Party concerned is obliged to implement the Convention in an appropriate way so as to prevent unfair, inequitable or prohibitively expensive cost orders being imposed on a member of the public in such appeal cases.*"[703]

---

700 Economic Commission for Europe (ECE). Meeting of the parties to the Convention on access to information, public participation in decision-making and access to justice in environmental matters. Third meeting, Riga, 11–13 June 2008. Item 6(b) of the provisional agenda. Procedures and mechanisms facilitating the implementation of the Convention: Compliance mechanism. ECE/MP.PP/2008/5/Add.3. 2 April 2008, www.unece.org/fileadmin/DAM/env/pp/compliance/C2005-11/Update/ece_mp_pp_2008_5_add_3_e.pdf accessed 29 March 2014.

701 United Nations Economic Commission for Europe (UNECE) (2013). The Aarhus Convention: an Implementation Guide, www.unece.org/fileadmin/DAM/env/pp/ppdm/Aarhus_Implementation_Guide_second_edition_-_text_only.pdf accessed 14 March 2014, p. 218.

702 ACCC/C/2008/24 (Spain), ECE/MP.PP/C.1/2009/8/Add.1, 8 February 2011, §§99–100, www.unece.org/fileadmin/DAM/env/pp/compliance/CC-26/ece_mp.pp_c.1_2009_8_add.1_e.pdf accessed 21 March 2014.

703 ACCC/C/2008/24 (Spain), ECE/MP.PP/C.1/2009/8/Add.1, 8 February 2011, §108, www.unece.org/fileadmin/DAM/env/pp/compliance/CC-26/ece_mp.pp_c.1_2009_8_add.1_e.pdf accessed 21 March 2014.

Based on this, the Committee recommends that: "*(a)(vi) adequate, timely and effective remedies, including injunctive relief, which are fair, equitable, and not prohibitively expensive be made available at first and second instance in administrative appellate courts for members of the public in environmental matters; (b) to develop a capacity-building programme and provide training on the implementation of the Aarhus Convention for central, local and regional authorities responsible for Aarhus-related issues, including provincial commissions granting free legal aid, and for judges, prosecutors and lawyers; and to develop an awareness-raising programme on Aarhus rights for the public.*"[704]

Another interesting communication is *ACCC/C/2009/36 (Spain)*,[705] in which the Spanish non-governmental organisation Plataforma Contra la Contaminación del Almendralejo (the Communicant) submitted a communication to the Committee alleging a general failure of the Party concerned to implement several provisions of the Convention.

In the findings of this communication, the Compliance Committee notes that the concerned Party's system of legal aid appeared to be very restrictive for small NGOs. The Committee also finds that by setting high financial requirements for an entity to qualify as a "public utility entity" enabling it to receive free legal aid, the Party's system was contradictory. It also finds that "*instituting a system of legal aid which excluded small NGOs from receiving such aid provided sufficient evidence to conclude that the Party concerned did not take into consideration the establishment of appropriate assistance mechanisms to remove or reduce financial barriers to access to justice as required by Article 9, paragraph 5, and also failed to provide for adequate and effective remedies, as required by Article 9, paragraph 4.*"[706] Therefore, the Committee concludes that the Party concerned failed to comply with Article 9(4) and (5) of the Convention.

Apart from the situations in the communications discussed above, some examples on how to overcome some of the financial barriers to access to justice include a no-cost alternative to courts, shifting fees for court expenses to the violator, reducing court costs and finding alternatives to bond requirements.[707] To establish a legal assistance system that provide free or low-cost legal advice to individuals or NGOs is also a good way. For instance, the Czech Republic,

704 ACCC/C/2008/24 (Spain), ECE/MP.PP/C.1/2009/8/Add.1, 8 February 2011, §109, www.unece.org/fileadmin/DAM/env/pp/compliance/CC-26/ece_mp.pp_c.1_2009_8_add.1_e.pdf accessed 21 March 2014.

705 ACCC/C/2009/36 (Spain), ECE/MP.PP/C.1/2010/4/Add.2, 8 February 2011, www.unece.org/fileadmin/DAM/env/pp/compliance/CC-28/ece_mp.pp_c.1_2010_4_add.2_eng.pdf accessed 22 March 2014.

706 ACCC/C/2009/36 (Spain), ECE/MP.PP/C.1/2010/4/Add.2, 8 February 2011, §66, www.unece.org/fileadmin/DAM/env/pp/compliance/CC-28/ece_mp.pp_c.1_2010_4_add.2_eng.pdf accessed 22 March 2014.

707 United Nations Economic Commission for Europe (UNECE) (2013). The Aarhus Convention: an Implementation Guide, www.unece.org/fileadmin/DAM/env/pp/ppdm/Aarhus_Implementation_Guide_second_edition_-_text_only.pdf accessed 14 March 2014, p. 219.

Hungary, the Netherlands, Slovakia, the United Kingdom and Ukraine have privately funded or university-based legal assistance centres.[708]

5.3.2.5. Influence of the Aarhus Convention on EU Law on Access to Justice

At the EU level, the provisions of Article 6 of the Directive 2003/4/EC (Directive 2003/4/EC of the European Parliament and of the Council of 28 January 2003 on public access to environmental information and repealing Council Directive 90/313/EEC),[709] largely track the relevant provisions of the Aarhus Convention and in general require that access to judicial or administrative review has to be provided for any person who considers that his/her request for information has been unreasonably refused or ignored, has been inadequately answered or otherwise not dealt with.[710] Article 6(2) of the Directive states that the Member States may provide that third parties incriminated by the disclosure of information may also have access to legal recourse.

In addition, the objective of Article 1(b) of Directive 2003/35/EC (Directive 2003/35/EC of the European Parliament and of the Council of 26 May 2003 providing for public participation in respect of the drawing up of certain plans and programs relating to the environment and amending with regards to public participation and access to justice Council Directive 85/337/EEC and 96/61/EC)[711] is to contribute to the implementation of the Aarhus Convention obligations by improving public participation and providing for provisions on access to justice.[712] Provisions on access to justice in Articles 3(7) and 4(4) of Directive 2003/35/EC[713] entirely follow the idea of the Aarhus Convention.

---

708 United Nations Economic Commission for Europe (UNECE) (2013). The Aarhus Convention: an Implementation Guide, www.unece.org/fileadmin/DAM/env/pp/ppdm/Aarhus_Implementation_Guide_second_edition_-_text_only.pdf accessed 14 March 2014, p. 219.

709 Directive 2003/4/EC of the European Parliament and of the Council of 28 January 2003 on public access to environmental information and repealing Council Directive 90/313/EEC, OJ L41/26, http://eur-lex.europa.eu/LexUriServ/LexUriServ.do?uri=OJ:L:2003:041:0026:0032:EN:PDF accessed 1 November 2013.

710 Kostic, M. (2006). *The Right of Access to Environmental Information in the Sense of the Aarhus Convention: European Streams and Legal Framework in Serbia and Montenegro.* CPRINT Beograd, p. 135.

711 Directive 2003/35/EC of the European Parliament and of the Council of 26 May 2003 providing for public participation in respect of the drawing up of certain plans and programs relating to the environment and amending with regards to public participation and access to justice Council Directive 85/337/EEC and 96/61/EC [2003] OJ L156/17, http://eur-lex.europa.eu/LexUriServ/LexUriServ.do?uri=OJ:L:2003:156:0017:0024:EN:PDF accessed 28 October 2013.

712 Kostic, M. (2006). *The Right of Access to Environmental Information in the Sense of the Aarhus Convention: European Streams and Legal Framework in Serbia and Montenegro.* CPRINT Beograd, p. 135.

713 Directive 2003/35/EC of the European Parliament and of the Council of 26 May 2003 providing for public participation in respect of the drawing up of certain plans and programs relating to the environment and amending with regards to public participation and access to justice Council Directive 85/337/EEC and 96/61/EC [2003] OJ L156/17,

Access to justice in this Directive is reserved for organisations qualified as "public concerned" that claim a "sufficient interest" or an "impairment of a right".[714] The "public concerned" means the public affected or likely to be affected by, or having an interest in, the taking of a decision on the issuing or the updating of a permit or of permit conditions.[715]

Furthermore, the European Commission presented a Proposal for a Directive of the European Parliament and of the Council on access to justice in environmental matters. The proposal requires Member States to take all necessary measures 18 months after the entry into force of the directive.[716] The final provisions fix the date of entry into force for 1 January 2005. This proposal was part of the "Aarhus package", also consisting of the Proposal for a decision to ratify the Convention and a Proposal for a Regulation to apply the provisions of the Convention to Community institutions and bodies.[717]

Within this context, the realisation of access to justice largely depends on the related specific provisions at the domestic level. In theory, the right to access to justice can be protected by the Constitution. Judicial review is one procedural technique by which decisions of public bodies exercising environmental responsibilities can be challenged in court and a means by which the courts supervise public bodies in the exercise of their powers or the carrying out of their duties.[718] Most environmental acts can be subject to judicial review.[719] In European countries, environmental or general administrative laws provide possibilities for private persons to challenge acts or omissions by public authorities which contravene provisions of national environmental law. In practice, in determining whether public interest groups or NGOs have standing, the court may consider a number of factors including the merits of the challenge, the importance of vindicating the rule of law, the importance of the issues raised and the nature of the breach.[720] The national law may give standing to

---

http://eur-lex.europa.eu/LexUriServ/LexUriServ.do?uri=OJ:L:2003:156:0017:0024:EN:PDF accessed 28 October 2013.

714 Article 10(a), Directive 85/337/EEC as amended by Directive 2003/35/EC and Article 15(a) of Directive 96/61/EC as amended by Directive 2003/35/EC.

715 Article 1(2), Directive 85/337/EEC as amended by Directive 2003/55/EC and Article 2(14) of Directive 96/61/EC as amended by Directive 2003/35/EC.

716 Proposal for a Directive of the European Parliament and of the Council on access to justice in environmental matters, 2003/0246 (COD), http://eur-lex.europa.eu/legal-content/EN/TXT/?uri=CELEX:52003PC0624 accessed 28 November 2013.

717 The EU & the Aarhus Convention: in the EU Member States, in the Community Institutions and Bodies, http://ec.europa.eu/environment/aarhus/legislation.htm accessed 28 November 2013.

718 Woolf, H. Jowell, J. & Le Sueur, A.P. (1999). *De Smith, Woolf and Jowell's Principles of Judicial Review*. London: Sweet and Maxwell. Part I.

719 Lavrysen, L. (2010). The Aarhus Convention between environmental protection and human rights. *Liège, Strasbourg, Brussels: parcours des droits de l'homme*. Limal: Anthemis, pp. 647–671.

720 Economic Commission for Europe (2008). Meeting of the parties to the convention on access to information, public participation in decision-making and access to justice in environmental matters. Third meeting Riga, 11–13 June 2008. Item 6(a) of the

community groups or individuals to challenge a government decision on resource development.[721] However, the scope of actually "reviewable" acts is influenced by the limited number of potential plaintiffs in some areas.[722] If the legislation and/or practice of the courts of a country is based on the (strictly applied) doctrine of "impairment of rights", the group of "reviewable" acts is thereby limited.[723] Legal standing is one of the key factors for the realisation of access to justice, especially in environmental cases. Among the numerous possible ways to qualify standing, two key positions can be identified: on the one side, a restrictive approach, meaning that a person has standing only in cases which concern him or her directly and privately in a very narrow sense; and on the other side, a more generous, expansive approach, where *locus standi* does not depend on the connection between the subject and interest pursued at all.[724] The EU Member States are found somewhere between these two positions, but there has been a general – albeit slow and heterogeneous tendency among them to move from the first position towards the latter in cases concerning the environment.[725]

There are some interesting cases[726] at the EU level, as pointed out in *Plaumann v. Commission:*[727] *"Persons other than those to whom a decision is*

---

provisional agenda procedures and mechanisms facilitating the implementation of the Convention: reports on implementation. ECE/MP.PP/2008/4. 21 May 2008, www.unece.org/fileadmin/DAM/env/documents/2008/pp/mop3/ece_mp_pp_2008_4_e.pdf accessed 28 November 2013.

721 Economic Commission for Europe (2008). Meeting of the parties to the convention on access to information, public participation in decision-making and access to justice in environmental matters. Third meeting Riga, 11–13 June 2008. Item 6(a) of the provisional agenda procedures and mechanisms facilitating the implementation of the Convention: reports on implementation. ECE/MP.PP/2008/4. 21 May 2008, www.unece.org/fileadmin/DAM/env/documents/2008/pp/mop3/ece_mp_pp_2008_4_e.pdf accessed 28 November 2013.

722 Lavrysen, L. (2010). The Aarhus Convention between environmental protection and human rights. *Liège, Strasbourg, Brussels: parcours des droits de l'homme.* Limal: Anthemis, pp. 647–671.

723 Lavrysen, L. (2010). The Aarhus Convention between environmental protection and human rights. *Liège, Strasbourg, Brussels: parcours des droits de l'homme.* Limal: Anthemis, pp. 647–671.

724 Ebbesson, J. (2002). Comparative introduction. In: Ebbesson, J. (Ed.). *Access to Justice in Environmental Matters in the EU.* Leiden: Kluwer Law International, p. 24.

725 Ebbesson, J. (2002). Comparative introduction. In: Ebbesson, J. (Ed.). *Access to Justice in Environmental Matters in the EU.* Leiden: Kluwer Law International, p. 24.

726 e.g. Plaumann v. Commission, Case C-25/26, Judgment of the Court of 15 July 1963, http://curia.europa.eu/juris/liste.jsf?pro=&nat=or&oqp=&dates=&lg=&language=en&jur=C%2CT%2CF&cit=none%252CC%252CCJ%252CR%252C2008E%252C%252C%252C%252C%252C%252C%252C%252C%252C%252Ctrue%252Cfalse%252Cfalse&num=c-25%252F62&td=%3BALL&pcs=Oor&avg=&page=1&mat=or&jge=&for=&cid=157950 accessed 8 July 2014; Stichting Greenpeace Council and Others v. Commission, C-32/95P, Judgment of the Court of 2 April 1998, http://curia.europa.eu/juris/liste.jsf?pro=&nat=or&oqp=&dates=&lg=&language=en&jur=C%2CT%2CF&cit=none%252CC%252CCJ%252CR%252C2008E%252C%252C%252C%252C%252C%252C%252C%252C%252C%252Ctrue%252Cfalse%252Cfalse&num=c-321%252F95p&td=%3BALL&pcs=Oor&avg=&page=1&mat=or&jge=&for=&cid=157950 accessed 8 July 2014.

727 Plaumann v. Commission, Case C-25/26, Judgment of the Court of 15 July 1963, http://curia.europa.eu/juris/liste.jsf?pro=&nat=or&oqp=&dates=&lg=&language=en&jur=C

addressed may only claim to be individually concerned if that decisions affects them by reason of certain attributes which are peculiar to them or by reason of circumstances in which they are differentiated from all other persons and by virtue of these factors distinguishes them individually just as in the case of the person addressed." However, most of the time, it is impossible to single out the extent to which decisions exclusively relate to only one person. Owing to the complexity of the right to access to justice at the EU level, the two cases below will further explain this right in the case law of the CJEU.

In *Djurgården-Lilla Värtans Miljöskyddsförening (an association for environmental protection) v. Stockholms kommun genom dess marknämnd (Municipality of Stockholm)*,[728] the Stockholm regional authority made a decision to build a project, which would have a significant effect the environment, particularly with respect to groundwater. The Swedish environmental association appealed against the decision. According to Swedish law only an NGO with at least 2,000 members may bring an appeal against a decision adopted on an environmental matter. The Court of Justice of the European Union considered that the requirement in Swedish law was too restrictive in relation to EU Directive 85/337/EEC and the Aarhus Convention. The Court held that the national rules must ensure wide access to justice according to the Directive and the Aarhus Convention. In addition, the national rules must render effective provisions of Directive 85/337/EEC on judicial remedies.[729] From the situation in this case, we can see that the number that may set requirements for NGOs under national law, but in light of the integral role that NGOs play in the implementation of the Directive and the Convention, Parties could not impose some requirements which are stricter than the minimum standards set by the Directive and the Convention.

The second case is *Lesoochranárske zoskupenie VLK (an environmental NGO) v. Ministerstvo životného prostredia Slovenskej republiky (Ministry of the Environment of the Slovak Republic)*,[730] which concerned an environmental association's request to be a "party" to the administrative proceedings relating to the grant of derogations to the system of protection for species such as

%2CT%2CF&cit=none%252CC%252CCJ%252CR%252C2008E%252C%252C%252C%252C%252C%252C%252C%252C%252C%252Ctrue%252Cfalse%252Cfalse&num=c-25%252F62&td=%3BALL&pcs=Oor&avg=&page=1&mat=or&jge=&for=&cid=157950 accessed 8 July 2014.

728 Djurgården-Lilla Värtans Miljöskyddsförening v. Stockholms kommun genom dess marknämnd, Case C-263/08, Judgment of the Court (Second Chamber) of 15 October 2009, http://curia.europa.eu/juris/liste.jsf?language=en&jur=C,T,F&num=263/08&td=ALL accessed 13 April 2014.

729 Schoukens, H. (2013). Access to justice in conservation related matters in the EU: the added value of the Aarhus Convention in the quest to environmental justice. Guest lecture in the department of public international law, Ghent University, 27 November 2013.

730 Lesoochranárske zoskupenie VLK v. Ministerstvo životného prostredia Slovenskej republiky, Case C-240/09, Judgment of the Court (Grand Chamber) of 8 March 2011, http://curia.europa.eu/juris/liste.jsf?language=en&num=c-240/09 accessed 13 April 2014.

the brown bear, access to protected countryside areas, or the use of chemical substances in such areas. The Ministry of the Environment rejected the request. The administrative appeal was then brought by the environmental NGO against the rejection. It is noted that the EU has exercised its powers and adopted provisions to implement obligations deriving from the Aarhus Convention. The dispute in this case concerned "*whether an environmental protection association may be a 'party' to administrative proceedings concerning, in particular, the grant of derogations to the system of protection for species such as the brown bear. That species is mentioned in Annex IV (a) to the Habitats Directive, so that, under Article 12 thereof, it is subject to a system of strict protection from which derogations may be granted only under the conditions laid down in Article 16 of that directive.*"[731] As far as a species protected by the Habitats Directive is concerned, in order to ensure effective judicial protection in the fields covered by EU environmental law, the national court shall interpret its national law in a way which, to the fullest extent possible, is consistent with the objectives laid down in Article 9(3) of the Aarhus Convention. The other aspect of the case is not relevant in this book. The situation mentioned above indicates that although the Aarhus Convention does not apply to the Habitats Directive, the national courts must interpret environmental laws in a way which to the fullest extent possible give effects to the Articles of the Aarhus Convention.

Therefore, the Aarhus Convention sets the minimum standards for the implementation of EU law on right to access to justice. In addition, the EU Member States are also bound by the ECHR and in particular Articles 6 and 13 mentioned above. It is not necessary to further examine the relevant cases on the right to access to justice at the EU for the reason that the baseline would be similar with what has been discussed in the ECtHR, the ACCC and the relevant Directives in the EU level.

5.3.2.6. Right to Access to Justice in Protected Areas Conservation Law in Europe

5.3.2.6.1. The Bern Convention

There is no specific provision on the right to access to justice in the Bern Convention. As indicated above, if there is any infringement on the right to access to justice in Europe, the relevant provision(s) from the European Convention on Human Rights and the Aarhus Convention can be applied.

---

731 Lesoochranárske zoskupenie VLK v. Ministerstvo životného prostredia Slovenskej republiky, Case C-240/09, Judgment of the Court (Grand Chamber) of 8 March 2011, §37, http://curia.europa.eu/juris/liste.jsf?language=en&num=c-240/09 accessed 13 April 2014.

5.3.2.6.2. The Birds Directive and the Habitats Directive

The Birds Directive and the Habitats Directive do not provide any provision addressing the right to access to justice. However, if there is any infringement of the right to access to justice, some relevant provisions from the ECHR, the Aarhus Convention can be applied.

5.3.2.6.3. Case Law of the Court of Justice of the European Union

Because there is no provision addressing the right to access to justice in the Bern Convention and the two Directives mentioned above, there is no case law directly following the Convention and the Directives in the Court of Justice of the European Communities. Only some indirect cases link to the Habitats Directive, for instance, *Lesoochranárske zoskupenie VLK (an environmental NGO) v. Ministerstvo životného prostredia Slovenskej republiky (Ministry of the Environment of the Slovak Republic)* (see 5.3.2.5).

5.3.3. ANALYSIS AND INTERIM CONCLUSION

It is widely recognised that access to justice is one of the most basic human rights, without which the realisation of many other human rights becomes difficult.[732] States should ensure that their judicial institutions are effective to enhance access to environmental justice for the public.[733] However, there are different understandings and implementation for access to justice in China and in Europe, even if in the different States in Europe.

5.3.3.1. Differences in Access to Justice in China and in Europe

According to what has been discussed above, some differences of access to justice in China and in Europe will be analysed below.

5.3.3.1.1. Different Cultural Background for Access to Justice

Chinese traditional ideas have a negative view on litigation (see 5.3.1). Various other options are used for Chinese to pursue justice. More practically, guided by

732 Bhagwati, P.H. (2002). Democratization of remedies and access to justice. In: the First South Asian Regional Judicial Symposium on Access to Justice, New Delhi, 1–3 November 2002.

733 Kibugi, R. (2011). Enhanced access to environmental justice in Kenya. In: Benidickson, J., Boer, B., Benjamin, A.H. & Morrow, K. (Eds.). *Environmental Law and Sustainability after Rio*. The IUCN Academy of Environmental Law Series. Cheltenham (UK) and Northampton (USA): Edward Elgar Publishing, p. 159.

the modern principle called "efficiency in priority, fairness in balance",[734] people in China prefer mediation in environmental disputes rather than access to justice for the following reasons. Firstly, they regard mediation as a faster and more affordable dispute resolution. Secondly, compared to legal standing in the court, they could freely express their ideas when mediating some disputes. Thirdly, by mediating, they could get some more flexible and effective results. However, with the improvement of the existing legal system and the development of awareness of Chinese people, access to justice for environmental disputes is becoming popular.

In Europe, culture does not "affect" access to justice in Europe, and the ECHR provides two provisions on access to justice (see 5.3.2.1). The Aarhus Convention and the case law from the ACCC reflect the important roles of right to access to justice in environmental matters. All these provide some requirements and guidelines for the realisation of the right to access to justice in environmental matters in the European countries.

5.3.3.1.2. Different Historical Stages of Access to Justice

It is difficult to point out a specific time when access to justice became popular in China, but some progress was made after the year 2000 (see 5.3.1). The newly modified "Environmental Protection Law of the People's Republic of China" (2014 version) reflects that the legal standing of public interest litigation is expanded for individuals in China (see 5.3.1.1).

In Europe, the ECHR, which was signed in 1950, provided two provisions on access to justice (see 5.3.2.1). In 1998, the Aarhus Convention further addressed the right to access to justice in environmental matters. It is quite obvious that the historical stages of access to justice in China and in Europe are different.

5.3.3.1.3. Different "Supporters" of Access to Justice

Similar to other procedural human rights mentioned above, there is no independent human rights law in China at present. However, environmental law, administrative law, civil law and even criminal law in China provide some provisions relevant to the legal standing of access to justice. If individuals or NGOs want to appeal to the People's Court, some provisions from these laws will

---

734 It was one of the outcomes of a study of the "Chinese market economy and the design of social welfare institutions" in 1986, carried out by the Civil Affairs Ministry of the State Council. This new principle was soon formally adopted by the Chinese Communist Party, the ruling party, in 1987 at its thirteenth Party Conference. It was identical to Deng Xiaoping's well-known slogan to "let some people get rich first". At the end of the planned economy, commercial activities were considered to have a high political risk with uncertain gain, and people who were permitted to undertake commercial activities by this policy were allowed to use greater resources.

be applied according to different disputes. Notably, 134 environmental tribunals have been established since 1989 in China (see 5.3.1.2). Besides these, disputes on environmental issues could also be appealed to administrative tribunals, civil tribunals and criminal tribunals in China.

In Europe, the ECHR, the ECtHR, the Aarhus Convention, the ACCC, some Directives and the CJEU establish a right to access to justice in different degrees (see 5.3.2).

We can conclude that various laws and tribunals will be available for access to justice in environmental matters in China, if the legal standing is expanded. Besides various "supporters" of access to justice in environmental matters in Europe, the ECHR and ECtHR work as fundamental "supporters" to guarantee the right to access to justice.

5.3.3.2. Similarities in Access to Justice Between China and Europe

Apart from the differences, there are also some similarities in China and in Europe. Firstly, the developmental tendencies of access to justice in environmental matters are similar in China and in Europe. The legal standing of public interest litigation will be expanded for individuals in the newly modified environmental protection law in China (see 5.3.1.1). The laws and regulations began to pay more attention to access to justice in China. This is also the similar developmental trend in Europe. As a result of different legal traditions, systems and circumstances, it is sometimes difficult to compare the quality of access to justice in environmental matters in different Member States in the European Union.[735] It is even more difficult to ascertain the standard and quality of access to justice in environmental matters in different countries in Europe. Overall, it must be pointed out that the number of environmental public interest actions has grown considerably compared to the situation in the 1980s in Europe.[736] From the ECHR to the Aarhus Convention, from the Aarhus Convention to the Directives at the EU level, the right to access to justice attracts more attention than before, although the legal standing largely depends on the national States. Secondly, protected areas conservation regulations in China and protected areas conservation law in Europe keep silent on access to justice. However, in the European system, people have more possibilities to access administrative or

[735] Verschuuren, J., Bastmeijer, K. & van Lanen, J. (2000). Complaint Procedures and Access to Justice for Citizens and NGOs in the Field of the Environment within the European Union. Report discussed at the EU-IMPEL (European Union Network for the Implementation and Enforcement of Environmental Law) workshop, The Hague, the Netherlands, 10–11 May 2000, https://www.elaw.org/system/files/E.U.--IMPEL.Network%28Complaint.procedures.and.Access.to.Justice.for.citizens.and.NGO%29.pdf accessed 13 April 2014, p. 9.

[736] De Sadeleer, N., Roller, G. & Dross, M. (2005). *Access to Justice in Environmental Matters and the Role of NGOs: Empirical Findings and Legal Appraisal.* Groningen: Europa Law Publishing, p. 169.

judicial procedures to challenge the acts or omissions made by the government (see 5.3.1 and 5.3.2).

5.3.3.3. *Some Lessons for China*

A key issue for individuals and NGOs is how to get a "permit" to have a right to access to justice. Capacity-building is an essential problem not only for individuals, NGOs, judges, but also for the existing legal systems.

Nevertheless, the European Convention on Human Rights, the Aarhus Convention and some EU Directives provide some important guidelines for access to justice. The Aarhus Convention is open to accession by States outside Europe, which thus are not parties to the ECHR.[737] The similarity of the language suggests that, despite the autonomy of the Aarhus Convention vis-à-vis the ECHR, the case law of the European Court of Human Rights provides a binding interpretation on what qualifies as independent and impartial under the Aarhus Convention as well.[738] All the guidelines or bottom lines from the relevant provisions and case law can be useful for China. At least, any person "who considers" that his or her request has been wrongly denied shall be ensured access to review.[739] All these aim at achieving justice when balancing the interests from different parties.

As for the application to protected areas, the principle of social equity and justice requires that stakeholders, particularly those holding or claiming rights over land, sea or resources, should be respected and engaged in protected area design, establishment and management, and should have legal recourse if their rights are violated.[740] In addition, the principle requires the fair and equitable distribution of costs and benefits among the social groups and individuals involved in or affected by the establishment and management of formal protected areas.[741] Local people and communities near or in protected areas, as an affected and vulnerable group, have a right to access to justice, which means that with

---

737 The USA and Canada, which are not parties to the ECHR, did not sign the Aarhus Convention. Yet, they may accede to it in accordance with Article 19(2). Moreover, Article 19(3) of the Aarhus Convention makes it possible also for states which are not members of the UNECE to accede the Convention upon approval by the Meeting of the Parties. These states will not be parties to the ECHR. Neither is the European Communities a party to the ECHR. For detailed information see Ebbesson, J. (2002). Comparative introduction. In: Ebbesson, J. (Ed.). *Access to Justice in Environmental Matters in the EU.* Leiden: Kluwer Law International, p. 16.

738 Ebbesson, J. (2002). Comparative introduction. In: Ebbesson, J. (Ed.). *Access to Justice in Environmental Matters in the EU.* Leiden: Kluwer Law International, p. 16.

739 Ebbesson, J. (2002). European community. In: Ebbesson, J. (Ed.). *Access to Justice in Environmental Matters in the EU.* Leiden: Kluwer Law International, p. 61.

740 Lausche, B. (2011). *Guidelines for Protected Area Legislation*, Gland (Switzerland): IUCN, http://data.iucn.org/dbtw-wpd/edocs/EPLP-081.pdf accessed 8 July 2012, pp. 46–47.

741 Lausche, B. (2011). *Guidelines for Protected Area Legislation*, Gland (Switzerland): IUCN, http://data.iucn.org/dbtw-wpd/edocs/EPLP-081.pdf accessed 8 July 2012, pp. 46–47.

the support of appropriate legal systems, they have an ability to appeal to a court against a decision. Protected areas legislation could include provisions for appeal of administrative decisions authorised by the law.[742] In addition, provisions may recognise the legal standing of citizens and NGOs to bring a legal challenge for violation of their rights or to enforce the law through third-party claims.[743]

742 Lausche, B. (2011). *Guidelines for Protected Area Legislation*, Gland (Switzerland): IUCN, http://data.iucn.org/dbtw-wpd/edocs/EPLP-081.pdf accessed 8 July 2012, pp. 46–47.

743 Lausche, B. (2011). *Guidelines for Protected Area Legislation*, Gland (Switzerland): IUCN, http://data.iucn.org/dbtw-wpd/edocs/EPLP-081.pdf accessed 8 July 2012, pp. 46–47.

CHAPTER 6
CONCLUSIONS FOR PART II

The introduction and discussion on the relationship between the four human rights and protected areas pointed out that the global human rights texts do not explicitly mention environmental protection, let alone protected areas conservation. However, indigenous peoples, as a most relevant group for environmental protection, are already empowered with some rights relevant to environmental protection, although some rights were only included in soft law instruments. The main reason for this is that most early human rights instruments were adopted earlier than environmental instruments. Nevertheless, recent changes in human rights instruments and organs have reflected a developmental tendency towards more concern for environmental protection. For instance, the ILO Convention No. 169 states the right of indigenous peoples to "*participate in the use, management and conservation*" of the natural resources pertaining to their lands.[1] Article 29(1) of the United Nations Declaration on the Rights of Indigenous Peoples strongly holds that "*indigenous peoples have the right to the conservation and protection of the environment.*"[2] In addition, the CERD has applied the principle of free, prior and informed consent (FPIC) in nature conservation (see 5.1.1.1.2).

However, in practice, non-indigenous local people and communities that are concerned with environmental protection should also be taken into account. This is also the main reason why this book uses the term "local people and communities" which has been explained in the introduction chapter (see 1.1.2.1).

Ellen Desmet concludes that: "*except in the European human rights system, attention for the impact of nature conservation at the international level has been almost exclusively focused on the situation of indigenous peoples.*"[3] However, in general, the European human rights organs have been reluctant to pronounce

---

1 Article 15(1), International Labor Organization Convention No. 169: Indigenous and Tribal Peoples Convention, adopted on 27 June 1989 and entered into force on 5 September 1991, 28 ILM 1382, www.ilo.org/indigenous/Conventions/no169/lang--en/index.htm accessed 1 October 2012.

2 Preamble, §11, United Nations Declaration on the Rights of Indigenous Peoples (UNDRIP) was issued on 13 September 2007, UN Doc. A/RES/61/295, www.un.org/esa/socdev/unpfii/documents/DRIPS_en.pdf accessed 30 October 2012.

3 Desmet, E. (2011). *Indigenous Rights Entwined with Nature Conservation*. Antwerp: Intersentia, p. 648.

themselves on the conflict between conservation measures and the interests of individuals or minorities, given the complexity and sensitivity of the issue at stake.[4] A wide margin of appreciation has been left to the national States.[5]

According to what has been introduced and explored, some similar conflicts can be found both in China and in Europe (see 4.4). It is noted that the conflicts regarding human rights protection and protected areas conservation in different countries cannot be easily judged from their "appearance", normally they are the mixed products of political, economic, cultural, historical and legal factors. Similarly, the differences between the existing legal system concerning human rights protection and environmental protection, especially for protected areas conservation, largely depend on several features, which can mainly be summarised as the different traditional cultural background, the different historical stage, the different legal basis and the different knowledge levels of citizens.

It is accepted that it is not enough simply to compare legal words on page for the reason that law both drives and is influenced by the culture of the home country.[6] As for the different traditional cultural background, due to the ancient Confucian concept of social harmony, more attention was paid to the communities' rights rather than individual rights (see 3.1.3.2), in this sense, most of property rights in China belong to the collective; while according to the Roman concepts of *ius* and *dominium* (see 4.1.4), western countries focus a lot on an individual's own right. As explored above, property concepts are "thick" language with social, cultural, economic and even political constructs resonance. It seems that it is impossible to reach an agreement on what property or property rights are in different countries, even if in the different countries in the European region (see 4.1.1), one of the main reasons is the different cultural background. Similarly, three main schools of Chinese traditional ideas (see 5.3.1 "Confucianism, Legalism and Taoism") led the Chinese to try to find other methods to solve conflicts rather than going to court. In addition, the principle of "efficiency in priority, fairness in balance" (see 5.3.3) guides the Chinese to explore a more efficient way to solve most of the conflicts, compared with going to court. Concerning the different historical stages and legal basis in China and in Europe, due to the shorter history of open information and public participation in China, we cannot expect these procedural rights to reach the same level of protection and scope as what European countries have already had for several years. Regarding the different knowledge levels of citizens, "elite democracy"

4 Desmet, E. (2011). *Indigenous Rights Entwined with Nature Conservation.* Antwerp: Intersentia, p. 352.

5 Desmet, E. (2011). *Indigenous Rights Entwined with Nature Conservation.* Antwerp: Intersentia, p. 352.

6 Eberle, J.E. (2009). The method and role of comparative law. *Washington University Global Studies Law Review,* 8(3), http://law.wustl.edu/WUGSLR/Issues/Volume8_3/Eberle.pdf accessed 7 May 2014, p. 452.

and "participatory democracy" (see 5.2.4) may explain the main reason for the differences of public participation in a developing country like China and in European developed countries. These two theories could also be regarded as a foundation for the development of public participation. It is impossible to simply evaluate which one is better or more advanced; however, they are really needed by different societies based on the different knowledge levels of citizens.

Furthermore, when comparing the different legal systems in China and in Europe, it is obvious that there is no independent human rights law in China. However, some recent policies and laws do pay attention to the four human rights in China. In addition, there is no case law on these rights in China; China cannot easily modify the relevant law according to the development of society. When conflict occurs, there might sometimes be a lack of official support from a legal perspective, not only for an individual or a group of victims but also for lawyers and judges if victim wishes to go to court. Conversely, the ECHR, the ECtHR, the Aarhus Convention and the case law from the ACCC and the Directives at the EU are the "supporters" of the four human rights. Some keys for solving the conflicts regarding human rights protection and environmental protection can be found in some case law, if there is no direct answer from the existing laws in Europe. Therefore, some minimum criteria which have been established through the jurisprudence of the European Court of Human Rights would be valuable for improving the existing legal system and for helping to solve the potential conflicts in China.

Undoubtedly, both in theory and in practice, European countries have a relatively more comprehensive legal system to solve the conflicts regarding human rights protection and environmental protection. It is fair to say that it will take a longer time to achieve this in China. It could not have happened in China only in the last few decades for the reason that if China were to take a longer time to solve potential conflicts regarding human rights protection and protected areas conservation, other problems would arise. For instance there would not be so many protected areas in China and the surface of protected areas would not be as big as nowadays within such a short time. This would also reflect the advantage of collective property rights (see 4.4). If there are not that many protected areas in China and the surface is not big enough, biodiversity conservation will be worse than in the present situation. Broadly speaking, there needs to be a balance between legal expectation and legitimate efficiency. Some legal expectations are common sense, especially at the international level; however, it also depends on different situations in different countries. Legitimate efficiency largely depends on and is limited to the development stages of policy, economy, culture and law in a specific country. As for the Chinese situation, since a lot of protected areas have been established and some progress has been made as to biodiversity conservation, we shall devote more attention to stimulate the potential roles of local people and communities in protected areas conservation.

It is the right time to pay more attention to human rights protection. As reflected in *Taşkın and Others v. Turkey*[7] (see 5.2.3.2.3), the most important contribution existing human rights law has to offer with regard to environmental protection and sustainable development is the "empowerment" of individuals and groups affected by "environmental problems". Therefore, empowering local people and communities and conserving protected areas from a human rights perspective would be helpful to achieve sustainable development in China at this stage.

7 ECtHR, Taşkın and Others v. Turkey (2004), App. No. 46117/99, Judgment of 10 November 2004, 30 March 2005 (Final), http://hudoc.echr.coe.int/sites/eng/pages/search.aspx?i=001-67401#{%22itemid%22:[%22001-67401%22]} accessed 5 November 2013.

PART III

IMPLEMENTATION AND GENERAL CONCLUSION

CHAPTER 7

IMPLEMENTING A HUMAN RIGHTS-BASED APPROACH IN PROTECTED AREAS CONSERVATION IN CHINA

Based on what has been discussed in Part I and Part II, this chapter will explore how to implement a human rights-based approach in protected areas conservation in China. Since there is no independent human rights law in China, adopting a human rights-based approach in protected areas conservation means that the law and regulation on protected areas conservation shall take the existing human rights protection at the universal level into account.

7.1. EMPOWERING RIGHTS IN LEGISLATION ON PROTECTED AREAS

If an approach targets all elements, it is far more likely to ensure rights.[1] A human rights-based approach calls for people and institutions that are in power to fulfil their responsibilities toward those people with less rights and power. For the achievement of a human rights-based approach to conservation, a common idea is to support right-holders to be involved in conservation activities and decision-making. Concerning a human rights-based approach to conserving protected areas, it is better to make sure that conservation is undertaken with decency, which means protected areas conservation without humiliating or harming people.

7.1.1. A STAKEHOLDER ANALYSIS

Applying a human rights-based approach also requires that a stakeholder analysis identifies the different actors – the people or organisations that are

---

1 Schuijers, L. (2011). Application of rights-based approach to conservation: the problem of fragmentation and the need for a coordinated response. *Macquarie Journal of International and Comparative Environmental Law*, 7(1), p. 29.

vital to the success or failure of the protected areas.[2] Laws will either forge a compromise between the different interests and therefore become relatively vague and have less influence and control over outcomes; or they will be specific and will come to represent one type of interest while denying others; as such, those whose interests are not protected will accept it less.[3] While the community is dissatisfied with this bargain it can impose constraints through laws, or it can apply force or sanctions to ensure that the collective interest is not ignored.[4]

The following table shows the changing perception of protected areas from different perspectives.

Table 6. The changing perception of protected areas[5]

	As it was (19th century) Protected areas were:	As it is becoming (21st century) Protected areas are:
Objectives	– set aside for conservation – established mainly for spectacular wildlife and scenic protection – managed mainly for visitors and tourists – valued as wilderness – about protection	– run also with social and economic objectives – often set up for scientific, economic cultural reasons – managed more with local people in mind – valued for the cultural importance of "wildness" – also about restoration and rehabilitation
Governance	– run by central government	– run by many partners
Local people	– planned and managed against peoples – managed without regard to local opinions	– run with, for, and in some cases by local people – managed to meet the needs for local people
Wider context	– developed separately – managed as "islands"	– planned as part of national, regional and international systems – developed as "networks" (strictly protected areas, buffered and linked by green corridors)

2 Hesselink, F.J. *et al.* (2007). *Communication, Education and Public Awareness: a Toolkit for the Convention on Biological Convention.* Montreal: Secretariat of the Convention on Biological Diversity, www.cbd.int/cepa/toolkit/2008/doc/CBD-Toolkit-Complete.pdf accessed 3 March 2012.

3 Van Rooij, B. (2006). Implementation of Chinese environmental law: regular enforcement and political campaigns. *Development and Change*, 37(1), pp. 57–74.

4 See generally Coyle S. & Morrow, K. (2004). *The Philosophical Foundations of Environmental Law, Property, Rights and Nature.* Oxford: Hart Publishing; Raff, M. (2005). Toward an ecologically sustainable property concept. In: Cooke, E. (Ed.). *Modern Studies in Property Law* (III). Oxford: Hart Publishing.

5 Phillips, A. (2003). Turning ideas on their head – the new paradigm for protected areas. *The George Wright Forum*, 20 (2), www.uvm.edu/conservationlectures/vermont.pdf accessed 1 March 2013, pp. 8–32.

	As it was (19th century) Protected areas were:	As it is becoming (21st century) Protected areas are:
Perceptions	– viewed primarily as a national asset – viewed only as a national concern	– viewed also as a community asset – viewed also as an international concern
Management	– managed reactively within short timescale	– managed adaptively in long-term perspective
Techniques	– managed in a technocratic way	– managed with political considerations
Finance	– paid for by taxpayer	– paid for by many sources
Management	– managed by scientists and natural resource experts	– managed by multi-skilled individuals
Skills	– expert lead	– drawing on local knowledge

More importantly, the table above indicates two important developmental tendencies: the funding resources and the roles of local people in protected areas conservation. These are also key challenges which China urgently wants to solve (see 1.1.4.1). The table above also further confirms that local people and communities, as the most vulnerable groups, need more attention and protection from various aspects.

7.1.2. EMPOWERING RIGHTS FROM A SUBSTANTIAL PERSPECTIVE

From the perspective of substantial human right protection in protected areas conservation, because of different social, economic, policy, cultural and legal circumstances, it is impossible to judge which forms of property rights are better than others. Different forms of property rights are irreplaceable at certain different stages of society. Property rights are not granted in a vacuum but over a set of existing institutions and thus represent the meeting of formal, State-based and customary or informal local arrangements.[6] This duality in the nature of property translated into unresolved tensions about whether the rights of the landowner are only constrained by clearly specified legal accountability, or whether there are broader social responsibilities reflected in the term "care" that form part of owners' responsibilities that accompany their property rights.[7]

6 Larson, A.M., Cronkleton, P., Barry, D. & Pacheco, P. (2008). *Tenure Rights and Beyond: Community Access to Forest Resources in Latin America.* Occasional Paper No. 50, Bogor (Indonesia): CIFOR, www.pefc.org/images/stories/documents/external/OP-50.pdf accessed 4 August 2012.

7 Shepheard, M. & Martin, P. (2012). The political discourse of land stewardship reframed as a statutory duty. In: Jessup, B. & Rubenstein, K. (Ed.). *Environmental Discourses in Public and International Law.* Cambridge: Cambridge University Press, p. 78.

Furthermore, the legislator shall be aware that the proportionality principle, for instance, when imposing burdens on private property or collective property, the goal must be important enough to justify the measure. That is to say, the goal shall aim to guarantee the general interest (see 4.3.2.2). Also, reasonable compensation, as a better solution for a fair balance and an element of the proportionality principle, shall be provided. In other words, compensation for sacrificing property interests in the public interest: if an administrative action imposes a significant burden on private property thereby treating the proprietor differently and sacrificing his individual interest for the better of the general interest, and if the law does not provide a duty to compensate, then a judge-made law compensation must be provided.[8] There is a similar requirement for collective property rights; the main difference is a duty to compensate for a group of people. If there is no judge-made law in some legal systems in some countries, more specifically local regulations should be made. It would be better to empower the right-holders a right to compensation, not only providing clear standards but also providing procedures for payments and negotiations, no matter the manner in which their land has been taken, whether it is through expropriation or not, in a legal or illegal manner. A true change that would link compensation to land market value seems difficult to accomplish.[9] First, there may not be sufficient support to make such a change in the national legislation, and second, as long as the land market is not well developed, it remains difficult to determine a fair price on which to base such compensation.[10] This is particular true in China with diverse situations in different regions, thus it would take a longer time to achieve a fair price for compensation.

7.1.3. EMPOWERING RIGHTS FROM A PROCEDURAL PERSPECTIVE

Only talking about property right without any procedural rights is neither rationale nor viable. As indicated in the introduction chapter (see 1.1.4.3), "*low levels of consultation and representation triggered high levels of resistance*" for protected areas. Indeed, procedural human rights can be a useful toolbox to solve the potential conflicts, and procedural human rights of local people and

8 Winter, G. (2005). Conflicts between ownership rights and the implementation of the 'Natura 2000' Network. In: Paques, M. (Ed.). *Natura 2000 and Property Rights: International and National Reports*. Brussels: Etablissements Emile Bruylant, p. 106.

9 Van Rooij, B. (2010). Land loss and conflict in China: illustrated by cases from Yunnan province. In: Ubink, J.M., Hoekema, A.J. & Assies, W.J. (Eds.). *Legalizing Land Rights – Local Practices, State Responses and Tenure Security in Africa, Asia and Latin America*. Leiden: Leiden University Press, p. 447.

10 Ding, C.R. (2007). Policy and praxis of land acquisition in China. *Land Use Policy*, 24(1), pp. 1–13.

communities could make a great contribution for protected areas conservation. The first and key step is to empower local people and communities. It aims to enable them to access information, voice their opinion, devote their local knowledge, and assume greater roles in protected areas conservation activities. It often leads to positive changes concerning the guarantee of their livelihoods and the conservation for protected areas. However, determining what weight should be given to their opinions is a vexing question.[11]

Historically, the Chinese have tended to guide social behaviour rather by using moral precepts and customs than by formal laws.[12] Only recently, China has made great effort at environmental law making and enforcing regulations and has developed a relatively comprehensive environmental protection regulatory framework.[13] Such methods may be insufficient.

Much more progress needs to be made. Direct work on changing the power relations and empowering the relevant parties, especially local people and communities, in legislation is urgent.[14] Such empowerment first requires enhancing their access to the legal system, strengthening the role of civil society, while work should also focus on general development activities such as literacy training, strengthening community organisation, and legal awareness promotion.[15]

One of the key points of empowering rights in legislation in China is how to divide the power or interests for the different relevant parties and find a balance between human rights protection and protected areas conservation.[16]

---

11 Gilmour, D.A., Durst, P.B. & Shono, K. (2007). *Reaching Consensus, Multi-stakeholder Processes in Forestry: Experiences from the Asia-Pacific Region.* Bangkok: Food and Agriculture Organization of the United Nations Regional Office for Asia and the Pacific, ftp://ftp. fao.org/docrep/fao/010/ai390e/ai390e00.pdf accessed 15 December 2013.

12 Beyer, S. (2006). Environmental law and policy in the people's republic of China. *Chinese Journal of International Law*, 5(1), p. 185.

13 Cun-kuan, B., Yong-sen, L. *et al.* (2004). Framework and operational procedure for implementing strategic environmental assessment in China. *Environmental Impact Assessment Review*, 24(1), pp. 27–46; Gu, L. & Sheate, W.R. (2005). Institutional challenges for EIA implementation in China: a case study of development versus environmental protection. *Environmental Management*, 36(1), pp. 125–142; Beyer, S. (2006). *Environmental law and policy in the people's republic of China.* Oxford: Oxford University Press; Van Rooij, B. (2006) Implementation of Chinese environmental law: regular enforcement and political campaigns. *Development and Change*, 37(1), pp. 57–74; Zhu, T. & Lam, K.C. (2009). *Environmental Impact Assessment in China, Research Centre for Strategic Environmental Assessment.* Nanjing: Nankai University Press.

14 He, M. & Cliquet, A. (2013). Sustainable development through a rights-based approach to conserve protected areas in China. *China-EU Law Journal.* DOI 10.1007/s 12689-013-0031-7. http://link.springer.com/article/10.1007%2Fs12689-013-0031-7 accessed 4 November 2013.

15 Ubink, J.M., Hoekema, A.J. & Assies, W.J. (2010). *Legalizing Land Rights: Local Practices, State Responses and Tenure Security in Africa, Asia and Latin America.* Leiden: Leiden University Press, p. 25.

16 He, M. & Cliquet, A. (2013). Sustainable development through a rights-based approach to conserve protected areas in China. *China-EU Law Journal.* DOI 10.1007/s 12689-013-0031-7. http://link.springer.com/article/10.1007%2Fs12689-013-0031-7 accessed 4 November 2013.

Broadly speaking, nature conservation and human rights protection can be achieved in a relevant high position at the same time rather than they are like a zero-sum game.[17] Thus, to create an institutional framework becomes an important issue. Firstly, it is necessary to establish an accountability system of the local governments and the relevant departments. The local governments and relevant departments play an irreplaceable role in safeguarding the interests of local people and communities. Secondly, a dynamic management of protected areas could be useful. The local governments may need to change the policy depending on the different local situations or the different periods but the final goal is to clarify rights and duties and to balance the conflicts regarding human rights protection and protected areas conservation. For instance, China can learn from the successful experience from abroad to establish a contract system with the local people and communities to safeguard their interests. If all the relevant parties have signed the "management contract", they are bound by the contract; the relevant party (parties) who lost the interests shall get a reasonable compensation from the benefit party (parties). Even if various measures will be taken by different local governments according to different real situations in different regions, some "universal minimum" (or "baselines and principles") of what would be acceptable and useful (see Part II) cannot be violated.

7.1.3.1. Empowering the Right to Information

As for empowering the right to information, applying the principle of access to information through legislation promotes transparency of government decision-making.[18] Transparency enhances legitimacy, accountability and overall performance with respect to establishing and managing protected areas systems and sites.[19] Enough information is provided to understand and monitor institutions and their decision-making processes. We need a perfect information disclosure system for a better foundation of public participation.[20] When laws require more extensive environmental studies and mandate sharing environmental information with the public, governments will find that a consensus exists for environmental stewardship mandates.[21]

17 He, M. & Cliquet, A. (2013). Sustainable development through a rights-based approach to conserve protected areas in China. *China-EU Law Journal.* DOI 10.1007/s 12689-013-0031-7. http://link.springer.com/article/10.1007%2Fs12689-013-0031-7 accessed 4 November 2013.

18 Lausche, B. (2011). *Guidelines for Protected Area Legislation*, Gland (Switzerland): IUCN, http://data.iucn.org/dbtw-wpd/edocs/EPLP-081.pdf accessed 8 July 2012, p. 45.

19 Lausche, B. (2011). *Guidelines for Protected Area Legislation*, Gland (Switzerland): IUCN, http://data.iucn.org/dbtw-wpd/edocs/EPLP-081.pdf accessed 8 July 2012, p. 45.

20 Wang, H. (2009). Public participation in environmental management from the perspective of China. Discussion Papers in Social Responsibility, www.socialresponsibility.biz accessed 8 August 2012.

21 Robinson, N.A. (2012). Keynote address: a cannon for the anthropocene. In: "Rule of Law for Nature" Conference, Oslo University, Oslo, Norway, 9–11 May 2012.

Besides these, it is widely accepted that some reasonable restrictions on the right to information are necessary in a democratic society (see 5.1.3.2.2 and 5.1.3.4.3). It means that there are some reasonable restrictions on this right; and more importantly it means that people shall have the right to know what the restrictions are.

7.1.3.2. Empowering the Right to Participation

With regards to the right to participation, a distinction must be made between "shallow" forms of participation (e.g. passive engagement of stakeholders to "inform" them about what the decision will be, or consultations that do not include real opportunities to influence decisions), and "meaningful" participation.[22] A right to participation implies actively engaging with concerned parties, including marginalised or vulnerable right-holders, through transparent processes including appropriate power-sharing arrangements.[23] The importance of "co-learning" between local and scientific knowledge can be developed through local participation. Local participation may reduce a costly level of conflict in protected areas through increased legitimacy of the protection process of protected areas.[24] Decisions where public participation is particularly important and should be emphasised in legislation, include designating or amending a protected area, designating site management authorities, developing and approving a management plan, configuring and laying out a strategy for a protected area system plan, and reviewing a draft environmental and social impact assessment regarding proposed actions of the protected areas agency.[25] Clearly, more information is needed and participation is also required in the assessment of projects and plans which may have a possible negative effects on the protected areas.[26]

22 Springer, J., Campese, J. & Painter, M. (2011). Conservation and human rights: key issues and contexts scoping paper for the conservation initiative on human rights. Published in October 2011 https://community.iucn.org/cihr/Resources/Scoping%20Paper%20_Oct%20final.pdf accessed 30 October 2011, p. 21.

23 Regarding "degrees" of participation or power-sharing, see various versions of the "ladder or participation" (originally from Arnstein 1969), or the continuum of power-sharing arrangements from government-management to community-management in the context of co-management. See Springer, J., Campese, J. & Painter, M. (2011). Conservation and human rights: key issues and contexts scoping paper for the conservation initiative on human rights. Published in October 2011 https://community.iucn.org/cihr/Resources/Scoping%20 Paper%20_Oct%20final.pdf accessed 30 October 2011, p. 21.

24 Daugstad, K. The participatory dimension in nature conservation processes: examples of ideology and practice from Norway, http://download.springer.com/static/pdf/881/chp%253A 10.1007%252F978-90-481-9932-7_4.pdf?auth66=1379691801_f410c70c246033b6f9687fe81e 0b796d&ext=.pdf accessed 9 August 2013.

25 Lausche, B. (2011). *Guidelines for Protected Area Legislation*, Gland (Switzerland): IUCN, http://data.iucn.org/dbtw-wpd/edocs/EPLP-081.pdf accessed 8 July 2012, p. 45.

26 He, M. & Cliquet, A. (2013). Sustainable development through a rights-based approach to conserve protected areas in China. *China-EU Law Journal*. DOI 10.1007/s 12689-013-0031-7. http://link.springer.com/article/10.1007%2Fs12689-013-0031-7 accessed 4 November 2013.

Moreover, participatory processes can occur at multiple levels (from projects to national and international policy) and should not be exclusively government or NGO led; rather, community-led processes should also be supported and respected.[27] Some NGOs have the capacity to serve as facilitators of communication and cooperation between governments and local communities, or between local communities or governments and the private sector. Such role of facilitator may enable a more positive relationship among the stakeholders. In a conflict situation, NGOs are often well suited as mediators because they can be perceived as more neutral than protected areas managers or other government officials.[28] In other cases, NGOs may negotiate on behalf of certain interest groups, such as local communities.[29] Partnerships between NGOs and local communities may help to increase their effectiveness in confronting the power of other interests that might operate contrary to the interests of the objectives of the protected areas. All of these aim to solve the conflicts and to achieve a multiplicity of goals, namely to support the full and effective participation and involvement of local people and communities in all planning and management phases and properly take into account their natural, social, environmental and cultural concerns and interests.

Furthermore, as indicated above (see Part II), the Aarhus Convention is considered to be the most advanced environmental agreement in providing standards for public participation.[30] The Aarhus Convention itself is not geographically limited to European States, but is open for accession by any State willing to introduce environmental democracy.[31] Certainly, there are some differences in social, cultural, legal and political perspectives between China and Member States in the Convention, but China could nevertheless adopt similar laws or principles to safeguard the Chinese government's positive obligation in protected areas conservation and to guarantee peoples' right in protected areas

---

27 Springer, J., Campese, J. & Painter, M. (2011). Conservation and human rights: key issues and contexts scoping paper for the conservation initiative on human rights. Published in October 2011 https://community.iucn.org/cihr/Resources/Scoping%20Paper%20_Oct%20final.pdf accessed 30 October 2011, p. 22.

28 McNeely, J.A., Lockwood, M. & Chapman, J. (2006). Building support for protected areas. In: Lockwood, M., Kothari, A. & Worboys, G. (Eds.). *Managing Protected Areas: a Global Guide*. London: Earthscan, p. 665.

29 McNeely, J.A., Lockwood, M. & Chapman, J. (2006). Building support for protected areas. In: Lockwood, M., Kothari, A. & Worboys, G. (Eds.). *Managing Protected Areas: a Global Guide*. London: Earthscan, p. 665.

30 Boyle, A. & Boer, B. (2013). Human rights and the environment. In: the Thirteenth Informal ASEM (Asia-Europe Meeting) Seminar on Human Rights, Copenhagen, Denmark, 21–23 October 2013, http://asef.org/images/docs/13th%20Informal%20ASEM%20Seminar%20-%20Background%20paper%20%28FINAL%29.pdf accessed 1 November 2013, p. 41.

31 The Convention is open for accession to all UNECE-Member States and those States having been granted consultative status with the UNECE, such as USA and Canada. Moreover, Article 19(2) foresees the admission of any other State subject to the approval by the Meeting of Parties.

conservation. And indeed, at least, some "spirits" of the Aarhus Convention could be good lessons for China to improve the legal system and practice.

7.1.3.3. Empowering the Right to Access to Justice

Regarding the right to access to justice, legislative changes should be combined with measures that help to enhance implementation.[32] Such measures should be a combination of improving the implementation of legislation and regulation, increasing possibilities for the public, especially for the vulnerable people, to have a real right to access to justice from both substantial and procedural perspectives. Limited to the procedural perspective in this book, to provide the public formal legal standing and to increase their awareness to guarantee their rights is the first step that should be taken in China. In this way, the public could have more capacity to go to a court; at least they could have more effective channels to guarantee their appropriate interests.

Last but not least, to empower rights means "empowerment" and "rights" from both the inner angle (for instance the support from law and policy) and the external angle (for instance the legal capacity of local people and communities). It means that special laws and regulations should not neglect to include environmental education.[33] It can explain public rights, obligations of environmental education and the investment use of an environmental education fund, the affiliation of each department and a division for a monitoring sector with respective responsibilities for environmental education and execution.[34] This will promote the realisation of empowerment.

7.2. SAFEGUARDING RIGHTS IN THE ENFORCEMENT OF LEGISLATION ON PROTECTED AREAS

The aim of a good human rights-based approach is to ultimately increase the likelihood that rights are realised – ideally, to the level of certainty.[35] If there is no legislative framework that provides for enforcement remedies and deterrents

32 Ubink, J.M., Hoekema, A.J. & Assies, W.J. (2010). *Legalizing Land Rights: Local Practices, State Responses and Tenure Security in Africa, Asia and Latin America*. Leiden: Leiden University Press, p. 25.

33 He, M. & Cliquet, A. (2013). Sustainable development through a rights-based approach to conserve protected areas in China. *China-EU Law Journal*. DOI 10.1007/s 12689-013-0031-7. http://link.springer.com/article/10.1007%2Fs12689-013-0031-7 accessed 4 November 2013.

34 Wang, H. (2009). Public participation in environmental management from the perspective of China. Discussion Papers in Social Responsibility, www.socialresponsibility.biz accessed 8 August 2012.

35 Schuijers, L. (2011). Application of rights-based approach to conservation: the problem of fragmentation and the need for a coordinated response. *Macquarie Journal of International and Comparative Environmental Law*, 7(1), p. 29.

for breaching rights, then once again rights cannot be ensured, at least in a long-term capacity.[36] In other words, changes in legislation alone will not be sufficient to decrease current conflicts regarding human rights protection and protected areas conservation. When new rights are granted, or the existing rights are recognised, safeguarding rights in the enforcement of legislation will be the second step.

7.2.1. SAFEGUARDING RIGHTS IN THE ENFORCEMENT FROM A SUBSTANTIAL PERSPECTIVE

Generally, in China the success or failure of laws depends on how effectively they are enforced, especially at the local level.[37] Securing property rights requires the community as a whole to support an owner or user in defending their interest. This implies a social consensus about responsibility and freedom to exploit in which way and to what extent safeguard property rights.[38]

7.2.2. SAFEGUARDING RIGHTS IN THE ENFORCEMENT FROM A PROCEDURAL PERSPECTIVE

7.2.2.1. To Provide Information

The first step is to provide information to the relevant parties by various channels, especially for specific information regarding legal rights, claims and duties of potentially affected persons.[39] It is very important to let the relevant parties, especially the vulnerable parties, know which rights they can enjoy, which duties they must bear and how to guarantee their rights and interests.[40]

---

36 Schuijers, L. (2011). Application of rights-based approach to conservation: the problem of fragmentation and the need for a coordinated response. *Macquarie Journal of International and Comparative Environmental Law*, 7(1), p. 29.

37 Beyer, S. (2006). Environmental law and policy in the people's republic of China. *Chinese Journal of International Law*, 5(1), p. 185.

38 Martin, P. & Verbeek, M. (2002). Property rights and Property Responsibility. In: Land and Water Australia (Ed.). *Property: Rights and Responsibilities – Current Australian Thinking.* Canberra: Land and Water Australia, p. 1.

39 He, M. & Cliquet, A. (2013). Sustainable development through a rights-based approach to conserve protected areas in China. *China-EU Law Journal.* DOI 10.1007/s 12689-013-0031-7. http://link.springer.com/article/10.1007%2Fs12689-013-0031-7 accessed 4 November 2013.

40 He, M. & Cliquet, A. (2013). Sustainable development through a rights-based approach to conserve protected areas in China. *China-EU Law Journal.* DOI 10.1007/s 12689-013-0031-7. http://link.springer.com/article/10.1007%2Fs12689-013-0031-7 accessed 4 November 2013.

It is noted that in a time of rapid change, access to information is uneven, and many NGOs have been mobilised to help redress this imbalance.[41] Actually, many NGOs are best characterised as organisations designed to collect, process and transmit information, especially to influence public opinion or change government behaviour. In this sense, NGOs have been major contributors to protected areas in virtually all countries because they often publish newsletters, issue press releases and publish various kinds of books, field guides and other products to spread the related information to the public.

7.2.2.2. To Ensure Participation

The second step is to ensure participation with a goal of changing stakeholders' actions from infringement to involvement. If uncertain activities would infringe upon the rights of the relevant parties, the involvement of the related parties is meaningful for both the sustainable development of conservation activities and the interests of the related parties. Active participation would link people who have different interests and may help in acknowledging the needs of all stakeholders in the early stages of a potential infringement. Active dialogue and common understanding of stakeholders and their needs would be an irreplaceable step for solving these infringements or conflicts. The levels of participation are frequently portrayed as steps on a ladder, moving from informing, to information seeking, to consultation, and then to deciding together, and acting together, and finally seeking a possible remedy if it is necessary.[42] In this way, all the relevant parties could act together in the informed decision-making process and more importantly take their own appropriate responsibility for implementing decisions. In practice, NGOs could provide an outlet for those who "do not have a voice"; in other words marginalised members of society who do not belong to powerful associations nor occupy high-ranking positions.[43] This potential power from environmental NGOs in China could make a great contribution to protected areas conservation and management.

Ongoing engagement and consultation with stakeholders to create opportunities and channels for dialogue between duty-bearers and rights-holders can significantly increase the probability of realising sustainable outcomes.[44]

---

41 McNeely, J.A., Lockwood, M. & Chapman, J. (2006). Building support for protected areas. In: Lockwood, M., Kothari, A. & Worboys, G. (Eds.). *Managing Protected Areas: a Global Guide*. London: Earthscan, p. 665.

42 He, M. & Cliquet, A. (2013). Sustainable development through a rights-based approach to conserve protected areas in China. *China-EU Law Journal*. DOI 10.1007/s 12689-013-0031-7. http://link.springer.com/article/10.1007%2Fs12689-013-0031-7 accessed 4 November 2013.

43 Public participation and sustainable development on-line module, www.docstoc.com/docs/44508222/Public-Participation-and-Sustainable-Development-On-Line-Module accessed 25 October 2013, p. 7.

44 Berman, G. (2008). Undertaking a Human Rights-based Approach: a Guide for Basic Programming – Documenting Lessons Learned for Human Rights-based Programming: an

As pointed out above, Article 8(j) of the CBD requires that a State must as far as possible and appropriate, "*subject to its national legislation, respect, preserve and maintain knowledge innovations and practices of indigenous and local communities embodying traditional lifestyles relevant for the conservation of and sustainable use if biological diversity and promote their wider application with the approval and involvement of the holders of such knowledge, innovations and practices and encourage the equitable sharing of the benefits arising from the utilization of such knowledge, innovation and practices.*" The traditional knowledge should be obtained only from individuals who hold it and have the authority to release it. For instance, natural scientists or administrative officers who manage protected areas sometimes lack a thorough understanding of traditional ecological knowledge or characteristics of local areas, thus they are unable to respond properly to potential conflicts. Traditional ecological knowledge possessed by local people and communities can be extremely beneficial in the scientific understanding of ecosystem functioning and biological interactions.[45] However, strengthening this local involvement in the governance and conservation of protected areas raises questions about the willingness and ability of local communities to prioritise conservation issues over economic and rural development.[46] This is also the reason that China needs more time to involve local people and communities to participate in the governance and conservation in protected areas based on the stage of economic and rural development. In Europe, public participation focuses more on "early" and "effective" factors. The key issue is how to promote initiatives of the citizens, how to improve their capacity, especially for the local people and communities, and how to realise "early" and "effective" public participation in practice in China.

To promote public participation in protected areas management is not only the inherent requirement of achieving human rights protection, but also an important method to improve the level of protected areas management.[47] All men and women should have a voice in decision-making, either directly or through legitimate intermediate institutions that represent their intention. This kind of broad participation is built on fostering dialogue and achieving

---

Asia-pacific Perspective – Implications for Policy, Planning and Programming. Bangkok: UNESCO Asia and Pacific Regional Bureau for Education, http://unesdoc.unesco.org/images/0017/001791/179186e.pdf accessed 14 September 2012, p. 33.

45 Robinson, J.G. & Redford, K.H. (2004). Jack of all trades, master of none: Inherent contradictions among ICD approaches. In: McShane, T.O. & Wells, M.P., *Getting Biodiversity Projects to Work: towards More Effective Conservation and Development.* New York: Colombia University Press, pp. 10–34.

46 Fauchald, O.K. & Gulbrandsen, L.H. (2012). The Norwegian reform of protected areas management: a grand experiment with delegation of authority? *Local Environment: the International Journal of Justice And Sustainability*, 17(2), DOI 10.1080/13549839.2012.660910, www.fni.no/doc&pdf/OKF-LHG-LE-2012.pdf accessed 11 October 2013.

47 He, M. & Cliquet, A. (2013). Sustainable development through a rights-based approach to conserve protected areas in China. *China-EU Law Journal.* DOI 10.1007/s 12689–013–0031–7. http://link.springer.com/article/10.1007%2Fs12689–013–0031–7 accessed 4 November 2013.

collective agreements on management objectives and strategy, activities and tools among different parties. This has been proved by some good examples in practice. For instance, the Global Environment Fund (GEF) has made a proposal on Protected Areas Management in China in August 1995; ten protected areas in five provinces have adopted community co-management.[48] The core goal is to sustainably manage the natural resources and to increase the economic benefits for all the relevant parties.[49] It has achieved a better benefit from ecological, economic and social perspectives.

7.2.2.3. To Explore the Corresponding Environmental Education

Exploring the corresponding environmental education according to different regions and groups is the third step.[50] In order to increase public environmental protection awareness, educational methods of multi-objectives and multi-forms should be used.[51] Interesting and vivid forms of education will be more effective to make environmental protection become an important social morality standard.[52] Notably, Article 3(3) of the Aarhus Convention calls on the Contracting Parties to promote environmental education and environmental awareness among the public. It is fair to say that today average environmental awareness and concern of the general public in China is higher than before due to years of environmental education, the enforcement of environmental laws and environmental practice. However, there is still a lot of room for improvement in the rural areas in China.

7.2.2.4. To Stimulate the Enthusiasm of the Relevant Parties

Stimulating the enthusiasm of the relevant parties by balancing their interests will be the fourth step.[53] This phase involves shifting from legal passive

48 www.globalenvironmentfund.com/ accessed 5 May 2012.

49 He, M. & Cliquet, A. (2013). Sustainable development through a rights-based approach to conserve protected areas in China. *China-EU Law Journal*. DOI 10.1007/s 12689-013-0031-7. http://link.springer.com/article/10.1007%2Fs12689-013-0031-7 accessed 4 November 2013.

50 He, M. & Cliquet, A. (2013). Sustainable development through a rights-based approach to conserve protected areas in China. *China-EU Law Journal*. DOI 10.1007/s 12689-013-0031-7. http://link.springer.com/article/10.1007%2Fs12689-013-0031-7 accessed 4 November 2013.

51 Wang, H. (2009). Public participation in environmental management from the perspective of China. Discussion Papers in Social Responsibility, www.socialresponsibility.biz accessed 8 August 2012.

52 Xiong, Y. (熊鹰) (2007). *Effect Analysis of Government Environmental Regulation and Public Participation on Enterprise Pollution Behavior.* (政府环境管制、公众参与与对企业污染行为的影响分析). Doctorate Dissertation of Nanjing Agricultural University (南京农业大学博士论文), pp. 106–107.

53 He, M. & Cliquet, A. (2013). Sustainable development through a rights-based approach to conserve protected areas in China. *China-EU Law Journal*. DOI 10.1007/s 12689-013-0031-7. http://link.springer.com/article/10.1007%2Fs12689-013-0031-7 accessed 4 November 2013.

conservation of protected areas to initiative protection, especially for local residents.[54] The number and influence of environmental NGOs in China have increased in the past three decades.[55] NGOs can help the government and relevant departments to handle the complex people-protected areas conflicts and to facilitate genuine bottom-up participation in China.[56] However, at a time when NGOs and other lobbying groups become more and more professional, it is important to make sure that influence and access to participation is not merely shifted from the executive branches of government to powerful and influential NGOs pursuing their specific interests with little public mandate.[57] This is another problem that should be taken into account later.

Therefore, safeguarding rights in the enforcement is a way to guarantee that a goal will be achieved and results in a win-win outcome. Then, evaluation will be necessary to assess how this process is going on.

7.3. MONITORING AND EVALUATING APPLICATION OF THE HUMAN RIGHTS-BASED APPROACH

There is a risk that commitments made in legal instruments will remain an empty promise without effective monitoring and accountability.[58] In general terms, monitoring is used to check that objectives and targets have been achieved, to identify new issues and potential impacts and as a feedback mechanism to modify and improve practices.[59]

Domestic environmental laws can be most effective if they have designated an authority and created an appropriate institutional framework to enforce the law, including the establishment of a "watchdog" to monitor and verify that

---

54 He, M. & Cliquet, A. (2013). Sustainable development through a rights-based approach to conserve protected areas in China. *China-EU Law Journal*. DOI 10.1007/s 12689-013-0031-7. http://link.springer.com/article/10.1007%2Fs12689-013-0031-7 accessed 4 November 2013.

55 He, M. & Cliquet, A. (2013). Sustainable development through a rights-based approach to conserve protected areas in China. *China-EU Law Journal*. DOI 10.1007/s 12689-013-0031-7. http://link.springer.com/article/10.1007%2Fs12689-013-0031-7 accessed 4 November 2013.

56 He, M. & Cliquet, A. (2013). Sustainable development through a rights-based approach to conserve protected areas in China. *China-EU Law Journal*. DOI 10.1007/s 12689-013-0031-7. http://link.springer.com/article/10.1007%2Fs12689-013-0031-7 accessed 4 November 2013.

57 Pedersen, O.W. (2008). European environmental human rights and environmental rights: a long time coming? *Georgetown International Environmental Law Review*, 21, p. 99.

58 He, M. & Cliquet, A. (2013). Sustainable development through a rights-based approach to conserve protected areas in China. *China-EU Law Journal*. DOI 10.1007/s 12689-013-0031-7. http://link.springer.com/article/10.1007%2Fs12689-013-0031-7 accessed 4 November 2013.

59 The Energy & Biodiversity Initiative (EBI). Biodiversity indicators for monitoring impacts and conservation actions. www.theebi.org/pdfs/indicators.pdf accessed 28 February 2014.

the decision-making process is transparent, participatory and accountable.[60] Environmental impact assessment is of vital importance. However, when investigating and studying the activities that might infringe human rights, the impact assessment on human rights cannot be ignored. The Committee on Economic, Social and Cultural Rights has already encouraged states "*to introduce 'human rights impact assessments', comparable to environmental impact assessments, to ensure that the provisions of the Covenant are given due attention in all legislative and administrative policy and decision-making processes.*"[61] According to the Human Rights Impact Resource Centre, the goal of a human rights impact assessment is to "*measure the impact of policies, programmes, projects and interventions on human rights.*"[62] This goal would be useful to assess actions that will have a direct or indirect impact on human rights. Undoubtedly, protected areas conservation and certain activities such as project development in or near protected areas could have an impact on human rights. In this sense, the impact assessment on human rights is an irreplaceable step to implement a human rights-based approach to conserve protected areas.

Specifically, just as what has been discussed in the section of "the decision-making process must involve appropriate investigations and studies" (see 5.2.3.2.2), after some appropriate investigations and studies, we may predict and evaluate if these activities (for instance in order to establish or enlarge a protected area or an infrastructure project in or near a protected area) would infringe which parties' rights or interests. And then, some possible measures for reasonable compensation or guaranteeing the relevant rights could be taken, in order to achieve a balance between human rights protection and protected areas conservation.

When evaluating the rights in the enforcement of legislation on protected areas, it is necessary to assess the baseline and indicator context, as to ensure which rights are being respected and protected for the vulnerable groups.[63] Specifics may vary, but it is important to "map" the lines of authority that apply to the implementation of any specific environmental policy in any given locality.[64] The historical, cultural and social complexities in which the long-term

60 Razzaque, J. Field (the Foundation for International Environmental Law and Development), http://pubs.iied.org/pdfs/G00466.pdf accessed 1 October 2013.

61 UNESC (United Nations Economic and Social Council) (2001). Concluding observations of the Committee on Economic, Social and Cultural Rights: Germany. UN Doc. E/C.12/1Add.68, §32, www.institut-fuer-menschenrechte.de/fileadmin/user_upload/PDF-Dateien/Pakte_Konventionen/ICESCR/icescr_state_report_germany_4_2000_cobs_2001_en.pdf accessed 12 March 2014.

62 Human Rights Impact Resource Centre. *Human Rights Impact Assessment Guide*, www.humanrightsimpact.org/hria-guide accessed 12 March 2014.

63 He, M. & Cliquet, A. (2013). Sustainable development through a rights-based approach to conserve protected areas in China. *China-EU Law Journal*. DOI 10.1007/s 12689-013-0031-7. http://link.springer.com/article/10.1007%2Fs12689-013-0031-7 accessed 4 November 2013.

64 Lieberthal, K. (1997) China's governing system and its impact on environmental policy implementation. *China Environment Series*, 1, pp. 3–8.

perspective is grounded are understood and taken into account effectively. It is necessary to clarify specific objectives for different protected areas, as well as partnerships, and associated adaptive management initiatives, and meanwhile, to ensure consistency with international conventions, national legislation and agreements, and traditional or "modern" best practices. A full set of indicators for assessing human rights and protected areas should include:[65] (1) structural indicators, which measure whether appropriate legal, regulatory, and institutional structures are in place that are considered necessary or useful for the realisation of conservation with justice; (2) process indicators, which provide information on the processes by which the aims of conservation with justice have been respected in the design, implementation, and conclusion of the project or activity; and (3) outcome indicators, which provide information on the extent of realisation of conservation consistent with human rights. Regularly engaging in monitoring and evaluation can be an effective way to change in response to findings as part of an adaptive management strategy.

As for the Chinese situation, the conservation of protected areas is a big challenge as a result of issues such as an increasing vast population and the limitation of per capita land resources.[66] In the case of large protected areas, there might be a heavy economic burden on the local government, especially when these large protected areas were newly established. It is possible that a serious conflict between the exploration and protection for natural resources can occur, especially in the eastern developed region.[67] In the north-western developing region with a smaller population, if there is a large core area, it could also cause a conflict between protection and grazing.[68] Notably, Article 2 of the Bern Convention also indicates that measures on protected areas conservation are to take into account economic, social and cultural requirements and regional and local characteristics. Although this convention is about Europe, it points out the main concerns in protected areas conservation. In this sense, different protected areas in different regions would lead to different concerns as to monitoring and evaluation.

Thus, the baseline and indicator for assessing rights when evaluating the enforcement will be different depending on different regions, but the guideline is

---

65 Greiber, T. *et al.* (2009). Conservation with justice – a human rights based approach. Gland (Switzerland): IUCN Environmental Law Centre, http://data.iucn.org/dbtw-wpd/edocs/eplp-071.pdf accessed 28 October 2011, p. 27.

66 He, M. & Cliquet, A. (2013). Sustainable development through a rights-based approach to conserve protected areas in China. *China-EU Law Journal.* DOI 10.1007/s 12689-013-0031-7. http://link.springer.com/article/10.1007%2Fs12689-013-0031-7 accessed 4 November 2013.

67 He, M. & Cliquet, A. (2013). Sustainable development through a rights-based approach to conserve protected areas in China. *China-EU Law Journal.* DOI 10.1007/s 12689-013-0031-7. http://link.springer.com/article/10.1007%2Fs12689-013-0031-7 accessed 4 November 2013.

68 Cui, G.Y. (2004). Some scientific issues need to be solved in protected areas. *Beijing Forest University Newspaper,* 26 (6).

the same, which is to promote the win-win outcome for human rights protection and protected areas conservation.

7.4. PROVIDING A LEGAL REMEDY

Without effective and adequate remedies, access to justice would matter little.[69] Similarly, rights are not realisable unless someone is accountable for them, and unless the person whose rights have been breached has effective access to a justice system that will hold that someone to account.[70]

If the implementation does not go well, a legal remedy could help to solve the conflicts.[71] The first possibility includes compensation for owners or users. There are different kinds of compensation.

(1) *A financial indemnity.* Preferably, full compensation should be awarded to all claimants before the government takes possession of the land.[72] For instance, the local government gives a financial indemnity to farmers for their farmland used for a forest protected area. When the State expropriates collectively-owned agricultural land for one of the permissible public purposes designated herein, it must provide compensation to the owners and land-use right-holders of all affected land.[73] The amount of compensation in China is determined by statute. Current compensation standards can be found in the "Land Management Law" (2004 version).[74] Under this law, compensation for arable land expropriation includes: (a) compensation for the loss of land; (b) compensation for young crops

---

69 Ebbesson, J. (2011). Access to justice at the national level: impact of the Aarhus Convention and European Union law. In: Pallemaerts, M. (Ed.). *The Aarhus Convention at Ten: Interactions and Tensions between Conventional International Law and EU Environmental Law.* Groningen: Europa Law Publishing, p. 260.

70 Schuijers, L. (2011). Application of rights-based approach to conservation: the problem of fragmentation and the need for a coordinated response. *Macquarie Journal of International and Comparative Environmental Law*, 7(1), p. 37.

71 He, M. & Cliquet, A. (2013). Sustainable development through a rights-based approach to conserve protected areas in China. *China-EU Law Journal.* DOI 10.1007/s 12689-013-0031-7. http://link.springer.com/article/10.1007%2Fs12689-013-0031-7 accessed 4 November 2013.

72 Veit, P.G., Nshala, R., Ochieng' Odhiambo, M. & Manyindo, J. (2008). *Protected Areas and Property Rights - Democratizing Eminent Domain in East Africa.* World Resources Institute. http://pdf.wri.org/protected_areas_and_property_rights.pdf accessed 4 August 2012.

73 United States' Congressional-Executive Commission on China (2004). *Access to Justice in China: Roundtable before the Congressional-Executive Commission on China.* In: One Hundred Eighth Congress, second session, 12 July 2004. Washington D.C.: United States Government Printing Office, http://babel.hathitrust.org/cgi/pt?id=umn.31951d024064594;view=1up;seq=11 accessed 18 November 2013, pp. 52–53.

74 The "Land Management Law of the People's Republic of China" [中华人民共和国土地管理法] was issued in 1986 and amended in 1998, and later amended on 28 August 2004, for detailed information see (1998 version) www.zhb.gov.cn/ztbd/rdzl/2010sdn/zcfg/201001/t20100113_184226.htm, and (2004 version) www.china.com.cn/chinese/law/647616.htmaccessed 3 January 2012.

and fixtures; and (c) a resettlement subsidy.[75] The Land Management Law (2004 version)[76] also provides that farmers should get at least six times the average annual output of the last three years and an additional amount of at least four times the average annual output for farmers made to relocate.[77] China's statutory minimal compensation levels for land acquisition are based on the idea that farmers should be compensated sufficiently to provide them with the standard of living they previously had for a set number of years into the future.[78] Where the owner of the land to be expropriated, or one or more farm households possessing use rights to the land to be expropriated, or both, dispute the amount of compensation that the executing State agency has determined, they may appeal to the higher level of the People's Government for administrative review of the determination, or make a direct filing of a complaint with the People's Court.[79] Besides access to an administrative tribunal, access to a civil tribunal would be a supplementary channel if necessary.

Although the implementing regulation of the 2004 Land Management Law requires the State to allocate land compensation to the collective, it does not state how the collective should deal with such land compensation after the State delivers it to the collective.[80] The forthcoming policy directive on land takings should fill this vacuum by explicitly requiring the collective to

---

75 Article 47 of the "Land Management Law of the People's Republic of China" [中华人民共和国土地管理法] was issued in 1986 and amended in 1998, and later amended on 28 August 2004, for detailed information see (1998 version) www.zhb.gov.cn/ztbd/rdzl/2010sdn/zcfg/201001/t20100113_184226.htm, and (2004 version) www.china.com.cn/chinese/law/647616.htm accessed 3 January 2012.

76 Article 47.1 of the "Land Management Law of the People's Republic of China" [中华人民共和国土地管理法] was issued in 1986 and amended in 1998, and later amended on 28 August 2004, for detailed information see (1998 version) www.zhb.gov.cn/ztbd/rdzl/2010sdn/zcfg/201001/t20100113_184226.htm, and (2004 version) www.china.com.cn/chinese/law/647616.htm accessed 3 January 2012.

77 Article 47.1 of the "Land Management Law of the People's Republic of China" [中华人民共和国土地管理法] was issued in 1986 and amended in 1998, and later amended on 28 August 2004, for detailed information see (1998 version) www.zhb.gov.cn/ztbd/rdzl/2010sdn/zcfg/201001/t20100113_184226.htm, and (2004 version) www.china.com.cn/chinese/law/647616.htm accessed 3 January 2012.

78 Van Rooij, B. (2007). The return of the landlord: Chinese land acquisition conflicts as illustrated by peri-urban Kunming, www.jlp.bham.ac.uk/volumes/55/vanrooij-art.pdf accessed 12 September 2012, p. 220.

79 United States' Congressional-Executive Commission on China (2004). *Property seizure in China: round-table before the Congressional-Executive Commission on China*. In: One Hundred Eighth Congress, second session, 12 July 2004. Washington D.C.: United States Government Printing Office, http://hdl.handle.net/2027/umn.31951d02406427h accessed 8 August 2012, pp. 52–53.

80 United States' Congressional-Executive Commission on China (2004). *Property seizure in China: round-table before the Congressional-Executive Commission on China*. In: One Hundred Eighth Congress, second session, 12 July 2004. Washington D.C.: United States Government Printing Office, http://hdl.handle.net/2027/umn.31951d02406427h accessed 8 August 2012, p. 55.

distribute all or most land compensation to the affected households.[81] The recommended approach to increase the amount of compensation would be to require compensation based on a fair market value, while including a statutory minimum level of compensation for all cases of takings. Under this approach, the fair market value standard would be applied in areas where it is possible to determine a market value for the land rights – most likely in suburban or more economically developed areas – while the minimum compensation standard would apply in areas where fair market value could not be easily determined.[82]

(2) *Compensation by the beneficiaries.* For instance, development areas located in the downstream river provide compensation to the poor areas located in the headwater region;[83] or asking for compensation fees from the beneficiaries of projects, such as beneficiaries of industrial water and domestic water; wood processing, trafficking, hunting, tourism and other commercial activities of the scenic areas.

Other forms of compensation include resettlement, benefit-sharing and job training.[84] For instance, in the case of the Wolong Nature Reserve in Sichuan, China,[85] a "win-win" alternative was achieved by providing non-agricultural employment opportunities for local populations around the reserve, simultaneously reducing pressure on the giant panda habitat from fuel wood collection and agriculture while improving local livelihoods.

Another possibility for providing a legal remedy is prosecution where violation amounts to a crime. Increasingly, national law is imposing criminal liability on those who have negative impacts on the environment or seriously infringe the rights of others.[86] More than ten Articles from the "Criminal Law

81 United States' Congressional-Executive Commission on China (2004). *Property seizure in China: round-table before the Congressional-Executive Commission on China.* In: One Hundred Eighth Congress, second session, 12 July 2004. Washington D.C.: United States Government Printing Office, http://hdl.handle.net/2027/umn.31951d02406427h accessed 8 August 2012, p. 55.

82 United States' Congressional-Executive Commission on China (2004). *Property seizure in China: round-table before the Congressional-Executive Commission on China.* In: One Hundred Eighth Congress, second session, 12 July 2004. Washington D.C.: United States Government Printing Office, http://hdl.handle.net/2027/umn.31951d02406427h accessed 8 August 2012, p. 52.

83 He, M. & Cliquet, A. (2013). Sustainable development through a rights-based approach to conserve protected areas in China. *China-EU Law Journal.* DOI 10.1007/s 12689-013-0031-7. http://link.springer.com/article/10.1007%2Fs12689-013-0031-7 accessed 4 November 2013.

84 He, M. & Cliquet, A. (2013). Sustainable development through a rights-based approach to conserve protected areas in China. *China-EU Law Journal.* DOI 10.1007/s 12689-013-0031-7. http://link.springer.com/article/10.1007%2Fs12689-013-0031-7 accessed 4 November 2013.

85 Vina, A.S. *et al.* (2007). Temporal changes in giant panda habitat connectivity across boundaries of Wo-long Nature Reserve, China. *Ecological Applications*, 17, www.uiowa.edu/~geog/faculty/linderman/documents/i1051-0761-17-4-1019.pdf accessed 4 August 2012, pp. 1019–1030.

86 Greiber, T. *et al.* (2009). Conservation with justice – a human rights based approach. Gland (Switzerland): IUCN Environmental Law Centre, http://data.iucn.org/dbtw-wpd/edocs/eplp-071.pdf accessed 28 October 2011, p. 34.

of the People's Republic of China (2011 Revision)"[87] have provided different punishments for different crimes on the environment. For instance, Article 341 states: "*whoever illegally catches or kills precious and endangered species of wildlife under special State protection or illegally purchases, transports or sells such species of wildlife as well as the products thereof shall be sentenced to fixed-term imprisonment of not more than five years or criminal detention and shall also be fined; if the circumstances are serious, he shall be sentenced to fixed-term imprisonment of not less than five years but not more than 10 years and shall also be fined; if the circumstances are especially serious, he shall be sentenced to fixed-term imprisonment of not less than 10 years and shall also be fined or be sentenced to confiscation of property.*"

In addition, it is impossible to ignore the importance of dedicated conservation NGOs in appealing to the courts. After the first NGO for environmental protection was set up in 1978 in China, more and more NGOs were established. They play an important role in protecting specific animals and areas, organising public participation, providing practical suggestions to the governments and promoting sustainable development.[88] Environmental NGOs are the vanguard of the growing non-governmental activity in China today,[89] and thus the question is not only whether non-governmental actors can shape the future of environmental protection in China but also whether they can play a role in creating a broader change in the context of the ongoing transformation of State-society relations in China.[90] Access to procedural justice for environmental NGOs providing them with legal standing is thus an important goal.[91]

Although there are several different channels for individuals and NGOs to guarantee their rights if there is any infringement with regards to protected areas conservation, access to procedural justice for both individuals and environmental NGOs is expected to go forward.

When these four parts are implemented, they might help solve the conflicts and promote cooperation between human rights protection and protected areas conservation in China, both on paper and in the field.

---

87 The "Criminal Law of the People's Republic of China (2011 Revision)" [中华人民共和国刑法 （2011修正版）] was issued on 14 March 1997 and amended on 25 February 2011, www.szxingshi.com/95w.html accessed 8 January 2012.

88 www.epi88.com/master/News_View.asp?NewsID=1760&page=2 accessed 8 June 2012.

89 He, M. (2014). Human rights protection in ecological conservation in China: progress, problems and prospects. *IUCN Academy of Environmental Law E Journal*, 5, pp. 110–116.

90 Economy, E.C. (2004). *The River Runs Black. The Environmental Challenge to China's Future*. Ithaca: Cornell University Press, p. 56.

91 He, M. & Cliquet, A. (2013). Sustainable development through a rights-based approach to conserve protected areas in China. *China-EU Law Journal*. DOI 10.1007/s 12689-013-0031-7. http://link.springer.com/article/10.1007%2Fs12689-013-0031-7 accessed 4 November 2013.

CHAPTER 8
GENERAL CONCLUSION AND OUTLOOK

7.1. GENERAL CONCLUSION

It is widely acknowledged that protected areas are not only a means for the protection of the natural environment, but also a means for achieving harmony between humans and nature. Increasingly, it is also recognised that protected areas cannot be seen in isolation from the communities that have inhabited or used their resources, nor can many of them be seen only as wildlife conservation sites, given that these communities may perceive the same areas as cultural landscapes or areas for essential survival.[1] Various sections of society may value the same area differently, and there is no single "right" way to achieve conservation.[2] As Brockington, Igoe and Schmidt-Soltau[3] state, "*the ultimate challenge facing conservationists today is not only to reconcile errors of the past but also to determine how to shape human interactions with nature in landscapes of which people are a part.*" The conservation and management of protected areas have long discussed "balancing" the needs of different stakeholders when in reality win-win situations are difficult to realise.[4]

This book has explored how to adopt a rights-based approach to conserve protected areas to achieve a better balance between human rights protection and protected areas conservation in China. It has provided adequate answers to three sub-research questions: (1) What is the added value of a human rights-based approach to conservation? (2) How to solve the potential conflicts regarding human rights protection and protected areas conservation in China according to some principal lessons learned from Europe? (3) Based on the experiences and

---

1 Lockwood, M., Kothari, A. & Worboys, G. (Eds.) (2006). *Managing Protected Areas: a Global Guide*. London: Earthscan, p. 44.

2 Lockwood, M., Kothari, A. & Worboys, G. (Eds.) (2006). *Managing Protected Areas: a Global Guide*. London: Earthscan, p. 44.

3 Brockington, D., Igoe, J. & Schmidt-Soltau, K. (2006). Conservation, human rights and poverty reduction, *Conservation Biology*, 20, pp. 250–252.

4 Rees, S.E. *et al.* (2010). Is there a win-win scenario for marine nature conservation? A case study of Lyme Bay. *Ocean & Coastal Management*, 53, pp. 135–145; McShane, T.O. *et al.* (2011). Hard choices: making trade-offs between biodiversity conservation and human well-being. *Biological Conservation*, 144, pp. 966–972.

lessons learned from the legal systems and case law in Europe, how to implement a human rights-based approach in protected areas conservation in China?

Rather than predicting the developmental tendency between human rights protection and environmental protection or debating whether a right to an environment would be widely accepted or not, it would be practical to find a better balanced approach to solve the existing conflicts regarding human rights protection and environmental protection based on the existing linkages between these two issues at the international level. In essence, a human rights-based approach could be regarded as both a means and an end: protecting the environment, in particular conserving protected areas, is ultimately about making sure that everyone's human rights are met. Environmental protection, especially protected areas conservation, could also best be achieved by empowering people to better secure and fulfil their rights. These are of vital importance for the four human rights to be protected, which have been discussed in this book. The key to solve the conflicts regarding human rights protection and protected areas conservation lies in harmony between human and nature, the mutual exchange and coordinated development of human rights and nature rights.

As for the second sub-research question, this book has made a clarification and a comparative study on four human rights in China and in Europe. We cannot easily judge that human rights (for instance right to property, right to information, right to participation and right to access to justice discussed in this book) are not protected at all in China, we only can conclude that compared to Europe, the development stages of human rights in China are relative lower and the scope of human rights or the understanding of human rights in China is different from what we saw in Europe. However, all these differences do not happen in a vacuum, there are several factors causing the differences.

Nevertheless, on the one hand, China's modernisation has already reduced the number of Chinese living in absolute poverty from six hundred million to two hundred million.[5] On the other hand, as mentioned in this book, the number and the surface of protected areas are remarkably increasing; this tendency also reflects that a great progress has been made in environmental protection in China. The chief economist of the International Energy Agency, Fatih Birol, gave a talk in New York in late 2006. He was asked which country, in his view, had the most environmentally conscious government. Most people expected him to mention one or two Scandinavian countries, or perhaps even the UK. Instead, he named China, to the surprise of everyone in the room.[6] As introduced in this book, several laws, regulations and policy instruments on

5 Mahbubani, K. (2008). *The New Asian Hemisphere: the Irresistible Shift of Global Power to the East*. Public Affairs Publishing House, p. 1.

6 Mahbubani, K. (2008). *The New Asian Hemisphere: the Irresistible Shift of Global Power to the East*. Public Affairs Publishing House, pp. 190–191.

human rights protection and protected areas conservation have been adopted from the different levels of governments in China, especially since 2010. We have seen that today China is better than a decade ago; all the tendencies demonstrate that the situation will be greatly improved to well balance human rights protection and environmental protection.

There is a popular saying in China, "*we spent more than 30 years to establish the existing legal system, we will spend a few years to improve the existing legal system to better balance all the interests*". Similarly, as indicated above, in order to effectively conserve biodiversity, a big number of protected areas with a large surface have been established over the past years, although this needs further improvement. Some conflicts regarding human rights protection and protected areas conservation are waiting to be solved. Conflicts in themselves should not necessarily be regarded as negative because, if handled carefully, they can be a very productive way of highlighting problems, increasing understanding and promoting the creation of sustainable solutions.[7] At this moment, we need a better balanced approach to shift these conflicts in a constructive way. We are on the road to learn some good experiences from abroad. The lessons learned from Europe in this book, which could be regarded as some baselines or principles, could help China to solve the potential conflicts based on its own economic, political, cultural and legal circumstances. Nevertheless, no matter in which corner of the world, conservation understood as "sustainable use" is essential to promote livelihood security and to fight against poverty – themes central to human rights.[8]

With regards to the third sub-research question, according to Chinese laws, it is the local governments that are responsible for local environmental quality in China, while the central government and provincial governments provide regulations and policy guidance.[9] This is reasonable because it consists of a huge area with differences in the various regions. It is also the reason that this book only provides some baselines or principles to solve the potential conflicts. Environmental enforcement by the local governments, however, is often limited in China for technical, financial, and institutional reasons.[10] How to implement

---

7 Young, J. *et al.* (2005). Towards sustainable land use: identifying and managing the conflicts between human activities and biodiversity conservation in Europe. *Biodiversity and Conservation*, 14, DOI 10.1007/s10531-004-0536-z, p. 1656.

8 Lockwood, M., Kothari, A. & Worboys, G. (Eds.) (2006). *Managing Protected Areas: a Global Guide*. London: Earthscan, p. 140.

9 Wang, H. (2011). Stakeholder dialogue as an institutional strategy for sustainable development in China: the case of community environmental round-tables. The World Bank Development Research Group Environment and Energy Team, www-wds.worldbank.org/external/default/WDSContentServer/IW3P/IB/2011/08/15/000158349_20110815113133/Rendered/PDF/WPS5759.pdf accessed 21 October 2013, p. 6.

10 Wang, H. (2011). Stakeholder dialogue as an institutional strategy for sustainable development in China: the case of community environmental round-tables. The World Bank Development Research Group Environment and Energy Team, www-wds.worldbank.org/

a human rights-based approach to conserve protected areas in practice depends on various aspects. Moreover, how to implement a human rights-based approach to conserve a specific protected area in China needs further research.

Nevertheless, no single measure can be used to achieve the win-win relationship between human rights protection and environmental protection. Only with the meaningful involvement[11] of all levels of governance (see 1.1.5), from local communities to the international community of States and non-States actors, can the "art" of finding a balance between human rights protection and environmental protection be achieved. What we could do now is, to do it with hope step by step, in spite of the present difficulties.

7.2. A WAY FORWARD (LIMITATIONS OF THE RESEARCH)

As indicated above, there is no single "right" way to achieve satisfying conclusion for various parties. The mentioned considerations in this book are the main and key part of the answer. A few limitations of this research should be highlighted.

Firstly, in order to better conserve a protected area, the relevant authorities may need to take into account the following: land tenure system, including ownership, grazing rights, and customary rights; environmental regulation, including biodiversity and environmental impact assessment; existing intellectual property rights; human rights obligations; national development policies, including a poverty reduction strategy and a reasonable benefit-sharing; and other national policies, such as the national water policy and the national energy policy.[12] A human rights-based approach to conserve protected areas only tries to solve the potential conflicts regarding human rights protection and protected areas conservation. A rights-based approach is useful for assigning responsibilities, duties, and obligations as well as distributing benefits among different actors involved.[13] The approach would also stimulate the potential

external/default/WDSContentServer/IW3P/IB/2011/08/15/000158349_20110815113133/Rendered/PDF/WPS5759.pdf accessed 21 October 2013, p. 6.

11 Meaningful Involvement means that: (1) potentially affected community residents have an appropriate opportunity to participate in decisions about a proposed activity that will affect their environment and/or health; (2) the public's contribution can influence the regulatory agency's decision; (3) the concerns of all participants involved will be considered in the decision-making process; and (4) the decision-makers seek out and facilitate the involvement of those potentially affected. See US Environmental Protection Agency (2003). Toolkit for assessing potential allegations of environmental injustice, www.epa.gov/compliance/recent/ej.html accessed 18 December 2012.

12 Razzaque, J. & Blanco, E. (2009). Ecosystem services and human well-being in a globalized world: assessing the role of law. *Human Rights Quarterly*, 31, p. 719.

13 Razzaque, J. & Blanco, E. (2009). Ecosystem services and human well-being in a globalized world: assessing the role of law. *Human Rights Quarterly*, 31, p. 720.

roles of local people and communities and environmental NGOs in protected areas conservation. Their roles not only refer to devoting their enthusiasm and knowledge to help the relevant authorities to do some practical work,[14] but also contain that they could work as a "watchdog" to oppose any project that would destroy or damage protected areas. In a word, the human rights-based approach could be regarded as a part of a systematic way to achieve the harmonious relationship between human rights protection and protected areas conservation.

Secondly, the human rights-based approach aims to empower rights. However, "rights" are not limited to the four human rights discussed in this book. Many other human rights shall also be taken into account in practice. For instance, the spiritual and cultural values of protected areas are important as other values for many local people and communities. The right to enjoy one's own culture could be regarded as the second stage for realising the rights of local people and communities. It is also an interesting human right for further research.

Thirdly, empowering rights means "empowerment" and "rights" (see 7.1.3.3). "Empowerment" is a long term process. A significant danger of the larger involvement of local communities in protected areas management is that various individual and sectional interests are fully capable of turning this good idea to their own ends.[15] The challenge is to be able to shift out these detrimental interests from the local people who genuinely depend for their survival upon the natural resources of the protected areas, and empower the latter to be able to live with dignity.[16] This will be an ongoing process as people move in and out of local communities.[17] Certainly, one of the developmental tendencies in China is that problems are coming up. However, what we could do is to try to solve the most urgent one to achieve a relative balance at present. Therefore, this book only proposed some principal suggestions from Europe to solve the potential urgent problems in China.

Fourth, this book only devotes the attention to the ECHR, the Aarhus Convention and some protected areas conservation law in Europe. The laws in the EU level are the supplementary material to assess. As for the case law in Europe, what we may be witnessing is an unstopped process of complementing

14 It was approved in "What if we change - Hope in a Changing Climate" by John D. Liu. Published on 17 January 2013, www.youtube.com/watch?v=6iJKiFSQLn4&list=PLDknVzuz N8BRkIT3b4LBGHFHXKq2u82yA accessed 12 January 2014. This video shows how positive nature restoration can be for the local population, more importantly it also indirectly reflects how positive nature will be if local people and communities were meaningfully involved with a good guide.

15 Lockwood, M., Kothari, A. & Worboys, G. (Eds.) (2006). *Managing Protected Areas: a Global Guide*. London: Earthscan, p. 670.

16 Lockwood, M., Kothari, A. & Worboys, G. (Eds.) (2006). *Managing Protected Areas: a Global Guide*. London: Earthscan, p. 670.

17 Lockwood, M., Kothari, A. & Worboys, G. (Eds.) (2006). *Managing Protected Areas: a Global Guide*. London: Earthscan, p. 670.

"step by step" the content of some "traditional" rights guaranteed in the ECHR as a result of a growing awareness and concern for environmental issues, making the classical statement real that the European Convention on human rights is a living instrument to be interpreted and applied in the context of present-day conditions.[18] The case law from the ACCC also provides some interesting guidelines for the research question. Compared with other interesting legal instruments and case law from other agencies, for instance the Treaty of Lisbon[19] and the human rights case law from the CJEU, the above-mentioned could show a broader picture to propose the answer from a longer historical perspective. The other interesting legal instruments and case law from other agencies will be interesting materials for the further research.

Fifth, how a human rights-based approach to conserving a specific protected area in practice in China should be adopted needs further research. Field research would be the next step forward.

18 Garcia San José, D. (2005). *Environmental Protection and the European Convention on Human Rights*. Council of Europe Publishing, p. 59.

19 The Treaty of Lisbon (initially known as the Reform Treaty) is an international agreement which amends the two treaties which form the constitutional basis of the European Union (EU). The Lisbon Treaty was signed by the EU Member States on 13 December 2007 and entered into force on 1 December 2009, http://europa.eu/lisbon_treaty/full_text/index_en.htm accessed 12 March 2014.

REFERENCES

BOOKS AND MONOGRAPHS

Acreman, M.C., Barbier, E.B. & Knowler, D. (1997). *Economic Valuation of Wetlands: a Guide for Policy Makers and Planners*. Gland (Switzerland): Ramsar Convention Bureau.

Alexandre, K. & Shelton, D.L. (2004). *International Environmental Law* (third edition). New York (USA): Transnational Publishers.

Amend, S. & Amend, T. (Eds.) (1995). *National Parks without People? The South American Experience*. Quito, Ecuador: IUCN.

André, P., Enserink, B., Connor, D. & Croal, P. (2006). *Public Participation International Best Practice Principles*. (Special publication series no. 4). Fargo (USA): International Association for Impact Assessment.

Anton, D.K. & Shelton, D.L. (2011). *Environmental Protection and Human Rights*. Cambridge: Cambridge University Press.

Argumedo, A. & Pimbert, M. (2008). *Protecting Farmers' Rights with Indigenous Bio-cultural Heritage Territories: the Experience of the Potato Park*. International Institute for Environment and Development, Asociacion.

Barbier, E.B. (1989). *The Economic Value of Ecosystems: 1 –Tropical Wetlands*. LEEC Gatekeeper Series 89–02. London: London Environmental Economics Centre.

Berman, G. (2008). *Undertaking a Human Rights-based Approach: a Guide for Basic Programming – Documenting Lessons Learned for Human Rights-based Programming: an Asia-pacific Perspective – Implications for Policy, Planning and Programming*. Bangkok: UNESCO Asia and Pacific Regional Bureau for Education.

Beyer, S. (2006). *Environmental Law and Policy in the People's Republic of China*. Oxford: Oxford University Press.

Blomley, T., *et al.* (2009). *From Needs to Rights: Lessons Learned from the Application of Rights Based Approaches to Natural Resource Governance in Ghana, Uganda and Nepal*. Washington, DC: Rights and Resources Initiative.

Birnie, P., Boyle, A. & Redgwell, C. (2009). *International Law and the Environment* (third edition). Oxford: Oxford University Press.

Boesen, J. & Martin, T. (2007). *Applying a Human Rights-based Approach – an Inspirational Guide for Civil Society*. Copenhagen: Danish Institute for Human Rights.

Borrini-Feyerabend, G., *et al.* (2013). *Governance of Protected Areas: from Understanding to Action*. Best Practice Protected Area Guidelines Series No. 20. Gland (Switzerland): IUCN.

Borrini-Feyerabend, G. (1996). *Collaborative Management of Protected Areas, Tailoring the Approach to the Context*. Gland (Switzerland): IUCN.

Borrini-Feyerabend, G., Kothari, A. & Oviedo, G. (2004). *Indigenous and Local Communities and protected areas: towards Equity and Enhanced Conservation.* IUCN Best Practice Guidelines for Protected Area Series no. 11. Gland (Switzerland): IUCN.

Bryant, R.W.G. (1972). *Land Private Property, Public Control.* Montreal: Harvest House.

Clerk, A. & Kohler, P. (2005). *Property Law: Commentary and Materials.* Cambridge: Cambridge University Press.

Conservation of Arctic Flora and Fauna. (2002). *Protected Areas of the Arctic: Conserving a Full Range of Values.* Canada: CAFF (Conservation of Arctic Flora and Fauna) Secretariat, Department of Foreign Affairs.

Coyle S. & Morrow, K. (2004). *The Philosophical Foundations of Environmental Law, Property, Rights and Nature.* Oxford: Hart Publishing.

De Cosse, P.J., Thompson, P.M., Ahmad, I.U., Sharma, R.A. & Mazumder, A.H. (2012). *Protected Area Co-management Where People and Poverty Intersect – Lessons from Nishorgo in Bangladesh.* Bangladesh: United States Agency for International Development.

De Sadeleer, N., Roller, G. & Dross, M. (2005). *Access to Justice in Environmental Matters and the Role of NGOs: Empirical Findings and Legal Appraisal.* Groningen: Europa Law Publishing.

Desmet, E. (2011). *Indigenous Rights Entwined with Nature Conservation.* Antwerp: Intersentia.

Economy, E.C. (2004). *The River Runs Black: the Environmental Challenge to China's Future.* Ithaca: Cornell University Press.

Edmonds, R.L. (Ed.) (1994). *Patterns of China's Lost Harmony: a Survey of the Country's Environmental Degradation and Protection.* London: Routledge.

EEA (European Environment Agency) (2012). *Environmental Indicator Report 2012 – Ecosystem Resilience and Resource Efficiency in a Green Economy in Europe.* Luxembourg: Publications Office of the European Union.

Ely, Y.W. (1997). *The Guardian of Every Other Rights: a Constitutional History of Property Rights.* Oxford: Oxford University Press.

European Union (2013). *The Economic Benefits of the Natura 2000 Network.* Luxembourg: Publications Office of the European Union.

Fischer, F. (2000). *Citizens, Experts and the Environment: the Politics of Local Knowledge.* London: Duke University Press.

Fu, Y.F. (付延芳) (2012). *Discussion on the Legal Guarantee of Harmonious Development between Natural Reserve and Local Communities* (论自然保护区与当地社区和谐发展的法律保障). Master Dissertation in China University of Political Science and Law (中国政法大学硕士学位论文).

Fung, A., Graham, M. & Weil, D. (2007). *Full Disclosure: the Perils and Promise of Transparency.* New York: Cambridge University Press.

Gantionler, S., Rayment, M., Bassi, S., Kettunen, M., McConville A., Landgrebe, R., Gerdes, H. & ten Brink, P. (2010). *Costs and Socio-Economic Benefits Associated with the Natura 2000 Network.* Brussels: Institute for European Environmental Policy/GHK/Ecologic.

Garcia San José, D. (2005). *Environmental Protection and the European Convention on Human Rights.* Strasbourg (France): Council of Europe Publishing.

GEF (Global Environment Facility) (2005). *Making a Visible Difference in Our World.* Washington D.C.: GEF.

GEF (Global Environment Facility) (2005). *People and Protected Areas.* Washington D.C: GEF.

Gilbert, J. (2006). *Indigenous Peoples' Land Rights under International Law: from Victims to Actors.* New York: Transnational Publishers.

Gilmour, D.A., Durst, P.B. & Shono, K. (2007). *Reaching Consensus, Multi-stakeholder Processes in Forestry: Experiences from the Asia-Pacific Region.* Bangkok: Food and Agriculture Organization of the United Nations Regional Office for Asia and the Pacific.

Gillespie, A. (2007). *Protected Areas and International Environmental Law.* Leiden (Netherlands): Martinus Nijhoff Publishers.

Gillespie, A. (2011). *Conservation, Biodiversity and International Law.* Cheltenham (UK) and Northampton (USA): Edward Elgar Publishing.

Greiber, T. *et al.* (2009). *Conservation with justice – a human rights-based approach.* Gland (Switzerland): IUCN Environmental Law Centre.

Guo, C.R. (郭昌荣) (2012). *Research on Protected Areas Management from the Perspective of the Theory of Property Rights* (产权理论视野下自然保护区管理体制研究). Master dissertation in Kunming Technology University (昆明理工大学硕士学位论文).

Habermas, J. (1996). *Between Facts and Norms; Contributions to a Discourse Theory of Law and Democracy.* (Trans: Regh, W.). Boston: The MIT (Massachusetts Institute of Technology) Press.

Hayward, T. (2005). *Constitutional Environmental Rights.* Oxford: Oxford University Press.

Hesselink, F.J. *et al.* (2007). *Communication, Education And Public Awareness: a Toolkit for the Convention on Biological Convention.* Montreal: Secretariat of the Convention on Biological Diversity.

ICJ (International Commission of Jurists) (2010). *Access to Justice: Human Rights Abuses Involving Corporations – People's Republic of China*, Geneva: ICJ.

International Alliance of Indigenous – Tribal Peoples of the Tropical Forest (1996). *Indigenous Peoples, Forests, and Biodiversity.* Copenhagen: IWGIA.

International Fund for Agricultural Development (2010). *Rural Poverty Report 2011.* Rome: International Fund for Agricultural Development.

IUCN (1993). *Parks for Life: Report of the IVth World Congress on National Parks and Protected Areas.* Gland (Switzerland): IUCN.

IUCN (2002). *Sustainable Tourism in Protected Areas: Guidelines for Planning and Management.* Gland (Switzerland): IUCN.

Jin, R.L. (1990). *Environmental Law Science.* Beijing: Peking University Press.

Kapur, A. & Duvvury, N. (2006). *A Human Rights-based Approach to Realizing the Economic and Social Rights of Poor and Social Rights of Poor and Marginalized Women: a Synthesis of Lessons Learned.* International Center for Research on Women (ICRW).

Kostic, M. (2006). *The Right of Access to Environmental Information in the Sense of the Aarhus Convention: European Streams and Legal Framework in Serbia and Montenegro.* CPRINT Beograd.

Larson, A.M., Cronkleton, P., Barry, D. & Pacheco, P. (2008). *Tenure Rights and Beyond: Community Access to Forest Resources in Latin America*. Occasional Paper No. 50, Bogor (Indonesia): CIFOR.

Lausche, B. (2011). *Guidelines for Protected Area Legislation*. Gland (Switzerland): IUCN.

Lechie, S. (Ed.) (2007). *Housing, Land and Property Restitution Rights of Refugees and Displaced Persons: Laws, Cases And Materials*. Cambridge: Cambridge University Press.

Lee, M. (2005). *EU Environmental Law: Challenges, Change and Decision-making*. Oxford: Hart Publishing.

Leib, E.J. & He, B. (Eds.) (2006). *The Search for Deliberative Democracy in China*. New York: Palgrave Macmillan.

Leopold, A. (1968). *A Sand County Almanac and Sketches Here and There*. Oxford: Oxford University Press.

Liu, J. (刘杰) (2005). *The Right to Know and Laws on Information Disclosure* (知情权与信息公开法). Beijing: Qinghua University Press (北京: 清华大学出版社有限公司).

Lockwood, M., Worboys, G. & Kothari, A. (Eds.) (2006). *Managing Protected Areas: a Global Guide*. London: Earthscan.

Lucas, P.H.C. (1992). *Protected Landscapes – a Guide for Policy-Makers and Planners*. Gland (Switzerland): IUCN.

Mackinnon, J. & Xie, Y. (2008). *Regional Action Plan for the Protected Areas of East Asia*. Bangkok(Thailand): IUCN.

Mahbubani, K. (2008). *The New Asian Hemisphere: the Irresistible Shift of Global Power to the East*. Public Affairs Publishing House.

McNeely, J.A. & Miller, K.R. (1984). *National parks, Conservation and Development: the Role of Protected Areas in Sustaining Society*. Washington D.C.: Smithsonian Institute Press.

McNeely, J.A. & Pitt, D. (Eds.) (1985). *Culture and Conservation: the Human Dimension in Environmental Planning*. London: Croom Helm.

Millennium Ecosystem Assessment (2005). *Ecosystems and Human Well-being: Biodiversity Synthesis*. Washington D.C.: World Resources Institute.

Millennium Ecosystem Assessment (2005). *Ecosystems and Human Well-being: General Synthesis*. Washington D.C.: Island Press.

Ministry of Environmental Protection (MEP) (2011). *Report of Environmental Conditions of China in 2010*. Beijing: Ministry of Environmental Protection.

Mulongoy, K.J. & Gidda, S.B. (2008). *The Value of Nature: Economic, Cultural and Social Benefits of Protected Areas*. Montreal: Secretariat of the Conservation on Biological Diversity.

Neumann, R.P. (1998). *Imposing Wilderness: Struggles over Livelihood and Nature Preservation in Africa*. Berkeley: University of California Press.

PATF (Protected Area Task Force) (2004). *Evaluation and Policy Recommendations to the Protected Area System of China*. Protected Area Task Force report to the China Council for International Cooperation on Environment and Development (CCICED). Beijing: State Environmental Protection Administration.

Paques, M. (2005) (Ed.). *Natura 2000 and Property Rights: International and National Reports*. Brussels: Etablissements Emile Bruylant.

Qi, D. (齐玎) (2012). *Access to Environmental Justice: Environmental Groups Participating in Environmental Public Interest Litigation* (接近环境正义：环保团体参与环境公益诉讼问题研究). Master Dissertation in Fudan University (复旦大学硕士论文).

Reid, K. (2004). *A Practitioner's Guide to the European Convention on Human Rights* (second edition). London: Sweet & Maxwell.

Renn, O., Webler, T. & Wiedemann, P. (Eds.) (1995). *Fairness and Competence in Citizen Participation: Evaluating Models for Environmental Discourse.* Dordrecht: Kluwer.

Ribot, J.C. (2002). *Democratic Decentralization of Natural Resources: Institutionalizing Popular Participation.* Washington D.C.: World Resource Institute.

Richards, C., Blackstock, K. & Carter, C. (2004). *Practical Approaches to Participation.* SERG (Socio-Economic Research Group) Policy Brief No. 1. Macauley Land Use Research Institute.

Roe, D. (Ed.) (2010). *Linking Biodiversity Conservation and Poverty Reduction: a State of Knowledge Review.* CBD Technical Series No. 44. Montreal: Secretariat of the Convention on Biological Diversity.

Robertson, A.H. & Merrills, J.G. (1993). *Human Rights in Europe: a Study of the European Convention on Human Rights* (third edition). Manchester: Manchester University Press.

Sands, P. (2003). *International Environmental Law* (second edition). Cambridge: Cambridge University Press.

Scodari, P.F. (1990). *Wetlands Protection: the Role of Economics.* Washington D.C.: Environmental Law Institute Monograph.

Sepúlveda, M., van Banning, T., Gudmundsdóttir, G.D., Chamoun, C. & van Genugten, W. (2010). *Human Rights Reference Handbook.* Iceland: The Icelandic Human Rights Centre.

Singer, J.W. (2000). *Entitlement: The Paradoxes of Property.* New Haven: Yale University Press.

Singh, B. (2006). *Rights Based Approach and Housing for the Urban Poor: an Analysis of the Slum Rehabilitation Schemes in Mumbai.* Munich: GRIN Publishing.

Ssenyonjo, M. (2009). *Economic, Social and Cultural Rights in International Law.* Oxford: Hart Publishing.

State Environmental Protection Bureau (1996). *National Environmental Statistics of China in 1995.* Beijing: State Environmental Protection Bureau.

State Forestry Administration (国家林业局) (2007). *Research on the Legislation for Protected Areas in China* (《中国自然保护区立法研究》). China Forestry Publishing House (中国林业出版社).

Stec, S. & Casey- Lefkowitz, S. (2000). *The Aarhus Convention – an Implementation Guide.* United Nations Publication.

Task Force on Economic Benefits of Protected Areas of the World Commission on Protected Areas (WCPA) of IUCN, in collaboration with the Economics Service Unit of IUCN (1998). *Economic Values of Protected Areas: Guidelines for Protected Areas Managers.* Gland (Switzerland): IUCN.

Ubink, J.M., Hoekema, A.J. & Assies, W.J. (Eds.) (2010). *Legalising Land Rights – Local Practices, State Responses and Tenure Security in Africa, Asia and Latin America.* Leiden: Leiden University Press.

UNDP (United Nations Development Programme) (2000). *Human Development Report 2000*. Oxford: Oxford University Press.

United States' Congressional-Executive Commission on China (2004). *Property Seizure in China: Roundtable before the Congressional-Executive Commission on China*. In: One Hundred Eighth Congress, second session, 12 July 2004. Washington D.C.: United States Government Printing Office.

United States' Congressional-Executive Commission on China (2004). *Access to Justice in China: Roundtable before the Congressional-Executive Commission on China*. In: One Hundred Eighth Congress, second session, 12 July 2004. Washington D.C.: United States Government Printing Office,

Underkuffler, L.S. (Ed.) (2003). *The Idea of Property: Its Meaning and Power*. Oxford: Oxford University Press.

Vatn, A. (2005). *Institutions and the Environment*. Cheltenham (UK) and Northampton (USA): Edward Elgar Publishing.

Veit, P.G., Nshala, R., Ochieng' Odhiambo. M. & Manyindo, J. (2008). *Protected Areas and Property Rights – Democratizing Eminent Domain in East Africa*. World Resources Institute.

Wang, C. (王超) (2013). *Study on Legal System for Public Participation in Promoting Ecological Progress* (公众参与生态文明建设法制制度研究). Master Dissertation in Environment and Resources Protection Law of Central South University of Forestry and Technology (中南林业科技大学环境资源保护法硕士学位论文).

Wang, D.Q. & He, K.J. (王权典，何克军) (Ed.) (2012). *The Innovation for Rule of Law on Protected Areas and the Methods for the Reformation on Forest – Based on Field Work on the Construction for a Protected Areas Model Province in Guangdong* (自然保护区法制创新与"林改"方略–基于广东自然保护区示范省建设实施探索). Beijing: China Legal Publishing House (中国法制出版社).

Warren, C. (2002). *Managing Scotland's Environment*. Edinburgh: Edinburgh University Press.

WFFPDSFA (Wild Fauna and Flora Protection Division of the State Forestry Administration) (2003). *Chinese Nature Reserve Policy Research*. Beijing: China Forestry Publishing House.

Williams, I., Enemark, S., Wallace, J. & Rajabifard., A. (2010). *Land Administration for Sustainable Development*. ESRI Press Academic.

Woolf, H. *et al.* (1999). *De Smith, Woolf and Jowell's Principles of Judicial Review*. London: Sweet and Maxwell.

WWF (World Wide Fund for Nature) International (2008). *Indigenous Peoples and Conservation: WWF Statement of Principles*. Gland (Switzerland): WWF International.

Xiong, Y. (熊鹰) (2007). *Effect Analysis of Government Environmental Regulation and Public Participation on Enterprise Pollution Behavior*. (政府环境管制、公众参与与对企业污染行为的影响分析). Doctorate Dissertation of Nanjing Agricultural University (南京农业大学博士论文).

Zhao, L.L. (赵丽丽) (2009). *The Community-based Management on Fishery in China* (中国基于社区的渔业管理研究). Doctoral Dissertation of Ocean University of China (中国海洋大学).

Zhang, X.L. (张小利) (2007). *Economic Analysis on Poverty Elimination by Tourism Effect* (旅游扶贫效应的经济分析). Dissertation for Master Degree in Fudan University. (复旦大学硕士学位论文).

Zhou, G.J. (卓光俊) (2012). *Public Participation System for Environmental Protection in China* (我国环境保护中的公众参与制度研究). Doctoral Dissertation of Chongqing University (重庆大学博士论文).

Zhou, H.H. (2003). *Our Country's Experience with and Consideration of Open Government Affairs*. Beijing: China Law Press.

Zhou, S.X. (2006). *Forestry in China: Historical Transitions and Industry Developments*. Singapore: Thomson Learning.

Zhu, T. & Lam, K.C. (2009). *Environmental Impact Assessment in China, Research Centre for Strategic Environmental Assessment*. Nanjing: Nankai University Press.

BOOK CHAPTERS

Alkema, E.A. (2000). The concept of property – in particular in the European Convention on Human Rights. In: Loof, J.P., Ploeger, H. & van der Steur, A. (Eds.). *The Right to Property: the Influence of Article 1 Protocol No. 1 ECHR on Several Fields of Domestic Law*. Maastricht: Shaker Publishing.

Anderson, M.R. (1996). Human rights approaches to environmental protection: an overview. In: Boyle, A. E. & Anderson, M.R. (Eds.). *Human Rights Approach to Environmental Protection*. Oxford: Clarendon Press.

Andrusevych, A. (2013). Environmental human rights protection in the European Court of Human Rights. In: Stec, S. (Ed.). *Handbook on Access to Justice under the Aarhus Convention*. Szentendre (Hungary): The Regional Environmental Center for Central and Eastern Europe.

Arambiza, E. (1995). The Kaa-Iya protected area of the Grand Chaco: a case collaborations between indigenous peoples and conservationists. In: Gray, A. (Ed.). *Indigenous Peoples and Biodiversity Conservation in Latin America*. Copenhagen: EKs-Skolen Trykkrei APS.

Belcher, B. (2013). Forests, poverty and conservation: an overview of the issues. In: Roe, D., Elliott, J., Sandbrook, C. & Walpole, M. (Eds.). *Biodiversity Conservation and Poverty Alleviation: Exploring the Evidence for a Link*. Chichester (UK): John Wiley & Sons.

Bolshakova, M., Dusik, J. & Toth Nagy, M. (1998). Chapter 2: public participation in environmental decision-making. In: *Doors to Democracy: a Pan-European Assessment of Current Trends and Practices in Public Participation in Environmental Matters*. Szentendre (Hungary): The Regional Environmental Center for Central and Eastern Europe.

Bosselmann, K. (2011). Property rights and sustainability: can they be reconciled? In: Grinlinton, D. & Taylor, P. (Eds.). *Property Rights and Sustainability – the Evolution of Property Rights to Meet Ecological Challenges*. Leiden: Martinus Nijhoff Publishers.

Boyle, A. (2013). Relationship between International Environmental Law and other Branches of International Law. In: Bodansky, D., Brunnee, J. & Hey, E. (Eds.). *The Oxford Handbook of International Environmental Law.* Oxford: Oxford University Press.

Brunnee, J. (2009). Climate change, global environmental justice and international environmental law. In: Ebbesson, J. & Okowa, P. (Eds.). *Environmental Law and Justice in Context.* Cambridge: Cambridge University Press.

Campese, J. (2009). Human rights-based approaches to conservation: an overview of concepts and questions. In: Campese, J., *et al.* (Eds.). *Human Rights-based Approaches: Exploring Issues and Opportunities for Conservation.* Bogor (Indonesia): CIFOR and IUCN.

Černý, P. (2010). Practical application of Article 9 of the Aarhus Convention in 10 EU countries – comparative remarks. In: ENELO (European Network of Environmental Law Organizations). *Access to Justice in Environmental Matters.* Co-sponsored by the European Commission – LIFE+programme and the Ministry of Housing, Spatial Planning and the Environment of the Netherlands.

Ciriacy-Wantrup, S.V. & Bishop, R.C. (2003). 'Common property' as a concept in natural resources policy. In: Larson, B.A. (Ed.). *Property Rights and Environmental Problems.* Farnham (UK): Ashgate Publishing.

Dejeant-Pons, M. (2002). Human rights to environmental procedural rights. In: Dejeant-Pons, M. & Pallemaerts, M. (Eds.). *Human Rights and the Environment.* Strasbourg (France): Council of Europe Publishing.

Du, Q. (2009). Public participation and the challenges of environmental justice in China. In: Ebbesson, J. & Okowa, P. (Eds.). *Environmental Law and Justice in Context.* Cambridge (UK): Cambridge University Press.

Du Plessis, A. (2011). Local agenda 21: a rights-based approach to local environmental governance. In: Benidickson, J., Boer, B., Benjamin, A.H. & Morrow, K. (Eds.). *Environmental Law and Sustainability after Rio.* The IUCN Academy of Environmental Law Series. Cheltenham (UK) and Northampton (USA): Edward Elgar Publishing.

Dumashie, D. (2010). The marine cadastre: a rights based approach to marine conservation in England. In: Falque, M. & Lamotte, H. (Eds.). *Biodiversity, Property Rights, Economics and Environment.* Brussels: Bruylant.

Ebbesson, J. (2002). Comparative introduction. In: Ebbesson, J. (Ed.). *Access to Justice in Environmental Matters in the EU.* Leiden: Kluwer Law International.

Ebbesson, J. (2002). European community. In: Ebbesson, J. (Ed.). *Access to Justice in Environmental Matters in the EU.* Leiden: Kluwer Law International.

Ebbesson, J. (2011). Access to justice at the national level: impact of the Aarhus Convention and European Union law. In: Pallemaerts, M. (Ed.). *The Aarhus Convention at Ten: Interactions and Tensions between Conventional International Law and EU Environmental Law.* Groningen: Europa Law Publishing.

Eissen, M.-A. (1993). The principle of proportionality in the case-law of the European Court of Human Rights. In: Macdonald, R.S.J., Matscher, F. & Petzold, H. (Eds.). *The European System for the Protection of Human Rights.* Leiden: Martinus Nijhoff Publishers.

Eide, A. (2001). Economic, social and cultural rights as human rights. In: Eide, A., Krause, C. & Rosas, A. (Eds.). *Economic, Social and Cultural Rights: A Textbook* (second revised edition). Leiden: Martinus Nijhoff Publishers.

Führ, M., Gebers, B., Ormond, T. & Roller, G. (1995). Access to justice: legal standing for environmental associations in the European Union. In: Robinson, D. & Dunkeley, J. (Eds.). *Public Interest Perspectives in Environmental Law.* London: Wiley Chancery.

García-Ureta, A. & Lazkano, Í. (2014). Instruments for sites active management of Natura 2000: balancing between stakeholders and nature conservation? In: Born, C.-H., Cliquet, A., Schoukens, H., Misonne, D. & Van Hoorick, G. (Eds.). *The Habitats Directive in its EU Environmental Law Context: European Nature's Best Hope?* Oxford: Routledge.

George, R. (2007). Reflections on the protection of property under the European Convention on Human Rights. In: Breitenmoser, S., *et al.* (Eds.). *Human Rights, Democracy and the Rule of Law: Liber Amicorum Luzius Wildhaber.* Berlin: Nomos Publishers.

Godden, L. (2010). Governing common resources: environmental markets and property in water. In: Mcharg, A., *et al.* (Eds.). *Property and the Law in Energy and Natural Resources.* Oxford: Oxford University Press.

Graham, N. (2012). Dephysicalisation and entitlement: legal and cultural discourses of place as property. In: Jessup, B. & Rubenstein, K. (Ed.). *Environmental Discourses in Public and International Law.* Cambridge: Cambridge University Press.

Grinlinton, D. (2011). Evolution, adaptation and invention: property rights in natural resources in a changing world. In: Grinlinton D. & Taylor, P. (Eds.). *Property Rights and Sustainability – the Evolution of Property Rights to Meet Ecological Challenges.* Leiden: Martinus Nijhoff Publishers.

Horsley, J.P. (2007). Toward a more open China. In: Florini, A. (Ed.). *The Right to Know: Transparency for an Open World.* New York: Columbia University Press.

Jendroska, J. (2011). Public participation in environmental decision-making: interactions between the Convention and EU Law and other key legal issues in its implementation in the light of the opinions of the Aarhus Convention Compliance Committee. In: Pallemaerts, M. (Ed.). *The Aarhus Convention at Ten: Interactions and Tensions between Conventional International Law and EU Environmental Law.* Groningen: Europa Law Publishing.

Kibugi, R. (2011). Enhanced access to environmental justice in Kenya. In: Benidickson, J., Boer, B., Benjamin, A.H. & Morrow, K. (Eds.). *Environmental Law and Sustainability after Rio.* The IUCN Academy of Environmental Law Series. Cheltenham (UK) and Northampton (USA): Edward Elgar Publishing.

Kiss, A. (1992). An introductory note on a human right to environment. In: Weiss, E.B. (Ed.). *Environmental Change and International Law.* Tokyo (Japan): United Nations University Press.

Kritikos, M. (2011). Shaping transnational public participation norms in the field of modern biotechnology: time for a global good governance approach? In: Pallemaerts, M. (Ed.). *The Aarhus Convention at Ten: Interactions and Tensions between Conventional International Law and EU Environmental Law.* Groningen: Europa Law Publishing.

Kothari, U. (2001). Power, knowledge and social control in participatory development. In: Cooke, B. & Kothari, U. (Eds.). *Participation: the New Tyranny?* London: Zed Books.

Last, K. (2005). Property Rights and Natura 2000 in Great Britain. In: Paques, M. (Ed.). *Natura 2000 and Property Rights: International and National Reports.* Brussels: Etablissements Emile Bruylant (2005).

Lavrysen, L. (2010). The Aarhus Convention between environmental protection and human rights. In: *Liège, Strasbourg, Brussels: parcours des droits de l'homme.* Limal: Anthemis.

Li, P., Prosterman, R., Ye, J.P., Wu, J. & van Rooij, B. (2010). Land reform and tenure security in China: history and current challenges. In: Ubink, J.M., Hoekema, A.J. & Assies, W.J. (Eds.). *Legalizing Land Rights – Local Practices, State Responses and Tenure Security in Africa, Asia and Latin America.* Leiden: Leiden University Press.

Loof, J.P., Ploeger, H. & van der Steur, A. (2000). The right to property in European human rights and its influence on several fields of domestic law. In: Loof, J.P., Ploeger, H. & van der Steur, A. (Eds.). *The Right to Property: the Influence of Article 1 Protocol No. 1 ECHR on Several Fields of Domestic Law.* Maastricht: Shaker Publishing.

Martin, P. & Verbeek, M. (2002). Property rights and Property Responsibility. In: Land and Water Australia (Ed.). *Property: Rights and Responsibilities – Current Australian Thinking.* Canberra: Land and Water Australia.

McNeely, J.A. (1995). Partnerships for conservation: an introduction. In: McNeely, J.A. (Ed.). *Expanding Partnerships in Conservation.* Washington D.C.: Island Press.

McNeely, J.A., Lockwood, M. & Chapman, J. (2006). Building support for protected areas. In: Lockwood, M., Kothari, A. & Worboys, G. (Eds.). *Managing Protected Areas: a Global Guide.* London: Earthscan.

Miao, H. (2000). Community participation mechanism of China's nature reserve. In: China Man and Biosphere Committee (Eds.). *Study of Sustainable Management Policies for China's Nature reserve.* Beijing: Scientific and Technical Documents Publishing House.

Morrow, K. (2011). The Courts and public participation in environmental decision-making. In: Benidickson, J., Boer, B., Benjamin, A.H. & Morrow, K. (Eds.). *Environmental Law and Sustainability after Rio.* The IUCN Academy of Environmental Law Series. Cheltenham (UK) and Northampton (USA): Edward Elgar Publishing.

Narain, S. & Agarwal, A. (2007). Harvesting the rain: fighting ecological poverty through participatory democracy. In: Boyce, J.K., Narain, S. & Stanton, E.A. (Eds.). *Reclaiming Nature: Environmental Justice and Ecological Restoration.* London: Anthem Press.

Obradovic, D. (2011). EU rules on public participation in environmental decision-making operating at the European and National Levels. In: Pallemaerts, M. (Ed.). *The Aarhus Convention at Ten: Interactions and Tensions between Conventional International Law and EU Environmental Law.* Groningen: Europa Law Publishing.

Pallemaerts, M. (2002). Introduction: human rights and environmental protection. In: Dejeant-Pons, M & Pallemaerts, M. (Eds.). *Human Rights and the Environment.* Strasbourg (France): Council of Europe Publishing.

Pallemaerts, M. (2011). Access to environmental justice at EU Level: has the 'Aarhus Regulation' improved the situation? In: Pallemaerts, M. (Ed.). *The Aarhus Convention at Ten: Interactions and Tensions between Conventional International Law and EU Environmental Law.* Groningen: Europa Law Publishing.

Pathak, R.S. (1992). The human rights system as a conceptual framework for environmental law. In: Weiss, E.B. (Ed.). *Environmental Change and International Law.* Tokyo (Japan): United Nations University Press.

Pechota, V. (1981). The development of the Covenant on civil and political rights. In: Henkin, L. (Ed.). *The International Bill of Rights: the Covenant on Civil and Political Rights.* New York: Columbia University Press.

Petts, J. (1999). Public participation and environmental impact assessment. In: Petts, J. (Ed.). *Handbook of Environmental Impact Assessment.* London: Blackwell Science.

Ploeger, H.D. & Stolker, C.J.J.M. (2000). In search of the importance of Article 1 Protocol No. 1 ECHR to private law. In: Loof, J.P., Ploeger, H. & van der Steur, A. (Eds.). *The Right to Property: the Influence of Article 1 Protocol No. 1 ECHR on Several Fields of Domestic Law.* Maastricht: Shaker Publishing.

Pimber, M.L. & Pretty, J.N. (1997). Parks people and professionals: putting "participation" into protected area management. In: Ghimire, K.B. & Pimber, M.P. (Eds.). *Social Change and Conservation: Environmental Politics and Impacts of National Parks and Protected Areas.* London: Earthscan.

Raff, M. (2005). Toward an ecologically sustainable property concept. In: Cooke, E. (Ed.). *Modern Studies in Property Law* (III). Oxford: Hart Publishing.

Razzaque, J. (2013). Information, public participation and access to justice in environmental matters. In: Alam, S., *et al.* (Eds.). *Routledge Handbook of International Environmental Law.* London and New York: Routledge.

Robinson, J.G. & Redford, K.H. (2004). Jack of all trades, master of none: inherent contradictions among ICD approaches. In: McShane, T.O. & Wells, M.P. *Getting Biodiversity Projects to Work: towards More Effective Conservation and Development.* New York: Colombia University Press.

Rosas, A. (1992). Property rights. In: Rosas, A. & Helgesen, J. (Eds.). *The Strength of Diversity: Human Rights and Pluralist Democracy.* Leiden: Martinus Nijhoff Publishers.

Sagel-Grande, H.I. (2000). Property rights and ownership in eastern and western Europe and Article 1 Protocol No. 1 European Convention on Human Rights. In: Loof, J.P., Ploeger, H. & van der Steur, A. (Eds.). *The Right to Property: the Influence of Article 1 Protocol No. 1 ECHR on Several Fields of Domestic Law.* Maastricht: Shaker Publishing.

Scherl, L.M. (2006). Social justice and human rights in conservation: an ethical consideration for future policies and actions. In: IUCN. *Policy Matters – Poverty, Wealth and Conservation.* No. 14, the IUCN Commission on Environmental, Economic and Social Policy (CEESP).

Schermers, H.G. (1988). The international protection of the right of property. In: Matscher, F. & Petzold, H. (Eds.). *Protecting Human Rights: the European Dimension* (Studies in honour of Gerard J. Wiarda). Koln/Berlin/Bonn/Munchen: Carl Heymanns.

Shelton, D.L. (2011). Human rights and the environment: substantive rights. In: Fitzmaurice, M., Ong, D.M. & Merkouris, P. (Eds.). *Research Handbook on International Environmental Law.* Cheltenham (UK) and Northampton (USA): Edward Elgar Publishing.

Shelton, D.L. (2001). Environmental rights. In: Alston, P. (Ed.). *Peoples' Rights.* Oxford: Oxford University Press.

Shelton, D.L. (2012). Using law and equity for the poor and the environment. In: Bouthillier, Y.L., Cohen, M.A., Marquez, J.J.G., Mumma, A. & Smith, S. (Eds.). *Poverty Alleviation and Environmental Law.* The IUCN Academy of Environmental Law Series. Cheltenham (UK) and Northampton (USA): Edward Elgar Publishing.

Shepheard, M. & Martin, P. (2012). The political discourse of land stewardship reframed as a statutory duty. In: Jessup, B. & Rubenstein, K. (Ed.). *Environmental Discourses in Public and International Law.* Cambridge: Cambridge University Press.

Shue, H. (1984). The interdependence of duties. In: Alston, P. & Tomaševski, K. (Eds.). *The Right to Food.* Leiden: Martinus Nijhoff Publishers.

Soupajärvi, L. (2003). Competing industries and contested nature in Finnish lapland after World War II. In: Möller, S. & Pehkonen, S. (Eds.). *Encountering the North: Cultural Geography, International Relations and Northern Landscapes.* Farnham (UK): Ashgate Publishing.

Stec, S. (1998). Chapter 3: Access to Justice in Environmental Matters. In: *Doors to Democracy: a Pan-European Assessment of Current Trends and Practices in Public Participation in Environmental Matters.* Szentendre (Hungary): The Regional Environmental Center for Central and Eastern Europe.

Tava, I.V. (2013). The role of non-governmental organizations, peoples and courts in implementing international environmental laws. In: Alam, S., Hossain Bhuiyan, M.J., Chowdhury, T.M.R. & Techera, E.J. (Eds.). *Routledge Handbook of International Environmental Law.* London and New York: Routledge.

Turton, D. (2002). The mursi and the elephant question. In: Chatty, D. & Colchester, M. (Eds.). *Conservation and Mobile Indigenous Peoples: Displacement, Forced Settlement and Sustainable Development.* Oxford: Berghahn Books.

Twining, W. (2009). Law, justice and rights: some implications of a global perspective. In: Ebbesson, J. & Okowa, P. (Eds.). *Environmental Law and Justice in Context.* Cambridge: Cambridge University Press.

van Rooij, B. (2010). Land loss and conflict in China: illustrated by cases from Yunnan province. In: Ubink, J.M., Hoekema, A.J. & Assies, W.J. (Eds.). *Legalising Land Rights – Local Practices, State Responses and Tenure Security in Africa, Asia and Latin America.* Leiden University Press.

Winter, G. (2005). Conflicts between ownership rights and the implementation of the 'Natura 2000' Network. In: Paques, M. (Ed.). *Natura 2000 and Property Rights: International and National Reports.* Brussels: Etablissements Emile Bruylant.

Zhuge, R. (2000). Questionnaire survey on local participation into efforts of nature conservation and resources management in nature reserve of China. In: China Man and Biosphere Committee (Eds.). *Study of Sustainable Management Policies for China's Nature Reserve.* Beijing: Scientific and Technical Documents Publishing House.

JOURNAL ARTICLES

Adams, M.W. & Hutton, J. (2007). People, parks and poverty: political ecology and biodiversity conservation. *Conservation and Society*, 5(2).

Adams, W.M., Aveling, R., Brockington, D., Dickson, B., Elliott, J., Hutton, J., Roe, D., Vira, B. & Wolmer, W. (2004). Biodiversity conservation and the eradication of poverty. *Science*, 306.

Adams, W. (2001). If community conservation is the answer in Africa, what is the question? *Oryx*, 35(3).

Alcorn, J.B. & Royo, A.G. (2007). Conservation's engagement with human rights: "traction", "slippage", or avoidance? *Policy Matters*, 15.

Allendorf, T.D., Smith, J.L.D. & Anderson, D.H. (2007). Residents' perceptions of Royal Bardia national park, Nepal. *Landscape and Urban Planning*, 82.

Andresen, S. & Hey, E. (2005). The effectiveness and legitimacy of international environmental institutions. *International Environmental Agreements: Politics, Law and Economics*, 5(3).

Aminzadeh, S.C. (2006). A moral imperative: the human rights implications of climate change. *Hastings International and Comparative Law Review*, 30.

Andrew-Essien, E. & Bisong, F. (2009). Conflicts, conservation and natural resource use in protected area systems: an analysis of recurrent issues. *European Journal of Scientific Research*, 25(1).

Anderson, D. (1999). Compensation for interference with property. *European Human Rights Law Review*, 9.

Atapattu, S. (2002). The right to a healthy life or the right to die polluted? The emergence of a human right to a healthy environment under international law. *Tulane Environmental Law Journal*, 16(65).

Atapattu, S. (2004). The public health impact of global environmental problems and the role of international law. *American Journal of Law & Medicine*, 30(2&3).

Barbier, E.B. (1993). Valuing tropical wetland benefits: economic methodologies and applications. *Geographical Journal*, 1(59).

Bardhan, P. (2002). Decentralization of governance and development. *Journal of Economic Perspectives*, 16(4).

Bajracharya, S.B., Furley, P.A. & Newton, A.C. (2006). Impacts of community-based conservation on local communities in the Annapurna conservation area, Nepal. *Biodiversity and Conservation*, 15(8).

Barrett, C.B., Travis, A.J. & Dasgupta, P. (2011). On biodiversity conservation and poverty traps. *Proceedings of National Academy of Sciences of the United States of America*, 108.

Beierle, T.C. (2002). The quality of stakeholder-based decisions. *Risk Analysis*, 22(4).

Berkes, F. (2007). Community-based conservation in a globalized world. *Proceeding of National Academy of Sciences of the United States of America*, 104(39).

Beyer, S. (2006). Environmental law and policy in the people's republic of China. *Chinese Journal of International Law*, 5(1).

Blahna, D.J. & Yonts-Shepard, S. (1989). Public involvement in resource planning: toward bridging the gap between policy and implementation. *Society and Natural Resources*, 2.

Boyle, A. (2012). Human rights and the environment: where next? *The European Journal of International Law*, 23(3).

Brockington, D., Igoe, J. & Schmidt-Soltau, K. (2006). Conservation, human rights and poverty reduction. *Conservation Biology*, 20.

Brody, S.D. (2003). Measuring the effects of stakeholder participation on the quality of local plans based on the principles of collaborative ecosystem management. *Journal of Planning Education and Research*, 22.

Brosius, P. (2004). Indigenous Peoples and Protected Areas. *Conservation Biology*, 18(3).

Bruch, E. C. & Czebiniak, R. (2002). Globalizing environmental governance: making the leap from regional initiatives on transparency, participation, and accountability in environmental matters. *Environmental Law Reporter*, 32.

Castro, A.P. & Nielsen, E. (2001). Indigenous people and co-management: implications for conflicts management. *Environmental Science & Policy*, 4.

Cai, S. (蔡守秋) (2012). On strengthening the construction for environmental court (《论加强环境法庭的建设》). *Research on Front Issues in Environmental Law* (《环境法前沿问题研究》).

Carvalho, A.M. & Frazao-Moreira, A. (2011). Importance of local knowledge in plant resources management and conservation in two protected areas from Tras-os-Montes, Portugal. *Journal of Ethnobiology and Ethnomedicine*, 7(36).

Chávez, B.V. & Bernal, A.S. (2008). Planning hydroelectric power plants with the public: a case of organizational and social learning in Mexico. *Impact Assessment and Project Appraisal*, 26(3).

Chess, C. & Purcell, K. (1999). Public participation and the environment – do we know what works. *Environmental Science and Technology*, 33.

Coad, L., *et al.* (2009). Progress towards the convention on biological diversity terrestrial 2010 and marine 2012 targets for protected area coverage. *Parks*, 17.

Cun-kuan, B., Yong-sen, L., *et al.* (2004). Framework and operational procedure for implementing strategic environmental assessment in China. *Environmental Impact Assessment Review*, 24(1).

Daniels, A.E. (2002). Indigenous peoples and neotropical forest conservation: impacts of the protected area systems on traditional cultures. *Macalester Environmental Review*, 23 September 2002, http://lueci.clas.ufl.edu/southworth/grad-application/2002_Daniels%20-%20Neotropical%20forest%20conservation%20-%20indigenous%20peoples%20&%20protected%20areas.pdf.

Dearden, P., Bennett, M. & Johnston, J. (2005). Trends in global protected area governance 1992–2002. *Environmental Management*, 36(1).

Defries, R., Hansen, A., Turner, B.L., Reid, R. & Liu, J.G. (2007). Land use change around protected areas: management to balance human needs and ecological function. *Ecological Applications*, 17(4).

Del Furia, L. & Wallace-Jones, J. (2000). The effectiveness of provisions and quality of practices concerning public participation in EIA in Italy. *Environmental Impact Assessment Review*, 20(4).

Desmet, E. (2010). Balancing conflicting goods: the European human rights jurisprudence on environmental protection. *Journal for European Environmental & Planning Law*, 7(3).

Ding, C.R. (2007). Policy and praxis of land acquisition in China. *Land Use Policy*, 24(1).

Eberle, J.E. (2009). The method and role of comparative law. *Washington University Global Studies Law Review*, 8(3).

Economy, E.C. (2007). The great leap backward? *Foreign Affairs*, 86(5).

Elvin, M. (1998). The environmental legacy of imperial China. *The China Quarterly*, 156.

Estes, A.B., Kuemmerle, T., Kushnir, H., Radeloff, V.C. & Shugart, H.H. (2012). Landcover change and human population trends in the greater Serengeti ecosystem from 1984–2003. *Biological Conservation*, 147(1).

Fauchald, O.K. & Gulbrandsen, L.H. (2012). The Norwegian reform of protected areas management: a grand experiment with delegation of authority? *Local Environment: the International Journal of Justice And Sustainability*, 17(2).

Fitzmaurice, M. (1999). The right of the child to a clean environment. *Southern Illinois University Law Journal*, 23.

Fraga, J. (2006). Local perspectives in conservation politics: the case of the Ria Lagartos Biosphere Reserve, Yucatan Mexico. *Landscapes Urban Plan*, 74.

Gao, S. (高硕) (2013). Investigation and reflection of local indigenous people's compensation in nature reserves: based on Sanjiang national protected area (关于自然保护区原住民补偿问题的调查与思考 – – 基于对黑龙江三江国家级自然保护区的调查). *Journal of Northeast Forestry University* (东北林业大学学报), 41(7) (第41卷第7期).

Garie´py, M. (1991). Toward a dual-influence system: assessing the effects of public participation in environmental impact assessment for hydro-Quebec projects. *Environmental Impact Assessment Review*, 11.

Gauthier, M., Simard, L. & Waaub, J.P. (2011). Public participation in strategic environmental assessment: critical review and the Quebec (Canada) approach. *Environmental Impact Assessment Review*, 31.

Gillingham, S. (2003). People and protected areas: a case study of local perceptions of wildlife, crop damage and conflict, *Oryx*, 37(3).

Giorgetta, S. (2002). The right to a healthy environment, human rights and sustainable development. *International Environmental Agreements: Politics, Law and Economics*, 2.

Goelz, J.D. (2009). China's environmental problems: is a specialized court the solution? *Pacific Rim Law & Policy Journal Association*, 10(1).

Greer, S. (2004). "Balancing" and the European Court of human rights: a contribution to the Habermas-Alexy debate. *Cambridge Law Journal*, 63(2).

Gu, L. & Sheate, W.R. (2005). Institutional challenges for EIA implementation in China: a case study of development versus environmental protection. *Environmental Management*, 36(1).

Han, N. (2000). A policy study on sustainable management for China's nature reserves. *Journal of Nature Resource*, 15(3).

Hansen, A.J. & DeFries, R. (2007). Ecological mechanisms linking protected areas to surrounding lands. *Ecological Applications*, 17.

Hartley, N. & Wood, C. (2005). Public participation in environmental impact assessment – implementing the Aarhus Convention. *Environmental Impact Assessment Review*, 25.

He, M. (2014). Human rights protection in ecological conservation in China: progress, problems and prospects. *IUCN Academy of Environmental Law E Journal*, 5.

He, M. & Cliquet, A. (2013). Sustainable development through a rights-based approach to conserve protected areas in China. *China-EU Law Journal.* DOI 10.1007/s 12689-013-0031-7. http://link.springer.com/article/10.1007%2Fs12689-013-0031-7.

He, G.M., *et al.* (2008). Distribution of economic benefits from ecotourism: a case study of Wolong nature reserve for Giant Pandas in China. *Environmental Management,* 42.

Herrold, B. & Beijing, L. (2008). An Overview of Property Development in China. *SGLA (Sino-Global Legal Alliance) Law Journal,* 1(2).

Hoekstra, J.M., Boucher, T.M., Ricketts, T.H. & Roberts, C. (2005). Confronting a biome crisis: global disparities of habitat loss and protection. *Ecology Letters,* 8.

Honore, A.H. (1961). Ownership. *Oxford Estates in Jurisprudence,* 107.

Hull, V., *et al.* (2011). Evaluating the efficacy of zoning designations for protected area management. *Biological Conservation,* 144.

Jack, B. (2006). The European Community and biodiversity loss: missing the target? *Review of European Community and International Environmental Law,* 15(3).

Jans, J.H. (2000). Proportionality revisited. *Legal Issues of Economic Integration,* 27.

Jim, C.Y. & Xu, S.S.W. (2004) Recent Protected-area Designation in China: an Evaluation of Administrative and Statutory Procedures. *The Geographical Journal,* 170.

Jim, C.Y., *et al.* (2002). Stifled stakeholders and subdued participation: interpreting local responses toward Shimentai Nature Reserve in South China. *Environmental Management,* 30 (3).

Johnson, C. & Forsyth, T. (2002). In the eyes of the sate: negotiating a "human rights-based approach" to forest conservation in Thailand. *World Development,* 30(9).

Jones, P.J.S. & Burgess, J. (2005). Building partnership capacity for the collaborative management of marine protected areas in the UK: a preliminary analysis. *Journal of Environmental Management,* 77(3).

Jones-Walters, L. & Civic, K. (2013). European protected areas: past, present and future. *Journal for Nature Conservation,* 21.

Kabeer, N. (2002). Citizenship, affiliation and exclusion: perspectives from the South. *IDS (Institute of Development Studies) Bulletin,* 33(2).

Keulartz, J. (2009). European nature conservation and restoration policy – problems and perspectives. *The Journal of the Society for Ecological Restoration International,* 17(4).

Khalesi, A.M. (2013). Principles and content of right to environment (in the light of international documents and conventions). *Advances in Applied Science Research,* 4(4).

Kravchenko, S. (2009). Is access to environmental information a fundamental human right? *Oregon Review of International Law,* 11.

Koontz, T.M. & Thomas, C.W. (2006). What do we know and need to know about the environmental outcomes of collaborative management? *Public Administration Review,* 66.

Kothari, A. (2006). Protected areas and people: the future of the past. *Parks,* 17(2).

Lee, M. & Abbot, C. (2003). The usual suspects? public participation under the Aarhus Convention. *The Modern Law Review,* 66(1).

Li, Y.F. (2004) The legal system for the public participation and environmental protection. *Zhejiang Social Science,* 2.

Li, W.X., Liu, J.Y. & Li, D.D. (2012). Getting their voices heard: Three cases of public participation in environmental protection in China. *Journal of Environmental Management*, 98.

Liang, Q., Wang, X.H. & Lees, B. (2011). Community participation in the management of marine protected areas in China. *Labour and Management in Development Journal*, 11.

Lieberthal, K. (1997) China's governing system and its impact on environmental policy implementation. *China Environment Series*, 1.

Liu, W.J. (2011). Approaching democracy through transparency: a comparative law study on Chinese open government information. *American University International Law Review*, 26(4).

Lockie, S., Franetovich, M., Sharma, S. & Rolfe, J. (2008). Democratization versus engagement? social and economic impact assessment and community participation in the coal mining industry of the Bowen Basin, Australia. *Impact Assessment and Project Appraisal*, 26(3).

Locke, H. & Dearden, P. (2005). Rethinking protected area categories and the new paradigm. *Environmental Conservation*, 32(1).

Lockwood, M. (2010). Good governance for terrestrial protected areas: a framework, principles and performance outcomes. *Journal of Environmental Management*, 91.

Lu, Y., *et al.* (2003). A framework for evaluating the effectiveness of protected areas: the case of Wolong Biosphere Reserve. *Landscapes Urban Plan*, 63.

MacKinnon, K. (2001). Editorial. *Parks*, 11(2).

Maikhuri, R.K., Nautiyal, S., Rao, K.S. & Saxena, K.G. (2001). Conservation policy-people conflicts: a case study from Nanda Devi Biosphere Reserve (a world heritage site), India. *Forest Policy and Economics*, 2(3, 4).

McAllister, S.T. (1998). Human rights and the environment: the Convention on access to information, public participation in decision making, and access to justice in environmental matters. *Colorado Journal of International Environmental Law Yearbook*, 9.

McDonald, R.I. & Boucher, T.M. (2011). Global development and the future of the protected area strategy. *Biological Conservation*, 144.

McDonagh, M. (2013). The right to information in international human rights law. *Human Rights Law Review.* DOI 10.1093/hrlr/ngs045, http://hrlr.oxfordjournals.org/content/early/2013/02/20/hrlr.ngs045.full.pdf+html

McNeely, J.A. (1994). Protected areas for the 21st century: working to provide benefits to society. *Biodiversity and Conservation*, 3.

Mcshane, T.O., *et al.* (2011). Hard choices: making trade-offs between biodiversity conservation and human well-being. *Biological Conservation*, 144.

Morgera, E. (2005). An update on the Aarhus Convention and its continued global relevance. *Review of European Community and International Environmental Law*, 14(2).

Miao, G.P. & West, R.A. (2004). Chinese collective forestlands: contributions and constraints. *International Forestry Review*, 6.

Momtaz, S. & Gladstone, W. (2008). Ban on commercial fishing in the estuarine waters of New South Wales, Australia: community consultation and social impacts. *Environmental Impact Assessment Review*, 28(2–3).

Mowery, L.A. (2002). Earth rights, human rights: can international environmental human rights affect corporate accountability? *Fordham Environmental Law Journal*, 13.

Newig, J. (2007). Does public participation in environmental decisions lead to improved environmental quality? Towards an analytical framework. *Communication, Cooperation, Participation(International Journal of Sustainability Communication)*, 1.

Newmark, W.D., Leonard, N.L., Sariko, H.I. & Gamassa, D.G.M. (1993). Conservation attitudes of local people living adjacent to 5 protected areas in Tanzania. *Biological Conservation*, 63.

Ormsby, A. & Kaplin, B.A. (2005). A framework for understanding community resident perceptions of Masoala National Park. *Madagascar Environmental Conservation*, 32 (2).

Pedersen, O.W. (2008). European environmental human rights and environmental rights: a long time coming? *The Georgetown International Environmental Law Review*, 21.

Peterlin, M., Kross B.C. & Kontic, B. (2006). Information in an EIA process and the influence thereof on public opinion. *Journal of Environmental Assessment Policy and Management*, 8(2).

Peukert, W. (1981). Protection of ownership under Article 1 of First Protocol to the European Convention on Human Rights. *Human Rights Law Journal*, 3, 37(43).

Phan, P.N. (2005) Enriching the land or the political elite? Lessons from China on democratization of the urban renewal process. *Pacific Rim Law and Policy Journal*, 14.

Phillips, A. (2003). Turning ideas on their head – the new paradigm for protected areas. *The George Wright Forum*, 20(2).

Pirk, S. (2002). Expanding public participation in environmental justice: methods, legislation, litigation and beyond. *Journal of Environmental Law and Litigation*, 17(1).

Pomeroy, R.S. & Berkes, F. (1997). Two to tango: the role of government in fisheries co-management. *Marine Policy*, 21(5).

Popovic, N.A.F. (1993). The right to participate in decisions that affect the environment. *Pace Environmental Law Review*, 10(2).

Prosterman, R., Schwarzwalder, B. & Y, J.P. (2000). Implementation of 30-year land use rights for farmers under China's 1998 land management law: an analysis and recommendations based on a 17-province survey. *Pacific Rim Law & Policy Journal*, 9.

Qi, S.J. & Zhou, Y.Y. (齐树洁，周一颜) (2013). Judicial reforms and access to justice: after civil procedural law amended (《司法改革与接近正义 – – 写在民事诉讼法修改之后》). *Journal of Heilongjiang Administrative Cadre College of Politics and Law*(黑龙江省政法管理干部学院学报), 1.

Qiu, W., Wang, B., Jones, P.J.S. & Axmacher, J.C. (2009). Challenges in developing China's marine protected areas system. *Marine Policy*, 33(4).

Rao, K.S., Maikhuri, R.K. & Saxena, K.G. (2003). Local people's knowledge, aptitude and perceptions of planning and management issues in Nanda Devi Biosphere Reserve, India. *Environmental Management*, 31 (2).

Reed, M.S. (2008) Stakeholder participation for environmental management: a literature review. *Biological Conservation*, 141.

Reed, M.S., Fraser, E.D.G. & Dougill, A.J. (2006). An adaptive learning process for developing and applying sustainability indicators with local communities. *Ecological Economics*, 59.

Rees, S.E., *et al.* (2010). Is there a win-win scenario for marine nature conservation? A case study of Lyme Bay. *Ocean & Coastal Management*, 53.

Razzaque, J. & Blanco, E. (2009). Ecosystem services and human well-being in a globalized world: assessing the role of law. *Human Rights Quarterly*, 31.

Robinson, J.R., *et al.* (1996). Public access to environmental information: a means to what end? *Journal of Environmental Law*, 8 (1).

Robinson, N.A. (2012). Ensuring access to justice through environmental courts. *Pace Environmental Law Review*, 29.

Rowe, G. & Frewer, L.J. (2004). Evaluating public-participation exercises: a research agenda. *Science, Technology & Human Values*, 29.

Sachs, J.D., Baillie, J.E.M., Sutherland, W.J., Armsworth, P.R., Ash, N., Beddington, J., Blackburn, T.M., Collen, B., Gardiner, B. & Gaston, K.J. (2009). Biodiversity conservation and the millennium development goals. *Science*, 325.

Schlager, E. & Ostrom, E. (1992). Property rights regimes and natural resources: a conceptual analysis. *Land Economics*, 68(3).

Schmidt, P.M. & Peterson, M.J. (2009). Biodiversity conservation and indigenous land management in the era of self-determination. *Conservation Biology*, 23(6).

Schuijers, L. (2011). Application of rights-based approach to conservation: the problem of fragmentation and the need for a coordinated response. *Macquarie Journal of International and Comparative Environmental Law*, 7(1).

Schwarzwalder, B., *et al.* (2002). An update on China's rural land tenure reforms: analysis and recommendations based upon a seventeen-province survey. *Columbia Journal of Asian Law*, 16.

Shelton, D.L. (1991). Human rights, environmental rights, and the right to environment. *Stanford Journal of International Law*, 28.

Soutullo, A., De Castro, M. & Urios, V. (2008). Linking political and scientifically derived targets for global biodiversity conservation: implications for the expansion of the global network of protected areas. *Diversity and Distributions*, 14.

Soveroski, M. (2007). Environmental rights versus environmental wrongs: forum over substance? *Review of European Community & International Environmental Law*, 16(3).

Stewart, T.R., Dennis, R.L. & Ely, D.W. (1984). Citizen participation and judgment in policy analysis – a case-study of urban air quality policy. *Policy Science*, 17.

Stewart, J.M.P. & Sinclair, A.J. (2007). Meaningful public participation in environmental assessment: perspectives from Canadian participants, proponents and government. *Journal of Environmental Assessment Policy and Management*, 9(2).

Stringer, L., Dougill, A., Fraser, E.D.G., Hubacek, K., Prell, C. & Reed, M. (2006). Unpacking 'participation' in the adaptive management of socio-ecological systems: a critical review. *Ecology and Society*, 11.

Subrahmanyan, A. (2004). Land use in China: the impact of the economic revolution. *China Law & Practice*, 18(9).

Sun, Y.H. & Chen, S.Y. (2004). Arguments for the new Law of protected areas. *Environmental Protection*, 3.

Tallis, H., Kareiva, P., Marvier, M., Chang, A. (2008). An ecosystem services framework to support both practical conservation and economic development. *Proceedings of National Academy of Sciences of the United States of America*, 105.

Taylor, P. E. (1997). From environmental to ecological human rights: a new dynamic in international law? *Georgetown International Environmental Law Review*, 10(309).

Trakolis, D. (2001). Local people's perceptions of planning and management issues in prespes lakes national park, Greece. *Journal of Environmental Management*, 61.

van de Venis, J. (2011). A human right to a clean and healthy environment: dream or reality in Europe? *Environmental Law Network International*, 1.

Van Rooij, B. (2006). Implementation of Chinese environmental law: regular enforcement and political campaigns. *Development and Change*, 37(1).

Vina, A.S., *et al.* (2007). Temporal changes in giant panda habitat connectivity across boundaries of Wo-long Nature Reserve, China. *Ecological Applications*, 17.

Wallner, A., Bauer, N. & Hunziker, M. (2007). Perceptions and evaluations of biosphere reserves by local residents in Switzerland and Ukraine. *Landscape and Urban Planning*, 83.

Wang, A. (2006). The role of law in environmental protection in China: recent developments. *Vermont Journal of Environmental Law*, 195.

Wätzold, F. & Schwerdtner, K. (2005). Why be wasteful when preserving a valuable resource? A review Article on the cost-effectiveness of European biodiversity conservation policy. *Biological Conservation*, 123(3).

Weladji, R. (2003). Conflict between people and protected areas. *Oryx*, 37(1).

West, P., Igoe, J. & Brockington, D. (2006). Parks and peoples: the social impact of protected areas. *Annual Review of Anthropology*, 35.

Wiesmann, U., Liechti, K. & Rist, S. (2005). Between conservation and development: concretizing the first World Natural Heritage Site in the Alps through participatory processes. *Mountain Research and Development*, 25(2).

Wirth, D.A. (1996). Public participation in international processes: environmental case studies at the national and international levels. *Colorado Journal of International Law and Policy*, 7.

Wissel, S. & Wätzold, F. (2010). A conceptual analysis of the application of tradable permits to biodiversity conservation. *Conservation Biology*, 24(2).

Wong, B. (2000). Traditional Chinese philosophy and dispute resolution. *Hong Kong Law Journal*, 30.

Wu, G. (2011). China in 2010: dilemmas of "scientific development". *Asian Survey*, 51 (1).

Wu, R.D., *et al.* (2011). The performance of nature reserves in capturing the biological diversity on Hainan Island, China. Environmental Science and Pollution Research, 18.

Wu, R.D., *et al.* (2011). Effective-ness of China's nature reserves in representing ecological diversity. Frontiers in Ecology and the Environment, 9.

Wu, X., Xu, H., Jiang, M. & Liu, L. (2002). Harmonized development of nature reserve and local community. *Rural Eco-Environment*, 18(2).

Wu, J.K. (吴进科) (2007). Chinese traditional no litigation ideas and harmony society construction (我国传统无讼思想与构建和谐社会). *Enterprise Civilization* (企业文明), 10.

Wu, Y. & Tian, B. (吴勇，田犇) (2012). Improvement of public participation system in the east dongting lake nature reserve (论东洞庭湖自然保护区公众参与机制的完善). *Journal of Wuling* (武陵学刊), 37(3).

Xiao, J.H. & Zhou, X.F. (肖建华、周训芳) (2009). Collective land management in protected areas and community co-management contract (自然保护区集体土地管理与社区共管契约). *Seeker* (求索), 2.

Xu, J.C. & David, R.M. (2007). Rethinking the Effectiveness of Public Protected Areas in Southwestern China. *Conservation Biology*, 21(2).

Xu, J.C. & Ribot, J.C. (2004). Decentralization and accountability in forest management: case from Yunnan, southwest China. *European Journal of Development Research*, 16(1).

Xu, J.Y., *et al.* (2006). Local people's perceptions as decision support for protected area management in Wolong Biosphere reserve, China. *Journal of Environmental Management*, 78.

Xu, L. (2002). Current situation and development of Nature Reserves in Yunnan Province, China. *Forest Inventory and Planning*, 27(4).

Young, J., *et al.* (2005). Towards sustainable land use: identifying and managing the conflicts between human activities and biodiversity conservation in Europe. *Biodiversity and Conservation*, 14.

Young, J.C., *et al.* (2013). Does stakeholder involvement really benefit biodiversity conservation?. *Biological Conservation*, 158.

Young, J., Butler, J.R.A., Jordan, A. & Watt, A.D. (2012). Less government intervention in biodiversity management: risks and opportunities. *Biological Conservation*, 21(4).

Yu, G.Z. & Jiang, Z.-G. (2003). Buffer zones: Pattern, function and design principles. *Biodiversity Science*, 11.

Zeng, C.L. (曾彩琳) (2012). Research on legal system of right protection of residents of nature reserves in China (我国自然保护区地居民权利保障法律制度研究). *Journal of Dalian University of Technology (Social Sciences)* (大连理工大学学报（社会科学版）), 33(3).

Zhang, K.M. & Wen, Z.G. (2008). Review and challenges of politicizes of environmental protection and sustainable development in China. *Journal of Environmental Management*, 88.

Zhao, H.X., Qu, F.T., Zhu, P. & Shi, X.P. (2010). Resource and environmental issues in transitional China: a perspective from the interaction among market, government and society. *Chinese Journal of Population Resources and Environment*, 8(2).

Zhou, D.Q. & Grumbine, R.E. (2011). National parks in China: experiments with protecting nature and human livelihoods in Yunnan province, People's Republic of China (PRC). *Biological Conservation*, 144.

Zhu, K.L., *et al.* (2006). The rural land question in China: analysis and recommendations based on a 17-Province in 2003 Survey. *Journal of International Law & Politics*, 38.

Zube, E.H. & Busch, M.L. (1990). Park–people relationships: an international review. *Landscapes Urban Plan*, 19.

CONFERENCE PAPERS

Bjerler, N. (2004). Do Europeans have a right to environment?. In: International Environmental Law – agora session of the Inaugural Conference of the European Society of International Law, Florence, Italy, 13–15 May 2004, www.esil-sedi.eu/sites/default/files/Bjerler_0.PDF

Bhagwati, P.H. (2002). Democratization of remedies and access to justice. In: the First South Asian Regional Judicial Symposium on Access to Justice, New Delhi, 1–3 November 2002.

Boyle, A. & Boer, B. (2013). Human rights and the environment. In: the Thirteenth Informal ASEM Seminar on Human Rights, Asia-Europe Meeting, Copenhagen, Denmark, 21–23 October 2013, http://asef.org/images/docs/13th%20Informal%20ASEM%20Seminar%20-%20Background%20paper%20%28FINAL%29.pdf

Bruch, C. (2000). Regional opportunities for improving environmental governance through access to information, public participation and access to justice. In: the Eighth Session of the African Ministerial Conference on Environment (AMCE), Abuja, Nigeria, 3–6 April 2000, www.eli.org/pdf/africa/csamcen00.pdf

Campese, J., *et al.* (2008). Rights and conservation in a diverse and sustainable world: a journey at the 2008 IUCN World Conservation Congress. In: A Congress Forum Journey Report, Barcelona, Spain, 5–14 October 2008, http://cmsdata.iucn.org/downloads/rights_and_conservation_journey_report_1_2.pdf

Cao, M.D. & Wang, F.Y. (曹明德，王凤远) (2009). The theoretical basis of environmental public interest litigation – the necessity and obstacles of the environmental public interest litigation by ENGO in China (《ENGO环境公益诉讼的理论依据 – 兼论中国ENGO环境公益诉讼的必要性及主要困境》). In: Ecological Civilization and Environmental Protection Law – National Environmental and Resources Law Symposium in 2009 (生态文明与环境资源法 – 2009年全国环境资源法学研讨会论文集), Kunming (昆明), 3 – 6 August 2009.

Chaudhry, P. (2012). Ethnic minority development in China and ASEAN countries. In: the sixth China – ASEAN Forum on Social Development and Poverty Reduction in 2012. UNDP & IPRCC, www.cn.undp.org/content/dam/china/docs/Publications/UNDP-CH-HD-Publications-Ethnic-Minority-Development-in-China-and-ASEAN-countries.pdf

Council of Europe (2004). Naturaopa: the 25 years of the Bern Convention. No. 101, http://128.121.10.98/coe/pdfopener?smd=1&md=1&did=594649

Deloges, C. & Gauthier, M. (1997). Community forest and forest resource conflicts: an overview. In: The XI World Forestry Congress, Antalya, Turkey.

Directorate of Culture and Cultural and Natural Heritage (2011). Improving the case-file system of the Bern Convention. Convention on the Conservation of European Wildlife and Natural Habitats Standing Committee. In: thirty-first meeting, Strasbourg, 29 November – 2 December 2011, https://wcd.coe.int/com.instranet.InstraServlet?command=com.instranet.CmdBlobGet&InstranetImage=1956319&SecMode=1&DocId=1811880&Usage=2

Ebbesson, J. (2009). Draft paper on: Participatory and procedural rights in environmental matters: state of play. In: High Level Expert Meeting on the New Future of Human Rights and Environment: Moving the Global Agenda Forward

Co-organized by UNEP and OHCHR, Nairobi, 30 November – 1 December 2009, www.unep.org/environmentalgovernance/LinkClick.aspx?fileticket=vZU4Z-_S4Vo%3d&tabid=2046&language=en-US

Economic Commission for Europe (2005). Findings and Recommendations with regards to compliance by Ukraine with the obligations under the Aarhus Convention in the case of Bystre deep-water navigation canal construction (submission ACCC/S/2004/01 by Romania and communication ACCC/C/2004/03 by Ecopravo-Lviv (Ukraine)). Adopted by the Aarhus Convention's Compliance Committee on 18 February 2005. ECE/MP.PP/C.1/2005/2/Add.3. 14 March 2005, www.unece.org/fileadmin/DAM/env/pp/compliance/C2004-03/S01C03findings.pdf

Economic Commission for Europe (ECE) (2006). Meeting of the parties to the Convention on access to information, public participation in decision-making and access to justice in environmental matters. Twelfth meeting, Geneva, 14–16 June 2006. ECE/MP.PP/C.1/2006/4/Add.2. 28 July 2006, www.unece.org/fileadmin/DAM/env/documents/2006/pp/ece.mp.pp.c.1.2006.4.add.2.e.pdf

Economic Commission for Europe (ECE) (2007). Meeting of the parties to the Convention on access to information, public participation in decision-making and access to justice in environmental matters. Sixteenth meeting, Geneva, 13–15 June 2007, www.unece.org/fileadmin/DAM/env/documents/2008/pp/mop3/ece_mp_pp_2008_5_add_1_e.pdf

Economic Commission for Europe (2008). Meeting of the parties to the convention on access to information, public participation in decision-making and access to justice in environmental matters. Third meeting Riga, 11–13 June 2008. Item 6(a) of the provisional agenda procedures and mechanisms facilitating the implementation of the Convention: reports on implementation. ECE/MP.PP/2008/4. 21 May 2008, www.unece.org/fileadmin/DAM/env/documents/2008/pp/mop3/ece_mp_pp_2008_4_e.pdf

Economic Commission for Europe (ECE) (2008). Meeting of the parties to the Convention on access to information, public participation in decision-making and access to justice in environmental matters. Third meeting, Riga, 11–13 June 2008. Item 6(b) of the provisional agenda. Procedures and mechanisms facilitating the implementation of the Convention: Compliance mechanism. ECE/MP.PP/2008/5/Add.3. 2 April 2008, www.unece.org/fileadmin/DAM/env/pp/compliance/C2005-11/Update/ece_mp_pp_2008_5_add_3_e.pdf

Engel, J.R. (2009). Faustian pact or new covenant with Earth? In: the Conference Property Rights and Sustainability, University of Auckland, Auckland, New Zealand, 16–18 April 2009.

Hu, Y.Q. (2009). One year of openness: environmental information disclosure laws in China and Pollution Information Transparency Index (PITI). In: the IUCN Colloquium, Wuhan, China, www.greenlawchina.org/2009/05/one-year-of-openness-greenlaw-and-the-first-anniversary-of-chinas-open-information-regulations/

Joint UNEP-OHCHR (2002). Human rights and environment issues in multilateral treaties adopted between 1991 and 2001. Background Paper No. 1. In: Expert Seminar on Human Rights and the Environment, Geneva, Swiss, 4–16 January 2002, paras 15 and 16, www.unhchr.ch/environment/bp1.html

Jiang, Z.M. (江泽民) (1997). Hold high the great banner of Deng Xiaoping theory, for an all-around advancement of the cause of building socialism with Chinese characteristics in the 21st Century (高举邓小平理论伟大旗帜，把建设有中国特色社会主义事业全面推向二十一世纪). In: The Fifteenth National Congress of the Communist Party of China (中国共产党第十五次全国代表大会). www.fas.org/news/china/1997/970912-prc.htm, http://news.xinhuanet.com/zilia/2003-01/20content_697189.htm

Miao, H., Ouyang, Z., Wang, X. & Song, M. (2000). Management of communities in natural reserves: challenge and solutions. In: The Fourth National Conservation and Sustainable Use of Biological Diversity Seminar Proceedings, http://cpfd.cnki.com.cn/Article/CPFDTOTAL-ZKYS200011001009.htm, www.brim.ac.cn/book/book235_594.pdf

Peng, L. (彭莉) (2004). Research on the joint management of the communities in the protected areas (自然保护区中社区"共管"问题初探). In: The Annual Meeting and Academic Seminar of Environmental and Natural Resources Law under China Law Society (中国法学会环境资源法学研究会). Chongqing China (中国重庆), July 2004, www.riel.whu.edu.cn/Article.asp?id=26422

Robinson, N.A. (2012). Keynote address: a cannon for the anthropocene. In: "Rule of Law for Nature" Conference, Oslo University, 9–11 May 2012.

Schmidt-Soltan, K. & Brockington, D. (2004). The social impacts of protected areas. In: the First Global Workshop of World Conservation Congress, Bangkok, 20 November 2004, www.social-impact-of-conservation.net/

Shelton, D.L. (2009). Human rights and environment: past, present and future linkages and the value of a declaration. In: High Level Meeting on the New Future of Human Rights and Environment: Moving the Global Agenda Forward, Co-organized by UNEP and OHCHR, Nairobi, 30 November – 1 December 2009.

Tyler, T. (2014). Legitimacy in everyday life. In: the seminar Procedural Justice and the Courts: Normative Dimensions. Ghent University, Belgium. 17 January 2014.

United States' Congressional-Executive Commission on China (2004). Access to Justice in China: Roundtable before the Congressional-Executive Commission on China. In: One Hundred Eighth Congress, second session, 12 July 2004. Washington D.C.: United States Government Printing Office, http://babel.hathitrust.org/cgi/pt?id=umn.31951d024064594;view=1up;seq=11

Verschuuren, J., Bastmeijer, K. & van Lanen, J. (2000). Complaint procedures and access to justice for citizens and NGOs in the field of the environment within the European Union. In: The EU-IMPEL (European Union Network for the Implementation and Enforcement of Environmental Law) workshop, The Hague, the Netherlands, 10–11 May 2000, https://www.elaw.org/system/files/E.U.--IMPEL.Network%28Complaint.procedures.and.Access.to.Justice.for.citizens.and.NGO%29.pdf

Wang, C.F. (2010). The role of environmental litigation in protecting environmental rights and improving environment. In: the Workshop on Business, Human Rights and Access to Justice in China, Hong Kong, 5–6 March 2010.

Wu, R.D. (2013). Review of Chinese nature reserves data in the WDPA. In: National Workshop in China, www.unep-wcmc.org/medialibrary/2013/02/19/2aa7df96/Review%20of%20Chinese%20nature%20reserves%20data%20in%20the%20WDPA-%20Yunnan%20University.pdf

REPORTS AND OTHER PAPERS

A human rights approach to development – primer for development practitioners (draft) (2003), www.google.be/url?sa=t&rct=j&q=A+Human+Rights+Approach+to+Development+---+Primer+for+Development+Practioners+%28Draft+July+2003&source=web&cd=1&cad=rja&ved=0CCkQFjAA&url=http%3A%2F%2Fwww.crin.org%2Fdocs%2Fresources%2Fpublications%2Fhrbap%2FRBA_training_UNDP_primer.doc&ei=cDCZUMTMCuqM0AXXgYHoDA&usg=AFQjCNGCZTn74rZPh47TvAJ8ansmb7ev7g

AEETC (Asia-Europe Environmental Technology Centre) (2002). Public Involvement in Environmental Issues in the ASEM (Asia-Europe Meeting) – Background and Overview, published by Asia-Europe Environmental Technology Centre, Helsinki: Edita Prima, http://bch.cbd.int/protocol/outreach/ASEM.pdf

Andrusevych, A., Alge, T. & Clemens, C. (Eds.) (2008). Case law of the Aarhus Convention Compliance Committee (2004–2008), http://doku.cac.at/case_law_accc.pdf

Andrusevych, A., Alge, T. & Clemens, C. (Eds.) (2011). Case law of the Aarhus Convention Compliance Committee (2004–2011), http://rac.org.ua/fileadmin/user_upload/publications/ACCC_Case_Law_Electronic_Advanced_Version.pdf

Annan, K. (2010). The Aarhus Convention, an Implementation Guide, http://live.unece.org/environmentalpolicy/treaties/publicparticipation/publications/guidance/2000/aarhus-convention implementation-guide/aarhus convention-implementation-guide.html

Brandom, K. & Bruner, A. (2008). Local benefits of protected areas: perspectives and experiences of conservation International. In: Secretariat of the Convention on Biological Diversity. Protected Areas in Today's World: Their Values and Benefits for the Welfare of the Planet. Technical Series No. 36, Montreal: Secretariat of the Convention on Biological Diversity, https://www.cbd.int/doc/publications/cbd-ts-36-en.pdf

Bowen-Jones, E. (2012). Tackling human-wildlife conflicts: a prerequisite for linking conservation and poverty alleviation: a decision-makers guide to financial and institutional mechanisms. Poverty and Conservation Learning Group Discussion Paper No. 6, http://povertyandconservation.info/sites/default/files/PCLG%20HWC%20discussion%20paper_0.pdf

Bulletin on Environment in China in 2010 (2010年中国环境状况公报) (2011). The establishment and management on protected areas in China in 2010 (2010年自然保护区建设与管理情况). Published on 3 June 2011, http://sts.mep. gov.cn/zrbhq/zrbhqgzjb/201106/t20110603_211638.htm

Burke, E. (1791). Reflections on the Revolution in France. www.constitution.org/eb/rev_fran.htm. and www.fordham.edu/halsall/mod/1791burke.asp

Care Danmark (2009). Right-based approach guidelines (draft). Published in April 2009, www.careclimatechange.org/files/toolkit/CDK_Rights-Based_Guidelines.pdf

Changbaishan Protected Area Net (长白山自然保护区网). The introduction on Changbaishan protected area (长白山自然保护区介绍), http://211.103.250.141/publicfiles//business/htmlfiles/cbsbhq/jqgk/index.html

China Dialogue (中外对话) (2012). The environmental information disclosure in most regions of China cannot get a satisfied result (中国大部分地区环境信息公开不及格). Posted on 18 January 2012, www.chinadialogue.net/weblogs/4/weblog_posts/436?lang=en

China Youth Daily (中国青年报) (2011). Friends of Nature, an environmental NGOs in China, asked the Ministry of Environmental Protection to release some important information (民间环保组织"自然之友"就长江上游珍稀特有鱼类国家级自然保护区调整向环境保护部申请信息公开). Published on 13 May 2011, http://env.people.com.cn/GB/14625045.html

China Environmental Newspaper (中国环境报) (2010). Strengthen protected areas management and promote ecological civilization (加强自然保护区管理，促进生态文明建设), www.clapv.org/weiquanwenxian_content.asp?id=175

China Green Times (2009). How to reform the collective ownership of forest in protected areas. Posted on 26 May 2009, www.caf.ac.cn/news/xwzx/201001/2010-01-08-10-57.html

China Talk (中国访谈) (2013). Chinese protected areas legislation: civilian' activities (中国自然保护地法立法：民间在行动). Published on 23 January 2013, http://fangtan.china.com.cn/2013-01/23/content_27770395.htm

China Youth Daily (中国青年报) (2012). The Ministry of Environmental Protection: forbid to explore hydropower. Posted on 20 January 2012, http://env.people.com.cn/GB/16928251.html

CLAPV (Center for Legal Assistance to Pollution Victims) (2010). Access to environmental information in China: evaluation of local compliance, www.article19.org/data/files/pdfs/reports/access-to-environmental-information-in-china-evaluation-of-local-compliance.pdf

Clem, W. (2010). Half of websites miss the mark. Published in South China Morning. Post on 23 February 2010, www.scmp.com/portal/site/SCMP/menuitem.2af62ecb329d3d7733492d9253a0a0a0/?vgnextoid=12f549df716f6210VgnVCM100000360a0a0aRCRD

Council of Europe. Nature ecological networks and emerald network. www.coe.int/t/dg4/cultureheritage/nature/econetworks/default_en.asp

Cook, P. (1999). Non-discrimination and diversity: the rights of indigenous children (access to basic service and legal protection). A paper submitted to the CRC Day of Discussion on the rights of indigenous Children, International Institute for Child Rights and Development, www.crin.org/docs/resources/treaties/crc.34/IICRD_University_of_Victoria_Canada.pdf

China News (中国新闻网) (2008). 68 Villagers of Yu Yao, Zhejiang Successfully Sue Municipal Government Over Open Information Case (《浙江余姚68名村民信息公开案告赢市政府》). Issued on 10 October 2008, www.chinanews.com.cn/sh/news/2008/10-10/1407244.shtml

CIEL (Center for International Environmental Law) (2012). Human rights & environment in the Rio+20 UN Conference on Sustainable Development, www.ciel.org/Publications/Rio+20_IssueBrief_Feb2012.pdf

Conservation, human rights & protected areas governance: a field-based workshop in the Baviaanskloof Mega-Reserve (2007). South Africa, 6-7 July 2007, http://cmsdata.iucn.org/downloads/bav_workshop.pdf

Cui, G.Y. (2004). Some scientific issues need to be solved in protected areas. *Beijing Forest University Newspaper*, 26(6).

Daugstad, K. The Participatory Dimension in Nature Conservation Processes: Examples of Ideology and Practice from Norway, http://download.springer.com/static/pdf/881/chp%253A10.1007%252F978-90-481-9932-7_4.pdf?auth66=1379691801_f410c70c246033b6f9687fe81e0b796d&ext=.pdf

De Sadeleer, N. (2002). Access to justice in environmental matters. ENV.A.3/ETU/2002/0030. Final Report, www.ucastverejnosti.cz/dokumenty/studie-aarhus-zeme-eu.pdf

DETR (Department of Environment Transport Regions) (2000). Public participation in making local environmental decisions: the Aarhus Convention Newcastle workshop, www.unece.org/fileadmin/DAM/env/pp/ecases/handbook.pdf

EEA (European Environment Agency) (2010). 10 messages for 2010 Protected Areas. Published on 16 March, 2010, www.eea.europa.eu/publications/10-messages-for-2010-2014

EEA (European Environment Agency) (2012). Protected areas have increased to cover one fifth of Europe's land. Published on 23 October 2012, www.eea.europa.eu/highlights/protected-areas-have-increased-to

EEA (European Environment Agency) (2012). Protected areas in Europe – an overview. Published on 22 October 2012, www.eea.europa.eu/publications/protected-areas-in-europe-2012

EEA (European Environment Agency) (2013). Is there a protected area near you? find out on UN Biodiversity Day. Published on 22 May 2013, www.eea.europa.eu/highlights/is-there-a-protected-area

Energy & Biodiversity Initiative (EBI). Biodiversity indicators for monitoring impacts and conservation actions, www.theebi.org/pdfs/indicators.pdf

European Commission (2000). Managing Natura 2000 sites, the provisions of Article 6 of the Habitats Directive 92/43/CEE. http://ec.europa.eu/environment/nature/natura2000/management/docs/art6/provision_of_art6_en.pdf

European Communities (2009). Natura 2000 – Europe's Nature for You. Luxembourg: Office for Official Publications of the European Communities, http://ec.europa.eu/environment/nature/info/pubs/docs/europe_nature_for_you/en.pdf

European Commission (2010). Communication from the commission to the European parliament, the Council, the European Economic and Social Committee and the committee of the regions: options for an EU vision and target for biodiversity beyond 2010. Issued on 19 January 2010, http://ec.europa.eu/environment/nature/biodiversity/policy/pdf/communication_2010_0004.pdf

European Commission (2010). Public participation in nature conservation – making it happen, Science for Environment Policy, DG Environment News Alert Service. Published on 30 September 2010, http://ec.europa.eu/environment/integration/research/newsalert/pdf/211na5.pdf

Eurostat (2010). Employment in Europe 2010 – Statistical annex, http://ec.europa.eu/employment_social/eie/statistical_annex_key_employment_indicators_en.html

EIPP (European Institute for Public Participation) (2009). Public participation in Europe: an international perspective, www.participationinstitute.org/wpcontent/uploads/2009/06/pp_in_e_report_03_06.pdf

EU (European Union) (2013). The economic benefits of the Natura 2000 network: synthesis report, http://ec.europa.eu/environment/nature/natura2000/financing/docs/ENV-12-018_LR_Final1.pdf

Ewing, M., Hough, A. & Amajirionwu, M. (2007). Environmental RTDI programme 2000–2006: assessing access to information, participation, and justice in environmental decision-making in Ireland. Prepared for the Environmental Protection Agency by Centre for Sustainability, Institute of Technology, Sligo in Partnership with Department of Law, University College Cork COMHAR, the Sustainable Development Council, www.environmentaldemocracy.ie/pdf/finalreport.pdf

Feiring, B. (2013). Indigenous peoples' rights to lands, territories and resources, published in May 2013, www.landcoalition.org/sites/default/files/DraftILC IndigenousPeoplesPeerReview.pdf

Filmer-Wilson, E. & Anderson, M. (2005). Integrating human rights into energy and environment programming: a reference paper. Prepared for UNDP. Published in May 2005, www.hurilink.org/tools/Integrating_HRs_into_Energy_and_Environment_Programming.pdf

freedominfo.org (2009). European Court of Human Rights: right to information essential to free expression. Posted on 14 April 2009, www.freedominfo.org/2009/04/european-court-of-human-rights-right-to-information-essential-to-free-expression/

Fritz, K. (2009). National parks in China: a new model for nature conservation, http://digitalcollections.sit.edu/cgi/viewcontent.cgi?article=1708&context=isp_collection

First Financial Daily (第一财经报) (2011). Chinese protected areas: closed or open? (中国自然保护区：封闭还是开发). Posted on 13 April 2011, www.forestry.gov.cn/portal/bhxh/s/651/content-472781.html accessed in May, 2011, in Chinese.

Fonseca, H. (2004). Protected areas: protected against whom? Oilwatch & World Rainforest Movement www.forestpeoples.org/topics/convention-biological-diversity-cbd/publication/2011/protected-areas-protected-against-whom

Forest Peoples Programme (2012). Press release: indigenous peoples insist on human rights-based approaches and respect for traditional knowledge and practices in Rio+20 outcomes. Published on 20 June 2012, www.forestpeoples.org/topics/sustainable-livelihoods/news/2012/06/press-release-indigenous-peoples-insist-rights-based-app

Gao, X.Y. (高筱妤) (2012). The obstacles and strategies for Chinese environmental NGOs participating environmental public interest litigation (我国环保NGO参与环境公益诉讼的障碍及方略). Published on 12 December 2012, www.hicourt.gov.cn/theory/artilce_list.asp?id=7578&l_class=4

GI-ESCR (The Global Initiative for Economic, Social and Cultural Rights) (2014). A GI-ESCR practitioner's guide, http://globalinitiative-escr.org/wp-content/uploads/2014/03/GI-ESCR-Practitioners-Guide-Human-Rights-Environment-and-Climate-Change.pdf

Gong, Y.D. (2006). Public hearings: driving the engine of democracy in China. Posted in China Daily, www.chinadaily.com.cn/china/2006-10/05/content_701880.htm.

Government of India Ministry of Environment and Forests (2008). National Biodiversity Action Plan. http://envfor.nic.in/downloads/public-information/NBAP-iyb.pdf

Guidelines for the judgment in environmental issues in Yunnan Province (云南出台环保案"审判指南"). Posted on 18 May 2009, http://fiance.ifeng.com/huanbao/fgbz/20090518/673278.shtml

Harris-Curtis, E., Marleyn, O. & Bakewell, O. (2005) The implications for Northern NGOs of adopting human rights-based approaches. Occasional Papers Series 41, International NGO Training and Resource Center (INTRAC). www.intrac.org/docs/OPS%2041.pdf

Horsley, J.P. (2007). China adopts first nationwide open government information regulations, www.law.yale.edu/documents/pdf/Intellectual_Life/Ch_China_Adopts_1st_OGI_Regulations.pdf

Horsley, J.P. (2009). Public participation in the People's Republic: developing a more participatory governance model in China, www.law.yale.edu/documents/pdf/Intellectual_Life/CL-PP-PP_in_the__PRC_FINAL_91609.pdf

Horsley, J.P. (2010). Update on China's open government information regulations: surprising public demand yielding some positive results. Posted 23 April 2010, www.freedominfo.org/2010/04/update-on-china-open-government-information-regulations

Human rights-based approach – Statement of Common Understanding, www.unicef.org/sowc04/files/AnnexB.pdf

Human rights & environment in the Rio+20 UN Conference on Sustainable Development (2012). Posted on 15 February 2012, https://docs.google.com/viewer?a=v&q=cache:duwmOANP1DkJ:www.ciel.org/Publications/Rio%2B20_IssueBrief_Feb2012.pdf+human+rights+%26+environment+in+the+rio%2B20+UN+conference+on+sustainable+development&hl=nl&gl=be&pid=bl&srcid=ADGEESgb9- b4D3DEx8PYYQBZcQ7z2S5d1umIbUmFJjqhxetn6rfeeOa 5GLs2tim9n3fRY3a0EyrLFoGY00iHbYkMnMMZbU1QFUxbXYPjDT6KIfoFlN1n8Av1DiRVFGR9Lnc3acqLqmuf&sig=AHIEtbTHPwEWsU6nSdAA-I9QDPtPfefk4w

Human Rights Impact Resource Centre. Human Rights Impact Assessment Guide, www.humanrightsimpact.org/hria-guide

International Business Leaders Forum and International Finance Corporation (2007). Guide to human rights impact assessment and management road-testing draft. Published in June 2007, www.iblf.org/resources/general.jsp?id=123946

IBON International (2012). Reforming global sustainable development governance: a rights-based agenda. IBON International Working Paper, http://rio20.net/wp-content/uploads/2012/02/DRAFT_Reforming-international-susdev-governance-a-rights-based-agenda1.pdf

IUCN & WWF (1999). Principles and guidelines on indigenous and traditional peoples and protected areas: joint policy statement, www.wwf.fi/wwf/www/uploads/pdf/indigenous_people_policy.pdf

IUCN arborvitae (2008). Human rights-based approaches to forest conservation. The IUCN Forest Conservation Programme Newsletter, No. 36, www.rightsandresources.org/documents/files/doc_786.pdf

IUCN (2008). Governance of natural resources, equality and human rights, www.iucn.org/about/work/initiatives/sp_cprihome/sp_cpri_themes_/sp_cpri_natural_resources

IUCN (2012). Nature + people and governance –key messages from the IUCN congress forum. Posted on 12 September 2012, www.iucnworldconservationcongress.org/about/theme_and_slogan/people/?11038/Nature-people-and-governance---Key-messages

IUCN. Rights and Conservation Journey, www.iucn.org/congress_08/forum/journeys/rights_conservation/

IWGIA (International Work Group for Indigenous Affairs) (2011). Update 2011- China. www.iwgia.org/regions/asia/china/859-update-2011-china

IWGIA (International Work Group for Indigenous Affairs). Country profile: China. The concept of indigenous peoples in Asia – a resource book/ country profiles. www.iwgia.org/images/stories/sections/regions/asia/documents/short-country-profiles/china.pdf

Justice and Environment (2011). The most recent (2008–2011) case law of the Aarhus Convention Compliance Committee, www.justiceandenvironment.org/_files/file/2011%20ACCC%281%29.pdf

Kravchenko, S. (2007). Using human rights instruments for biodiversity conservation. IUCN Commission on Environmental, Economic & Social Policy. Issued on 15 July 2007, http://cmsdata.iucn.org/downloads/pm15.pdf

Kunming Daily (昆明日报) (2011). The land of protected areas in yunnan province will occupy more than 8% of provincial land in next 5 or 10 Years (云南自然保护区在5至10年内将达土地面积的8%). Posted on 23 December 2011, http://trip. house.sina.com.cn/News/2011–12–23/12655.html

Legal Blog: Judicial Studies (2008). Access to justice in China. Published on 7 November 2008, http://seiya.fyfz.cn/b/659795

Li, L. (2006). Topics about environment at the National People's Congress. *China Environment News*, 8, published on 6 March 2006 (in Chinese).

Li, Y. (李莹) (2014). Environmental trial must go in a professional way (环境审判必须走专业化道路). Published in China Environment News (中国环境报) on 14 July 2014

Liu, Y.D. (2005). Strategies on the increase of tourism tax revenues in Zhangjiajie, www.hnce.cn/news/Article_Print.asp?ArticleID=377

Liu, Y.W. (2006). Zhangjiajie tourism development with a promising future, www.zjj-trip.com/news/NewsInfo.aspx?ID=3568&pageUp=5

International Labor Office (2009). Report of the Committee of experts on the application of conventions and recommendations, www.ilo.org/wcmsp5/groups/public/---ed_norm/---relconf/documents/meetingdocument/wcms_103484.pdf

Luttrel, C. & Quiroz, S. (2007) Linkages between human rights-based approaches and environment. Published in October 2007, www.poverty-wellbeing.net/resources/sharewebResource_en_1545.pdf

Mason, M. (2010). Information disclosure and environmental rights: the Aarhus Convention, global environmental politics, 10(3), http://eprints.lse.ac.uk/29135/1/information%20disclosure%20and%20environmental%20rights%20%28LSERO%29.pdf

Mitlin, D. & Patel, S. (2005). Re-interpreting the human rights-based approach – a grassroots perspective on rights and development. A ESRC Research Group, Global Poverty Research Group (GPRG), Economic & Social Research Council (ESRC), www.gprg.org/

Nature Conservation Legislation Research Group (2012). The recommended framework for "protected area law of China". Issued on 14 September 2012, www.unep-wcmc.org/medialibrary/2012/10/03/f6c87f81/Main%20recommendations%20to%20PA%20Law%20of%20China-en.pdf

Natura 2000 (2010). Natura 2000 – addressing conflicts and promoting benefits, http://ec.europa.eu/environment/nature/natura2000/management/docs/conflict_solving2010.pdf

OECD (Organization for Economic Cooperation and Development) (1976). Recommendation of equal right of access in relation to trans-frontier pollution. Posted on 11 May 1976, www.dipublico.com.ar/english

OHCHR (2002). Draft guidelines: a human rights approach to poverty reduction strategies. Published on 10 September 2002, www1.umn.edu/humanrts/instree/povertyreductionguidelines.html

OHCHR (2011). Analytical study on the relationship between human rights and the environment (OHCHR 2011 Report). Published on 16 December 2011, UN Document, A/HRC/19/34, para. 2, www.ohchr.org/Documents/HRBodies/HRCouncil/RegularSession/Session19/A-HRC-19–34_en.pdf

OHCHR. Applying a human rights-based approach to climate change negotiations, policies and measures, www.ohchr.org/Documents/Issues/ClimateChange/InfoNoteHRBA.pdf

Orest Nowosad National Institutions Team. A human rights-based approach to development: strategies and challenges, http://nhri.ohchr.org/EN/Regional/Africa/4thConferenceDocuments/Novosad%20Development.pdf

Pan, Y. (2006). Reflections on Chinese environmental problems (《中国环境问题的思考》). Posted on the website of the Ministry of Environmental Protection of the People's Republic of China on 12 December 2006, www.sepa.gov.cn/info/ldjh/200701/t20070118_99754.htm

Parnell, M. Public participation in environmental decision-making, www.edo.org.au/edosa/research/aialpaper.htm

Renmin Net (人民网) (2009). The win-win road for Chinese protected areas (中国自然保护区寻求双赢之路). Published on 18 July 2009, http://env.people.com.cn/GB/9676896.html

People's Daily (人民日报) (2003). Human rights progress in China in 2003 (2003 中国人权事业的进展), www.people.com.cn/GB/shizheng/1026/2418866.html

People's Net (人民网), The first "measures on public participation in environmental issues was issued, it strengthens democracy in decision-making" （第一部环境问题中的公共参与措施颁布，加强决策民主）. Posted on 22 February 2006, http://env.people.com.cn/GB/1072/4130691.html, in Chinese.

Picolotti, R. & Taillant, J.D. (Eds.) (2010). Linking human rights and the environment. www.uapress.arizona.edu/Books/bid1492.htm

Portalewska, A. (2012). Free, prior and informed consent: protecting indigenous peoples' rights to self-determination, participation and decision-making. Published on 27 November 2012, www.culturalsurvival.org/publications/cultural-survival-quarterly/free-prior-and-informed-consent-protecting-indigenous

Poverty and Conservation Learning Group (2007). Towards an integrated system for measuring the social impact of protected areas. UNEP-World Conservation

Monitoring Centre: Vision 2020; WCPA/CEESP Taskforce on Protected Areas, Equity and Livelihoods, http://povertyandconservation.info/sites/default/files/Towards%20an%20integrated%20system%20for%20measuring%20the%20social%20impact%20of%20Protected%20Areas.pdf

Public participation and sustainable development on-line module, www.docstoc.com/docs/44508222/Public-Participation-and-Sustainable-Development-On-Line-Module

Razzaque, J. FIELD (the Foundation for International Environmental Law and Development), http://pubs.iied.org/pdfs/G00466.pdf

Roe, D. *et al.* (2010). Conservation and human rights: the need for international standards. Published in May 2010. IIED (International Institute for Environment and Development), www.iied.org/pubs/display.php?o=17066IIED

Schoukens, H. (2013). Access to justice in conservation related matters in the EU: the added value of the Aarhus Convention in the quest to environmental justice. Guest lecture in the department of public international law, Ghent University, 27 November 2013.

Secretariat of the Convention on Biological Diversity (2008). Protected areas in today's world: their values and benefits for the welfare of the planet. Technical Series No. 36, Montreal, https://www.cbd.int/doc/publications/cbd-ts-36-en.pdf

Shelton, D.L. (2002). Human rights, health & environmental protection: linkages in law & practice (A Background Paper for the World Health Organization). Health and Human Rights Working Paper Series No. 1, www.who.int/hhr/Series_1%20%20Sheltonpaper_rev1.pdf

Shelton, D.L. A rights-based approach to public participation and local management of natural resources. http://pub.iges.or.jp/modules/envirolib/upload/1503/attach/3ws-26-dinah.pdf

Shelton, D.L. (2010). Linkages between human rights and environmental protection, www.ttenvironmentalcommission.org/lectureseries/2010/dinah_shelton.pdf

Springer, J., Campese, J. & Painter, M. (2011). Conservation and human rights: key issues and contexts scoping paper for the conservation initiative on human rights. Published in October 2011, https://community.iucn.org/cihr/Resources/Scoping%20Paper%20_Oct%20final.pdf Statement on a Common Understanding of a Human Rights-Based Approach to Development Cooperation (Statement of Common Understanding). Issued in May 2003, www.hrea.org/index.php?base_id=104&language_id=1&erc_doc_id=3107&category_id=44&category_type=3&group=

Taillant, J.D. (2000). Environmental discrimination. Center for Human Rights and Development (CHRD), www.cedha.org.ar/en/documents

Theis, J. (2004). Promoting human rights-based approaches – experiences and ideas from Asia and the Pacific. CRIN (Child Rights International Network), www.crin.org/hrbap/index.asp?action=theme.themeItem&subtheme=6&item=4780

Tomicevic, J. & Bjedov, I. (2012). Understanding linkages between public participation and management of protected areas – case study of Serbia. In: Ishwaran, N. (Ed.). The Biosphere. Published on 14 March 2012, www.intechopen.com/books/the-biosphere/understanding-linkages-between-public-participation-and-management-of-protected-areas-case-study-of-.

Tsukhishvili, N. The case law of the European Court of Human Rights (ECHR): the right of access to public information. Institute for Development of Freedom of

Information (IDFI). Published on February 2013, www.idfi.ge/uploadedFiles/files/ECHR%20Case%20Laws%20Analysis%281%29.pdf
UN (1949). Survey of international law in relation to the work of the international law Commission: preparatory work within the purview of Article 18, paragraph 1, of the international law Commission – memorandum submitted by the Secretary-General, GAOR A/CN.4/Rev., paras 3–14, http://legal.un.org/ilc/documentation/english/a_cn4_1_rev1.pdf
UN (2003). The human rights based approach to development cooperation towards a common understanding among UN Agencies, www.undp.org/content/dam/aplaws/publication/en/publications/environment-energy/www-ee-library/external-publications/un-the-human-rights-based-approach-to-development-cooperation/UN_Common_Understanding_on_Human_Rights-Based_Approach_to_Development_Cooperation_and_Programming.pdf
UN (2011). United Nations final report of the study on indigenous peoples and the right to participate in decision-making: report of the expert mechanism on the rights of indigenous peoples. Issued on 17 August 2011, www2.ohchr.org/english/bodies/hrcouncil/docs/18session/A-HRC-18-42_en.pdf
UNESC (United Nations Economic and Social Council) (2001). Concluding observations of the Committee on Economic, Social and Cultural Rights: Germany. UN Doc.E/C.12/1Add.68,www.institut-fuer-menschenrechte.de/fileadmin/user_upload/PDF-Dateien/Pakte_Konventionen/ICESCR/icescr_state_report_germany_4_2000_cobs_2001_en.pdf
UNECE (United Nations Economic Commission for Europe) and UNEP (United Nations Environment Programme) (2006). Your right to a healthy environment: a simplified guide to the Aarhus convention on access to information, public participation in decision-making and access to justice in environmental matters, www.unece.org/fileadmin/DAM/env/documents/2006/pp/ece%20mp%20pp%205_E.pdf
UNDP (2006). Applying a human rights-based approach to development cooperation and programming: a UNDP capacity development resource. Capacity development group, Bureau for development policy, http://hurilink.org/tools/Applying_a_HR_approach_to_UNDP_Technical_Cooperation--unr_revision.pdf
UNDP. Ecosystems and biodiversity, http://web.undp. org/biodiversity/protected_areas.shtml
UNEP (United Nations Environment Programme). High level expert meeting on the future of human rights and environment: moving the global agenda forward, www.unep.org/environmentalgovernance/Events/HumanRightsandEnvironment/tabid/2046/Default.aspx
UNEP (2011). Guidelines for the Development of National Legislation on Access to Information, Public Participation and Access to Justice in Environmental Matters was adopted at the eleventh Special Session of United Nations Environment Programme Governing Council/Global Ministerial Environmental Forum in Bali, Indonesia, www.unep.org/civil-society/Portals/24105/documents/Guidelines/GUIDELINES_TO_ACCESS_TO_ENV_INFO_2.pdf
UNESCO (United Nations Educational, Scientific and Cultural Organization)/ UNCF (United Nations Children's Fund) (2007). A human rights-based approach to education, http://unesdoc.unesco.org/images/0015/001548/154861e.pdf

UNFPA (The United Nations Population Fund Agency), Human rights principles, www.unfpa.org/rights/principles.htm

US Environmental Protection Agency (2003). Toolkit for assessing potential allegations of environmental injustice, www.epa.gov/compliance/recent/ej.html

van Rooij, B. (2007). The return of the landlord: Chinese land acquisition conflicts as illustrated by peri-urban Kunming, www.jlp.bham.ac.uk/volumes/55/vanrooij-art.pdf

Voorhoof, D. & Fathaigh, R. Ó. (2013). The press and NGOs' right of access to official documents under strict scrutiny of the European Court of Human Rights. Strasbourg Observers. Published on 3 December 2013, http://strasbourgobservers.com/2013/12/03/the-press-and-ngos-right-of-access-to-official-documents-under-strict-scrutiny-of-the-european-court-of-human-rights-2/

Vucic, M. (2011). The right to environmental information as a techniques for the protection of the environment, www.doiserbia.nb.rs/img/doi/0025–8555/2011/0025–85551103449V.pdf

Wang, H. (2009). Public participation in environmental management from the perspective of China. Discussion Papers in Social Responsibility, www.socialresponsibility.biz

Wang, H. (2011). Stakeholder dialogue as an institutional strategy for sustainable development in China: the case of community environmental round-tables. The World Bank Development Research Group Environment and Energy Team, www-wds.worldbank.org/external/default/WDSContentServer/IW3P/IB/2011/08/15/000158349_20110815113133/Rendered/PDF/WPS5759.pdf

Wangyi News (网易新闻). The environment and resource tribunal was newly established at the supreme of People's Court: its name has been changed for several times (最高法院成立环境资源审判庭："名字曾经改了好几次"). Published on 30 June 2014, http://news.163.com/14/0630/09/9VVQHKB600014AED.html

Washington Post (2008). China to all land leasing, transfer. Published on 20 October 2008.

Washington Times (2009). China resolves pollution case, avoids suit. Posted on 2 September 2009, www.washingtontimes.com/news/2009/sep/02/china-resolves-pollution-case-avoids-suit

Wen, J.B. (温家宝) (2004). Report on the work of the government (政府工作报告). Section III, www.peopledaily.com.cn/GB/shizheng/1024/2394441.html

World Databases on Protected Areas (WDPA) (2012). Statistics, www.wdpa.org/Statistics.aspx

WWF (World Wide Fund for Nature) China (2004). The minutes of the symposium on the co-management with the community in protected areas in China. Issued on 19 May 2004, www.wwfchina.org/pressdetail.php?id=257

Wu, W.Z. (武卫政) (2008). Safeguarding a right in environmental issues urgently needs to find away out (环境维权亟待走出困境). Posted in People's Daily (《人民日报》) on 22 January 2008.

Xinhua Net (新华网) (2013). The Progress in China's Human Rights in 2012 (2012年中国人权事业的进展). Posted on 14 May 2013, http://news.xinhuanet.com/politics/2013–05/14/c_115758619.htm

Xinhua Net (新华网) (2010). Guiyang: environmental organization can sue the administrative omission concerning environmental resources (《贵阳：环保组织可对涉及环境资源行政不作为提起诉讼》). Posted on 15 January 2010, www.gz.xinhuanet.com/2008htm/xwzx/2010-01/15/content_18774216.htm

Xian, P. (2006). Experts discussing the public participation in environmental protection legislation – the scope of participation should be broader and the participants should be pluralism, www.clapv.org/NewsContent.asp?id=532

Xu, J.C. & Melick, D. (2007). Towards community-driven conservation in southwest China: reconciling state and local perceptions. ICRAF (International Center for Research in AgroForestry) Working Paper No. 52, www.worldagroforestry.org/downloads/publications/PDFs/WP15421.PDFY

Yusuf, S. (2012). Pursuing the right for today, securing the environment for tomorrow. UNISCI (Research Unit on International Security and Cooperation) Discussion Paper No. 29, www.redalyc.org/pdf/767/76724487011.pdf

Zhang, S.J. & Lu, L. (张式军 卢磊) (2006). On legal guarantee for realization of access to justice in environmental matters: some ideas on improving Article 6 in "Environmental Protection Law of the People's Republic of China" (论环境诉权实现的法律保障 – – 对完善《环境保护法》第六条的思考). Published on 4 May 2006, www.procedurallaw.cn/msss/zdwz/200807/t20080724_49656.html

Zhang, X. (张鑫) (2005). Who should hold the key for an environmental litigation (《环境诉讼启动钥匙该谁拿》). Posted in Legal Daily (《法制日报》) on 3 November 2005.

Zhang, Y.R. (张艳蕊) Promoting Environmental Protection through Environmental Civil Public Interest Litigation (通过环境民事公益诉讼促进环境保护). Published on 25 January 2013, http://theory.people.com.cn/n/2013/0125/c40531-20326493.html

CASES AND OTHER MATERIALS

CASES FROM EUROPEAN COMMISSION/COURT OF HUMAN RIGHTS (ECMHR/ECTHR)

1979 – ECtHR, Airey v. Ireland (1979), App. No. 6289/73, Judgment of 9 October 1979 (http://hudoc.echr.coe.int/sites/eng/pages/search.aspx?i=001-60486#{%22fulltext%22:[%22airey%20v%20ireland%22],%22itemid%22:[%22001-57420%22]})

1979 – ECtHR, Marckx v. Belgium (1979), App. No. 6833/74, Judgment of 13 June 1979 (http://hudoc.echr.coe.int/sites/eng/pages/search.aspx?i=001-57534#{%22itemid%22:[%22001-57534%22]})

1979 – ECtHR, Sunday Times v. the United Kingdom (1979), App. No. 6538/74, Judgment of 26 April 1979 (http://hudoc.echr.coe.int/sites/eng/pages/search.aspx?i=001-57584#{%22itemid%22:[%22001-57584%22]})

1982 – ECtHR, Sporrong and Lönnroth v. Sweden (1982), App. Nos. 7151/75; 7152/75, Judgment of 23 September 1982 (http://hudoc.echr.coe.int/sites/eng/pages/search.aspx?i=001-57580#{%22itemid%22:[%22001-57580%22]})

1985 – ECtHR, Herrick v. the United Kingdom (1985), App. No. 11185/84, Commission decision of 11 March 1985 (http://echr.ketse.com/doc/11185.84-en-19850311/)
1986 – ECtHR, Agosi v. the United Kingdom (1986), App. No. 9118/80, Judgment of 24 October 1986 (http://echr.ketse.com/doc/9118.80-en-19861024/)
1986 – ECtHR, James and Others v. the United Kingdom (1986), App. No. 8793/79, Judgment of 21 February 1986 (http://sim.law.uu.nl/SIM/CaseLaw/Hof.nsf/1d4d0dd240bfee7ec12568490035df05/0ef9f8927a96c5a5c1256640004c2410?OpenDocument)
1986 – ECtHR, Lithgow and Others v. the United Kingdom (1986), App. Nos. 9006/80, 9262/81, 9263/81, 9265/81, 9266/81, 9313/81, 9405/81, Judgment of 8 July 1986 (http://hudoc.echr.coe.int/sites/eng/pages/search.aspx?i=001-57526#{%22itemid%22:[%22001-57526%22]})
1987 – ECtHR, Leander v. Sweden (1987), App. No. 9248/81, Judgment of 26 March 1987 (http://hudoc.echr.coe.int/sites/eng/pages/search.aspx?i=001-57519#{%22itemid%22:[%22001-57519%22]})
1991 – ECtHR, Wiesinger v. Austria (1990), App. No. 11796/85, Judgment of 30 October 1991 (http://sim.law.uu.nl/sim/caselaw/Hof.nsf/e4ca7ef017f8c045c1256849004787f5/e682cdf930183cd3c1256640004c1b27?OpenDocument)
1991 – ECtHR, Observer and Guardian v. the United Kingdom (1991), App. No. 13585/88, Judgment of 26 November 1991 (http://hudoc.echr.coe.int/sites/eng/pages/search.aspx?i=001-57705#{%22itemid%22:[%22001-57705%22]})
1991 – ECtHR, Pine Valley Developments Ltd. and Others v. Ireland (1991), App. No. 1274/87, Judgment of 29 November 1991 (http://echr.ketse.com/doc/12742.87-en-19930209/)
1991 – ECtHR, Fredin v. Sweden (1991), App. No. 12033/86, Judgment of 18 February 1991 (http://sim.law.uu.nl/sim/caselaw/Hof.nsf/2422ec00f1ace923c1256681002b47f1/a3f2e913fcf974fec1256640004c18e0?OpenDocument)
1991 – ECtHR, Oerlemans v. Netherlands (1991), App. No. 12565/86, Judgment of 27 November 1991 (http://echr.ketse.com/doc/12565.86-en-19911127/view/)
1992 – ECtHR, Claesson and Others v. Sweden (1992), App. No. 13903/88, Judgment of 1 July 1992 (http://echr.ketse.com/doc/13903.88-en-19920701/view/)
1994 – ECtHR, The Holy Monasteries v. Greece (1994), App. Nos. 13092/87; 13984/88, Judgment of 9 December (http://hudoc.echr.coe.int/sites/fra/pages/search.aspx?i=001-57906#{%22itemid%22:[%22001-57906%22]})
1994 – ECtHR, Stran Greek Refineries and Andreadis Stratis v. Greece (1994), App. No. 13427/87, Judgment of 9 December 1994 (http://hudoc.echr.coe.int/sites/eng/pages/search.aspx?i=001-57913#{%22itemid%22:[%22001-57913%22]})
1995 – ECtHR, Gasus Dosier-und Fordertechnik GmbH v. the Netherlands (1995), App. No. 15375/89, Judgment of 23 February 1995 (http://hudoc.echr.coe.int/sites/eng/pages/search.aspx?i=001-57918#{%22itemid%22:[%22001-57918%22]})
1995 – ECtHR, Loizidou v. Turkey (1995), App. No. 15318/89, Judgment of 23 March 1995 (http://hudoc.echr.coe.int/sites/eng/pages/search.aspx?i=001-57920)
1996 – ECtHR, Tsomtsos and Others v. Greece (1996), App. No. 20680/92, Judgment of 15 November 1996 (http://echr.ketse.com/doc/20680.92-en-19961115/)
1996 – ECtHR, Katikaridis and Others v. Greece (1996), App. No. 31423/96, Judgment of 15 November 1996 (http://echr.ketse.com/doc/19385.92-en-19961115/)

1996 – ECtHR, Buckley v. the United Kingdom (1996), App. No. 20348/92, Judgment of 29 September 1996 (http://hudoc.echr.coe.int/sites/eng/pages/search.aspx?i=001-58076#{%22itemid%22:[%22001-58076%22]})
1996 – ECtHR, Mateos e Silva, Ltd and Others v. Portugal (1996), App. No. 15777/89, Judgment of 16 September 1996 (http://echr.ketse.com/doc/15777.89-en-19960916/)
1996 – ECtHR, Gunther v. Sweden (1996), App. No. 26265/92, Commission decision of 27 November 1996 (http://echr.ketse.com/doc/26265.92-en-19961127/)
1998 – ECtHR, Anna Marina Guerra and 39 Others v. Italy (1998), App. No. 14967/89, Judgment of 19 February 1998 (http://hudoc.echr.coe.int/sites/eng/pages/search.aspx?i=001-58135)
1999 – ECtHR, Papachelas v. Greece (1999), App. No. 31423/96, Judgment of 25 March 1999 (http://hudoc.echr.coe.int/sites/fra/pages/search.aspx?i=001-58291#{%22itemid%22:[%22001-58291%22]})
1999 – ECtHR, Chassagnou and Others v. France (1999), App. Nos. 25088/94, 28331/95 and 28443/95, Judgment of 29 April 1999 (http://hudoc.echr.coe.int/sites/eng/pages/search.aspx?i=001-58288#{%22itemid%22:[%22001-58288%22]})
1999 – ECtHR, Iatridis v. Greece (1999), App. No. 31107/96, Judgement of 25 March 1999 (http://hudoc.echr.coe.int/sites/eng/pages/search.aspx?i=001-58227#{%22itemid%22:[%22001-58227%22]})
1999 – ECtHR, Spacek, s.r.o., v. the Czech Republic (1999), App. No. 26449/95, Judgment of 9 November 1999 (http://echr.ketse.com/doc/26449.95-en-19991109/)
2000 – ECtHR, Kudla v. Poland (2000), App. No. 20577/05, Judgment of 26 October 2000 (http://hudoc.echr.coe.int/sites/eng/Pages/search.aspx#{%22appno%22:[%2230210/96%22],%22itemid%22:[%22001-58920%22]})
2001 – ECtHR, Chapman v. the United Kingdom (2001), App. No. 27238/95, Judgment of 18 January 2001 (http://hudoc.echr.coe.int/sites/eng/pages/search.aspx?i=001-59154#{%22itemid%22:[%22001-59154%22]})
2001 – ECtHR, Thoma v. Luxembourg (2001), App. No. 38432/97, Judgment of 29 June 2001 (http://hudoc.echr.coe.int/sites/eng/pages/search.aspx?i=001-59363#{%22itemid%22:[%22001-59363%22]})
2001 – ECtHR, Tsironis v. Greece (2001), App. No. 44584/98, Judgment of 6 December 2001 (http://echr.ketse.com/doc/44584.98-en-20011206/)
2002 – ECtHR, Al-Nashif v. Bulgaria (2002), App. No. 50963/99, Judgment of 20 June 2002 (http://hudoc.echr.coe.int/sites/eng/Pages/search.aspx#{%22fulltext%22:[%22Al-Nashif%20v.%20Bulgaria%22],%22documentcollectionid2%22:[%22GRANDCHAMBER%22,%22CHAMBER%22],%22itemid%22:[%22001-60522%22]})
2002 – ECtHR, Christine Goodwin v. the United Kingdom (2002), App. No. 28957/95, Judgment of 11 July 2002 (http://hudoc.echr.coe.int/sites/fra/pages/search.aspx?i=001-60596#{%22itemid%22:[%22001-60596%22]})
2002 – ECtHR, Jokela v. Finland (2002), App. No. 28856/95, Judgment of 21 May 2002 (http://echr.ketse.com/doc/28856.95-en-20020521/)
2002 – ECtHR, Posti and Rahko v. Finland (2002), App. No. 27824/95, Judgment of 24 September 2002 (http://sim.law.uu.nl/sim/caselaw/Hof.nsf/1d4d0dd240bfee7ec12568490035df05/bb445d6738ec3a2d41256c3f002f588e?OpenDocument)

2002 - ECtHR, Stafford v. the United Kingdom (2002), App. No. 46295/99, Judgment of 28 May 2002 (http://hudoc.echr.coe.int/sites/eng/pages/search.aspx?i=001-60486#{%22itemid%22:[%22001-60486%22]})

2004 - ECtHR, Taşkın and Others v. Turkey (2004), App. No. 46117/99, Judgment of 10 November 2004, 30 March 2005 (final) (http://hudoc.echr.coe.int/sites/eng/pages/search.aspx?i=001-67401#{%22itemid%22:[%22001-67401%22]})

2004 - ECtHR, Vides Aizsardzibas Klubs v. Latvia (2004), App. No. 57829/00, Judgment of 27 May 2004 (https://wcd.coe.int/ViewDoc.jsp?id=1025311&Site=COE)

2005 - ECtHR, Saliba v. Malta (2005), App. No. 4251/02, Judgment of 8 November 2005 (http://echr.ketse.com/doc/4251.02-en-20051108/)

2006 - ECtHR, Lazaridi v. Greece (2006), App. No. 31282/04, Judgment of 13 July 2006 (http://sim.law.uu.nl/sim/caselaw/Hof.nsf/1d4d0dd240bfee7ec12568490035df05/47ce77ee58527b39c12571b0003ebca4?OpenDocument)

2006 - ECtHR, Hutten-Czapska v. Poland (2006), App. No. 35014/97, Judgment of 19 June 2006 (http://hudoc.echr.coe.int/sites/eng/pages/search.aspx?i=001-75882#{%22itemid%22:[%22001-75882%22]})

2006 - ECtHR, Matky v. Czech Republic (2006), App. No. 19101/03, Judgement of 10 July 2006 (http://hudoc.echr.coe.int/sites/eng/pages/search.aspx?i=001-76707#{%22itemid%22:[%22001-76707%22]})

2006 - ECtHR, Nikas and Nika v. Greece (2006), App. No. 31273/04, Judgment of 13 July 2006 (http://echr.ketse.com/doc/31273.04-en-20060713/)

2008 - ECtHR, Turgut and Others v. Turkey (2008), App. No. 1411/03, Judgment of 8 July 2008 (http://echr.ketse.com/doc/1411.03-en-20080708/)

2009 - ECtHR, Devecioğlu v. Turkey (2009), App. No. 17203/03, Judgement of 4 May 2009 (http://echr.ketse.com/doc/17203.03-en-20081113/view/)

2009 - ECtHR, Kenedi v. Hungary (2009). App. No. 31475/05, Judgment of 26 August 2009 (http://hudoc.echr.coe.int/sites/eng/pages/search.aspx?i=001-92663#{%22itemid%22:[%22001-92663%22]})

2009 - ECtHR, Társaság a Szabadságjogokért v. Hungary (2009), App. No. 37374/05, Judgement of 14 July 2009 (http://hudoc.echr.coe.int/sites/eng/pages/search.aspx?i=001-92171#{%22itemid%22:[%22001-92171%22]})

2010 - ECtHR, Ivan Atanasov v. Bulgaria (2010), App. No. 12853/03, Judgment of 2 December 2010, 11 April 2011 (final) (http://hudoc.echr.coe.int/sites/eng/Pages/search.aspx#{%22fulltext%22:[%22\%22right%20to%20participation\%22%22],%22documentcollectionid2%22:[%22GRANDCHAMBER%22,%22CHAMBER%22],%22itemid%22:[%22001-101958%22]})

2011 - ECtHR, Dubetska and Others v. Ukraine (2011), App. No. 30499/03, Judgment of 10 February 2011, 10 May 2011 (final) (http://hudoc.echr.coe.int/sites/eng/pages/search.aspx?i=001-103273#{%22itemid%22:[%22001-103273%22]})

2013 - ECtHR, Österreichische Vereinigung zur Erhaltung, Stärkung und Schaffung eines wirtschaftlich gesunden land- und forstwirtschaftlichen Grundbesitzes v. Austria (2013), App. No. 39534/07, Judgement of 28 November 2013 (http://hudoc.echr.coe.int/sites/eng/pages/search.aspx?i=001-139084#{%22itemid%22:[%22001-139084%22]})

2014 - ECtHR, Sace Elektrik Ticaret Ve Sanayi A.Ş. v. Turkey (2014), App. No. 20577/05, Judgment of 22 January 2014 (Final) (http://hudoc.echr.coe.int/sites/eng/Pages/

search.aspx#{%22fulltext%22:[%22\%22effective%20right%20of%20access%20to%20a%20court\%22%22],%22documentcollectionid2%22:[%22GRANDCHAMBER%22,%22CHAMBER%22],%22itemid%22:[%22001-127105%22]})

COMMUNICATIONS FROM THE AARHUS CONVENTION COMPLIANCE COMMITTEE

2004 – ACCC/C/2004/04 (Hungary), ECE/MP.PP/C.1/2005/2/Add.4, 14 March 2005 (www.unece.org/fileadmin/DAM/env/pp/compliance/C2004-04/C04findings.pdf)

2004 – ACCC/C/2004/03 (Ukraine), ECE/MP.PP/C.1/2005/2/Add.3. 14 March 2005 (www.unece.org/fileadmin/DAM/env/documents/2005/pp/c.1/ece.mp.pp.c1.2005.2.Add.3.e.pdf)

2005 – ACCC/C/2005/12 (Albania), ECE/MP.PP/C.1/2007/4/Add.1, 31 July 2007 (www.unece.org/env/pp/compliance/Compliancecommittee/12TableAlbania.html)

2006 – ACCC/C/2006/18 (Denmark), ECE/MP.PP/2008/5/Add.4, 29 April 2008 (www.unece.org/fileadmin/DAM/env/documents/2008/pp/mop3/ece_mp_pp_2008_5_add_4_e.pdf)

2007 – ACCC/C/2007/21 (European Community), ECE/MP.PP/C.1/2009/2/Add.1, 8 February 2011 (www.unece.org/fileadmin/DAM/env/pp/compliance/CC-23/ece_mp.pp_c.1_2009_2_add.1_eng.pdf)

2007 – ACCC/C/2007/22 (France), ECE/MP.PP/C.1/2009/4/Add.1, 8 February 2011 (www.unece.org/fileadmin/DAM/env/pp/compliance/C2008-22/Findings/ece_mp.pp_c.1_2009_4_add.1_eng.pdf)

2008 – ACCC/C/2008/29 (Poland), ECE/MP.PP/C.1/2009/6/Add.2, 25 September 2009 (www.unece.org/fileadmin/DAM/env/pp/compliance/CC-25/ece_mp.pp_c.1_2009_6_add.2_e.pdf)

2008 – ACCC/C/2008/24 (Spain), ECE/MP.PP/C.1/2009/8/Add.1, 8 February 2011 (www.unece.org/fileadmin/DAM/env/pp/compliance/CC-26/ece_mp.pp_c.1_2009_8_add.1_e.pdf)

2009 – ACCC/C/2009/37 (Belarus), ECE/MP.PP/2011/11/Add.2, 12 May 2011 (www.unece.org/fileadmin/DAM/env/pp/compliance/C2009-37/Findings/ece_mp.pp_2011_11_eng_add2.pdf)

2009 – ACCC/C/2009/36 (Spain), ECE/MP.PP/C.1/2010/4/Add.2, 8 February 2011 (www.unece.org/fileadmin/DAM/env/pp/compliance/CC-28/ece_mp.pp_c.1_2010_4_add.2_eng.pdf)

CASES FROM COURT OF JUSTICE OF THE EUROPEAN UNION

1963 – Plaumann v. Commission, Case C-25/26, Judgment of the Court of 15 July 1963 (http://curia.europa.eu/juris/liste.jsf?pro=&nat=or&oqp=&dates=&lg=&language=en&jur=C%2CT%2CF&cit=none%252CC%252CCJ%252CR%252C2008E%252C%252C%252C%252C%252C%252C%252C%252C%252C%252Ctrue%252Cfalse%252Cfalse&num=c-25%252F62&td=%3BALL&pcs=Oor&avg=&page=1&mat=or&jge=&for=&cid=157950)

1998 – Stichting Greenpeace Council and Others v. Commission, C-32/95P, Judgment of the Court of 2 April 1998 (http://curia.europa.eu/juris/liste.jsf?pro=&nat=or&oqp=&dates=&lg=&language=en&jur=C%2CT%2CF&cit=none%252CC%252CCJ%252CR%252C2008E%252C%252C%252C%252C%252C%252C%252C%252C%252C%252Ctrue%252Cfalse%252Cfalse&num=c-321%252F95p&td=%3BALL&pcs=Oor&avg=&page=1&mat=or&jge=&for=&cid=157950)

2003 – Commission of the European Communities v. Kingdom of Belgium, Case C-415/01, Judgment of the Court (Sixth Chamber) of 27 February 2003 (http://curia.europa.eu/juris/liste.jsf?language=en&num=C-415/01)

2004 – Waddenvereniging and Vogelbeschermingsvereniging, Case C-127/02, Judgment of the Court (Grand Chamber) of 7 September 2004 (http://curia.europa.eu/juris/liste.jsf?pro=&nat=or&oqp=&dates=&lg=&language=en&jur=C%2CT%2CF&cit=none%252CC%252CCJ%252CR%252C2008E%252C%252C%252C%252C%252C%252C%252C%252C%252C%252Ctrue%252Cfalse%252Cfalse&num=127%252F02&td=%3BALL&pcs=Oor&avg=&page=1&mat=or&jge=&for=&cid=420788)

2009 – Djurgården-Lilla Värtans Miljöskyddsförening v. Stockholms kommun genom dess marknämnd, Case C-263/08, Judgment of the Court (Second Chamber) of 15 October 2009 (http://curia.europa.eu/juris/liste.jsf?language=en&jur=C,T,F&num=263/08&td=ALL)

2010 – Terre Wallonne ASBL v. Région Wallonne, Case C-105/09, Inter-Environment Wallonie ASBL v. Région Wallonne, Case C-110/09, Joined Case Judgment of the Court (Fourth Chamber) of 17 June 2010 (http://curia.europa.eu/juris/document/document.jsf?text=&docid=83020&pageIndex=0&doclang=EN&mode=lst&dir=&occ=first&part=1&cid=135853)

2011 – Lesoochranárske zoskupenie VLK v. Ministerstvo životného prostredia Slovenskej republiky, Case C-240/09, Judgment of the Court (Grand Chamber) of 8 March 2011 (http://curia.europa.eu/juris/liste.jsf?language=en&num=c-240/09)

2012 – Peter Sweetman and Others v. An Bord Pleanala, Case C-258/11, Peter Sweetman and others v. An Bord Pleanala, Case C-258/11, Judgment of the Court (Third Chamber) of 11 April 2013 (http://curia.europa.eu/juris/liste.jsf?pro=&nat=or&oqp=&dates=&lg=&language=en&jur=C%2CT%2CF&cit=none%252CC%252CCJ%252CR%252C2008E%252C%252C%252C%252C%252C%252C%252C%252C%252C%252Ctrue%252Cfalse%252Cfalse&num=258%252F11&td=%3BALL&pcs=Oor&avg=&page=1&mat=or&jge=&for=&cid=383224)

2014 – Cascina Tre Pini S.s. v. Ministero dell' Ambiente e della Tutela del Territorio e del Mare and Others, Case C-301/12, Judgment of the Court (Second Chamber) of 3 April 2014 (http://curia.europa.eu/juris/liste.jsf?language=en&jur=C,T,F&num=C-301/12&td=ALL)

CHINESE CASES

1721 People v. Rongping Chemical Plant (屏南县溪坪村张长建等1721人诉容屏联营化工厂环境污染损害赔偿纠纷案), Fujian Provincial High People's Court (福建省高级人民法院), 2003 (www.fsou.com/html/text/fnl/1175258/117525863.html)

All-China Environment Federation (ACEF) v. Jiangyin Container Ltd. (中华环保联合会诉江苏省江阴港集装箱有限公司环境污染侵权案), The Intermediate People's Court in Wuxi City of Jiangsu Province (江苏省无锡市中级人民法院), 6 July 2009 (http://blog.voc.com.cn/blog.php?do=showone&type=blog&itemid=726395)

All-China Environment Federation (ACEF) v. The Land Resources Bureau in Qingzhen City (中华环保联合会诉贵州省清镇市国土资源管理局), The Intermediate People's Court in Qingzhen City of Guizhou Province (贵州省清镇市国土资源管理局), 29 July 2009 (www.jcrb.com/zhuanti/fzzt/lpsh/gyss/201001/t20100112_300833.html)

LEGAL AND POLICY INSTRUMENTS

INTERNATIONAL INSTRUMENTS

1948 – Universal Declaration of Human Rights, adopted on 10 December 1948, UN Doc. A/810 AT 71, UNGA Res. 217 A (III) (www.un.org/en/documents/udhr/)

1957 – International Labor Organization Convention No. 107, adopted on 26 June 1957 and entered into force on 2 June 1959 (www.ilo.org/indigenous/Conventions/no107/lang--en/index.htm)

1965 – International Convention on the Elimination of All Forms of Racial Discrimination, signed on 21 December 1965 and entered into force on 4 January 1969, 660 UNTS 195 (www.ohchr.org/EN/ProfessionalInterest/Pages/CERD.aspx)

1966 – International Covenant on Civil and Political Rights, issued on 16 December 1966, and went into force on 23 March 1976, 999 UNTS 171 (www.ohchr.org/en/professionalinterest/pages/ccpr.aspx)

1966 – International Covenant on Economic, Social and Cultural Rights, adopted on 16 December 1966, and went into force 3 January 1976, 993 UNTS 3 (www.ohchr.org/EN/ProfessionalInterest/Pages/CESCR.aspx)

1971 – Convention on Wetlands of International Importance (Ramsar Convention), adopted on 2 February 1971 and amended by the Paris Protocol on 3 December 1982, 11 ILM (1972) 963 (www.ramsar.org/cda/en/ramsar-documents-texts/main/ramsar/1-31-38_4000_0__)

1971 – UNESCO's Man and the Biosphere Programme, issued in 1971 (www.unesco.org/new/en/natural-sciences/environment/ecological-sciences/man-and-biosphere-programme/about-mab/)

1972 – Convention Concerning the Protection of the World Cultural and Natural Heritage (The World Heritage Convention), adopted on 16 November 1972, 11 ILM (1972) 1358 (http://portal.unesco.org/en/ev.php-URL_ID=13055&URL_DO=DO_TOPIC&URL_SECTION=201.htm)

1972 – Declaration of the United Nations Conference on the Human Environment (Stockholm Declaration), adopted on 16 June 1972, UN Doc. A/CONF.48/14/Rev.1 (www.unep.org/Documents.Multilingual/Default.asp?documentid=97&articleid=1503)

1972 – Action Plan for the Human Environment, 11 ILM (1972), 1416 (www.unep.org/Documents.multilingual/Default.asp?DocumentID=97&ArticleID=1505&l=en)

1973 – Convention on International Trade in Endangered Species of Wild Fauna and Flora (CITES), issued in 1973 and amended on 22 June 1979, 12 ILM (1973) 1055 (www.cites.org/eng/disc/text.php)

1976 – OECD (Organization for Economic Cooperation and Development) Recommendation of Equal Right of Access in Relation to Trans-frontier Pollution, issued on 11 May 1976 (www.dipublico.com.ar/english)

1979 – Convention on the Elimination of Discrimination Against Women, adopted and opened for signature on 18 December 1979 and entry into force 3 September 1981, 1249 UNTS 14 (www.ohchr.org/Documents/ProfessionalInterest/cedaw.pdf)

1981 – African Charter on Human and Peoples' Rights (also known as the Banjul Charter), adopted on 27 June 1981, OAU Doc. CAB/LEG/67/3/Rev.5 (1981), reprinted in 21 ILM 58 (1982) (www.achpr.org/files/instruments/achpr/banjul_charter.pdf)

1982 – United Nations Convention on the Law of the Sea, adopted on 10 December 1982 (www.un.org/depts/los/convention_agreements/convention_overview_convention.htm)

1982 – World Charter for Nature, adopted on 28 October 1982, A/RES/37/7 (www.un.org/documents/ga/res/37/a37r007.htm)

1987 – United Nations Report of the World Commission on Environment and Development: Our Common Future (Brundtland Report), adopted on 4 August 1987, A/42/427 (http://conspect.nl/pdf/Our_Common_Future-Brundtland_Report_1987.pdf)

1988 – Additional Protocol to the American Convention on Human Rights in the Area of Economic, Social and Cultural Rights ("Protocol of San Salvador"), adopted on 14 November 1988, OAS TS No. 69, reprinted in 28 ILM 156 (1989) (www.oas.org/juridico/english/treaties/a-52.html)

1989 – Convention on the Rights of the Child, signed on 20 November 1989 and entered into effective on 2 September 1990, 1577 UNTS 3 (www.unicef.org/crc/)

1989 – International Labor Organization Convention No. 169: Indigenous and Tribal Peoples Convention, adopted on 27 June 1989 and entered into force on 5 September 1991, 28 ILM 1382 (www.ilo.org/indigenous/Conventions/no169/lang--en/index.htm)

1990 – UN Convention on the Protection of the Rights of All Migrant Workers and Members of their Families, signed on 18 December 1990 and entered into force on 1 July 2003, 2220 UNTS 3 (www2.ohchr.org/english/bodies/cmw/cmw.htm)

1991 – Espoo Convention on Environmental Impact Assessment in a Trans-boundary Context, adopted on 25 February 1991 (www.unece.org/fileadmin/DAM/env/eia/documents/legaltexts/conventiontextenglish.pdf)

1992 – Rio Declaration on Environment and Development (United Nations Conference on Environment and Development, UNCED), adopted in June 1992, A/CONF.151/26 (www.unep. org/Documents.Multilingual/Default.asp?documentid=78&articleid=1163)

1992 – United Nations Framework Convention on Climate Change (UNFCCC), adopted on 9 May 1992 and entered into force 21 March 1994, 1771 UNTS 107; 31 ILM 849 (http://unfccc.int/2860.php)
1992 – Convention Biological Diversity (CBD), opened for signature on 5 June 1992 and entered into force on 29 December 1993, [1993] ATS 32/1760 UNTS 79/31 ILM 818 (1992) (www.cbd.int/)
1992 – Agenda 21, action plan adopted at the United Nations Conference on Environment and Development in Rio de Janeiro in June 1992 (http://sustainabledevelopment.un.org/content/documents/Agenda21.pdf)
1992 – Convention on the Trans-boundary Effects of Industrial Accidents, adopted on 17 March 1992, ECE/CP. TEIA/15/Add.1 (www.unece.org/env/teia.html)
1992 – Kari-Oca Declaration, signed during the World Conference of Indigenous Peoples on Territory, Environment and Development at Kari-Oca, Brazil on 30 May 1992 and reaffirmed at Bali, Indonesia on 4 June 2002 (www.dialoguebetweennations.com/ir/english/kariocakimberley/KODeclaration.html)
1992 – Indigenous Peoples Earth Charter, signed at Kari-Oca (Brazil) Conference on 25–30 May 1992 (www.dialoguebetweennations.com/ir/english/kariocakimberley/KOCharter.html)
1993 – United Nations Vienna Declaration and Programme of Action, adopted on 25 June 1993 (www.ohchr.org/en/professionalinterest/pages/vienna.aspx)
1996 – Arctic Council, issued in 1996 (www.arctic-council.org/index.php/en/)
1996 – Joint Communique (Canada-Demark-Finland-Iceland-Norway-the Russian Federation-Sweden-United States) and Declaration on the Establishment of the Arctic Council, adopted on 19 September 1996 at Ottawa, reprinted in 35 ILM 1382 (http://1997–2001.state.gov/www/global/oes/oceans/arctic_council.html)
1997 – International Atomic Energy Agency (IAEA) Joint Convention on the Safety of Spent Fuel Management and on the Safety of Radioactive Waste Management, opened for signature on 29 September 1997 and entered into force on 18 June 2001 (www.iaea.org/Publications/Documents/Conventions/jointconv.html)
1997 – General Recommendation No. 23: Indigenous Peoples, issued on 18 August 1997 (www.unhchr.ch/tbs/doc.nsf/0/73984290dfea022b802565160056fe1c)
1998 – Rotterdam Convention on the Prior Informed Consent Procedure for Certain Hazardous Chemicals and Pesticides in International Trade, adopted on 10 September 1998 and revised in 2011 (www.pic.int/TheConvention/Overview/TextoftheConvention/tabid/1048/language/en-US/Default.aspx)
1998 – Convention on Access to Information, Public Participation in Decision-making and Access to Justice in Environmental Matters (Aarhus Convention), adopted on 25 June 1998 and entered into force since 30 October 2001, 2161 UNTS 447 (http://ec.europa.eu/environment/aarhus/)
1999 – Declaration of Bizkaia on the Right to the Environment, adopted on 24 September 1999, 30 C/INF.11 (http://unesdoc.unesco.org/images/0011/001173/117321e.pdf)
2001 – The Stockholm Convention on Persistent Organic Pollutants, signed on 22 May 2001 and effective from May 2004 (www.pops.int/documents/convtext/convtext_en.pdf)

2002 – Johannesburg Declaration on Sustainable Development, adopted in September 2002, A/CONF.199/20 (www.unescap.org/esd/environment/rio20/pages/Download/johannesburgdeclaration.pdf)

2003 – Statement on a Common Understanding of a Human Rights-Based Approach to Development Cooperation (Statement of Common Understanding), issued in May 2003 (www.hrea.org/index.php?base_id=104&language_id=1&erc_doc_id=3107&category_id=44&category_type=3&group=)

2004 – Akwe: Kon Guidelines for the Conduct of Cultural, Environmental and Social Impact Assessment regarding Developments Proposed to Take Place on, or which are Likely to Impact on, Sacred Sites and on Lands and Waters Traditionally Occupied or Used by Indigenous and Local Communities, issued in 2004 (https://www.cbd.int/doc/publications/akwe-brochure-en.pdf)

2004 – Programme of Work on Protected Areas, issued in 2004 (www.cbd.int/doc/publications/pa-text-en.pdf)

2004 – Seventh Meeting of the Conference of the Parties to the Convention on Biological Diversity (COP 7), issued in February 2004 (www.cbd.int/decisions/?m=COP-07&ID=7765&LG=0)

2007 – United Nations Declaration on the Rights of Indigenous Peoples, issued on 13 September 2007, UN Doc. A/RES/61/295 (www.un.org/esa/socdev/unpfii/documents/DRIPS_en.pdf)

2009 – Report of the Special Rapporteur on the Situation of Human Rights and Fundamental Freedoms of Indigenous Peoples, issued on 5 October 2009 (www.refworld.org/docid/4ae5b9f02.html)

2009 – Report of the Committee of Experts on the Application of Conventions and Recommendations adopted by International Labor Office in 2009 (www.ilo.org/wcmsp5/groups/public/---ed_norm/---relconf/documents/meeting document/wcms_103484.pdf)

2010 – Nagoya Protocol to the Convention on Biological Diversity, adopted on 29 October 2010 (www.cbd.int/abs/doc/protocol/nagoya-protocol-en.pdf)

2011 – The Tkarihwaire: Ri Code of Ethical Conduct to Ensure Respect for the Cultural and Intellectual Heritage of Indigenous and Local Communities, adopted in 2011 (www.cbd.int/traditional/code/ethicalconduct-brochure-en.pdf)

2011 – Permanent Forum on Indigenous Issues, Report on the tenth session, issued in May 2011 (www.un.org/esa/socdev/unpfii/documents/session_10_report_EN.pdf)

2011 – United Nations Final Report of the Study on Indigenous Peoples and the Right to Participate in Decision-making: Report of the Expert Mechanism on the Rights of Indigenous Peoples, issued on 17 August 2011 (www2.ohchr.org/english/bodies/hrcouncil/docs/18session/A-HRC-18–42_en.pdf)

2012 – Food and Agriculture Organization Voluntary Guidelines on the Responsible Governance of Tenure Guidelines, issued in 2012 (www.fao.org/docrep/016/i2801e/i2801e.pdf)

2012 – United Nations Conference on Sustainable Development (UNCSD, Rio 2012 or Rio+20), held in Rio de Janeiro on 20–22 June 2012, A/CONF.216/16 (www.uncsd2012.org/)

2012 – The Special Rapporteur on the Rights of Indigenous Peoples, issued on 6 July 2012 (http://unsr.jamesanaya.org/annual-reports/report-to-the-human-rights-council-a-hrc-21-47-6-july-2012)
2012 – United Nations Final Draft of the Guiding Principles on Extreme Poverty and Human Rights, issued on 18 July 2012 (www.ohchr.org/Documents/Issues/Poverty/A-HRC-21-39_en.pdf)

REGIONAL INSTRUMENTS

Africa

1981 – African Charter on Human and People's Rights (also known as the Banjul Charter), adopted on 27 June 1981 and entered into force 21 October 1986 (www.achpr.org/files/instruments/achpr/banjul_charter.pdf)

America

1948 – American Declaration of the Rights and Duties of Man, adopted in 1948 (www1.umn.edu/humanrts/oasinstr/zoas2dec.htm)
1969 – American Convention on Human Rights, adopted on 22 November 1969 and entered into force on 18 July 1978, 1144 UNTS 123 (www.hrcr.org/docs/American_Convention/oashr5.html)
1988 – Additional Protocol to the American Convention on Human Rights in the Area of Economic, Social and Cultural Rights ("Protocol of San Salvador"), adopted on 14 November 1988 (www.oas.org/juridico/english/treaties/a-52.html)
1994 – North American Convention on Environmental Cooperation, came into effective on 1 January 1994 (www.cec.org/Page.asp?PageID=1226&SiteNodeID=567&AA_SiteLanguageID=1)

Asia

1981 – Protection of Migratory Birds and Their Habitat Agreement (China – Japan), issued on 3 March 1981
1990 – Cooperation Agreement on Natural Environment (China – Mongolia), issued on 6 May 1990
1994 – Agreement on the Establishment of a Natural Reserve with Mongolia and Russia, issued on 29 March 1994

Europe

1950 – Convention for the Protection of Human Rights and Fundamental Freedoms (European Convention on Human Rights), drafted in 1950 and entered into force on 3 September 1953, 213 UNTS (www.echr.coe.int/Documents/Convention_ENG.pdf)

1952 – Protocol to the Convention for the Protection of Human Rights and Fundamental Freedoms, amended by Protocol No. 11 in 1952 (http://conventions.coe.int/Treaty/en/Treaties/Html/009.htm,) Paris, 20.III.1952

1979 – Birds Directive (Directive 79/409/EEC of 2 April 1979 on the Convention of Wild Birds), replaced by 2009 Bird Directive (http://ec.europa.eu/environment/nature/legislation/birdsdirective/index_en.htm)

1979 – Convention on the Conservation of European Wildlife and Natural Habitats (Bern Convention), issued in 1979 and entered into effective on 1 June 1982, BH756.txt;1284 UNTS 209 (http://conventions.coe.int/Treaty/Commun/QueVoulezVous.asp?NT=104&CM=8&DF=&CL=ENG)

1979 – Recommendation 854 (1979) on Access by the Public to Government Records and Freedom of Information, issued on 1 February 1979 by the Parliamentary Assembly of the Council of Europe (http://assembly.coe.int/main.asp?Link=/documents/adoptedtext/ta79/erec854.htm)

1982 – Council Directive of 24 June 1982 on the Major-Accident Hazards of Certain Industrial Activities (82/501/EEC), issued on 24 June 1982 and replaced by 87/216/EEC, signed on 19 March 1987 (http://eur-lex.europa.eu/LexUriServ/LexUriServ.do?uri=CELEX:31982L0501:EN:HTML)

1985 – Council Directive 85/337/EEC of 27 June 1985 on the Assessment of Certain Public and Private Projects on the Environment, issued on 27 June 1985, recently recast as Directive 2010/75/EU on Industrial Emissions (http://ec.europa.eu/environment/eia/full-legal-text/85337.htm)

1990 – Council Directive 90/313/EEC of 7 June 1990 on the Freedom of Access to Information on the Environment, issued on 7 June 1990, replaced by the Directive 2003/4/EC on Public Access to Environmental Information in 2003 (www.sazp. sk/slovak/struktura/ceev/EIA/twin/englishtwin/legislation/directives/Access%20to%20Environmental%20Information.pdf)

1991 – Geneva Protocol Concerning the Control of Emission of Volatile Organic Compounds or Their Trans-boundary Fluxes, issued on 18 November 1991 (www.unece.org/env/lrtap/vola_h1.html)

1992 – Convention for the Protection of the Marine Environment of the North-East Atlantic (the OSPAR Convention), adopted on 22 September 1992 (www.ospar.org/content/content.asp?menu=01481200000000_000000_000000)

1992 – Habitats Directive (Directive 92/43/EEC of 21 May 1992 on the Conservation of Natural Habitats and of Wild Fauna and Flora) (http://ec.europa.eu/environment/nature.legislation.habitatsdirective.index_en.htm)

1992 – Helsinki Convention on Protection and Use of Trans-boundary Watercourses and International Lakes, adopted on 17 March 1992 (www.unece.org/fileadmin/DAM/env/water/pdf/watercon.pdf)

1995 – Protocol Concerning Specially Protected Zones and Biological Diversity in the Mediterranean, adopted on 10 June 1995 and entered into force on 12 December 1999 (http://ec.europa.eu/world/agreements/prepareCreateTreatiesWorkspace/treatiesGeneralData.do?step=0&redirect=true&treatyId=598)

1996 – Council Directive 96/61/EC of 24 September 1996 Concerning Integrated Pollution Prevention and Control, issued on 24 September 1996, recently recast as Directive 2010/75/EU on Industrial Emissions (http://eur-lex.europa.eu/LexUriServ/LexUriServ.do?uri=CELEX:31996L0061:en:HTML)

1999 – Council of Europe, Future action to be taken by the Council of Europe in the field of environment protection, Parliamentary Assembly Recommendation 1431 (1999) (http://assembly.coe.int/Main.asp?link=/Documents/AdoptedText/ta99/EREC1431.htm)

2000 – Directive 2000/60/EC of the European Parliament and of the Council of 23 October 2000 Establishing a Framework for Community Action in the Field of Water Policy, issued on 23 October 2000 (http://eur-lex.europa.eu/LexUriServ/LexUriServ.do?uri=OJ:L:2000:327:0001:0072:en:PDF)

2001 – Directive 2001/42/EC of the European Parliament and of the Council of 27 June 2001 on the Assessment of the Effects of Certain Plans and Programs on the Environment, issued on 27 June 2001 and entered into effective 21 July 2001 (www.ecolex.org/ecolex/ledge/view/RecordDetails;jsessionid=05602270319C24F8AA6403BAB3123F46?id=LEX-FAOC034996&index=documents)

2003 – Directive 2003/4/EC of the European Parliament and of the Council of 28 January 2003 on Public Access to Environmental Information, issued on 28 January 2003 (http://eur-lex.europa.eu/LexUriServ/LexUriServ.do?uri=OJ:L:2003:041:0026:0032:EN:PDF)

2003 – Directive 2003/35/EC of the European Parliament and of the Council of 26 May 2003 Providing for Public Participation in Respect of the Drawing up of Certain Plans and Programs relating to the Environment and Amending with regards to Public Participation and Access to Justice Council Directive 85/337/EEC and 96/61/EC, issued on 26 May 2003 (http://eur-lex.europa.eu/LexUriServ/LexUriServ.do?uri=OJ:L:2003:156:0017:0024:EN:PDF)

2003 – Council of Europe, Environment and human rights, Parliamentary Assembly Recommendation 1614 (2003) (http://assembly.coe.int/Main.asp?link=/Documents/AdoptedText/ta03/EREC1614.htm)

2009 – Council of European Convention on Access to Official Documents, issued on 18 June 2009, CETS No. 205, http://conventions.coe.int/Treaty/EN/Treaties/Html/205.htm

2010 – Directive 2010/75/EU on Industrial Emissions (Integrated Pollution Prevention and Control), issued on 24 November 2010 (http://eur-lex.europa.eu/LexUriServ/LexUriServ.do?uri=OJ:L:2010:334:0017:0119:en:PDF)

NATIONAL INSTRUMENTS

China

1951 – Provisional Regulations on Safeguarding State Secrets [保守国家机密暂行条例], promulgated in 1951 and remained in effect until 1989, when the Law on Guarding State Secrets was enacted.

1959 – Instruction on Positive Development of Hunting [关于狩猎积极发展的说明], formulated by the Forest Ministry. (Expired)

1962 – Instruction on Positive Protecting and Reasonable Utilizing Wild Animal Resources [关于积极保护和合理使用野生动物资源的说明], issued by the State Council. (Expired)

1963 – Regulation for Forest Protection [森林保护条例], issued by the State Council. (Expired)

1973 – Provisional Regulation on Management of Nature Reserves (draft) [自然保护区暂行条例（草案）], formulated by the Forest Ministry. (Expired)

1980 – Notification for Managing, Planning and Scientific Investigation for Protected Areas [关于管理、规划和科学研究自然保护区的说明], issued by the Forest Ministry. (Expired)

1982 – Constitution of the People's Republic of China [中华人民共和国宪法], adopted in 1982 and newly amended on 14 March 2004 (http://guoqing.china.com.cn/2012-01/31/content_24516030.htm)

1982 – Marine Environmental Protection Law of the People's Republic of China [中华人民共和国海洋环境保护法], adopted on 23 August 1982 and revised on 25 December 1999 (www.novexcn.com/marine_environemental_prot.html and www.mlr.gov.cn/mlrenglish/laws/200710/t20071012_656329.htm)

1984 – Forest Law of the People's Republic of China [中华人民共和国森林法], adopted in 1984 and amended on 29 April 1998 (www.china.org.cn/english/environment/207457.htm)

1984 – Water Pollution Prevention and Control Law of the People's Republic of China [中华人民共和国水污染防治法], issued on 11 May 1984 and amended on 28 February 2008 and entered into force on 1 June 2008 (www.lawinfochina.com/display.aspx?lib=law&id=6722)

1985 – Grassland Law of the People's Republic of China [中华人民共和国草原法], adopted in 1985, revised on 28 December 2002. The revised version went into effect on 1 March 2003 (www.eduzhai.net/yingyu/615/763/yingyu_247335.html)

1986 – General Principles of the Civil Law of the People's Republic of China [中华人民共和国民法通则], adopted in 1986 and entered into force on 1 January 1987 (www.china.com.cn/policy/txt/2012-01/14/content_24405953.htm)

1986 – Land Management Law of the People's Republic of China [中华人民共和国土地管理法], issued in 1986 and amended in 1998, and later amended on 28 August 2004 (www.china.com.cn/chinese/law/647616.htm)

1987 – Chinese Program for Nature Conservation [中国自然保护纲要], issued in 1987 (www.chinabaike.com/article/baike/1000/2008/200805111455370.html)

1987 – Law of the People's Republic of China on the Prevention and Control of Atmospheric Pollution [中国人民共和国大气污染防治法], issued in 1987 and revised on 29 April 2000 (www.lawinfochina.com/display.aspx?lib=law&id=6722)

1988 – Law of the People's Republic of China on Guarding State Secrets [中华人民共和国保守国家秘密法], promulgated on 5 September 1988 and entered into effective on 1 May 1989, later revised on 29 April 2010 and entered into effect on 1 October 2010 (www.lawinfochina.com/law/display.asp?id=1191)

1989 – Administrative Procedural Law of the People's Republic of China [中华人民共和国行政诉讼法], adopted on 4 April 1989 and entered into effective on 1 October 1990, later revised on 1 November 2014 (www.npc.gov.cn/wxzl/gongbao/2014-12/23/content_1892467.htm)

1989 – Environmental Protection Law of the People's Republic of China [中华人民共和国环境保护法], entered into effective on 26 December 1989, later revised on 24 April 2014 and entered into force on 1 January 2015 (www.law-lib.com/law/law_view.asp?id=6229; http://edu.sina.com.cn/en/2014-05-20/144680376.shtml)
1989 – Mineral Resources Law of the People's Republic of China [中华人民共和国矿产资源保护法], adopted in 1989 and amended on 29 August 1996 (www.china.org.cn/environment/2007-08/20/content_1034342.htm)
1990 – Regulations of the People's Republic of China on the prevention of pollution damage to the marine environment by land-sourced pollutions [中华人民共和国防治陆源污染物污染损害海洋环境管理条例], entered into effect on 1 August 1990 (http://dinrac.nowpap.org/documents/law/China/Regulations_on_Prevention_of_Pollution_Damage_to_Marine_Environment_by_Land-Based_Pollutants_China.pdf)
1991 – Civil Procedural Law of the People's Republic of China [中华人民共和国民事诉讼法], adopted on 9 April 1991 and amended on 31 August 2012 (www.kd325.com/ShowArticle.shtml?ID=201051016355390786.htm)
1992 – Law of the People's Republic of China on the Protection of Rights and Interests of Women [中华人民共和国妇女权益保障法], adopted on 3 April 1992 and amended on 28 August 2005 (www.china.org.cn/english/government/207405.htm)
1994 – Chinese Agenda 21 [中国21世纪议程], issued in 1994 (www.unescap.org/drpad/vc/conference/ex_cn_1_ca21.htm; www.acca21.org.cn/english/index.html)
1994 – Regulations of the People's Republic of China on Nature Reserves [中华人民共和国自然保护区条例], entered into effect on 1 December 1994 (www.asianlii.org/cn/legis/cen/laws/ronr333/)
1995 – Land Management Approach in Nature Reserve [自然保护区土地管理办法], issued on 24 July 1995 (www.mlr.gov.cn/zwgk/flfg/tdglflfg/200406/t20040625_585545.htm)
1995 – Law of the People's Republic of China on Prevention of Environmental Pollution Caused by Solid Waste [中华人民共和国固体废物污染环境防治法], issued in 1995, amended on 29 December 2004 and entered into effect on 1 April 2005 (www.lawinfochina.com/display.aspx?lib=law&id=119)
1995 – Marine Protected Areas Management Measures [海洋自然保护区管理办法], issued on 24 July 1995 (http://biodiv.coi.gov.cn/fg/hy/02.htm)
1996 – Decision of the State Council on Several Issues Concerning Environmental Protection [国务院关于环境保护若干问题的决定], issued on 3 August 1996 (www.lawinfochina.com/display.aspx?lib=law&id=6372)
1996 – Law on Administrative Penalty [中华人民共和国行政处罚法], promulgated by National People's Congress on 17 March 1996, and entered into effect on 1 October 1996 (www.npc.gov.cn/englishnpc/Law/2007-12/11/content_1383613.htm)
1996 – Law of the People's Republic of China on Prevention and Control of Pollution from Environmental Noise [中华人民共和国噪声污染防治法], issued on 29 October 1996 and entered into effect on 1 March 1997 (www.lawinfochina.com/display.aspx?lib=law&id=544)
1997 – Aquatic Animals and Plants Nature Reserve Management Approach of the People's Republic of China [中华人民共和国水生动植物自然保护区管理办法], issued on 17 October 1997 (http://zfs.mep.gov.cn/gz/bmgz/qtgz/199710/t19971017_81935.htm)

1997 – Chinese Nature Reserve Development Planning Outline (1996–2010) [中国自然保护区发展规划纲要], issued on 24 November 1997 (www.zhb.gov.cn/ztbd/rdzl/2010sdn/bhcj/201001/t20100113_184243.htm)

1998 – Law on the Organization of Villagers' Committees [村民委员会组织法], promulgated on 4 November 1998, and entered into effect on 4 November 1998 (www.chinalawedu.com/news/23223/23228/22926.htm)

1997 – Regulations of the People's Republic of China on the Protection of Wild Plants [中华人民共和国野生植物保护条例], entered into force on 1 January 1997 (www.xj.xinhuanet.com/shengtai/2004-04/23/content_2026071.htm)

2000 – Conservation Action Plan for Wetlands in China [中国湿地保护行动计划], issued on 8 November 2000 (http://lianghui.china.com.cn/chinese/2000/Nov/10342.htm)

2000 – Legislation Law of the People's Republic of China [中华人民共和国立法法], issued on 15 March 2000 (http://english.gov.cn/laws/2005-08/20/content_29724.htm)

2001 – National Wildlife Conservation and Natural Reserve Construction General Plan [全国野生动植物保护及自然保护区建设工程总体规划], issued in 2001 (www.beinet.net.cn/zcfg/gh/qggh/200802/P020080423597945791148.pdf)

2001 – Law of the People's Republic of China on Prevention and Control of Desertification [中华人民共和国防沙治沙法], entered into effect on 31 August 2001 (www.china.org.cn/china/LegislationsForm2001-2010/2011-02/14/content_21915867.htm)

2001 – Program for the Development of Chinese Women (2001–2010) [中国妇女发展纲要(2001–2010)], published on 22 May 2001 (www.china.org.cn/english/features/cw/140979.htm)

2001 – Regulations on the Procedures for Formulating Rules [行政法规制定程序条例], promulgated on 16 November 2001 and entered into effect on 1 January 2002 (www.gov.cn/english/laws/2005-08/24/content_25827.htm)

2002 – Rules on Open Government Information of Guangzhou Municipality [广州市政府信息公开规定], promulgated on 6 November 2002 and entered into effect on 1 January 2003 (www.people.com.cn/item/flfgk/dffg/1992/D442053199204.html)

2002 – Law on Environmental Impact Assessment of the People's Republic of China [中华人民共和国环境影响评价法], adopted in 2002 and entered into effect on 1 September 2003 (www.people.com.cn/GB/shehui/212/3572/3574/20021029/853043.html)

2002 – Regulation on the adjustment for boundaries and functional areas of national nature reserves and changing their name [国家级自然保护区范围调整和功能区调整及更改名称管理规定], issued on 29 January 2002 (www.gov.cn/gongbao/content/2002/content_61943.htm). Expired and replaced by "Regulation on the Adjustment for National Nature Reserves" [国家级自然保护区调整管理规定] on 2 December 2013, http://vip. chinalawinfo.com/newlaw2002/slc/slc.asp?db=chl&gid=214332

2002 – Guangzhou Municipal Provisions on Open Government Information [广州市信息公开条例], issued on 6 November 2002 and entered into effect on 1 January 2003 (www.freedominfo.org/documents/provisions.pdf)

2003 – Cleaner Production Promotion Law of the People's Republic of China [中华人民共和国清洁生产促进法], entered into effect on 1 January 2003 and amended on 29 February 2012 (www.chinacp. org.cn/eng/cppolicystrategy/cp_law2002.html)

2003 – Law of the People's Republic of China on Land Contract in Rural Areas [中华人民共和国农村土地承包法], went into effect on 1 March 2003 (http://english.gov.cn/laws/2005-10/09/content_75300.htm)

2004 – Measures of Shenzhen Municipality for Online Open Government Information [深圳市政府信息网上公开办法], entered into effect on 1 April 2004 (www.chinacourt.org/flwk/show1.php?file_id=92369)

2003 – People's Republic of China Law on the Prevention and Control of Radioactive Pollution [中华人民共和国放射性污染防治法], adopted on 28 June 2003 and entered into effect on 1 October 2003 (www.china.org.cn/china/LegislationsForm2001-2010/2011-02/14/content_21915263.htm)

2006 – Guangzhou Municipal Measures on Public Participation in Formulating Rules [广州市规章制定公众参与办法], adopted on 27 June 2006 and entered into effective on 1 January 2007 (www.law.yale.edu/documents/pdf/Intellectual_Life/CL-PP-Final_GZ_PP_MeasuresFinal__tr9-4-09_%28Eng%29.pdf)

2007 – Law of the People's Republic of China on Property Rights [中华人民共和国物权法], entered into effect on 1 October 2007 (www.lehmanlaw.com/fileadmin/lehmanlaw_com/laws___regulations/Propoerty_Rights_Law_of_the_PRC__LLX__03162007.pdf)

2007 – Measures on Open Environmental Information (for trial implementation) [环境信息公开办法（试行）], adopted on 8 February 2007 and entered into effect on 1 May 2008 (www.epa.gov/ogc/china/open_environmental.pdf)

2007 – Notification on Further Intensifying the Degree of Public Participation in Matters Related to Government Legislative Work from the Legislative Affairs Office of the State Council [国务院法制办关于进一步提高政府立法工作公众参与程度有关事项的通知], issued on 31 March 2007 (www.chinabaike.com/law/zy/bw/bs/fzb/1376475.html)

2007 – Regulations of the People's Republic of China on Open Government Information [中华人民共和国政府信息公开条例], adopted on 17 January 2007 and entered into effect on 1 May 2008 (www.law.yale.edu/documents/pdf/Intellectual_Life/Ch_OGI_Regualtions_Eng_Final_051607.pdf)

2007 – Urban and Rural Planning Law of the People's Republic of China [中华人民共和国城乡规划法], issued on 28 October 2007 and entered into effect on 1 January 2008 (www.lawinfochina.com/display.aspx?lib=law&id=6495)

2008 – Opinions of the General Office of the State Council on Various Issues of Implementing the Open Government Information Regulations of the People's Republic of China [国务院办公厅关于贯彻落实中华人民共和国政府信息公开条例的各种问题的意见], issued on 29 April 2008 (www.law.yale.edu/documents/pdf/Intellectual_Life/CL-OGI-State_Council_Opinions-English.pdf)

2008 – Water Pollution Prevention and Control Law of the People's Republic of China [中华人民共和国水污染防治法], issued on 28 February 2008 and entered into force on 1 June 2008 (www.lawinfochina.com/display.aspx?lib=law&id=6722)

2009 – Measures of Hunan Province to Implement the Regulations of the People's Republic of China on Open Government Information [湖南省关于执行中华人民共和国政府信息公开条例的办法], adopted by the 40th Standing Committee of the Provincial People's Government on 27 October 2009, and entered into effect on 1 January 2010 (www.law.yale.edu/documents/pdf/Intellectual_Life/CL-OGI_Hunan_OGI_Measures_%28Eng_FINAL%29.pdf)

2009 – Regulation of the People's Republic of China on Environmental Impact Assessment of Planning [中华人民共和国规划环境影响评价条例], adopted on 12 August 2009 and entered into force on 1 October 2009 (www.lawinfochina.com/ProductsServices/index.shtm)

2009 – Supreme People's Court Issues Notice of Six Provisions on Judicial Transparency and Certain Provisions on Acceptance by the People's Courts of Supervision by the Media and Public Opinion [《最高人民法院印发《关于司法公开的六项规定》和《关于人民法院接受新闻媒体舆论监督的若干规定》的通知》]. Issued on 8 December 2009 (www.chinacourt.org/flwk/show.php?file_id=140270)

2010 – Guiyang Regulations on Promoting Ecological Civilization Construction [贵阳市促进生态文明建设条例], issued on 8 January 2010 (www.ghb.gov.cn/doc/201029/52054307.shtml)

2010 – Hubei Xingdoushan National Nature Reserve Management Regulation in Enshi Tujia and Miao autonomous prefecture [湖北省人民代表大会民族宗教侨务外事委员会关于《恩施土家族苗族自治州湖北星斗山国家级自然保护区管理条例》], issued on 30 July 2010 (www.hppc.gov.cn/list-hyzl.asp?id=164)

2010 – Interim Management Measures on the Special Marine Protected Areas [海洋特别保护区管理暂行办法], issued on 31 August 2010 (www.soa.gov.cn/oa/governmentaffairs/guojiahaiyangjuwenjian/hyhjbh/webinfo/2010/11/1289376295103759.htm)

2010 – Notification on Well Managing Protected Areas from the General Office of the State Council[国务院办公厅关于做好自然保护区管理有关工作的通知], issued in December 2010 (www.gzhjbh.gov.cn/hjpj/tzwj/45214.shtml)

2010 – Notification on the National Major Functional Zonation Plan of China from the State Council [国务院关于印发全国主体功能区规划的通知], issued on 21 December 2010 (www.gov.cn/zwgk/2011-06/08/content_1879180.htm)

2010 – Opinions of the General Office of the State Council on Improving the Work of Disclosing Government Information upon Request [国务院关于完善依申请而信息公开工作的意见], issued on 12 January 2010 (www.law.yale.edu/documents/pdf/Intellectual_Life/CL-OGI_SCGO_Opinions_on_OGI_Request_2010_%28Eng%29.pdf)

2010 – Regulation for Promoting Ecological Civilization Construction in Guiyang [贵阳市促进生态文明建设条例], issued on 8 January 2010 and entered into effective on 1 March 2010 (www.gz.xinhuanet.com/2008htm/xwzx/2010-01/15/content_18774216.htm)

2010 – Regulations on Comprehensive Scientific Survey for Protected Areas (Trial) [自然保护区综合科学考察规程（试行）], issued in 2010 (http://wenku.baidu.com/view/844713da5022aaea998f0ff8.html)

2010 – Strategy and Action Plan for Biodiversity Preservation in China (2011–2030) [中国生物多样性保护战略与行动计划 (2011–2030)], issued on 17 September 2010 (www.mep. gov.cn/gkml/hbb/bwj/201009/t20100921_194841.htm)

2011 – Criminal Law of the People's Republic of China (2011 Revision) [中华人民共和国刑法 (2011修正版)], issued on 14 March 1997 and amended on 25 February 2011 (www.szxingshi.com/95w.html)

2011 – Rules on Several Issues of Adjudicating Open Government Information Administrative Litigation [政府信息公开条例司法解释], passed the Supreme

People's Court on 29 July 2010 and entered into force on 13 August 2010 (http://lvshi.sz.bendibao.com/news/2011817/315374.shtm)

2011 – Supreme People's Court, Rules on Several Issues of Adjudicating Open Government Information Administrative Litigation [最高人民法院关于审理政府信息公开行政案件若干问题的规定], passed by the Judicial Committee of the Supreme People's Court on 29 July 2011 and entered into force on 13 August 2011, fashi [2011] No. 17 (http://lvshi.sz.bendibao.com/news/2011817/315374.shtm)

2012 – National Human Rights Action Plan of China (2012–2015) [国家人权行动计划(2012–2015)], issued in 2012 (http://news.xinhuanet.com/politics/2012-06/11/c_112186014.htm)

2012 – Notification on Further to Strengthen Hydropower Construction and Environmental Protection [关于进一步加强水电建设环境保护的通知], issued on 6 January 2012 (www.mep. gov.cn/gkml/hbb/bgt/201201/t20120117_222665.htm)

2013 – Management Rules on Wetland Protection" [湿地保护管理规定], issued by the State Forestry Administration on 28 March 2013 and entered into force on 1 May 2013 (www.forestry.gov.cn/portal/main/s/72/content-594660.html)

2013 – Regulation on the Adjustment for National Nature Reserves [国家级自然保护区调整管理规定], issued and entered into effective on 2 December 2013 (http://vip. chinalawinfo.com/newlaw2002/slc/slc.asp?db=chl&gid=214332)

2014 – Implementation Regulations of the People's Republic of China on Guarding State Secrets [中华人民共和国保守国家秘密法实施条例], issued in February 2014 and went to effective on 1 March 2014 (http://news.163.com/14/0203/02/9K4HVN5800014AED.html)

2015 – Measures on Right to Participation in Environmental Protection [环境保护公众参与办法], issued on 2 July 2015 and entered into force on 1 September 2015 (www.zhb.gov.cn/gkml/hbb/bl/201507/t20150720_306928.htm)

2015 – Overall Plan for the Reform of Ecological Civilization System [生态文明体制改革总体方案], issued on 21 September 2015 (http://news.xinhuanet.com/politics/2015-09/21/c_1116632281.htm)

www.ingramcontent.com/pod-product-compliance
Ingram Content Group UK Ltd.
Pitfield, Milton Keynes, MK11 3LW, UK
UKHW051919100926
8556IPUK00021B/1256

9 781780 683881